The *Dictionary* is an historical reference work for students of the Renaissance conceived as a great cultural and intellectual age; therefore the great bulk of the entries is given over to biographical sketches of artists, humanists, philosophers, etc., and to characterizations of their works or achievement. But since the political and social context of the age is of great importance, the compilers have added a considerable amount of material on leading political and military figures and events, social evolution, the history of the principal Italian cities, etc. Nor are the Reformation and Counter Reformation ignored, although they have little intrinsic connection with the Renaissance. The same may be said of the expansion of Europe: it has little direct relationship with the Renaissance, but contact with strange lands and strange traditions did have a stimulating and emancipating impact upon the European mind. Pains have been taken to cover European enterprise overseas, especially to include those explorers and travelers who wrote accounts of their journeyings, because they helped to shape the prevailing notions of geography, cosmology and history.

Referring to the objections that have been raised against the idea of Renaissance in the period 1350-1600, the authors answer the skeptics and iconoclasts, and demonstrate that an examination of the history of art, thought and scholarship, of music and literature, of social and political forms amply justifies the Burckhardtian notion of the Renaissance.

Frederick M. Schweitzer teaches at Manhattan College and H. E. Wedeck at Brooklyn College, both in New York.

DICTIONARY
OF THE
RENAISSANCE

DICTIONARY
OF THE
RENAISSANCE

edited by

FREDERICK M. SCHWEITZER,

Department of History, Manhattan College

and

HARRY E. WEDECK,

Department of Classics, Brooklyn College

PHILOSOPHICAL LIBRARY
NEW YORK

INTRODUCTION

I

The *Renaissance* is the most famous term in historical discourse. It gained its currency from the celebrated book of Jacob Burckhardt, *The Civilization of the Renaissance in Italy*, published little more than a century ago. Since then an enormous amount of thought and writing has been expended on the concept of the Renaissance. There has been a severe reaction against Burckhardt's view. Much of the criticism stems from a belief in the overriding continuum of all history, an excessive reaction—it would seem—to the readiness with which Burckhardtians set their period off from what preceded, as though the Renaissance had nothing in common with and no roots whatsoever in the medieval era. Burckhardt's chief offense does not seem to be his elevation of the Renaissance to so shining and lovely an eminence —his crime there was no more than the exaggeration of an enthusiast; rather, it was his aspersions on medieval civilization and medieval man, somnolent beneath that obscuring "veil." Burckhardt was ignorant of the Middle Ages—a statement still made but unjust to the man who had written on medieval history and Gothic art. His depreciation of the Middle Ages was a reasoned conclusion based on knowledge; to refer to his "ignorance" of medieval civilization is only to say that he knew nothing of the medieval scholarship and research done since his time.

That research has greatly expanded our knowledge and understanding of the Middle Ages. One of its results has been the delight with which medievalists cite examples of Renaissance individualism, classicism, etc., long before the supposed onset of the Renaissance. Some scholars have carried the principle of continuity so far as to deny all originality or special character to the Renaissance, asserting that it was no more than a phase of the Middle Ages, the denouement of the marvelous twelfth and thirteenth centuries or even that the Renaissance never existed. The fallacy of establishing continuity in this manner is obvious: It may be that Peter Abelard was decidedly an individualist or that an English don, Magister Gregorius, enthusiastically admired and measured Roman antiquities like any Renaissance archaeologist, but they constitute no more than isolated instances and, moreover, did not conform to any widely accepted ideal or norm for doing such things. The establishment of such an ideal came only with Petrarch.

Other factors have strengthened the principle of continuity and thus undermined the concept of the Renaissance. In the last two generations much of our history—and our most decisive history in the sense of shaping our general views and interpretation of the past—has been written by economic and social historians. Quite properly they see their subject in long spans: the economic historian must see his subject in terms of great tides of economic progress and decline, to which all else is pegged. Further, the Renaissance was a period, if not of economic decline, of stasis, of what Henri Pirenne called "a cessation of all advance." Accordingly, economic historians would tend to discount the notion of a Renaissance and carry a great many of us along with them in their abandonment of it. Parenthetically, one may wonder whether the Renaissance was culturally a great age precisely because an economic peak had just been passed.

Another factor in the barrage of criticism of the Renaissance concept has been historical specialization. An intensive study of the social evolution of one town or city over a period of a generation will lead a scholar to say that "my findings indicate that Renaissance society was not as Burckhardt described it, but . . ." Too often a general statement or conclusion about the Renaissance as a whole will be made on so narrow a basis: the result is distortion and a false perspective. A corollary to the misinterpretation stemming from the specialist in Renaissance studies is the dicta of medievalists: they are authorities on their subject, but with the same mantle they will often make pronouncements on the Renaissance where their knowledge is ordinarily insufficient to warrant such judgments. The result is often deleterious to historical studies. Others, with their eyes on today's dilemmas, have read into the Renaissance whatever they were seeking there.

The concept of the Renaissance having come under such heavy attack, it will be appropriate here to adduce some of the criteria by which one may assert, with a degree of confidence, that there indeed was a Renaissance, an era extending from about 1300 to 1600 that was reasonably homogeneous and that possessed a distinct set of characteristics peculiar to itself.

One thing in our favor is that so many of the men of the time were convinced that they were living in a new and great age. A sense of liberation and exaltation, of achievement and enlightenment, of renewal and revival, pervades the literature of fourteenth- and fifteenth-century Italy, as Hans Baron's books and articles have shown. One wonders why those assertions and opinions are so frequently discounted or ignored, while the claims of scientists and publicists of the later sixteenth and seventeenth centuries—about the uniqueness and superiority of their age and the supreme importance of its achievements—are so readily accepted by historians seeking to establish the "scientific revolution" as the onset of modern times, and to reduce the Renaissance to a side show within an "age of religion."

II

The great duel that racked Italy and Germany in the medieval period had an outcome which neither of the combatants could have anticipated. The real winner was a third party, the communes of the Po Valley and Tuscany. There occurred in Italy a double cancellation of authority when the Hohenstaufen defeat and the dismemberment of the Imperial power were followed by the Papacy's experience of, in Toynbee's words, "the nemesis of victory," namely the Babylonian Captivity and the Great Schism. Hence, by the fourteenth century the communes of Italy, unlike their counterparts north of the Alps, could flourish relatively unhampered by ecclesiastical or imperial pretension. They had been spawned by the economic revival that began in the eleventh, or perhaps as early as the tenth century, which continued until the early fourteenth century, and which was centered in the Mediterranean.

By 1300 Italian society bore little resemblance to that of the feudal age. Because feudalism had never been too thoroughly established in Italy, because some degree of civic life had never died out, and because the economic revival came early and centered in the peninsula, the social transformation of Italy came nearest to being complete. Fully admitting that the bulk of the population—the agricultural peasant and even the urban workers—lived much the same life later as earlier, it is nevertheless true that there emerged several new social categories that were anomalies in the medieval social order. They were the capitalist merchants, entrepreneurs and financiers, the absolute princes and their civil servants, the humanists, and the artists. From them derived the characteristic features of the Renaissance and to them the era owed its distinctive achievements. Thus, the economic revival had created a new social environment in Italy, one that was urban, commercial, and lay, in which neither feudal lord nor ecclesiastical prince was able to set the tone of society or give direction to its affairs. The economic revival of the eleventh through the thirteenth centuries affected all Europe and brought similar social changes in its wake, but north of the Alps the old order managed to preserve itself without much difficulty: there the merchant deferred to the noble lord, lay and ecclesiastical, who continued to dominate and set the tone for transalpine society. Hence the new culture was generated in Italy and from there was carried to the rest of Europe.

III

Renaissance individualism was, in many respects, nothing more than the recognition of, or taking advantage of, the social environment. It is not necessary to assert that individualism was unknown to the Middle Ages or that it was a Renaissance invention. Yet the Renaissance social matrix provided scope for the individual's following his star—or at least following an alternate authority or tradition—as the medieval age, with its sense of one's place and its duties, could not. The new social classes, since they were new, were less bound by tradition and custom. Reference has frequently been made to the individualism that characterized the *devotio moderna* of the Netherlands: it was a lay piety that sought a personal relationship with God and encouraged private judgment. There was also, of course, the individualism of the merchant who deferred to no guild regulations or ecclesiastical prohibitions, and who, as W. K. Ferguson remarked, "stressed the direct communion of man with Mammon."

More important than the citation of examples of individualism, it needs to be said that the development of one's genius and individuality, or the following of one's ambitions, received in the writings of Petrarch an ideological rationale, one which was reinforced by the contagious example of his life. His ideals of *virtù* and *fama* suggest the individualism permitted, or even generated, by Renaissance society. As norms of behavior—even if limited to a minority, as Petrarch and his humanist followers did limit them—*virtù* and *fama* are inconsistent with medieval conceptions of community.

By the end of the fourteenth century, individualism had the force of a social imperative. The trend fundamental to the thought and philosophy of the age, according to Ernst Cassirer, was toward "delimitation and articulation, toward distinction and individuation." The Florentine Platonists and Paduan Aristotelians strengthened individualism, for the two philosophical schools concurred in opposing the Averroist doctrine of the soul's merging, at death, with a great collective over-soul. In this life, it was felt, a man was *made,* not *born.* To be a member of the Renaissance aristocracy of *virtù,* one need not, said Castiglione, be of noble blood. It is education that is decisive: *"Educatio superat omnia"* was a Renaissance motto. For the Renaissance was one of the ages that took—at least until 1520—a Pelagian view of human nature. It was wondrous what man by dint of *virtù, ars,* and *studium* could do, although it was never forgotten how much "Fortune" could undo. In the writings of Pico is to be found one of the most eloquent of all tributes to human powers and potentialities, free and plastic, untrammeled by astrological or other impediments; he marks the increasingly stronger insistence on the principle of the freedom of the will that is central to the philosophy and thought of the Renaissance.

IV

Having introduced a few of the economic and social criteria for positing the existence of the Renaissance, we may turn to the political. One of the most notorious individualists during the Renaissance was the prince. It was the prince who ultimately filled the vacuum created in Italy by the demise of the Empire and the eclipse of the Papacy; the communes, unable in nearly every instance to make municipal institutions work, turned themselves over or fell victim to despotic rulers—whether it was concealed and mild despotism as in the Florence of the Medici or open and brutal as in the Milan of the Visconti. Illegitimate rulers and usurpers, they had to be virtuosos in gaining and staying in power; and cruelty and deceit followed as inevitable corollaries of the origin and character of their rule. So, too, to some extent, did patronage of the arts. North of the Alps the age-old formal political structures had remained intact, with the result that power remained dynastic and legitimate, and political life was less sanguinary. These (significant) differences apart, rulers north and south alike carried on the systematic consolidation and centralization of power, coupling it with territorial acquisitions at the expense of their lesser neighbors. The Renaissance, in fact, saw the creation of the sovereign state, an entity hardly known in the Middle Ages with its congeries of imperial, ecclesiastical, royal, baronial, and municipal interlocking and overlapping political entities. Leviathan did not receive its name, nor the legal code, international law, by which it was to be guided in its relations with others like itself, until the seventeenth century; but the process of consolidation and centralization under prince or king, employing those modern instruments of state— the professional army and corps of civil servants—went on apace in the fourteenth and fifteenth centuries. By the reign of Pope Sixtus IV, 1471-1484, the Papacy had re-established its position in Italy, with the outcome that by 1500 the peninsula was parcelled out among the five giants: Milan, Venice, Florence, the Papal States, and the Kingdom of Naples and Sicily. Outside of Italy similar steps were being taken by Ferdinand and Isabella in Spain, Edward IV and the Tudors in England, Charles VII and Louis XI in France, and the greater princes of Germany. A concomitant development was the appearance of resident ambassadors and all the machinery of diplomacy, that is, the beginnings of that pattern of international relations which was fully evolved by the end of the Thirty Years' War. Internally, attempts were made—not always successful, but nowhere wholly unsuccessful— to establish the *Corpus Juris Civilis* as the law of the land. In the political realm, as elsewhere, one notices close parallels among the various states of Europe, although Italy is almost always in the vanguard by a considerable margin.

V

Another lineament of the Renaissance, again suggesting that it was a distinct and self-contained age, was the protracted decline of the ecumenical authority of the Papacy and the Church. That decline was closely related to the political evolution just referred to, for one of the first things the prince would wish to subsume under his indivisible sovereignty was, as he took it to be, his slice of the international Church. By the early sixteenth century the kings of France and Spain were administrative heads of the Church in their realms as much as Henry VIII ever hoped to be in his. Quarrels between kings and popes over investiture, ecclesiastical courts, revenues and similar matters had a long history before the Renaissance. Such struggles had gone on throughout the Middle Ages. But after 1300 it was decidedly the kings who were winning out. They succeeded, for example, in siphoning off more and more revenues of the Church with the result that the magnificent ecclesiastical structures of the late fifteenth and sixteenth centuries were often paid for by selling church lands, and by more questionable financial expedients. It would be an exaggeration to say that the Church by 1500 had fallen into desperate financial straits, but it certainly had experienced a sharp diminution of revenues in the face of mounting expenses.

What struck contemporaries, however, was the moral decline of the Papacy and the clergy of Europe. The Papacy had become just another Italian princeling long before Machiavelli stated the fact outright. The Avignonese papacy, in the shadow of France, had forfeited much of its moral sway over the minds and hearts of Christians: jobbery in ecclesiastical offices became so notorious that, it was said, a mule, with the right request hanging from its neck and enough gold in its pack, could procure a bishopric. The wealth, sensuality and degradation of individual prelates and friars called forth a chorus of criticism and a literature of mockery which swelled to new proportions in the time of the Great Schism, when the two (and for a time three) popes hurled anathemas at each other and divided Christendom into two ecclesiastical camps.

The extreme centralism of the papal monarchy joined to the debacles of the Papacy in the fourteenth century generated the reform program known as the Conciliar Movement. It took the form of a constitutional struggle within the Church that had as its aims the creation of a constitutional papal monarchy to be controlled through frequent Church councils, and "the reform of the Church in head and members." The conciliarists did succeed finally in ending the schism when Martin V was elevated; but he led the Church into the ways of lavish patronage of the arts and learning and along the path of worldly splendor. He was in fact the first of the Renaissance Popes and no reformer at all. After having stimulated a considerable ferment over the governance of the Church and the relationship of secular and ecclesiastical authority, the Conciliar Movement was defeated by the Papacy it helped revive and by its own excesses. The attempt to reform abuses, with some few exceptions such as that of Cardinal Nicholas of Cusa in his diocese of Brixen, came to nothing. There appeared those warrior-nepotist popes from Sixtus IV to Julius II who did much to preserve the Papacy as a temporal power in the jungle of Italian wars and politics, but nothing—or worse—to restore the spiritual character of their office. For the rest of the sixteenth century, and in a more fundamental sense, the Papacy and the Church were on the defensive.

Another inescapable feature of the religious life of the age is the number and tenacity of heresies: Wycliffe and Lollardy, Hus, Beguines and Beghards, Flagellants, Guglielmites, Dolcinists, Sagerellists, Luciferans—the list is so long as to make those of the sixteenth century seem a continuation of a persistent phenomenon. One of the most hateful heretics in the view of the popes was Marsilius of Padua, who initiated no popular movement, but whose Defensor Pacis of 1324 struck at the roots of all papal and ecclesiastical authority. That protagonist of the laity and of the secular state denied every power to the priesthood except transubstantiation: priests have no power to remit sin; papal headship of the Church has no historical, legal or Biblical basis; general councils should include laymen and are superior to the Pope; all power derives from the people; unorthodox religious views ought to be tolerated—the priesthood has the right neither to judge nor to punish heretics, for each man is answerable to Christ alone. Expressions of such individualism and laicism are to be found in religious movements throughout the Renaissance, and one of the most striking examples is the *devotio moderna* of the Netherlands and northern France. Such new religious associations as the Brethren of the Common Life remained within the pale of orthodoxy; yet by their attachment to a personal, mystical, lay and Bible-reading form of piety, they underscore the view that the religious life of Europe was departing from its age-old forms.

VI

Another criterion for the existence of the Renaissance as a coherent period of European history is the development of science. The history of science has come into its own in the last generation, and part of that new interest has been an examination of science in the Renaissance. Frequently, Renaissance men have been found deficient as scientists, and their deficiencies have proved to be one of the most devastating weapons in the hands of anti-Renaissance scholars. Two scholars in particular—the late George Sarton and Lynn Thorndike—have found not merely that scientific advance in the fourteenth and fifteenth centuries failed to maintain the pace of the twelfth and thirteenth centuries, but that the age that began with Petrarch was one of abrupt decline in the sciences and retrogression in civilization generally. Blamed was the bookish mentality of the humanists who depended on antiquity and their sacrosanct classical texts instead of looking to experiment and the observation of physical objects and phenomena.

In the case of Sarton at least, the wheel has come round full circle. In 1929 he could thump the Renaissance as the triumph of style over knowledge, truth and morality, and assert that its achievement of beauty was a "sham." By 1953 he thought otherwise. No longer a trough between two lofty peaks, Renaissance science was now seen as marking a new thrust forward. He went so far as to speak of Renaissance achievements as "revolutionary."

This rejuvenation of Renaissance science—and thereby to a considerable extent of the Renaissance as a whole—owed much to the research completed by the 1950's. It was now seen that the greatest barrier to scientific progress, viz., the divorce between theoretical and applied science, or better, between theoretical scientists and practical artisans and technicians, was overcome in the Renaissance. Further, it has been found that nonscientists, particularly artists and craftsmen, contributed much to science and technology; among numerous inventions by persons who were little more than handymen may be mentioned the printing press, while specific fields of inquiry, e.g. zoology, botany, anatomy, owe much—even their very foundations—to artists like Leonardo and Dürer. Still more fundamental to the progress of science was the reorientation of outlook that may be traced in the history of thought and philosophy from Nicholas of Cusa to Johannes Kepler: if the haunted-house view of nature prevalent in the Middle Ages (despite the rationalizing tendency of Thomism) was not banished forever by 1600, without doubt there had been born a new concept of nature which postulated forces that were operative in nature, that were rational, proportional, and immanent.

As for the humanists, they seem now not to have been so antiscientific as earlier thought. If their deference to the authority of the ancients was an obstacle, their enthusiasm for lost manuscripts brought to light additional authors and treatises, especially from the Greek corpus, which supplemented and which often were not consistent in significant matters with those long known. This wider span of authorities and the differences among them helped to undermine the authority of the ancients and thus to open the way to new observation and experiment. Moreover, the humanists provided better texts and a method for attaining a more accurate reading of them. Their revival of Plato was conducive to the explanation of natural phenomena in simple and mathematical terms. As for Aristotle having so stultifying an effect upon the march of science, it has been shown that out of a "constructive criticism" of the Aristotelian texts at the University of Padua there developed the method of formulating a hypothesis and of demonstrating its proof, i.e., the development of the scientific method. To this achievement Galileo was profoundly indebted; indeed, as John Herman Randall, Jr., has said, "the whole literature of scientific method in the seventeenth century is a series of footnotes to Aristotle."

Thus, while no complete break with medieval science is evident, there are enough new beginnings, innovations and achievements to justify our speaking of a distinct phase in the history of science, and insisting upon its place in the larger cultural complex, the Renaissance itself. We may go further and say that Zabarella of the school of Padua was the emancipator of natural science in precisely the same sense that Machiavelli was of political science.

VII

Reference was made above to the classical revival. This has been an intrinsic part of the concept of the Renaissance, at least since Georg Voigt's great work *The Revival of Classical Antiquity, or the First Century of Humanism*, 1859. To some, Renaissance and classical revival are synonymous, but, as one scholar remarked in a humorous essay, "others snort and cite Thorndike on the superficiality of Italian Neo-Platonism, reel off a list of classical authors known continuously in Western Europe, and comment on the Greek studies of the Arabs in Spain." From the enormous amount of work done on the classical heritage, it is now abundantly clear that the medieval classicist's use of the ancient authors was no more than the adaptation of materials suitable for Christian ends. Einhard, for example, pillaged Suetonius of whole phrases for his biography of a Christian ruler in the same spirit that builders quarried ancient ruins. The humanists approached piously, not as wreckers. They had harsh words for such a one as Pope Nicholas V, who ordered Roman antiquities swept aside to make way for new structures. They sought to adopt as their own the antique way of life, the style, and the values that were set like so many precious jewels in the classical corpus of literature. Ancient literature commended itself to Petrarch and his followers for much the same reason that the *Corpus Juris Civilis* had commended itself to Irnerius and the revivers of Roman law in twelfth-century Bologna: Roman jurisprudence was relevant to a social context that was neither feudal nor ecclesiastical, but urban, commercial and lay. So too, if more intensely, Petrarch found in the classics a mirror to hold up to his own age and an answering chord to his own consciousness. It is no exaggeration, then, to claim that the stage of the classical revival that began with Petrarch was distinct in character and significance from the medieval series of revivals; for with the Renaissance there came, in the larger sense, the end of that practically complete cultural allegiance, as we may call it, of even the most powerful and original minds to the Church and the Christian faith, an allegiance that had lasted a millennium. The humanist pursuit of antique civilization as an ideal and model for imitation in many aspects of life, and as a rival in significant ways of Christian civilization, was peculiar to the Renaissance and important in conferring upon the age a special character and homogeneity that mark it off from its predecessor and successor.

VIII

The history of the visual arts is too vast a subject to treat here except briefly. Suffice it to say that the marvelous flowering of the arts—which no student of the period has ever denied—was made possible, but not determined, by the economic revival to which reference was made earlier. Merchants and bankers furnished the cash, but also what is equally indispensable to any flourishing of the arts, intelligent patronage.

It has been remarked that Renaissance art was anthropometric and anthropomorphic, and thus clearly identified with classical art and clearly distinguished from Gothic forms. Man was the measure of all things artistic; art was in the image of man. In his structures, for example, the architect sought to relate the units to each other and to the whole organically, as are the parts of the human body. The architect also assumed that there was a fundamental unit of measure or "module" for man and all natural forms; every dimension of a given man was thought to be proportionate to the module. Hence, in his buildings the architect employed the module, the diameter of a column or pilaster, of which every length in the structure was an exact multiple or division. This Neo-Platonic conception was carried even to the point of town planning, e.g. in the width of streets, in the dimensions of gardens and public squares, and in the design of a city's walls. Truly the Renaissance architect lived in, and dreamed of, a city of men; so too his colleagues in the sister arts.

Artist nowadays is a magical word. The artist is a kind of oracle in our culture. Such he has been since the Renaissance, when there occurred, with regard to the place of the artist in society, one of the most significant transformations. Whereas in the medieval period the artist was no more than a craftsman who had his place in the appropriate guild and performed his task like any other artisan, he is now regarded as one of a special breed of mankind, those who have the genius to create or invent works of truth and beauty that awe and inspire, and that constitute collectively "a criticism of life." For a medieval architect to think himself a creator would have been to blaspheme, to think himself a genius would have been to be sinfully wanting in humility. Whatever he managed to do was by the grace of God, as were the accomplishments of other producers, whether intellectual, artistic or manual. But in the Renaissance, man occupied a different place in the cosmos. He, according to Pico, was still God's creature, but in the celebrated *Oration on the Dignity of Man,* Pico has God speak to the progenitor of the human race in the following terms:

> Neither a fixed abode nor a form that is thine alone nor any function peculiar to thyself have we given thee, Adam, to the end that according to thy longing and according to thy judgment thou mayest have and possess what abode, what form, and what functions thou thyself shalt desire. The nature of all other beings is limited and constrained within the bounds of laws prescribed by Us. Thou, constrained by no limits, in accordance with thine own free will, in whose hand We have placed thee, shalt ordain for thyself the limits of thy nature. We have set thee at the world's center that thou mayest from thence more easily observe whatever is in the world. We have made thee neither of heaven nor of earth, neither mortal nor immortal, so that with freedom of choice and with honor, as thou the maker and molder of thyself, thou mayest fashion thyself in whatever shape thou shalt prefer. Thou shalt have the power to degenerate into the lower forms of life, which are brutish. Thou shalt have the power, out of thy soul's judgment, to be reborn into the higher forms, which are divine.

Man, too, was a creator. It is not surprising, then, that Michelangelo should be hailed as "the divine one" or that the Holy Roman Emperor Charles V should stoop to retrieve the brush of his court painter, Titian. The artist had left the guild to join the elite. Our conceptions of the artist, originality, creation, genius—in a word, our theories of the arts—derive directly from the Renaissance; in its notion of the artist and the role of the arts, the Renaissance makes a clear contrast with the Middle Ages.

IX

What is said above about the visual arts and the new position enjoyed by the artist applies to the field of music. Moreover, our contention that the Renaissance existed, that it was an especially brilliant and creative age must be borne in upon anyone who studies its music. Renaissance music has been studied diligently and often profoundly, yet the general historian of the age has, with very few exceptions, taken no notice of the findings of the specialists. It is often pointed out, for example, that Castiglione required manifold musical accomplishments of his Courtier; it is not said, however, that the disposition to experiment, to set aside the rules and start afresh in music was very strong in the Renaissance and that the outcome was an age of monumental achievements.

It is not possible to credit the Renaissance with the invention of polyphony, but certainly the perfection of that form did come in the Renaissance; more important, harmony as a science—and a necessary science for the composer of polyphonic music who will do something more than lay his voices one over the other— was a Renaissance creation. Others were polyphonic choral singing and the antiphonal use of two or more choruses, the modern system of notation, and the stops for the organ—one of many improvements and inventions of instruments which could be mentioned. Instrumental music came into its own during the Renaissance, in part, owing to these inventions; by the end of the sixteenth century the violin made its appearance, so too the first music especially for violin, the *Sonatas* of 1587 by Andrea Gabrieli. That astonishingly versatile genius Leonardo was an accomplished musician; he also addressed himself to the improvement of the lute and the violin's parent, the viol.

That individualism we have noted in the Renaissance may be traced in the field of music also: the virtuoso was born of the Renaissance. Other developments may be mentioned: the expansion of the musical range from less than three to nearly five octaves, and the discovery and exploitation by some musical Columbus of the bass voice. Numbered among new musical forms were the oratorio and, above all, the opera.

The invention of the opera by the Camerata group at Florence suggests another important aspect of Renaissance music. It has frequently been pointed out that no ancient music survived and, therefore, that Renaissance music was untouched by the classical revival. If the Renaissance had no body of ancient music, it did have a corpus of ancient writing—literary, philosophical, theoretical—on music that included Plato and Aristotle, Lasus of Hermione, Aristoxenus of Tarentum, and various references to the Pythagoreans.

The Camerati sought to create a dramatic form based on the Greek drama; Greek music was monodic, and was subordinate to and inseparable from the poetry (and dance) of the drama. Hence the Camerata reaction against the polyphonists, "Goths" as the Camerati dubbed them: polyphonic music obscured the poetry. Out of their efforts to purge away that obscuration came the recitative—in effect the aria—based upon the Greek melodic declamation. So was born the *"dramma per musica"* or opera. Ballet also had classical inspiration. Enough has been said to demonstrate the power for creation of the classical tradition and that the period of the Renaissance was a truly great age in the history of music; perhaps it was the greatest of all.

X

One other aspect of the period merits our notice as an indication of the uniformity and coherence of the Renaissance, viz., the dispersion of the new culture from Italy to the rest of Europe from about 1490 on. The 1490's would seem to be a rather late date, since by 1400 it was clear that northern Europe was falling behind Italy in art and learning, while not long after the turn of the century much excitement was generated by Italian achievements. Yet until well into the fifteenth century France retained her wonted intellectual and cultural hegemony over northern and western Europe, and aside from some not very important anticipations, it was not until the end of the century that northerners sought in earnest to ransack the Italian treasure house. The direct contact with Italy initiated by the French invasion of 1494 was, of course, of the first importance, but other considerations seem to have been of at least equal moment.

Reference has already been made to the economic revival and the social transformation it wrought in Italy and, to a lesser extent, in transalpine Europe. By the fourteenth century in Italy, a merchant oligarch class had gained economic and political predominance, in response to which a new urban, lay and increasingly secular culture arose, bringing with it new standards and ideas in conduct, education, government and, above all, in the arts and scholarship. In northern Europe the feudal nobility and the ecclesiastical community were not so completely displaced. On the contrary, the first two estates with the monarchy still dominated society and gave direction to practically every aspect of its life until the sixteenth century. Hence, the slowness with which the new culture of Italy found acceptance: an urban, lay, quasi-pagan culture could have little appeal in the north. Transalpine scholars were not attracted by the ideal of a return to antiquity, but rather were preoccupied with the creation of a more perfect Christian society. The profoundly ethical character of the northern Renaissance, once it began, is well known. It was only when the new culture took on a decidedly religious character that it became attractive to northern scholars and patrons; "hence the key position," as Hans Baron has said, "of Florentine Neoplatonism, the phase of the Italian development in which humanistic culture, more than any other, seemed capable of providing a religious-motivated approach to antiquity and a devout philosophy of life." The Florentine pilgrimages of Colet, Lefèbvre d'Étaples, Reuchlin, and others, and the reverence prevalent in the north for Ficino and Pico, confirm this assertion.

Thus, the appeal for the north of the new learning was chiefly that of an improved educational instrument. A more perfect Christian society—as Colet was the first to see—could best be attained by education; that is, education which, first, utilized the classics for its curriculum in order to acquire that precision of thought and expression which only the classics could bestow, and, second, imparted a true knowledge of the Bible and of the Latin and Greek Fathers by following the humanist canons of history, philology and textual criticism—in a word, the *pietas litterata*. Once the educational possibilities of the new culture were recognized, northerners rushed to appropriate Italy's treasures; by 1520 that movement had reached high tide; by the end of the century it was of prime importance for the young artist, scholar, musician, man of letters, or gentleman to sojourn in Italy.

In claiming the spread of the new culture from Italy as support for our contention of the unity and coherence of the Renaissance epoch, there is no intention to deny considerable diversity among the countries of Europe in their reception of the new dispensation. Speaking of England, E. F. Jacob has noted "the gentle, religious and on the whole rather unadventurous humanism of these islands, free from the asperities evinced by the more ruthless and thorough-going Italian minds; a humanism loath to break entirely with the Middle Ages." By contrast, the humanism of Germany was intent, in certain areas, upon making such a break. Additional variation may be found for other areas, but it is variation within uniformity.

XI

Finally, as to the relation of the Renaissance to the Reformation and the Counter Reformation: it will be seen that the *Dictionary* contains numerous entries pertaining to the two great religious movements of the sixteenth century. Without the Renaissance there would in all probability have been no Reformation, although, in the judgment of the present author, the Reformation was essentially antithetical to the Renaissance; if the Reformation grew out of the Renaissance, it soon diverged from it and became a mass movement. Goethe complained, it is worthwhile to recall, that Luther and Calvin introduced the mob into the citadel where they should have feared to tread.

The German canon and humanist scholar, Rufus Mutianus, is a perfect symbol of the relation of Renaissance and Reformation. He was the leader of the circle of German humanists that produced the celebrated *Epistles of Obscure Men,* had been the school chum of Erasmus at Deventer, was the friend of Pico, and had taken his law degree at Bologna; upon his return from Italy he dedicated himself to "God and the Saints and the study of all Antiquity." Inscribed above his scholar's door was *Beata Tranquillitas.* But it was all pillaged and overthrown when a Lutheran mob shattered his *tranquillitas* in 1524. Indeed, the Reformation and Counter Reformation together so shackled the expansive spirit of the Renaissance that, although much that survives into the seventeenth century is of the Renaissance in origin and character, it is only broken fragments of the whole that survive. The fragments become part of a new synthesis, the Baroque.

The chilling history of the Counter-Reformation Papacy, Inquisition, and Index is well known, as is the triumph of the spirit of reaction at the Council of Trent. It may be added here that Henry VIII—at an earlier date—did as much as he could to crush the Renaissance flowering in England. The King imprisoned Polydore Vergil, decapitated More, Fisher, and Surrey, sent Vives to prison and finally let him go to the Continent, where Erasmus felt it better to stay after several visits to England. There is little more to Henry's credit than that he had one of the most complete collections of musical instruments in Europe, although in the writings of such scholars as Douglas Bush and Fritz Caspari a better case is being built up for the King, e.g., as the founder of many educational institutions to accommodate the new learning. Nevertheless, he—and the two Lord Protectors and Mary after him—so arrested the cultural life of England that it did not recover until well into Elizabeth's reign. With so chequered a history in England as elsewhere, it is a wonder that the Renaissance lasted as long as it did. At any rate, it is to the immortal glory of the Renaissance that never have art, literature, scholarship and learning flourished more or been more highly esteemed than then.

A word of acknowledgment and gratitude is due to my colleagues, Harold E. Hazelton and Brother Patrick Stephen, F.S.C., for their penetrating criticisms and helpful advice, and to Ernest V. Speranza for assistance on Spanish entries; to Mrs. Rose Morse of Philosophical Library for her kindness and assistance; and, not least of all, to my wife Esperanza and son Manfred for their assistance in proofreading and for their patience.

FREDERICK M. SCHWEITZER
Department of History
Manhattan College

DICTIONARY
OF THE
RENAISSANCE

A

AACHEN, HANS VON
(1552-1615). German artist. Court painter to Emperor Rudolph II. Executed Biblical and mythological pictures, portraits.

AANDE
A term meaning *breath*. Used in the fifteenth century.

ABAD, ALONSO
Born c. 1526. Spanish conquistador. Led an expedition to Argentina. Ruler of Santiago.

ABBATE, NICCOLO DEL
(1509-1571). Painter. Lived at Fontainebleau from 1552. Executed religious and mythological murals.

ABBEY-LUBBER
A term of contempt used by anti-Catholics in the sixteenth century. In *The Burnynge of Paules Church* (1563) the expression is explained as *one who was idle, well fed, a loiterer, disinclined to work.*

ABBOT, GEORGE
(1562-1633). Archbishop of Canterbury. Collaborated in translation of New Testament in King James version of the Bible. As a Puritan he came into conflict with the king.

ABECEDARY
An alphabet book, a primer. In use during the fifteenth and sixteenth centuries and later.

1

ABELIN, JOHANN PHILIPP
(died c. 1637). German historian. Projected world history entitled *Theatrum Europaeum.*

ABELL, THOMAS
(executed 1540). English priest and chaplain to Catherine of Aragon. Author of *Invicta Veritas* published in 1533. Opposed Henry VIII's ecclesiastical claims and the divorce of Queen Catherine; was imprisoned in the Tower, executed for treason, beatified in 1886.

ABENCERRAJE Y LA HERMOSA JARIFA
Spanish romantic narrative, anonymous, of early sixteenth century. Theme derived from Moorish cycle dealing with events c. 1485. Protagonists are Abindarráez, Moor: his bride Jarifa: Spanish knight Narváez. This tale constitutes beginning of Spanish *novela.*

ABINGDON SCHOOL
In Berkshire, England. English public school. Founded in pre-Norman times. Re-endowed by John Roysse in 1563.

ABJECT
As a noun, this term means *a servile person, an outcast.* Shakespeare, in *Richard III,* mentions *the Queen's abjects.*

ABOAB, ISAAC
(1433-1493). Spanish rabbi. Author of Biblical commentaries. Teacher of Isaac Abravanel. He led a delegation of eminent Spanish Jews to King John II of Portugal to negotiate an agreement by which they should be allowed to settle in Portugal; this was at the time when Ferdinand and Isabella began the expulsion of Jews, 1492.

ABOLETE
Obsolete. The term occurs in John Skelton's *Why come ye not to courte?* (1522): "practyse such abolete sciens."

ABRAHAM DE BALMES
(died c. 1523). Italian Jewish scholar. Physician to Cardinal Grimini in Padua. Author of a grammar. Translated into Latin Aristotle's *Posterior Analytics:* published in 1520. Translated Averroës from Hebrew into Latin and scientific treatises in Arabic into Latin. Wrote on medical subjects. Lectured on philosophy at Padua.

2

ABRAHAM DE LUNEL

Sixteenth century. Jewish scholar and philologist of Provence. Embraced Christianity and thus was able to become professor of Hebrew at Avignon.

ABRAVANEL, ISAAC

(1437-1508). Spanish Jew, he was a theologian, Biblical commentator, and financier, attached to the Court of Alfonso V of Portugal. Forced to flee from Portugal to Spain and then to Naples, where he entered the royal service. Banished by French rulers. Fled to Venice, where he remained until his death. Buried in Padua. Author of *Wells of Salvation, The Salvation of the Anointed, Proclaiming Salvation.*

ABRAVANEL, JUDAH

(c. 1460-1530). Portuguese physician and scholar. Born in Lisbon: died in Venice. Lived in contact with three cultures: Jewish, Spanish, Italian. Together with father, Isaac Abravanel, fled in 1483 from Portugal to Spain: then, in 1492, to Italy. Practiced medicine: interested in philosophy, mathematics, astronomy. Lectured at Universities of Naples and Rome. Thought to have been a friend of Pico della Mirandola. Chief work: *Dialoghi di Amore.* Translated into Hebrew, Latin, French, Spanish, English, it was a landmark in the history of aesthetics: important contribution to metaphysics and ethics; it was a mixture of Jewish teachings and Neo-Platonic mysticism, and as such had a wide influence, e.g., upon Camoens and Cervantes.

ABREU, DIEGO DE

(died 1553). Spanish conquistador. Associated with the Rio de la Plata.

ABSEY BOOK

A hornbook. A term used by Shakespeare in *King John* (1596): "And then comes answer like an absey-book."

ABSONISM

Incongruity in the use of language. Thomas Nashe, in *Strange News* (1592): "Everie third line hath some of this over-rackt absonisme."

ACADEMIA DE LOS NOCTURNOS

Valencian literary academy (1591-1594). Guillén de Castro

3

(1569-1631) revived Academy under name of Montaneses del Parnaso: 1616.

ACADEMIES
In the fifteenth century academies were established as follows: At Ravenna: Informi. At Faenza: Smarriti. At Perugia: Insensati. At Urbino: Assorditi. At Naples: Sereni, Ardenti, Incogniti. At Florence: Platonic. At Rome: the Sapienza.

ACADEMY
Inspired by Plato's Academy, there were a great many academies founded in the fifteenth and sixteenth centuries, of which Ficino's Platonic Academy at Florence was the most famous. A new type of institution for a new era, the academies were half literary club and half learned society; they were especially important for the study and diffusion of Platonism. Dedicated to the idea of the contemplative life, they resembled the religious associations of laymen that gave rise to the *Devotio Moderna* in France and the Lowlands, only with classical scholarship and philosophy added to religious interests. The Venetian Academy, associated with Aldus Manutius, was a center for the study of Greek literature, that of Rome for archaelogy. The Florentine Camerata circle, the center where opera was created, was essentially an academy; Italian drama also was fostered by the academies. In France there were similar institutions, one developing into the *Collège de France;* the *Pléiade* was an outgrowth of Baïf's foundation of the *académie de poesie et musique.* In Germany there were many similar bodies, known as sodalities.

Academies of art fall into two distinct groups. Studio academies were gatherings of mature and beginning artists in a private workshop for the purpose of drawing after sculptural or living models. Such was the Academy of B. Bandinelli in 1531, the earliest artistic enterprise known under the name of academy: also the Academy of Carracci in Bologna, after 1590.

Official academies differed from private academies in their wider aims and their greater pretensions. They were designed to raise the level of medieval craftsmen to that of the creative artist by freeing him from the jurisdiction of the guilds. The protection of the monarch was invoked: the result often being the subservience of the artist to the Crown.

The pedagogical aim of the academy came gradually to the

fore. In medieval times, the artist had received his elementary education in the *bottega,* his master's workshop.

All official academies trace their origin back to the *Accademia del Disegno,* founded in 1563 by Giorgio Vasari. Its immediate successor was the *Accademia di San Luca* in Rome, established in 1593.

ACADEMY OF GENEVA
Pedagogical institution founded by John Calvin in 1559. Seminary for prospective Protestant ministers. Also offered public lectures in Greek, Hebrew, philosophy, theology.

ACADEMY OF NAPLES
Established during reign of Alfonso of Aragon (1442-1458). The guiding spirit was Antonio of Palermo, called Beccadelli (1394-1471). Later, academy was organized as club.

ACCADEMIA DEI LINCEI
This Italian academy was founded in 1609.

ACCADEMIA DELLA CRUSCA
An Italian academy founded in 1582.

ACCADEMIA PLATONICA
Italian academy founded in Florence: 1470. Inspired by Plato's Academy.

ACCIAIUOLI, DONATO
(1428-1478): Italian humanist scholar of Florence. Statesman and diplomat. Author of biographies of Scipio, Hannibal, Charlemagne. Translated Bruni's history of Florence into Italian.

ACCOLTI, BENEDICTUS
(c. 1415-c. 1466): Italian humanist historian and jurist. Chancellor of Republic of Florence. Wrote a Latin account of First Crusade and Conquest of Jerusalem: source for Tasso's *Jerusalem Delivered.*

ACCOLTI, BERNARDO
(1465-1536): Italian poet. Noted for reciting extempore verses. He enjoyed a great reputation in his day and a stipend from Pope Leo X.

ACCORAMBONI, VITTORIA
(1557-1585): An Italian Helen of Troy. Noted for her beauty

and unscrupulousness. Assassinated. She appears in the dramatist John Webster's play *Vittoria Accoramboni or The White Devil*: published in 1612.

ACHILLINI, ALESSANDRO
(1463-1518): Italian physician, anatomist. He taught at Bologna and Padua. Author of *Humani Corporis Anatomia*: published in 1516. Also wrote *Annotationes Anatomiae*. He was a moderate Averroist in philosophy and the opponent of Pomponazzi.

ACIDALIUS, VALENS
(1567-1595): German humanist scholar and philologist. Neo-Latin poet. He wrote commentaries on classical authors, including Tacitus and Plautus. He had studied in Italy.

ACONZIO, JACOPO
(c. 1492-c. 1565): Italian writer. Spent many years in England. Author of *The Stratagems of Satan;* intended to reconcile all Christian sects, it was dedicated to Queen Elizabeth. In addition to theology he also wrote on philosophy and law.

ACOSTA, CRISTOVAL D'
Sixteenth century. Spanish Jesuit. Royal physician to hospital of Cochin, China. Author of five books, among them *Tratado de las Drogas Medicinas de las Indias*: published in 1575.

ACOSTA, JOSÉ DE
(1539-1600): Spanish Jesuit missionary, poet, cosmologist, historian; brother of the above. Author of *De Natura Novi Orbis, Historia natural y moral de las Indias,* a seminal work, and a great many catechetical works.

ACOSTA, URIEL
(1585-1647): Born in Portugal, of Marrano descent; educated in the Catholic tradition, he decided to enter the priesthood. Tortured by doubts, however, he fled to Holland. Embraced Judaism but defied Jewish orthodoxy. Banished repeatedly: ostracized for seven years. Committed suicide. Subject of many novels and dramas. Wrote autobiography: *Exemplar Humanae Vitae,* a fascinating human document.

ACT OF SIX ARTICLES
This act, pushed through Parliament in 1539 by Henry VIII, was

called by Protestants *The Whip with Six Strings.* It reaffirmed transubstantiation, auricular confession, communion in one kind, clerical celibacy, and also provided the death penalty for denial of these doctrines as heresy; replaced papal by royal leadership of the church, failure to recognize which was punishable by death as treason.

ACT OF SUPREMACY, ENGLISH
An act of Parliament that named the king and his successors Protector and sole Supreme Head of the Church and Clergy of England. This act was the most radical step taken by Henry VIII in the English Reformation. It was promulgated in 1534.

ACTS OF UNIFORMITY
Promulgated in 1549: required Prayer Book acceptance by subjects of King Edward VI of England.

Promulgated in 1552. Required acceptance of second Prayer Book, more distinctly Protestant than the first, by subjects of Edward VI.

Promulgated in 1559. Made acceptance of revised Prayer Book obligatory on subjects of Queen Elizabeth I. The Act confirmed England's place on the side of the Reformation in Europe.

ACUÑA, HERNANDO DE
(c. 1500-1580): Spanish diplomat, poet, and soldier. Translated from French into Spanish *Le Chevalier Délibéré*, poem by Olivier de la Marche, as well as other works on chivalry, the subject of much of his own poetry.

ADAM, DANIEL
(1545-1599): Czech historian of Prague, where he was professor. Author of *Historical Calendar*, of an historical dictionary, and a chronicle of the city of Prague.

ADAMS, WILL
(c. 1575-1620): English navigator. First Englishman to visit Japan. Settled, married in Japan. Kept by Japanese as expert shipwright, navigator, and mathematician. Sailed to Cochin China, Siam to promote trade. His *Letters* give an interesting account of an early Westerner seeking to introduce Western technology to the Orient.

ADAM VON FULDA
(born c. 1450): German musicologist and Franciscan monk. Wrote *De Musica:* published in 1490. He composed motets.

ADDLED PARLIAMENT
In James I's reign, this was his second Parliament. It sat from April 5 to June 7, 1614 and was dissolved without achieving any legislation. So called because of its violent quarrels with the king over the royal prerogative.

ADELPHUS, JOHANNES
Sixteenth century. Also known as Mueling. Physician attached to the circle of Strassburg humanists whose leader was Sebastian Brant. Translated Ficino. Edited medical literature. Compiled facetious stories. Produced historical work on the Emperor Frederick I Barbarossa.

ADIAPHORISTIC CONTROVERSY
Seventeenth century debate arising out of the Augsburg Interim. Melanchthon had accepted the Interim as regards things *indifferent:* adiaphora.

ADMIRALTY
The British Admiralty was founded in London in 1512 by Henry VIII, the real founder of the Royal Navy.

ADMIRALTY ISLANDS
In the Bismarck Archipelago, in the Southwest Pacific Ocean. Discovered by Dutch in 1616.

ADMONET NOS
A Bull issued by Pope Pius V in 1567. The Bull opposed nepotism.

ADORNMENT
The Renaissance woman favored blond hair or used false hair made of silk. Beautifying means in vogue were abundant: waters, powders, paints, unguents, plasters—for teeth, cheeks, eyelids. All kinds of exotic and concocted perfumes were put under contribution by ladies of the courts, matrons, and all women involved in social activities. Also cleanliness was demanded, both personally and domestically. As an epithet of contempt and barbarism, the term *Germanic* was in common use; it could mean anything from unclean to uncultured.

ADRETS, BARON DES, FRANÇOIS DE BEAUMONT
(1513-1587): French soldier. Notorious for cruelty. Abjured Huguenot faith. Made war upon Protestants during the brutal civil and religious wars in France.

ADRIAN CASTELLENSIS
(died c. 1518): Author of *True Philosophy:* published in 1507. Bishop of Hereford, England.

ADRIANI, GIOVANNI BATTISTA
(1513-1579): Italian statesman of Florence, secretary to the Republic of 1527-30. Author of a history covering the years from 1536 to 1574, written while he was professor of rhetoric at Florence; he also wrote an account of ancient painting.

ADURE
Burn up. Used in the fifteenth century. The past participle, adjusted, was used in the sense of dried up: especially in relation to the four humors of the body.

A. E. I. O. U.
Anagram of Emperor Frederick III (1415-1493): *Austriae est imperare orbi universo: It is the fate of Austria to rule the world.*

AERTZEN, PETER
(c. 1509-c. 1575): Called *Lange Pier*, "Long Pete." Dutch artist of Amsterdam. Noted for religious paintings and scenes of rustic life.

AFONSO DA PAIVA
Portuguese explorer. On the basis of the intelligence about Prester John brought back by Afonso de Aveiro, he was sent out to reach the famous king of legend via the Mediterranean and Egypt, where he died. His companion, Covilhan, wrote an important account of the trip, (important because his reportings were drawn upon in planning the voyage of Vasco da Gama).

AFONSO DE AVEIRO
Fifteenth century. Portuguese traveler. Founded a factory in Guinea, at Benin, in 1486, where he heard from the natives of a great king whom he and the Portuguese took to be Prester John. This report stimulated King John II to send out the expeditions of Afonso da Paiva and Vasco da Gama.

AGARIC

A tree fungus. In Renaissance pharmacy, 'female agaric' was widely used as a cathartic, while the 'male agaric' was used as a styptic to coagulate blood.

AGEMATE

A person of the same age. Stanyhurst, in the *Aeneis* (1583): "My sire his agemate."

AGNADELLO, BATTLE OF

In 1509 the Venetians were defeated by the forces of the League of Cambrai, the Emperor Maximilian I and Louis XII of France at this battle. The Venetians lost all their possessions on the mainland for a short time.

AGNESE, BATTISTA

Sixteenth century. Italian cartographer of Genoa. Produced colorful and artistic atlases of Atlantic Ocean, Pacific, Indian, the best of his day; also chart of planetary system. *Battista Agnese fecit Venetiis* identifies his work.

AGNOLO, BACCIO D'

(1462-1543): Florentine sculptor and architect. Designed the Campanile of San Spirito in Florence. Also villas, palazzos; carved church decorations. He had studied in Rome and came under the influence of Raphael and Bramante.

AGORE-BLOOD

Dripping with clotting blood. In North's translation of Plutarch's *Lives* (1580): "rivers running all agore-blood."

AGOSTINI, PAOLO

(1593-1629): Italian musician. Conductor in St. Peter's, Rome. Composed sacred music, *Agnus Dei* for eight voices.

AGOSTINO VENEZIANO

(c. 1490-c. 1540). Italian engraver of works by Raphael, Michelangelo, Dürer and others. He worked in Venice, Florence and Rome; very few of his plates have survived.

AGOSTINO DI DUCCIO

(1418-c. 1485): Sculptor. Followed the style of early Florentine Renaissance, did interior decorations for Malatesta Temple at Rimini.

AGRICOLA, GEORG BAUER

(c. 1490-1555): German mineralogist. Father of mineralogy. Author of *De Re Metallica:* 1556, filled with the keen observations on metallurgy, chemistry, mining, etc., of this practical man and technician. Translated into English by Herbert Hoover, 1912.

AGRICOLA, JOHANNES

(1494-1566):German reformer. Involved in bitter controversy with Luther. Later, influential and active at the court of Brandenburg.

AGRICOLA, MICHAEL

Sixteenth century. Finnish Bishop. Prepared a number of elementary books for religious instruction. Translated New Testament in 1548: also about a quarter of the Old Testament. Agricola was a student at Wittenberg, where he was influenced by his teachers Luther and Melanchthon.

AGRICOLA, RODOLPHUS

(1444-1485): Original name, Roelof Huysman, called "the father of German humanism." He wrote very little and taught only briefly, although he possessed great learning and artistic gifts. He had spent ten years in Italy and upon his return to Germany set the style of the universal man and the Italianate German. He had mastered Greek, was an accomplished Latin stylist, musician and draughtsman, a fascinating talker and personality. His background is similar to Erasmus': born in the Lowlands and educated in the spirit of the *devotio moderna* by the Brothers of the Common Life in their school at Deventer. As professor of Greek at Heidelberg, 1482-1485, he taught the classical languages as ends in themselves rather than as mere handmaids to theological and biblical studies. He did recognize the importance of Latin and Greek for the understanding of the Bible —and urged that Hebrew studies also be established for that purpose; but in his championing of Latin as the language of all learning and even of everyday life, he typifies the reception of Italian humanism in Germany. He translated Lucian and Isocrates, wrote *De Inventione Dialecta* on rhetoric.

AGRIPPA VON NETTESHEIM, HEINRICH CORNELIUS

(1486-1535): German philosopher, physician, astrologer and magician, soldier, secretary to Maximilian I, and later historian to Emperor Charles V; he traveled extensively in France, the

Netherlands, England, Spain, and Italy, and taught briefly at Pavia. His magical and cabalistic doctrines were condemned by the Church; his published works and teachings caused him to be hounded by the Inquisition and to resign several teaching positions, even though he remained a Catholic and was highly critical of the Reformation. His religious views resemble Erasmus', his contemporary, in that he desired a return to a primitive Christianity, peeling away all the Scholastic and other accretions; hence, as with Erasmus, he tended to be condemned by all parties. He was a productive writer. In his *De occulta philosophia* his point of departure is that magic is the supreme science and constitutes the true path to the knowledge of God and nature; it is a piece of Neo-Platonic-Christian theosophy. This work is complemented by his *Incertitudine et vanitate scientarum,* a strongly skeptical assault on the science of his own day and a bristling attack on pretentious scholars, whether scientific or philosophical; the *Incertitudine* makes Agrippa an important figure in the history of skepticism, his position recalling in some ways that of Nicholas Cusanus in *De docta ignorantia.* Among his other works is a panegyric on woman. His stature as a thinker and his central place in the intellectual travail of the early sixteenth century are coming to be recognized, and he is less often dismissed as a charlatan.

AGUILAR, JERÓNIMO DE
(1489?-1531): Spanish conquistador. Was with Balboa in Darien. Participated in expedition to Central America, Mexico. He learned the Mayan language; the chief use to which he put his knowledge was to serve as interpreter of Cortés.

AGUISE
Dress, adorn. Used by Spenser in *The Faerie Queene* (1596): "Sometimes her head she fondly would aguise/With gaudy girlonds."

AINSWORTH, HENRY
(1571-c. 1623). English theologian, Oriental scholar, Biblical exegete, and an outstanding exponent of civil and religious liberty. Joined Brownists in Holland. Wrote a defense of Brownists.

AIRESVITORIA, ANRIQUE
(Early sixteenth century). Portuguese dramatist. Author of a tragedy entitled *Vingança de Agamenon,* 1528; based upon

Sophocles' *Electra*, it testifies to the growing strength of humanism in Portugal. As a very early Portuguese tragedy it is a milestone in the development of the Portuguese drama that reached its zenith in the latter part of the sixteenth century as the national theatre did in Spain and England.

ALAMANNI, LUIGI
(1495-1556): Italian poet forced to flee after conspiracy against Medici and lived in France, patronized by Francis I. Influenced *La Pléiade*. Author of epigrams, lyrics, eclogues, satires, elegies, sonnets. His first volume of poems was published in Venice in 1542. Author of *Gyrone il Cortese*: chivalric romance, imitative of Ariosto's *Orlando Furioso*, and *The Cultivation of the Fields*, inspired by Vergil's *Georgics*.

ALAMORT
A form of French: *à la mort*. Mortally sick, dispirited. In Shakespeare's *Taming of the Shrew* (1596) the expression occurs: "What sweeting, all-amort?"

ALARCÓN, HERNANDO DE
Sixteenth century. Spanish explorer. With Coronado in America. Explored Gulf of California.

ALATINO, MOSES
(Born 1529). Italian Jewish scholar, physician, who enjoyed the patronage and protection of Cardinal Luigi d'Este of Ferrara. Translated and wrote commentary on Aristotle. Also translated into Latin Galen's commentary on Hippocrates.

ALBANIAN
The oldest fragment of written Albanian is found in the writing of the Orthodox Bishop of Durrës: dating from 1462.

ALBANIAN BOOK
The first Albanian printed book is the *Dizionario Latino-Epirota*, by Francesco Blanco: published in 1635.

ALBERT I OF HOHENZOLLERN
(1490-1568): First Duke of Prussia. Last Grand Master of the Teutonic Order, which he secularized. Follower of Martin Luther. Introduced the Reformation in Prussia. His portrait was painted by Lucas Cranach.

ALBERT III
(1443-1500): Called Albert the Bold. Duke of Saxony. Subject of German drama by Koppel-Elfeld.

ALBERTI, LEANDRO
(1479-1553): Italian geographer, historian. Born in Bologna. Traveled throughout Italy on geographical investigations. Author of a *History of Bologna, De Viris Illustribus,* a *Description of Italy,* and a history of the Dominican order.

ALBERTI, LEONE BATTISTA
(c. 1404-1472): Florentine painter, sculptor, architect, musician, one of the earliest and most important Renaissance theorists of the arts: based on Vitruvius, his work was extremely influential, his ideas repeated hundreds of times, extended and rounded out most notably by Leonardo and Dürer. The artist's practice must be based on theory; this was stated many times over. There were two fundamental concerns: accuracy of representation and beauty. Under the first heading the artist became a student of mathematics and perspective, anatomy, zoology, etc. Beauty, on the other hand, was synonymous with harmony and proportion, symmetry, abundance, variety, composition, and unity; all of these attributes of beauty were derived from the human body, itself a reflection of the divine harmony and proportion of the universe. Such theorizing stimulated the elevation of the painter, sculptor, architect, and goldsmith from the humble ranks of the medieval guild to the exalted status of the artist, man of genius and creator, which he became in the Renaissance. The Renaissance ideal of the universal man owed much to this theory of the arts: to be a painter required one to be also a scientist acquainted with several fields as well as a man of taste, master of humane and philosophical learning. Alberti himself illustrates the tendency of his theory. His classicism—in architecture and letters— was of the purest sort. He wrote a much read *Trattado della famiglia,* on the family, in which he conceived of the family as the foundation of morality and the state; he urged that rearing a family—as in antiquity—was a duty owed to one's homeland.

ALBERTINELLI, MARIOTTO
(1474-1515): Painter of Florence. Executed pictures with

14

religious motifs. He collaborated frequently with Fra Bartolomeo, who influenced him greatly.

ALBERT OF BRANDENBURG
(1490-1545): Elector and Archbishop of Mainz. Against the abuses of the sale of indulgences promoted by him and by Pope Leo X, Luther made his famous protest. Patron of learning. Liberal Catholic prince during Reformation struggles.

ALBERT THE PIOUS
(1559-1621): Archduke of Austria. Son of the Emperor Maximilian II. Stadholder of the Netherlands from 1599 to 1621. Defeated by the Dutch. Negotiated a twelve-years' truce, with the Netherlands, in 1609. Patron of the arts and of the University of Louvain.

ALBUQUERQUE, ALFONSO DE
(1453-1515): Responsible for the victory of the Portuguese in the East Indies. Organized Portuguese Empire in the Orient. Took Goa, which became the principal Portuguese outpost in the East, in 1510. He also secured control of Ceylon, Malacca, the Malabar Coast of India. Died at sea. Wrote commentaries.

ALCALÁ DE HENARES, UNIVERSITY OF
Founded by Cardinal Ximénes de Cisneros in 1508. Intended as a citadel for the philosophy of Duns Scotus, it soon became the home of the new learning in Spain, because there was no long-standing intellectual tradition for humanist protagonists to contend with. Provision was made for the study of Greek, Hebrew, and Aramaic. Boasting its own printing press, the university was responsible for the publication of several important grammars and dictionaries in addition to the Complutensian (the Latin for Alcalá) Polyglot Bible. It was for the purpose of theological studies and biblical exegesis that the new learning was established here as elsewhere (but much more hesitantly) in the Iberian peninsula.

ALCAZABA, SÍMON DE
(died 1535): Portuguese explorer. In Spanish service. Participated in expedition to the Molucca Islands.

ALCÁZARQUIVER, BATTLE OF
King Sebastian of Portugal defeated and killed by Moslems in 1578 in Morocco.

ALCHEMUSY
A reflector to catch the sun's rays: used in divination.

ALCIATUS, ANDREAS
(1492-1550): Italian historical jurist. Wrote on weights and measures: *De Ponderibus et Mensuris*: published in 1530, and a treatise on nature of crime, evidence, function of judges: published in 1542. Also versified moral precepts, in Latin. Wrote *De Verborum Significatione*: deals with terms in jurisprudence: published in 1546. He exemplified the humanist concern to purify the text of the spurious and of accretions, especially is this noticeable in his *Annotations on the Corpus Juris Civilis*. Treatise on symbolism, published in 1535, *Emblematum Libellus*. He taught widely in Italy and France and moved in the humanist circles of Erasmus, More, Bembo and Vasari.

ALCYONIUS, PETRUS
(1487-1527): Italian humanist. Pupil of Musurus. Taught Greek in Florence. Author of *Medices Legatus de Exilio*: a dialogue pervaded by classical scholarship on the advantages of exile.

ALDEGREVER, HEINRICH
(1502-c. 1555): German painter. Executed copperplate engravings. Treated religious, mythological, ornamental themes. One of the Kleinmeister or German Little Masters, greatly influenced by Dürer.

ALDRINGER, JOHANN, COUNT VON
(1588-1634): General in Imperial German army. Under Wallenstein in Thirty Years' War. Commander of army of Catholic League. Fought successfully against Swedish forces.

ALDROVANDUS, ULYSSES
(1522-1605): Italian naturalist and founder of the Bologna Botanical Gardens. Called by his contemporaries Pontifex Maximus of Natural History. Wrote on ornithology, anatomy. His chief work was the multi-volumed *Natural History*.

ALDUS MANUTIUS
(1450-1515). Founder of the celebrated Aldine press at Venice. By the time of his death there had been published twenty-seven *editiones principes* of Greek authors, done with a scholar's zeal for accuracy and completeness. He utilized a circle of scholars—

many of whom were Greek refugees—as editors, proofreaders, and collators. There grew up out of Aldus' publishing activity the Venetian Academy, where scholars and learned gentlemen met, founded by him in 1502 as *Accademia aldina.* Its by-laws were in Greek and made it mandatory that Greek be spoken at its meetings. Erasmus was for a while associated with Aldus, who printed *In Praise of Folly.* He is credited with a more elegant, cleaner type and was the inventor of *italic;* it was the italics that enabled him to produce the compact editions of Greek works that were authoritative texts and moderate in cost.

ALEANDER, HIERONYMUS
(1480-1542). Italian humanist. Rector of University of Paris. Represented papacy in Reformation. Appealed to Charles V to bring Luther to punitive justice. Planned bonfire of Luther's books. Prepared Edict of Worms. Produced Greek-Latin lexicon. One-time friend and later critic of Erasmus.

ALEANDER, HIERONYMUS
(1574-1649): Italian philosopher and antiquarian. Grandnephew of the above. Friend of Rubens. Author of *Antiquae Tabulae Marmoreae;* published in 1616 in Rome. A survey of ancient mythology and astrology. One of the founders of the Academy of Roman Humorists, the *Humorosi.*

ALEMÁN, MATEO
(1547-1614?): Spanish author of picaresque genre of novel, and adventurer. Born in Seville. Studied medicine. In 1608 fled to Mexico, where he spent rest of life. Wrote *Guzmán de Alfarache.* In first fifty-four years it went through twenty-six editions. Influenced novels of Spain, France, Germany. Praised by Lessing.

ALESIUS, ALEXANDER
(1500-1565): Scottish theologian and physician. Preached Lutheranism in England and Germany. Fled to Germany. Rector of University of Leipzig.

ALESSI, GALEAZZO
(1512-1572): Italian architect of Perugia, disciple of Michelangelo. Died in Genoa where he did most of his work: churches, palaces, villas, all in the style of High Renaissance.

17

ALEXANDER VI
(1430-1503). Pope (1492-1503). Corrupt pontificate. Nepotism and simony were rife. In conflict with Savonarola: Savonarola executed in 1498. Active in European power politics. The Renaissance Papacy at its worst.

ALEXANDER, SIR WILLIAM, EARL OF STIRLING
(1567?-1640): Scottish poet and dramatist. Author of a series of sonnets, elegies, songs entitled *Aurora*. Long poem called *Doomsday*. Also dramas, in Senecan tone, entitled *Monarchical Tragedies of Croesus, Darius, Alexander, Julius Caesar*. He also composed madrigals, founded a colony in Canada and wrote a book entitled *Encouragement to Colonies*.

ALEXANDER AB ALEXANDRO
(died 1523): Italian jurist of Naples. He was the first to edit fragments of the *Twelve Tables*, the earliest codification of Roman law. He also wrote *Gerialium Dierum Libri Sex:* published in Paris in 1586.

ALEXANDRISTS
Materialistic philosophers who followed the Aristotelian commentator of the third century, Alexander of Aphrodisias, in their interpretation of Aristotle. They denied personal immortality. Their leader was Pietro Pomponazzi (1462-1525).

ALEXIANS
They were lay brothers, in Belgium and Germany, who tended the sick and buried the dead, especially during periods of plague.

ALFARROBEIRA, BATTLE OF
In 1449, in this battle, Peter the regent of Portugal was defeated and killed by Alfonso V, who now was of age and ruled in his own right.

ALFIN
In the fifteenth and sixteenth centuries, a term for a bishop in the game of chess.

ALFINGER, AMBROSE
Traveler. In 1531 headed an expedition to South America, in search of El Dorado. Killed by Indians, c. 1532.

18

ALFONSO II, THE MAGNANIMOUS

(died 1458). King of Aragon, Sicily, and by conquest, of Naples, where he ruled as a typical Renaissance prince: a lavish patron of architecture and scholarship, he filled his court with artists and learned men from northern Italy. His humanist flatterers bestowed his famous sobriquet upon him; to them, and genuinely it seems, he was magnanimous as well as munificent; to others he was notoriously harsh and vengeful. His illegitimate son Ferrante I, died 1494, succeeded as king of Naples and continued in his father's footsteps.

ALGARDI, ALESSANDRO

(1602-1653): Italian architect and sculptor. Executed large-scale sculptures. Belongs to the Central Italian baroque school.

ALIAGA, LUIS DE

(1560-1630): Spanish Dominican monk. Instrumental in the expulsion of Moriscos in 1609.

ALKABETZ, SOLOMON

(1500-1580): Cabalist and liturgical poet, Jewish mystic, cabalistic commentator on books of the Bible. Author of Sabbath eve hymn *Come My Beloved*. Died in Safed, Palestine.

ALKMAAR, SIEGE OF

An episode of the Dutch Revolt against Spain. The Spaniards under the Duke of Alva besieged the Dutch at Alkmaar. The Dutch opened the dykes and forced the Spaniards into retreat, in 1573.

ALLEGRI, GREGORIO

(1582-1652): Italian composer. Produced the *Miserere:* sung annually in the Sistine Chapel during Holy Week.

ALLEN, THOMAS

(1542-1632): English mathematician, astrologer, philosopher, antiquary. He enjoyed the protection of the Earl of Leicester and was acquainted with Dr. John Dee. Collected manuscripts—historical, astronomical, philosophical, mathematical.

ALLEN, WILLIAM

(1532-1594): English prelate and apologetic writer. Cardinal. Encouraged religious opposition and plots against Queen Elizabeth. Founder of the Jesuit seminary of Douai for the training of English priests.

ALLORI, ALESSANDRO
(1535-1607): Painter of Florence. Executed frescoes, altarpieces, portraits. Noted for Tuscan mannerism. Called Alessandro Bronzino after his master.

ALLORI, CHRISTOFANO
(1577-1621): Son of above, painter. Worked in Florence. Belongs in the transition period of early baroque realism. Noted for his many portraits.

ALLOTT, ROBERT
Early seventeenth century. English anthologist whose collection, *England's Parnassus*, c. 1600, included "the Choycest Flowers of our Modern Poets" which every courtier should know.

ALMAGRO, DIEGO DE
(1472?-1538). Spanish conquistador. On expedition with Pizarro. Participated in conquest of Peru. On expedition to Chile. In conflict with Hernando Pizarro. Executed.

ALMEIDA, FRANCISCO DE
(c. 1450-1510). Portuguese conquistador. First viceroy of Portuguese India, 1505-1509. Established trading posts in Cochin and East Indies.

ALMEIDA, LOURENÇO
Portuguese explorer in Africa. First Portuguese in Ceylon. Killed off Chaul, India, in 1508.

ALMONER
An official in a monastery or household of a noble, who distributed alms. Wolsey had been almoner to Henry VII.

ALONSO DE LEDESMA
(1552-1623): Spanish poet. Initiator of *conceptismo*: exaggerated, witty subtlety cultivated by Spanish baroque writers. Frequently combined with style of *culturanismo*. Author of *Conceptos Espirituales*.

ALONSO DE OJEDA
(c. 1465-1515). Spanish explorer. Accompanied Columbus to

Hispaniola. Explored the coast of South America with Amerigo Vespucci. Founded colony at Darien.

ALPAGO, ANDREA
(Sixteenth century): Italian philosopher and physician. A student and admirer of Avicenna, whose manuscripts he tracked down, edited and translated.

ALTARPIECES
In the sixteenth century the altarpiece was a simple picture attached to a wall behind the altar or set into an architectural frame. These altarpieces, during the baroque period, became highly elaborate, frequently combining in extravagant design architecture, painting, and sculpture. Examples are the *Sistine Madonna* by Raphael and Titian's *Assumption of the Virgin*.

ALTDORFER, ALBRECHT
(1480-1538). German artist, architect, engraver. Produced *Holy Family*. Called one of the German Little Masters. Leader of the Danubian school. After Albrecht Dürer, most important artist of early Renaissance in Southern Germany, especially noteworthy as the earliest German painter of landscapes.

ALTENSTAIG, JOANNES
Sixteenth century. German pedagogue of Mandelheim. Author of *Vocabularius:* a grammar survey for Renaissance students. Published in 1515. As logician, author of *Dialectica:* published in 1514.

ALTHANIR, ANDREAS or ALTHAMER
(c. 1500-1539): German humanist and Lutheran. In 1529 he published an annotated edition of Tacitus' *De Germania*: it included a study of German antiquities and travel through Germany. He also wrote the first Lutheran *Catechism*, 1528.

ALUNNO, FRANCESCO
(c. 1485-1556): Italian scholar of Ferrara. Composed the first dictionary of the vernacular language; arranged by subject matter it was entitled *The Riches of the Italian Language*. His object was to demonstrate that all human concepts were and could be expressed in the Tuscan language, that Latin was not so necessary for the expression of nuance, etc. He culled examples from Petrarch, Boccaccio, Dante, Bembo. A later work,

21

entitled *Della Fabrica del Mondo Libri X*, was first published in 1548, a kind of Renaissance Bartlett.

ALVA, FERNANDO ALVÁREZ DE TOLEDO, DUKE OF

(1508-1583): A ruthless Spanish commander under Charles V and Philip II. Suppressed revolt in the Low Countries in 1567. Established Council of Blood or Council of Troubles: 1567-1573. The Council was a tribunal intended to crush opposition in the Low Countries. Defeated William of Orange. Ultimately he was unsuccessful in the Netherlands and was recalled. Led expedition that conquered Portugal, in 1580-1581.

ALVARADO, ALONSO DE

(c. 1490-1554). Spanish soldier. With Cortés in Mexico. In Peru. Governor. Killed during revolt.

ALVARADO, PEDRO DE

(1485?-1541): Spanish conquistador. Accompanied Cortés and participated in conquest of Mexico. On expedition to Guatemala, which he conquered and became governor from 1530 to 1534.

ÁLVARES, FATHER FRANCISCO

Sixteenth century. Portuguese missionary. Spent many years in Abyssinia. Author of *True Relation of Prester John:* published in 1540.

ÁLVARES, JORGE

Portuguese traveler. First European since the fourteenth century to reach China: 1513.

ÁLVAREZ DE VILLASANDINO, ALFONSO

(died 1425): Castilian troubadour, adventurer and celebrated character of Burgos. Prolific satirical poet. Wrote for royal or wealthy patrons. Many of his poems appear in Baena's *Cancionero*, a collection of Castilian poetry compiled c. 1500.

ALVISE DA CADAMOSTO

Fifteenth century. Venetian captain. Made an expedition along the African coast in 1455.

ALVIXE

Sixteenth century. Italian sculptor of Padua. Worked in bronze. Self-styled Master of Sculpture. Executed *Horse Running:* medallions.

AMADAS, PHILIP
(1550-1618). English sailor. On expedition with Sir Walter Raleigh to America and West Indies.

AMADEO, GIOVANNI ANTONIO
(c. 1447-1522). Italian sculptor and architect of Pavia. Helped to design Milanese Duomo, the Certosa of Pavia, and the Chapel of the Colleoni, the family of condottieri, at Bergamo. He followed in the style of Bramante and did most of his work at Milan for Ludovico il Moro.

AMANS, NICOLAUS
Sixteenth century. Logician. Wrote on Aristotelian logic.

AMATO, GIOVANNI ANTONIO D'
(1475-1555). Italian painter of Naples. Specialized in religious themes, imitated the manner of Pietro Perugino.

AMATORY POETS
Among erotic poets of the Renaissance are Antonius Panormitas, author of *Hermaphroditus*: Ramusius Arminensis, author of *Carmina:* Pacificus Maximus Asculanus, author of *Carmina:* Joannes Jovianus Pontanus, author of *Amores.*

AMATUS LUSITANUS
(1510-1568). Portuguese Jewish physician. Forced to seek religious refuge in many cities of Europe: finally settled in Greece. Court physician in Italy; he also lectured on anatomy and medicinal plants at Ferrara; his dissections there revealed the function of the valves in the circulation of the blood. Wrote extensively on medical subjects. Precursor of William Harvey.

AMBERGER, CHRISTOPH
(c. 1500-1561). Painter of Augsburg. Specialized in portraits. Belongs in the South German Renaissance school. His work is reminiscent of Holbein, e.g., his famous portrait of the Emperor Charles V.

AMBOISE, CONSPIRACY OF
Conspiracy was formed by Condé and the Huguenots. Directed by La Renaudie, in 1560. The purpose was to end the influence of the Guises on Francis II, and included an attempt to kidnap the king. The conspiracy was abortive and was ruthlessly sup-

pressed; it did much to touch off the murderous French civil
and religious wars which began soon thereafter.

AMBOISE, FRANCOIS D'
(1550-1620). French writer. Statesman. Translated treatises by
Piccolomini and Landi. Wrote on emblems.

AMBROGIO DE' PREDIS
(c. 1455–c. 1506). Italian painter, miniaturist, portraitist of Milan.
He worked under Leonardo, who greatly influenced him, so
much so that their works are hard to distinguish from each other.
He is remembered for his *Girl with Cherries* and portrait of
Emperor Maximilian I and his wife Bianca—the daughter of
Ambrogio's patron, Duke Francesco Sforza of Milan.

AMBROSIAN REPUBLIC OF MILAN
St. Ambrose was Bishop of Milan in the fourth century and the
city's patron saint. The Ambrosian Republic was proclaimed
when the Visconti ducal house died out in 1447 and was overthrown by Francesco Sforza, who became duke in 1450.

AMBROSIANS
A name given to an Order founded under the patronage of St.
Ambrose by Alexander Givelli, Antonio Petrasancta, and Albert
Besazzi.

In 1579 St. Charles Borromeo reformed the discipline of the
Order. In 1589 Pope Sixtus V united the Brothers of St. Barna-
bas to the Congregation of St. Ambrose. In 1650, under Innocent
X, the Order was dissolved.

AMES, WILLIAM
(1576-1633). English Puritan and controversialist who fled to
Holland. Author of treatises in Latin on theological subjects.

AMMAN, JOST
(1539-1591). Swiss engraver, painter, and glass artist in the tradition of the German Little Masters (*Kleinmeister*). Worked in
Nuremberg. Executed woodcuts to illustrate Bible. Also copperplate engravings. Produced collection of woodcuts descriptive
of various crafts: *Recueil des Métiers*.

AMMANATI, BARTOLOMEO
(1511-1592). Sculptor, architect of Florence. Worked as sculptor.

Imitated Michelangelo, was a rival of Cellini. As architect, built in the late Renaissance style.

AMSDORF, NICOLAS VON
(1483-1565). German Lutheran theologian. Participated in translation of the Bible, a violent controversialist, associated with founding of university of Jena.

AMSTERDAM, BANK OF
This bank was founded in 1609.

AMYOT, JACQUES
(1513-1593). French humanist scholar. Bishop of Auxerre. Translated Plutarch's *Lives* and other classical texts into French; Sir Thomas North's famous English translation of Plutarch, utilized by Shakespeare, was based upon Amyot's.

ANABAPTISTS
Name of several Christian sects that postulated adult baptism. Inspired by the 'prophet' Muenzer. Began in Münster, in 1521: spread to Zürich among the followers of Zwingli, in 1523. Attempted the establishment in Germany of a community with property held in common, in 1534. Persecuted as dangerous to the stability of the state. In the form established by John of Leyden, it took the form of a "Zion" without law, property or marriage. During the Reformation, the term Anabaptist was used in an abusive sense. The movement first reached England in 1549; it was fundamentally anarchist.

ANABAPTISTS, MASSACRE OF
In 1535 the Anabaptists of Munich were massacred.

ANAPES
Literally, *from Naples.* Descriptive of cloth: e.g., fustian anapes.

ANCENIS, PEACE OF
In 1468 Louis XI of France dictated this peace to Francis II, Duke of Brittany; it confirmed the possession of Normandy by the crown.

ANCHIETA, JOSÉ DE
(1534-1597). Spanish missionary in Brazil among Indians, learned at least one of the native languages; for his numerous writings,

in Spanish and Portuguese, he is declared to be "the first Brazilian writer".

ANCONA
Port of Adriatic coast. Location of one of the oldest Jewish communities in Italy.

ANCRE, MARQUIS D'
(died 1617). Original name Concino Concini. Italian soldier of fortune. Attached to the French court of Marie de Médicis. Marshal of France. Assassinated by order of Louis XIII, his wife executed as a sorceress. Subject of drama by Alfred de Vigny and of novel by François Mauriac.

ANDAGOYA, PASCUAL DE
(died 1548). Spanish explorer. In 1522 sailed to the coast of Columbia.

ANDERNACH, GUNTHER VON
(died 1574). German scholar, translated medical treatises. Professor at Paris. Later, lived in Strassburg. Author of *De Medicina Veteri et Novo:* published in 1571.

ANDRAE, LAURENTIUS
(c. 1470-1552). Swedish statesman. Studied in Germany. Chancellor of Gustavus Vasa. Helped to make royal power independent of papal authority and superior to power of nobles. Assisted in the translation of the Swedish Bible.

ANDREA DA SALVERNO, SABATINE
(c. 1490-1530). Italian painter. The chief influences upon his work were the Umbrian school and Raphael. All of his known work, entirely of religious subjects, is to be found in Naples and his native Salerno.

ANDREA DEL SARTO
(1487-1531). Italian painter of Florence. Attached to court of Francis I, in Paris. Skilled in chiaroscuro. His works include frescoes, portraits, paintings: *Annunciation, Pietà.* Called by Italians *Il Pittore Senza Errori.* J. A. Symonds' estimate includes these comments: "Andrea del Sarto not unworthily represents the golden age of Florence. There is no affectation, no false taste, no trickery in his style."

ANDREANI, ANDREA
(c. 1540-1623). Italian wood engraver. Born in Mantua. Noted for *The Triumph of Julius Caesar* and treatments of religious themes.

ANDREAS, JACOBUS
(1528-1590). Professor of theology at University of Leipzig. Reformer. Wrote on post-Reformation education: *Oratio de Studio Sacrarum Litterarum:* published in 1577.

ANDRÉ DE LA VIGNE
(c. 1457-c. 1527). French poet. Secretary to the Duke of Savoy. In the retinue of Charles VIII's expedition to Italy. Author of *Vergier d'Honneur* and the *Moralité de l'Aveugle et du Boiteux.*

ANDRELINI, PAOLO FAUSTO
(1462-1518). Italian Neo-Latin poet of Forli. Educated at Bologna. Received poet's laurel in Rome for Latin poem entitled *Livia.* Professor of rhetoric, poetry, and astronomy at the University of Paris. Attached to the court of Charles VIII and afterwards of Louis XII. Friend of Erasmus. Author of Christian-Stoic poem in hexameters entitled *Carmen de Virtutibus cum Moralibus tum Intellectualibus:* published in 1509. Author of popular Renaissance text: *Epistulae Proverbiales.* Contains excerpts from and comments upon classical authors which have contemporary relevance. As such it is a typical Renaissance reference work, guide to usage, and source of ideas. Also wrote *De Fuga Balbi ex Urbe Parisia:* published in Paris in 1496. Contains material on Italian and French humanists.

ANDREOLI, GIORGIO
(c. 1465-c. 1555). Italian worker in ceramics. Noted for introducing lustre on pottery; much of his work is in the British Museum.

ANDREWES, LANCELOT
(1555-1625). Anglican Bishop of Winchester. Collaborated in translation of the Authorized Version of the Bible. Opposed Puritanism. A prodigy of learning and piety.

ANDROUET DU CERCEAU, JACQUES
(c. 1515-1584). French architect. Worked in Paris. Executed architectural etchings, ornamental designs. Wrote on architec-

tural theory. Worked on Louvre. Helped to introduce Italian Renaissance into France. His son Jacques (died 1614) was also an architect, as were two other sons; they worked on the Tuileries, Louvre.

ANGELA DE MERCI, SAINT
(c. 1474-1540). Italian nun. Founded order of Ursulines at Brescia to educate the young and care for the sick.

ANGELICO, FRA
(1382-1455). Celebrated Florentine painter of religious subjects and Dominican friar. His work did not go far in accommodating the new realism and naturalism of Masaccio; although his work does show Masaccio's influence, he is more notable for a traditional, gentle piety and angelic spirituality; Vasari relates that he would pray before he began a work, that when he painted a crucifixion the tears ran down his cheeks.

ANGELO DI COSTANZA
(1507-1591). Neapolitan scholar. Author of a *History of the Kingdom of Naples,* 1572. Imitated the linguistic purism of Bembo.

ANGELUS DE CLAVASIO
(1411-1495). Vicar-General of the Franciscan Order. Author of *Summa Angelica de Casibus Conscientialibus:* a kind of dictionary of theology and morals. It also contains juristic items. Burned by Martin Luther, who condemned the legal matter of the *Summa,* in 1520.

ANGERIANUS, HIERONYMUS
Sixteenth century. Neapolitan poet. Author of eclogues, published in 1535. Also poems on love, studies.

ANGLICAN CHURCH
Established by Augustine in 597. Variantly called Episcopal Church, Church of England. Separated from Catholic Church in 1534 by Henry VIII, restored by Mary, in the 1550's, returned to the Henrician compromise in the long reign of Elizabeth I.

ANGLICUS SUDOR
Sweating sickness. An epidemic disease that first appeared in England in 1485. Epidemics of this disease recurred in 1506, 1518, 1528, 1529, 1551.

ANGOLA
Territory in Africa. Discovered by Portuguese navigator Diogo Cão (fl. 1480).

ANGUISCIOLA, SOFONISBA
(1527-1625). Italian painter of Cremona. She did religious subjects but specialized in portraits, including her own remarkable self-portrait. She went to Spain to paint portraits of Philip II and the royal family, for which she received an annual pension. Died blind in Genoa, where she spent last years of her life as patroness of the arts.

ANIMUCCIA, GIOVANNI
(c. 1500-1571). Italian composer. Chapel master at St. Peter's. Called Father of the Oratorio. Composed sacred music, influenced Palestrina.

ANNATES
A papal source of revenue. A considerable portion of the annual value of a benefice, paid originally as a gift of the "first fruits" of the office; spread over several years, it often became permanent, equivalent to a tax.

ANNE OF BRITTANY
(1477-1514). Wife successively of Charles VIII of France and Louis XII. As heiress of Brittany, her marriage united the duchy to France. Louis XII divorced his first wife in order to marry Anne; he had procured a papal dispensation to do so. This was a precedent which Henry VIII's emissaries cited at Rome but to no avail.

ANNE OF DENMARK
(1574-1619). Queen of James I of England. Participated in royal performances of masques.

ANSELMO DEL BANCO
Renaissance loan-broker. Founder, reputedly, of Venetian Jewish community.

ANTICO
Italian sculptor. His original name was Ilario Bonacolsi. Worked in Padua from 1460 to 1528. Executed small sculptures, especially in bronze.

ANTIGUA
Island in West Indies. Discovered by Christopher Columbus in 1493.

ANTI-JEWISH POLICY
Pope Paul IV (1476-1559) and Pope Paul V (1504-1572) restricted Jews to Rome, Avignon, Ancona. In 1597, under Spanish rule, Milan expelled Jews. They moved to other cities, particularly Padua and Verona.

ANTINOMIAN CONTROVERSIES
Antinomianism was associated with certain types of ethical thought at variance with Mosaic Law. Controversies on this subject raged violently through the sixteenth and seventeenth centuries. Best known was in Germany, involving Luther, Melanchthon, and Johannes Agricola, German Reformer. Ended by the Formula of Concord: 1577.

ANTONELLO DA MESSINA
(c. 1430-c. 1485). Italian painter: native of Sicily. Worked in Venice. Reputedly, introduced Flemish methods of oil painting into Italy. Works include: *Salvator Mundi, Crucifixion, St. Jerome in his Study* and the famous *St. Sebastian.* With his altarpieces and superb portraits, he was a leader in early Venetian Renaissance.

ANTONIO
Prior of Crato. Claimant to throne of Portugal, but of illegitimate birth. On the death of King Cardinal Henry in 1580 Antonio made repeated attempts, with the help of French and English, for kingship, but was defeated by Philip II of Spain, who also had a claim to the throne. Died in 1595.

ANTONIO DA MONZA
Franciscan friar. Illuminator. Executed missal for Pope Alexander VI (1492-1503).

ANTONIO DA MOTA
Sixteenth century. Portuguese navigator. In company with Francisco Zeimoto and Antonio Peixoto, he was the first European to reach Japan, from Siam, in 1542.

ANTONIO DE BERRIO
Spanish explorer in South America. In military service in Italy,

North Africa. In search of El Dorado. In 1584, to the Orinocu River. Governor of El Dorado. Crossed from Andes to the Atlantic Ocean.

ANTONIO DE ESLABA
Sixteenth century. Spanish novelist. Author of *Winter Nights:* published in 1609. Series of tales in a *Decameron* framework.

ANTONIO DE MIRANDA
Portuguese explorer. Sent on a mission: reached Siam in 1511.

ANTONIO DI SALVI
(1450-1527). Italian goldsmith.

ANTONIO DI SAN GALLO
(Fifteenth century). Florentine sculptor, furniture maker and woodworker.

ANTONIO FEDERIGHI DEI TOLOMEI
(c. 1420-1490). Italian sculptor of Siena. Executed the colossal statuary of the portals of Siena's Cathedral and other features of its façade.

ANTONIUS DE FANTIS
Sixteenth century. Physician, logician. Wrote a commentary on Sirectus: published in Venice in 1588.

ANTWERP SCHOOL
This was an art school that developed in Antwerp. From 1480 to 1505 painters came to Antwerp from Bruges, Cologne, Westphalia. Antwerp superseded Bruges as an art centre. Among the artists associated with Antwerp were Quentin Massys, Mabuse, Hendrik Bles, Peter Brueghel, Rubens, Van Dyck.

ANTWERP, TRUCE OF
The United Provinces of the Netherlands gained independence of Spain, freedom to conduct Indian trade, right to exclude Catholicism from their dominions. The truce was signed in 1609: intended to last for twelve years.

APIANUS, PETRUS
(c. 1501-1552). Latinized name of Peter Bienewitz. German geographer, astronomer, cartographer. Author of *Cosmographicus Liber*, 1524, and *Astrononoicum Caesareum*, 1540. Among the

first to produce a map of America, he also was a pioneer in the study of comets and he invented several mathematical instruments.

APOLLONIO DE' BONFRATELLI
Italian illuminator. Executed miniatures for Pope Pius IV, in 1564.

APOMECOMETRY
The science of measuring distance. A term in use until the sixteenth century.

APOSTOLIUS, MICHAEL
(1422-1486). Greek rhetorician, theologian of Constantinople. After fall of city in 1453 he moved to Italy. Sponsored by Cardinal Bessarion. Opposed Aristotelianism and urged Platonism. Taught Greek. Compiled collection of ancient proverbs: published in 1538. The head of a large family that was often indigent, he typifies the expatriate Greek scholar who, having no great gifts, beat out a living as editor, translator and teacher.

AQUILANO, SERAFINO
(1466-1500). Italian-Jewish poet and singer. Attached to court of Cesare Borgia, among others. His favorite form was the sonnet; so successful was he at it that he was compared to Petrarch.

ARABIC PRINTING PRESS
First established at Fano, in Italy, under Pope Julius II, and consecrated under Leo X in 1514. A knowledge of Arabic was indispensable to the Renaissance scholar, since many of the classical manuscripts and the ablest commentaries upon them came to him from the Islamic world.

ARAGONESE LINE
Alfonso V: 1416-1458. King of Aragon, Naples, Sicily. John II: 1458-1479. King of Aragon, Sicily. Ferrante I: 1479-1494. King of Naples. Ferdinand II: 1479-1516. King of Aragon. By a marriage tie, their claim to southern Italy descended from the Hohenstaufen.

ARANZIO, JULIUS CAESAR
(1530-1589). Italian anatomist. Professor for thirty-two years at the University of Bologna. Conducted anatomical investigations

of the brain, eyes, the tongue, the human fetus, etc. and contributed much to the development of anatomy.

ARASON, JÓN
(1484-1550). Finnish Bishop. Author of religious poem entitled *Ljómur*. Also wrote poems on contemporary subjects. Brought to Iceland the first printing press.

ARBALEST
In 1535 the English abandoned the arbalest as a weapon of war.

ARBUTHNOT, ALEXANDER
(1538-1585). Scottish jurist and Protestant theologian. Printer of first Bible issued in Scotland, in 1575. He also wrote a history of Scotland.

ARCADELT, JACOB
(1514-post 1557). Flemish musician, composer of polyphonic music. Lived in Rome, Paris. Composer of masses. In 1539 published madrigals. Master of the choir of St. Mark's, Venice. Noted also for secular music.

ARCA, NICCOLO DELL'
(died 1494). Sculptor. Died in Bologna. Belonged to early Renaissance school, most of his work was on tombs.

ARCHAEOLOGY, BEGINNINGS OF IN RENAISSANCE
Biondo in his *Roma Instaurata* was a pioneer in his reconstruction of the physical features of the ancient city. Brunelleschi and Donatello also had a hand in the development of the discipline when they went on their famous expedition to Rome to measure and plot the layout of its ancient buildings, monuments, and squares. By the sixteenth century the collection of antiquities (not only works of art) became a fad. The interest in Greek antiquities was snuffed out by the Turkish conquests. Epigraphy and excavation—Raphael as conservator of antiquities proposed extensive and systematic diggings in his report of 1519 to Pope Leo X—have their beginnings in the Renaissance. Some German scholars, most notably Konrad Peutinger of Augsburg, 1465-1547, also contributed as collectors of coins, metals, sculptures, inscriptions, and manuscripts. Rome was the principal center for archaeology; the Roman Academy, under papal auspices, was the chief center for discussions and investigations. Ancient ruins

to Petrarch, Cyriac of Ancona, c. 1455, and the sixteenth-century Spanish bishop Antonio Agustin seemed to be so many ghosts beckoning them to the lost world of antiquity; the romance with which ruins were invested may be seen in the many sketches and wood cuts in which they appear, and particularly in the strange love story *Hypneratomachia Polifili* (late fifteenth century) in which the pair experience the vicissitudes of love amid evocative ruins.

ARCHANGEL
City in Northern Russia, at the mouth of the Dvina River, near the White Sea. Founded in 1584.

ARCHANGEL PASSAGE
Discovered in 1553 by English navigator, Richard Chancellor, died 1556, on his way to the White Sea and to the Orient by the northern route which he hoped to find.

ARETINO, PIETRO
(1492-1556). "The Scourge of Princes," satirist, publicist, poet, and Bohemian man of the world; free-lance satirist and virtuoso in making and breaking reputations among the great, artist of blackmail: fear of his merciless pen enabled him to gain patronage and live in princely style on the Grand Canal in Venice. Scurrilous, indecent in his writings and in his life, his Venetian establishment was the scene of sexual orgies and aberrations. His extreme paganism and obscenity make him practically unique among Renaissance scamps; he was the subject of several memorable portraits by Titian. He wrote a superb Italian, sinuous and compelling, unpedantic, if not popular; he was the one literary genius that Venice produced, although he was born at Arezzo.

AREVALO, RODRIGUEZ SANCHEZ DE
(1404-1470). Spanish bishop and writer who spent most of his life in Rome in the Papal service. In the time of Paul II he was castellon of the Castel Sant'Angelo and thus jailer of the humanist Platina, who appears as interlocutor in the bishop's *De falso et vero bono*. Never a humanist himself, he became the friend of Bessarion and was held in respect in Roman humanist circles. He wrote several works, in Latin, Italian, Spanish; the most notable being a treatise on morality, *Speculum vitae humanae*.

ARGENSOLA, BARTOLOMÉ LEONARDO DE and
LUPERCIO LEONARDO DE
(1565-1631), (1564-1613). Spanish poets, brothers. Called "The Spanish Horaces." Bartolomé was the author of *Conquest of Moluccas:* issued in 1609. Lupercio wrote dramas, history, poems.

ARGOSY
A medieval merchant ship. A term derived from the city of Ragusa. A Ragusee was a ship from Ragusa. In the sixteenth century, in England, Ragusa was also called Aragouse, Arragosa: hence argosy.

ARGYROPULOS OF CONSTANTINOPLE, JOANNES
(1416-1486). Greek scholar. He had been teacher to the Imperial School of Constantinople before 1453, and had had several western students before coming to Italy, where he appeared as early as 1441, teaching Greek at Padua, at Florence from 1456 to 1471 where he enjoyed Medici patronage, at Rome from 1471 to his death. He translated Aristotle and lectured on Thucydides. A famous occasion was, when he heard Reuchlin read and translate a passage of Thucydides, his exclamation, "Lo! through our exile, Greece has flown across the Alps."

ARIAS DE AVILA, PEDRO
(c. 1440-1531?). Called Pedrarias. Spanish administrator. Governor of Darien. Infamously cruel. Executed Balboa. Founded Panama City.

ARIASMONTANO, BENITO
(c. 1527-1598). Spanish scholar and theologian of the Counter Reformation. At the Council of Trent. Died in Seville. Attached to the court of Philip II of Spain. Published Polyglot Bible: called the Antwerp Polyglot. Issued in 1569-1573.

ARIOSTO, LODOVICO
(1474-1533). Italian poet. In diplomatic and military service. Governor of Garfagnana. Retired to Ferrara, where he was director of the Este theatre. Author of epic poem of chivalry entitled *Orlando Furioso.* Published in 1516, it was intended as a glorification of the Este family. Also wrote odes, Latin poems, satires, sonnets, comedies, miscellaneous pieces.

ARISTOTELIAN INFLUENCE

The Renaissance is still in many respects an Aristotelian age which in part continued the trends of medieval Aristotelianism, and in part gave it a new direction under the influence of classical humanism. The development of the scientific method at Padua owed much to Aristotle.

ARMADA, SPANISH

In 1587 Captain Drake plundered Cadiz and caused havoc in Lisbon Bay. Off Cape St. Vincent he intercepted a squadron of Spanish transports from the Mediterranean.

In retaliation, a fleet was assembled by King Philip II of Spain, with the intention of invading England; it consisted of about 130 ships and was to convoy the army of the duke of Parma across the Channel from the Netherlands. The Spanish Armada was ready in May, but a storm postponed the departure until July 12, 1588.

The English fleet under Lord Howard engaged the Armada and caused great destruction, the rendezvous with Parma never took place. A storm wrecked the remnants of the Spanish fleet, as it tried to escape by sailing north around Scotland and west of Ireland. Only about half the fleet returned.

ARMINIANISM

Religious movement founded by Dutch theologian Jacobus Arminius (Harmensen). 1560-1609. The emphasis of Arminianism is on human free will: man can resist grace and is not predestined to damnation or salvation as the orthodox Calvinists of the Dutch Reformed Church believed.

ARMINIUS, JACOBUS or HARMENSEN

(1560-1609). Dutch theologian, who criticized the orthodox Calvinist position of the Dutch Reformed Church and advocated a more moderate doctrine of election. After his death, his ideas were organized into the systematic body of doctrine, Arminianism.

ARMOR, REDUCTION OF

Gustavus Adolphus (1594-1632) took away from his soldiers all their limb armor, leaving them with only a light cuirass.

ARMOR, REPUGNANCE TO

In the sixteenth century the common soldier had no liking for his armor, and was eager for its abolition. The soldier had to pay for his own armor, or a deduction was made from his pay. Secondly, the fatigue of wearing armor was intolerable. Again, it afforded little protection now that firearms were growing common and it produced physical deformities. Both French and German soldiers maintained this view. Hence the French soldier assumed armor only at the moment of battle. The German soldiery of Charles V, in their first campaigns against French armies, appeared equipped in buff leather coats instead of armor.

ARMORED KNIGHT
During the sixteenth century the effectiveness of knights in armor, in battle engagements, began to diminish. But although they were made the object of ridicule by Cervantes, the knights in armor did not disappear, for armor was essential for court and public ceremony.

ARNAULD, ANTOINE
(1560-1619). Celebrated French jurist. He and his many children after him were antagonists of the Jesuits—he accused them of disloyalty to France in a speech which they dubbed his "original sin"—and were sympathetic to, or adherents of, Jansenism.

ARNDT, JOHANN
(1555-1621). German mystic and Protestant theologian. Noted for his great work *True Christianity*, which had wide circulation and great influence.

ARNOLD, BARTHOLOMAUS
(1463-1532). Bartholomäus von Usingen. German logician and humanist. Wrote *Compendium Novum Totius Logicae*. He taught at Erfurt where Luther was among his students; he remained within the Church, to Luther's great exasperation.

ARNOLD VON HARFF
Fifteenth century. German traveler. Made a journey to the Levant, 1497-1499, as a member of a caravan bound for Mecca; he wrote an account of his trip entitled *Journey of a Pilgrim to the Holy Land and the Orient*.

ARNOLD VON LUYDE
(died 1540). Logician of Tongres. Wrote commentary on Aristotle's *Organon*: published in 1507.

ARNOLFINI, GIOVANNI

(Fifteenth century). Lucchese wool merchant and agent for the merchant house of Marco Guidecon of Laccor; immortalized with his wife in a painting by Jan van Eyck, 1434.

ARQUEBUS

Literally, in German, a *hook-gun*. This small arm was invented by the Spaniards in the mid-fifteenth century.

ARQUES, BATTLE OF

In this battle Henry IV of France, in conflict with the Duke of Mayenne, claimant to the throne, defeated the Duke in 1589. In 1590 Charles X, Cardinal of Bourbon, assumed the throne for a time, expelling Henry IV.

ARRAIS, FREI AMADOR

(1530-1600). Portuguese bishop. Author of *Dialogues:* published in 1589.

ARRAS, TREATY OF

There were two treaties of Arras: (1) In 1435 between Charles VII of France and Duke Philip the Good of Burgundy; by its terms, Burgundy renounced its alliance with England in favor of one with France; thereby France was enabled to expel the English from the Continent—in the last phase of the Hundred Years' War—by 1453, by which time England retained only Calais. (2) In 1482, a treaty settlement between Louis XI of France and the governments of the Netherlands following the death of the Burgundian heiress, Mary of Burgundy. Her husband Maximilian, Archduke of Austria and later Emperor, agreed reluctantly to the treaty, 1483, which ceded Artois and Franche Comté—as his daughter's (Margaret of Austria) dowry on her marriage to Louis' son Charles—to France.

ARREBOE, ANDERS CHRISTENSEN

(1587-1637). Danish poet and bishop. Author of *Hexaemeron:* a narrative poem, published in 1661; he introduced the alexandrine meter to the national literature.

ARSENAL OF VENICE, THE

The government-operated shipyard founded c. 1100 by the doge was one of the tourist marvels of the Renaissance world; frequently rebuilt and expanded, it occupied about thirty acres and was surrounded by formidable walls. The largest and most efficient factory in Europe, it employed 1,000 to 1,600 men (*arsenalotti*) and in the sixteenth century could produce a hundred fully equipped galleys for war against the Turks in two months. The Venetian government carefully supervised the design, construction, and use of ships, specifying their retirement after a given period of service, etc.; interchangeable standard parts were required; by design merchantmen were readily convertible to warships. All ships were owned by the state: merchants bid competitively to rent them for each journey.

ARS NOVA
The style of music, in Italy and France, in the fourteenth and early fifteenth centuries; "the new art," as distinguished from the *Ars Antiqua,* was characterized by a soft, cantabile melodic style and was less decidedly church music. Depending upon one's predilections, one may call the *Ars Nova* the musical style of the late middle ages or of the early Renaissance; the term itself derives from the title of the treatise-manifesto by the friend of Petrarch, Philippe de Vitry, c. 1321.

ART OF ILLUMINATION
Among notable Renaissance book illuminations are: *Smeralda Horace:* 1472, Florence. *Breviary* of S. Croce Franciscan Convent: Florence: late fifteenth century.

ARTICLES OF RELIGION, ENGLISH
Six were published by Henry VIII of England, in 1536. Forty-two were published without Parliamentary consent in 1552. In 1563, these were reduced to thirty-nine: received Parliamentary authority: 1571. They constitute the doctrinal basis of Anglicanism.

ARTUSI, GIOVANNI MARIA
(c. 1550-1613): Italian musicologist. Wrote a number of treatises on musical theory and composition, a sharp critic of Monteverdi.

ASCARELLI, DEBORAH
Sixteenth century. Italian-Jewish authoress, poet. Translated Hebrew liturgical hymns into Italian. She was deeply learned in the corpus of Hebrew literature.

ASCENSION ISLAND
Discovered by Portuguese navigator João da Nova on Ascension Day. 1501.

ASCHAM, ROGER
(c. 1515-1568). English humanist, Latin and Greek scholar, Latin secretary to Queen Mary of England. Secretary to Queen Elizabeth whose tutor he had been. Author of *The Schoolmaster*: educational treatise published in 1570. Also *Toxophilus*: treatise on archery: 1545.

ASELLI, GASPARO
(1581-1626). Professor of anatomy and surgery at Padua. Discovered lacteal vessels. His work was severely taken to task by William Harvey.

ASKE, ROBERT
English leader, in 1536, of Pilgrimage of Grace, a revolt against Henry VIII's religious changes. Executed: 1537.

ASPER, HANS
(1499-1571). Swiss artist. Executed miniatures, woodcuts; best known for his portraits, e.g., *Zwingli;* he imitated Holbein closely.

ASPERTINI, AMICO
(1474-1552). Italian painter and sculptor. Born in Bologna. Executed *St. Augustine administering Baptism, Martyrdom of Saints Valerian and Tibursius;* he also did mythological and historical works, e.g., *The Rape of the Sabines.*

ASPERTINI, GUIDO
(c. 1467-c. 1502). Brother of Amico Aspertini. Italian painter. Born in Bologna. Studied with Ercole of Ferrara. Executed *Crucifixion, Lucretia.*

ASPETTI, TIZIANO
(1565-1607). Sculptor of Padua and nephew of Titian. Died in Venice where he did most of his work. Executed large-scale sculptures and small bronzes, religious and mythological subjects.

ASSASSINATION OF WALLENSTEIN
In 1634 Wallenstein, the Imperial general, was assassinated by

Captain Devereux, probably at the behest of the Emperor Ferdinand II, who distrusted his ambitious general and thought he had no more need of him since the war (Thirty Years' War) would soon end.

ASSELYN, JAN
(1610-1660). Dutch painter. Died in Amsterdam. Known as Crabettje. Noted for landscapes with figures. Usually his motifs are Italian or classical.

ASSEMBLY OF MOULINS
Held in 1566. At meeting of Estates of Moulins Charles IX promulgated far-reaching reforms of the French legal and administrative system.

ASTROLABE, MARINERS'
Adapted from astronomers' astrolabe c. 1480 by German navigator and geographer Martin Behaim (1459-1507). Much used, and much improved, in the age of discoveries, it was not replaced until the invention of the sextant in the eighteenth century.

ASTROLOGICAL PORTENT
Early in 1524 there was widespread fear throughout Europe of another universal deluge. This fear was associated with the conjunction of the planets, in Pisces, in that year.

ASUNDEN LAKE, BATTLE OF
Christian II of Denmark invaded Sweden and defeated the Swedes at Lake Asunden in 1520.

ATHENS
In 1458 Athens was occupied by the Turks.

ATLAS
The Ptolemy Atlas, printed in 1513, is the first modern atlas.

ATLAS OF AMERICA
The first atlas entirely devoted to America was Wytfliet's *Descriptionis Ptolemaicae Augmentum:* published in Louvain in 1597.

ATTAVANTE FIORENTINO, GABRIEL DEGLI
(1452-c. 1510). Most famous of Florentine illuminators. Some thirty-one illuminated codices have been preserved under his

41

name. Noted for artistic taste, glowing colors, decorations. Worked on both secular and religious books. Among his productions are: Urbino Bible, missals, gradual, Corvinus Breviary. Much of his work was commissioned by Vespasiano da Bisticci, the Florentine bookseller.

AUBERBACH, BONIDACIUS
(1495-1562). Jurist. Professor at Basel.

AUBIGNÉ, THÉODORE AGRIPPA D'
(1552-1630). French Huguenot poet. Attached to court of Henry IV. Lived in Geneva. Noted for *Les Tragiques.* Also wrote *Histoire Universelle,* a history of the Huguenot movement, 1553-1602, *Les Aventures du Baron de Foeneste:* satirical novel. Also sonnets, odes.

AUDIGUIER, VITAL D'
(1569-1624). French man of letters, poet, novelist. Translated Cervantes into French. Also author of letters and discourses on poetry and philosophy. He had renounced the life of the soldier for literature, but wrote much on duels, etc.

AUGSBURG, CONFESSION OF
Principal statement of the Lutheran creed during Reformation. Written by Melanchthon. Presented to Emperor Charles V at Diet of Augsburg: 1530, it was an attempt at conciliation. With approval of Luther, creed signed by Protestant notables. Both Latin and German texts. Unaltered Augsburg Confession is foundation of Lutheran confessional literature.

AUGSBURG, DIET OF
An imperial diet held under Charles V, at which the Protestants presented the *Augsburg Confession,* drawn up by Philip Melanchthon. It set forth the Protestant tenets, without prejudice to Catholics. From Strassburg, where Zwingli's teaching had had an impact, the *Confession of Four Cities* was submitted: it resembled the *Augsburg Confession.* The diet decreed the abolition of innovations and affirmed the Edict of Worms, which proclaimed Martin Luther a heretic. The result of the diet was the creation of two opposing parties among the Germans. The diet was held in 1530.

AUGSBURG INTERIM
Temporary agreement in religious matters beween Catholics and

Lutherans. Made at Diet of Augsburg in 1548. Though it com-
promised Reformation doctrines, it was to be binding on Lutherans. Rejected by most Lutheran cities, especially Magdeburg.
Terminated in Treaty of Passau in 1552.

AUGSBURG, RELIGIOUS PEACE OF
A settlement of the Catholic-Lutheran controversy, reached at
the Diet of Augsburg in 1555. All adherents of the Augsburg
Confession were acknowledged as Lutherans and given legal
status and religious freedom. The religion of the ruler was to
be the religion of his subjects: *cuius regio, eius religio.* All dis-
senters were given the right to emigrate. Ostensibly a victory
for the Protestants, the Peace contained an "ecclesiastical reserva-
tion" of the forfeiture of the estates of Catholic prelates who became Protestants after 1552. The settlement ignored Calvinists.

AUGUSTINE DE ZARATE
Sixteenth century. Spanish historian. Wrote on the destruction of
the Inca Empire and the conquest of Peru: published in 1555.
He was an official in the government of Charles V for the Netherlands and afterwards for the possessions in the New World.

AUGUSTINUS, ANTONIUS
(1517-1586). Archbishop of Tarragona, Spain. Noted classical
and legal scholar and archaeologist. He studied law at Bologna
under Alciatus and published a collation of the *Digest* and other
legal studies: emendations to the canonical collection of Gratian:
De Emendatione Gratiani Libri Duo. Published 1607. His reputation for learning was such that he was known as a "repository
of all antiquarian knowledge."

AULIC COUNCIL
Privy Council. Established by the Emperor Maximilian I in
1505. Later it became Council of State of Austria.

AURIFABER, ANDREAS GOLDSCHMIDT
(1514-1559). German physician, philosopher and theologian. He
had studied in Italy; on his return he taught at Wittenberg, then
at Königsberg.

AURISPA, GIOVANNI
(c. 1370-c. 1455). Sicilian humanist, most successful of Italian
collectors of Greek manuscripts. He set off on grand tours comb-

43

ing the Byzantine Empire from 1405 to 1413 and again from 1421 to 1423 with such success that he garnered 238 manuscripts, including works of Aeschylus, Sophocles, and Apollonius of Rhodes.

AUSTRIA AND TURKS
A conflict that extended from 1593 to 1606. The Prince of Transylvania aided the Emperor, Ferdinand of Hapsburg, against the Turks. Part of an age-old contest that ran from the fourteenth into the eighteenth century.

AUSTRIAN ART
In the sixteenth century Late Gothic and Renaissance overlapped in Austrian art. After 1500, Renaissance forms were introduced from Italy, but developed in the Late Gothic spirit. The distinction between Early and High Renaissance, valid for Italy, is not applicable to Austria at this period.

During the first half of the sixteenth century, art destined for the court and for wealthy patrons took precedence over religious art. The reign of Maximilian I (1493-1515) was a period of particular splendor. It was distinguished by a notable school of painting, centering in the Danube Valley, that created an independent art of landscape and drawing. The Danube School, originating chiefly between Passau and Vienna, had as participants Rueland Frueauf the Younger, Marx Reichlich, Jörg Kolderer, Lucas Cranach, Albrecht and Erhard Altdorfer.

The most prominent monument of Renaissance sculpture in Austria is the tomb of Maximilian I at Innsbruck.

The Late Renaissance extends to the latter half of the sixteenth century. It nationalized Italian forms. Austria was open to the influence of the South during the Counter-Reformation. Italian artists received many commissions. The international culture of court and nobility during the reign of the Emperor Rudolph II (1576-1612) sponsored Italian and Netherlands artists.

AUTHORIZED VERSION OF THE BIBLE, THE
Made by order of King James I of England. King named a committee of translators who were 'the best learned in both the Universities.' First published in 1611. Replaced Bishops' Bible and Geneva Bible. Has had an incalculable influence upon English literary style.

AUTO-DA-FÉ
Act of Faith. A public ceremony and announcement, accompanied by its execution, of sentence of the Inquisition. Associated largely with Spain, Portugal, and their colonies. The first recorded Auto-da-Fé was held by Torquemada in Seville, in 1481.

AVANTIUS, JULIUS CAESAR
Sixteenth century. Italian anatomist. Wrote on embryology and gynecology. Work appeared in 1564.

AVENTIUS, JOANNES THURMAIR
(1477-1534). German humanist. Historian. Taught the princes of Bavaria. He wrote a great guide and miscellany of theology and philosophy based upon the classical philosophers and the Latin Fathers, entitled *Encyclopaedia Arbisque Doctrinarum,* 1517. Compiled *Rudimenta Grammaticae;* published in 1542. Best Latin grammar of its time. Author of a history of Bavaria entitled *Annales Boiorum.* He was a sharp critic of abuses and of certain traditions, e.g., pilgrimages in the Church.

AVERCAMP, HENDRIK VAN
(1585-1634). Dutch painter of Amsterdam. Noted for winter landscapes with figures, seascapes also. His works are very rare.

AVERULINO, ANTONIO, IL FILARETE
(died 1469). Florentine sculptor, architect. Worked in bronze. Executed a Marcus Aurelius, bas-relief: *Triumph of Caesar: Madonna and Child.* Did most of his work for the Sforza of Milan.

AVILA, GIL GONZÁLEZ DE
(1577-1658). Spanish historian; he had studied at Rome. Royal historiographer of Castile. Prolific author and editor of Spanish history and antiquities.

AVILA, HERNANDO DE
(Late sixteenth century). Spanish painter and sculptor at the court of Philip II.

AVILA Y ZUNIGA, LUIS DE
(c. 1490-1550). Spanish general, historian, diplomat and dramatist. Wrote on Charles V's campaigns in Germany during 1546-1547.

AVONT, PIETER VAN
(1600-1652). Flemish painter, offspring of a family of many

painters, among them his four brothers. Executed landscapes with many figures in the style of Jan Brueghel the Younger.

AYALA, BALTHASAR
(1543-1612). Spanish jurist. Head of military court of Philip II in Flanders. Author of treatise on nature of war, treatment of prisoners, international law, discipline, punishments: published in 1597, half a century before a similar work by Hugo Grotius.

AYLLON, LUCAS VASQUEZ DE
In 1520-1521 led expedition along the coast of the Carolinas. In 1526 founded colony near Jamestown.

AYOLAS, JUAN DE
(died c. 1537). Spanish conquistador. Explored Rio de la Plata region.

AYRER, JACOB
(died 1605). German dramatist and Imperial notary for Nuremberg. Prolific writer. Part of the same tradition as Hans Sachs. He produced thirty tragedies and comedies and a history of Bamberg.

AYTON, SIR ROBERT
(1570-1638). Scottish poet. Traveled widely on the Continent. Attached to court of James VI of Scotland, whom he followed to England when he became James I; he continued to enjoy royal patronage under Charles I. Studied in Paris. Diplomat. A friend of Ben Jonson. Wrote a superb English, devoid of Scottish dialect.

AZALUS PIACENZA, POMPILUS
Sixteenth century. Author of *Liber de Omnibus Rebus Naturalibus:* published in 1544.

AZPILCUETA, MARTIN
(1493-1586). Spanish theologian and jurist. Author of *Tractatus de Reditibus Beneficiorum Ecclesiasticorum,* one of several works on the reform of the Church, an enterprise to which he devoted much of his life. He also taught for many years at Coimbra in Portugal, and he wrote a treatise on music.

AZURARA, GOMES EANNES DE
(died 1474). Portuguese chronicler. As official keeper of im-

portant archives he had access to superb source material. This he utilized for his chronicles of the reigns of King John, of Alfonso V, of the discovery and conquest of Guinea, of the career of Duarte de Menezes, one of the heroes of Portuguese exploration of the African coast.

B

BABINGTON, ANTONY
(1561-1586). English conspirator. Page to Mary Queen of Scots. Imprisoned in 1586 as leader of conspiracy to murder Queen Elizabeth and bring Mary to the throne of England. He was executed.

BABLAKE SCHOOL
In Coventry, England. English public school. Founded by Queen Isabella: 1344. Refounded in 1560.

BACCIO D'AGNOLO, BARTOLOMEO
(1462-1543). Florentine architect. Raised the Campanile of S. Spirito and many other structures, ecclesiastical, public, private, at Florence. He was decisively influenced by Bramante.

BACKER, JAKOB ADRIANSZ
(1608-1651). Dutch painter. Noted for portraits and genre scenes, strongly influenced by Rembrandt but also by a study trip to Italy.

BACKHOFEN, HANS
(1450-1518). German sculptor. Died in Mainz. Important sculptor of funeral monuments. Belongs to the transitional period from the Gothic to the Renaissance.

BACON, FRANCIS, LORD VERULAM, VISCOUNT ST. ALBANS
(1561-1626). English statesman, philosopher, scientist. Attempted unsuccessfully to win the favor of Queen Elizabeth. On the accession of James I, however, he advanced rapidly, becoming Lord Chancellor in 1618. Charged with bribery, he was imprisoned and banished from court. Later, he was released and pardoned.

Bacon is the author of essays, history, and chiefly of the scientific treatise the *Novum Organum:* 1626. Bacon expounded and advocated the inductive method of reasoning; he did much to "rehabilitate nature" as a subject of inquiry and speculation.

BACON, SIR NICHOLAS

(1509-1579). English statesman. Father of Francis Bacon. Lost royal favor during Mary's reign. Under Queen Elizabeth, he became Lord Keeper of the Great Seal.

BACQUET, JEAN

(died 1597). French jurist and royal official. Wrote on legal questions: disinheritance, bastardy, escheat; a profound student of Roman and feudal law and one of the pioneers of modern historiography.

BADEN

Here, in 1526, a public disputation took place. The participants were John Eck, John Faber, Thomas Münzer. The issue: Lutheran and Zwinglian doctrines.

BAFFIN, WILLIAM

(c. 1584-1622). English navigator. While in search of Northwest Passage, discovered Baffin Bay and Baffin Island. Killed at siege of Ormuz, in Persia. Left account of his experiences in *Voyages.* First to determine longitude by lunar observation.

BAGLIONI FAMILY OF PERUGIA, THE

Despotic rulers of Perugia in the fifteenth century. They are typical of the lesser despots of Italy in the ferocity and cruelty with which they maintained themselves in power until their destruction at the hands of the popes of the 1520's and 1530's. The struggles for power among the Baglioni, and between them and the Oddi family, are echoed in some of the scenes painted by Raphael, a native of Perugia.

BAGLIONI, GIOVANNI, IL SORDO DEL BAROZZO

(1571-1644). Italian painter, writer. Paintings in St. Peter's. Author of *Lives of Painters, Sculptors, Architects:* published in 1642.

BAGNACAVALLO, BARTOLOMMEO RAMENGHI, IL

(1484-1542). Italian painter. Pupil of Raphael. Executed *Madonna with Saints, Crucifixion.*

BAÏF, JEAN ANTOINE DE
(1532-1589). French poet. Member of La Pléiade. Engaged in adapting classical metrical forms to French poetry. Founder of first French academy of music and poetry.

BAIUS, MICHAEL
(1513-1589). Flemish theologian of the Catholic Church, Chancellor of the University of Louvain, sent to the Council of Trent. His doctrines on the nature of sin and grace anticipate Jansenism and were condemned by Pope Pius V. Baius abjured his errors and died a Catholic.

BAKOCZ, THOMAS
(c. 1442-1521). Hungarian Cardinal. Statesman. Chancellor of Hungary. Reduced peasants to serfdom.

BALASSA, VALENTINE
(1551-1594). Hungarian poet. First lyric poet in Hungarian literature. Died in battle against the Turks. Disciple of Petrarch. Wrote religious and patriotic poems, songs of military life, love lyrics.

BALBI, GASPARO
Sixteenth century. Venetian traveler, merchant. Traveled in Southern Asia from 1579 to 1583. Published an account of the East Indies stressing trading possibilities and giving more accurate general description of the region than was available up to then.

BALBOA, VASCO NUÑEZ DA
(1475-1517). Spanish navigator. Sailed to America. Discovered Pacific Ocean in 1513 after having crossed the Isthmus of Panama. Took possession of it and all the shores it touched in the name of Spain. Made journeys of exploration to Central America. Accused of treason: executed by a jealous commander sent out from Spain to replace him.

BALBUENA, BERNARDO DE
(1568-1627). Spanish poet. Lived in New World. Wrote pastoral tales, epic, series of eclogues. La Grandeza Mexicana, which appeared in 1604, is a description of Mexico City.

51

BALDI, BERNARDINO

(1553-1617). Italian philologist and mathematician. An incredibly learned man, he left hundreds of manuscripts on a great variety of subjects, e.g., Aristotle, biographies of several notable figures, Biblical studies, history, etc.

BALDOVINETTI, ALESSIO

(1427-1499). Painter of Florence. Produced frescoes, easel pictures in the style of later stages of early Florentine Renaissance. One of the first to experiment with oil painting. Teacher of Ghirlandaio. He did a vast amount of other work, e.g., mosaics, vases, shields, etc.

BALDWIN, WILLIAM

Sixteenth century. English playwright. Poet. Contributor to *A Mirror for Magistrates.*

BALE, JOHN

(1495-1563). English cleric, poet, and biographer. Fled to Germany: recalled by Edward VI, fled again under Mary, recalled by Elizabeth. As bishop in Leicester, opposed Catholics. Called "Bilious Bale." Wrote Latin catalogues of British writers, beginning with Adam. Also author of plays. Wrote polemical tracts in support of Protestantism.

BALEN, HENDRIK VAN

(1575-1632). Flemish painter of Antwerp. Taught Van Dyck. Executed the figures in the works of Joos de Momper, Jan Brueghel the Elder, and Franz Snyders. He had studied at Rome —as many contemporaries did as a matter of course, so much so that they constituted a society known as Romanists, of whom Balen was a member. Three of his eleven children became painters.

BALLARD, JOHN

(died 1586). English Jesuit. Collaborated in Babington's plot. Executed.

BALLATE

Dance-songs popular in Italy during the Renaissance.

BALNAVES, HENRY

(c. 1500-1579). Scottish Protestant reformer. Secretary of State in 1543. Imprisoned as Protestant, in France. Author of *The Confession of Faith, Treatise on Justification,* and contributor to the *Book of Discipline;* he was one of the builders of Presbyterianism. Released from prison: returned to Scotland.

BALSAMO, GIACOMO DE

Illuminator of Milan. In 1470-1489 he executed four graduals and eight antiphonaries.

BANCHIERI, ADRIANO

(c. 1567-1634). Italian musician and musical theorist. Composed sacred pieces, as well as the music for the comedy *La pazzia senile.* Wrote treatises on music, founder of *Accademia de Floridi* of Bologna.

BANDELLO, MATEO

(c. 1480-c. 1562). Italian writer of romances in the tradition of Boccaccio, utilizing Italian traditions and legends, e.g., of Romeo and Juliet. His work became a mine of sources for others to work.

BANDE NERE, GIOVANNI DELLE

Sixteenth century. Member of the Medicean family. Famous military captain.

BANDINELLI, BACCIO

(1493-1560). Italian sculptor and painter of Florence. Under the patronage of Pope Clement VII. The great passion of his life seems to have been a jealous antagonism for Cellini and Michelangelo. Executed large-scale sculptures. Produced a *Hercules and Cacus,* statutes of Hercules, *Laocoön,* satyrs, *Neptune,* river-gods, bas-reliefs. Symonds: "Nothing Greek about them but their names, their nakedness, and their association with myths."

BANNATYNE, GEORGE

(1545-1608). Scottish anthologist. Left a manuscript compiled during the plague of 1568 of Scottish poetry of the later Middle Ages and down to the sixteenth century. In his honor Sir Walter Scott founded the Bannatyne Club to publish Scottish antiquities.

BAPTISTA MANTUANUS

(1448-1516). Original name Baptista Spagnolo. Of Spanish birth. Studied at Mantua, Padua. He was tutor to the children of Gonzaga, the ducal house of Mantua; he also celebrated the house of Gonzaga in his poetical works. Entered Carmelite monastery renouncing his earlier life of extravagance and indulgence. In 1513, became General of Carmelite Order. Wrote on philosophy, theology, rhetoric. Reputedly produced some 55,000 verses, especially ten *Eclogues* that became a highly popular textbook. Among his contemporaries he was ranked with Vergil. His influence as a poet was felt in Germany, in France, where the *Pléiade* circle knew him well, and in England, among the sixteenth century bucolic poets.

BAPTIST CHURCH

First English Baptist Church formed in Amsterdam in 1609. In London, in 1611.

BARBARI, JACOPO DE

(c. 1455- c. 1515). Venetian painter. Died in Brussels. Brought knowledge of Venetian painting of the school of Bellini to Germany, by means of his religious and mythological paintings. He was a friend of Dürer.

BARBARO, ERMOLAO or HERMELAUS BARBARUS

(1454-1493). Venetian scholar, humanist, translator, and diplomat. As professor at the university of Padua, he was a critic of the scholastic curriculum, insisting that Aristotle was to be known in the original Greek, not through the old translations, still less the Scholastic commentaries. He, as had his father, served Venice as ambassador at Italian and transalpine courts. He wrote a manual of advice, *De officio legati*, for a friend entering the diplomatic service. Written in elegant Ciceronian Latin, it describes the new diplomacy of the new sovereign state; "the first duty of an ambassador," he says, "is exactly the same as that of any other servant of government, that is, to do, say, advise and think whatever may best serve the preservation and aggrandizement of his own state."

BARBARO, FRANCESCO

(1398-1454). Venetian humanist, grandfather of Ermolao, friend of Poggio with whom he shared an enthusiasm for hunting up

54

manuscripts. He is remembered for collecting, collating and emending Greek manuscripts.

BARBARO, JOSAFAT
(died 1494). Venetian merchant. Sent as ambassador to Persia to attempt to form an alliance against the Turks.

BARBAROSSA
Two brothers: Horush (c. 1473-1518) and Khair ad-Din (1483-1546). Turkish pirates, based in Algeria, who terrorized Christian shipping in Mediterranean. Horush killed by Spaniards. Brother died in Constantinople, full of honors as admiral of the Turkish fleet and twice the victor over Andrea Doria.

BARBERS AND BARBER SURGEONS
In 1462 Edward IV of England granted barbers a charter of incorporation. The charter referred to 'Barbers of our city of London exercising the Mystery or the Art of Surgery.' They were at first called *barbitonsors* or *barbisarsors*. Later, they were given the designation of *tonsores chirurgici*. In 1505 their profession was mentioned in the official register in France, and was termed Chirurgia Tonsoria. Unlike medicine, surgery was recognized as no more than a craft.

BARBOU
French family of printers. Sixteenth century. Jean Barbou issued works of the poet Marot in 1539. Hugues Barbou, in Limoges, produced an edition of Cicero's *Letters* in 1580. The firm lasted into the nineteenth century.

BARCELONA, TREATY OF
Negotiated between the Pope, Clement VII, and the Emperor Charles V in 1529. The result: the Medici were restored to Florence and the Spanish ascendancy in Italy was fixed.

BARCLAY, ALEXANDER
(1474-1552). Scottish poet. Traveled in France, Italy. Benedictine monk: then Franciscan. Became rector of All Hallows, London, upon suppression of monasteries. Translated the *Narrenschiff* of Brant as *The Ship of Fools*, 1509.

BARCLAY, JOHN
(1582-1621). Scottish writer and satirical poet. Born in France. Author of *Euphormionis Satyricon:* published in 1605. Politico-

satirical romance, directed against Jesuits, under whom he had been educated. Also wrote *Argenis:* political allegory. Published in 1621.

BARDI, GIOVANNI DE'
(1534-1612). Florentine nobleman, musician and musicologist. It was around him, and meetings at his palace, that the *Camerata* group formed: out of its sessions the opera developed.

BARENTZ, WILLEM
(died 1597). Dutch navigator. Led three expeditions as far as Nova Zembla, in quest of Northeast passage to Orient. In 1596 he discovered Spitzbergen Archipelago. Barents Sea and Barents Island were named after him.

BARET, JOHN
(born 1511). French jurist and magistrate. Author of *Alvearie, or Triple Dictionaire,* in English, Latin and French. Published in 1573. He also published legal studies.

BARGAGLI, ESCIPIONE
(1540-1612). Italian scholar of Siena. Outstanding personality of city. Most famous work is *Delle Imprese:* on emblematic literature; he also wrote a study of the Sienese dialect.

BARGAGLI, GIROLAMO
(died 1586). Professor of Roman law at Siena, brother of the above. Member of the Accademia degl' Intronati of Siena. Author of a book on games: *Dialogo de' Guochi:* published in Venice in 1572.

BARLAEUS, CASPAR, or BAERLE
(1584-1648). Dutch scholar. Poet. Historian. Author of *Epithalamia,* among them *Paradisus,* that describes the nuptials of Adam and Eve. Also wrote *Orationum Liber:* published in 1643: on trade, political philosophy, theology, the Spanish Armada. He taught logic, medicine, philosophy at the Universities of Leiden and Amsterdam; his Calvinist faith compelled him to flee for safety several times in the course of his life.

BARLETTI, MARIANO SANTO DE
(1490-1550). Italian physician. Pupil of Giovanni de Vigo (1460-1525). Lithotomist. Author of *De Lapide ex Vesica per Incisionem*

Extrahendo. Published in Rome in 1522. He also wrote the *Life and Deeds of Scanderbeg,* the Albanian king and hero.

BARLOW, WILLIAM
(died 1625). English mathematician, courtier to James I who made him Archdeacon of Salisbury. Wrote on magnetism and the use of the compass for navigation.

BARNABITES
Catholic Order. Popular name of Congregation of Clerks Regular of St. Paul. Founded in 1530 by St. Anthony Mary Zaccaria (died 1539). Purpose of Order was to preach, catechize, and give missions in conformity with Epistles of St. Paul.

BARNES, BARNABE
(c. 1569-1609). English lyric poet. Wrote sonnets, tragedy: *The Devil's Charter.* Also *Parthenophil and Parthenophe: Sonnettes, Madrigals, Elegies, and Odes,* 1593, an extravagantly fanciful work.

BARNET, BATTLE OF
One of the battles in the Wars of the Roses: fought in 1471. Edward IV, Yorkist, defeated and killed the Earl of Warwick, the Kingmaker, his kinsman and former ally.

BARNEVELDT, JAN VAN OLDEN
(1547-1619). Dutch republican statesman who championed Dutch independence, and opposed the monarchist party of Maurice of Nassau. Supported Remonstrants against Maurice and the orthodox Calvinists. Arranged treaty with Spain, in 1609. Illegally arrested in 1618, he was charged with treason and executed.

BARNFIELD, RICHARD
(1574-1627). English poet. Author of pastoral poems. Noted for *The Affectionate Shepherd:* published in 1594. Two of his poems were long attributed to Shakespeare.

BAROCCIO, FEDERIGO
(1528-1612). Italian painter and engraver of Urbino. Influenced by Raphael, Correggio. Most of his painting was on religious subjects; they are characterized by an intensity suggestive of the Baroque.

BAROMETER
Earliest form of instrument invented in 1644 by Evangelista Torricelli (1608-1647). Torricelli was an Italian physicist and mathematician. Secretary to Galileo. Professor at Academy of Florence.

BARONET
Title created by King James I of England: 1611.

BARONIUS, CAESAR
(1538-1607). Ecclesiastical historian and disciple of St. Philip Neri. In 1557 he joined the Oratory in Rome. Vatican librarian. Known for his *Annales Ecclesiastici:* twelve volumes appeared between 1588 and 1607 that cover from the time of Christ to the reign of Innocent III; distinctively favorable to the popes, it is nevertheless a remarkably objective work.

BAROZZI, GIACOMO
(1507-1573). Italian architect. Giacomo da Vignola. Author of a treatise on the Five Orders of Architecture, based upon Vitruvius. Worked in France, Bologna, Rome. After Michelangelo, the chief achitect of St. Peter's. He is important for the transition to Baroque architecture; although he was a close student of classical forms, he insisted upon freedom and originality in their use. His design of the mother church of the Jesuits, Church of the Gesu of Rome, is notable for its sumptuous interior and is said to have established "the Jesuit style." He was the greatest architect of the later sixteenth century.

BARRAT
Fraud: distress. In the fifteenth and sixteenth centuries a barrator was an ecclesiastic who bought and sold preferment, or a dishonest judge.

BARRETO, FRANCISCO
Sixteenth century. Portuguese Governor of India. In 1569 led an expedition to Mozambique. In conflict with native tribes. Died of fever. On his order Camoens was forced to depart for Macao, an incident to which reference is made in the *Lusiades* and in a later satirical work by Camoens, *Disparates da India.*

BARROW, HENRY

(died 1593). English reformer. Proposed reformation in Anglican Church. His followers were known as Barrowists.

BARROW, ISAAC

(1630-1677). English mathematician, theologian, and linguist, Professor at Cambridge. Taught Isaac Newton. Author of *Methods of Tangents:* also *Sermons* and theological works.

BARTAS, SEIGNEUR DU, GUILLAUME DE SALUSTE

(1544-1590). French Huguenot poet, diplomat and soldier. Author of *La Semaine ou Création du Monde:* didactic epic poem on Creation. Work influenced Milton. In six years thirty editions were published; it was translated into Latin, German, Italian, and English. Also wrote *La Seconde Semaine:* universal history, incomplete.

BARTHOLIN, KASPAR

(1585-1629). Danish physician and man of universal learning. Author of fifty works on philosophy, history, literary criticism, medicine, anatomy and theology; he traveled widely in Europe.

BARTHOLOMEW'S DAY, MASSACRE OF SAINT

Massacre of Protestants by Catholics in Paris on St. Bartholomew's Day, August 24, 1572. Among the victims were Ramus, Coligny, La Place. Result was renewal of civil war. Blame rests chiefly with the regent, Catherine de' Medici and her indefinite policies.

BARTISCH, GEORGE

(1535-1606). German ophthalmologist. Removed the practice of ophthalmology from itinerant quacks and elevated it to the dignity of a medical specialty. Advanced from position of an unlettered barber surgeon to the status of court oculist to the Elector of Saxony. Author of *Augensdienst:* published in Dresden in 1583. Among the first oculists to base his theories on anatomy, physiology, and optics.

BARTOLOMMEO DELLA PORTA, FRA

(c. 1470-1517): Italian painter of Florence. Adherent of Savonarola, whose portrait he painted. Entered Dominican convent, shortly after Savonarola's death. Teacher of Raphael. Works: *Christ at Emmaus, Madonna and Saints, Last Judgment.* An excellent craftsman and a consummate colorist, on the testimony of J.A. Symonds. Bartolommeo's contribution to Italian art lies in his composition and coloring. Nature, he adds, made Fra Bartolommeo the painter of adoration. Together with Andrea del Sarto, he represents the peak of Renaissance painting in Florence. Executed religious subjects only.

BARTOLOMMEO DELLA ROCCA
(1467-1504). Called Cocles. Italian occultist. Mendicant barber who undertook the study of physiognomy, chiromancy and astrology. Wrote a compendious work on the subjects, entitled *Anastasis*. Translated into English, French, German.

BARTOLOMMEO DI RICCI
(1490-1569). Teacher in Ravenna and Ferrara. Author of *Apparatus Latinae Locutionis:* a Latin dictionary with illustrative quotations from the classics. Published in 1535.

BARTOLUS OF SASSOFERATO
(1314-1357). "The prince of jurists," the founder of the leading school of Roman law studies of the fourteenth and fifteenth centuries. He taught law at Perugia; he and his followers, the Bartolists, sought to elaborate the Roman law—incorporating the legal principles of the Church, practices and conceptions of the Italian towns and the transalpine states—into a code for all Christendom. Humanist scholars were severely critical of the Bartolist school as unhistorical.

BARTON, ELIZABETH
(c. 1506-1534). English prophetess and mystical seer. Called The Nun of Kent and The Maid of Kent. Executed for treason during Henry VIII's religious revolution, for predicting dire consequences if Henry divorced Queen Catherine.

BARZENA, ALONSO
(1528-1598). Spanish missionary. Called The Apostle of Peru. Born in Cordova. In 1559, to the New World. Wrote on languages of South America.

BASAITI, MARCO
(Sixteenth century). Venetian painter. Spent most of his life in Venice. Executed religious subjects with landscape backgrounds, one of the first Venetian painters to work in oils.

BASCIO, MATTEO DA
(1495-1552). Franciscan monk. Adhered rigidly to the rule of St. Francis. Tended plague-stricken peasants.

BASELARD
A dagger, usually worn at the belt. In use for several centuries, from the fourteenth on.

BASEL, COUNCIL OF
This Council ran from 1431-39 at the high tide of the Conciliar Movement; its attempts to impose limitations on the papal monarchy were discredited as heresy.

BASEL, PEACE OF
This treaty ended the war between Maximilian I and the Swiss, in 1499.

BASIUS ASCENIUS, JODOCUS
(1462-1535). An eminent printer at Paris; he had studied at Ferrara, was for some time professor of Greek at Lyons, and edited several of the classical authors. He wrote a life of Thomas à Kempis and a satire on women, the *Novicula Itultarum Mulierum.*

BASMAISON ROYGUET, JEAN DE
(Sixteenth century). French jurist, remembered for his moderation in cases involving Huguenots. He wrote a treatise on fiefs and one on feudal custom.

BASQUE
The oldest Basque literary monument is a series of poems written by Bernard Dechepare, a priest, in 1545.

BASSANO
Venetian family of painters in sixteenth century. Members were: the founder of the family workshop, Francesco the Elder (c. 1470-1541), Jacopo (1510-1592). Executed religious subjects in genre form, landscapes with figures, peasant scenes, portraits. Francesco the Younger (1549-1592). Leandro (1558-1623). Both Francesco and Leandro painted large-scale religious pictures, landscapes, portraits.

BASSANO, JACOPO
(1510-1592). Italian painter of Venice. Specialized in genre themes, portraits. His works include Biblical scenes, e.g., *The*

Good Samaritan. Also portraits of Ariosto and Tasso. Founded school that specialized in rural themes: cattle, markets.

BASSE, WILLIAM
(died c. 1653). English poet. Author of bucolic works *Urania, Polyhymnia,* wrote an elegy on Shakespeare, and a long poem of epic deeds, *Sword and Buckler.*

BASSEN, BARTHOLOMAUS VAN DER
(1600-1652). Dutch painter and architect. Died at The Hague. Produced richly peopled interiors, Dutch churches; much of his painting is notable for architectural backgrounds.

BASSOMPIERRE, FRANÇOIS, BARON DE
(1579-1649). Marshal of France and protagonist of Henry IV. In conflict with Huguenots. Opposed to Richelieu. Author of *Memoirs,* written while he was imprisoned in the Bastille at Richelieu's order.

BASTIDAS, RODRIGO DE
(c. 1460-1526). Spanish explorer in South America. Founded Santa Maria, Colombia, in 1525. Had accompanied Balboa and was a friend to the Indians.

BATHORY, STEPHEN
(1533-1586). Prince of Transylvania. Elected King of Poland in 1575. In conflict with Russia: 1579-1582, he defeated Ivan the Terrible several times and sought to make Russia a client state of Poland. He brought the Jesuits into Poland to reform the Church and stamp out heresy.

BATTELL, ANDREW
(1565-1640). English traveler. To Rio de la Plata. Captured by Indians. Imprisoned by Portuguese. Sent to the Congo. Traded with Portuguese. Returned, after eighteen years, to England. Left a narrative of his experiences, *The Strange Adventures of A. Battell, Prisoner in Angola.*

BATTISTA DA IMOLA, FRA
Fifteenth century. Italian traveler. In 1482 headed a delegation to Abyssinia and Eritrea, sent out for missionary purposes by Pope Sixtus IV; he left a written account of his itinerary.

BAUHIN, GASPARD

(1560-1624). Swiss botanist and physician. Professor at Basel. Author of *Theatrum Anatomicum:* published in 1621. Also wrote treatise on botany: *Prodromus Theatri Botanica.* Published in 1620. His classifications of plants by genus and species anticipated the work of Linnaeus.

BAUHIN, JEAN

(1541-1613). Swiss botanist, elder brother of the above. Wrote history of plants: uncompleted.

BAYARD, SEIGNEUR

(c. 1474-1524). Pierre du Terrail. French heroic figure. Personified perfect knighthood and the ideal of chivalry. Known as *Chevalier sans peur et sans reproche.* Participated in Italian campaigns. Killed in battle in Italy. He was brave but also intelligent.

BAZZI, GIOVANNI

(c. 1477-1549). Called Il Sodoma. Italian painter. Produced series of frescoes at Monte Oliveto on the life of St. Benedict; like all his work, they exhibit a delicate and ethereal religious sentiment. He was the most gifted disciple of Leonardo.

BÉARN

This region in the Pyrenees was united to France in 1620.

BEAUFORT, MARGARET

(1443-1509). Countess of Richmond and Derby. Granddaughter of John of Gaunt, she married Edmund Tudor and was mother of Henry VII. Called Lady Margaret. Philanthropist. Sponsored education: endowed professorial chairs and with the help of her confessor, John Fisher, founded Christ's College and St. John's College at Cambridge.

BEAUMONT, FRANCIS

(1584-1616). English dramatist. Collaborated with John Fletcher (1579-1625) in numerous comedies and tragedies, among them: *The Knight of the Burning Pestle, The Coxcomb, Philaster.*

BEAUMONT, SIR JOHN

(1583-1627). English poet. Author of *The Crown of Thorns:*

sacred poem. Not extant. Also *Bosworth Field:* historical piece celebrating the victory of Henry VII over Richard III.

BEAUNE, FLORIMOND DE

(1601-1652). French mathematician. Noted for studies in the field of integral calculus, anticipating Newton and Leibnitz.

BEBEL, HEINRICH

(1472-1518). German humanist, patriot, friend of Erasmus, popular poet, social critic. Compiled collection of German proverbs: translated into Latin: *Facetiae,* and numerous works on history, politics, poetry. Among his students was Melanchthon; he was crowned poet laureate by Emperor Maximilian.

BECCADELLI, ANTONIO, IL PANORMITA

(1394-1471). Italian humanist poet and chief figure of the Academy of Naples founded by Alfonso the Magnanimous, whom he commemorated in an anecdotal *Words and Deeds of Alfonso the Great.* He is chiefly remembered for his poetical jumble of licentious, satirical and panegyrical verse, the *Hermaphroditus,* 1425.

BECCAFUMI, DOMENICO

(1486-1551). Il Meccherino. Sienese painter, sculptor, engraver. Treated scenes from Old Testament. Noted for frescoes, marble figures, sculptural pieces. His work, especially after his stay at Rome, shows strongly the influence of Raphael and Michelangelo.

BECCARI, ANTONIO

(Fifteenth century). Italian Hellenist. He traveled to England and enjoyed the patronage of "good Duke Humphrey" of Gloucester and later, upon his return to Italy, of Ermolao Barbaro. He made numerous translations, e.g., from Aristotle and Plutarch. He was a member of a famous family that produced several humanists. Author of the first complete pastoral drama: *Il Sacrificio,* published in 1554.

BECERRA, GASPAR

(1520-1570). Spanish sculptor, architect and painter, studied under Vasari, executed commission for Philip II of Spain.

BECK, LEONARD

(born 1542). German artist. Born at Augsburg. Made designs for woodcuts. Member of circle of artists attached to **Emperor Maximilian.**

BEDMAR, ALFONSO DE CUEVA, MARQUIS DE
(1572-1655). Spanish ambassador to Venice. In 1618 conspired to destroy Venetian Republic and annex it to Spain. Exposed. Went to Flanders: became cardinal. Subject of Thomas Otway's play *Venice Preserved.*

BEDWELL, WILLIAM
(c. 1561-1632). English Orientalist of St. John's College, Cambridge. Introduced Arabic studies in England. Lexicographer. Wrote Arabic lexicon. Also translated Arabic texts on mathematics. He also was a member of the group of scholars who made the King James Version of the Bible.

BEGARELLI, ANTONIO
(1479-c. 1565). Italian sculptor of Modena. Executed large-scale figures, groups in clay. Most of his work was religious, commissioned by ecclesiastical patrons. He did, however, do a *Hercules* for Duke Ercole II of Modena. His nephew Ludovico (c. 1529-1577) followed in his footsteps as a sculptor.

BEGGARS
A term of contempt applied to Dutch petitioners for reforms in the Spanish government of the Netherlands in 1566, the starting point of the Dutch Revolt. The expression was subsequently associated with all Hollanders who fought against Spain in the wars of independence.

BEGGARS OF THE SEA
Privateers chartered by William the Silent in 1569 were so called. The Dutch seamen fought against the Spanish during the Dutch Revolt: 1568-1576, and were most effective against the Duke of Alva, who was capable of fighting only a land war.

BEHAIM, MARTIN
(1459?-1507). German cosmographer, navigator, astronomer, and mathematician. Traveled as merchant through Europe. Made improvements in the astrolabe and other navigational devices and also constructed a terrestrial globe. Appears in German fiction.

BEHAM, BARTHEL
(1502-1540). Painter, engraver. Painter to Duke William of

Bavaria who sent him to Italy to study. Executed portraits, superb copperplate engravings.

BEHAM, HANS SEBALD

(1500-1555). German artist of Nuremberg, brother of the above. Executed ornamental engravings, noted for their depiction of the life of the day. He and his brother were among the finest of the German Little Masters or *Kleinmeister*.

BELAIN, PIERRE, SIEUR D'ESNAMBUC

(c. 1570-1636). Founded first French colonies in St. Christopher, West Indies, also in Martinique.

BELGA, BENIGNUS BOSSIUS

Sixteenth century. Belgian engraver. Worked in Rome after 1550. Engraved some of Raphael's paintings.

BELGIC CONFESSION

The Reformed creed of thirty-seven articles, prepared in 1561 by Guido de Bres. In amended form, adopted by various synods from 1566 to 1581: finally, by the Synod of Dort, in 1619. Authoritative doctrinal statement of Reformed Churches of Holland and Belgium.

BELGRADE

The city of Belgrade was captured by the Turks in 1521. It had been under Turkish pressure for many years, e.g., in 1456 when John Hunyadi forced Mohammed II to raise his siege of the city.

BELLANO, BARTOLOMEO

(1434?-1497?). Italian sculptor and architect of Padua. Executed tombs, statues, bas-reliefs with biblical themes, in bronze and marble in the style of Donatello.

BELLARMINO, ROBERTO, SAINT

(c. 1542-1621). Italian diplomat, theologian, papal champion, one of the architects of Catholic Reform. Archbishop of Capua. Cardinal. Entered Jesuit Order. Noted for his integrity. Engaged in theological disputes with James I of England and others. Author of *De Controversiis Christianae Fidei:* on Protestant position. Published in Rome in 1581. Also produced autobiography, in Latin. Wrote *De Officio Principis Christiani:* published in 1619. Friend and admirer of Galileo, with whose condemnation he had nothing to do, although he was a member of the Inquisition.

BELLAUD DE LA BELLAUDIÈRE, LOUIS
(1532-1588). Provençal poet. His poems display intense love for Provence; e.g., *Don-don infernal*: published in 1588. He was something of a vagabond in the Villon tradition; he was embroiled in the civil and religious strife, and was imprisoned for two years.

BELLEGAMBE, JEAN
(c. 1489-post 1535). Painter. Belongs in the early Brabantine-French Renaissance. Most of his work was religious; his canvases are often crowded with many figures.

BELLENDEN, JOHN
Sixteenth century. Scottish writer, translator, and poet. Attached to court of James V. Theologian. Translated part of Livy. Also Boece's *Historia Scotorum* into Scottish idiom, in 1533. His antagonism for the Reformation in Scotland led to his exile to the Continent.

BELLENDEN, WILLIAM
(c. 1555-1633). Scottish classical scholar. Professor in Paris and friend of James I of England, who was his patron. Author of *De Statu Libri Tres*: published in 1616. Also wrote *De Tribus Luminibus Romanorum*: published in 1634. He greatly admired Cicero: all his published works deal with Cicero, Roman history and politics at the end of the Republic, and the origin and nature of monarchy as seen in the Roman sources, especially Cicero.

BELLI, VALERIO
(1465?-1546). Italian engraver. Executed medallions. Worked in bronze. Much of his work was commissioned by Popes Leo X and Clement VII.

BELLINI, GENTILE
(c. 1426-1507). Italian painter. Produced work for the Venetian State and was sent by it to Constantinople. Introduced oil painting in murals. Chief works: Portraits, series of pageants and *Preaching of St. Mark*, most notable production. At Constantinople, executed the famous portrait *Mohammed II*.

BELLINI, GIOVANNI
(1428-1516). Italian painter of Venice. Represents the Venetian

Renaissance at its peak. Executed religious subjects, portraits, altarpieces; the teacher of Giorgione and Titian.

BELLINI, JACOPO

(c. 1400-1464). Italian painter of Venice, father of Gentile and Giovanni. His sketch book (c. 1430) is among the most valuable sources for the history of Venetian art. He was the founder of the Bellini family tradition in painting and of the family's workshop. J. A. Symonds: "Bright costumes, distinct and sunny landscapes, broad backgrounds of architecture, large skies, polished armor, gilded cornices, young faces of fisher boys and country girls."

BELMONTE, JACOB ISRAEL

(1570-1629). Poet: born in Madeira. A founder of the Amsterdam Portuguese-Jewish Community. His poem *Job* is an account of the Inquisition in the Iberian peninsula.

BELON, PIERRE

(1517-1564). French naturalist and favorite of Henry II and Charles IX. Studied medicine. Pupil of Valerius Gordus the botanist. Traveled for three years in Asia Minor, Arabia, Egypt. Planted the first cedar trees in France. Author of travel book. Also wrote treatises on birds, herbs, fishes, works which make him a pioneer in comparative anatomy. He was assassinated in Paris, a victim of the civil and religious strife.

BEMBO DA CREMONA, BONIFACIO

Painter, illuminator. Worked c. 1440 to 1478. Decorated many manuscripts. Patronized by the Sforza court of Milan. Noted for his portraits.

BEMBO, PIETRO

(1470-1547). Venetian nobleman, educated in the humanist tradition of Guarino at the University of Ferrara, papal secretary to Leo X during whose reign Bembo was at the zenith of his fame as veritable literary dictator and as the "strictest of Ciceronians"; wrote a defense of the Italian vernacular; made a Cardinal in 1538. He was commissioned by the Venetian government to write a Latin history of that state; entitled *Historia rerum Venetorum,* it was a continuation of a fifteenth-century work by Sabellicio. Bembo was famous in his lifetime as an expounder of Platonic love, especially in his *Gli Asolani;* he appears as one of the speakers in Castligione's *Il Cortegiano* where he is made to express the Platonic notions of love and of the soul.

BENALCÁZAR, SEBASTIÁN DE
(c. 1479-1551). Spanish conquistador, ruthless and ambitious. Accompanied Columbus on third journey, attached to Pizarro in the conquest of Peru. Participated in conquest of Colombia and Ecuador, founder of Quito and Guayaquil.

BENATIUS, JACOBUS
Sixteenth century. Professor at the University of Bologna. Lectured on medicine and astrology.

BENAVIDES, MARCUS
(1489-1582). Jurist of Padua. He stood high in the esteem of Emperor Charles V and Pope Pius IV. He was a collector of art, protector and friend to a circle of artists and writers, and author of an *Epitome virorum illustrium*.

BENEDETTI, ALEXANDER
(c. 1460-1525). Teacher of anatomy at Padua. In his lectures, he stressed the necessity for dissection and the direct observation of nature; he wrote several works on anatomy and medicine.

BENEDETTI, GIOVANNI BATTISTA
(1530-1590). Venetian mathematician, pioneer in analytical geometry. He was an antagonist of Aristotelian physics and is credited with the conclusion that bodies of different weight fall at different speeds because of air resistance. He wrote several works on geometry, mathematics and physics, in one of which he was the penetrating critic of Euclid.

BENEDETTO DA MAJANO
(1442-1497). Italian sculptor and architect of the Florentine school. Noted for pulpits, altarpieces and other church furnishings.

BENEGNO, GIORGIO
Sixteenth century. Archbishop of Nazareth. Logician. Author of *Praecepta Dialectices:* published in Rome in 1520.

BENINCASA, URSULA
(1547-1618). Italian nun. Founded Order of Theatine nuns: Order

of Oblate Sisters of the Immaculate Conception of the Blessed
Virgin Mary.

BENING, ALEXANDER
(died 1519). Flemish illuminator. In 1469 he became member of
Ghent Guild of Painters. Father of Simon and Paul Bening, most
famous Flemish miniaturists of sixteenth century. Among the
rulers whose patronage they enjoyed was Charles V.

BENIVIENI, ANTONIO
(c. 1440-1502). Florentine surgeon and pathological anatomist.
Performed autopsies to determine cause of death. His one work,
De abditis nonnullis ac mirandis marborum et sanatorius causis,
was published shortly after his death.

BENSON, AMBROSIUS
(died 1550). Painter of Lombard origin. Died in Bruges. Noted
for religious subjects, portraits, including one of St. Anthony
of Padua.

BENTIVOGLIO FAMILY, THE
Despotic rulers of Bologna during fifteenth century. The struggle
to establish their lordship was completed by Giovanni II, who
ruled from 1462 to 1506, when Pope Julius II conquered the
city and added it to the Papal States. The Bentivoglio were
typical of the *signori* in their lavish patronage of the arts and
of learning.

BENTIVOGLIO, GUIDO
(1579-1644). Italian diplomat, historian, cardinal. Author of a
history of the wars in the Netherlands against Spanish rule; published in 1629. Also wrote *Memoirs* and letters, important sources
for Dutch Revolt.

BEOLCO, ANGELO, IL RUZZANTE
(1502-1542). Italian poet, actor of Padua. Wrote and produced
comedies in which comic element derives from Italian dialects
and pantomime. Beginning in the tradition of the *commedia dell'
arte*, he is said to have developed the masked comedy.

BERANDA, PAMVA
(died 1632). Ukrainian author of *Slavena-Rossky* Lexicon.

BERENGARIO DA CARPI, GIACOMO
(1470-1550). Italian anatomist and surgeon. Professor at Bologna from 1502 to 1522. Author of *De Fractura Cranii:* published in Bologna in 1518. Wrote a commentary on the *Anatomy* of Mondino: published in Venice in 1521. Also a treatise on the heart, *Isogogae:* published in 1523. He was the first to undertake a systematic view of the textures of which the human body is composed. He was also among the first to illustrate an anatomical text with figures. He is most notable, however, as an early dissenter from Galen, a serious matter for which one might even be arrested.

BERGER, LUIS
(1590-1643). Spanish Jesuit. At age of twenty-six, set out to Buenos Aires on mission to Indians. Used his skills in music and painting to convey theological conceptions and to persuade natives to be baptized.

BERGERAC SAVIENIEN, CYRANO DE
(1619-1655). French writer. Author of satirical romances, e.g., *Histoire Comique des États de la Lune et du Soleil.* He appears in Edmond Rostand's play *Cyrano de Bergerac,* much idealized; his own character was that of a swashbuckler who gained renown for many duels fought over insults to his nose.

BERGOMOTIUS, LAURENTIUS
Fifteenth century. Italian musician. Composed *laude.*

BERLICHINGEN, GOTTFRIED VON
(1480-1562). German knight and adventurer. At siege of Landshut, in 1504, lost arm. Called Götz with the Iron Hand. Imprisoned twice. In service of Charles V. Fought against French, Turks. Subject of plays in German, French: one by Goethe which drew on Götz's memoirs. He is a symbol of towering, instinctive courage and the absence of mental torment or introspection.

BERNARDES, FATHER DIOGO
(c. 1530-c. 1605). Portuguese poet. Spent years in captivity in North Africa. Author of *Various Rhymes to the Good Jesus:* published in 1594. Also *Flowers of the River Lima:* appeared in 1596. Chief poet of the Renaissance in Portugal, given a pension by Philip II of Spain, who was also King of Portugal after 1580.

BERNARDI, GIOVANNI DA CASTELBOLOGNESE
(1496-1553). Italian sculptor and medal artist. Executed plaques in bronze, medallions in gold, etc., for the Este, Charles V and Pope Clement VII.

BERNARDINO DA MILANO
(Fifteenth century). Italian sculptor and architect. Executed bronze casts for the sculptor Giovanni Francesco Rustici (1474-1554). He also had a hand in the layout of the main square of Vicenza.

BERNARDINO DA SIENA, SAINT
(1380-1444). Observant Franciscan monk and preacher of repentance. A passionate concern for his salvation and that of mankind, and an equally passionate sense of sin, led him to abandon his legal studies and refuse ecclesiastical preferment in order to dedicate himself to a long career of itinerant preaching. He went to Guarino for lessons in rhetoric; beyond that, however, he was untouched by humanism. His career testifies—as does Savonarola's—to the puritanical-revivalist current that persisted throughout the Renaissance. He was canonized six years after his death by Nicholas V.

BERNARD VON BREYDENBACH
Fifteenth century. German traveler. Canon of Mainz. Made a pilgrimage to the Holy Land. Wrote an account, illustrated: published in 1483-1484.

BERNERS, JOHN BOURCHIER, LORD
(1467-1533). English writer, statesman. Chancellor of the Exchequer. Made a classic translation of Froissart's *Chronicles,* a work which Shakespeare drew upon directly or indirectly in his *Histories.* Also the romance of *Huon of Bordeaux* and other works of chivalry.

BERNI, FRANCESCO
(1497-1536). Italian poet. Noted for burlesque poetry: named after him *poesia bernesca.* This was a Tuscan genre, practiced by Della Casa, Varchi, Mauro, Dolce, Firenzuola. He also recast Boiardo's unfinished *Orlando Innamorato.* He was center of a circle of wits at Rome; there is a tradition that he was poisoned by Duke Alessandro of Florence.

BERNINI, GIOVANNI
(1598-1680). Italian architect and sculptor of the Baroque age; he did the baldachino over the altar of St. Peter's as well as the colonnades of its piazza.

BEROALDO, FILIPPO
(1453-1505). Italian humanist of Bologna. Professor of literature. Cultivated the style of the Latin Apuleius. Author of *Varia Opuscula:* published in 1509. A collection of orations, epigrams, study of Pythagorean symbols. He also left an account of the French invasions of Charles VIII and Louis XII. His son and namesake (1472-1518) was librarian of the Vatican collection under Leo X and editor of Tacitus.

BERQUIN, LOUIS DE
(died 1529). French reformer. Heretic. Supported Lutheran doctrines. Executed. He was a friend of Erasmus and moved in humanist circles.

BERRUGUETE, ALONSO
(c.1480-1561). Spanish sculptor, painter and architect. Pupil of Michelangelo and notable for bringing to Spain the influence of his master and the High Renaissance. Court sculptor, painter, and chamberlain to Charles V.

BERTAUT, JEAN
(1552-1611). Bishop of Séez. French poet of light and airy verse. Follower of Ronsard. He is supposed to have helped convert Henry IV to Catholicism.

BERTIUS, P.
(1565-1625). Geographer and historiographer to King Louis XIII. Friend of Lipsius and Grotius. Edited Ptolemy. Also wrote *De Aggeribus et Pontibus:* a history of building of dams and bridges, from antiquity to his own times. Published in 1629.

BERTOLDO DI GIOVANNI
(c. 1420-c. 1491). Sculptor and metals artist of Florence. Executed reliefs, small bronzes for San Marco of Florence. He was the disciple of Donatello, intimate friend of Lorenzo the Magnificent, and one of the teachers of Michelangelo.

BESSARION, CARDINAL, NICENO
(died 1472). Byzantine scholar and monk who came to Italy in

the train of the Emperor, John Paleologus, for the Council of Ferrara-Florence, 1431-1434, at which time the two Churches were reconciled and on which occasion Pope Eugenius IV made Bessarion a Cardinal. He was instrumental in furthering Greek studies in Italy; he is most important as the defender of Plato in a much-read apologia, and thus paved the way for the vogue of Plato and the establishment of the Florentine Platonic Academy. Twice he came close to being elected pope, but owing to his Greek origin was passed over, in 1471 in favor of the infamous Sixtus IV.

BESSARION'S LIBRARY
In 1468 Cardinal Bessarion donated his collection of Greek and Roman authors to the Church of Saint Mark, in Venice.

BETHLEN GÁBOR
(1580-1629). Prince of Transylvania. King of Hungary. Protestant. Opposed Austrian Hapsburgs. In 1621 he made peace with Emperor Ferdinand II and renounced royal title. Called 'one of the three great Magyars.' Appears in Hungarian fiction much idealized, in reality was a supple opportunist.

BETTI, BENEDETTO
Sixteenth century. Florentine humanist scholar. Delivered funeral oration on Duke Cosimo I de' Medici. Published in 1574.

BETUSSI, GIUSEPPE
(died 1573). Trevisan author and scholar. Author of treatise on Platonic and ideal love, supported by opinions of Dante, Boccaccio, Castiglione. Also translated into Italian Boccaccio's *De Claris Mulieribus*. A merry scamp, he led an adventurous life and authored many works, e.g., a life of Boccaccio, works on aesthetics, and a verse translation of part of the *Aeneid*.

BEUKELAER, JOACHIM
(c. 1535-1573). Painter of Antwerp. Noted for still life, kitchen interiors, market places, religious scenes.

BEUTER, PEDRO ANTONIO
Early sixteenth century. Spanish theologian, historian, papal nuncio. Wrote *Crónica Generale d'Hispagna:* kings of Aragon, Castile, Navarre, conquest of Moors, history of El Cid, and history of his native Valencia. He was trained in the humanist

methods of textual analysis and was famous for his exposure of the forgeries of Annio da Viterbo.

BEYER, ABSOLON PEDERSSON
(c. 1529-c. 1574). Norwegian scholar. Educated at Copenhagen and Wittenberg. Taught at Bergen. Lutheran humanist. Author of a *Description of Norway*. Also wrote *Diary, Liber Bergensis Capituli*, a work on the history of Bergen. His wife was burnt as a witch in 1590.

BEZA, THEODORE
(1519-1605). French scholar and Calvinist theologian. Friend of Calvin. Leader of Reformation in France. Prolific author of religious treatises in French and Latin, and professor of Greek at Lausanne and then at Geneva; he also participated in Greek and Latin editions of the New Testament. Successor to Calvin at Geneva.

BEZONIAN
A raw recruit: a beggar: a rascal. Originally, *besonio:* from the Italian *bisogno*, need, want. Applied to ill-equipped soldiers who came to Italy from Spain in the fifteenth and sixteenth centuries.

BIANCHI, MARCO ANTONIO
(1498-1548). Paduan jurist. Wrote *Practica Criminalis*: on accusation, witnesses, evidence, sentencing: a compendium of Renaissance law: published in 1556. Also treatise on homicide considered from legal and moral aspects: published in 1546, and several other works on law and jurisprudence.

BIARD, PIERRE
(c. 1567-1622). French missionary. In charge of first Jesuit mission to Canada, in 1611. Wrote *Relation de la Nouvelle France*, the record of his violent experiences in Canada, including a lengthy imprisonment; it was published in 1616.

BIBAGO, ABRAHAM
(died after 1489). Spanish-Jewish philosopher, exegete, religious disputant. Author of *Way of Faith*, a defense of Judaism. Grounded in Christian and Islamic learning as well as Jewish thought, he was a defender of Maimonides and of Averroës.

BIBLE IN ITALY
First translation of Bible into Italian by Niccolò Malermi. Published in Venice in 1493.

BIBLIANDER, THEODORUS
(1504-1564). Swiss theologian and Orientalist. Professor of Hebrew and later of theology at Zurich. Wrote commentary on Koran and Mohammedan faith, published in 1543. He was an Erasmian Reformer; he also helped to edit the Zurich Bible.

BICCHERNA TABLETS
A series of illuminated tablets associated with Siena. Contained tax records, contracts, and other civic memoranda. Date from thirteenth century to fifteenth century. Artists engaged in this work included: Giovanni di Paolo (c. 1403-1482), Sano di Pietro, Lorenzo di Pietro (c. 1412-1480), Benvenuto di Giovanni (1436-c. 1518), Neroccio di Bartolomeo (1447-1500), Domenico Beccafumi (1486-1551).

BICOCCA, BATTLE OF LA
The French under Francis I were defeated by the forces of the Pope, England, and Charles V, in 1522.

BIDERMAN, JAKOB
(1578-1639). German Jesuit, dramatist, poet and author of many works of philosophy and theology. Wrote Latin tragedies, verse. In his day he was famed for great sanctity and immense learning.

BIEL, GABRIEL
(died 1495). Professor of philosophy at Tübingen. Logician. Occamist nominalist. Wrote a commentary on the *Sententiae* of Petrus Lombardus: also a treatise on money, a work which made him an outstanding early monetary theorist; his theological thought influenced Luther and Melanchthon.

BIJNS, ANNA
(1494-1575). Flemish poetess who wrote in Dutch, member of a lay sisterhood. Champion of orthodoxy. Attacked Lutheranism and the social upheaval created by the Reformation. Attack presented in poetic diatribes. Also wrote love lyrics, religious poems.

BILNEY, THOMAS
(c. 1495-1531). English martyr. In almost all essential points he

76

was a Roman Catholic. He was an Erasmian in that he greatly admired his edition of the New Testament. Charged before Cardinal Wolsey: recanted. Imprisoned in Tower one year, released, returned to Cambridge; there he relapsed into heresy in regard to transubstantiation and was burnt as a heretic. Among his friends were Matthew Parker and Hugh Latimer.

BINCK, JAKOB
(c. 1500-c. 1565). German painter of Cologne who probably studied under Dürer. He became portrait painter to the court of Christian VIII of Denmark.

BIONDO, FLAVIO
(c. 1380-1463). Apostolic secretary at the papal court, historian of Rome, Italy, and the medieval past. He utilized and developed methods of textual criticism and historical judgment; the periodization of Antiquity-Middle Ages-Renaissance owes something to him. A humanist whose note was critical rather than rhetorical, he emphasized facts and chronology. Biondo was a pathfinder in archaeology: in his *Roma instaurata* he laid out painstakingly the topography of the ancient city. He showed the true antiquarian's temperament in his denunciation of Pope Nicholas V who ordered sites cleared of ruins to make way for new construction.

BIONDO, MICHELANGELO
(1493-1565). Italian physician, attached to the court of Paul III. Wrote on physiognomy, astrology, navigation, the memory, and made translations and summaries of ancient Greek medical works.

BIRAGUE, RENÉ DE
(1507-1583). French statesman, chancellor. Cardinal. Born in Milan. Adviser of Catherine de' Medici. Accused of being one of the instigators of the Massacre of St. Bartholomew's Day; at any rate he had a righteous hatred of Protestants.

BIRINGUCCIO, VANNOCCIO
(1480-c. 1538). Italian chemist and metallurgist of Siena. Fled from city. In service of Florence, Venice, the dukes of Parma and Ferrara. Head of papal foundry in Rome and director of munitions under Pope Paul III. Author of *De La Pirotechnia*. Published posthumously in Venice in 1540. He produced the first

printed book on general technology, illustrated with woodcuts, and describing contemporary industrial processes such as gun-casting and manufacture of glass.

BIRK, SIXT
(1500-1554). German dramatist of Augsburg. Author of plays: *Susanna, Sapientia Salomonis,* and others of biblical inspiration. He was a school teacher and then director of the Institute of his native city.

BIRO DE DEVA, MATTHEW
(died 1546). Theologian. First Hungarian to accept Zwinglianism.

BISSOLO, PIER FRANCESCO
(1464-c. 1550). Painter of Venice. Assistant and disciple of Giovanni Bellini, inspired by Titian. Worked on religious themes. A lesser figure of the Venetian Renaissance.

BLACKWELL, ADAM
(1539-1613). Scottish writer, protagonist of Mary, Queen of Scots. He was educated at Paris and Toulouse, and taught philosophy at Paris. In his *Apology for Kings* he made his defense of Mary and denounced the views of his compatriot Buchanan. He also wrote prose and verse of pious edification.

BLAEU, WILLEM JANSZOON
(1571-1638). Dutch cartographer and cartographical publisher, mathematician, astronomer, student of Tycho Brahe. The English edition of his sea atlas, *The Light of Navigation,* appeared in Amsterdam in 1612. His printing was one of the best of his day and was continued by his descendants. He was famous for his folio editions.

BLAHOSLAV, JAN
(1523-1571). Czech writer and theologian. He had studied at Wittenberg, where he came to know Luther; he did much to establish educational institutions among his coreligionists. He established a printing press in Moravia. Began translation of the New Testament, published beginning in 1565; it became part of the standard Bible for Bohemian Brethren.

BLANDRATA, GIORGIO
(c. 1515-c. 1588). Italian physician. Also polemical writer. In-

troduced Unitarianism in Poland, Transylvania. Forced to flee to Geneva, where he was the theological antagonist of Calvin. Became physician to the Prince of Transylvania. Strangled by a relative while asleep.

BLASPHEMY EDICT
This edict was promulgated by the Emperor Maximilian in 1495. It contained reference to syphilis and is an important document in the effort to trace the origin of the disease to Columbus' expeditions.

BLASTUS, NICOLAS
(died 1500). Greek typographer, editor, calligraphist. Migrated to Venice. Worked in collaboration with Zacharias Callierges, beginning in 1493.

BLES, HENRI
(1480-1554?). Met de Bles. Painter of Bouvines. Noted for spacious religious landscapes with figures. Significant for development of landscape painting. Relatively few works can be attributed to him with any assurance.

BLOEMAERT, ABRAHAM
(1564-1651). Dutch painter. Known for religious and mythological themes, landscapes. He was among the most Italianate of the Dutch painters. His father, Andreas, had been a sculptor, architect and engineer; his son, Henry, continued the family tradition as a painter.

BLOIS, FRANÇOIS LOUIS DE or BLOSIO
(1506-1566). Flemish mystic. Benedictine monk. Author of Latin works exalting the spiritual and ascetic life, among them *Institutio Spiritualis*.

BLOIS, TREATY OF
This treaty was signed in 1505 by King Ferdinand of Spain and Louis XII of France. France surrendered its old claim to Naples to Spain; a short-lived settlement and pause in the Italian Wars.

BLOOD
Circulation of blood discovered in 1615 by William Harvey (1578-1657). Harvey was physician to King James I of England. Studied under Galileo at Padua. It climaxed a century of dissection and of the study of the heart.

BLUE-COAT SCHOOL
English public school in London. Founded by King Edward VI in 1553.

BLUNDELL, PETER
(1520-1601). English clothier. Founded and endowed public school. Blundell's School dates from 1604.

BOAISTUAN, PIERRE
(1506-1566). French writer. Author of *Histoires Prodigieuses*: published in Paris in 1575. His outlook and interests were typical of the Renaissance era: he wrote on "the excellence and dignity of man" as well as an inquiry into the idea of the Christian ruler and the origin of the kingdoms of Europe.

BOCCACCINO, BOCCACCIO
(c. 1447-1525). Italian painter of Cremona. Executed frescoes of religious subjects. He was the butt of many jokes, according to Vasari. His son Camilo was also a painter.

BOCCACCIO, GIOVANNI
(1313-1375). Author of the celebrated *Decameron*, 1354. His father was an agent of the Florentine banking firm, the Bardi, at their branch in Paris, where the son was born of a liaison with a French woman. Intended for a business career, he was sent to Florence and then to the court at Naples to learn the trade. His apprenticeship was more to love and letters than to business; with the bankruptcy of the Bardi, he returned to Florence and devoted himself to classical studies and imaginative literature. Unlike his friend Petrarch, Boccaccio greatly admired Dante, whose biography he wrote and on whose *Divine Comedy* he gave public lectures at Florence, paid by the city, in 1373. He too "rescued" ancient manuscripts, most notably Tacitus; he too had his Laura, "Fiametta". When he was nearly fifty he went through a religious crisis and intended for a while to become a monk. Persuaded instead by Petrarch to rededicate himself to classical studies, he produced several important works, most notably *The Genealogy of the Gods*, the first handbook of mythology. Unlike Petrarch, Boccaccio managed to learn Greek.

BOCCALINI, TRAIANO
(1556-1613). Literary critic and political satirist. Defender of Tasso. Author of *News from Parnassus*: published in 1612; *Politi-*

cal Touchstone: published in 1614. Both contain violent attacks on the Spanish tyranny inflicted upon Italy. He was probably assassinated at Venice by one of his many enemies.

BOCK, JEROME

(1498-1554). German botanist and Protestant pastor. He was learned in the humanities, theology and medicine. His chief importance is as one of the founders of the new botany: his illustrated *Neu Kreuterbuch*, 1539, was remarkable for its classification and descriptions of plants as well as its illustrations. He had been director of the botanical gardens at Zweibrücken.

BOCSKA, STEPHEN

(1557-1600). Hungarian leader who followed alternately a pro-Turkish and pro-Hapsburg policy in trying to establish the independence of Transylvania. In conflict with the Emperor Rudolph II. Traditionally, he was poisoned as he was about to renew wars with Hapsburgs.

BODENHAM, JOHN

(floruit 1600). English scholar. Edited a number of miscellaneous works: *Belvedere, Wits Commonwealth, England's Helicon, Wits Theater*, compilations of wit and sententious sayings.

BODIN, JEAN

(1530-1596). French social and political philosopher, economist, one of the seminal minds of France. In an age of civil and religious wars he was an advocate of religious toleration, one of the *politiques*. His great work was *The Six Books of a Commonwealth*, an inquiry into the nature of the state and of society as well as a milestone in historiography and the philosophy of history: he thought the laws of God and nature were the only restraints upon the sovereign power, and that physical environment has a profound impact upon the laws, customs, beliefs and character of a people and also upon the course of events. Much Mercantilist doctrine will be found already developed in his writings; he was a pioneer in the understanding of inflation (there was a great price rise in the course of the sixteenth century). Bodin had studied the civil law at Toulouse and was a successful practicing lawyer. He also wrote on witchcraft, believing strongly in the reality of necromancy, hexes, etc.

BODLEIAN LIBRARY

In Oxford University. Founded in 1598 and opened in 1602, by Sir Thomas Bodley (1545-1613), a courtier of Queen Elizabeth; his enterprise had begun as an attempt to restore "good Duke Humphrey" of Gloucester's collection which had been destroyed during the Reformation.

BOECE, HECTOR

(1465-1536). Scottish historian. Friend of Erasmus. Principal of Aberdeen University. Author of *Historia Scotorum ab illius gentis Origine*: contains much legendary material and does not measure up to humanist standards in treating sources.

BOECE DE BOOT

(died 1634). Physician to Emperor Rudolf II. Noted as a naturalist. Author of *De Gemmarum et Lapidum Historia:* a study of precious stones, the technique of cutting and polishing: illustrated with woodcuts. Published in 1636.

BOEHME, JOHANNES

(First half of sixteenth century). German scholar of Bavaria. Author of first compendium of scientific ethnography: *Mores, Leges et Ritus Omnium Gentium*. Published in Leyden in 1541. This work was so popular that it was translated into English, French, Italian. He also wrote a history of Swabia.

BOGERMAN, REYNER

(c. 1475-1555). Frisian poet. Author of didactic verses.

BOHEMIAN REVOLT

The Protestants of Bohemia, in conflict with Catholic governors, revolted in 1617 against Holy Roman Emperor Matthias (1557-1619). Uprising occurred in Prague in 1618 and was the first episode of the Thirty Years' War.

BOHIER, NICOLAS DE

(1469-1539). French jurist. Professor of law at Bourges and president of one of the provincial *parlements*. He wrote, in Latin, *Tractatus de Seditiosis:* published in 1515, *Boerii Consilia:* published in Venice in 1574, and other works on law, jurisprudence, and public office.

BÖHME, JAKOB, PHILOSOPHUS TEUTONICUS

(1575-1642). German philosopher of a pantheistic tendency:

mystic. Claimed to possess revelations which he wrote out symbolically and poetically. Influenced German philosophical and religious thought and Quakerism in England. His chief work is *Aurora*. Also wrote *Mysterium Magnum*.

BOIARDO, MATTEO MARIA
(1440-1494). Leading epic poet of Quattrocento, member of the Este court at Ferrara and governor of Modena. Lyric poet in Latin and Italian. His *Canzoniere* became the most outstanding contribution of the fifteenth century. Author of unfinished epic *Orlando Innamorato:* material derived from Carolingian and Breton cycles, intermixed with classical and Italian elements.

BOLEYN, ANNE
(c.1507-1536). Married Henry VIII of England in 1533, his second wife, mother of Elizabeth I. Beheaded.

BOLOGNA, CONCORDAT OF, 1516
An agreement between Francis I of France and the Pope, whereby royal power over the Church was extended and consolidated; it helps to explain why Protestantism had little appeal to the kings of France.

BOLOGNA, ANTONIO
(Fifteenth century). Italian poet at the Neapolitan court of Alfonso the Magnanimous.

BOLOGNA, GIAN
(1524-1608). Italian sculptor. Born at Douai, Florentine by education. Executed mythological and religious subjects. J.A. Symonds: "That he was a greater sculptor than his immediate predecessors will be affirmed by all who have studied his bronze *Mercury*, the *Venus of Petraja*, and the *Neptune* on the fountain of Bologna." His sculptures suggest the transition to Italian baroque. Also called Giovanni da Bologna and Il Fiammingo. He was greatly influenced by Michelangelo, after whose death he had no rival.

BOLOGNA, SCHOOL OF
The founders of what is called the Eclectic School of Bologna were Agostino and Annibale Carracci: born in Bologna between 1555 and 1560. They established the Academy of Painting in Bologna in 1589. In opposition to the prevalent imitation of

Caravaggio, the Bolognese school followed Raphael and Correggio. The most famous work of the Carracci is the painting of the gallery in the Farnese Palace in Rome. Executed by Annibale and Agostino in 1600.

BOLSEC, JEROME
(Died 1585). French priest and ex-Carmelite. Attacked Calvin's doctrine of Predestination. Imprisoned in 1551 and then banished from Geneva. After many vicissitudes he returned to France and Catholicism and became an antagonist of Protestantism. He wrote highly critical biographies of Calvin and Beza and studies of their ideas.

BOLTON SCHOOL
English public school. Founded in 1524 by William Haighe. Rebuilt and endowed by Robert Lever: 1641.

BOLTRAFFIO, GIOVANNI ANTONIO
(1467-1516). Italian painter of the school of Milan at the height of its fame under Sforza patronage. Pupil of Leonardo da Vinci. Executed altarpieces and portraits. Noted for chiaroscuro.

BONA OF SAVOY
The widow of Duke Galeazzo Maria Sforza of Milan. In 1476, after the Duke was killed, she took control of the government, but was ousted by Ludovico il Moro, her brother-in-law.

BONATTI, GUIDO
(1235-1296). Italian astrologer. Wrote a work that mixes astronomy and astrology, and which was known to Dante, *Liber astronomicus;* in his day he was famous for his predictions.

BONAVENTURA, ANTERUS MARIA DE S.
(Late fifteenth and early sixteenth century). Franciscan Minorite friar of Brescia and musical theorist. His *Regula musicae planae,* 1497, was a standard work until late in the sixteenth century and was reissued many times.

BONAVENTURE DES PÉRIERS
Author of *Cymbalum Mundi:* published in 1537. In 1539 Bonaventure des Périers was condemned by the Sorbonne. In 1558 he published *Nouvelles Récréations et Joyeux Devis.*

84

BOND OF ASSOCIATION
A plot organized against Queen Elizabeth of England in 1584.

BONET DE LATTES
(Early sixteenth century). French-Jewish physician and astrologer. Papal physician to Alexander VI and successors. Author of astrological calendar, *Prognosticon*. He did make a contribution to astronomy in the form of an "astronomical ring" for measuring the altitude of the heavenly bodies and telling time better.

BONETUS, NICOLAUS
Logician. Professor in Venice. Author of *Topica:* published in 1505.

BONFINI, ANTONIO
(1434-1504). Italian humanist and historian. Attached to the court of King Matthias of Hungary (1458-1490). Author of *Rerum Hungaricarum Decades:* for centuries a source book on Hungarian history up to 1495. Translated Greek historians into Latin as well as other Greek works.

BONIFAZIO DE PITATI DA VERONA
(1487-1553). Italian painter. Died in Venice. Belongs to Venetian Renaissance. Noted for religious narrative themes: emphatic use of color. He was one of three Bonifazios who were of a Veronese family of painters. They established themselves in Venice in the early sixteenth century, the other two being a brother and a son to the present artist.

BONIRELLI, GUIDUBALDO
(1563-1608). Author of *Phyllis of Scyros,* a pastoral, published in 1607.

BONNER, EDMUND
(c. 1500-1569). Bishop of London. In service of Henry VIII. Protégé and lieutenant of Wolsey; he was later the friend of Bishop Gardner. Sentenced several Protestant martyrs. Deprived of bishopric under Edward VI. Restored under Mary. Participated in religious persecutions. Under Elizabeth deposed, imprisoned. He is described as cruel and hateful, one of the worst of villains in Foxe's *Book of Martyrs.*

BONNET DE BÉZIERS
(floruit 1616-1657). Provençal writer. Jurist. Wrote popular

plays for the annual Ascension Day performances: e.g., *Judgment of Paris:* appeared in 1616.

BONNIVARD, FRANÇOIS DE
(1496-1570). Swiss prelate, statesman. Imprisoned in Castle of Chillon from 1532 to 1536 for supporting the revolt against the Duke of Savoy. Subject of Byron's *The Prisoner of Chillon.* He authored a chronicle history of Geneva, published in the nineteenth century.

BONSIGNORI, FRANCISCO
(1455-1519). Italian painter of Verona. He did religious scenes and portraits of contemporaries. The chief influences upon him were Giovanni Bellini and Mantegna.

BOOK AUCTION
The first book auction occurred when George Doussa's library went on sale in Leyden, Holland. 1604.

BOOK ILLUMINATORS
Among the prominent artists who worked in this field were: Francesco d'Antonio del Cherico, worked from 1455 to 1485, Gherardo (1444?-1497), Monte di Giovanni detto Fora (1448-1529), Francesco Pesellino (1422-1457), Bartolomeo d'Antonio, Giovanni d'Antonio, Antonio Sinibaldi, the brothers Boccardi, Attavante degli Attavanti, all more or less contemporary.

BOOK OF CONCORD
Definitive collection of Lutheran Confessional documents. Published in 1580.

BOOK OF RATES
A book of rates was a list of commodities and their value. Used in the sixteenth and seventeenth centuries for import and export purposes. In England it had to have Parliamentary approval, and was a source of friction between Parliament and the Stuarts.

BOORDE, ANDREW or BORDE
(c. 1490-1549). English physician. Traveler. With a dispensation to leave his diocese, he went to France to study medicine. Traveled in Spain. Traveled through East, to Rhodes, Jerusalem. Died in prison, in London. Author of *Itinerary of*

England, Handbook of Europe and encyclopedic compilations on hygiene, beards, general knowledge, that are spiced with wit.

BOR, PIETER CHRISTIAANSZOON
(1559-1635). Dutch chronicler and historian. Author of *Wars of the Netherlands* and other historical works. His works are still useful for he wrote in an impartial spirit and, having access to the Dutch archives, reproduced many Dutch, Spanish and Italian documents.

BORA, CATHERINE VON
(1499-1552). Wife of Martin Luther. Cistercian nun. Fled to Wittenberg, where she married Luther in 1525. Subject of German drama and novel.

BORCHT, HENDRIK VAN DER
(1583-1660). Flemish painter and engraver. Died in Antwerp. Noted for flowers and still life. He had traveled to Italy and England with his son of the same name, who was also a painter and engraver.

BORDONE, BENEDETTO
(died 1539). Venetian illuminator and wood engraver of artistic school dominated by Mantegna and Bellini. Worked in Padua. Executed missal, gospel-book, psalter. He may have done the wood engravings for the *Hypnerotomachia Poliphilo*.

BORDONE, PARIS
(1500-1570). Painter. Died in Venice. Noted for allegorical and historical subjects, also portraits. Titian was his master as is suggested by his use of color. Belongs to Venetian Renaissance: he settled in Venice after stays at the royal court of France and the Fuggers of Bavaria.

BORELLI, GIOVANNI ALFONSO
(c. 1606-1679). Italian mathematician, astronomer and physicist. Professor at Pisa, Messina. He pointed out that comets travel along parabolic courses. Author of *De Motu Animalium*.

BORGHINI, RAFFAELLO
(1541-1588). Florentine writer, author of the pastoral comedy *Diana pietosa*, of prose comedies, various verse and a treatise on painting and sculpture, *Il Riposo*.

BORGHINI, VINCENZO

(1515-1580). Florentine philologist and antiquary. Author of critical study of the *Decameron*. In accordance with suggestions made by the Council of Trent, Borghini proposed emendations and expurgations for a new version. He wrote short stories of his own, some studies of Dante, as well as an account of Florentine antiquity.

BORGIA, CESARE

(1476-1507). Of Spanish descent, one of the celebrated infamous figures of the Renaissance. His attempt—with the blessing and aid of his father, Pope Alexander VI—to create a great state for himself in the Romagna nearly succeeded. In alliance with Charles VIII—which brought him a French bride and the title duke of Valentinois—and taking advantage of the French invasion of 1494, he made headway in achieving his ambition. His name is a byword for treachery and ruthlessness, and these arts he certainly practiced, yet he also had a capacity for decent government as well as a personal refinement and magnetism. He lost out on the death of his father; his efforts to create a new state in central Italy were reaped by Pope Julius II, who expanded and consolidated the Papal States. Borgia died in an obscure battle in Spain. He and Ferdinand of Aragon are set forth by Machiavelli in *The Prince* as exemplary practitioners of the political arts.

BORGIA, FRANCESCO, SAINT

(1510-1572). Member of Spanish branch of Borgia. Third General of Society of Jesus. Promoted foreign missions.

BORGIA, LUCREZIA

(1480-1519). Duchess of Ferrara. Married thrice: to Giovanni Sforza, annulled in 1497. The second marriage was to Alfonso of Aragon, who was murdered by order of her brother Cesare Borgia, 1500. Her third husband was Alfonso d'Este, 1501. She maintained a court that was a distinguished cultural centre for all the arts. Daughter of Pope Alexander VI. Had reputation, now believed unwarranted, for sinister machinations.

BORRO, GIROLAMO

(1512-1592). Italian humanist and member of a famous family of Arezzo. Taught philosophy at Pisa when Galileo was a student at the university. Author of dialogue on physics, astronomy, and analogous scientific subjects.

BORROMEO, FEDERIGO

(1564-1631). Italian cardinal, archbishop of Milan, 1595-1631. He founded the Ambrosian Library, Milan, 1609.

BORROMEO, SAINT CHARLES

(1538-1584). Italian prelate, cardinal, archbishop of Milan 1563 to his death; one of the greatest figures of the Counter Reformation; dominant at Council of Trent in later sessions. Vigorous in reforming his archdiocese and maintaining discipline, he was in danger of assassination. Founded hospitals, libraries, colleges, seminaries, also an academy of learned and pious men, whose memorials and proceedings—the *Noctes Vaticanae*—he himself wrote. A reflection of the Counter Reformation spirit is his removal of elaborate tombs, decorations, ornaments, banners, arms, etc., from his cathedral; he also divided it in half so that the sexes would be segregated. He inspired the great ecclesiastical figure in Manzoni's *The Betrothed.* Of noble birth, his uncle was Pope Pius IV, his nephew Federigo, above.

BORSO D'ESTE, DUKE OF FERRARA

Fifteenth century. He was typical of the despotic rulers who were munificent patrons of the arts and learning; his death provoked almost divine analogies. Panegyric published, in Latin hexameters, called *Borseid,* was all too typical of the effusive laudation humanists felt it proper to lavish on princes and their houses.

BORUP, MORTEN

(1446-1526). Danish poet. Wrote in Latin. Author of *Carmena Vernale, Marmora Danica,* and many other volumes of poetry. He was rector of the Latin school of Aarbus.

BOSCÁN ALMOGÁVER, JUAN

(1493?-1542). Catalan lyric poet. Born and died in Barcelona. Of noble lineage, he was attached to court of Charles V. Boscán introduced into Spanish literature the Italian ottava rima, the metrical form of all Spanish epic poets of the Renaissance. He also made the sonnet and the terza rima into standard Spanish forms. His poems were published in 1543: include more than ninety *sonetos.* He also translated Castiglione's *El Cortesano,* in

1534. The influence of Petrarch, Tasso, Bembo, and Poliziano may be found in his work.

BOSCH, HIERONYMUS

(c. 1462-1516). Flemish painter. Subjects are religious, macabre Satanic scenes, horrific figures. Known particularly for his *Temptation of St. Anthony*. Philip II of Spain took great delight in the bizarre fancifulness of Bosch's works.

BOSSCHAERT, AMBROSIUS

(c. 1570-1645). Dutch painter. Died at Utrecht. Noted for flower pictures.

BOSWORTH FIELD, BATTLE OF, 1485

Fought between Richard III and Henry Tudor, the Earl of Richmond, who won out, killing Richard III, and became Henry VII; marks the establishment of the Tudor dynasty in England.

BOTANICAL GARDEN

A botanical garden, for medical purposes, was founded at Pisa in 1543. The first botanical garden attached to a medical school was inaugurated at Padua, in 1545.

BOTERO, GIOVANNO

(1543-1617). Italian political writer. Author of a treatise on political science: *Ragion di Stato*, published in 1619. Intended to refute Machiavelli. Deals with the use of the militia, functions of the navy, labor and agriculture, currency, population. His work *Causa della grandezza e magnificenza delle città* is notable for its use of economic data as a criterion for political and historical judgment.

BOTHWELL, JAMES HEPBURN, EARL OF

(c. 1536-1578). Scottish noble. Third husband of Mary Queen of Scots. Imprisoned. Fled to France. Accomplice in murder of Darnley. In conflict with nobles, fled to Norway. Imprisoned. Died insane.

BOTTAZZO, GIOVANNI JACOPO

(Sixteenth century). Minor Italian poet. Wrote *Dialogi Maritimi:* published in 1547. Dialogues on geography, influence of winds, celestial spheres, conquests of Alexander the Great. A compendium of Renaissance views of cosmography.

BOTTICELLI, SANDRO
(c. 1444-1510): Italian painter of Florence. Attached to distinguished Florentine families. Studied at school of Fra Lippo Lippi. Helped in decoration of Sistine Chapel. Chief works: *Adoration of the Magi, Birth of Venus, Mars and Venus*. Also illustrated with eighty-four drawings, Dante's *Divina Commedia*. He was touched deeply by the sermons of Savonarola. The fact that he painted the Virgin and Venus with the same sad face has fascinated generations of students.

BOUCHER, JEAN
(1548-1624). French priest. Member of Catholic League during French civil and religious wars. Author of nine sermons denying claims to kingship of Henry IV of France. One of the most passionate enemies of the Huguenots and prolific author of religious polemic.

BOULENGER, JULES CÉSAR
(1558-1628): French historian and Jesuit. Author of *De Pictura, Plastice, Statuaria Libri Duo:* a treatise on art techniques, art schools, museums. Published in 1627. He also wrote a Latin history of the period 1500 to 1610.

BOURBON, HOUSE OF
Henry IV: 1589-1610. Ruler of Navarre, came to French throne on extinction of the house of Valois in 1589, the death of Henry III. Louis XIII: 1610-1643.

BOURBON, CHARLES
(1490-1527). Created Constable of France for heroism at the Battle of Marignano: 1515. Deserted the king of France for Emperor Charles V. Supported expulsion of French from Italy. Participated in Battle of Pavia: 1525, when French were defeated. Attacked and sacked Rome with Spanish and German troops: 1527. He was mortally wounded, reputedly by Benvenuto Cellini, the bombardier on the parapet of Castel Sant'Angelo.

BOURBON, NICOLAS, THE ELDER
(1505-c.1548). French poet. Humanist. Wrote Latin verse: *Nugae* and was tutor to the daughter of Margaret of Navarre. He was the foremost Hellenist of his generation in France.

BOURBON, NICOLAS, THE YOUNGER

(1574-1644). French poet. Neo-Latinist. Author of *Dirae in parricidam:* curses on murderer of Henry IV. He was professor of rhetoric and of Greek literature at various universities of France.

BOURDICHON, JEAN

(1457-1521). French painter, illuminator. Commissioned in 1478 to decorate Royal Chapel. In 1484 granted title of *Painctre du Roy*. Portrait painter: but also designed lamps, reliquaries, coins. Famed for his Book of Hours—*Heures d'Anne de Bretagne* (1508). He also did a Book of Hours for King Charles VIII.

BOURDIGNE, JEAN DE

(died 1547). Cleric and doctor of law of Angers. Author of chronicle of Anjou and Maine, beginning with the Creation. Published in 1529. Full of legendary matter, but also contains much of historical value.

BOURGES

By the Pragmatic Sanction of Bourges of 1438, Charles VII had gained extensive power over the Church in France. By the Revocation of the Pragmatic Sanction of Bourges, Louis XI of France negotiated, in 1461, reconciliation with Papacy, but restored very little real authority over the Church in France.

BOURNE, WILLIAM

(c. 1535-1582). English self-taught mathematician and student of navigation. Born in Gravesend. Author of *A Regiment of the Sea*: published in London in 1577, and other works on naval strategy and navigation.

BOUSSARD, GEOFFROY

(c.1439-1522). French theologian. Rector of the University of Paris in 1487. Edited *Ecclesiastical History* of Eusebius. He had visited Italy: his scholarly editing and Biblical commentaries show the influence of humanist textual methods.

BOUTS, DIRK

(c. 1420-1475). Dutch painter. Died in Louvain. In spite of certain Gothic details, his paintings belong to early Renaissance school. Executed religious paintings, portraits, landscapes; his

92

works have a resemblance to the Van Eycks', with whom he probably worked.

BOVILLUS, CAROLUS
(c. 1470-1550). French philosopher and mathematician, logician. Author of commentaries on principles of logic. His most important work was *De sapiente*, where, following Pico and Nicholas of Cusa, he places man at the center of the universe: man is a part of nature but also is above nature by virtue of his consciousness. He was a disciple of Lefèbve d'Étaples and author of numerous works.

BOYD, M. W.
He led an adventurous life as a student of the civil law under Ayons in France, a participant on the side of Henry III in the French civil and religious wars, and as swordsman, translator, Greek conversationalist and roustabout.

BOYD, ZACHARY
(c. 1585-1653). Scottish cleric. Professor in France at the Protestant school of Saumur. Rector of Glasgow University. Author of *The Last Battle of the Soul in Death:* published in 1629. Also metrical renderings of Biblical history: called *Boyd's Bible* or *Zion's Flowers.* He preached before Oliver Cromwell, "railing at him to his face." He later came to admire the Protector.

BOYLE, RICHARD, FIRST EARL OF CORK
(1566-1643). Helped emigration of English Protestants to Ireland. Favored by Queen Elizabeth. Promoted building and other civic activities. He had studied at Corpus Christi College, Cambridge, and taught common law in the Middle Temple. Later he was antagonist of Strafford.

BOYLE, ROBERT
(1627-1691). Considered the Father of Modern Chemistry. Formulated Boyle's Law of gases, explaining the relationship of temperature and pressure to volume. Born into wealth, he lost his fortune, spent his life investigating fields of specific gravity, electricity, crystallography. First in England to use a sealed thermometer. Discovered the importance of air in the transmission of sound. One of the original members of the Royal Society. Author of *New Experiments Physico-Mechanical Touching the Spring of the Air and its Effects.* Published in 1660.

The Sceptical Chemist appeared in 1661. The *Origin of Forms and Qualities according to the Corpuscular Philosophy* was published in 1666.

BOZIUS, THOMAS or BOZIO

(1548-1610). Italian canonist, scholar, historian. Member of the Congregation of the Oratory of St. Philip Neri. Author of book attacking Machiavelli: *De Antiquo et Novo Italiae Statu Libri Quattuor adversus Macchiavellum:* published in Rome in 1596. He collaborated with Baronius to publish the *Annales Ecclesiastici* and the *Annales Antiquitatum.* Bozius also invented the rumor of Martin Luther's suicide.

BRACCIO, ALESSANDRO

(died 1503). Florentine poet, writer, public official. He was secretary to the Republic and, at the time of his death, ambassador to the Papacy. He wrote Latin poetry; he also made translations of classical writers into Italian.

BRACELLI, GIACOMO

(died c. 1466). Italian humanist and historian, chancellor of Genoa for more than half a century. His principal work was a history of the Genoese wars with Alfonso V of Aragon, *De Bello Hispano.* He also wrote a *Liguriae discriptio* and *De claris Genuensibus libellus.*

BRADSHAW, JOHN

(1602-1659). English jurist. Regicide. Friend of Milton. Presided at trial of King Charles I. Buried in Westminster Abbey, disinterred: gibbeted.

BRAHE, TYCHO

(1546-1601). Danish astronomer who rejected most of the Copernican system, although he was not an adherent of Ptolemy or Aristotle, except in the sense that he thought the position of the earth fixed (geostatic). His importance was as an observer: he collected great quantities of astronomical data at the Uraniborg observatory (located on an island in the Danish Sound and under the patronage of King Frederick II). By dint of improved instruments, many designed by himself, and ceaseless diligence, his tables and records were more accurate than anything known before or to be known for nearly a century. He thus laid the groundwork for further advance in astronomy, e.g., Kepler's elliptical orbits, although he seemed to have no inkling of such developments.

BRAMANTE, DONATO D'AGNOLO

(1444-1514). Also called Lazzari. Italian achitect. Born near Urbino. Lived in Milan. In service of Ludovico Sforza. In 1499, went to Rome: employed by Popes Alexander VI and Julius II. Bramante's was the original design for rebuilding St. Peter's. J.A. Symonds: "He exercised the profoundest influence over both successors and contemporaries." Created architectural style known as Bramantesque, strictly classical in its simplicity and monumental character. He was a close student of ancient architecture and had made many pilgrimages to survey and measure ruins.

BRAMANTINO, BARTOLOMEO SUARDI

(1455-1530). Italian painter and architect of Milan. Imitated Bramante. Executed easel pictures, frescoes, noted for the highly wrought architectural backdrops of his painting. He was attached to the Sforza court at Milan. His works include the *Ecce Homo* and *Adoration of the Magi.*

BRANCALUPO, RUDOLFO

Court illuminator for King Ferdinand I of Spain. Executed St. Augustine's *Commentary on the Psalms,* in 1480.

BRANDOLINI, AURELIO

(c. 1440-1497). Italian humanist. Attached to the court of King Matthias of Hungary (1458-1490). Famous as an improviser in Latin verse; he wrote in Latin prose on rhetoric and philosophy.

BRANDOLINI, RAFFAELLO

(c. 1465-c. 1520). Latin poet and humanist, brother or cousin of the above. Remarkable for his facility in improvising, composed and delivered the panegyric of Charles VIII when he entered Naples in 1495; later he went to Rome to sing the praise of Pope Leo X and the Medici family.

BRANT, SEBASTIAN

(1458-1521). German humanist and Chancellor of the city of Strassburg, author of the *Narrenschiff* or *Ship of Fools.* First printed in 1494, it went through countless editions that included striking woodcuts. A satire on the foibles of humanity, including the clergy. It shows how far the clergy had fallen in popular esteem. It bypasses, by ignoring rather than by rebuttal, the whole mechanism of salvation according to Pope and Church. Beneath its persiflage and satire, the book is pervaded by a moral earnestness by which man is exhorted to fix upon God as the true goal of his life and never to let anything violate that intimate relationship. The book extolls wisdom and virtue, the examples of which are drawn from antiquity, e.g., Hercules, Pythagoras, Socrates, Plato, Penelope, and Virgil. The book is one of the most important examples of a humanistic work that paved the way for the Reformation. As a discourse on human folly it may be compared to Erasmus' famous work; Katherine Anne Porter's novel, *Ship of Fools*, was inspired by Brant.

BRASAVOLA, ANTONIUS MUSA
(1500-1555). Italian physician, scientist. Physician to Pope Paul III and several other popes as well as kings of his time. Author of treatise on medicinal herbs: in dialogue form, and a work of commentary and annotations on Hippocrates.

BRASSICANUS, IOANNES ALEXANDER
(1500-1539). German humanist. Wrote triumphal ode to Charles V, after the capture of Francis I on battlefield of Pavia: *In Gallum Nuper Proligatum atque Captum Vincente ac Triumphante Carolo Caesare V Carmen*. He edited a series of classical and Christian texts; his father, of the same name, (died c. 1514) was also a humanist and he wrote a Latin grammar.

BRAVO
A word meaning brave and valorous; in the Renaissance it came to mean a daring villain, hired soldier or reckless assassin. The word's history suggests the seamy side of the Renaissance when murder and assassination became a fine art also.

BRAVO, FRANCISCO
Sixteenth century. Spanish physician who practiced in Mexico. Author of *Opera Medicinalia:* published in 1570, in Mexico. Possibly earliest medical publication in New World.

BREA, LODOVICO
(died c. 1523). Italian painter of Nice. He did religious subjects as did other members of the same family: principally his brother or son, Francesco.

BREDA, COMPROMISE OF
The Compromise or League of Breda consisted of a group of the nobility of Holland in sympathy with Calvinism. Organized in 1565. Petitioned the Inquisition to suspend the laws directed against heretics. One of the preliminary steps to the Dutch Revolt.

BREDERO, GERBRAND ADRIAANSZOON
(1585-1618). Dutch comic poet, playwright. Began as painter. In close touch with Dutch people. Wrote farces: e.g. *The Farce of the Cow and the Miller.*
Also comedy: *The Spanish Brabant Man.*
He continued the tradition of folk song, but adapted it to Renaissance poetical forms. His comic realism is suggestive of Cervantes.

BREDERODE, COUNT HENDRIK VAN
(1531-1568). Flemish statesman in the service of Philip II. He was one of the petitioners for reform and redress in 1566. He sought to arm Antwerp against Alva; Spanish might compelled him to flee to Germany.

BREECHES BIBLE
Published by Calvinists at Geneva in 1558. So called because in *Genesis* 3.7 Adam and Eve 'made themselves breeches.'

BREENBERGH, BARTOLOMAUS
(1599-1659). Dutch painter. He visited and studied in Italy, where he developed the capacity for naturalistic depiction and landscapes. He had been a student of Bul; he did most of his work in Amsterdam.

BREGNO, ANDREA
(1418-1503). Italian sculptor and architect, he worked principally at Rome in the service of popes and ecclesiastical princes and did sepulchral monuments. His namesake and possibly of the same family was the sculptor ANTONIO, fifteenth century, who worked in Venice and did the tomb of the doge, Francesco Foscari. The two brothers, LORENZO and GIOVANNI BATTISTA, early sixteenth century, sculptors and architects, were probably of the same family. They belonged to the Lombard School and were notable for the church domes they did, mostly in Venetia.

BRENTWOOD SCHOOL
English public school. Founded by Sir Antony Browne: 1557.

BRENZ, JOHANN
(1499-1570). Swabian reformer and Lutheran controversialist. Follower of Luther. He wrote *Syngramma Suevicum*, 1525, a discourse on the Lutheran conception of the eucharist. His Biblical expositions followed the humanist canon of textual analysis.

BRENZ, SAMUEL FRIEDRICH
(Late sixteenth, early seventeenth century). Converted Jew. Author of pamphlet on Judaic customs: published in Nuremberg, in 1614. He became a righteous anti-Jewish writer and got into heated controversy with such works as *The Jewish Serpent's Skin Stripped*.

BRERELY, ROGER
(1586-1637). English poet, cleric. A Puritan, he founded a group, vaguely defined and hardly constituting a sect, known as the Gringhtonion Familists. It remained within the fold of Calvinist orthodoxy but came into conflict with the Anglican Church.

BRESCIA, FRA ANTONIO DA
(Beginning of sixteenth century). Italian engraver on stone. Gold and silversmith. Painter. His brother GIOVANNI was also an engraver and goldsmith.

BRESCIANO DA SIENA, ANDREA
(Fl. early sixteenth century). Italian painter of Siena, noted for his religious subjects. He shows the influence of Andrea del Sarto and of Raphael. He also did portraits.

BRESSIUS, MAURITIUS
(Late sixteenth century). French mathematician and astronomer. Delivered address before Pope Clement VIII pledging loyalty of Henry IV: *Oratio ad Clement VIII pro Enrico IV Franciae.* Published in 1597. He was professor of mathematics at the Collège de France and published an important work on astronomical geometry.

BRETON, NICHOLAS
(c. 1545-c. 1626). Prolific and facile English poet. Pamphleteer in prose and verse. Produced satires and humorous, religious, lyrical, pastoral pieces. He himself tells us that he "spent a few

years" at Oxford; his discourse on bright Wit and slight Will was typical of a subject which fascinated the Renaissance mind.

BREU, JORG
(1475-1536). Painter of Augsburg. Highly realistic religious works that greatly influenced the elder Holbein. He is said to have transcribed the Italian Renaissance manner in painting for Northern Europe. Jorg Breu the Younger, his son, was also a painter of religious subjects; he followed the tradition established by his father.

BREWSTER, WILLIAM
(c. 1560-1644). Elder Brewster. Leader of the Pilgrims who came over in the Mayflower in 1620. Born in Nottinghamshire, removed to Holland in 1609, engaging in the publication of Puritan literature. In 1619 he secured a patent from the Virginia Company for a tract of land in America. He was the Ruling Elder of the Plymouth Colony. Left *Memoirs of Elder Brewster.*

BREYTKOPF, GREGORIUS
(died 1529). Prussian theologian, humanist, logician. Called Laticephalus. Wrote on Aristotelian logic: *De Inventione Medii:* published in 1509. Also *De Proprietatibus Modalibus.* Most of his life as a productive scholar was spent at Leipzig.

BRICE, GERMAIN
(before 1500-1538). French scholar, cleric and Neo-Latin poet. Author of *Carmina,* a naval epic entitled *Chordigera* and various religious works: controversy, edification, scholarship and history.

BRICOT, THOMAS
(Late thirteenth century). French professor of theology at Paris. He wrote on logic, Aristotle and scholastic philosophy. His *Textus Abbreviatus Logices* was republished as late as 1492. His work was not forgotten until well into the sixteenth century.

BRIDGE OF SIGHS
In Venice. Erected in 1597.

BRIDGES
Bridges have involved not mere technical but architectural skill as well. The Renaissance bridge revived the ancient principles of bridge building. The artistic and technical theory was mainly developed in the treatise of Andrea Palladio (1508-1580), based

on Vitruvius' *De Architectura*. Among the most remarkable Renaissance bridges is the Ponte S. Trintà, in Florence: erected in 1567 by Bartolommeo Ammanati (1511-1592).

BRIGGS, HENRY
(c. 1561-1631). English mathematician. Professor of Geometry at Gresham College and then at Oxford. Pioneer in development of logarithms; suggested the base of ten. Wrote *Arithmetica Logarithmica*.

BRIGHT, TIMOTHY
(c. 1551-1615). English physician, cleric. Originated modern system of shorthand, which he called *Characterie*. Granted patent by Queen Elizabeth I to teach his method. He wrote a *Treatise on Melancholy* which is supposed to have influenced Shakespeare; he also wrote several works on medicine and hygiene.

BRILL, MATTYS
(1550-1583). Flemish painter. Worked in Rome, having come to Italy as a young man. He was noted for his landscapes.

BRILL, PAUL
(1554-1626). Dutch painter. Brother of the above. Died in Rome. Important as landscape painter. Executed easel pictures, frescoes. He seems to have worked some time in France, at Fontainebleau, and then joined his brother at Rome.

BRINKLOW, HENRY
(Died 1545). English satirical writer. Author of a tract against oppression of the poor: *Complaynt of Roderigo Mors*, his pseudonym, 1542: he attacks the enclosures, the abuse of commercial rights and oppression of the peasantry; he was a former monk of Grey Friars, married and became a well-to-do mercer; hence his writings are spiced with anti-papal and anti-clerical jibes.

BRIOSCO, ANDREA, IL RICCIO
(c. 1470-1532). Sculptor of Padua. Executed candelabra, plaques and medallions in bronze. Also worked as architect.

BRISSOT, PIERRE
(1478-1522). French physician. He was one of the earliest to break with the traditions of Arabo-Galenic medicine. He wrote a treatise on pleurisy: he spent his last years at the Portuguese

court, where he is said to have cured the king of the same disease.

BRISTOL GRAMMAR SCHOOL
English public school. Chartered in 1532.

BRISTOL, JOHN DIGBY, FIRST EARL OF
(1580-1653). English diplomat. Envoy to Spain. Imprisoned in the Tower of London: released. In exile in France.

BRITO, FREI BERNARDO DE
(1568-1617). Portuguese historian and Cistercian monk. Having studied at Rome, he returned to Portugal to write the history of his Order and, by royal commission, the history of the kingdom; his principal work, *Monarchia Lusitana,* is animated by a patriotic hatred for the Spanish occupation and was continued after his death by other members of the Order.

BRITTANY
Northwest region of France. Had been autonomous in Middle Ages under its duke; by marriage to the heiress Anne, it became a possession of the crown; she was first married to Charles VIII; his successor, Louis XII, divorced his first wife in order to marry Anne.

BROCENSE, EL
Nickname of the Spanish humanist, Francisco Sánchez de las Brozas (1523-1601).

BROCHMAND, JESPER or RASMUSSEN
(1585-1652). Danish cleric. Bishop of Zealand and professor at the university of Copenhagen. Wrote extensively on theological subjects. His *Universae Theologiae Systema* became a textbook in many universities throughout Europe. In Danish he wrote several devotional books.

BROKE, ARTHUR
(died 1563). English writer. Translator. Produced the first English version of the Romeo and Juliet theme, published in 1562, and the source of Shakespeare's tragedy.

BROME, RICHARD
(died 1652). English playwright. Friend of Ben Jonson, Dekker, Ford. Collaborated with Thomas Heywood. Wrote some fifteen

plays. Among his romantic and realistic comedies are: *The Jovial Crew, The City Wit, The Northern Lass, The Lancashire Witches, The Court Beggar, The Antipodes, The English Moor.* One of the most prolific playwrights of the age. He owed everything to Jonson: his conception of comedy, of comic types, etc.

BROMSGROVE SCHOOL
English public school. Reorganized by King Edward VI in 1553.

BRONZINO, ANGELO
(1502-1572). Painter of Florence. Symonds says: "His portraits form a gallery of great interest for the historian of Duke Cosimo's reign": they include the duke and duchess as well as Dante, Petrarch and Boccaccio. Bronzino also produced religious pieces, mythological works, frescoes.

BROSAMER, HANS
(ante 1490-1554). German painter, engraver. Died at Erfurt. Noted for woodcuts, etchings of copperplate; one of the German Little Masters.

BROSSE, SALOMON DE
(c. 1571-1626). French architect. Attached to court of Marie de Médicis. Constructed Luxembourg Palace, Palais de Justice, aqueduct of Arcueil.

BROUWER, ADRIAEN
(c. 1605-1638). Dutch painter; he had studied with Franz Hals. Noted for landscapes and genre pieces. Works include: *The Smoker, The Drinker, Tavern Interior* and other scenes from rustic life. Led a riotous life and so died young, nevertheless executed a great number of works.

BROWNE, ROBERT
(c. 1550-c. 1633). English preacher. Founder of religious sect called Brownists. Attacked Established Church. Fled to Holland. Returned: reconciled to the Elizabethan settlement and became a bishop. He was concerned with matters of ecclesiastical organization and control rather than doctrine. Brownists later known as Congregationalists.

BROWNE, WILLIAM
(1591-1643). English poet. His chief work is *Britannia's Pastorals.* Also wrote miscellaneous poems. He was an imitator of Spenser.

BRUCIOLI, ANTONIO
(Died 1556). Italian humanist and Biblical commentator. One of the first to translate the Old and New Testaments into the Tuscan tongue. Published in 1544 in Venice, where he was forced to flee on accusation of Lutheranism and of opposition to the Medici.

BRUDUS, DIONYSIUS
(1478-1522). Portuguese physician. Fled from Portugal to escape persecution on charges of heresy. Court physician to King Manuel. Professor at the University of Paris. Author of a critique of Pierre Brissot on bloodletting.

BRUDUS, MANUEL
(Late sixteenth century). Portuguese physician, son of the above. Wrote on fevers and diet. Fled from Portugal to Venice to escape the Inquisition. Author of *De Ratione Victus*, published in Venice in 1544, and other medical works.

BRUEGHEL, JAN
(1568-1625). Son of Pieter the Elder. He is known as Velvet Brueghel and as Flower Brueghel; a friend and collaborator of Rubens; noted for landscapes.

BRUEGHEL, PIETER
(c. 1525-1569). The Elder. Flemish painter, influenced by Bosch. Called Peasant Brueghel. Subjects deal with bucolic and peasant activities, also depicted Biblical episodes and the merciless activities in the Lowlands of the Inquisition. He had visited Italy; his work is characterized by realism and close observation and the painstaking execution of minute details.

BRUEGHEL, PIETER
(c. 1564-1637). The Younger. Known as Hell Brueghel. Flemish painter. Subjects deal with rural activities, also Satanic and demoniac infernal horrors.

BRUEYS, CLAUDE
(1570-1650). Provençal poet. Author of *Jardin deys Musos provensalos:* appeared in 1628. Gained popularity for his comedies and carnival songs, all of which evoke the spirit of his homeland and preserve its customs and special character as well as its language.

BRUGES

During Renaissance Bruges was the headquarters of almost all the leading Flemish illuminators and the center of the school of Flemish painting, as well as one of the largest commercial cities from the twelfth to the sixteenth century. Its turbulent political life and the silting up of its harbor explain its economic decline and the rise of Antwerp in the sixteenth century.

BRÜGGEMANN, HANS

(c. 1480-c. 1540). German painter, sculptor, woodcarver, known to have been in Schleswig in 1521. Artist of late Gothic period in North Germany. He did religious subjects but is better remembered for his depiction of the hard, pathetic lives of the peasantry.

BRULÉ, ÉTIENNE

(c. 1592-1632). French explorer, lieutenant of Champlain. Traveled in West of America and other regions. Lived with American Indians. Dealt in furs. Murdered by Indians.

BRULIFER, STEPHANUS

(Died 1489). French logician, Franciscan monk and doctor of theology at Paris. Author of *Epitomata in Formalitates Iuxta Doctrinam Scoti,* published in Venice in 1501, and other theological works, including a study of St. Bonaventura.

BRÜLOW, KASPAR

(1585-1627). German dramatist. His Latin plays include *Andromeda, Gaius Julius Caesar,* etc., produced at the Academy Theatre of Strassburg, the city where he spent most of his life in an educational post.

BRUNELLESCHI, FILIPPO

(1377-1446). Florentine architect and sculptor, first great architect of the Renaissance. He was beaten out in the competition for the famous doors of Florence's Baptistery by Lorenzo Ghiberti. He made a famous expedition with Donatello to Rome to study, measure and sketch classical structures. Two of his best-known works are the dome of the cathedral of Florence and the Pazzi Chapel; the octagonal ribbed dome and the perfectly round Chapel (the circle was the Neo-Platonic symbol of perfection) demonstrate that he was no slavish copier of his ancient models.

BRUNFELS, OTTO

(c. 1461-1534). German botanist, herbalist and physician. Called Father of Botany. His herbal, *Herbarum vivae icones*, was one of the first to be printed, was especially well illustrated and a milestone in the history of botany, first description of plants indigenous to Germany. In 1530 published a catalogue of famous physicians.

BRUNI, ANTONIO

(1593-1635). Italian poet. Counselor and secretary of Francesco Maria II della Rovere, Duke of Urbino. Author of a series of *Erotic Epistles*, in *terza rima;* subjects are historical and mythological. He enjoyed great fame with the publication of his *canzoniere, Selva di Parnaso.*

BRUNI, LEONARDO

(1370-1444). Born at Arezzo, studied at Florence under Chrysoloras, classical teacher at Florence, secretary to Popes Innocent VIII and "John XXIII"; he accompanied John to Council of Constance where the pope was deposed, whereupon Bruni resigned and became Chancellor of Florence; in the course of his life he held many high offices in the government of Florence. His Latin *History of the Florentine People,* to 1404, was the first of the distinctively humanist histories. He had a high esteem for republican institutions, those of ancient Rome and the contemporary Italian communes. To political liberty and widespread political experience and responsibility he attributed ancient Roman and contemporary Florentine greatness; his work came to look like the epitaph of Florentine freedom, written as it was on the eve of the Medici ascendancy. He was also a translator of Plato, Aristotle, and Plutarch.

BRUNO, GIORDANO

(c. 1548-1600). Italian philosopher; there is a strange mixture of poetry and science in his speculations. He detested dogmatism. Forced to leave the Dominican Order: 1576. The following years were spent in travel, lecturing and writing. Bruno supported the Copernican theory. He postulated an infinite universe, of infinite duration and a plurality of worlds. He rejected transubstantiation and the immaculate conception. Arrested by the Inquisition, he was burned at the stake. While in England, during the years 1583-1585, Bruno associated with John Florio, Sir

Philip Sidney, Dr. John Dee and probably William Gilbert. Influenced subsequent philosophy: Leibnitz, Spinoza, Hegel. Author of *De Nomade, De Umbris Idearum*. Also *Degli Eroici Furori*, Renaissance cosmography and theory of love. He also was a satirist and poet.

BRUNSCHWIG, HIERONYMUS
(c. 1450-c. 1534). German physician of Strassburg; he studied at Bologna, Padua and Paris. He was a pioneer in bringing medical theory and surgical practice together in his *Buch des Chirurgien*, 1497. He also wrote works on drugs, distillations and the plague.

BRUYN, BARTHEL
(1493-1555). Painter. Died in Cologne and the last important figure of its school. Noted for religious subjects, portraits. Began in the Flemish style but veered more and more toward Italian realism.

BRY, JEAN DE
(1561-1623). Flemish engraver and printer-publisher. Settled in Frankfurt. He visited London and was a friend of Hakluyt, published art works.

BRY, THEODORE DE
(1528-1598). Flemish engraver of Liège, father of the above. Settled in Frankfurt. Introduced into book illustration the technique of engraving. A very valuable set of his prints depicts Spanish rule in the New World. Also established a printing press.

BRYSKETT, LODOWICK
(c. 1545-c. 1612). Poet, translator, official in Ireland. Son of Italian immigrant, educated at Cambridge. Friend of Sir Philip Sidney, with whom he traveled in Europe. Friend of Edmund Spenser. Translated an Italian work by Baptisto Giraldous, *A Discourse of Civil Life*: published in 1606. Some of his other works include conversations with Sidney and other memorabilia.

BUCENTAUR or BUCINTORO
The richly decorated Venetian barge of state from which the doge threw the ring in the annual ceremony by which Venice was married to the sea. The popes and several Italian princes, e.g., the Sforza of Milan and the Este of Ferrara, also owned lavish barges for use on state occasions.

BUCER, MARTIN
(1491-1551). German Protestant reformer of Strassburg and one time Dominican friar. Mediator between followers of Zwingli and Lutherans. At Diet of Ratisbon, in 1541, he attempted reconciliation between Roman Catholics and Protestants; upon his failure to do so, he came to England on the invitation of Cranmer. Professor of theology at Cambridge. Spread Reformation in England.

BUCHANAN, GEORGE
(1506-1582). Scottish poet and scholar. Distinguished for his Latinity. Wrote satire against Franciscans. Imprisoned. Escaped to France. One of the teachers of Montaigne. Returning to Scotland, supported Calvinists. Tutor to James VI of Scotland. Author of a number of tragedies, Latin poems. Also produced history of Scotland: *Rerum Scoticarum Historia*, 1582. His *De jure regni apud Scotos* is memorable for its fierce defense of tyrannicide and of the right of resistance, 1579.

BUCHNER, HULDRICH
German poet. Author of series of poems on Renaissance notables of Germany, including poets, statesmen, philosophers, lawyers, physicians, theologians: entitled *Anagrammatismorum Pleiades*. Personalities include: Dasypodius, Chytraeus, Camerarius, Fabricius, Lipsius, Reusner, Egenolph. Published in 1601.

BUCKINGHAM, GEORGE VILLIERS, DUKE OF
(1592-1628). Favorite of King James I of England. Dissolute and wealthy. Mismanaged marriage proposals between Spanish Infanta and Prince Charles; he utilized the failure to promote war between England and Spain. He arranged the marriage of the Prince with Henrietta Maria of France, and also sought to bring England into the Thirty Years' War on behalf of the Protestants of Bohemia. Buckingham was impeached by the Commons, but was saved by the King. He was notoriously involved in an affair with the Queen of France. Assassinated.

BUDÉ, GUILLAUME or BUDAEUS
(1468-1540). Trained as a lawyer, he was one of the first French humanists to bring the methods of the new learning to the elucidation of Roman law, for unlike so many humanists he did not have a thorough-going contempt for the legal pro-

fession. His *Notes on the Pandects* of Justinian appeared in 1508. He was among the giants of French scholarship, among his more important works were a treatise on Roman coinage and his *On Philology*, 1530. He was the friend of Erasmus, librarian and secretary to King Francis I; he sought to encourage classical studies, especially Greek and his *Commentarii Linguae Graecae* was published in 1529. He was instrumental in founding the Royal Library, which later became the Bibliothèque Nationale, and he persuaded the king to establish the Collège de France. Humanist religious concerns may be seen in his treatise *Transitus*, an inquiry into the relationship of Hellenism and Christianity.

BUGENHAGEN, JOHANN

(1485-1558). German reformer and onetime priest. Friend of Martin Luther and Melanchthon. Organized many Protestant churches. Taught at the University of Wittenberg and aided Luther in translation of the Bible. Published funeral oration of Luther. Organized Danish Church on Lutheran lines; his chief importance was in the ecclesiastical and educational organization of the Lutheran Church.

BUGIARDINI, GIULIANO

(1475-1554). Italian painter of Florence. Friend of Michelangelo, who influenced his work, as did Raphael and Leonardo.

BUGLIONI, BENEDETTO

(1461-1521). Florentine sculptor of terracotta in the manner of the Della Robbias.

BUGLIONI, SANTI

(1494-1576). Florentine sculptor, disciple of the above, from whom he took his name. He worked in terracotta and collaborated with Giovanni della Robbia; he also did a ciborium and similar ecclesiastical pieces.

BUIL, BERNARDO

(c. 1450-1520). Benedictine monk. Accompanied Columbus to America. Later, in conjunction with Columbus' enemies, made charges against him.

BULL, JOHN

(c. 1563-1628). English musician and composer. Organist to King James I. As a Catholic, fled to Brussels. Organist at Antwerp Cathedral. Reputedly composed English National Anthem. He was famous as a virtuoso of the virginal and organ, and left many compositions for those instruments.

BULLANT, JEAN
(c. 1515-1578). French architect. Architect to Henry II of France and Catherine de' Medici. Worked on Tuileries. He had studied classical architecture at Rome.

BULLINGER, HEINRICH
(1504-1574). Swiss reformer at Zurich. Successor of Zwingli in struggle with Catholics. Author of a *History of the Reformation*. Headed Reformation movement in German Switzerland. Participated in promulgation of first Helvetic Confession: 1536. Helped to bring an accommodation between his followers and Calvinists; was the friend and collaborator of Calvin.

BULLOKAR, JOHN
(c. 1580-c 1640). English physician, lexicographer. Published an English dictionary in 1616; it went through several editions.

BULLOKAR, WILLIAM
(c. 1520-c. 1590). Phonetist and orthographic reformer. He wrote a grammar but chiefly a *Book at Large* where he sought to settle the "quarrels in the teacher and lothsomness in the learner" that grew out of an irrational system of pronunciation. He ran into opposition as have his successors in such reforms. He also published translations from the Latin, e.g., Aesop's *Fables*.

BUONCONSIGLIO, GIOVANNI, IL MARESCALO
(Died c. 1536). Venetian painter. He did mostly religious subjects. The chief influence upon him was Giovanni Bellini, but the sense of depth and plasticity are his own.

BUONI, TOMASO
Lucchese scholar and cleric. Published series of *Lettere Argute* in 1603, addressed to contemporary literary figures. Contain discussions on academic problems in literature, philosophy and related areas.

BUONTALENTI, BERNARDO
(1536-1608). Florentine architect, sculptor, painter and miniaturist. Possibly last important artist of Italy who was also an illumi-

nator. He was patronized by the Medici Duke of Florence, Cosimo I, for whom he built splendid residences; he marks the transition to Baroque.

BURBAGE, RICHARD
(c. 1567-1619). English actor. Called Roscius. Built famous Globe Theatre. Among his theatrical partners was Shakespeare himself.

BURGHLEY, WILLIAM CECIL, LORD
(1520-1598). English statesman. Secretary of State: 1550-1553. Conformed to Catholicism during Queen Mary's reign, when he was out of favor and out of office. Chief Secretary of State in Elizabeth's reign. Exercised a cautious, opportunistic policy at home and abroad. Lord High Treasurer from 1572 to his death. Instrumental in execution of Mary, Queen of Scots. He was essentially a *politique*.

BURKMAIR, HANS
(1473-1531). German painter and engraver of Augsburg. Friend of Albrecht Dürer. Did a series of woodcuts with scenes from the Emperor's life for Emperor Maximilian I. Master of chiaroscuro, he was instrumental in introducing Italian Renaissance style into Germany. Works include frescoes, landscapes, religious motifs, portraits.

BURTON, ROBERT
(1577-1640). English scholar and cleric. Wrote comedy in Latin: *Philosophaster*. Noted especially for *The Anatomy of Melancholy:* ostensibly an analysis of various phases of melancholy, but actually an encyclopedic miscellany.

BUSBECQ, AUGIER GHISELIN DE
(1522-1592). Humanist. Flemish statesman in the service of the Hapsburgs. Ambassador of Emperor Ferdinand I to Turks. Wrote an account of the Turkish government and military system in form of letters: *Legationis Turcicae Epistulae Quattuor:* published in 1589. A learned scholar, graceful Latinist and collector of manuscripts, coins and other antiquities.

BUXTORF, JOHANN
(1564-1629). German Hebraist and Biblical scholar. Professor of Hebrew at Basel, a chair held by his descendants for three

generations. Died of plague. Compiled a Chaldaic, Talmudic Rabbinic lexicon and a concordance to the Hebrew Bible.

BYE PLOT
Called The Surprising Treason. It aimed at the incarceration of King James I of England. Exposed in 1603. The Main Plot of the same year sought to depose James in favor of his cousin, Arabella Stuart.

BYRD, WILLIAM
(c. 1540-1623). English composer. Founded the school of Elizabethan madrigalists. Composed sacred music also. He was organist to Queen Elizabeth, with whom he stood in high favor.

C

CABBALA AND CABBALISTS, THE

The medieval system of Jewish theosophy which many Renaissance scholars regarded as a talisman for reconciling ancient philosophy and Christian doctrines; it was supposed to have dated from the age of Abraham, but was no older for the most part than the thirteenth century. It exercised great influence on the thought of Pico, who translated cabbalistic works into Latin, and of Reuchlin who wrote the cabbalistic theses *De Verbo Mirifico* and *De Arte Cabbalistica*, c. 1500.

CABEZÓN, ANTONIO DE

(1510-1566). Blind composer, court organist and harpsichordist to Charles V and Philip II of Spain; one of the earliest keyboard composers. He composed popular as well as liturgical music.

CABEZÓN, HERNANDO DE

(Died 1602). Son of the above, successor to his father's place at court.

CABEZÓN, JUAN DE

(Sixteenth century). Brother of the above, also a composer.

CABOT, GIOVANNI

(1458-1498). John Cabot. Italian-born explorer. Entered Mecca. In 1490, settled in England. Commissioned by Henry VII to undertake a voyage of exploration to East: 1497. Sighted Cape Breton Island. Discovered Newfoundland: 1497. On basis of this voyage, England later claimed land in America.

CABRAL, PEDRO ALVARES

(c. 1460-c. 1526). Portuguese explorer. Sent by Emmanuel I of Portugal to East Indies on trade mission. Took westward course and landed on coast of Brazil. Despite storms, loss of ships, made Calicut, India.

CABRILLO, JUAN RODRIGUEZ

(died 1543). Spanish explorer. In America: in Mexico with Cortés. Present at capture of Mexico City in 1521. Explored Mexican coast.

CACCINI, GIULIO

(c. 1558-c. 1618). Italian composer. Produced *Euridice* in 1600: one of the first operas; he and Peri had produced *Daphne* in 1597. He knew Plato and Aristoxenus on music and was a pioneer in the development of the recitative and monody.

CADAMOSTO, ALVISE DA

(c. 1432-c. 1511). Venetian navigator. Explored west coast of Africa. Discovered Cape Verde Islands in 1456. Wrote an account of his voyages.

CADIZ, NAVAL BATTLE OF

Sir Francis Drake, informed of Philip of Spain's preparations for invasion of England, sailed into Cadiz harbor and sank thirty-seven ships, in 1587.

CADORE, BATTLE OF

The Emperor Maximilian I engaged with the Venetians. He was assisted by French and Spaniards, but was defeated, 1509.

CAEPOLLA, BARTOLOMMEUS

(died 1474). Italian jurist, studied Roman law at Bologna, taught at Ferrara and Padua. He sought to mold and adapt Roman law to the needs of his own time, in the Bartolist tradition.

CAESARIUS, JOHANNES

(1460-1551). German humanist and philosopher. Author of treatise on dialectics, entitled *Dialectica:* published in 1567. He was the friend of Reuchlin and Erasmus, learned in Greek, had a hand in the *Letters of Obscure Men,* and wrote or edited numerous works in the humanities and science.

114

CAIADO, HENRIQUE
(died c. 1508). Portuguese jurist, poet and Latinist. He published one volume of Latin poetry, *Eclogas, Silvas e Epigramas*, 1501. He traveled much in Italy, studied at Padua, lived a wild life and died of alcoholism.

CAIUS AND GONVILLE COLLEGE
Cambridge University. Founded as Gonville Hall by Edmund Gonville (died 1351) in 1348. Assumed present name under Royal Charter in 1557.

CAIUS, JOHN
(1510-1593). English physician. Studied under Vesalius at Padua. Physician to Edward VI and Queen Elizabeth. Wrote on scientific and antiquarian subjects. Refounded Gonville and Caius College at Cambridge, 1557.

CAJETAN, CARDINAL THOMAS OF THIENE, SAINT
(1480-1547). Italian prelate and reformer, one of the architects of the Counter Reformation. Co-founder of Oratory of Divine Love, later called Theatines.

CAJETANUS, THOMAS DE VIO
(c. 1469-1534). Cardinal and scholar. In Lutheran controversy, Luther was brought before Cajetanus to undergo questioning in an attempt to reconcile Luther's teachings with those of the Church. Wrote commentary on Aristotelian logic, made translations of parts of the Bible.

CALAIS
French seaport. Recovered from England by French in 1558. It was the last portion of France to be held by England.

CALCAGNI, ANTONIO
(1536-1593). Italian sculptor. Executed bronze casts: an *Apollo*, a *Venus* for Marcello Melchiorri, also religious scenes, e.g., *Descent from the Cross*, as well as tombs of princes and ecclesiastics.

CALCAGNINI, CELIO
(1479-1541). Italian humanist writer on many subjects, e.g., astronomy, rhetoric, Egyptology and philosophy; also served as ambassador of the Este house of Ferrara. He was a friend of Erasmus.

CALCAR, JOOS VAN

(c. 1499-1546) Italian painter. Died in Naples. Produced genre pieces in the style of Venetian colorists. Disciple of Raphael and Titian. He is credited by some authorities with the splendid illustrations for Vesalius' famous anatomy.

CALCOS ISLANDS

In British West Indies. Discovered c. 1512.

CALEPIN

A dictionary, especially a polyglot dictionary. The term is derived from Ambrogio Calepino of Calepio, Italy. He was an Augustinian monk who in 1502 published a Latin dictionary, of which an edition in eight languages was published in 1609.

CALEPINO, AMBROGIO

(1435-1511). Italian Augustinian monk, humanist, lexicographer. Author of a huge Latin-Italian dictionary: *Cornucopia,* published in 1502. Dictionary became so popular that it was edited and extended by Forcellini and others until it included eleven languages.

CALIPHATE

Egyptian Caliphate extinguished by Ottoman conquest: 1517. Thereafter the Ottoman threat to Europe was great.

CALIXTUS III

(1378-1458). First Spanish pope, 1455-58, since Damasus I. On entering pontificate, began crusade against Turks. Organized fleet that sailed in 1456, gained victory, but in the end his crusade came to nothing owing to quarrels among participants. Introduced ringing of angelus. Painted by Sano di Pietros.

CALIXTUS, GEORG

(1586-1656). Lutheran theologian. He attempted to restore Christendom by removing unimportant differences among sects. His attempts made him suspect to all as a "syncretist"; his proposals were put forth in his *Desidarium concordiae ecclesiastical.*

CALLIERGES, ZACHARIAS

(floruit c. 1525). Greek scholar and printer. Founded printing press in Venice. Noted for beauty of Greek type. Issued *Commentary on Aristotle,* works of Galen. Moved to Rome, where he

116

continued his work. Issued Pindar, Theocritus, Thomas Magister. He also wrote learned works on such subjects as etymology.

CALLOT, JACQUES
(1592-1635). French painter, engraver. Took themes for his highly realistic etching sequences from the campaigns in which he participated. Executed extensive works of historical importance. The greatest original graphic artist of the baroque period. First made etching a significant art. Among his works are *Pont-Neuf, Les Gueux, Madonna of the Impruneta, Caprices, Misères de Guerre.* He had studied in Rome, went to Florence to serve its Medici duke, Cosimo II, upon whose death he returned to Lorraine and its ducal court. Later executed etchings for Louis XIII of France.

CALMO, ANDREA
(1510-1571). Venetian comic writer and poet. His works were collected under name of Cherebizzi in 1601. Written in Venetian patois, they offer commentary on contemporary mores: also imaginary letters packed with literary and scholarly allusions. His work was often bizarre and fantastic.

CALVAERT, DIONYS
(1540-1619). Flemish painter. After achieving fame in his homeland he went to Rome and Bologna, spending most of his maturity in Italy. Executed historical themes, landscapes. Founder of school of painting in Bologna that produced Dominiquino, Albano and Guido Reni and noted for the meticulous execution of detail.

CALVIN, JOHN
(1509-1564). Religious reformer. Born at Noyon, Picardy. Trained as a lawyer, of middle-class origin. Educated for the Church. In 1536 published *Institutes of Christian Religion.* Settled in Geneva, where he established a theocracy. Influenced the controversy between the Guises and the Huguenots in France. His contributions were the systematization of Protestant doctrine and the organization of its ecclesiastical discipline. Called the Protestant Pope.

CALVISIUS, SETHUS
(1556-1615). German musician, composer, astronomer, and mathematician. He composed motets and wrote treatises on

music, one of which, *Exercitationes musicae duae,* included what was probably the first history of music ever written, *De initio et progressu musices,* published 1600.

CAM, DIOGO
(floruit 1480-1486). Portuguese navigator. Discovered mouth of Congo in 1484. Also explored coast of West Africa.

CAMBIASI or CAMBIASO, LUCA
(1527-1585). Genoese painter. Died in Madrid, where he had been invited by Philip II to contribute to the Escorial. Produced religious subjects, frescoes, mythological paintings. Modified mannerist style.

CAMBINI, ANDREA
(died late 15th C.) Italian historian, died at Florence. Author of a history of the Ottoman Empire, until the conquest of Constantinople. Published in 1538.

CAMBRAI, LEAGUE OF
This league was organized among Louis XII of France, Ferdinand of Spain, Emperor Maximilian I, Pope Julius II, and other Italian states to wage a revengeful war to dismember the hated Venetian state, in 1508-1510.

CAMBRAI, TREATY OF
By this treaty, the Emperor Charles V ceded ducal Burgundy, while Francis I of France gave up Naples. This treaty was also called The Ladies' Peace, *Paix des Dames,* as the negotiations were arranged by Margaret, mother of Charles V, and Louise of Savoy, mother of Francis I: 1529. It marked the end of the first phase of the struggle between the emperor and Francis I.

CAMBRIDGE UNIVERSITY PRESS
Founded in 1583 by Thomas Thomas (1553-1588).

CAMDEN, WILLIAM
(1551-1623). English scholar, antiquary, historian. Headmaster of Westminster School. Author of *Britannia*: Latin survey of English history. Published in 1586. Also compiled, in Latin, collection of epitaphs in Westminster Abbey, collection of early English historians. Wrote *Annals of Reign of Elizabeth.* The Camden Society was founded in his honor, one of the giants of English scholarship.

CAMERARIUS, JOACHIM

(1500-1574). One of the greatest classical scholars of sixteenth-century Germany. Professor of Greek at Tübingen, Nuremberg. Supported the Reformation. Friend of Melanchthon. Edited Homer and other classical texts, also made Latin translations of Greek texts. Author of biographies, and compiled reference works for the study of the classics, e.g., on numismatics. Wrote treatise on symbolism derived from a study of Dante: published in Nuremberg in 1590. Author of *History of the Orthodox Brethren in Bohemia and Poland.* Also wrote pedagogical treatise based on Melanchthon's theology: published in 1566. His attempts to reach an accommodation between Lutheranism and Catholicism, once with Francis I of France and later with Emperor Maximilian II, came to nothing.

CAMERATA DE'BARDI OF FLORENCE

A circle of artists, poets, musicians, and classicists that met in the palace of the count, Giovanni Bardi, in the late sixteenth century; it included Vincenzo Galilei (father of the scientist), Giulio Caccini, Jacopo Corsi, Piero Strozzi, Jacopo Peri, and Ottavio Rinuccini. They reacted against what they conceived as the over-elaborate polyphonic music and, guided by their knowledge of Greek monodic music and inspired by Greek ideals of simplicity and expressiveness, created the operatic form. The first opera *Daphne,* to which many of the group contributed, although Peri was the principal composer and Rinuccini the librettist, was given at Corsi's palace in 1597.

CAMERON, JOHN

(1579-1623). Scottish theologian and reformer. Principal of Glasgow University. Professor of divinity at Saumur and Montauban in France. Calvinist. Founder of party within the French Protestant Church called Amyraldians from Amyraut, one of his followers. The Cameronites adhered to a more moderate, semi-Pelagian view of grace, salvation and human nature than did Calvinists. Author of theological treatises, in Latin and French. Stabbed to death.

CAMILLO, GIULIO

(c. 1480-c. 1544). Called Delminio. Born at Forli. Taught at Bologna. Pupil of Pico della Mirandola. Attached to the court of Francis I of France. Engaged in controversy with Erasmus. Classical and Oriental scholar and cabbalist. Author of *The Idea of the Theatre:* contains discussions on mythology, philosophy, pseudo-philosophy in the form of a theatrical allegory. Posthumously published in 1550.

CAMINHA, PEDRO DE ANDRADE

(c. 1520-1589). Portuguese court poet, related to the royal house of Bragança. Wrote sonnets pervaded by a mystical strain. An enemy of Camões, whom he satirized in several epigrams. His poetry has been found "decadent": his sheltered life and highly personal poetry make the sharpest contrast with those of Camões.

CAMÕES, LUIZ VAZ DE or CAMOENS

(c. 1524-1580). Portuguese poet. Attached to the court at Lisbon, banished for an amorous escapade. Led an adventurous life. Fought in Morocco. Lost an eye. Soldier in India. Imprisoned. Returned to Portugal, reinstated. In 1570 secured the patronage of King Sebastian. Author of *Os Lusiades,* or *The Sons of Lusus,* published in 1572. The finest Renaissance epic in the vernacular on a contemporary subject on the classical model in style, structure, etc. It is the story of Vasco da Gama's expedition. Camões himself was an explorer and fits the Portuguese heroic ideal of the *fidalgo.* Also wrote epigrams, sonnets, lyrics, comedies.

CAMPAGNA, GIROLAMO

(1550-1623). Architect and sculptor. Died in Venice, where he did most of his work. Large-scale religious sculptures, funeral monuments, etc. Belongs in the early baroque period.

CAMPAGNOLA, DOMENICO

(1500-c. 1564). Italian painter and engraver of Padua. Reputedly, aide to Titian. Produced frescoes, woodcuts, engravings, sketches. Noted for *Holy Family, Birth of Christ.*

CAMPAGNOLA, GIULIO

(1482-post 1513). Italian painter, miniaturist, and engraver. Executed original copperplate engravings in a soft stippled technique in the tradition of Bellini and of Georgione. Did all his work in his native city of Padua; some of his work was commissioned by Aldus Manutius.

CAMPALONGO, EMILIO

(1550-1609) Italian physician, professor of medicine at Padua.

120

Follower of views of medical reformer Pierre Brissot (1478-1522) and author of several works on medical subjects.

CAMPANA, PEDRO

(1503-1580). Pieter van Kempener. Painter. Died in Brussels. He studied and worked for about a decade in Italy, then about 1537 he settled in Seville. Executed dramatic, religious themes for the cathedral of Seville.

CAMPANELLA, TOMMASO

(1568-1639). Italian Dominican monk. Political philosopher. Opposed to Aristotelianism. His conception of science was similar in many respects to that of Bacon. Imprisoned on charge of heresy, fled to France. While in prison, produced *De Civitate Solis:* conception of Utopia founded on Plato's *Republic.* Also author of some eighty other works. Wrote *De Sensu Rerum et Magia Libri IV:* published in 1620. J. A. Symonds: "The audacious Titan of the modern age."

CAMPEGGIO, CARDINAL LORENZO

(c. 1472-1539). Italian prelate. Papal legate. On mission to England, became Bishop of Salisbury by order of Henry VIII. He had been sent by Pope Clement VII to delay and temporize in the matter of Henry's divorce from Catherine of Aragon; his legatine court only aggravated the king and discredited Wolsey.

CAMPHUYSEN, DIRK RAFELSZOON

(1586-1627). Poet. Wrote religious poems: simple, vigorous, ascetic. Had been professor of theology at Utrecht, was expelled for his Arminianism, led an aberrant life and died mysteriously.

CAMPI, BERNARDINO

(1522-c. 1590). Italian painter of Cremona. Executed frescoes with Biblical themes.

CAMPI, CAVALLERE ANTONIO

(died 1591). Italian painter, architect, and historian of Cremona, brother of the above. Executed still life, portraits.

CAMPI, GIULIO

(c. 1500-c. 1572). Italian painter, architect of Cremona, father of the above. Founded school of painters at Cremona. Executed altarpieces, frescoes.

CAMPI, VINCENZO

(1532-1591) Son of the above, painter of portraits and still life.

CAMPION, EDMUND

(1540-1581) English Jesuit. Student at Oxford, his brilliance gained him the favor of Queen Elizabeth and the patronage of Leicester. Professor of rhetoric at Prague University. Charged with conspiracy against throne, executed as traitor within two years of his return to England as a missionary. Wrote treatise entitled *Imitation:* also *Compendium of Rhetoric;* his *History of Ireland* was one of the great historical works of the age.

CAMPION, THOMAS

(1567-1619). English poet, musician, physician. Composed court music. Wrote Latin epigrams, elegies. Also English lyrics. Wrote treatises on prosody.

CANANO, GIOVANNI BATISTA

(1515-1579). Italian anatomist, physician to Pope Julius III. Discovered muscle known as *palmaris brevis* and the valves of the veins. Author of *Muscularum Humani Corporis Picturata Dissectio:* published in 1541. Also wrote *Liber Primus* of a projected comprehensive treatise on anatomy. His text was illustrated with diagrams of the muscles. He devoted most of his life to teaching anatomy at Ferrara.

CANCIONERO GENERAL

Largest and most important Castilian poetic anthology. Published in 1511. Compiled by Hernando del Castillo, it contains some 1000 poems contributed by more than 100 poets, love lyrics, ballads, satire, didactic and devotional pieces.

CANDID, ELIA, DE WITTE

(Sixteenth century) Dutch sculptor. Little is known of his life except that he learned and practiced his art in Florence. He worked in bronze and did an *Aeolus* and a *Perseus.* His son, PETER, (1548-1628) accompanied his father to Florence and was inspired to become a painter. He assisted Vasari. The Italian influence is strong in the works of father and son.

CANISIUS, PETER, SAINT

(1521-1597). German theologian. Founded first Jesuit house in Cologne. Promoted Catholicism in Germany, Poland. Wrote

Summa Doctrinae Christianae: published in 1555; it was a catechism in German and Latin and a very persuasive weapon in the hands of Jesuit missionaries to Protestant lands; it was modeled on a similar work by Luther.

CANNON-BALLS
Iron cannon-balls were first cast in the reign of Louis XI (1461-1483) in France.

CANO, JUAN SEBASTIÁN DEL
(died 1526). Spanish navigator. First navigator who circumnagivated the globe. Accompanied Magellan. After death of Magellan, led expedition.

CANTER, WILLEM
(1542-1575). Dutch scholar of Utrecht. Worked in Louvain on Greek dramatists. Edited Aeschylus, Sophocles, Euripides. He had studied at several universities in Italy and France. He was a prodigy of learning. He published numerous learned works on and editions of the classics. He wore himself out on his studies and thus died at so young an age.

CANTIUNCULA, CLAUDIUS
(1490-1565). Jurist. Professor of law at Basel from 1518 to 1524, and thereafter at other universities. He wrote extensively on civil and common law and on the power of popes, councils and the Holy Roman Emperors.

CAPARRA, NICCOLO GROSSO
(Late fifteenth century). Called Il Fabbro, Metalworker of Florence. His lanterns and other decorative works are found in the Medici and other Florentine Palaces.

CAPELLA, GALEATUS
(1487-1537). Milanese historian, secretary to Jerome Morone, then to Duke Francisco Sforza II. Author of *Nuper in Italia de Bello Mediolanesi seu de Refus*, published in 1533, a history of Milan 1520-1531; he also wrote an account of Sultan Suleiman the Magnificent.

CAPELLO, BIANCA
(1542?-1587). Italian beauty, mistress of Francesco de' Medici, whom she later married. Became Grand Duchess of Tuscany.

123

Involved in murderous intrigue. Died suddenly, probably of colic. Bronzino did two fine portraits of her.

CAPILUPI, CAMILLO

(1504-1548). Writer in prose and verse, made translations, member of the Gonzaga court of Mantua.

CAPILUPI, IPPOLITO

(1511-1579). Humanist scholar, poet, translator, councilor to the house of Gonzaga of Mantua.

CAPILUPI, LELIO

(1497-1563). Italian humanist, brother of the above. Acquired a reputation for his vernacular Petrarchan sonnets, Latin poems and his macaronic works in which he mixed Latin and Italian words and added Latin endings, etc.

CAPITO, WOLFGANG FABRICIUS

(1478-1541). German Catholic priest. Benedictine. Professor of theology at Basel. Supported Reformation. Leader of Reformation movement in Strassburg. Participated in Tetrapolitan Confession of 1530 and worked, unsuccessfully, for an accord between Lutheranism and Zwinglianism.

CAPIVACCIUS, HIERONYMUS

(Died 1589). Italian physician. Wrote on philosophy: *De Differentiis Doctrinarum Logicis, Philosophis, Atque Medicis Pernecessarium*. Student of the contagion of plague.

CAPORALI, GIACOMO AND BARTOLOMEO

(Fifteenth century). Brothers who worked in second half of century. Representatives of Perugian school of illumination. Executed missals in 1469 and 1496.

CAPORALI, GIAN BATTISTA

(1476-1560). Italian miniaturist, painter, architect, son of Bartolomeo. Executed missal illuminations and other works. He wrote a commentary on Vitruvius.

CAPPONI, NICCOLO

Gonfalonier of the Republic formed in Florence in 1527, re-elected in 1528; his attempt to reach a negotiated settlement with the Medici—who had been expelled—in order to avoid a siege of

Florence caused a revulsion against him and he fell from power in 1529; the Republic fell to the Medici in 1530.

CAPREOLUS, ELIAS
(Died 1519). Italian jurist and historian of Brescia. He wrote a history of Brescia and a *Confirmation* of Christian doctrine.

CAPREOLUS, JOHANNES
(c. 1380-1444). Logician, scholastic philosopher. Author of *Quaestiones in Libros Sententiarum:* published in Venice in 1589. A defender of St. Thomas, he attacked the Occamists and Scottists.

CAPRETTO, PIETRO
(Sixteenth century). Italian musician. Composed *laude.*

CAPUCHIN ORDER
Religious Order founded in 1528 by Italian monk, Matteo di Bassi (c. 1495-1552), branched off from the Franciscan Order.

CARA, MARCHETTO
(fl. 1495-1525). Musician at the Gonzaga court of Mantua from 1495 to 1525. Composed *laude,* also polyphonic secular music, much of which was printed by Petrucci.

CARACCIOLI, SER GIOVANNI, PRINCE OF MELFI
(1480-1550). Italian statesman, Marshal of France, fought in the wars against Spain and the Hapsburgs.

CARACCIOLO, GIOVANNI BATTISTA
(c. 1570-c. 1637). Neapolitan painter, disciple of Caravaggio. After a sojourn in Rome he returned to Naples, where he did almost all his work, predominantly religious scenes.

CARAVAGGIO, MICHELANGELO AMERIGHI DA
(1569-1609). Italian painter. Worked in Rome. Founded Roman naturalist school: he was an outspoken critic of the older Ideal-Antique tradition in painting. After killing a companion, obliged to leave Rome. Among his paintings are: *Gipsy Fortuneteller, Card Players, Entombment of Christ, Death of Mary.* Also executed portraits. He never ceased to be a tempestuous personage, much of his vigor and zest expressing themselves in his violent colors and imaginative scenes.

CARAVAGGIO, POLIDORO CALDARA DA

(c. 1495-1546). Italian painter. Died at Messina. His subjects were mythological and religious. He also executed frescoes, graffiti, bas-reliefs in the antique manner, making frequent use of allegory. Did most of his work at Rome, where he came under the influence of Raphael.

CARDANUS, HIERONYMUS or GEROLAMO

(1501-1576). Italian scholar, physician, mathematician, philosopher, astrologer, educated in medicine at Padua. Author of *Proxeneta*: citizenship, functions and characteristics of rulers, governors and governed, obligations of citizens. He was a prolific writer and wrote on many subjects, e.g., rhetoric, astronomy, physics: *De Subtilitate Rerum:* published in 1557. Also autobiography: *De Propria Vita.* His son, GIOVANNI BATTISTA (1534-1560), was an eminent physician but was executed as a criminal.

CARDUCCI, BARTOLOMMEO

(1560-1608). Florentine painter, sculptor and architect. In service of Philip II and Philip III of Spain. Executed frescoes, altarpieces. Noted for *Descent from the Cross, Adoration of the Kings;* contributed to the Escorial.

CARDUCCI, VINCENZO

(c. 1568-1638). Florentine painter, brother of the above. Worked in Spain. Attached to court of Philip III and Philip IV. Wrote dialogue on painting, the *Diálogos de las excelencias de la pintuna.*

CAREW, RICHARD

(1555-1620). English poet, antiquarian, friend of Raleigh, William Camden, Henry Spelman.

CAREW, THOMAS

(c. 1595-c. 1645). English Cavalier poet. Attached to court of Charles I. Friend of many contemporary dramatists, among them Ben Jonson; also of poet Sir John Suckling and the philosopher Lord Herbert of Cherbury. Noted for his lyrics.

CARLINE

Small silver coin current in Sicily during the Renaissance.

CARLISLE GRAMMAR SCHOOL
In north of England. English public school. Probably founded by Henry I in 1122. Refounded by Henry VIII in 1541.

CARLOS, DON
(1545-1568). Heir of Philip II of Spain. Charged with plotting against father. Imprisoned. Died in prison. Subject of *Don Carlos*, tragedy by Schiller. Also theme of dramas by Alfieri, Otway, André Chénier.

CARLSTADT, ANDREAS RUDOLF BODENSTEIN
(c. 1480-1541). German reformer. Professor at Basel. At first attached to Martin Luther, although Carlstadt was always more radical than he. Expelled from Saxony. In Wittenberg, under Luther's protection. Involved in endless doctrinal controversies. Fled to Zürich. Attached to Zwingli.

CARMELITES, ORDER OF
The Order of the *Carmes Déschaussés* was founded by St. John of the Cross in 1568.

CARO, ANNIBALE
(1507-1568). Italian poet, translator of the *Aeneid*. Wrote madrigals, sonnets, eclogues. Friend of Bembo, Cellini, and Varchi. Produced a bitter literary *Apologia*, in reply to the critic Castelvetro.

CARO, JOSEPH BEN EPHRAIM
(1488-1575). Rabbinical scholar. Born in Toledo, died in Palestine. Author of standard Jewish code: *Prepared Table*, published in 1564. Treatise on daily duties, festivals, rituals, civil law.

CAROTO, GIOVANNI
(c. 1488-c. 1562). Veronese painter, brother of Giovanni Francesco (below), with whom he frequently collaborated.

CAROTO, GIOVANNI FRANCESCO
(c. 1480-1555). Italian painter of Verona. Pupil of Mantegna. Executed frescoes, panels, chiefly of religious subjects; noted for the luminescence of the atmosphere against which he places his figures.

CARPACCIO, VITTORE
(c. 1455-c. 1525). Italian painter of Venice, influenced chiefly by

Bellini. Painted *History of Saint Ursula* in a series of scenes. Similarly, *Life of Saint George,* in series of nine episodes. Noted for his *Presentation in the Temple,* and *The Two Courtesans.* Notable for bright colors, a glistening luminosity and extensive detail; he conveys much of the public life of Venice in his day, the festivals and processions, etc. He also painted rather fanciful scenes from the East.

CARPI, UGO DA
(1455-1523). Italian painter and engraver. Died in Rome. Introduced chiaroscuro technique of the woodcut into Italy. His works, e.g., the *Diogenes* engraving, have a compelling power to them.

CARRACCI, AGOSTINO
(1557-1602). Italian painter and engraver. He was the principal founder of the center for discussions of painting and the arts, the *Accademia dei Desiderari.* He and the Accademia were strong classicists and opposed the anticlassicism of Caravaggio and his school.

CARRACCI, ANNIBALE
(1560-1609). Italian painter, brother of the above. Died in Rome. Artist and founder of Roman school of baroque painting. Religious and mythological themes, landscapes, frescoes. He was the most influential painter of the family, in Italy and Europe at large.

CARRACCI, LUDOVICO
(1555-1619). Italian painter of Bologna, cousin of the above. Studied in Venice. Taught painting. Noted for his *Transfiguration.* Executed altarpieces and frescoes. His studio was the nucleus of the *Accademia dei Desiderari.*

CARRANZA, BARTOLOMÉ DE
(1503-1576). Spanish theologian. Dominican. Professor of theology at Valladolid. Adviser to Charles V, Philip II. Imprisoned by Inquisition, charged with heresy in 1559. Removed to castle in Rome. Recalled, died shortly after.

CARRILLO Y SOTOMAYOR, LUIS DE
(1583?-1610). Spanish scholar, poet, soldier, of a refined and aristocratic temperament. Born in Cordova. Attached to court in

128

Naples. Translated Ovid and Seneca. Exponent of *culturanismo:* expressed literary doctrines in *Libro de la Erudición Poética.* Advocated allusive, classical, subtle, cryptic style, suggestive of Góngora, and practiced it in his volume of poems, *Fábula de Acis y Galatea.*

CARTARI, VINCENZO
(1520-1570). Italian Renaissance scholar and poet. Author of *Imagines Deorum:* published in 1581; a study of the pagan pantheon, religious ceremonies, etc.

CARTIER, JACQUES
(1491-1557). French explorer. Sailed to India three times. In 1534 discovered the Saint Lawrence River, Canada.

CARTWRIGHT, THOMAS
(1535-1603). English religious leader: exegete. Puritan professor of divinity. Imprisoned for nonconformity to Church of England. Migrated to continent.

CARTWRIGHT, WILLIAM
(1611-1643). English poet, playwright, theologian. Author of many poems: lyrics, occasional pieces. Among his plays is *The Ordinary,* one of the few of his works that has lasted, most of them were stilted.

CARVER, JOHN
(c.1576-1621). English leader of Pilgrim Fathers. Chartered Mayflower. First governor of Plymouth colony.

CARY, LUCIUS, VISCOUNT FALKLAND
(c. 1610-1643). Scottish noble, poet. In service of Holland. On return, devoted himself to classical study. Author of poems. Also *Discourses of Infallibility.* Killed in battle at Newbury.

CASA DE CONTRATACIÓN
House of Commerce at Seville; it was a board of trade, a commercial court and a clearing-house for colonial trade; the instrument of royal control set up by Spain to regulate colonial trade, 1503.

CASA GIOCOSA, LA
The Happy House. School founded by Vittorino da Feltre in 1425. Training ground for many notable Renaissance figures.

CASA, GIOVANNI DELLA

(1500-1556). Archbishop of Benevento, poet, man of letters. Author of standard work on courtesy, *The Galateo,* directed to young Renaissance gentlemen: published in 1598. Translated into many languages.

CASALA PILGRIM

The Casala Pilgrim was a sixteenth-century guide to the Holy Land.

CASAUBON, ISAAC

(1559-1614). French classical scholar, theologian. Born in Geneva. Huguenot. Professor of Greek at Geneva, Montpellier. Lectured on Plautus, Terence, Homer. Worked in Royal Library, in Paris. Migrated to England, remained for the rest of his life and entered the Church of England. Edited many Greek and Latin authors, among them: Polybius, Athenaeus, Persius, Suetonius.

CASKET LETTERS

A number of letters exchanged with the Earl of Bothwell that reputedly but not definitively implicated Mary Queen of Scots in a plot resulting in the murder of her husband Lord Darnley.

CASSERIO, GIULIO

(1552-1616). Italian anatomist of Piacenza. Taught anatomy and surgery privately at Padua. Author of treatises on the organs of hearing, the larynx, as well as more general anatomical works.

CASTAGNO, ANDREA DEL

(c. 1390-1457). Florentine painter. He followed the tradition of Masaccio; his work is characterized by much the same kind of naturalism and realism as his master's. He was known as *degl'Impiccatti*—the hanged man—for his first painting; it was of the hanged Peruzzi and Albizzi political leaders, 1435, enemies of the Medici.

CASTALION, SÉBASTIEN

(1515-1562). Châtillon. French Protestant theologian. Translated Bible into French and Latin in 1551. Disagreed with Calvin over doctrine and over the execution of Servetus. Noted for his support of religious tolerance. Held the chair of Greek literature at Basel.

CASTANHEDA, FERNAO LOPES DE

(died 1599). Portuguese historian. Lived many years in India. Wrote an account in seven volumes of the conquests in India by the Portuguese. He also tells of Portuguese trade and administration and other matters in which he had a hand.

CASTELEIN, MATTHIJS DE

(c. 1488-1550). Flemish poet, dramatist. Member of *Chambers of Rhetoric*. Author of plays: treatise on versification.

CASTELLI, ADRIANO, or CASTELLESI

(c. 1458-1517). Cardinal. Author of *De Sermone Latino et Modis Latine Loquendi*. A dictionary of Latin usage, reinforced by quotations from classical writers, published in 1587. Of dubious character, he was the intimate friend of Pope Alexander VI.

CASTELLION, SÉBASTIEN

(c. 1515-1563). French humanist. Protestant theologian. Migrated to Basel. Professor of Greek. Made two translations of the Bible: one into French, the other into Latin. Author of *De Haereticis: 1554*, in which he advocated religious liberty. He came into conflict with Calvin at Geneva, where he was head of the College, and fled to Basel.

CASTELLO, BERNARDO

(1557-1629). Genoese portrait and historical painter, designer. Friend of Tasso. Illustrated Tasso's *Jerusalem Delivered* in 1592.

CASTELLO, GIOVANNI BATTISTA

(c. 1500-c. 1569). Born near Bergamo, but a painter of the Genoese school where he did most of his work, historical and religious subjects; also an architect and sculptor. Invited to Spain by Philip II, but died there within a few years of his arrival.

CASTELNAU, MICHEL DE

(c. 1520-1592). French soldier. Ambassador to English court. He played an important role in the great matters of his day, e.g., the struggle between Mary, Queen of Scots, and Elizabeth, the French civil and religious wars, the Dutch Revolt; hence the importance of his *Mémoires*.

CASTELVETRO, LODOVICO

(1505-1571). Italian scholar, philologist, literary critic. Accused of heresy, fled from Italy in 1561 to France, Switzerland and finally to the court of Maximilian II.

CASTIGLIONE, BALDASSARE

(1478-1529). Of noble birth, educated in the humanist school of Mantua, author of the celebrated *Book of the Courtier*, which owed much to his stay at the ducal palace of Urbino. He proclaimed the ideal of the gentleman, a blending of feudal knightly and classical ideals with those suggested by his own time and place. His ideal of civility, refinement, grace, taste, learning, of physical, mental, and spiritual vigor—in a word, of *virtù*—was very attractive, and even necessary, in an age typified by the Sforza who in the course of three generations rose from peasants to princes and required instruction in the proprieties. A noble spirit, not noble blood, was required of Castiglione's Courtier. There were many such works before and after Castiglione's; his work, going through many editions, was frequently imitated; he was the subject of a memorable portrait by Raphael.

CASTIGLIONE, SABBA DA

(1485-1554). Italian savant, collector. Author of work on his artist friends, among them Leonardo da Vinci and Michelangelo. Procurator general of the Order of Malta. He retired to Faenza to devote himself to pious works and to teach the poor.

CASTILE LINE

John II: 1406-1454. Henry IV: 1454-1474. Isabella: 1474-1504.

CASTILLEJO, CRISTÓBAL DE

(1490?-1556). Spanish court poet. Born in Ciudad Rodrigo, died in Vienna. Attached to court of Ferdinand of Aragon, afterwards Emperor Charles V, and his brother Ferdinand. Priest. Spent most of his life in Vienna. Last years were marked by ill-fortune and sickness. Supported traditional Spanish verse forms. Author of polemical verse, erotic pieces—*Sermón de Amores*—, and *Diálogo de Mujeres;* his best work is probably the *Diálogo de la vida de la corte.*

CASTILLO SOLÓRZANO, ALONSO DE

(1584-1649). Spanish picaresque novelist and dramatist. Began career in 1619 in Madrid. Wrote numerous tales imitative of *Decameron:* novels, plays. Noted for tales, widely imitated by French: e.g. *La Niña de los Embustes, Las Harpías de Madrid.*

CASTRITIUS, MATTHIAS

Sixteenth century. Musician of Durnstadt. Chronicler of German Emperors, Hohenstaufen and Hapsburg houses: *De Heroicis Virtutibus Memorabilibus Principum Germaniae Libri V.* Published in 1565.

CASTRO y BELLVIS, GUILLÉN DE

(1569-1631). Spanish dramatist. Author of some fifty plays. Born in Valencia, died in Madrid. Of noble family, he held civil and military posts. Member of *Academia de los Nocturnos*: 1591-1594. Friend and imitator of Lope de Vega. His plays are romantic, historical, mythological, religious. He was the first to dramatize El Cid legend, and also the Don Quixote themes and scenes. The foremost playwright of the Valencian school.

CASTRO, JOAO DE

(1500-1548). Portuguese navigator. Led expeditions against the Moors in the service of Charles V in Tunis. Commanded fleet against Mediterranean pirates. On expedition to India: Portuguese viceroy. He had a humanist education and humanist tastes, and was a friend of Camões.

CASTRO, RODRIGO DE

(1546-1628). Noted Portuguese physician who settled in Hamburg. Wrote on obstetrics and gynecology, in 1603. Also described the plague in Hamburg in 1596.

CATEAU-CAMBRÉSIS, PEACE OF

This peace, negotiated in 1559, ended conflicts between French under Henry II and Spaniards under Philip II. England had supported the Spaniards and lost Calais. France regained territory taken by Spaniards. It constituted no more than a truce in the long struggle between France and Spain for the hegemony of Europe.

CATENA, VINCENZO

(1470-1531). Italian painter of Venice. Noted for portraits and religious themes; influenced first by Giovanni Bellini, but later in his career shows a close resemblance to Giorgione.

CATESBY, ROBERT

(1573-1605). English conspirator. Participated in rebellion of Earl of Essex. Also implicated in Rye Plot of 1603. Aimed at compulsion of James I to grant religious concessions to Catholics. Planned Gunpowder Plot. Killed while being arrested.

CATHERINE DE'MEDICI
(1519-1589). Queen of France and Regent during minority of her three sons, a)Francis II, b)Charles IX, c)Henry III, when the French civil and religious wars raged. Provoked hostilities between Catholics and Huguenots. Responsible for Massacre of St. Bartholomew's Day in 1572, not by plotting it, but because she did not prevent it. She had little capacity for government and was little more than a schemer.

CATHERINE OF ARAGON
(1485-1536). Daughter of Ferdinand and Isabella. First wife of Henry VIII of England. Mother of Mary Tudor, "Bloody Mary." Until 1527, Catherine was treated honorably by the king. Then he secured a divorce in 1533. Catherine, remaining in England, spent her latter years in austerity.

CATHERINE OF SAN CELSO
(died 1511). Also known as Imperia. Notorious Renaissance courtesan.

CATHOLIC LEAGUE
Founded in South Germany in opposition to Protestant Union. Leader was Maximilian of Bavaria. Pope also was a member, while Spain made treaty of alliance with League. Army of the League participated extensively in early phases of Thirty Years' War. The term also identified the party led by the duke of Guise in the French civil and religious wars of the late sixteenth century.

CATHOLICON
A Breton—Latin—French vocabulary. Of historical interest. Published in 1464.

CATS, JACOB
(1577-1660). Dutch statesman, prolific poet. Ambassador to England in 1627 and in 1652. Author of didactic and moralizing poems; one of his favorite subjects was happy marriage and domestic bliss; also autobiography.

CATTANEO, DANESE
(1509-1573). Italian sculptor and architect of Venice. Executed

bas-reliefs, the tomb of Bembo and decorations for the library of St. Mark's. He was a student of Sansovino in Rome and a friend of Tasso; he published a volume of love poems.

CAUBRAITH, ROBERT
Sixteenth century. Scottish logician. Wrote on logical modes, published in Paris in 1510.

CAUS, SALOMON DE
(1576-c. 1626). French engineer, physicist and architect. Fled France, as a Protestant, for England and Germany, where he did most of his work.

CAVALCANTI, ANDREA
(1412-1462). Called Il Buggiano. Italian sculptor. Associated with Brunelleschi and the Cathedral of Florence, some of whose interior, e.g., the pulpit, includes his sculpture and bas-reliefs.

CAVALCANTI, BARTOLOMEO
(1503-1562). Scholar and politician. Died in Padua. Hostile to the Medici. Took refuge with Cardinal Ippolito d'Este of Ferrara and later went to Rome. Wrote on Plato's *Republic*, Aristotle's *Politics*, and their application to the contemporary state. Wrote *Rhetorica*, based on Aristotle, published in 1559.

CAVALIERI, EMILIO DE
(1550?-1602). Italian musician. Attached to the court of the Medici as inspector of arts. Member of the Florentine Camerata group and among those who originated *basso continuo* accompaniment. Wrote dramatic compositions, among them *Il Satiro*.

CAVALIERI, FRANCESCO BUONAVENTURA
(1598-1647). Italian mathematician. Member of the Order of Jesuits of St. Jerome in Milan. Pupil and friend of Galileo. Professor in Bologna. Wrote on spherical trigonometry and related subjects in numerous works, the most important of which was *Geometria indivisibilibus*.

CAVALLETTO, GIOVANNI BATTISTA
Italian illuminator of Bologna. Belonged to the Bologna Guild of Drapers, on testimony of extant illuminated membership-book, dated 1523.

CAVALLI, MARINO
Sixteenth century. Ambassador of Venetian Republic to Francis I of France, and later to Emperor Charles V. Left accounts of his embassies, especially the one to France: it is an outstanding example of the *relazione* demanded by the Venetian government of its ambassadors.

CAVAZZOLA, PAOLO MORANDO
(1486-1522). Painter of Verona. Executed frescoes, easel pictures in the late stages of the Early Renaissance; noted for his rich colors and nobility of expression, e.g., in his *Portrait of a Gentleman.*

CAVENDISH, GEORGE
(1500-1560). English writer. In the service of Wolsey, whose *Life* he later wrote; it is one of the greatest biographies of the Renaissance.

CAVENDISH, THOMAS
(c. 1555-1592). English navigator. Third sailor to circumnavigate the globe. On expedition to Virginia. Reached the Strait of Magellan. Returned via Cape of Good Hope to England. Reached Philippine Islands, Moluccas, Java. Second expedition was disastrous. Died at sea off Ascension.

CAVICEO, JACOPO
(1443-1511). Italian novelist and priest. Author of *Il Peregrino:* allegorical romance with Romeo and Juliet theme. It went through many editions and was translated into French and Spanish; he was an imitator and utilized many of the literary devices of Boccaccio.

CAWDREY, ROBERT
Early seventeenth century. English lexicographer. Author of a lexicon of difficult expressions, totaling about 2,500 entries. He was a schoolmaster and many of his entries reflected that fact; he, however, plagiarized the works of previous compilers.

CAXTON, WILLIAM
(c. 1422-c. 1491). First English printer. Merchant in Low Countries. Learned printing in Germany. Established printing press at Westminster. Produced first dated book printed in England: *The Dictes and Sayings of the Philosophers:* 1477. Many of the books he published he himself translated from French, Latin or Dutch;

as a publisher he did not measure up to the standards set by Aldus or Froben.

CAYET DE LA PALME, PIERRE VICTOR

(1525-1610). French historian and theologian. Huguenot apostate. Wrote history of reign of Henry IV of France.

CECIL, ROBERT, FIRST EARL OF SALISBURY

(c. 1563-1612). Called Crooked-backed Earl. English statesman. Secretary of State. Instrumental in placing James VI of Scotland on English throne. Son of Lord Burghley, the most famous minister of Queen Elizabeth; he served both Elizabeth and James.

CELESTINA, LA

The title of a Spanish drama or dramatized novel, in dialogue form. The full title is *Tragicomedia de Calixto y Melibea.* Called Celestina from the name of the principal character. It contains echoes of Plautus, Terence, Ovid, Plutarch. In literary excellence and influence, this Spanish production ranks with *Don Quijote.* There is doubt as to dates and authorship. The first edition was published in 1499, in sixteen acts. Later editions contain more acts. The author of the original play is assumed to have been Fernando de Rojas, a converted Jewish lawyer (died 1541). *La Celestina* is valuable for its revelation of early sixteenth-century life among the common people of Spain. In the sixteenth century, sixty-three editions appeared in Spain. There were also many translations and imitations in French, Italian, German, English.

CELLINI, BENVENUTO

(1500-1571). Florentine metals craftsman, sculptor, and author of a famous *Autobiography.* He revered Michelangelo whom he took as his model and mentor. In his *Autobiography,* bristling with egotism and self-confidence, he tells of his part as a gunner in the defense of Castel St. Angelo during the sack of Rome in 1527, of his imprisonment, fantastic escape, reincarceration, and eventual release from a papal jail, of his work in metals for popes and princes and the vexations that their patronage brought him, and of his casual murders and amours. His description of his stay and of his compatriots at the court of Francis I of France testifies how dependent, artistically, France still was upon Italy. He also wrote *Trattati* of a more technical nature on the goldsmith's art, casting and sculpture, and design. His most famous works are the *Saltcellar*, done for Francis I, and *Perseus with the head of Medusa*, for Cosimo I, the Medici duke of Florence. His literary style, his art, his character: all suggest the exuberant phase of the Renaissance in which he lived.

CELTES, CONRADUS PROTUCIUS, KONRAD PICKEL
(1459-1508). German humanist. Neo-Latin poet, playwright. Friend of Emperor Maximilian. Professor at Ingolstadt and Vienna. Organized and encouraged study of classics by founding sodalities, or academies, in Cracow, Budapest, and Heidelberg. Discovered dramas of the medieval nun Hrotswitha. Edited classical texts. Author of *Ars Versificandi, Amores,* historical works.

CENCI, BEATRICE
(1577-1599). Italian. Daughter of ruthless and vicious father, of an ancient family of Roman nobility. Plotted with brother death of father, Francesco Cenci (1548-1598). Father was killed in bed by hired assassin. Members of Cenci family arrested, unsuccessful in securing papal pardon from Pope Clement VIII. Executed in 1599. The life of Beatrice Cenci has been used in various literary genres, particularly in a tragedy by P. B. Shelley.

CENNINI, BERNARDO
In 1471 Cennini printed at his press in Florence Servius' commentary on Vergil's *Bucolics.* In 1472, the *Aeneid* and the *Georgics* were issued. Cennini was the first Italian printer to cast his own type.

CENNINI, CENNINO
(c. 1370-1440). Florentine painter none of whose works survive; remembered for his technical manual on painting, which embodied Giotto's methods and was widely read, *Libro dell' Arte.*

CENSORSHIP
Censorship of printed books began in Mainz in 1486. In many ways printing made censorship by the prince or by the church easier, as shops had to be licensed, etc.

CENTORIO DEGLI HORTENSII, ASCANIO
(Sixteenth century). Italian soldier, poet and historian. Author of history of Transylvanian wars of mid-sixteenth century, Mar-

tinazzi, Transylvanian leader, Ottoman victories under Suleiman I. Published in 1566.

CENTUM GRAVAMINA
One hundred items of complaints about papal administration. Drawn up at the Diet of Worms in 1521.

CENTURIES OF MAGDEBURG
A series of Protestant attacks on Catholicism. Published in Basel between 1559 and 1574.

CERDAGNE AND ROUSSILLON
The territory of Cerdagne and the province of Roussillon, both in the region of the Pyrenees, were acquired by Louis XI of France in 1462.

CERTON, PIERRE
(died 1572). French musician. Attached to choir of Sainte Chapelle. Produced many compositions, religious and secular. He was a disciple of Josquin des Prés and composed in the polyphonic mode.

CERTON, SALMON
(1550-1610). French poet and secretary to Henry IV, translator of Homer.

CERTOSA, LA
A Carthusian convent in Italy, near Pavia. Noted for Renaissance architecture.

CERVANTES SAAVEDRA, MIGUEL DE
(1547-1616). Greatest novelist of Spain. Born in Alcalá de Henares, died in Madrid. Studied briefly under Madrid humanist Juan López de Hoyos. Largely self-schooled, traveled in Italy, impressed by Italian art and literature. Served at Battle of Lepanto, wounded in 1571. Captured by pirates, sold as slave in Algiers, ransomed in 1580. Published pastoral romance, *La Galatea,* in 1585. Became tax collector of revenues to finance the Armada; irregularities in his accounts caused his imprisonment; he was imprisoned several times for debt. In prison, he began *Don Quijote,* satirical novel, synthesis of chivalric romance and picaresque realism. Also *Novelas Ejemplares,* twelve short stories, comedies. Also *Viaje del Parnaso,* published in 1614, versified critique of contemporary writers.

CERVONI DA COLLE, GIOVANNI

Sixteenth century. Florentine scholar. Wrote commentary on Petrarch's sonnet *Amor, Fortuna*. Published in 1550.

CESALPINO, ANDREAS

(1519-1603). Italian anatomist, botanist. Professor of medicine at Pisa. Personal physician to Pope Clement VIII. Director of Botanical Garden at Pisa. Called The Pope of Philosophers. Wrote on minerals, plants, astronomy, occult subjects. Author of *De Plantis*: published in 1538, which, by seeking to establish a "natural system" for the plant world, led to the creation of scientific botany. He also made important contributions to the study of the lungs and of the circulation of the blood. Also *Peripatetic Questions*: a commentary on Aristotle. Called by Linacre *Primus Verus Systematicus*.

CESARE DA SESTO

(1477-1523). Italian painter of the school of Leonardo da Vinci; little is known of his life beyond the fact that he worked at Rome and at Milan, where he died. Almost all of his paintings, of which there are few, depict the life of the Virgin.

CESARI, GIUSEPPE, IL CAVALIERE D'ARPINO

(1568-1640). Roman painter of the "idealist" as opposed to the "naturalist" school of his day; he rose from penury to great wealth by dint of papal patronage—Clement VII made him a "knight of Christ." For all that he was an inferior artist.

CESPEDES, PABLO DE

(1538-1608). Spanish painter, sculptor, architect, writer of Cordova. He visited and studied in Italy several times, and he greatly admired Michelangelo whose influence is traceable in Cespedes' work. He had been educated in the humanist center, Alcalá de Henares, and wrote a treatise comparing ancient and modern painting, and one on architecture.

CETINA, GUTIERRE DE

(c. 1520-c. 1570). Spanish poet. Author of lyrics, madrigal; translator of poems of Petrarch. He traveled in Italy and Germany.

CEULEN, LUDOLPH VAN

(1540-1610). Dutch mathematician and military architect. Noted for calculations of π, Ludolph's number, for calculating the circumference of the circle.

CHABIB, JACOB BEN SOLOMON IBN
(1460-1516). Spanish Talmudist. Compiled and annotated portions of Babylonian Talmud. Settled in Salonika in 1492 when the Jews were expelled from Spain.

CHABOT, PHILIPPE DE
(1480-1543). French admiral. Close friend of Francis I. Banished, his property was confiscated in 1540 through instrumentality of the Duchess d'Étampes. He secured pardon, however, from the king.

CHALCONDYLAS, DEMETRIUS
(1424-1511). Greek scholar of Athens. Taught Greek in Padua, Milan, Florence. In Padua, first teacher of Greek to receive fixed salary. Prepared *editio princeps* of Homer, published in 1488. Also *Erotemata*, on grammar. Also *editiones principes* of Suidas and Isocrates, published by Aldus.

CHAMBIGES, MARTIN
(Died 1532). French architect whose style of building was a mixture of Gothic and classical elements.

CHAMBIGES, PIERRE
(died 1544). French architect, son of the above. He began the construction of the Château de Saint-Germain-en-Laye in 1539. He also designed Fontainebleau.

CHAMBRE ARDENTE, LA
Catholics in France proposed establishment of Inquisition in France. Opposition, however, came from the *Parlement* of Paris the supreme court. A special tribunal of the *Parlement*, called La Grande Chambre, was established to try heretics, in 1574. The tribunal acted so vigorously that it presently acquired the name of *La Chambre Ardente*.

CHAMPAGNE, PHILIPPE DE or CHAMPAIGNE
(1602-1674). Flemish painter. Born in Brussels. One of the great representatives of French classicism. Executed portraits—among them, of Richelieu and of Mazarin, and Louis XIII—and religious subjects.

CHAMPIER, SYMPHORIEN

(1472-1533). French physician, Platonic philosopher, historian, and poet. Prolific author on Celtic Gaul, Druidic practices, political administration: *Galliae Celticae Campus,* 1637, and especially on medical subjects. His son Claude and nephew Jean were also eminent physicians.

CHAMPLAIN, SAMUEL DE

(c. 1567-1635). French explorer. Visited West Indies, Mexico, Central America. On fur-trading expeditions. Lieutenant Governor of Canada. Instrumental in founding Quebec. Wrote a number of travel books based on his experiences: *The Travels of Sieur de Champlain:* published in 1613. Discovered Lake Champlain.

CHANCELLOR, RICHARD

(died 1556). English mariner. On a voyage to discover a northeast passage to India, he entered the White Sea and proceeded to Ivan the Terrible's court in Moscow. The voyage inaugurated commercial relations between England and Russia; he was a founder of the Muscovy Company.

CHANTAL, JEANNE FRANÇOISE, BARONNE DE

(1572-1641). French nun. Dedicated to charitable works. In 1610 she founded the Congregation of the Visitation of Our Lady and is associated with St. Francis de Sales.

CHAPMAN, GEORGE

(c. 1559-1634). English classical scholar, poet, and dramatist. There was a tradition that he was imprisoned in 1607 for a satire against the Scots. Wrote tragedies, comedies: *Bussy d'Ambois, The Widow's Tears.* Translated Homer: the rendering inspired a famous sonnet by John Keats.

CHAPMAN, WALTER, or CHEPMAN

(c. 1473-1538). Scottish lawyer, merchant, burgess. Under a patent granted by King James IV, he and Andrew Myllar set up first printing press in Scotland. Beginning c. 1507, they published a series of books, most of which were chivalrous romances and epic tales.

CHARLES V

(1500-1558). Holy Roman Emperor. Also, as King of Spain, Charles I. Grandson of Ferdinand and Isabella. He inherited Burgundy and the Netherlands in 1506. In 1520 he was crowned Emperor. He also ruled Milan, Naples, and Sicily and lands in eastern Europe. His consort was Isabella of Portugal, whom he married in 1525. During the Reformation, he sought to reach an accommodation with Lutherans and hoped that such a policy would prevail at the Council of Trent, but in Spain he persecuted heretics. Convened several diets to achieve religious settlement. At the Peace of Augsburg, reconciled to Protestants, in 1555. In conflict with France. Fought against Turks. Extended Spanish territory in the New World. Abdicated: entered monastery in 1557.

CHARLES VIII
(1408?-1470). King of Sweden: also Norway. In long conflict with Denmark. Fled to Germany: recalled to throne.

CHARLES IX
(1550-1611). King of Sweden. Restored Protestantism in country. In long conflict with Poland. Also at war with Denmark.

CHARLES VIII
(1470-1498). King of France. Anxious to revive Anjevin rule in Naples, he neglected French interests and allied himself with Milan. Entered Naples in 1495 but driven out same year by the forces of the Holy League under Gonzalo de Córdoba. His invasion signals the end of the golden age of the Italian Renaissance and of Italian independence.

CHARLES IX
(1550-1574). King of France. Under the domination of his mother, Catherine de Medici, throughout his reign. France, during his rule, was disrupted by violent religious and civil wars, marked by the Massacre of St. Bartholomew's Day: 1572.

CHARLES EMMANUEL I
(1562-1630). Duke of Savoy. Alternately in alliance with France and Spain. During his rule, the economy of the country deteriorated.

CHARLES OF VIANA
(1421-1461). Spanish prince. Inherited the throne of Navarre. Imprisoned by father: released: reconciled. Scholar, poet. Author of chronicle of the kings of Navarre.

CHARLES THE BOLD or THE RASH

(1433-1477). The last Duke of Burgundy. Married Margaret of York. Assumed rule in 1467. In conflict with Louis XI of France. In 1475 conquered Lorraine. Acquired Alsace from the Emperor Sigismund. Defeated by the Swiss in 1476. Defeated by Louis XI at Nancy in 1477. His death ended the Burgundian ascendancy and cultural great age.

CHARLES THE GREAT

(1543-1608). Duke of Lorraine. At court of Henry II of France, as youth. Member of Holy League. Participated in religious wars.

CHARLES THE WELL-SERVED

A term applied to the French King, Charles VII (1422-1461), well-served by Joan of Arc.

CHARRON, PIERRE

(1541-1603). French Catholic theologian and chaplain to Marguerite, Queen of Henry IV. Friend of Montaigne. Author of *De La Sagesse:* published in 1601. A treatise opposing all formal religions. Also wrote *Les Trois Vérités:* published in 1594. An echo of Montaigne's *Essays.*

CHARTERHOUSE SCHOOL

English public school. Founded in 1611 by Thomas Sutton (1532-1611). Formerly a Carthusian monastery.

CHASSANION, JEAN DE

(Sixteenth century). French historian, Protestant. Wrote *De Gigantibus:* published in 1580. Discusses giants in antiquity, in Scriptural and contemporary contexts, discoveries of remains of giants in France, Italy. His *History of Albigensianism,* the work for which he is principally known, appeared in 1595; another work emphasized the miraculous elements of Christianity. As an historian he was partial, as a philosopher he came perilously close to superstition.

CHASTELARD, PIERRE DE

(1540-1564). French poet and friend of Ronsard. Attached to court of Francis II. Infatuated with Mary, Queen of Scots. Followed her to Scotland. Subject of drama by Swinburne. His infatuation cost him his life: he was executed in Edinburgh, protesting his love for the "beautiful" but "cruel" Mary with his last breath.

CHASTELLAIN, GEORGES

(1403-1475). French chronicler and courtier to the Dukes of Burgundy. Author of *Recollection de Merveilleuses Advenues en Notre Temps*: published c. 1475. Also panegyrics in verse: *Épitaphe de Jacques de Lalaing: Épitaphe de Pierre de Brézé*. Little of the Renaissance or humanism can be found in his work, which is cast in the tradition of medieval chivalry.

CHASTENOY, PEACE OF

Peace negotiated in 1576 between Henry III of France and the Huguenots. Favorable terms were granted to the latter; it was a step toward the Edict of Nantes granted by Henry IV.

CHÂTILLON

The family name of three brothers. Gaspard, François d'Andelot, Cardinal Châtillon, Catholics who became Protestants. In conflict with the House of Guise during the years of French civil and religious wars of the later sixteenth century.

CHAUNDLER, THOMAS

Chancellor of Oxford from 1457 to 1461. Author of *Liber Apologeticus de Omni Statu Humanae Naturae*. Illustrated with miniatures. A Hellenist, he labored to establish the study of Greek in England.

CHAUVET, JACQUES

Professor at the University of Paris. Author of textbook on commercial arithmetic: published in 1578 in French. Also wrote on geometrical instruments and mensuration.

CHECHICKY, PETR or CHELČICKY

(1390-1460). Czech Hussite religious writer. Author of *Book of Interpretations of the Gospel for the Whole Year* and *The Net of True Faith*: guides to Christian living. His followers grouped themselves into the Bohemian Brethren.

CHEKE, SIR JOHN

(1514-1557). English classical scholar, "the Exchequer of Eloquence," did much to popularize the study of Greek. Gained political advancement under Edward VI and in the short reign of Lady Jane Grey. Deprived by Queen Mary. Went to Belgium. Brought back to Tower. Forced to abjure Protestantism. First Regius Professor of Greek at Cambridge University.

CHEMNITZ, MARTIN
(1522-1586). German Lutheran theologian, disciple of Melanchthon. Versed in mathematics, astrology. Leader of Lutheran Church of Lower Saxony. Influential in unifying Lutherans of Saxony and Swabia. His *Loci Theologici,* published in 1591, is a commentary on the *Loci Communes* of Melanchthon. He also wrote *De Vera Praesentia, De Duabus Naturis in Christo.* His greatest work is *Examen Concili Tridentini* (1565-1573): an analysis of the Roman Catholic position as set forth by the Council of Trent and a defense of Protestantism.

CHESTER CATHEDRAL
In England. Founded in 1093. Created Cathedral by Henry VIII in 1541.

CHETTLE, HENRY
(c. 1560-1607). English dramatist. Author of thirteen plays, e.g., *Robin Hood.* Also wrote elegy on Queen Elizabeth I.

CHIABRERA, GABRIELLO
(1552-1638). Italian poet, Greek scholar, student of the sciences, born in Savona. Imitated Pindar, Anacreon. Called the "Italian Pindar." Produced poetic epistles, lyrics, epics, satires in Italian. Noted for imitations of classical metres and metrical innovations. Enjoyed the patronage of Cosimo II of Tuscany, Charles Emmanuel of Savoy, and Pope Urban VIII.

CHIEREGATI, FRANCESCO
Bishop of Teramo. Nuncio of Pope Hadrian VI (1522-1523). Agent for enforcement of the Edict of Worms. In the midst of the Lutheran convulsions he sought to preach in Germany a crusade against the Turks.

CHIGI
Roman family of bankers and patrons of the arts. Agostino Chigi (c. 1465-1520), banker to Pope Leo X, built up one of the great fortunes of the age. Patron of Perugino, Peruzzi, Raphael and Aretino. Built Villa Farnese in Rome.

CHIGWELL SCHOOL
English public school in Essex. Founded in 1629 by Samuel Harsnett, Archbishop of York (1561-1631).

146

CHIOS
The island of Chios, occupied by the Genoese, fell to the Turks in 1566. The Genoese Eastern power thus came to an end.

CHIVALRIC ROMANCES
Prose narratives of knightly adventures. Originated in fourteenth century. Flourished during Renaissance: in Spain, in sixteenth century, called *libros de caballerías*. The themes of these tales were: Arthurian legends, the Carolingian cycle, the Crusades, classical mythology, Milesian tales, the Amadis de Gaulis cycle. They were pervaded by love motifs, supernatural elements, epic heroism. The romances glorified knightly virtues, chivalric concepts, and ethical mores. In time, they acquired a realistic, satirical tone, as in *Don Quijote*.

CHRIST CHURCH
College of Oxford University, founded in 1525 by Cardinal Wolsey and initially named Cardinal's College. After his fall it became King's College and then Christ Church (1546).

CHRISTIAN I
(1426-1481). King of Denmark and Norway. Founded house of Oldenburg. Established University of Copenhagen in 1479.

CHRISTIAN II
(1481-1559). Called the Cruel. King of Denmark and Norway and briefly of Sweden. Massacred Swedish nobility. Deposed. Imprisoned in 1532, where he remained until his death.

CHRISTIAN III
(1503-1559). King of Denmark and Norway. Called Father of the People. A staunch Lutheran, he introduced the Reformation into his country: 1536. The Danish Diet abolished Roman Catholicism and seized Church property for the crown.

CHRISTIAN IV
(1577-1648). King of Denmark and Norway. During his reign, Oslo was rebuilt; his designation of the capital as "Christiana" did not long survive his death. His invasion of Germany in behalf of the Protestants initiated the Danish phase of the Thirty Years' War.

CHRISTIAN ALPHABET
A manifesto of the Christian faith, in dialogue form. Drawn up

by Juan de Valdés for Giulia Gonzaga, Countess of Fondi (1499-1566).

CHRISTMANN, JACOB

(1554-1613). German Orientalist and mathematician, Professor of logic and also of Hebrew and Arabic at Heidelberg. Wrote treatises on astronomy, Oriental philosophy, mathematics, and chronology.

CHRIST'S COLLEGE

Cambridge University. Founded as God's House in 1448 by King Henry VI. Refounded by the Lady Margaret Beaufort in 1505.

CHRISTUS, PETRUS

(Fifteenth century). Dutch painter of religious subjects, interiors and portraits in the tradition of Jan van Eyck, under whom he may have studied.

CHRONICA HUNGARORUM

A History of Hungary. Appeared in 1473. The first printed book in Hungary.

CHRYSOLORAS, MANUEL

(c. 1355-1415). The Byzantine scholar who came to Italy on a diplomatic mission to plead for aid against the Turks. His mission failed, but his knowledge of the Greek classics roused great interest at Florence, to which he returned in 1396 to become a municipally paid lecturer. He introduced the meticulous, painstaking methods characteristic of Byzantine scholarship and gained a numerous band of eminent students, disciples, and admirers, e.g., Guarino, Bruni, Filelfo. Some historians, pointing to the important medieval elements in Petrarch's thought and outlook, have set the Italian aside as a transitional figure and urged that the full tide of the Renaissance begins with the arrival of Chrysoloras in Florence.

CHURCH DOCUMENT, CHURCH OF THE BOHEMIAN BRETHREN

Apologia Verae Doctrinae eorum qui vulgo appellantur Waldenses vel Picardi: Third edition: 1538. One of the earliest documents of the Church of the Bohemian Brethren. The members were Hussites and supporters of the Waldensian Reform Movement that resulted in the Czech Reformation: parallel to the German Reformation. The *Apologia* appeared in two German versions: one printed in Zurich, the other, with Luther's approval, in Wittenberg, in 1533.

CHURCH OF SCOTLAND
Presbyterian Church in Scotland that has largely maintained offiscal state connection. Constituted by action of First General Assembly of the Scotch Estates in 1560.

CHURCHYARD, THOMAS
(c. 1520-1604). English soldier, poet. Served under Earl of Surrey. Served in Netherlands, Scotland, Ireland. Contributed to Tottel's *Miscellany* and to *Mirror for Magistrates*. Corpus of writings gathered in *Churchyard's Chips*. One of his best known poems was his *Legend of Jane Shore*.

CHUTE, ANTHONY or CHEWT
(died c. 1595). Minor Elizabethan poet. His verses attacking Thomas Nashe brought a satirical reply from that poet.

CHYTRAEUS, DAVID, or KOCHHAFE
(1530-1600). Lutheran theologian and historian of Lutheranism. On his marriage, Melanchthon, Cisner and other friends celebrated the occasion poetically by publication of *Carmina et Epistolae de Coniugio:* issued in 1567. He wrote a history of Saxony from 1500-1595 and a survey of contemporary writers: *De Lectione Historiarum Recte Instituenda:* published in 1563.

CIAMPELLI, AGOSTINO
(1578-1640). Florentine painter in the service of Pope Clement VII; almost all his work is religious in subject matter.

CIARLA, RAFFAELLO
Sixteenth-century painter of Urbino, noted for his decoration of majolica vases; imitator of Raphael; patronized by Philip II of Spain.

CIARPI, BACCIO
(1578-1642). Florentine painter of historical subjects, worked at Rome.

CICERO, MARCUS TULLIUS
The Roman author who was the most profoundly revered of all the ancients during the Renaissance; recovery of portions of his works caused the greatest excitement. The humanists found

in him a high statement of the ideal of civic virtue; for them he reconciled perfectly the claims of the contemplative life with the responsibilities of the public life and devotion to the weal of the state. Leonardo Bruni wrote a biography, significantly entitled *Cicero novus,* 1415, where he presents the Cicero so beloved in the Renaissance.

CICERONIANISM

Based on the recognition of Cicero as the greatest master of Latin prose style. In some sense practically every learned man of the Renaissance was a Ciceronian; some writers elevated Cicero into an authority from whom there could be no deviation in matters of vocabulary, syntax, cadences, and constructions. Such was Bembo's position. Petrarch, Politian, and Erasmus urged that Cicero be imitated in no pedantic and literal way, for such was the negation of style: instead of being a portrait, a new work should bear no more than a family resemblance to its model. The triumph of an extreme Ciceronianism accounts for Latin becoming a dead language.

CICOGNARA, ANTONIO

Italian illuminator. In 1483 he decorated an antiphonary for Cremona Cathedral. He also designed ornate playing cards which, in the Renaissance, were also raised to the level of an art.

CICOGNINI, GIACINTO ANDREA

(1606-1660). Florentine poet. Author of *The Stone Guest:* published c. 1653. Comedy in Spanish style. First Italian treatment of the Don Juan legend.

CIGOLI, LODOVICO CARDI DA

(1559-1613). Italian architect, painter, man of letters. Worked in Florence. Among his paintings are: *Ecce Homo, Joseph,* and *Cain killing Abel,* also frescoes. Executed baroque themes. Wrote treatises on perspective and on the five orders of architecture.

CIMA DA CONEGLIANO, GIOVANNI

(1459-c. 1517). Italian painter who worked almost all his life in Venice. Executed altarpieces with splendid landscape backgrounds, and religious works generally; his style resembles that of Giovanni Bellini and Mantegna, under whom he probably studied.

CIMABUE, GIOVANNI

(c. 1240-c. 1302). Florentine painter, very few works can be attributed to him definitively. His *Madonna and Child Enthroned* in the Uffizi at Florence and his *Crucifix* in the Church of S. Domenico at Arezzo belong to the highly formalized Byzantine tradition of style, although there are some few signs of naturalism in the execution of the faces. Giotto is said to have been his pupil.

CINI, GIOVAMBATTISTA

(c. 1530-c. 1612). Orator, poet, dramatist of Casata. Wrote the life of Cosimo I, Grand Duke of Tuscany (1537-1574).

CINQ-MARS, HENRI COIFFIER DE RUZÉ, MARQUIS DE

(1620-1642). French courtier. Favorite of Louis XIII, introduced to the court by Richelieu. Conspired with Spanish aid against Richelieu and died on scaffold in 1642. Subject of novel by Alfred de Vigny and opera by Gounod.

CINQUECENTO

Italian-500. Also an abbreviation for *mil cinque cento*-1500. Used to designate the years beginning with 1500: that is, the sixteenth century. In art, the expression refers to Italian styles of High and Late Renaissance during the sixteenth century. In this century, the Renaissance reached its climax in Rome. Venice rose as the dominant school of painting, while Florence declined. In architecture notable names are those of Donato Lazzari, Bramante, Baldassare Peruzzi, Antonio San Gallo the Younger. Painting in the Cinquecento is associated with 'the grand manner.' Outstanding figures are Raphael and Leonardo da Vinci. The most homogeneous school of painting during this century was that of Venice. Prominent names of artists are those of Titian, Giorgione, Tintoretto, Veronese. In sculpture, Michelangelo's name is dominant. Jacopo Sansovino, Benvenuto Cellini, and Giovanni da Bologna also appear.

CIOMPI REBELLION OF 1378 IN FLORENCE

Ciompi refers to the lowest class in Florentine society, the industrial workers, especially the wool workers, who were denied the right to organize themselves into a guild and thus play a role in the government of the city. In the 1340's a severe economic crisis had discredited the merchant oligarchy, who gave way to the rule of the petty bourgeoisie; their hold on the government lasted for almost half a century during which time Florence came closest to being a democracy. Repeated efforts of the oligarchs to resume control failed, one of their attempts in 1378 backfired with the result that Michele di Lando, a young wool-comber, came to power. Thereupon the Ciompi were organized into three new guilds and given political rights comparable to the other twenty-one. The new guilds were the dyers, shirt-makers, and *popolo minuto* or little people—to this last group the term Ciompi came more definitely to be attached. Efforts to infringe Ciompi rights provoked a new wave of radical violence; it failed, with the outcome that the Ciompi guild was disbanded and was reduced again to a pitiful state. The petty bourgeoisie survived crises and conspiracies until 1382 when the merchant oligarchs came back into power; they held it until 1434 when the Medici ascendancy began.

CIOLI, VALERIO
(1529-1599). Italian sculptor. Worked for Duke Cosimo I of Florence, and executed sculptures for the tomb of Michelangelo, who was the principal influence on his work.

CIRCIGNANO, ANTONIO
(1560-1620). Italian painter, studied and worked chiefly at Rome, did religious subjects.

CIRCIGNANO, NICCOLÓ
(1519-c. 1590). Italian painter, father, teacher, collaborator of the above. He did religious subjects for ecclesiastical patrons.

CIRVELO, PEDRO
(born 1470). Spanish theologian. Mathematician. Wrote on astrology and magic.

CISNER, NICHOLAS
(1529-1583). German historian, professor of civil law at Heidelberg, Imperial official at Spires. He wrote Latin verses, several historical works, and edited Krantz's *History of Saxony*.

CITIES, BEAUTIFICATION OF
One of the features of Renaissance life in Italy was the beautification of cities. Perfectly proportioned buildings, spacious squares, parks, sculptural adornments reflected the interest and the deliberate desire to produce a physical atmosphere in harmony with the creation of intellectual and visual beauty.

CITTADINI, CELSO

(1553-1627). Italian man of letters and antiquarian. He collected many manuscripts of Petrarch, Boccaccio, Bembo and other Renaissance figures with a view to their preservation; also wrote on the origin of Tuscan.

CIVERCHIO, VINCENZO or VERCHIO

(died c. 1540). Italian painter, decorated the old cathedral of Brescia, did altarpieces and portraits.

CIVITALI, MATTEO

(1436-1501). Italian sculptor, engineer, architect, and printer of Lucca. Decorated the Cathedral of Lucca. Worked in Genoa. Executed tombs, altars; designed chapels. All his work is characterized by a deep intensity and often by an exaggeration of form and line that suggest the Baroque.

CLAESSON, ARNOLD

(1498-1564). Dutch painter.

CLAESZ, JAN

(died 1544). Dutch bookseller of Amsterdam. Met his death for publishing and selling works of Menno Simons (c. 1496-1561).

CLAESZ, PIETER

(1500-1576). Flemish painter. He was the first of a family that produced a great many painters; he and his descendants were known for their historical subjects, portraits, still lifes.

CLAPMARIUS, ARNOLDUS

(1574-1604). German jurist. Wrote on Renaissance political theory, foreign relations, qualifications of rulers: *De Arcanis Rerum Publicarum Libri Sex*. He had been a soldier, had traveled in Germany, the Lowlands, and England, and became professor of history at Altdorf.

CLAVIUS, CHRISTOPHER

(1537-1612). German mathematician, astronomer. Jesuit. At the instance of Pope Gregory XIII, made researches in calendar. He wrote several works on mathematics, including commentaries on Sacrobosco and Euclid; he contributed nothing to astronomy—he was a reactionary antagonist of the Copernican system.

CLEMENT VII

(1475-1534). Medici Pope, of weak character, incapable of making a decision. At first, he tried to make peace among the great powers of Europe. The Holy League of Cognac was formed in 1526 by Francis I, Venice, Milan, and the Pope. By 1527 the League was defeated and there occurred the Sack of Rome: Spanish and German troops broke into the city of Rome, plundering, murdering, creating ruin and pestilence and bringing to an end the Golden Age of the Renaissance in Italy. The Pope was made a prisoner for seven months by the victorious Emperor Charles V at the most critical time of Henry VIII's divorce from Catherine of Aragon. Pope favored Cellini. Machiavelli's *History of Florence* was dedicated to Clement. His portrait was painted by Sebastian del Piombo. Under him, Michelangelo built the Bibliotheca Laurenziana. The poet Francesco Berni wrote this verdict on Clement:

His reign was rich in seeking every way,
In change of mind and trying to be wise,
In ifs and buts and noes and ayes,
With nothing ever done, but always much to say.

CLEMENT VIII
(1536-1605). Pope. Succeeded in converting Henry IV to Catholicism. Contributed to internal peace of the Church in France. In his pontificate, Giordano Bruno executed: also Beatrice Cenci. Clement was a patron of Tasso. Charitable to the poor of Rome. Sponsored revision of the Vulgate: later called the Clementine Vulgate.

CLEVE, HENDRIK VAN or CLEEF
(Died 1589). Dutch painter. He had studied in Italy, noted for landscapes that are luminous and strongly chromatic. The one, with his brothers Marten and Willem, to establish the family tradition in painting.

CLEVE, JOOS VAN or CLEEF, THE ELDER
(1491-1560). The Elder. Painter of Antwerp. Influenced by Leonardo da Vinci. Remarkable as a colorist, thought to have gone to Madrid late in life at the call of Philip II.

CLEVE, JOOS VAN or CLEEF, THE YOUNGER
(c. 1520-c. 1556). Dutch painter, son of Willem. Painted portraits, secular and mythological as well as religious subjects in the Italian rather than Flemish manner, although he seems not to have visited Italy.

154

CLEVE, MARTEN VAN or CLEEF
(1527-1581). Dutch painter. Produced harshly realistic genre subjects, historical subjects.

CLEVE, WILLEM VAN or CLEEF
(Sixteenth century, died young) Dutch painter, brother of Hendrik. Few works can be identified definitively as his; he is said to have been a figure painter, principally of historical scenes.

CLICHTOVENS, JODUCUS
(1473-1543). Belgian Catholic theologian and logician. Wrote on problems in logic. His *Introductio* was published in Leyden in 1540. Also wrote on the mystic significance of numbers. In public debate and in lengthy treaties, he was an antagonist of Luther.

CLOTH OF GOLD, FIELD OF THE
Near Calais, France. Staged in elaborate surroundings, this was the scene of conference between Henry VIII of England and Francis I of France: 1520.

CLOUET, FRANÇOIS JANET
(ante 1522-c. 1580). French painter. Died in Paris. Court painter to Francis I and Henry II. Noted for his many portraits of French kings, princes, nobles and one of Mary, Queen of Scots.

CLOUET, JEAN
(c. 1480-1540). Painter, father of the above. Died in Paris. Court painter to Francis I and Louis XII. Excelled at portraits. Belongs to the transition period before the Renaissance became dominant in France. He was of Flemish extraction, but migrated to France.

CLOUET, JEAN
(Died c. 1490). Flemish painter to the dukes of Burgundy, a miniaturist. Possibly the father of the above.

CLOVIO, GIORGIO GIULIO
(1498-1578). Italian illuminator and painter. He was actually Croatian by birth. Migrated to Italy. Worked in Perugia, Rome, Florence. He completed the illuminations for an edition of the *Divine Comedy* begun by Giotto; he was himself the subject of a memorable portrait by El Greco. His work exhibits a remark-

able accuracy of anatomical detail—even for insects—attained by his use of a magnifying glass.

CLOWES, WILLIAM
(1540-1604). English surgeon. Served as military surgeon. Also surgeon to Queen Elizabeth. Author of surgical treatise *A Proved Practice for all Young Chirurgians*. Also work on syphilis: *Now an approved Treatise on the care of the French Pox by the Unctions*. Served as naval surgeon at the time of the Armada.

CLUSIUS, CAROLUS
(1526-1609). Charles L'Ecuse. Flemish physician, botanist and savant. Attached to the publishing house of Plantin. Traveled widely. Proficient in the classical as well as many European languages. Wrote on exotic plants: *Exoticorum Libri X*: published in 1605. Reputedly introduced the potato to Europe from Peru. He was a prolific author on a great variety of subjects from natural history to the conquest of Carthage.

CLUVERIUS, PHILIPP
(1580-1623). German geographer. Traveled in Norway, England, Scotland, Italy, France. Died in London. Originated historical geography, especially for the study of antiquity. He was a prodigy of erudition and is said to have known all the European languages.

COCHLAEUS, IOANNES
(1479-1562). Arch-enemy of Martin Luther. Compiled, from some sixty-one works of Luther, a polemical treatise entitled *Septiceps Lutherus:* published in 1564. Also wrote an iconoclastic biography of Luther.

CODEX ARGENTEUS
This codex is the only extant source of the ancient Gothic language. The manuscript, partly preserved at Uppsala University, was discovered in the 1550's and brought to Sweden as war booty, following the storming of Prague by Swedish armies in 1648.

COGNAC, LEAGUE OF
An alliance between Francis I of France and Venice, Milan, the Pope, and the Florentines in opposition to the Emperor Charles V and Spain. Formed in 1526. The League was thoroughly defeated.

COIMBRA
University of Coimbra in Portugal was originally founded in Lisbon in 1288. Transferred to Coimbra in 1537.

COITER, VOLCHER
(1534-c. 1576). Dutch anatomist. Studied in medical schools in Italy. Pioneer in pathological anatomy; some of his more important work was done on the spinal column and the fetal skeleton, of which he was the first to publish drawings.

COKE, SIR EDWARD
(1552-1634). English jurist. Held many high offices, including that of Chief Justice of the King's Bench. In the trials of Essex, Sir Walter Raleigh, and the Gunpowder Plot conspirators, Coke was the prosecutor. He insisted upon the judiciary's independence of the Crown, and, in the name of the common law, became the great antagonist of the royal prerogative. In drawing up the Petition of Right he was an active participant: 1628. Author of four notable *Institutes* and *Law Reports*.

COLA DI RIENZI
(1313-1354). Roman revolutionary, of humble origin, but a flaming spirit; he possessed an extensive knowledge of the classics. In the absence of the popes at Avignon he sought to rejuvenate the ancient Roman Empire and its capital by a popular revolution against the Roman nobles. As a notary in the papal service he awaited the auspicious moment; this seemed to come in May, 1347 when he assembled "the Roman people" who granted him great power and, later, the title "Tribune of the people." Initial success against the nobles did not last; before long the pope—whose place in Cola's schemes is not clear—turned against him, and before the year was out Cola fled. He spent several years at the court of the Emperor Charles IV but by 1354 was back in the papal service. He accompanied Cardinal Albornoz on an expedition to consolidate the Papal States, but soon resumed his revolutionary program. For a while he was virtual ruler of Rome (as "Senator"), but there was no real basis for his position. His extravagance and cruelty soon antagonized the people, who put him to death brutally at the foot of the Capitol. Cola shared with Petrarch, his contemporary, an intense enthusiasm for antiquity and had received from the poet a letter extolling the effort to restore ancient ways and institutions as

157

well as the expulsion of the "foreign tyrant," by which was meant the nobles; the people were "Roman."

COLARD, MANSION
(died 1484). Flemish printer. Writer, first printer in Bruges; he published twenty-one volumes.

COLET, JOHN
(c. 1467-1519). The founder of St. Paul's School, 1510, which used Linacre's grammar, commissioned by Colet. He appointed William Lilly, an accomplished Greek scholar as its first head. Greatly influenced by Erasmus, Colet's foundation marked the beginning of humanist education in England: classical literature dominated the curriculum, for Colet insisted the classics be known in their purity and excluded what he called medieval "blotterature." Typifing the northern Renaissance, the school was dedicated to the rearing of Christian gentlemen. Colet's career was of great significance as a bridge between Italy and England. He himself was no humanist, for he knew no Greek and his knowledge of the Bible, Plato, and Plotinus derived from Latin translations; but he did introduce the humanist methods of scholarship. He had made a two-year trip to Italy and Florence in the 1490's and made the acquaintance of Ficino and others of the Platonic Academy. It was the more definitely religious outlook of Ficino and the Academy that impressed Colet: the new learning of Italy was not an end in itself, but an instrument for the better understanding of the Bible and the Faith. Returned to England, he lectured at Oxford, from 1496 on, on St. Paul's Epistles; the lectures embody the new methods of scholarship and mark a decisive break with the Scholastics. Thus if Colet does not represent the first bridge between Italy and England, he was the first of any significance, for earlier contacts, e.g., that represented by "good duke Humphrey" in the 1440's came to very little.

COLIGNY, GASPARD DE
(1519-1572). French general, admiral. Leader of Huguenots. Prisoner in Spain: became Protestant. Helped Huguenots to settle in America. Killed in Massacre of St. Bartholomew's Day, 1572.

COLINS, ALEXANDER
(1526-1612). Sculptor. Belongs in the late Flemish Renaissance.

158

Sculptured reliefs for the tomb of Maximilian I as well as tombs of other Hapsburgs.

COLLE, RAFFAELLO DAL
(c. 1490-c. 1566). Italian painter of Tuscany. Executed religious and mythological themes. Friend and collaborator of Raphael and later of Vasari and Bronzino. Founded academy at Borgo San Sepolcro, his birthplace.

COLLÈGE DE COQUERET
French institution headed, in 1547, by the Hellenist Jean Dorat, who taught there most of the members who later formed *La Pléiade*.

COLLÈGE DE FRANCE
French institution established in 1530, on the suggestion of the humanist scholar, Budé, by Francis I; subsidized by the crown, it was originally known as the Collège des Lecteurs Royaux. An important center for humanist scholarship, it provided instruction in Latin, Greek, and Hebrew—the three "sacred" languages.

COLLÈGE DE GUYENNE AT BORDEAUX
The school attended by Montaigne and of which he complains in his *Essays*. It was modeled on Sturm's famous humanist school at Strassburg and was notable for an excessive concentration on the style of the ancients, ignoring their ideas. Among its teachers were Andreas de Gouvea, Cordier, and the Scots humanist, George Buchanan.

COLLEGIUM GERMANICUM
Jesuit institution, founded by Loyola, 1552; it was an important center of the Counter Reformation.

COLLEGIUM TRILINGUE OF LOUVAIN
Founded by Jerome Busleyden, died 1517; there were to be, as he directed in his will, three professors "to read and expound publicly to all comers, both Christian and other moral and approved authors, in the three languages, that is, in Latin, Greek and Hebrew." It met with opposition from the more traditional theologians at Louvain as did efforts to establish such an institution at other universities. Encouraged by Erasmus—in many ways its spiritual father—the Collegium flourished and was a milestone

159

in making provision for humanist study of the three languages. It was a model followed in part in the foundation of Corpus Christi College, Oxford, 1517, and the Collège de France, c. 1530.

COLLERYE, ROGER DE

(c. 1470-c. 1540). French poet and ecclesiastic. Founded club of gourmets and wits headed by the "Abbé des Fous." Author of satirical and comic lyrics: published in 1539.

COLOGNE, SCHOOL OF

This refers to the Gothic tradition of painting of the fourteenth to sixteenth centuries centered in Cologne. Stephen Lochner was the chief painter of the fifteenth century. His principal work is the *Altar of the Magi*. His successor was The Master of the Life of Mary. This name derives from a series of panels depicting the life of Mary. One of his pupils was The Master of the Lyversberg Passion. Other Masters were: The Master of the Legend of St. George: The Master of the Glorification of Mary: The Master of the Holy Kinship: The Master of St. Bartholomew: The Master of St. Severin: The Master of the Legend of St. Ursula. Bartholomeus Bruyn and his students brought the School of Cologne to an end. Bruyn, noted for his portraits, was born in 1493: died in Cologne in 1555. He effected the transition of the School of Cologne to the Italian manner of the Renaissance.

COLOMBE, JEAN

(1467-1529). French calligrapher and miniaturist. Executed, c. 1485, notable *Laval Hours*, now in the Bibliothèque Nationale at Paris. Patronized by the ducal house of Savoy, but worked chiefly at Bourges.

COLOMBE, MICHEL

(c. 1430-c. 1515). Sculptor, probably brother of the above. Belongs in the Early French Renaissance; he had studied the new Italian art forms at Bologna. He did the tomb of Duke Francis II of Brittany at Nîmes, and a bas-relief of *St. George and the Dragon*.

COLOMBO, REALDO

(c. 1516-1559). Italian anatomist of Padua and one of the founders of scientific anatomy. Pupil of Vesalius. Succeeded Vesalius at Padua. Author of *De Re Anatomica*. Published in 1559.

COLONNA FAMILY, THE

Ancient noble family of Rome that played an important role in her history from the twelfth through the sixteenth centuries; they were implacable foes of the Orsini family. The Colonna were leaders of the Ghibelline party in Italy and usually supported the Holy Roman Emperors against the popes and the Guelphs; one member of the family, however, ascended the papal throne as Martin V, 1417-1431. He was a Renaissance patron of the arts and learning as were several later members of the family; others were soldiers; Vittoria Colonna (1492-1547) was a gifted poetess and choice spirit of the age. The family still survives.

COLONNA, FABIUS

(1567-1650). Neapolitan lawyer and botanist who discovered, in Dioscorides, valerian as an aid in epilepsy. As a result, he published *Psytobasanos:* a history of plants, in 1592. He was a man of great learning in fields other than science, especially in music; he built an instrument on which the octave span was divided into seventeen notes.

COLONNA, FRANCESCO

(1449-1527). Italian scholar and Dominican. Author of one of the strangest imaginative works produced in the Renaissance, the *Hypnerotomachia,* 1467. It is the symbolic story of the star-crossed love of Polifilo for Polia; it is cast in scenes of rapturous, dreamlike fantasy in the gardens of Adonis and amid haunting antique ruins. At last true love triumphs in the Temple of Venus. There are echoes in the work of the *Roman de la Rose,* Dante, Boccaccio, *et al.*

COLONNA, VITTORIA

(1492-1547). Italian poetess. Friend of Michelangelo, Reginald Pole, and many of the humanists of her day. Her poems based largely on religious motifs. Addressed two sonnets to Pope Paul III, in 1541.

COLUCCI, BENEDETTO

(1438-c. 1491). Humanist of Pistoia. He completed his studies at Florence, returned to Pistoia to teach rhetoric and literature and then went to Bologna. He wrote about the civil disturbances of his own city and a work lauding the pacification that came with the Medici ascendancy, *De discardiis.*

COLUMBUS, CHRISTOPHER

(1446-1506). Discoverer of America. Born at or near Genoa, he settled in Lisbon. He urged the King of Portugal to send an expedition West, toward the Orient. Unsuccessful, he appealed to Spain in 1484 and secured financial support from Ferdinand and Isabella in 1492. Equipping three vessels—Santa Maria, Niña, and Pinta—he sailed from Palos on August 3, and on October 12, 1492 sighted Watling Island, one of the Bahamas group. Columbus sailed around Cuba and Haiti and returned to Palos in 1493. On his second voyage he set out with seventeen ships and 5000 men. He discovered Dominica and Jamaica. Made a settlement, called Isabella, on Haiti, in 1493. Isabella was the first European town in the New World. Columbus returned to Spain in 1496. On the third voyage, he left Spain in 1498: discovered Trinidad and the mouth of the Orinoco River. As the result of complaints from the new colonies, an official investigation, under Francisco de Bobadilla, was organized, in 1500. Columbus and his brothers were arrested, and sent in chains to Spain. Released, Columbus set out on a fourth voyage, in 1502: discovered Honduras, and sailed down to the Isthmus of Panama. Returned to Spain in 1504, he failed to regain lost honors. Columbus died at Valladolid.

COMMANDINO, FEDERICO

(1509-1575). Italian mathematician. Born in Urbino. Secretary to Pope Clement VII. Studied Greek and medicine at Padua. Devoted himself to mathematics. Translated Greek mathematical texts into Latin, among them were Euclid, Archimedes, and Hiero of Alexandria. Also wrote *Horologiorum Descripto:* published in 1562. Also *Liber de Centro Gravitatis Solidorum:* published in 1562.

COMMEDIA DELL' ARTE

The popular Italian drama, which flourished in the sixteenth century, in which the company played extempore from a repertoire of stereotyped plots and traditional characters. It utilized stylized masks, which may go back to those used in ancient Roman farces; among the most famous characters were Pulcinella of Naples and Stentorello of Florence.

COMMEDIA ERUDITA

Renaissance type of secular comedy, based on classical motifs, it flourished at Ferrara.

COMMERCE

In the fourteenth century trading corporations sprang up in Italy: *commenda* and *societas*. Genoese merchants, trading with Corsica, Cyprus, Chios, formed mercantile organizations called *maone*. Letters of exchange (*lettres de foire*) appeared in the trading centres of Europe. Money-lending became vastly profitable. In 1407 the Bank of St. George was founded in Genoa. During the Renaissance bookkeeping developed. In 1494 Luca Pacioli published a treatise on double entry. In 1484 Pietro Borghi published a manual on commercial arithmetic.

COMMINES, PHILIPPE DE

(c. 1445-1511). Intimate adviser to Duke Charles the Rash of Burgundy whom he abandoned in favor of the Duke's enemy, King Louis XI of France. With the king's death in 1483, Commines was forced to retire and subsequently wrote his *Mémoires*. They are characterized by a hard-headedness and realism in, e.g., his ridicule of chivalry and feudal warfare, in his preference for the diplomatic and subtle Louis to the headstrong and arrogant Charles, and in his commendation of ruse and indirection. Both Machiavelli and Guicciardini were in his debt.

COMMUNE

The municipalities, particularly of Northern Italy and also of the Netherlands, which were virtually independent of any outside power, although there was often a charter in which the commune acknowledged a king, emperor, magnate or prelate as suzerain and to whom it paid an annual sum for the rights of self-government, maintenance of an army and protecting walls, commercial rights, etc. The communes correspond roughly to the ancient city-state. In the great age of the communes, twelfth through fourteenth centuries, there was a fairly large governing class of merchants with power distributed among many offices held for short terms, and most were at least semi-democratic societies. In the course of the fourteenth century, and growing out of the endless factional quarrels and disorders, power came to be concentrated in fewer hands for longer periods of time, this process culminating in the despots (*signori*) of the fifteenth century. Florence preserved her communal institutions longest; perhaps her success in doing so is the chief explanation of the genius of her citizens in so many areas over so long a span of time.

COMPAÑÍAS DE TÍTULO
The eight royal troupes of actors organized in 1600 during reign of Philip III of Spain. The status of actors was regulated in order to conform to clerical objections to professional theatrical companies.

COMPIÈGNE, EDICT OF
This edict, issued in 1557 by Henry II of France, imposed the death penalty on Calvinists; the king sought to establish the Inquisition in France but was dissuaded by the *Parlement* of Paris.

COMPLAYNT OF SCOTLAND
A Scottish ballad that dates from the mid-sixteenth century.

COMPLUTENSIAN BIBLE
A polyglot version of monumental scholarship. Contained New Testament in Greek and Latin, and Old Testament in Hebrew, the Vulgate, the Septuagint, with Latin translation, and the Syriac. It was produced by the University of Alcalá de Henares (*Complutum*) under the patronage of Ximénez and published in 1522.

COMUNEROS
A Spanish term meaning *the bourgeois*. An organization of Spanish cities under the leadership of Juan de Padilla of Toledo that rose against the government of the Emperor Charles V (Charles I of Spain) whom the *comuneros* regarded as a foreigner and centralist. The *comuneros* dominated the Holy League formed in 1520 to defend the privileges of the towns. Defeated at Villalar in 1521. The chief participants were executed.

CONCEPTISMO
An exaggerated, witty subtlety cultivated by Spanish Baroque writers in seventeenth century. In prose, the great proponent was Baltasar García (1601-1658), author of *Agudeza y Arte de Ingenio*. Another notable practitioner was Francisco de Quevedo (1580-1645), author of *Aguja de Navegar Cultos:* 1631.

CONDELL, HENRY
(died 1627). Actor of the Globe Theatre. First editor of Shakespeare's plays.

CONDEMNATION OF ELIZABETH

Queen Elizabeth I of England was excommunicated by Pope Pius V in 1570 in the bull *Regnans in excelsis*. The Queen was deprived of her right to the throne and declared to be a heretic and persecutor of the true faith, her subjects anathematized if they obeyed her.

CONDIVI, ASCANIO

(c. 1520-1574). Italian painter. Pupil of Michelangelo. Wrote biography of his master, *Life*, 1553, which is one of the more important sources for its subject.

CONDOTTIERI

The leaders of mercenary troops in Italy in the fourteenth and fifteenth centuries. They were large-scale contractors as well as generals who rented out their forces to the highest bidder among princes and cities. Such mercenaries commended themselves to oligarchs and princes in a money-minded age; rulers preferred to trust the condottieri to arming their own citizens who might take the opportunity to rebel. Paid professional armies were as indispensable an arm of the new sovereign state as its paid professional officials were. Some of the most famous condottieri were Sir John de Hawkwood, died 1394, an Englishman in the service of Florence; Francesco Sforza who became so powerful that he gained the duchy of Milan for himself; Federigo da Montefeltro, the duke of Urbino, whose professional earnings enabled him to be a generous patron of the arts and learning, Francesco Carmagnola, who served Milan, Florence, and Venice in turn and came to be so distrusted that the Venetians summoned him before the Council of Ten and executed him for treason, 1432; Bartolomeo Colleoni, who fought many of Venice's wars and is commemorated by Verrochio's famous equestrian statue. The condottieri system was the negation of patriotism; in the era of foreign invasions and defeats after 1494 the system was discredited. Machiavelli, and others, attributed the might of the ancient Roman Republic to its citizen militia, and in his *Art of War*, 1521, he outlined a new military system modeled on the ancient ideal. Little came of it, but the era of the condottieri had ended.

CONINXLOO, GILLIS VAN

(1544-1609). Born in Antwerp. Died in Amsterdam. Painter. His subjects are heroic, romanticized murals, and landscapes. He had traveled extensively in Italy as well as France: few of his works have survived.

CONRADUS DE ZABERNIA
(Later fifteenth century). Alsatian musicologist. Author of *Opusculum de Monochordo*, c. 1470, a treatise on the use of the monochord; he also wrote on the best methods for singing choral music. He taught music at Heidelberg.

CONSPIRACY OF AMBOISE
A plot against the house of Guise, crushed in 1560. It triggered the French civil and religious wars.

CONSTABLE, HENRY
(1562-1613). English poet. Migrated to Paris. Attached to the French court. Died at Liège. Author of *Diana:* corpus of some seventy-five sonnets. He was a Catholic and sympathetic to the cause of Mary Queen of Scots and thus fled from England.

CONTADO
The surrounding territory of an Italian city, ruled by that city and from which it drew its agricultural goods.

CONTARINI, AMBROGIO
Fifteenth century. A Venetian merchant. Sent on diplomatic service to Persia, in 1474, to secure aid against the Turks. On his return, he traveled up the Volga as far as Moscow. He published an account of his four-year embassy.

CONTARINI, GASPARI
(1483-1542). Member of distinguished Venetian family. Author of a constitutional and social history of Venice. The family had produced eight doges as well as several artists and one cardinal.

CONVENTUALS
A group of the Franciscan Order who were not extreme in following the rule of St. Francis.

COOPER, JOHN
(1570-1627). Italianized his name to Giovanni Coperario after his stay in Italy. English composer and instrumentalist. Wrote lute-songs, masque music, madrigals, villanelles, organ music; was music master to the children of James I.

166

COOPER, THOMAS
(c. 1517-1594). English cleric. Author of *Thesaurus Linguae Romanae et Britannicae:* published in 1565. Called Cooper's Dictionary. The work so commended him to Elizabeth that she made him Bishop of Winchester; earlier he had been a fellow at Magdalen College, Oxford, where William Camden was one of his scholars. Cooper was born of a poverty-stricken tailor in Cot Street, Oxford; he is one of the few examples of a person rising from the social depths to the commanding heights. He also finished Thomas Lanquet's *Chronicle of the World,* which went through several editions and is a compendium of the historical notions prevalent in the age.

COORNHERT, DIRK VOLCKERTSZOON
(1522-1590). Dutch engraver, scholar, poet, scientist. Author of *Ethics.* Also translated *Odyssey,* Cicero, Seneca. Took part in and wrote a defense of the Dutch Revolt. An Arminian, he championed religious toleration.

COPERNICUS, NICHOLAS
(1473-1543). Mathematician and astronomer, of Polish birth, trained at Cracow, but the chief stimulus for his astronomical ideas derives from his stay at Padua. His heliostatic-heliocentric theory, retained the epicycles and deferents of Ptolemy and much else that was basic to the received astronomy. His famous treatise, *De revolutionibus orbium coelestium,* was published in 1543, although it had circulated in manuscript form as early as twenty years before. Historians of science now emphasize the conservative, rather than the radical, character of his doctrines; it is pointed out that his conception of science is shot through with mystical and Neo-Platonic notions, and that his theory was no more than "a modified form of the Ptolemaic system—assuming the same celestial machinery, but with one or two of the wheels interchanged through the transposition of the roles of the earth and the sun." (Butterfield).

CORAS, JEAN DE
(1513-1572). French jurist, victim of the St. Bartholomew Massacre of 1572. Professor of law at Toulouse. Wrote on the qualities of a good judge, a technical treatise on the legal aspects of marriage as well as a work on Pico della Mirandola.

CORBET, RICHARD

(1582-1635). English poet and prelate. Author of *Iter Boreale*: a poetic description of a vacation tour. Also *Journey into France* and *Fairies' Farewell*. His work is jovial and comic; he was strongly opposed to the Puritans.

CORDIER, MATHURIN

(1478-1564). French grammarian and teacher. Espoused Calvinism and fled to Geneva. Author of pedagogical texts.

CORDIERI, NICOLAS

(1567-1612). Sculptor, painter and engraver; born in Lorraine but reared and trained in Rome. Most of his work is to be found in the churches of Rome—statues of saints, etc.—and almost all of it shows the influence of Michelangelo whom Cordieri revered.

CORDUS, EURICIUS

(1486-1535). German humanist, physician, poet, botanist. Follower of Luther. Wrote Latin epigrams, a treatise on botany called *Botanologicon*. He had studied medicine at Ferrara.

CORDUS, VALERIUS

(1515-1544). German physician, botanist, pharmacologist. He was a student of Melanchthon and traveled widely in Germany and Italy. Author of first real pharmacopoeia used in Germany: published in 1535, entitled *Dispensatorium pharmacorum omnium*. Described some 500 new species of plants. Wrote commentary on Dioscorides. Discovered sulphuric ether in 1540.

CORENZIO, BELISARIO

(c. 1558-c. 1643). Neapolitan painter of Greek descent. According to tradition, pupil of Tintoretto in Venice. Executed frescoes.

CORNARIUS, IANUS

(1550-1558). German physician. He had studied medicine in Italy. Translated the *Oneirocritica* of Artemidorus: Greek treatise on dreams, into Latin. Made a monumental translation of Hippocrates after long years of collocating manuscripts.

CORNARO, CATERINA

(1454-1510). Venetian great lady of noble birth, Queen of Cyprus. Commanded to abdicate by the Venetian government, she established a sophisticated court at Treviso; patroness of the

168

arts and letters; Bembo was her friend, his *Gli Asolani* has reference to her court and its discussions of love.

CORNARO, LUIGI
(c. 1467-1566). Venetian noble and student of philosophy. Author of autobiography: *Discorsi della Vita Sobria*: published in 1558. Also: *Exhortation,* written in ninety-fifth year of his life. He is supposed to have attained so great an age by dieting and the practice of scientific hygiene.

CORNAZANO, ANTONIO
(1431-1500). Author of *I Proverbi*: a collection of sixteen stories. Wrote in Latin and Italian. Attached to the courts of Francesco Sforza, Bartolommeo Colleoni, Ercole I of Ferrara.

CORNEILLE DE LYONS
(Died c. 1574) French painter. He was court painter to Henry II and Catherine de' Medici and painted many portraits of the royal family.

CORNELISZ, JAKOB
(1477-1533). Dutch painter and engraver. Worked in Amsterdam, depicted religious subjects. He founded a family workshop where his son and brother worked with him.

CORNELISZ, LUCAS
(1493-c. 1552). Dutch painter. Royal painter to Henry VIII of England. Some of his portraits are still at Hampton Court.

CORNELISZOON VAN HAARLEM, CORNELIS
(1562-1638). Dutch painter. Worked in Haarlem. His subjects were typically landscapes with figures, still-life flowers, religious themes, and mythology.

CORNEUS, PETRUS PHILIPPUS DE or PIER FILIPPO CORNEO
(1420-1493). Perugian jurist. He taught civil law at Perugia, Ferrara, Pisa. Author of corpus on pleas and responses in civil and criminal law.

CORONADO, FRANCISCO VÁSQUEZ DE
(1510-1554). Spanish explorer in America. On expedition in Mexico. Discovered Grand Canyon. Explored California.

CORONADO, JUAN VÁSQUEZ DE
(c. 1525-1565). Spanish conquistador. In South America. Ex-

plored in Central America. Founded city of Cartago in 1563.

CORONEL, ANTONIUS

Sixteenth century. Logician of Segovia. Wrote commentary on Aristotelian categories: published in Paris in 1513. Also *Rosarium,* and a monograph entitled *Exponibilia et Fallaciae.*

CORREGGIO, ANTONIO ALLEGRI DA

(1494-1534). Leader of Renaissance school of painting in Parma. Noted for his chiaroscuro, his delicacy and vivaciousness, and anatomical fidelity. Executed religious and mythological themes, frescoes, easel pictures. His influence on Baroque art was nearly as great as Michelangelo's.

CORT, CORNELIS

(c. 1533-1578). Dutch engraver, employed by Titian; he spent most of his life in Italy.

CORTÉS, HERNÁN

(1485-1547). Spanish conqueror of Mexico. Born at Medellín. In 1504 he sailed to Santo Domingo. In command of expedition to the mainland. Served in the conquest of Cuba, in 1511. Founded Vera Cruz and entered Mexico City in 1519. Although expelled, he re-entered the city triumphantly in 1521. Was made Governor in 1523 but was deposed three years later. Recalled to Spain in 1528, and made Marquis of the Valley of Oaxaca. In 1530 he returned to Mexico. Died in obscurity in Spain, seeking redress against the Governor who had replaced him and with whom he had quarreled. Wrote *Cartas de Relación*: 1519-1529: Five letters, following the style of Julius Caesar, addressed to the Emperor Charles V and giving an account of the conquest.

CORVINA

Famous library of King Matthias of Hungary (1458-1490), established at Budapest. He was a Renaissance prince *par excellance,* patron of the arts and sciences; his library was one of the best in Europe.

CORYATE, THOMAS

(c. 1577-1617). English traveler, courtier of James I. Traveled through Europe. Visited Constantinople, the Holy Land, Persia, India. Author of a travel book: *Coryate's Crudities*: published in 1611.

170

COSA, JUAN DE LA
(1460?-1510). Spanish navigator. Accompanied Columbus as master of the Santa María, on two occasions: in 1492 and in 1493. Acted as pilot in South American expeditions. Killed by Indians. Executed the first large map (i.e., the oldest surviving) of the New World, in 1500. It is especially interesting in that it indicates a great land mass barring passage to the West.

COSSA, FRANCESCO
(1439-1480). Italian painter. Belongs to the Early Ferrarese Renaissance school. Much of his work was done on the Este palace at Ferrara; when he shifted to Bologna he became one of the founders of its school of painting.

COSTA, LORENZO
(1460-1535). Italian painter of the Ferrarese and Bolognese schools. Works include frescoes. Noted for his *Madonna and Child with the Bentivoglio Family.*

COTA DE MAGUAQUE, RODRIGO
(died c. 1495). Spanish poet. Author of *Dialogue between Love and an Old Knight;* possibly the author of *La Celestina.*

COTGRAVE, RANDLE
(died c. 1632). English lexicographer. Author of an early French-English dictionary: first edition published in 1611. He was secretary to William Cecil, Lord Burghley.

COTTA, POMPONIUS
Sixteenth century Milanese jurist. Author of address delivered in 1560 before Pope Pius IV on achievements of Faculty of Law of Milan.

COTTON, SIR ROBERT BRUCE
(1571-1631). English antiquary. Collector of records, coins, books, especially valuable for the Greek, Hebrew and Anglo-Saxon manuscripts. The Cottonian Collection is now in the British Museum.

COUCY, EDICT OF
This edict was issued by Francis I of France, 1535, granting freedom to heretics who recanted, with the exception of Sacramentarians: that is, Calvinist adherents; it was politically

171

motivated in that the king desired the alliance of the Protestant German princes.

COUNCIL OF BLOOD
Also known as the Council of Troubles. This was a tribunal set up by the Duke of Alva to crush opposition in the Netherlands: 1567-1573.

COUNCIL OF THE LATERAN
The Council was convened by Pope Julius II in 1512. The purpose was to reform ecclesiastical abuses; it made no headway whatsoever.

COUNCIL OF TRENT
See Trent, Council of.

COUNTER REFORMATION
To counteract the initial success of the Reformation, the Roman Catholic Church organized a campaign directed to the removal of abuses and the re-capture of lost territory. In the year 1545-1564 the Council of Trent achieved the first purpose. The Society of Jesus, the Inquisition, the *Index Librorum Prohibitorum,* the *Index Librorum Expurgatorum,* were all intended to accomplish the second objective. This Counter Reformation succeeded so well that many parts of Central Europe and of Southern Germany, that had turned to Protestantism, were regained for Roman Catholicism. The fact that the Church was on the defensive had a stultifying effect on art and thought, except in those instances where they could serve religious purposes.

COURTEYS, JEAN
(1511-1586). French enameler of Limoges, member of a family celebrated for its enamel work.

COURTEYS, PIERRE
(1520-1586). French enameler. Work preserved in the Louvre, Paris, and in other European museums. Noted for rich, lavishly detailed work.

COUSIN, JEAN
Father (c. 1490-1560). Son Jean (c. 1520-1590). French painters and sculptors. Noted for executions in stained glass.

COVARRUBIAS, ANTONIO ALONSO DE

(Died 1570) Spanish architect. The influences that came to bear on him were north European rather than Italian; architect to Charles V and Philip II. A striking portrait of him was done by El Greco.

COVARRUBIAS Y OROZCO, SEBASTIÁN DE

(1539-1613). Priest of Toledo. Canon at Cathedral of Cuenca. Wrote homiletic work entitled *Emblemas Morales* in 1610. Noted as compiler of *Tesoro de la Lengua Castellana o Española*, published in 1611. Best dictionary available during Golden Age of Spanish literature.

COVERDALE, MILES

(1488-1568). English cleric. In 1539 was published the Great Bible in English translation, a work to which Coverdale was a principal contributor. It was presented to Henry VIII by Thomas Cromwell, Coverdale's friend, as was Thomas More.

COVILHAM, PEDRO DE

(1450?-c. 1545). Portuguese navigator. With Afonso da Paiva, sent on mission in 1487 to discover the legendary kingdom of Prester John. Paiva died in Cairo. Covilham was kept prisoner in Abyssinia until his death.

COWELL, JOHN

(1554-1611). English jurist. Professor of law at Cambridge. Author of legal dictionary: *The Interpreter*: published in 1607. For its exaltation of the royal prerogative it was denounced by Sir Edward Coke before the House of Commons.

COX, RICHARD

(1500-1581) English reformer. Fled to Frankfurt during Mary's reign; made Bishop of Ely by Elizabeth. He translated the four Gospels and wrote theological works.

COXIE, MICHIEL

(1497-1592) Flemish painter, member of a family of numerous painters, spent much of his life in the service of Philip II of Spain.

COXIE, RAPHAEL

(1540-1616) Flemish painter, son of the above; his work suffers from too close an imitation of Michelangelo.

COZZARELLI, GIACOMO DI BARTOLOMEO
(1453-1515). Sienese sculptor and architect. Worked in bronze and terracotta.

COZZARELLI, GUIDOCCIO
(Later fifteenth century) Italian painter and miniaturist. He designed the *Sibilla Libica*.

CRABETH, DIRK PIETERSZ
(1501-1577). Dutch painter. Executed stained-glass windows in churches in Italy, France, Belgium. He was a member of a family of painters.

CRABETH, WOUTER PIETERSZ
(1509-c. 1590). Dutch painter, brother of the above. Executed stained-glass windows in churches in Belgium, France.

CRACOVIA, MATTHAEUS DE
Author of *Dialogus rationis et conscientiae*. Published in Mainz c. 1459. One of first printed books.

CRAIG, JOHN
(1512-1600). Scottish reformer. Dominican. Converted to Protestantism. Condemned by Inquisition. Escaped. Returned to Scotland as royal chaplain and lieutenant to John Knox. Drew up *Craig's Catechism*.

CRAIG, SIR THOMAS
(1538-1608). Scottish jurist. Poet: wrote in Latin. Author of *Jus Feudale*, published in 1608. Also wrote *De Unione Regnorum*: on relationship between England and Scotland and urged James I's claim to the English throne. His searching study of feudal law, and his recreation of the feudal structure of medieval society from it, make him a pioneer of modern historiography.

CRANACH, LUCAS
(1472-1553) German painter, engraver. Court painter to the dukes of Saxony at Wittenberg, where his shop was located. He became a Lutheran, painted portraits of Luther, Malanchthon, *et al.*, and served the Protestant cause in his art. His son Lucas continued the flourishing workshop.

CRANBROOK SCHOOL
In Kent. English public school. Founded c. 1520 by John Blubery. Granted Royal Charter in 1574.

CRANMER, THOMAS
(1489-1556). English ecclesiastic. Archbishop of Canterbury. Gained favor of Henry VIII by declaring marriage of Henry and Catherine of Aragon void: also nullified another marriage. In Henry's ecclesiastical revolution he participated willingly, being of a diffident, scholarly nature. He upheld the royal prerogative. Wrote the Thirty-Nine Articles of Religion and compiled First and Second Books of Common Prayer. On accession of Catholic Queen Mary, Cranmer was condemned for heresy and treason; excommunicated: burned at stake.

CRANSTOUN, DAVID
(Sixteenth century) Scottish logician of Glasgow, educated at Paris, where he became professor and spent most of his life. Author of a work on morals and one on logic.

CRASHAW, RICHARD
(c. 1613-1649). English religious poet. Fled on the outbreak of Puritan and Parliamentary strife. Converted to Catholicism in Paris. Wrote largely on sacred subjects. Died at Loretto. Author of *Epigrammatum Sacrorum Liber*: published in 1634, the *Steps to the Temple*, and *The Flaming Heart*, which was inspired by St. Teresa of Spain.

CRÉPY, TREATY OF
Or Crespy. This treaty ended hostilities between Francis I of France and the Emperor Charles V. Signed in 1544, it was another pause in the long struggle between France and the Hapsburgs.

CRESPI, GIOVANNI, IL CERANO
(1557-1632). Italian painter, architect, and sculptor of the Milanese school; his work suggests transition to Baroque.

CRETAN PRINTERS
Two Cretan printers, Callierges and Blastus, became noted for new Greek type: in use in 1499.

CRÉTIN, GUILLAUME
(1461-1525) Guillaume Dubois. French poet, one of the

175

Rhétoriqueurs. Chronicler, enjoyed the patronage of Francis I. Wrote panegyrics in verse: *Complaints sur la Mort de Feu Guillaume de Bissipat*. Also *Poésies*: published in 1526. Wrote the *Chronique française*.

CRICHTON, JAMES

(c. 1560-1582). Scottish scholar: prodigy. Called The Admirable Crichton. Reputedly versed in twelve languages. Served in French army; traveled and studied in Italy, where he disputed successfully with noted scholars and professors. Killed in street fight by, it is said, his own student, the son of a Mantuan nobleman.

CRILLON, LOUIS DES BALBES DE BERTON DE

(1541-1615). *L'Homme sans Peur*. French soldier of the Guise faction. Fought against Huguenots. Wounded at battle of Lepanto in 1571. Participated in the siege of La Rochelle in 1573; was one of the best commanders in the service of Henry IV.

CRISTOFORO DE' PREDIS

Illuminator of Milan. Executed *Lives of SS. Joachim and Anna*, in 1476, a missal, in 1476, a gradual, a Roman Breviary, and Vergil's *Aeneid*.

CRIVELLI, CARLO

(c. 1435-c. 1495). Italian painter. Worked only in tempera. Died in Venice. Executed sharply drawn religious pictures in the Early Renaissance style. Elaborate detail. Among his works are *Madonna and Child, Pietà, Crucifixion*.

CROATIAN-HUNGARIAN KINGS

During the Renaissance, many rulers of Croatia-Hungary, among them Matthias Corvinus, were interested in the artistic and intellectual activities of Italy. The rulers of this period were as follows: Matthias I Corvinus (1458-1490): Vladislav II (1490-1516): Louis II (1516-1526): John Zapolski (1526-1540): Ferdinand I (1527-1564): Maximilian (1564-1576): Rudolph (1576-1608): Mathias II (1608-1619): Ferdinand II (1619-1637): Ferdinand III (1637-1657). Beginning in 1526 the kings were Hapsburgs and usually Holy Roman Emperors.

CROKE, RICHARD

(c. 1489-1558). English classical scholar. Pupil of Erasmus and of many of the celebrated humanists of the day. Taught Greek at Cambridge: also Louvain, Leipzig. He edited several classical texts, e.g., Ausonius. He was sent to Italy to learn what the canonists thought of Henry's divorce from the Queen and took the opportunity to make transcriptions of the Church Fathers' writings.

CROMWELL, THOMAS
(1485-1540). English statesman. Son of a Putney brewer. Became assistant to Cardinal Wolsey and, after Wolsey's fall, Privy Councillor: 1531. Master of Jewels: 1532. Chancellor of the Exchequer: 1533. King's Secretary: 1534. Lord Privy Seal: 1536. Baron Cromwell: 1536. Lord Great Chamberlain: 1539. Earl of Essex: 1540. He was instrumental in implementing the Act of Supremacy, the suppression of monasteries, the confiscation of their property: 1536-1539. He made efforts to convert England to Protestantism and to increase power of Henry VIII. His arrangement of Henry's marriage with Anne of Cleves resulted in his loss of favor. Accused of treason, he was beheaded.

CROTUS, RUBIANUS
(c. 1480-after 1539). German humanist scholar. Accepted Reformation. Rector of University of Erfurt. Returned to Catholicism after a trip of three years to Italy. Contributed to *Epistolae Obscurorum Virorum,* and was a friend of Hutten.

CROWLEY, ROBERT
(c. 1518-1588). English writer, reformer, printer. Issued Welsh books. Archbishop of Hereford. Author of *A Way of Wealth,* published in 1550, and works of religious controversy.

CRUL, CORNELIS
(died 1551). Flemish poet. His work reveals ironical humor.

CRUQUIUS, JACOB DE
(Later sixteenth century). Dutch classical scholar. Professor of Latin at Bruges. Produced edition of Horace: begun in 1565, completed in 1578. He also wrote Latin verse.

CRUSIUS, MARTIN
(1526-1607). German historian and philologist, Philhellene humanist. Professor of classics at Tübingen. Promoted the union of the Greek Orthodox and Lutheran Churches. Introduced the study of modern Greek into Germany. First real philhellene in

the sixteenth century. Author of books directed to the study of modern Greece: *Turcograecia,* published in 1584: and *Germanograecia,* published in 1585 and numerous scholarly manuals, commentaries, scholia, etc.

CRUZ, AGOSTINHO DA
(1540-1629). Portuguese mystical poet and monk. Portugal's greatest mystical poet; he wrote sonnets, odes, eclogues that echo Petrarch, but are more notable for their profound and fervid religiosity. Sonorous and musical, they lend themselves to recitation.

CRUZ, FREI GASPAR DE
(Died 1570). Portuguese historian and Dominican missionary. He wrote of the Portuguese empire in the East and also of China, the first account of China, it has been said, since Marco Polo.

CRUZ, SAN JUAN DE LA
(1542-1591). Spanish mystical lyric poet. Named Juan de Yepes before entering Carmelite Order in 1563. Studied at Salamanca in 1568. Friend of St. Teresa de Ávila. Became a determined reformer; was abused and imprisoned, where he wrote much of his finest poetry. His chief work is *La Subida del Monte Carmelo* (1578-1583): eight *canciones,* with prose commentaries.

CUESTIÓN DE AMOR
Anonymous Spanish *novela sentimental:* c. 1510. Dialogue in mixed prose and verse. The theme is love and intrigue at the Spanish court in Naples.

CUEVA, JUAN DE LA
(1543-1610). Spanish poet and dramatist. Born and died in Sevilla. Wrote fourteen plays: published in 1583. Best known drama is *El Infamador:* swashbuckling adventure, 1581. First Spanish playwright to conceive of a national drama based on national history and traditions; the best known example is his *Los siete infantes de Lara.* His sources were Spanish chronicles and folk ballads. Also expounded theories of dramaturgy in versified *Ejemplar Poético,* published in 1606.

CUIUS REGIO, EIUS RELIGIO
The religion of the ruler is the religion of his subjects. This was

the principle of the Religious Peace of Augsburg, granted in 1555 by the Emperor Charles V. It recognized Catholicism and Lutheranism, but not Calvinism, in the Holy Roman Empire.

CUJAS, JACQUES

(1500-1590). French jurist and historical scholar. Author of summaries of Justinian Code, presented in short axioms, and student of French feudalism and feudal law. Out of the humanist criticism of the unhistorical approach to the *Corpus Juris Civilis* came the Renaissance historical school of jurisprudence, of which Cujas was a founder. He published editions of the Roman jurists, Ulpian and Paulus, that utilize the humanist techniques of historical and philological study.

CULPEPER, NICHOLAS

(1616-1654). English physician, astrologer. Author of *Herbal:* published in 1653. Had extensive popularity, as did other of his works, e.g., the *London Dispensatory* and the *Astrological Judgment.*

CUNHA, NUNHO DA

(1487-1539). Portuguese explorer. Went to East Indies. Governor of India. Secured possession of Basra for Portugal. Died on way home.

CUNHA, TRISTÃO DA

(c. 1460-1540). Portuguese explorer, father of the above. Made expeditions to Africa, India. Discovered Tristão da Cunha Island, in 1506, in the South Atlantic.

CUNNINGHAM, ALEXANDER, EARL OF GLENCAIRN

(died 1574). Scottish reformer. One of the principal promoters of the Reformation in Scotland, an antagonist of Mary, Queen of Scots. Destroyed monasteries in West of Scotland, 1561; he had gone to England to seek aid from Elizabeth against Mary and the French.

CUNNINGHAM, WILLIAM

(c. 1522-c. 1577). English physician, author, and engraver. Author of a mariner's manual—*The Cosmographical Glass:* published in 1559. It was illustrated by many fine maps, drawn by the author.

CUREUS, JOACHIM

(1532-1573). German physician. Practiced in Freistadt. Pupil of

179

Melanchthon. He was an enthusiastic Lutheran and the author of both religious and scientific works.

CURTIUS, FRANCISCUS
(died 1533). The Younger. Italian jurist. Adviser to Francis I, king of France. Author of *Tractatus Feudalis:* published in 1547; it is a detailed survey of feudal law: rights of lords, serfs, manorial obligations, etc.

CUSANUS, NICHOLAS or NICHOLAS OF CUSA
(1401-1464). German classical scholar, philosopher, and a theologian, Platonist, cosmologist and mathematician; made a Cardinal by Nicholas V, 1448. As a philosopher he has the distinction of having been the one systematic and original philosopher of the Renaissance; he made fundamental contributions to epistemology, setting forth in *De docta ignorantia* a thorough-going conception of the relativity of human knowledge; a critic of Aristotelian logic, he was a pioneer of quantification in physics; his ideas of proportion and harmony had a profound influence on Renaissance aesthetics, metaphysics, and mathematics. He was the fountain head of Renaissance philosophy.

He had been a pupil of the Brothers of the Common Life at Deventer, studied briefly at Heidelberg, then Padua where he took his doctorate in canon law, 1423, visited Rome, and went on to Cologne to study theology. He returned to Rome to become secretary to Cardinal Orsini and thus moved among the humanists. His studies brought him to doubt the validity of the Donation of Constantine, but fell short of proof. He also anticipated to some degree the heliocentric theory: while he made the assertion that the earth moves, he said no more than that; yet he did proclaim that Venus and Mercury revolve around the sun. He wrote several treatises on mathematics and one on statistics that greatly impressed Leonardo, who deeply admired Cusanus. Despite his achievements in science and mathematics, he was no experimentalist: he arrived at his conclusions theologically and metaphysically.

He was the champion of and played an active part in the Conciliar Movement; in his *De concordantia catholica*, he minimized the role and power of the papacy in the headship of the Church, sought the theological basis for the reconciliation of the Greek and Latin Churches, opposed the pretensions of the clergy, and urged religious toleration. He knew Greek and was learned in Plato—the first Westerner to be so; the Florentine Platonic revival owed much to him as did Ficino's conception of man. An avid hunter of manuscripts, he discovered twelve plays of Plautus in 1429, and, on an embassy to Constantinople in 1436, collected many Greek manuscripts. The library of this universal man, left to the Hospital that he founded at Cusa (Cues), survives, although not complete. An edition of his works was published by Lefèbvre d'Étaples in 1514. In the historical scholarship of a generation ago Cusanus was reckoned a humanist, lately he appears to be in the tradition of the medieval Franciscan mystics, without quibbling one may designate him an important transitional figure.

CUSPINIANUS, JOHANNES
(1473-1529). Viennese humanist. Diplomat. Physician to the Emperor Maximilian I. He wrote about the Roman imperial tradition, the history of Austria, the Turkish wars, etc.; he edited several classical works and wrote his memoirs.

CUYP, BENJAMIN
(1610-1652). Dutch painter. Specialized in peasant themes and some portraits. Taught by his uncle but shows more profoundly the influence of Rembrandt.

CUYP, JACOB GERRITSZOON
(1594-c. 1651). Dutch painter, uncle and teacher of the above. Noted for portraiture, landscapes, in the manner suggestive of Rembrandt.

CYPRUS
The Venetians acquired the island of Cyprus in 1489 from the Lusignan family and held it until the Turkish conquest, 1571.

CYRIAC OF ANCONA
(died c. 1457). Peripatetic antiquary and classical enthusiast. He was an Italian merchant who traveled much in Italy and the classical lands of the eastern Mediterranean area collecting antiquities and inscriptions, and making the earliest careful sketches of ancient sites and ruins. He advertised his finds and himself in extravagant letters to his friends and to the rulers of Italy, and thus did much to establish the vogue of archaeology. He served popes on diplomatic missions, worked (in the train of Cardinal Bessarion) for union of the Churches at the Council

of Florence in 1439, and, later, was an intimate acquaintance of Mohammed II.

CZECHOSLOVAKIA, ART OF, or BOHEMIA

In architecture, the sixteenth century marks the advent of the Renaissance in Bohemia. There was a strong influence of Italian Renaissance, brought into the country by many Italian architects working at the Hapsburg court of Ferdinand I. Examples of this architectural style are the Spanish Hall in the Hradcany, Belvedere, and Schwarzenberg Palaces. Czech Renaissance sculpture is characterized by fine decorative craftsmanship: in stucco ceilings, carved wood furniture, ornamental metalwork. As an example, there is the Singing Fountain in the garden of the Prague Castle. Grafitto painting was introduced by the Italians during the Renaissance. Both the interiors and the exteriors of public buildings were decorated in this manner. For instance, the Minuta House in Prague, and Schwarzenberg Palace.

D

DAMMONIS, INNOCENTIUS

Sixteenth century. Italian musician. Composed *laude*.

DANDIPRAT

A small coin in use in the sixteenth century. Figuratively, an insignificant fellow, a dwarf, a child.

D'ANGHIERA, PIETRO MARTIRE

(c. 1456-1526). Italian scholar, statesman, historian. He entered the service of Ferdinand and Isabella: consular diplomat and the dean of Cathedral of Granada. Wrote *De Rebus Oceanicis et Novo Orbe*: published in 1516. It contains one of the earliest full accounts of the discovery of America and the progress of exploration to the time of writing. Also volume of letters: *Opus Epistolarum*.

DANIEL, SAMUEL

(1562-1619). English poet, dramatist. In 1604 appointed Master of Queen's Revels. Groom to the Queen. Author of masques, Senecan plays, the epic, *The Civil Wars between the Two Houses of Lancaster and York* (1595-1609): poem in seven books. *Musophilus*: a versified defense of learning. *Defense of Rime*. His *History of England* was not published until 1631.

DANIELE DA VOLTERRA

(c. 1509-1556) Italian painter and sculptor. Follower of Michelangelo. He carved a famous bust of his master; his paintings are characterized by an intensity and torment suggestive of the baroque—most notably in the frescoes he did in the Farnese Palace.

183

DANIELLO, BERNARDINO LUCCHESE

(died 1565). Italian critic and littérateur. Taught classics at Padua. Produced notable commentary on Dante's *Divine Comedy*. Also *La Poetica*: poetic criticism: published in 1536, a study of Petrarch, 1541, and a translation in verse of Vergil's *Georgics*.

DANTE ALIGHIERI

(1265-1321). Dante was essentially a medieval figure, his conception of the ideal life, of love, of a Christian society, and of the dual governance of the world by Holy Roman Popes and Holy Roman Emperors are all part of the medieval world. His profound reverence for antiquity, its heroes and authors—especially Vergil, Aristotle, and Seneca, his depiction of flesh-and-blood characters in *The Divine Comedy*, his conscious literary artistry and fame as a man of letters make him a harbinger of the Renaissance.

DANTISCUS, JOANNES

(1485-1527). Polish Latin poet, diplomat, and prelate. Wrote satirical pieces: *De Nostrorum Temporum Calamitatibus*. He had traveled in Italy, Greece, and Palestine.

DANTI, VINCENZO

(1530-1576). Italian architect, sculptor and theorist of the arts. Executed statue of Pope Julius III, bas-reliefs: bronze serpent: *The Conquerer*, copied from Michelangelo whose influence upon him was profound. He wrote a treatise on "perfect proportions" in the arts.

DANUBIAN SODALITY

A club dedicated to the humanities. Founded by German scholar Conrad Celtes (1459-1508) along the same lines as the Italian academies.

DARCIUS, JOANNES or JEAN DARCI

(Early sixteenth century) Neo-Latin poet of Naples. Author of sporting book: *Venusini Canes*. Published in Paris in 1543.

D'ARGENTA, JACOPO FILIPPO MEDICI

Fifteenth century. Italian illuminator of Ferrarese school. Executed antiphonary, gradual, Xenophon's *Cyropaedia*, Pliny.

DARIOT, CLAUDE

(c. 1530-1594). French physician. Calvinist. Wrote on astrology.

DARNLEY, HENRY

(1545-1567). Pretender to English throne as successor to Queen Elizabeth. Dissolute. Second husband of Mary Queen of Scots. Father of James I. Murdered, reputedly, with connivance of Mary Queen of Scots.

DAUCHER, ADOLF

(c. 1460-c. 1523). German sculptor. Sculptor of Early Swabian Renaissance school. Among his patrons were the Fuggers, for whom he sculptured the choir in their chapel at Augsburg.

DAUNTSEY'S SCHOOL

In Wiltshire, England. English public school. Founded by Alderman William Dauntsey in 1543.

DAURAT, JEAN

(c. 1510-1588) French classical scholar. Taught as students at the Collège de Coqueret in Paris most of the group that later formed *La Pléiade* and was probably the inspiration of their purpose to refine the vernacular by imitating classical models.

DAVID, GERARD

(c. 1450-1523). Flemish artist. Active in Bruges. In 1501 became dean of Bruges Painters' Guild. After death of Memling, became leading painter of early Dutch Renaissance school. Subjects were religious, among them a *Pietà*. Noted for deep rich colors.

DAVIES, JOHN

(c. 1565-1618) English poet and writing master; wrote as epigrams, *The Scourge of Folly.*

DAVIES, SIR JOHN

(1569-1626). English statesman, poet. Attorney General for Ireland. Attempted to impose Anglicanism in Ulster. In favor with James I. Author of *Nosce Teipsum:* didactic poem on the immortality of the soul. *Orchestra:* poem on dancing. Published in 1596. *Astraea:* collection of poems in honor of Queen Elizabeth I. Published in 1599. Saintsbury: "Passages finely wrought and expressed in a stately music."

DÀVILA, ENRICO CATERINO

(1576-1631). Italian historian. In service of France, Venice. Shot by assassin. Author of *History of the Civil War of France:* 1558-

1598. He had spent most of his life in France having been a page to the Queen-Regent, Catherine de' Medici, and also fought in the wars that he later wrote about.

DAVIS, JOHN
(c. 1550-1605). English explorer. While in search of Northwest Passage, discovered Davis Strait, Greenland, in 1587. Also made expeditions to South Seas. Discovered Falkland Islands. Invented double quadrant: called Davis' Quadrant. He also wrote a navigator's manual, *The Seaman's Secrets.*

DAY, JOHN
(Late sixteenth century). English printer and writer. Member of Gonville and Caius College, Cambridge. Contemporary of Shakespeare. His shop published the first edition of Foxe's celebrated *Book of Martyrs,* 1562.

DAY OF BARRICADES
The Duke of Guise, Henri I de Lorraine, entered Paris, defying Henry III of Valois. At the same time a popular rising broke out, called the Day of Barricades: 1588.

DECEMBRIO, PIERO CANDIDO
(1392-1477). Italian classical scholar, pupil of Chrysoloras. Translator of Appian. Also translated some books of Homer's *Iliad.* Secretary to the last Visconti duke of Milan, Filippo Maria. Prolific author and translator.

DECIMAL NUMBERS
Developed by Simon Stevin (1548-1620), Dutch mathematician.

DECIMATOR, HENRICUS
(fl. c. 1580). German poet. Wrote Latin poems in classical form but on contemporary themes.

DECIO, AGOSTINO
Illuminator. Flourished in Duchy of Milan under Francesco II Sforza (1492-1535). Executed religious books at courts of Rodolfo II and Duke of Savoy.

DECORATION OF THE ROSE, THE HAT, AND THE SWORD
This papal distinction was conferred on Federigo da Montefeltro, Duke of Urbino (1422-1487). It was frequently used by Renaissance popes as a diplomatic weapon; traditionally it was granted once a year.

DEE, JOHN

(1527-1608). English alchemist, mathematician. Charged with thaumaturgic practices against Queen Mary of England. In favor with Queen Elizabeth I. Associated with Edward Kelley in crystal gazing and magic arts. Wrote in Latin on mathematics, alchemy, logic. Also *Monas Hieroglyphica*. He headed a circle of learned men similar to the academies in Italy, an unofficial Royal Society.

DEFENDER OF THE FAITH

Latin: *Fidei Defensor*. English royal title. First bestowed by Pope Leo X on Henry VIII in 1521, in recognition of his defense of the seven sacraments against Martin Luther. The king was theologically conservative and remained so all his life.

DEI, BENEDETTO

(1418-1492). Florentine merchant, traveler, publicist, and political informer. Wrote accounts of Africa and Asia, and especially of the Ottoman Empire. He was an agent of the Medici.

DE LA WARR, THOMAS WEST, BARON

(1577-1618). Governor of Colony of Virginia: 1610. To prevent collapse of colony, returned to England for aid. Died on way back to Virginia. He had served in the army of the independent states of the Netherlands, the United Provinces.

DELFINO, DOMENICO

(1490-1560) Italian lexicographer and encyclopedist. Author of an encyclopedic work in Italian; in it he discusses natural science, immortality of the soul, generation. Published in 1565.

DELFINO, FEDERIGO

(1477-1547) Italian physician and astronomer who taught at Venice and most notably at Padua. So successful was he in his medical practice that he was accused of being a magician. He wrote a number of treatises on the two subjects of his callings.

DELICADO, FRANCISCO

Andalusian priest and novelist. He studied and traveled much in Italy. His sojourn in Rome (1523-1527) is reflected in his picaresque novel entitled *Retrato de la Loçana Andaluza*: published in 1528. It describes Italian mores during Renaissance. He also edited an *Amadis* in 1533 and other works on or inspired by the ideal of chivalry.

DELLA CASA, GIOVANNI

(1503-1556). Italian prelate and poet. Archbishop of Benevento. Opposed Italian Reformation. Papal Secretary of State. Translated Thucydides. Author of *Il Galateo*, guide for gentlemen, and of a life of Bembo.

DELMEDIGO, GIUSEPPE SALAMONE

(1591-1655). Physician, mathematician, philosopher, and teacher. Disciple of Galileo as a student at Padua. Wandered from Candia in Crete, his native town, to Padua: then to Egypt, Turkey, Poland, Hamburg, Amsterdam, Frankfurt, Worms. Died in Prague. Only known works are *Palms*, dealing with the natural sciences, metaphysics: essays: letters. He is known to have been a critic of Aristotelian science.

DELMINO, GIULIO CAMILLO

(1485-1544). Italian scholar and man of letters, defender of Ciceronianism against Erasmus, his principal work was *Della imitazione*. He was learned in Oriental religions and languages.

DELONEY, THOMAS

(c. 1550-1600). English novelist. Author of *Jack of Newbury, The Gentle Craft, Thomas of Reading*. Sources for English social history.

DELORME, PHILIBERT or DE L'ORME

(c. 1517-1570). French architect, one of the greatest of the French Renaissance. Court architect to Henry II of France. Worker at Fontainebleau. Built many châteaux. Also Tuileries. He also wrote a treatise on architecture, *Nouvelles Inventiones pour bien bâtir*.

DEMARCATION, BULL OF

Issued by Pope Alexander VI in 1493 Divided discoveries in the known world between Spain and Portugal; laid down the principles followed in the treaty of Tordesillas of 1494.

DEMPSTER, THOMAS

(c. 1579-1625). Scottish classical scholar. Professor in Paris, Pisa, Bologna. Author of autobiography. Also *Historia Ecclesiastica*

Gentis Scotorum: published in Bologna where he spent the better part of his career. He published several works of classical scholarship and others on Christian antiquity.

DENCK, HANS

(c. 1495-1528). Anabaptist. Prominent and turbulent figure in the Reformation. Rector of school at Basel: also at Nuremberg. Ejected for preaching Anabaptism. Expelled from other German cities. Died at Basel. Compelled to publish a retraction of his radical theological ideas on, e.g., predestination, the nature of Christ, the Sacraments.

DE NOVA STELLA

On the new star: book published in 1573, by the astronomer Tycho Brahe. He sighted the new star in Cassiopeia on November 11, 1572.

DEPOSITION, BULLS OF

One issued by Pope Paul III, excommunicating King Henry VIII in 1535. Second bull issued by Pope Pius V, in 1570 excommunicating Queen Elizabeth I. As a papal weapon, it dates from the eleventh century.

DE ROSSI, VICENZO

(1525-1587). Italian sculptor. He worked principally in Florence, *Samson and the Philistine* for the main door of the Palazzo Vecchio, a *Vulcan* and a *Dying Adonis,* which is also attributed to Michelangelo. His work is mannerist and pompous.

DESIDERIO DA SETTIGNANO

(1428-1464). Italian sculptor of Florence. Pupil of Donatello. Executed tombs, decorative sculpture, busts. His masterpiece is the tomb of the humanist Carlo Marsuppini. Noted for his fineness of line and a characteristic charm and buoyancy.

DE SOTO, HERNANDO

(c. 1498-1542). Spanish explorer of North America. He had been a lieutenant of Pedrarias and of Pizarro; made governor of Cuba by Charles V. Set out on expedition to conquer Florida: explored for three years, in search of gold. Discovered Mississippi River in 1541. Died on banks of river.

DES PÉRIERS, BONAVENTURE

(c. 1500-1544). French humanist writer. Attached to the court of Margaret of Navarre. Author of *Cymbalum Mundi*: appeared in 1537. Dialogue satirizing contemporary religious mores and exhibiting a good deal of religious skepticism which was not, however, unique in Margaret's circle. Also wrote short stories. Reputedly committed suicide.

DES PORTES, PHILIPPES, ABBÉ DE THIRON

(1546-1606) French poet. Educated in Italy. Wrote amatory pieces, satires, religious poems. Collected works published in 1611. Favorite of Charles IX and Henry III, made his peace after some hesitation with Henry IV; was very popular in his day.

DES RUES, FRANÇOIS

(1575-1633). Author of popular historical works, e.g., on the French Marguerites and on the great cities of Europe.

D'ESTE, BEATRICE

(1475-1497) Duchess of Milan, as wife of Ludovico il Moro. Noted for her beauty, diplomatic and political skill, taste and patronage of the arts. The court of her family at Ferrara was culturally one of the most enlightened and advanced in Italy.

D'ESTE, ISABELLA

(1474-1539). Sister of the above, married Francisco Gonzaga of Mantua; she had all the gifts for diplomacy and statecraft, the capacity for intelligent patronage and keen judgment of the arts of her sister; she also was a great beauty—her portraits were done by Leonardo and Titian.

DEVAY, MÁTYÁS BIRÓ

(c. 1500-c. 1545). Hungarian Catholic priest. Accepted Reformation. Founded Reformed Church of Hungary following the doctrine of Luther. He was protected, patronized and financed by Count Nadasdy and thus able to establish the first printing press in Hungary. He thus published many of his own writings and a Hungarian translation of the New Testament.

DEVOTIO MODERNA

This term denotes a religious movement in the Netherlands and Rhine valley of the late fourteenth and fifteenth centuries; a similar movement, although it represented less of a departure from traditional religious forms, appeared in northern France.

Exemplified best by the lay Brothers of the Common Life and Augustinian Canons of Windesheim. Although it remained within the traditional ecclesiastical framework and won the approval and blessing of popes, the *devotio moderna* represents a considerable shift of emphasis away from the older forms of piety. Its followers sought a direct and personal relationship with God through mystical contemplation, the attainment of an informed piety through learning. It looked more to a knowledge of the sacred texts and the Christian classics (having somewhat of the same concern for purified and corrected texts and the copying of manuscripts as the humanists) than to the performance of ritual ceremony and the offices of the clergy. The Brothers' concern for an informed piety was a fillip to education; their schools, especially Deventer and Zwolle, were famous; among their pupils were Erasmus, Nicholas of Cusa, and Agricola, (died 1485). Although the *devotio moderna* is important for understanding the acceptance of Italian humanism north of the Alps, since, e.g., it utilized the classical authors as the basis for its curriculum, it should be remembered that the spirit of the movement was Christian rather than classical and that in many respects it was antithetical to Italian humanism. *The Imitation of Christ* contains the quintessence of the *devotio moderna*.

DIANE DE POITIERS
(1499-1566). Mistress of Henry II of France. Exerted great influence on governmental policies.

DIAZ, BARTOLOMEU
(c. 1450-1500). Portuguese explorer. Sailed round Africa. Discovered Table Mountain and cape named by King John II of Portugal Cape of Good Hope, in 1487-1488. First to open route to the Orient. On expedition to Brazil with Cabral. Died during storm.

DIAZ DEL CASTILLO, BERNAL
(1492-1581). Spanish conquistador. Member of influential family. Came to America in 1514: participated in expeditions of conquest. Served in Darien, Cuba, Yucatan, and with Cortés in Mexico. Diaz wrote his *Historia verdadera de la conquista de la nueva España*, written from the professional soldier's viewpoint, to exonerate Cortés from slurs on his character and leadership.

191

Diaz was over eighty when he wrote, the last survivor of Cōrtés' expedition.

DIGGES, LEONARD
(died c. 1571). English mathematician. Reputedly one of the inventors of the telescope. He wrote three treatises on geometry and its application to military problems.

DIGGES, THOMAS
(died 1595). English mathematician, son of the above. Wrote on mathematical and engineering subjects, as well as astronomy.

DINOTHUS, RICHARDUS
(died c. 1590). French Calvinist historian. Described historical mysteries, prodigies, and oddities as well as personalities and battle scenes in his histories of the French civil and religious wars and of the rise of Henry IV.

DIOGO DO COUTO
(1542-1616). Portuguese chronicler. In military service in India. Wrote an account of Portuguese discoveries in India: appeared in 1602.

DIONYSIUS DE LEUWIS THE CARTHUSIAN
(1402-1471). Called The Ecstatic Doctor. Prolific Flemish theologian, philosopher, exegete. He was associated briefly with Nicholas of Cusa; some of his works were later placed upon the Index.

DISSOLUTION OF MONASTERIES
In England. Under orders of Henry VIII, Thomas Cromwell was the instrument of dissolution. Monks owned eighth of cultivated land in England. Cromwell, visiting barely a third of the monasteries, reported that they were licentious and corrupt. By Act of 1536, smaller monasteries were dissolved. Act of 1539 dissolved the larger ones.

DIU, BATTLE OF
In this battle, in 1509, the Portuguese, under Francisco de Almeida, destroyed the Moslem fleet, clearing the way for the Portuguese ascendancy in the Indian Ocean.

DJEM, PRINCE
Brother of the Turkish Sultan Bayazid II and prisoner of the

papacy; captured in battle and turned over to Pope Innocent VIII, who tried to use him as a diplomatic counter to bring pressure to bear on the most feared enemy of Christendom. The Sultan feared Djem as a rival and sought to have him put to death. Nothing came of the efforts of either side and Djem eventually died in prison.

DLUGOSZ, JAN, LONGINUS
(1415-1480). Polish historian. Wrote voluminous *Historia Polonica*, detailed and accurate.

DODOENS, REMBERT
(1517-1585). Latinized name, Rembertus Dodonaeus. Flemish herbalist and botanist. Wrote *Cruydeboek*: published in 1554. Treats indigenous and foreign plants.

DOLCE, LODOVICO
(1506-1568) Venetian scholar. He produced translations, commentaries, imitations and plagiarisms of Greek and Roman classics, most notably Vergil, Catullus, Ovid and Cicero. He was a follower of Bembo in matters of style; he entered the quarrel over the use of the vulgar tongue in his *Osservazioni sulla volgar lingua*, where he takes the Bembist position that Italian did have literary uses proper to it. He also wrote a great number of miscellaneous works that are of little value, e.g., on precious stones.

DOLET, ÉTIENNE
(1509-1546?) French humanist, philologist, scholar and printer. Author of *Commentarii Linguae Latinae*, which he printed in his own shop; his printing of a French version of the Bible and of heretical works brought his condemnation as a heretic and his execution.

DOLZ, JOHANNES
(Early sixteenth century). Spanish writer and logician. Pupil of Caspar Lax. Author of *Termini*: a commentary on the first tractate of Petrus Hispanus: published in Paris c. 1510. He was rector of the Lexoniense College of Paris, where he spent most of his life and wrote his numerous works on logic and related fields.

193

DOMENICO VEZIANO

(c. 1400-1461) Florentine painter. Very few of his works survive; noted for the superb use of colors.

DOMINICUS DE FLANDRIA

(died 1500). Logician. Thomist. Wrote a commentary on Aristotelian logic.

DOMINIS, MARC ANTONIO DE

(1566-1624). Italian prelate, Jesuit, Archbishop. Became Anglican; recanted. Imprisoned by Inquisition. Relapsed and reimprisoned, where he died. Wrote on optics. Also *De Republica Ecclesiastica contra Primatum Papal*. He was well received in England by James I and published there an English translation of the *History of the Council of Trent* by his friend Paolo Sarpi.

DONATELLO, DONATO DI NICCOLÒ

(c. 1386-1466) Greatest Italian sculptor of the early Renaissance. Noted for a radical realism and austerity, he was a profound student of classical art and this had a softening and restraining effect on his art. Some of his best-known works were the *St. George, David* and the equestrian statue of the condottiere, *Gattamelata*.

DONI, ANTONIO FRANCISCO

(c. 1513-1574). Italian writer of Florence. Led an adventurous, roving life. His *Libreria* identified all the printed musical books of his age.

DONI, GIOVANNI BATTISTA

(1593-1647). Italian scholar who specialized in ancient music, on which he published a learned treatise. Invented a double lyre or "amphicord". In the papal service at Rome until he went to Florence to teach.

DORBELLUS, NICOLAUS or NICHOLAS DE ORBELLIS

(died 1455). French author of *Logicae Brevis Expositio*. The epithet DORBEL for a logic-mongering pedant and dry scholar in the Scholastic mold derives from him, a professor at Poitier of Scholastic philosophy. Similarly DUNCE derives from DUNS SCOTUS. Scholasticism was a prime target of the humanists.

DORCHESTER GRAMMAR SCHOOL

English public school. Refounded and endowed by Thomas Hardye in 1569.

DORIA, ANDREA

(1468-1560) Genoese admiral and ruler. He was descended of an ancient merchant family that had been prominent in Genoa's political life and in its acquisition of a maritime empire. He had been a condottiere in the service of Francis I of France; his desertion of the defeated Francis for the triumphant Emperor Charles V in 1528 enabled Doria to rule Genoa as a despot. He placed the fleet at the Emperor's disposal in the African wars, and, with the backing of his ally, mercilessly suppressed his political opponents. He recovered Corsica for his city in 1559 with the help of France, having once again deserted his ally.

D'ORLÉANS, LOUIS

(1542-1629) French advocate general, poet, jurist. He was the author of numerous works, many of them *recherché*; among them were juridical works, fanciful poetry, religious apology and panegyrics on behalf of Henry IV.

DORP, JOHANNES

Late fifteenth century Dutch logician. Author of *Summula Buridani* published in Leyden in 1510. He was one of the last of the Scholastic philosophers.

DORPIUS, MARTEN

(1480-1525) Dutch humanist scholar. A critic of Erasmus' Christian humanism and of his *Praise of Folly;* they were, however, reconciled to each other and Erasmus wrote Dorpius' epitaph. He was a professor of rhetoric and philosophy at Louvain, wrote a defense of Aristotelianism and a *Dialogue between Venus and Cupid.*

DOSSO, DOSSI GIOVANNI

(c. 1479-1542). Painter. Influenced by Georgione, Titian, Raphael. Imaginative and important painter of Renaissance school of Ferrara where he executed many of the works decorating the ducal palace. He was a friend of Ariosto. His brother, BATTISTA (died 1548) was also a painter.

DOTTORI, CARLO

(1618-1685). Author of mock heroic poem entitled *The Donkey*:

published in 1652, and numerous poems, dramas, and melo-dramas, and one tragedy, *Aristodemo*.

DOUAI BIBLE
First English Catholic translation: published in 1609-1610, pre-pared by the college established there for training English priests by Philip II of Spain.

DOUFFET, GERARD
(1594-1660). Dutch painter. Pupil of Rubens, but he had also studied in Rome, Venice and Naples. He painted religious as well as historical and mythological scenes, and also portraits.

DOUGLAS, DAVID
Sixteenth century. Scottish scholar. Author of *De Naturae Mira-bilibus Opusculum*, published in 1524. A treatise on meteorology and natural phenomena.

DOUGLAS, GAWAIN
(c. 1474-1522). Scottish poet and prelate. Dean of St. Giles, Edinburgh. Attached to Scottish court. Imprisoned, released. Subject of political and religious dissension in regard to prefer-ment. Author of *Palace of Honor, King Hart*, two allegories. Translated *Aeneid*. Also Ovid's *Remedia Amoris*.

DOURADO, FERNANDO VAZ
(born in 1520). Portuguese cartographer. Produced charts of the Indian Ocean, after extensive traveling in the East. His world atlases appeared in 1568 and 1571.

DOUSA, JANUS
(1545-1604) Dutch scholar, historian and general. Organized League of Beggars to oppose Philip II of Spain. Author of several historical works on the Lowlands, the Revolt from Spain, as well as commentaries upon Horace, Catullus, Juvenal and other Latin authors of antiquity, satirical poems and epigrams. He was a man of boundless energy and vast erudition.

DOVIZI, BERNARDO
(1470-1520). Man of letters, diplomat, made a cardinal by Pope Leo X, he had long been in the service of the Medici. On mis-sion to France. Author of a comedy entitled *Calandria*: highly popular, it was based on Plautus' *Menaechmi*. Portrait by Raphael.

DOWNES, ANDREW

(c. 1549-1628). English classical scholar, Regius Professor of Greek at Cambridge. Published lectures on Demosthenes, Lysias. Collaborated in revision of Authorized Version of Bible.

DRAKE, SIR FRANCIS

(1540-1596). Great Elizabethan seaman. Made expeditions to the Gulf of Mexico, West Indies. First English navigator to see the Pacific Ocean. Explored the Strait of Magellan. Reached the coast of California. Expeditions associated with plundering Spanish, on land and sea. After successfully and repeatedly attacking Spanish shipping, he sailed from Plymouth, in 1577, with five small ships, across the Atlantic Ocean and around Cape Horn. Reduced to three ships, Drake experienced many losses: one ship foundered: the other returned to England. Drake, however, continued in the *Golden Hind,* took much plunder at Valparaiso, reached the Golden Gate, struck across the Pacific, and via the Cape of Good Hope returned to England in 1580. The following year he was knighted. He raided Cartagena, destroyed the Spanish fleet in Cadiz harbor, and helped to defeat the Armada in 1588. In 1595 he sailed with Hawkins against the Spanish Main. Hawkins died off Puerto Rico. Drake died aboard ship of dysentery, off Portobello. Introduced to England the potato, and tobacco smoking equipment. He corresponds to a heroic type similar to that of the *hidalgo* of Spain, there being very little in him, except his zest, to identify him as a figure of the Renaissance.

DRAYTON, MICHAEL

(c. 1563-1631). English poet. Attached to court. Prolific writer. Author of sonnets; *The Shepherd's Garland*; odes; *Polyalbion*; a poetical gazetteer of all England; *The Harmony of the Church*; sacred poem; *Mortimeriades*.

DREBBELL, CORNELIUS

(1572-1634). Dutch inventor of special type of thermometer; he experimented with a primitive submarine and many more similar matters.

DRESSER, MATTHAEUS

(1536-1607). Professor of history and classical philology at the University of Leipzig. Author of *Explicatio Pia et Historica*: published in 1593. Contains a warning against danger from the Ottoman Empire.

He wrote historical works on Saxony and continued the *History of Saxony* begun by Fabricio. He had been a student of Luther and Melanchthon at Wittenberg, and he wrote from the Lutheran point of view.

DREUX, JEHAN
Late fifteenth-century Flemish miniaturist and illuminator who worked for dukes of Burgundy. There are many variants in the spelling of his name.

DREXELIO, JEREMIAH
(1581-1638) Jesuit of Augsburg. Professor of humanities and rhetoric. Prolific author. Court preacher to Elector of Bavaria. He wrote on many subjects, e.g., astrology, Hermes Trismegismus and devotional works.

DRINGENBERG, LEWIS
(Died 1490) German scholar of Westphalia. Rector and founder of influential school at Schlettstadt. He had been educated at Deventer in the spirit of the *devotio moderna,* and that spirit showed itself in his new school.

DRIVÈRE, JEREMIAS
(1504-1554) Belgian physician and philosopher, associated with the University of Louvain; he wrote numerous works on medicine which range from commentaries on Galen and Hippocrates to highly specialized studies of human maladies.

DROESHOUT, MARTIN
Sixteenth century. Flemish engraver. Noted for portrait of Shakespeare, an inferior work, but contemporary.

DRUMMOUND, WILLIAM OF HAWTHORNDEN
(1585-1649). Scottish poet. Associated with Ben Jonson. Imitated *la Pléiade;* and Italian and Spanish poets. Author of *Forth Festing:* address to James VI of Scotland. Produced elegies, sonnets, madrigals. Also prose tract, *Cypress Grove,* on death, and a history of Scotland from 1423 to 1542.

DRYANDER, FRANCISCO DE
The Anglicization of Francisco de ENCINAS, q.v.

DUAREN, FRANCISCUS

(1509-1559). French historical jurist of the school of Alciatus; he taught many years at Bourges where he was the colleague of Cujas. He wrote various commentaries and treatises on the *Digest* and *Codex* of the *Corpus Juris Civilis*. He expounded his method for legal study and analysis in *De ratione docende discendique iuris.*

DU BELLAY, GUILLAUME

(1491-1543). French statesman and general. On missions to England. Governor in Italy. Author of allegorical poem entitled *Peregrinatio Humana.*

DU BELLAY, JEAN

(1492-1560) Humanist prelate and patron of his nephew Joachim.

DU BELLAY, JOACHIM

(1522-1560). French poet, nephew of the above. Called Prince of the Sonnet. Also known as The French Ovid. Member of *La Pléiade.* Author of lyrics, *Divers Poèmes,* and especially sonnets, particularly volume entitled *Les Antiquités de Rome.* Also wrote *Xenia, Amores.* He wrote the manifesto of *La Pléiade* circle in his *Defense of the French Tongue.*

DUCCIO, AGOSTINO DI

(1418-1481?). Italian sculptor. Belongs in school of Donatello. Sculptured reliefs for the tombs and temple of the Malatesta at Rimini.

DU CHALARD, JOACHIM

(died c. 1562). French jurist of Limousin. Wrote survey and commentary on French laws that has reference to the reign of Charles IX; he called himself a "republican" and was the protagonist of a constitutional system.

DUCHESNE, JEAN

Translator. In 1474 translated into French Caesar's *De Bello Gallico.* Illuminated copies are preserved in Bodleian Library and in British Museum.

DUCHESNE, JOSEPH, SEIGNEUR DE LA VIOLETTE

(c. 1544-1609). Latinized name—Quercetanus. French Paracelsan.

Physician to Henry IV of France. Author of *De Materia Verae Medicinae Philosophorum Priscorum* and other works on medicine as well as a volume of French verse. He was a pioneer in the application of chemistry to medicine (it would seem to have been as much alchemy as chemistry); he had been much in Germany, where iatrochemistry dated from Paracelsus' time.

DU CHOUL, GUILLAUME
(Sixteenth century) French archaeologist and antiquarian. Interested in Roman antiquities, in France and Italy. His life-long study resulted in two books: one on Roman religion, the other on military science. He had gone to Italy to study the methods of archaeology; many of the sources for his two books were coins, inscriptions, etc. which he himself discovered in France.

DUFAY, GUILLAUME
(c. 1400-1474) Flemish composer and priest, chief founder of the polyphonic school of the Netherlands. He served Philip the Good, Duke of Burgundy as musical tutor to his son, Charles the Rash; he also spent many years in Italy, especially as a chorister of the papal chapel. Composed songs, motets, masses.

DUIVEKE
"Little Dove." The Dutch mistress of Christian II (1513-1523), King of Denmark. Daughter of Sigbrit Willems, she exercised great influence over the king.

DULLAERT, JOHANNES
(c. 1471-1518). Scholastic philosopher and logician of Ghent. Pupil of Johannes Majoris. Author of *Quaestiones:* published in Paris in 1506, and a work of Aristotelian commentary, 1509. He is thought to have been the teacher of the Spanish humanist Vives.

DULWICH COLLEGE
English public school. Founded as the College of God's Gift by Edward Alleyne (1566-1626), actor-manager, contemporary of Shakespeare.

DU MOULIN, CHARLES
(1500-1566). French Renaissance jurist. A Calvinist, he wrote on usury urging that, in keeping with divine law, it be moderate. He also wrote on contracts.

DUNBAR, WILLIAM
(1465?-1536?). Scottish poet. Franciscan friar. At court of James IV of Scotland. On diplomatic missions. Author of *The Two Maryit Wemen and the Wedo*: satire on woman, Chaucerian in style. *The Friars of Berwick*: a poetic version of a fabliau: also in Chaucerian tone. *The Golden Targe*. *The Flyting of Dunbar and Kennedy*. *Dance of the Seven Deadly Sins*. *The Thistle and the Rose*. Also many minor pieces. Declared to be the greatest Scots poet after Robert Burns.

DUPLESSIS-MORNAY, PHILIPPE
(1549-1623) Huguenot statesman. For his energetic leadership of the Calvinist cause in Europe for half a century he was called the Pope of the Huguenots. He was the friend and ally of Coligny and, after Coligny's murder in 1572, of Henry of Navarre (Henry IV); he also aided the Dutch and William of Orange against Spain. He is sometimes credited with the authorship of the *Vindiciae contra Tyrannos*: published in 1579, one of the most uncompromising indictments of tyranny—an invocation of the right of revolution.

DUPRAT, ANTOINE
(1463-1535). French Cardinal and statesman. Chancellor of France under Francis I. Candidate for Papacy. In his exaltation of the royal prerogative he anticipated the views of Cardinals Richelieu and Mazarin.

DU PRÉ, CLAUDE
(1550-1620). Lyonese jurist. Wrote treatise on French tribal origins: Celts and Gauls, national emergence of France. Published in 1601. He also wrote a dialogue on war which is typical of many humanist pleas for an end of Armageddon and the inauguration of the era of perpetual peace.

DUQUESNOY, FRANÇOIS or FRANÇOIS FLAMAND
(1594-1643) Flemish sculptor. Executed tombs, large ecclesiastical sculptures, statues of children. He worked much in Rome and in a style suggestive of Bernini.

DU QUESNOY, JEROME, THE ELDER
(1570-1641) Flemish sculptor, father of the above and JEROME THE YOUNGER, also a sculptor. His patron was the Duke of Brabant; his decoration of the ducal palace featured classical

motifs and was typified by the nymphs of the great fountain in the courtyard.

DURAND DE VILLEGAGNON, NICHOLAS
(1510-1571) French mariner and soldier. Leader of French Huguenots who sought to colonize Brazil in 1556. The colony fell to the Portuguese. Durand wrote an account of the venture as well as a work on theology.

DÜRER, ALBRECHT
(1471-1528). German artist, engraver of Nuremberg. He became a Lutheran. Leader of Renaissance painting in Germany; he had made two decisive trips to Italy, 1494, 1505. Court painter to Maximilian I and Charles V. Considered inventor of etching. Among his woodcuts are: *The Greater Passion, The Lesser Passion, The Apocalypse.* His paintings include: *Adam and Eve, Adoration of the Trinity.* He was an important theorist of the arts and student of anatomy and perspective; he argued that the great artist must theorize as well as practice, that only when theory and practice interpenetrate each other will great art be produced.

DURHAM SCHOOL
English public school. Reconstructed in 1414 by Cardinal Thomas Langley and again by Henry VIII in 1541.

DUTCH WAR OF INDEPENDENCE or DUTCH REVOLT
(1578-1648). In the Netherlands, Calvinism had become the religion in the Northern Provinces, while the South adhered to Catholicism. Philip II became simultaneously King of Spain in 1556 and ruler of the Netherlands. His tax policy, Spanish garrisons, fear of the introduction of the Inquisition led the Dutch nobles to form a protective league. Three hundred nobles presented a petition for the redress of grievances and assurance of security. The expression Beggars was first used in connection with this petition. Among the lower classes, revolt against the Spanish broke out. Some Dutch nobles, Count Egmont and William of Orange among them, deprecated these popular demonstrations, but they were overruled.

In 1567 Philip sent the Duke of Alva, with 20,000 troops, to the Netherlands. His policy was to be repressive and ruthless against all who resisted the royal authority. William of Orange and many

Hollanders left their country. Margaret of Parma, the Regent, resigned as a protest. Alva, however, held a Council of Blood. Count Egmont, a Flemish general, and Count Horn, a Flemish statesman, were executed.

War broke out between the Netherlands and Spain. William of Orange and his brother Louis invaded the Netherlands to aid the rebels. Insurrection spread. Alva was recalled in 1573. Antwerp was sacked in 1576 by the Spanish.

The Pacification of Ghent, negotiated in 1576, united all the provinces against the Spaniards. The Governor, Alexander Farnese, subdued the Southern Provinces, restoring political liberties. Seven Northern Provinces formed the Union of Utrecht, in 1579. Independence was proclaimed in 1581.

William of Orange was murdered in 1584. His son Maurice continued resistance until the Republic of the United Provinces and Spain negotiated a twelve-year truce in 1609. The treaty of Westphalia acknowledged the independence of the Republic of the United Provinces, in 1648. It is the first of the modern revolutionary upheavals, the first of the modern wars of independence.

DUVERGIER DE HAURANNE, JEAN

(1581-1643). French theologian. Friend of Cornelis Jansen and one of the builders of Jansenism. He was a theological antagonist of the Jesuits and an enemy of Richelieu who had him imprisoned.

DYCK, ANTHONY VAN

(1599-1641). Flemish Painter. Collaborated with Rubens. Worked in Genoa, Rome, Paris, Antwerp. From 1632, court painter in London, where he painted a famous portrait of Charles I. Executed portraits and religious pieces. His major importance rests in portraiture. Developed the group portrait to high degree of effectiveness. His use of color is superb, extremely sensitive. Founded a national school of portrait painting in England.

DYER, SIR EDWARD

(c. 1545-1607). English diplomat, traveler, courtier, poet. Friend of Sir Philip Sidney and member of Queen Elizabeth's court. Had great contemporary reputation. Known for his poem: *My mind to me a kingdom is.*

E

EBER, PAUL
(1511-1569). German Lutheran theologian and religious controversialist. Author of numerous works on theology and related subjects, e.g., a revised translation of Old Testament and a Biblical history. He taught grammar, philosophy and Greek at Wittenberg.

EBOLI, ANA DE MENDOZA, PRINCESS OF
(1540-1594). Intimate friend of King Philip II of Spain. Beautiful, refined and accomplished, she became involved in an intrigue and was banished from court. Appears in Schiller's drama *Don Carlos.*

EBOLI, RUY GOMEZ DE SILVA, PRINCE OF
(died 1572). Spanish statesman. Favorite of King Philip II of Spain.

ECCIUS DEDOLATUS
A satire that appeared during the Reformation. Attributed to Willibald Pirkheimer (1470-1539).

ECK, JOHANNES
(1486-1543). Taught at University of Ingolstadt. In Reformation history, associated with disputation in Leipzig. Eck represented University of Leipzig, rival of Luther's University of Wittenberg. Leipzig supported absolute claims of papacy, while Wittenberg supported Luther. By pressing Luther, he compelled him to realize for the first time how fundamentally antagonistic his views were to those of the Church; Eck was notorious for wish-

ing to see Luther excommunicated. Also wrote a treatise on logic: *Elementarius Dialecticae*: published in 1517.

ÉCOLE DES BEAUX ARTS
Endowed school of fine arts, Paris. Founded in 1648.

ÉCORCHEURS
In France, the *écorcheurs*, or scratchers, were armed bands that ravaged the country under Charles VI (1380-1422) and Charles VII (1422-1461) during the Hundred Years' War.

EDELS, SAMUED ELIEZER
(1551-1631). Jewish Talmudic scholar of Posen. He is associated with a new method for the study of the Talmud that featured the analysis of passages which seemed to be inconsistent with the work as a whole. He was also learned in philosophy and astronomy.

EDEN, RICHARD
(c. 1521-1577). English scholar, scientist. Wrote on exploration. Author of *The History of Travel in the West and East Indies*: published in 1555. His endeavor to bring together geographical and navigational knowledge in historical accounts and to translate and publish the works of others was similar to the effort of Hakluyt, and in some respects superior to the later worker in the field.

EDER, GEORG
(1524-1586). German Catholic theologian. Orator. Prolific writer. Author of *Oeconomia Bibliorum*: published in Cologne in 1571. He was an adviser of Emperor Ferdinand I, rector of the University of Vienna and a prolific author of religious polemics.

EDINBURGH UNIVERSITY
Founded in 1583.

EDWARD IV
(1442-1483). King of England. Exiled from England by Lancastrian Henry VI. Defeated Lancastrians in 1460. Crowned in 1461. Driven from throne: replaced by Henry VI, 1471. Returned to England: regained throne. Autocratic ruler. Patron of cultural, commercial activities; his rule resembles very closely that of the Tudors, especially was this true of the instruments of government that made the royal will effective throughout the realm.

EDWARD V

(1470-1483). King of England. Seized by uncle, Duke of Gloucester, and thrown into Tower of London. Deposed. Murdered in Tower. Gloucester became King as Richard III. He and his younger brother Richard were the celebrated "princes in the tower".

EDWARD VI

(1537-1553). King of England. Educated under Roger Ascham. Under the influence of his uncle, the Duke of Somerset and John Dudley, Duke of Northumberland, signed edict making Lady Jane Grey, husband of Northumberland's son, successor. The two Books of Common Prayer—largely the work of Cranmer—date from the period. His reign was the age of radical Protestantism in England, when Continental influences were paramount.

EDWARDS, RICHARD

(c. 1523-1566). English dramatist. Musician. Choir-master of Chapel Royal. Author of a play called *Damon and Pythias;* with music, it anticipates the operatic form. Also wrote *The Paradise of Dainty Devices.*

EGILSSON, JÓN

(1548-1634). Icelandic clergyman. Wrote annals of the bishops of Skálholt, a pioneer work for the history and culture of Iceland.

EGMONT, LAMORAL, COUNT OF

(1522-1568). Dutch statesman, general. Served in France and Spain. Opposed Spaniards in the Netherlands. Achieved victories over the French at St. Quentin and Gravelines. Allied himself with William of Orange, the Silent, to oppose the policies of the Duke of Alva. On mission to Spain, was arrested and condemned to death by the Council of Blood: executed, along with Count Horn. Their deaths helped provoke the revolt in the Netherlands. Egmont's tragedy is the theme of Goethe's drama *Egmont* (1788); his career and the Dutch Revolt inspired Beethoven's opera *Fidelio.*

EGNATIUS, JOHANNES BAPTISTA or GIAMBATTISTA CIPELLI

(1473-1553). Venetian humanist, orator, and scholar. Member of Aldine Academy. Editor and commentator of *Historiae Augustae Scriptores,* 1519. Professor of rhetoric and letters, author of numerous works: orations, poems, polemic, history, letters, etc.

ELECTORS OF THE PALATINATE
Frederick I (1425-1476): The Victorious.

Frederick II (1482-1556): The Wise. In conflict with the Turks, the Protector of Luther.

Frederick III (1515-1576): The Pious. Calvinist.

Frederick IV (1574-1610). The Upright. Lutheran.

Frederick V (1596-1632): "The Winter King." In exile, son-in-law of James I of England.

EL GRECO
See GRECO, EL.

ELIA, ANTONIO
Sixteenth century. Italian sculptor. Attached to Cardinal Hippolytus d'Este, Ambassador in Hungary. Executed a *Laocoön* in bronze.

ELIAE, PAULUS or POUL HELGESEN
(c. 1480-1523). Danish humanist, a leading figure of his generation in Denmark. Taught at University of Copenhagen. Sponsored by King Christian of Denmark (1513-1523). He played a leading role in the establishment of Lutheranism in his country; he wrote numerous works, among them a history of Denmark.

ELIJAH DI NOLA
Sixteenth century. Rabbi. Scholar. Lived in Rome.

ELIOT, SIR JOHN
(1592-1632). English statesman. In political controversy, antagonistic to king. He was the most important figure in the struggle with Charles I that ended with the Petition of Right of 1628. Confined to Tower. Author of a philosophical treatise entitled *The Monarchy of Man,* an exposition of his conception of constitutional monarchy. As a member of the gentry he may be said to typify the class that constituted the most formidable enemy of the Stuart monarchy.

ELIZABETH
(1602-1644). Queen of Spain. Wife of Philip IV. Daughter of Henry IV of France. Also known as Isabel.

ELIZABETH I
(1533-1603). Queen of England and Ireland. She studied under

exponents of the New Learning and the Reformation. In 1559 she decreed the English litany in Churches. Aided Protestants in Scotland, France, Netherlands. Promulgated Thirty-Nine Articles in 1563. Imprisoned her rival, Mary Queen of Scots, and signed her death warrant in 1587. One result was a Spanish attempt to invade England, in 1588. Elizabeth had many favorites, in succession. One of them, the Earl of Leicester, died in 1588. The Earl of Essex, another favorite, as Governor-General of Ireland, was unsuccessful in crushing revolt of the Earl of Tyrone. In 1601 Essex, attempting a revolt against the Queen, was executed; the motives for his treason have never been made clear.

Elizabeth, in her own person, was energetic and opportunistic. There was a streak of cruelty in her and insincerity, yet she was highly popular among her subjects, and her reign is associated with vast achievements in the arts and in exploration, in drama and science. Her secretaries and councilors served her long, faithfully and well; she had no need to execute any of them as her father had executed his. Her diplomatic skill, her *politique's* instinct for avoiding ultimate questions, went far to avoid civil war in England comparable to that which raged in France and also to keep England from being drawn irrevocably into the vortex of religious wars on the Continent.

ELIZABETHAN AGE
The reign of Queen Elizabeth I of England—from 1558 to 1603—coincides with great expansion in English life. A passion for the ancient Greek and Roman classics pervaded the intellectual level, while in other directions there manifested themselves a lust for discovery and adventure, a craving for beauty, and a longing for boundless self-expression. England had by this time reached the first rank as a nation. Her population had increased. Her economy flourished. The navy began to rival that of the Dutch. It was altogether fitting that the Queen should preside over this great cultural age, when the Renaissance in England reached its culmination, after its earlier promise had been unfulfilled in the reigns of Henry VIII, Edward VI and Mary.

ELIZABETH COLLEGE
In Guernsey, Channel Islands. Public school founded by Queen Elizabeth I: 1563.

ELIZABETH OF VALOIS

(1545-1568). Daughter of Henry II of France. Wife of Philip II of Spain. She had been destined to marry the ill-fated Don Carlos, heir to the throne, but married his father instead. Much legend grew up about her and she inspired works by Schiller, Alfieri, Verdi, and others.

ELPHINSTONE, WILLIAM

(1431-1514). Scottish bishop, diplomat, university official. He was educated at Glasgow and was for some time at Paris. Supported friendship with England. Instrumental in introducing printing press in Scotland. Founded Aberdeen University: 1506.

ELSHEIMER, ADAM

(1578-1610). German painter. Died in Rome. Small-scale landscapes, with mythological or religious figures and much atmosphere: moonlight and artificial light effects. Leading artist of early German Baroque movement. His paintings were small and minutely finished and detailed; he had gone to Rome early in his career to study the great Italian masters, but he did not follow them closely.

ELSTRACKE, REGINALD

(c. 1590-1630). Flemish engraver. Worked in England and chiefly for booksellers. Executed portraits of kings, nobles, royal secretaries, etc. of England and Scotland.

ELYE, ELIAS

(c. 1400-c. 1475). Swiss scholar and humanist; he introduced the printing press into Switzerland.

ELYOT, SIR THOMAS

(c. 1490-1546). English diplomat, writer. Ambassador to Emperor Charles V. Author of *The Boke of the Gouvernour,* published in 1531: on the education of princes, which shows the influence of Erasmus and the humanist ideal of the philosophic prince. Translated Isocrates, Plato, Eucolpius on *The Image of Governance,* and portions of Church Fathers. Wrote *Castle of Health*: medical text based on Galen and the ancient medical corpus. Compiled first Latin-English dictionary, 1538.

ELZEVIR

Family of Dutch publishers of the classics, noted for the beauty of their typography. Founded by Louis I (c. 1540-1617) at Leyden. Elzevir type named after family. The family business flourished until about 1680.

EMANUEL I

(1469-1521). King of Portugal, 1495. Called The Great, The Fortunate. Prepared code of laws. Patron of arts and science. Encouraged exploration and navigation, which had lapsed somewhat following the death of Prince Henry the Navigator, 1463.

EMANUEL SCHOOL

English public school. Founded by will of Anne Sackville, wife of Gregory Fiennes, Lord Dacre of the South: 1595.

EMBLEM

The emblem is an allegorical or symbolical device designed pictorially to convey an abstract concept. The vogue of emblems arose during the Renaissance, as a consequence of the prevalent preoccupation with hieroglyphics. A famous work was the *Hieroglyphica* of Harapollon; published by Aldus in 1505, it had circulated in manuscript form since 1419. It purported to be a Greek translation of an ancient Egyptian work: it was a highly fanciful and imaginative description of the intriguing hieroglyphic signs—animals, geometric symbols, etc. The humanists, e.g., Ficino and Pico, thought that ancient wisdom and love were expressed in these symbolic characters and thus they sought to unlock the secrets. There appeared many explanatory manuals called Books of Emblems. The interest was also a fillip to painting and other arts, and a knowledge of emblems is an important key to the study of Renaissance art, e.g., of Dürer's engraving of the Emperor Maximilian surrounded by emblematic animals.

EMILIO, PAOLO, OF VERONA

(c. 1460-1520). Italian humanist, he came to the University of Paris and became official historian to the French court. His humanist history of France, 1517, treats the legends of Trojan origins of the French, etc., in the critical manner of Polydore Vergil's history of England. He is an important bridge between Renaissance Italy and France.

EMMANUEL-PHILIBERT

(1525-1580). Duke of Savoy. Tête de Fer. Attached to the court of Charles V and then of Philip II. Commanded Emperor's forces. Gained victory over French at Battle of St. Quentin, in 1557, and also fought at Lepanto. Husband of Marguerite of Valois.

EMPSON, SIR RICHARD
(Died 1510). In the service of Henry VII, in the field of taxation. With Dudley he had an unsavory reputation for extortionate methods of tax collection; as a popular gesture Henry VIII had both of them executed.

ENCINA, JUAN DEL
(1468-1529). Spanish musician, dramatist, poet. Earliest important dramatic writer in history of Spanish theatre. Called *patriarca del teatro español.* Educated at Salamanca, became musical composer, attached to Duke of Alva: 1492. Inspired by Vergil's *Eclogues,* he wrote and composed *Eglogas*: pastoral-religious plays, which make use of singing and dancing, 1492. Cantor in Chapel of Pope Leo X at Rome. Ordained priest in 1519. He was active mostly in Rome, the great center for music during the Renaissance; his combining of music with drama is suggestive of the development of opera, which did not emerge, however, until c. 1600.

ENCINAS, FRANCISCO, DRYANDER
(1520-1552). Spanish Lutheran. He went to Wittenberg c. 1541 and became a trusted friend of Luther and Melanchthon. He translated the New Testament into Spanish; presenting it to the Emperor Charles V, he was imprisoned for his pains but managed to escape after a year. His brother Juan was burnt at the stake as a heretic in Rome, 1545.

ENCISCO, MARTIN FERNÁNDEZ DE
(c. 1470-1528). Spanish geographer. Settled in Santo Domingo. Founded Santa Maria, in Darien, in 1510. Wrote a geographical account of the Spanish New World, *Suma de Geografia,* 1519.

ENCOMIENDAS
The basic agricultural unit on estates organized by the Spanish in the New World; it resembles the medieval manor. Native villages were grouped under agents who looked after the religious and economic interests of the community and saw to it that labor services, etc., were rendered by the natives.

212

ENGELBRECHTSZ, CORNELIS
(1468-1533). Dutch painter of Leyden. Belongs to the Early Dutch Renaissance school. He did mostly religious subjects and is said to be the first painter of the Lowlands to paint in oil.

ENGELBREKTSSON, OLAF
Archbishop of Norway. As a Catholic, in opposition to King Christian, fled from country in 1537.

ENGLISH ART
Under Henry VII (1485-1509) secular decoration and portraiture came into vogue. The most notable work was that of foreigners, however, together with some minor English artists. Hans Holbein the Younger (1497-1543) was German. Antonio Mor (c. 1512-1575) was Dutch. Marc Gheeraedts the Younger (1561-1635) was Flemish. Daniel Mytens (c. 1590-1642) was Dutch. The most eminent was Anthony Van Dyck (1599-1641). Of native Englishmen, there were Nicholas Hilliard (1537-1619) and William Dobson (1610-1646) and a number of miniaturists, among them Isaac Oliver, John Hoskins, Alexander and Samuel Cooper. Art and culture in England were probably less transformed by Renaissance and Italian influences than was true in any major country of Western Europe. A generation ago English historians urged that the national culture was not touched in any way by Renaissance ideas.

ENRIQUEZ GÓMEZ, ANTONIO
(1602-c.1662). Spanish writer of Jewish origin. Fled to France to escape Inquisition. Wrote various works: political, lyrical, comic, etc.; among them the mystical epic poem entitled *La Culpa del Primer Peregrino*, the satirical romances mixing prose and verse were entitled *El Siglo Pitagórico*, and *El Sansón Nazareno*.

EPIDEMIOLOGY
During the fifteenth and the sixteenth centuries plagues and epidemics ravaged Europe. Among noted epidemiologists who studied conditions in this field were Luigi Mondella, professor at Padua (1462-1536), Johann Heurrnis (1543-1601), Antonio Musa Brassavole (1500-1555), Albertino Bottoni (died 1596), Ercole Sassania (1510-1598).

EPISCOPIUS, NICOLAUS or BISCHOFF

German publisher and editor, he had received a humanist education in philology. He married the daughter of the printer of Basel, Johannes Froben. On the latter's death in 1527 the firm became Froben and Episcopius. He was noted for the publication of the Fathers of the Church, with which he and Erasmus were associated until the latter's death in 1536.

EPISCOPIUS, SIMON

(1583-1643). Dutch theologian. Leader of Arminians or Remonstrants. Promulgated doctrinal theses in his *Institutiones Theologicae*.

EPISTULAE OBSCURORUM VIRORUM

Collection of letters in Latin, by Ulrich von Hutten, Reuchlin, Erasmus, Crotius, Rubienus. Published in 1515 and 1517. Reuchlin was the greatest student of Hebrew of the day.

EQUICOLA, MARIO

(1470-1525). Italian writer and courtier, secretary to Isabella d'Este Gonzaga. Author of treatise on the nature of love, human and divine, survey of history and literature. He also wrote a *Cronica de Mantua*.

ERASMISTAS, ERASMISMO

Erasmus had a far wider following in Spain than anywhere else in Europe; those who espoused his ideal of a reform of letters and piety were known as *erasmistas* and included Juan Luis Vives, Alfonso and Juan de Valdés, and Fray Luis de León. For a while the erasmistas constituted an influential party at the court of Charles V and in the Spanish universities, but with the Counter Reformation and the teachings of St. Ignatius de Loyola, orthodoxy was more narrowly defined and the erasmistas went on the defensive, some of them being forced to flee. They came to be known contemptuously as *alumbrados*, but nevertheless continued to exert some influence as may be seen in the writings of Gil Vicente and Torres Naharrio. The *Enquiridión o Manual del Caballero Cristiano* was translated into Spanish in 1521. In 1559 the works of Erasmus were placed on the Index. After the Jesuit Order was founded in 1534, traces of Erasmian influence continued to appear in mystical writers e.g., Fray Luis de León.

ERASMUS, DESIDERIUS

(1466-1536). The greatest figure of the northern Renaissance, the "Prince of Humanists". He was a many-sided genius, memorable for his satire *In Praise of Folly*, 1509; his editions and translations of the New Testament, numerous classical authors, the Greek and the Latin Fathers, particularly St. Jerome of whom he was especially fond and whom he resembled in several ways; also his Rabelaisian attack on monkish obscurantism and ecclesiastical abuses; his friendships—as revealed in his many letters, those newspapers of the day; and, in his last years, his tilting with Luther. His moderation and restraint, kindliness and sympathy made him ineffective as an antagonist of Luther or as a defender of the Church, to which he clung to the last. The greatest classical scholar of his age, he was above all a Christian. He wished to adapt classical civilization, or elements of it, to the ends and needs of a Christian society, not adopt it as a model for systematic imitation as Italian humanists tended to do. His opposition to Ciceronianism is symptomatic of his attitude toward antiquity and suggestive of his educational ideal. He demonstrated that the pagan Greek influence on Christianity was profound and also argued that many of the ancients urged a morality that was exemplary and readily consistent with Christian ethics. Thus the classical corpus, given its supreme capacity for inculcating good taste and stimulating lucid, accurate, precise thought and expression in the student, would serve ideally as the curriculum for Christian schools. It was necessary only to remove a few authors or works not suitable for Christian minds and to add the Christian classics, e.g., the Bible and the Latin Fathers. This was the basis of the *"pietas literata"*, of which Erasmus may be said to be the founder and which was the educational ideal of the Western World until the twentieth century. It is for education that Erasmus' career has its most permanent significance.

ERASTUS, THOMAS LÜBER

(1524-1583). German-Swiss theologian, physician. Follower of Zwingli. Professor of medicine in Switzerland. Set up Erastian Foundation for poor medical students. *Erastianism,* postulating state supremacy in religious matters, derives from his name. The Henrician-Elizabethan religious settlement in England—by which the monarch was recognized as "Supreme Head of the Church" —was Erastian, although Erastus' writings had no direct influence in the English religious revolution. It has been said that Erastus was no Erastian.

ERCILLA Y ZUNIGA, ALONZO DE

(1533-1594). Spanish courtier, poet, soldier. Born in Madrid. Favorite of Philip II. Spent seven years in South America: 1556-1563. As a result of his campaigns, composed epic poem on the history of Chile, called *La Araucana:* 1569-1589. The best example of epic of the Golden Age, it was much influenced by Tasso and Ariosto. He introduced Indian themes into Spanish literature.

ERCOLE

A fusion of romantic and classical narrative poetry: published in 1557, by Giovanni Battista Giraldi (1504-1573).

ERCONDELL, PETER

Frenchman: born in Normandy. Settled in England at end of sixteenth century. Taught French. Author of conversational handbook entitled *The French Garden,* published in 1605.

ERIC XIV

(1533-1577). King of Sweden. Patron of science and founder of literary academies. Fought seven years against Denmark. Infatuated with Queen Elizabeth of England. Became deranged, deposed, imprisoned.

ERIZZO, SEBASTIANO

(1525-1585). Nobleman and humanist man of letters of Venice. Member of the Council of Ten, the Venetian governing body. Numismatist. Wrote a voluminous study of ancient coins and medallions: published in 1568. Also author of a manual on classical rhetoric, a cycle of short stories, a translation of several of Plato's Dialogues and a work on Petrarch. From the fourteenth to the nineteenth century members of the family held high places in the Venetian government and were eminent as scholars and writers.

ERMAK, TIMOFIEF

(Died 1584). A Cossack leader who with his followers and under the auspices of the Czar at Moscow initiated the conquest of Siberia. Ermak is the subject of a drama, folk legends and songs.

ERPENIUS, THOMAS or VAN ERPEN

(1584-1624). Dutch Oriental scholar. Friend of Casaubon and Scaliger. Wrote a number of grammars: Arabic, Chaldean, Hebrew and wrote a prodigious number of scholarly works on oriental linguistics, Biblical exegesis, and classical philology.

ERRICO, SCIPIONE
(1592-1670). Italian writer of Messina. Wrote satires, comedies, heroic poems on destruction of Babylon, conquest of Constantinople, Trojan War. He also penned a diatribe against Paolo Sarpi.

ERSKINE, JOHN
(1509-1591). Scottish reformer. He is said to have been the first to have established the teaching of Greek in Scotland. Headed Reformed Church of Scotland in Northern Scotland. Participated in compilation of *Second Book of Discipline,* that appeared in 1578.

ERYTHROPILUS, RUPERTUS
Preacher in Hanover. Lutheran. Author of sermons against the Turks, the 'hereditary enemy of Christianity.' Published in 1595.

ESCORIAL, THE
In Spain, near Madrid. Palace built by King Philip II. Erected between 1563 and 1584. One of the greatest architectural piles of the late sixteenth century; it is an enormous somber structure of granite that includes a monastery, the royal residence, church, mausoleum, college, library and archives. It was a fitting symbol of the Spanish monarchy and the absolute and centralized government. Much of its magnificent art collection was made by Philip. Versailles is in many respects an imitation.

ESCUELA DE SALAMANCA
Two Salamancan schools: one in the eighteenth century, the other in the sixteenth century. The chief poet of the sixteenth century school was Fray Luis de León (1527-1591), humanist, erasmista and mystic. Followers were: Pedro Malón de Chaide (1530-1581) and Francisco de la Torre (born c. 1534). Characteristics of this school were emphasis on content, humanism, and mysticism.

ESCUELA SEVILLANA
Two schools: one in the eighteenth century, the other in the sixteenth century. The sixteenth century group was composed of humanists and poets. Leaders were Fernando de Herrera

(1534-1597), poet, and the educator Juan de Mal Lara (1524-1571).

Herrera produced theological work entitled *Anotaciones a las Obras de Garcilaso de la Vega*, in 1580. Mal Lara was chief of Escuela de Humanidades y Gramática. Other members of group were: Francisco de Medrano (1570-1607), Francisco Pacheco (1540?-1599), Baltasar del Alcázar (1530-1606), Francisco de Medina (died c. 1615), Juan de la Cueva (1543-1610). The school was neo-classic and aristocratic in orientation. It emphasized form and language. Represented transition between first stage of Renaissance, Italianate classicism, and final decadence.

ESPENCE, CLAUDE
(1511-1571). French cleric. Author of *Hodoiporicon:* on life and miracles of St. Godon, Abbot of Oye, the benefactions of Merovingian kings, and the progress of the Church during their reigns; Biblical studies, ecclesiastical discipline and religious apology, and a description of the ideal Christian prince.

ESPINEL, VICENTE
(1550-1624). Spanish novelist, poet, musician, soldier, priest. Died in Madrid. Educated at Salamanca. As youth, adventurous and dissolute. In military service in Italy, France. Translated Horace's *Ars Poetica*. Added fifth string to guitar. Wrote autobiographical picaresque novel: *Relaciones de la Vida del Escudero Marcos de Obregón:* published in 1618; Le Sage borrowed from novel in *Gil Blas*. Popularized, as poet, the *décima* or *espinela* verse forms.

ESSEX, EARL OF, ROBERT DEVEREUX
(1566-1601). Favorite of Queen Elizabeth I. Became Earl Marshal of England in 1597. Governor General of Ireland in 1599. Defeated by the Earl of Tyrone. Arrested: conspired against the Queen. The plot failed. Essex was executed. He had been a patron of literature and had himself composed sonnets.

ESTABLISHMENT OF UNIVERSITIES
During the Renaissance, German universities were established as follows: Grieswald, 1456; Freiburg, 1460; Basel, 1460; Ingolstadt, 1462; Tübingen, 1476; Mainz, 1476; Wittenberg, 1502; Frankfurt-in-the-Oder, 1506.

218

ESTIENNE, CHARLES

(1504-1564). French scholar, printer, brother of Robert. In 1554 published satire on prospective jurists: subjects dealt with are state of inebriation, feminine follies, public ignorance.

ESTIENNE, HENRI II

(1528-1598). French publisher of Geneva, scholar-printer, son of Robert, produced many editions of Greek and Roman texts. Also author of *Thesaurus Linguae Graecae*: published in 1572.

ESTIENNE, ROBERT

(1503-1559). The great scholar-printer of Paris, he carried on the tradition of Aldus in the publication of Greek works. His edition of the Vulgate Bible, 1538-1540, was a landmark of sixteenth-century publishing and scholarship. For it he was censured by the officials of the Sorbonne and had to leave Paris for Geneva. His edition, nevertheless, remained the principal scholarly edition for over two centuries. His famous Latin *Thesaurus* appeared in 1531, and was reprinted and expanded many times. Henri Estienne, his son, produced a Greek *Thesaurus*, 1572. From the late fifteenth century the family firm was celebrated for its magnificent editions of the classics.

ESTOUTEVILLE, GUILLAUME D', CARDINAL

(1403-1483). A great ecclesiastic in the service of Charles VII and Louis XI; it was chiefly he who negotiated the Pragmatic Sanction of Bourges and, at royal behest, reformed the University of Paris (c. 1450); his reform was not the introduction of Italian humanism, but was confined to purging abuses by clerics and to the introduction of new regulations.

ESTRÉES, GABRIELLE D'

(1573-1599). Mistress of Henry IV. 'She was completely woman in her tastes, her ambitions, even in her frailties.'—Sainte-Beuve.

ÉTAMPES, DUCHESSE D'

(1508-1580). Anne de Pisseleu. Mistress of Francis I of France. She took active part in politics.

ETON COLLEGE

English public school. Founded in 1440 by Henry VI.

EUPHUISM

Greek derivation, meaning good form, and identifying the English literary style that took its name from John Lyly's play, *Euphues,* 1579. It is characterized by excessive alliteration, classical allusions, antitheses and artificiality; it became the mode in the latter part of the sixteenth and early seventeenth centuries and is suggestive of the Baroque era. Echoes of it may be found in Shakespeare.

EUSEBIO DA SAN GEORGIO
(c. 1465-c. 1540). Italian painter, disciple of Perugino. He did principally religious scenes and shows the influence of Raphael's work.

EUSTACHIO, BARTOLOMEO
(c. 1500-1574). Italian anatomist. First described Eustachian Tubes. Considered among founders of modern anatomy. Author of *Tabulae Anatomicae:* illustrated. The plates are the first medical illustrations on copper.

EXPULSION OF THE JEWS
In 1492 Jews were massacred or expelled from Spain under orders of Torquemada. They sought refuge in Italy, Germany, Holland and Turkey. In 1496, Jews were massacred or expelled from Portugal by Manuel I.

EYB, ALBRECHT VON
(1420-1475). German humanist. Author of didactic, edifying works and a handbook for rhetoric that includes an anthology of classical Latinity; it is entitled *Margarita Poetica.* He also wrote *Ehebüchlein,* a marriage guide.

EYTZINGER, MICHAEL
(Sixteenth century). German diplomat, historian. He served as Imperial ambassador to the Council of Trent. Author of *Pentaplus Regnorum Mundi:* on federation of monarchies, church and state: published in 1579. He also wrote on the Dutch Revolt (he supported the Spanish cause ardently) with particular reference to the disorders in Belgium, the homeland of his forebears, entitled *De Leone belgico;* it is a long, painstaking, chronological outline.

F

FABER, FELIX
Fifteenth century. German Dominican monk. Traveled to the Holy Land on two occasions, in 1480 and 1483.

FABER DE WERDEA, JOHANNES
Logician. Wrote commentary on Petrus Hispanus: published in 1487.

FABIO, CALVO
Scholar of Ravenna. Commentator on Hippocrates. Teacher of Raphael. Lived more than ninety years. In sack of Rome, 1527, was dragged off by Spaniards. Died in hospital.

FABRIANO
In this city the earliest paper factory in Italy was reputedly established, dating from the twelfth century. Its school of painting is best known through Gentile da Fabriano.

FABRICIUS, GEORGIUS
(1516-1571). German philologist and poet. Wrote Latin poems in classical form but on contemporary themes. He was head of the College of Meissen and wrote a *Description of Rome* and the *Res Germaniae et Saxoniae memoribiles*.

FABRICIUS, HIERONYMUS
(1537-1619). Italian anatomist, embryologist, and surgeon. Professor at Padua. Taught William Harvey. Fabricius is noted for surgical techniques: also for his work in comparative anatomy. He had studied the veins and described their valves, although he did not realize what was their function. Author of *De Forma-*

tione Ovi et Pulli, published in Padua in 1621, as well as numerous other anatomical works.

FABRITIUS, CAREL
(1622-1654). Dutch painter of Delft, pupil of Rembrandt, teacher of Vermeer. Produced portraits and genre paintings. Very few examples of his work are preserved. His early death cut off a career that seemed to promise great accomplishments.

FABYAN, ROBERT or FABIAN
(c. 1450-1512). English historian. Wrote *The Concordance of Histories*: a simple, factual chronicle of English history.

FACINI, PIETRO
(c. 1560-1602). Bolognese painter who was noted for his skill as a colorist, for the vivacity and animation of his depictions and for his rivalry with Annibale Caracci.

FACINUS, GALEATIUS PONTICUS
(died c. 1506). Poet of Padua. Wrote amatory poems: also religious and eulogistic pieces. Produced a commentary on Silius Italicus.

FACIO, BARTOLOMEO
(c. 1400-1457). Italian humanist historian. He had been a student of Guarino of Verona. He was a teacher of the classics, an ambassador, the author of a work on the *Deeds* of Alfonso the Magnanimous, a history of art in Naples, and in his *De Viris illustribus* the biographer of eminent contemporaries.

FALCÃO, CRISTOVÃO
(born c. 1515). Portuguese bucolic poet. Author of *Chrisfal,* a poetic account of his amatory experiences; it is characterized by delicacy of sentiment and an elegiac tone.

FALCONE, NIELLO
(1600-1685). Italian painter. Founder of school of painters in Naples and was notable as a painter of battle scenes.

FALCONETTO, GIOVANNI MARIA
(c. 1458-1534). Italian architect of Verona, where he did most of his work; his brother was a painter of the Venetian school.

FALEO, BENEDETTO
Sixteenth century. Italian humanist. Wrote treatise on origin of Greek, Latin, Hebrew: published in 1520.

FALK, JOSHUA BEN ALEXANDER HAKOHEN
(c. 1550-1616). Polish Talmudist. Head of Lemberg Yeshivah. Author of commentary on Joseph Caro, entitled *Book of the Enlightenment of the Eyes* and numerous other works.

FALLETTI, GERONIMO, COUNT OF TRINO
(c. 1518-1564). Italian poet, historian. Ambassador of Duke of Ferrara to Charles V. Wrote account of Charles V and political and religious wars that ravaged Empire from 1524 to 1544; it was in verse. He wrote other historical works.

FALLOPIO, GABRIELLO
(c. 1523-1562). Italian anatomist. Chief pupil of Vesalius, and himself the teacher of Fabricius. Most illustrious Italian anatomist of sixteenth century. Taught anatomy at Padua. The first to discover and describe the function of Fallopian Tubes. Wrote treatise: *Observationes Anatomicae*: published in Venice in 1561; his collected works were published at Venice in 1584.

FANCELLI, DOMENICO ALESSANDRO
(1469-1519). Italian sculptor. Worked and died in Spain where he constituted an important bridge for the new art of Italy. Noted for religious and funerary statuary, especially the tomb of Ferdinand and Isabella.

FANCELLI, GIOVANNI
(flourished c. 1540). Italian sculptor. Executed bronze casts. Worked in Venice.

FANCELLI, LUCA
(1430-1495). Italian sculptor and architect in the service of the Gonzaga dukes of Mantua, where he built palaces and villas. He was also a military architect and hydraulic engineer.

FANCELLI, PANDOLFO
(Died 1526). Italian sculptor, father of DOMENICO. He too worked much in Spain.

FANINI
(c. 1530-1550). Protestant Italian of Faenza. At Ferrara, in 1550, he became the first martyr of Italian Protestantism.

FANO, BARTOLOMMEO DA

(c. 1460-c. 1534). Italian painter who belonged to the Roman school; his son POMPEO was also a painter.

FANO, IMMANUEL

(1548-1620). Italian rabbi and cabalist and member of a family of Italian Jews which has produced many distinguished rabbinical scholars since the sixteenth century.

FANSAGA, COSIMO

(1591-1678). Italian architect and sculptor. Died in Naples. Founder of Neapolitan school of baroque architecture.

FAREL, GUILLAUME

(1489-1565). French religious reformer and preacher; he had studied under Lefébvre d' Étaples. Settled in Switzerland, where he was instrumental in establishing Reformation. Banished along with Calvin. Became pastor at Neuchâtel. Continued activities toward spread of Reformation as a colleague of Calvin.

FARIA Y SOUSA, MANUEL DE

(1590-1649). Portuguese diplomat, poet and historian. He lived almost all his life at the time when Portugal lost its independence, having been annexed to Spain. He served the Spanish government and he wrote most of his works in Spanish. In poetry, produced sonnets, eclogues and wrote a treatise on poetry; they are all in the tradition of Góngora. His historical works include a *History of Portugal* and he also wrote a *Commentary* on the *Lusiades* of Camoens.

FARINATO, PAOLO

(c. 1525-1606). Italian painter, architect, engraver of Verona. Executed frescoes and oils. His father ORAZIO, born 1500, was also a painter and engraver.

FARISSOL, ABRAHAM BEN MORDECAI

(1451-1526). Hebrew scholar, geographer, translator, polemical writer. Friend of Christopher Columbus. Wrote Hebrew account of discovery of America, a defense of Judaism against Islam and Christianity, and Biblical commentaries.

FARMER, JOHN

(c. 1565-c. 1605). English musician. Known for his madrigals; they are reprinted in the *English Madrigal School, VIII.* He had been organist at Christ Church Cathedral at Dublin and then removed to London.

FARNABY, THOMAS
(1575-1647). English teacher, grammarian, literary critic, Latinist and Hellenist; he wrote several grammatical and literary works.

FARNESE, ALESSANDRO, DUKE OF PARMA
(1545-1592). Italian diplomat. Educated in Spain. Participated in the Battle of Lepanto. Fought against Henry IV of France. From 1577 to 1586, in the service of Philip II of Spain, in the Low Countries. In command of the Spanish armies during the years 1586-1592, where he died of wounds sustained at the Battle of Arros. It was his combination of competence as a general and skill as a diplomat and statesman that brought the southern provinces (Belgium) back to their allegiance.

FARNESE PALACE
In Rome. Designed by Antonio da Sangallo for Cardinal Alessandro Farnese, later Pope Paul III. Built c. 1513-1515. Michelangelo worked on building; it was finished by Giacomo della Porta; great heroes were painted in its main hall by Annibale Carracci and his followers. It was one of the most sumptuous palaces in Rome, much of the masonry was quarried from ancient monuments.

FARRANT, RICHARD
(c. 1530- c. 1585). English musician. Organist of Chapel Royal. Wrote anthems, morning and evening services, and other church music.

FAUCHET, CLAUDE
(1530-1601). French attorney and president of the *Cour des Monnaies*, historian and antiquarian. Wrote in a critical spirit on French history, literature, language. He also translated Tacitus into French as well as writing a study of the French magistracies.

FAUST, DR. JOHANN
(c. 1480-c. 1540). German astrologer, magician of Württemberg. Legend of his association with Mephistopheles has been treated in music and in drama: e.g. play by Christopher Marlowe: long dramatic poet by Goethe: opera by Gounod: the novel of

Thomas Mann. The legend first appeared in print in the *Volksbuch* of 1587.

FAVENTINUS, BENEDICTUS VICTORIUS
Logician of Bonn. Wrote commentaries on logic: published in Venice in 1504. Also *De Sensu Composito et Diviso*.

FAVRE, ANTOINE or ANTONIUS FABER
(1557-1624). French jurist. First President of Senate at Chambery. Wrote on Roman Law: *Coniecturarum Iuris Civilis Libri Tres*: published in 1581.

FAWKES, GUY
(1570-1606). English Catholic conspirator. Participated in Gunpowder Plot to blow up the Parliament. Guy Fawkes Day, November 5, is still celebrated in England.

FEDELES, FORTUNATO
(1550-1630). Italian physician of Palermo. First physician to treat of the legal aspects of medicine or forensic medicine. Discussed the theme in his *Relationes Medicorum:* published in 1602.

FEDERICI, CESARE
(Sixteenth century). Venetian merchant and traveler. Spent eighteen years in Southeast Asia, of which he wrote an account published in 1587, entitled *Voyage to the East Indies*.

FEDERIGO DA MONTEFELTRO, DUKE OF URBINO
(1422-1482). We are chiefly indebted to Vespasiano for our knowledge of Federigo, of whom he wrote "no other united as he did in his own person, the soldier and man of letters, or knew how to make intellect augment the force of battalions." His good faith as a condottiere was unique in Renaissance Italy. Consistently victorious in his campaigns he was in the service of King Alfonso and his son Ferrante of Naples for thirty-two years; in the service of the League of Lodi he manifested a concern for the peace of Italy that was quite unusual for his time. His great library at Urbino was assembled for him largely by Vespasiano. The superbly bound and illuminated manuscripts, Latin, Greek, Hebrew, and Italian, included the Roman and Greek authors, the Latin and Greek fathers, the Scholastics, and the "modern authors," e.g., Dante, Petrarch, Boccaccio and the humanists of his own day. Patron of humanist scholars, Federigo was a muni-

ficent patron of artists as well. Learned in architecture, his palace at Urbino was a monument to his knowledge and taste. He seems to have ruled well and justly, for only thus can one account for his holding his duchy without difficulty for forty years in the most turbulent corner of Italy, the Romagna. Not long after his death, his state was overwhelmed and eventually became part of the Papal States; most of the library ended up in the Vatican.

FEDERMANN, NICOLAS
(1501?-1542). German adventurer and explorer. Served in Venezuela from 1530 to 1532 and from 1536 to 1539 as an agent of the Welsar bankers. He went out in search of El Dorado in the course of which he ascended the Andes; he came into conflict with Quesada and other explorers and accomplished little that is significant in the history of exploration.

FELICE, MATTEO
(Fifteenth century). Court illuminator to Aragonese kings of Spain.

FELICIANO, FELICE, ANTIQUARIO
(Born c. 1420). Veronese antiquarian who collected inscriptions, medallions, etc., and wrote Latin epigrams.

FELICIANO, FRANCESCO
Sixteenth century Italian mathematician. Wrote treatise on science of numbers, arithmetical techniques, quadratics, square root.

FELSTED SCHOOL
English public school. Founded in 1564 by Richard, Lord Riche, Lord Chancellor of England (c. 1496-1567); he had been as attorney general the prosecutor of Thomas More.

FELTON, JOHN
(c. 1595-1628). Irish assassin of the Duke of Buckingham, the favorite of Charles I. On Duke's refusal to grant commission as captain, Felton assassinated him. Hanged.

FEMELIUS, CHRISTOPHER
Sixteenth century. Professor of mathematics at Erfurt. Wrote treatise on astronomical tables: published in 1599.

FENTON, EDWARD
(died 1603). English navigator. He fought against Shane O'Neill

in Ireland, was with Frobisher in search of Northwest Passage, led an expedition to the Molucca Islands and China in 1582, and commanded one of the English ships that fought the Armada.

FENTON, SIR GEOFFREY

(1539?-1608). Secretary of State for Ireland under Elizabeth and James I. Also translator: Translated *Golden Letters* of Spanish historian Guevara (c. 1490-1545), Bandello's tales, French romances of Pierre Boaisteau, and Guicciardini, *History of the Italian Wars.*

FEODOR I

(1557-1598). Tsar of Russia, son of last of Rurik line. During his weak reign the government was controlled by Boris Godunov, his brother-in-law and subject of Moussorgsky's opera.

FEODOR II

(1589-1605). Tsar of Russia. Son of Boris Godunov. Murdered by boyars. The age is known in Russian history as the time of troubles, and ended with the accession of the Romanovs in 1612.

FERDINAND I

(1423-1494). Ferrante. King of Naples. Notorious for his cruel, cynical character. In conflict with Pope Calixtus III. Reign marked by attack of Turks and revolt of nobles. He was the illegimate son of Alfonso the Magnanimous, whom he succeeded as King of Naples; he was a typical Renaissance prince in his cruelty and deviousness, and in his patronage of the arts and learning.

FERDINAND I

(1503-1564). Holy Roman Emperor, brother of Charles V, King of Bohemia and Hungary. In 1521 Ferdinand married Anna, sister of Louis II of Bohemia and Hungary. On the death of Louis, Ferdinand claimed the thrones of Bohemia and Hungary. The result was a conflict with John Zápolya, who, with the support of the Turks, claimed Hungary. Ferdinand finally bought off the Turks and became dual king, of both Bohemia and Hungary. Tried to reconcile Protestant and Catholic subjects.

FERDINAND II

(1578-1637). Holy Roman Emperor. King of Bohemia and Hungary. Hostile to Protestants: drove them from Bohemia. Reign marked by war with Protestants. With help of Catholic League, at first successful: but finally defeated by French and Swedish.

FERDINAND III
(1608-1657). Son of the above. Holy Roman Emperor. King of Hungary and Bohemia. Defeated the Swedes in 1634. In conflict with Protestants. Noted for scholarly and musical interests.

FERDINAND V
(1452-1516). Ferdinand of Aragon. Called The Catholic. His marriage to Isabella of Castile in 1469 resulted in the dynastic union of the two realms. He reorganized the league of towns and cities, the crusading orders, and the Inquisition so as to serve royal ends. In 1492 he took Granada from the Moors and in the same year expelled the Jews. At first he supported Columbus but deserted him later. As King of Naples, he was designated Ferdinand III. In 1508, member of the League of Cambrai against Venice. He is a symbol of wiliness and double dealing in diplomacy: to their great anger he repeatedly tricked and outwitted the kings of England and France. He was more Machiavellian than Cesare Borgia.

FERDINAND OF BRAGANZA
Portuguese noble who instigated revolt against King John II of Portugal. Revolt was suppressed in 1483: many participants were executed.

FERMAT, PIERRE DE
(1601-1665). French mathematician. First to apply differential calculus to tangential investigations. Shares with Pascal the discovery of calculation of probabilities and with Descartes the invention of analytical geometry. Also worked in optics.

FERNÁNDEZ, GREGORIO
(died 1636). Spanish sculptor. He did religious subjects, the strained expressions and agony of his figures are suggestive of the Baroque period.

FERNÁNDEZ, JUAN
(c. 1537-c. 1603). Spanish explorer. Sailed Pacific and Indian Oceans. Explored Peru and Chile.

FERNÁNDEZ DE CÓRDOBA, FRANCISCO
(died c. 1526). Spanish explorer. In Cuba. Died while fighting

against Maya in Yucatan. His expedition to Campeche and Yucatan in 1517 preceded, and helped to inspire, that of Cortés two years later. It is described by Bernal Diaz.

FERNÁNDEZ DE NAVARRETE, JUAN, EL MUDO

(c. 1526-1579). Spanish painter. He traveled much in Italy, staying for long periods in Florence and Rome. Titian had a profound influence upon him and he is called the "Spanish Titian." For the last decade of his life he was court painter to Philip II, for whom he painted numerous works for the Escorial, especially of religious subjects.

FERNÁNDEZ OVIEDO Y VALDÉS, GONZALO

(1478-1557). Spanish soldier, historian, governor of Cartagena. He wrote an *Historia general y natural des las Indias,* 1535. He wrote other works on his own family, the nobility of Spain and the royal court, where, in the time of Charles V, he enjoyed the post of historiographer of New Spain.

FERNEL, JEAN FRANÇOIS

(1497-1558). French scientist, physician and mathematician. Called The Modern Galen. While a medical student he experimented with exact measurement of a degree of the meridian: the result of his investigations was his *Cosmotheoria,* published in 1528. Fernel was court physician to Henry II and friend of Catherine de Medici. Author of *Universa Medicina,* published in 1554. Also wrote *De Abditis Rerum Causis:* published in Paris in 1560. Fernel correctly observed secondary symptoms of syphilis. Described epidemics in early sixteenth century.

FERRABOSCO, ALFONSO

(1544-1587). English composer, born in England of an Italian father who also was a musician. Under the patronage of Queen Elizabeth, he composed madrigals and other musical compositions.

FERRAR, NICHOLAS

(1592-1637). English theologian and physician. Founded religious community called Little Gidding or contemptuously, The Arminian Nunnery; he wrote its history. The community had some influence upon George Herbert and Richard Crashaw.

FERRARA

Ferrara came into the possession of the Guelph family, the Este, in 1240, who also acquired Modena and Reggio and held the three domains until the end of the sixteenth century. The fame of the Este for their patronage of art and learning and for their brilliant court began with Niccolo III (1393-1441); he, as were his successors in the main line of the house until it died out in 1597, was master of the art of playing off his powerful neighbors against each other and so preventing his small domain from being swallowed up. He reopened the University of Ferrara, which flourished in the fifteenth century. Other princes of the house are Lionello (1407-1450), the guitar virtuoso and patron of humanistic learning; his brother Borso (1413-1471), who acquired the ducal title from the pope and made Ferrara a center of book production by his establishment of a printing press; and the third brother Ercole I (1431-1505), who ruled Ferrara in its golden age. He was a generous patron of the arts and learning, but is chiefly remarkable for his translations of Seneca and Terence and other Roman playwrights whose works he staged in the palace courtyard. The first permanent theatre since antiquity was built at Ferrara. Music also flourished there: the masque was developed chiefly in Ferrara; the first performance of an opera occurred there. Ercole's wife, Leonora of Naples, brought tapestry-makers and embroiderers with her and established a center for these arts at the court. She, a gifted harpist, and her two brilliant daughters, Beatrice (1475-1497) and Isabella (1474-1539), were saluted as paragons of beauty, virtue and culture. Beatrice married Lodovico Il Moro of Milan, whose court she made the most lavish and magnificent of Europe; Isabella, in many ways her rival for fame, married Francesco Gonzaga of Mantua and is said to have exemplified by her character, taste, diplomatic and political skill, and gritty courage the lofty ideal and aspiration of the Renaissance. Ercole's son and successor was Alfonso I (1476-1534). He, like his forebears, was a successful condottiere. By dint of siding with the Emperor Charles V he preserved his duchy through the crises of the early sixteenth century. He was a patron of Ariosto, whose chivalrous epic idealizing woman and love reflects perfectly (as did Boiardo's a generation earlier) the atmosphere of the court—distinctly military but softened by the refining touch of sensitive women who conducted long discourses about the nature of love and passion.

231

Alfonso's brother and a cardinal was Ippolito I (1479-1520), the first patron of Ariosto, who dedicated the *Orlando Furioso* to him. Alfonso's two sons were both celebrated patrons: Ercole II (1508-1559) as duke and Ippolito II (1509-1572) as a cardinal and papal diplomat—it was he who built the sumptuous Villa d'Este at Tivoli. Ferrara was annexed to the Papal States in 1598.

FERRARA, ANDREA
Sixteenth century. Broadswordmaker. Had a reputation as an armorer at Belluno.

FERRARA BIBLE
A Spanish translation of the Bible, printed by Abraham Usque and Yomtov Athias in 1553.

FERRARI, DEFENDENTE
(1480-1535). Italian painter of Piedmont. Executed religious paintings, frescoes; most of them in monasteries and churches. Several of his works were commissioned by the duke of Savoy.

FERRARI, GAUDENZIO
(1484-1549). Italian painter. Born at Valduggia. Worked as Saronno, Vercelli, Milan. One of leading artists of Renaissance in Lombardy. Executed easel pictures and frescoes, in which he shows the influence of, among others, Leonardo da Vinci, under whom he had worked.

FERRARI, LODOVICO
(1522-1565). Italian mathematician. First solved equations of the fourth degree and also made other contributions to algebra.

FERREIRA, ANTÓNIO
(1528-1569). Portuguese poet and dramatist. Author of *Inês de Castro*: only complete and original sixteenth century Portuguese tragedy. Most of his work shows the influence of Italian models, especially his lyrical poems, the *Poemas Lusitanas*.

FERREIRA DE VASCONCELOS, JORGE
(1515-1585). Portuguese writer. Author of a romance: *Memorial of the Exploits of the Second Round Table*: published in 1567. Deals with the origins of chivalry: deeds of King Arthur: famous Portuguese tournament during reign of John III (1521-1557). Also wrote three dramas not intended for stage. His *Eufrosina,*

232

which appeared c. 1537, presents a prototype of the Castilian Don Juan.

FERRUCCI, ANDREA
(1465-1526). Italian sculptor. Died in Florence. He did a bust of Marsiglio Ficino. His work is characterized by the naturalism of the fifteenth century.

FESTA, COSTANZO
(Died 1545). Italian musician. Singer in the papal chorus. He composed religious music: masses, motets and a *Magnificat*. His polyphonic music is similar to, if simpler than, Palestrina's.

FESTIVITIES
In Renaissance Italy two forms of public display and entertainment were the mystery play, based on religious themes, and the procession. The procession was frequently, but not exclusively, of an ecclesiastical nature. There were directors of such festivities who traveled throughout Italy and were known as *festaiuli*. Parades of this type also took place in Spain, in Portugal, and in France. There were allegorical and historical dramatizations, chariots with living statuary, masked groups, triumphal processions depicting Roman and contemporary episodes, firework illuminations. Carnivals, involving dances and exhibitions, were likewise popular, especially in Venice and Florence. One such, the *Sempiterni*, held in Venice in 1541, was particularly lavish. Lorenzo the Magnificent's poems, the *Carnival Songs*, are among the most beautiful and delightful works of the age.

FETI, DOMENICO or FETTI
(1589-1624). Italian painter. Died in Venice. Treated mythological subjects poetically and scenes of daily life with Biblical and religious overtones, as well as purely religious works.

FICINO, MARSILIO
(1433-1499). Son of Cosimo de'Medici's physician; sponsored by the ruler of Florence, he dedicated himself to the study of Plato and all the relevant treatises and commentators; the fruit of his studies was his translation of the whole of Plato and Plotinus into Latin—the first time in the West; also Porphyry, Proclus, and Dionysius the Areopagite and the works attributed to Pythagoras and Hermes Trismegismus. He was the founder of the Florentine Platonic Academy and the intimate friend of Lorenzo the Mag-

nificent. His *Theologica Platonica*, in which he expressed his profound belief in the complete harmony of Platonism and Christianity, is one of the central texts for the study of the Renaissance. He coined the phrase "Platonic love" to denote his ideal of friendship and human relations. Central to the Renaissance philosophy of man, Platonic love was the ideal that bound together the members of the Academy.

FIELD OF CLOTH OF GOLD, 1520
A meeting between Francis I of France and Henry VIII of England. The purpose was the formation of an alliance against the Emperor Charles V. For three weeks the two kings and their consorts met near Calais, for conferences, banquets, and jousts, on a lavishly decorated Field.

FIERAVANTI, ARISTOTILE
(c. 1415-c. 1486). Italian architect. Born at Bologna. Constructed Cathedral of the Assumption and began that of St. Michael the Archangel in the reconstruction of the Kremlin under commission from Czar Ivan III. He worked in Hungary, as well as at Milan for the Sforza.

FIESCHI, GIOVANNI LUIGI, COUNT OF LAVAGNA
(c. 1523-1547). Politician and soldier of Genoa. Plotted overthrow of Doge of Genoa. Drowned during operations of plot. Subject of Schiller's drama *Fiesco*: 1783.

FIFTH MONARCHY MEN
A radical politico-religious group in England in the 1650's. Believed that the time was ripe for establishment of the Fifth Monarchy foretold in Biblical prophecy, which they took to mean the return of Jesus and the onset of His rule.

FIGUEROA, FRANCISCO DE
(c. 1535-c. 1620). Spanish poet. Noted for blank verse. Wrote *canciones*, elegies, sonnets, eclogue entitled *Tirsi*. He had traveled in Italy and Flanders: his *canciones* are written after Italian models.

FILARETE, ANTONIO DA
(c. 1400-c. 1470). Italian architect, sculptor. Died in Rome. Continued to incorporate Gothic elements in his buildings. His theoretical works on architecture were epoch-making. His sculp-

tures include a number of bronze reliefs for doors; he did a great bronze door for Pope Eugenius IV for the Basilica in the Vatican —it is the most purely classical of his works. He worked also in Florence, Rimini, Padua, and for the Sforza of Milan.

FILELFO, FRANCESCO
(1398-1481). Humanist scholar who went to Greece to learn its language and spent seven years as secretary to the Venetian ambassador at Constantinople, where he married the great-niece of Chrysoloras; on his return to Florence in 1427 he brought forty Greek manuscripts with him. At Florence he lectured on the classics at the university and read Dante aloud on days of holiday and celebration until, falling afoul of politics, he was exiled as a rebel on Cosimo de'Medici's return in 1434. Exile took Filelfo to Milan, then briefly to Naples and the patronage of Alfonso the Magnanimous. Returned to Milan, he wrote his *Sforziade* to honor the Sforza; it is an epic on the model of Vergil's *Aeneid*, and its fulsome praise is all too typical of the adulation which humanists felt appropriate to render to their princes. He wrote many satires and crossed swords with Poggio; finally allowed to return to Florence, he died shortly thereafter. His son, Gian Mario, 1426-1480, was more accomplished as a scamp than as a humanist.

FILIPPICHE
Philippics. An attack on the Spaniards. Published in 1615. Putative author—Alessandro Tassoni (1565-1635).

FILIPPO DE LURANO
Sixteenth century. Italian musician of Frottole. Composed *laude*.

FILIPPO DI MATTEO TORELLI
Italian book illuminator. Worked between 1440 and 1468. Executed Gospel-Book in 1466. Breviary, in 1470. Also copies of Petrarch, Dante.

FILMER, SIR ROBERT
(c. 1590-1653). English political writer and royalist. Supported the divine right of kings in a historical treatise entitled *Patriarcha;* he attacked Hobbes' contractual theory and urged instead the patriarchal theory to explain the origin of government.

FINCK, HEINRICH
(1445-1527). German musician. Composed motets, hymns. He was associated with the courts of Warsaw and Vienna.

FINCK, HERMANN
(1527-1558). German organist, composer and theorist. Composed songs. Author of treatise on music: *Practica Musica*. Published in 1556. He was educated at the University of Wittenberg and spent most of his career there.

FIOCCHI, ANDREA
(Died 1452). Florentine humanist, apostolic secretary to Eugenius IV. Wrote on Roman antiquities in his *De Romanorum magistratibus;* it is concerned with the early Empire.

FIORAVANTI, LEONARDO
(1518-1588). Italian physician. Author of compendium on senses, herbs, balsams, fish, insects, alchemy, tobacco: *Mirror of Universal Science*: published in 1564, and also other diverse works.

FIORENZO DI LORENZO
(1440-c. 1525). Italian painter of Perugia, where he did most of his work, religious subjects in the form of altarpieces and frescoes. He was probably the master of Perugino.

FIRENZUOLA, AGNOLO
(1493-1543). Florentine scholar, satirist, man of letters. Author of *Discorsi degli Animali*: a Renaissance imitation of Oriental and Aesopic fables. Also *Dialogo della Bellezze delle Donne,* in 1548. Also wrote two comedies and Petrarchan lyrical verse. He had been released from his monastic vows in 1526 and thereafter led the life of *bon vivant* and man of letters amidst aristocratic society.

FIRST BLAST AGAINST THE MONSTROUS REGIMENT OF WOMEN
A pamphlet by John Knox issued in 1556. Attacked Mary Tudor of England, Mary of Lorraine, the regent of Scotland, and her daughter Mary Queen of Scots. Nor did it endear him to Elizabeth of England upon her accession to the throne in 1558.

FIRST BOOK OF COMMON PRAYER
The first prayer book was introduced in England by Edward VI, in 1549; it was largely the work of Thomas Cranmer and was distinctly Protestant, though less so than its successor of 1552.

FISCHART, JOHANN

(1545-1591). German satirist. Poet. Protestant publicist. Author of more than fifty books. The best known is an imitation of Rabelais, entitled *Geschichtsklitterung*. He also wrote poetry, marked by eloquence, and symbolism. His religious satires include *Der Binenkorb* and *Das Jesuiten Hütlein*.

FISH, SIMON

(Sixteenth century.) English lawyer and pamphleteer. Author of a tract against the English clergy and the oppression of the poor: *Supplicacion of Beggars*: published in 1529, it is satirical and anti-Roman Catholic. Addressed to Henry VIII.

FISHER, SAINT JOHN

(1459-1535). English prelate and humanist enthusiast. Bishop of Rochester. Friend and fellow prisoner of Thomas More. Executed by Henry VIII for refusing to recognize the royal supremacy over the Church. Author of treatises against Lutheranism. Shortly before his death he had been made a cardinal.

FITCH, RALPH

(c. 1550-1611). English merchant. By way of the Euphrates he traveled to Bengal, Burma, Siam: 1583-1591. He left an account of his wanderings that, printed by Hakluyt, stimulated trade with the Orient. First European to visit Burma and Siam.

FLACIUS ILLYRICUS, MATTHIAS or VLACHICH or FRANKOWICH

(1520-1575). Italian Biblical scholar, historian, polemicist. He had a humanist education at Venice; was about to become a Franciscan monk when he was persuaded by his uncle—provincial of the order and sympathetic to Luther—to continue university studies at Tübingen in Germany; there he came under Luther's influence and subsequently became professor of Hebrew at Wittenberg. He was a rabid controversialist and condemned any attempted compromise with the Church, such as Melanchthon thought fitting; hence his rows and polemic against many Protestants as well as Catholics. He wrote many scholarly and historical works, among them the *Glossa-Compendiaria in Novum Testamentum, Clavis Scripturae Sacrae,* and the *Ecclesiastica Historia* or *Magdeburg Centuries*—the first history of the Church from a Protestant viewpoint and a cooperative work, although Flacius planned it and did most of the writing. (It took its name from the fact that each section of the work covered a century.) Written in Latin, it was soon translated into German; he stated its basic principle in the dictum, *"Historia est fundamentum doctrinae."*

FLAMINIO, MARCANTONIO

(1498-1550). Italian humanist and poet. Educated at Urbino. Author of a cycle of love poems entitled *Lusus Pastorales,* in which he imitated Petrarch; in later life his poetry took a more mystical and religious turn. He was deeply concerned about the reform of the Church.

FLEMISH ART

The art of all the provinces that now constitute the Kingdom of Belgium is called Flemish art. Flemish art generally applies to painting developed in Flanders from the fourteenth to the seventeenth century. The essential characteristic of this art is realism and detail. The flowering of Flemish art occurred in the fourteenth and fifteenth centuries in Bruges: in the seventeenth century, in Antwerp. In Bruges, in the fifteenth century, notable names are those of the painters Hubert and Jan van Eyck, whose themes were religious and portraiture: Peter Christus, who painted real life episodes. The school of Tournai was organized by Robert Campen and Roger van der Weyden. Dirk Bouts came to Flanders from Holland. Hugo van der Goes led the Flemish school into broader paths of realism. In the second half of the fifteenth century Hans Memling is important, painter of religious pictures and small portraits. The last great painter of the Bruges school was Ghecrardt David. By the beginning of the sixteenth century Antwerp succeeded Bruges as the centre of Flemish art. Sculpture, architecture, and painting began to be modified by Italian Renaissance influence. The first outstanding artist of this school was Quentin Massys. His work shows the increasing influence of Italian art. As landscape painters, Joachim Patinir and Hendrik Bles were distinguished. Hieronymous Bosch and Pieter Brueghel the Elder combined the traditional Flemish concern for painstaking detail with a macabre surrealism and a bizarre religiosity that are unique to the two painters. During the sixteenth century, Italian influence became progressively more pronounced, until Flemish and Italian elements merged. Among the Italianizers were Jan Gossart, Van Orley, Lancelot Blondeel, Jan Massys, Frans de Floris. The Italian influence was

238

so strong that many Flemish artists called themselves Romanists. As the beginning of the seventeenth century a taste for more naturalistic art developed. Copperplate engraving became popular in Antwerp.

FLEMISH ILLUMINATION
Earliest notice of book illumination refers to a ninth century Benedictine chronicle. In early centuries, style of illumination was partly Germanic, partly French or Burgundian. The scriptorium in the Benedictine Abbey of Stavelot was important from early times. By the fifteenth century, the art had reached its greatest height in the work of Pol de Limbourg, who did a famous *Book of the Hours* for the duke of Berry. Examples are a Book of Hours, of the Ghent-Bruges school, produced c. 1500, and many copies of Books of Hours preserved in libraries of Milan, Florence, Palermo, Turin, Naples.

FLEMMYNG, ROBERT
(Died 1483). English humanist and Bishop of Lincoln. Latin poet. Author of *Lucubraciunculae Tiburtinae.* Diocesan disputes induced him to go to Italy, where he spent several years and made the acquaintance of many humanists, including Platina, Pope Sixtus IV and Guarino, under whom he studied Greek. Most of his work was written in Italy and he may be said to typify English contact with Italy in the earlier stages of the Renaissance.

FLETCHER, GILES, THE ELDER
(1549-1611). English diplomat, poet. Envoy to Russia in 1588. Wrote an account of his embassy in 1591. Author of *Licia,* a collection of love poems, mostly in the sonnet form and a historical poem, *Richard III.*

FLETCHER, GILES, THE YOUNGER
(1588-1623). English poet. Son of the above. He was educated at Trinity College, Cambridge. Author of *Christ's Victory and Triumph*: published in 1610. Modeled on Spenser's *Faerie Queene;* it is a fine example of Baroque style and is said to have influenced Milton.

FLETCHER, JOHN
(1579-1625). English playwright. Collaborated with Francis Beaumont in some fifty plays: also with Shakespeare and Massinger.

239

Author of *Bonduca, Valentinian, The Faithful Shepherdess.* Died of plague. At least one of his plays, *The Pilgrim,* is modeled on Lope de Vega and suggests the vogue in England of Spanish drama, which was also enjoying a golden age.

FLETCHER, PHINEAS

(1582-1650). English poet, Son of Giles the Elder. Author of *The Purple Island:* published in 1633. Allegory of the physical body of man. Also wrote a masque, *Piscatory Eclogues, The Apollyonists:* a sacred poem. He followed Spenser closely in style and subject matter.

FLINCK, GOVAERT

(1615-1660). Dutch painter and disciple of Rembrandt. Died in Amsterdam. Executed portraits, historical paintings, genre pieces.

FLINTLOCKS

First flintlock was sometimes called snaphance; it superseded the matchlock. It was of Spanish origin. It was introduced c. 1625, whether first in Spain, England, or France is a matter of controversy.

FLODDEN FIELD, BATTLE OF

James IV of Scotland invaded England, in 1513, in the absence in France of Henry VIII and his forces. Queen Catherine, however, mustered an army commanded by the Earl of Surrey. At Flodden Field the Scotsmen were annihilated and the king was killed in battle.

FLOREBELLI MUTINENSIS, ANTONIO

(Sixteenth century.) Bishop of Modena. Author of *De Restituta in Anglia Religione Oratio:* published in 1555. Eulogy of marriage of Mary Tudor and Philip II of Spain in 1554.

FLORENCE

Florence was the centre of the Italian Renaissance until late in the fifteenth century. It was a lavish city, violent, powerful, brutal, and superlatively prosperous. It maintained its supremacy over the surrounding territory by military force. Its flourishing commercial life was founded on its guilds, its powerful *arti.* The Florentine merchants traded with France and Egypt, with Flanders and England, and dealt principally in wool, cloth and silk. The political power that controlled the city rested in the hands

240

of these rich merchants, who, beginning in 1434, fell under the
Medici ascendancy. And the Medici took full and ruthless advantage of the city's unending stream of wealth: the great wealth
which came to Florence as the financial and banking capital of
Europe. Florence was dominant artistically in painting and sculpture, in architecture, as well as in humanist-inspired works of
scholarship. It was the most luminous city of the age. Outstanding names compete for prominence: Poggio and Giotto, Bruni,
Masaccio, Donatello and Michelangelo, Ghiberti and Botticelli,
Pico della Mirandola, Ficino and Lorenzo the Magnificent. This
Athens of the Renaissance also produced Machiavelli and Guicciardini, among other historians and statesmen. Florence was, in
short, a turbulent city, politically and socially, intellectually and
artistically. Devout and licentious, earthy and nostalgic for the
classical past, bloody and scholarly, Florence was a city of contrasts: of Savonarola on the one hand and of Lorenzo the Magnificent on the other. Against cutthroats and assassins prepared to
execute any mission for hire were set the monks and ascetics.
Gay ladies contrasted with saintly nuns, the most lofty ideals
with dissolute iniquity. It is the same contrast which in greater
or lesser degree the Renaissance exhibited everywhere.

FLORENTINE PRINTERS
Among Renaissance printers who worked in Florence were: John
of Mainz, who started in 1472: Nicholas of Breslau, in 1477:
Antonio Miscomini, in 1481: Lorenzo Alopa of Venice.

FLORENTINE SCHOOL
This term applies to the painters, sculptors, architects, as well as
craftsmen in analogous fields who were citizens of Florence or associated with that city. Generally considered as the leading
school of the Italian Renaissance (1350-1550). The Florentine
School of painting is divided chronologically into schools of the
thirteenth century: *duocento,* fourteenth century: *trecento,* fifteenth century: *quattrocento,* sixteenth century: *cinquecento.*
Schools of the thirteenth and fourteenth centuries—late medieval
—are grouped together: dominated by Cimabue and Giotto. In
the fifteenth century Florence was the leader of the Renaissance.
The schools were of three classes: painters who continued the
late medieval tradition: progressive realists: narrative group. The
sixteenth century opened with da Vinci, Michelangelo, Andrea
del Sarto: then there was a rapid decline. The Florentine School

of sculpture challenged Pisan leadership in the fourteenth century and dominated Italy in the fifteenth century. Notable names include Andrea Pisano, Donatello, called The Father of Renaissance sculpture, Lorenzo Ghiberti, Luca della Robbia, Andrea del Verrocchio, Benedetto da Majano: all in the fifteenth century. In the sixteenth, Michelangelo and Benvenuto Cellini are outstanding.

FLORES, JUAN DE

(Late fifteenth-early sixteenth century). Spanish writer of *novelas sentimentals*. Noted for two novels: *Grimalte y Gradisa*: c. 1495: imitation of Boccaccio: and *Historia de Grisel y Mirabella*: c. 1495. Translated into Italian, French, English. He provided materials that were utilized by Ariosto, Lope de Vega, John Fletcher, and de Scudéry.

FLORIO, JOHN

(c. 1553-1625). English translator and scholar. Son of Italian refugee in London. Produced Italian-English dictionary: *A World of Words*: published in 1598. Also translated Montaigne's *Essays*, the standard translation until recently.

FLORIS, FRANS DE

(ante 1520-1570). Flemish painter. He had studied in Italy. All his work—portraits, religious and mythological scenes—exemplify the profound Italian influence dominant in the Lowlands in his lifetime; he is thus a Mannerist. William of Orange, as well as Dutch and Spanish nobles, were his patrons.

FLÖTNER, PETER

(c. 1485-1546). German sculptor, engraver. Executed plastic decorations, small sculptures, medallions, plaquettes. Designs for works of craft, ornamental works. He was a pioneer of the German Renaissance; his *Kunstbuch* was especially influential.

FOGLIANI, LUDOVICO, FOGLIANO, FOGLIANUS

(Died c. 1540). Musician and kappelmeister of Modena; author of the treatise *Music theorica*. His brother GIACOMO (1474-1548), was an organist and composer of madrigals and lauds.

FOLENGO, TEOFILO

(1491-1544). Italian comic poet, pseudonym was Merlinus Coccaius. He left his Benedictine monastery to be a wandering poet and the lover of his lady Girolama. His *Baldus,* 1517, is a Rabelaisian hero who espouses the natural life: his escapades provide full opportunity for parody and satire of the chivalric romances as well as realistic depiction of life. It is an epic in Italian, imitating Ariosto's *Orlando Furioso,* Vergil, and Dante; his style is "macaronic", i.e. the mixture of Italian and Latin words and the use of Latin suffixes for Italian words. His later piece of buffoonery, *Orlandino,* 1526, has particular reference to Ariosto's epic; it was condemned for its Lutheranism by the Inquisition. After about a decade of being poet and lover, Teofilo was readmitted to his monastery and gave himself over to writing works of devotion and piety. Both Rabelais and Cervantes knew his satirical works.

FOLZ, HANS
(c. 1450-1515). German Meistersinger and physician. Author of *Herzog von Burgund,* Lenten play. Also wrote tales, songs. He was responsible for several innovations in the Meistersinger musical tradition and succeeded in ending its "ancient manner."

FONDULIS, GIOVANNI
Fifteenth century. Italian sculptor. Executed bas-reliefs for city of Padua.

FONTANA, DOMENICO
(1543-1607). Italian architect. Attached to court of Pope Sixtus V. Worked on St. Peter's. Built Lateran Palace. Also Vatican Library. He left Rome, on the death of the Pope, for Naples where he built the royal palace. Several great engineering feats are to his credit, e.g., the redesign of the Neapolitan harbor and various aqueducts.

FONTANA, LAVINIA
(1552-c. 1614). Italian painter, the daughter of Prospero. Worked in Rome, Bologna. Noted for portraiture.

FONTANA, PROSPERO
(1512-1597). Italian painter. Worked in Bologna principally, but also helped to decorate the palace of Fontainebleau in France.

FONTOURA DA COSTA
Portuguese navigator. Wrote an account of a voyage to India: published in 1484.

FOPPA, CRISTOFORO

(died 1527). Called II Caradosso. Italian sculptor and medalist of Milan.

FOPPA, VICENZO

(c. 1429-1517). Italian painter. Lived and died in Brescia, but did most of his work in Milan and Pavia. His first works were in Gothic style: later, he tended toward style of Mantegna and Leonardo da Vinci. Founder of the Lombard school. Produced frescoes, easel pictures, religious subjects, a great many of which have not survived.

FORCADEL, ESTIENNE

(1534-1573). French jurist. Wrote dialogue on legal problems: *Necromantia Iurisperiti:* published in 1549. Also series of legal treatises: *Penus Iuris Civilis:* published in 1550.

FORKS

In the early sixteenth century, forks first came into use in Venice, whence the vogue spread to other cities. In the northern courts, e.g., that of Elizabeth of England in the later sixteenth century, they were still satirized as part and parcel of the *Italianate* gentleman.

FORMAN, SIMON

(1552-1611). English astrologer, necromancer and quack-doctor. Lived in London. Practiced medicine. Concocted love philtres. He was frequently involved in law suits, was imprisoned, but had influential friends; the University of Cambridge licensed him to practice medicine.

FORNOVA, BATTLE OF

In this battle, in 1495, Charles VIII of France, having invaded Italy and captured Naples the year before, was compelled to fight the forces of the League of Venice, organized to restore the Italian *status quo*. It included Pope Alexander VI, Ferdinand of Aragon and the Holy Roman Emperor Maximilian. Charles VIII barely won and fled over the Alps to France.

FORTESCUE, SIR JOHN

(c. 1394-c. 1476). Lord Chief Justice of England. Captured at Battle of Tewkesbury in 1471. Pardoned by Edward IV. Author of *On the Government of the Kingdom of England*. Also wrote juristic treatise, *De Laudibus Legum Angliae.* By his famous formula, *"politicum et regale,"* he designated England a limited monarchy and contrasted it with the absolutism of France.

FOSCARI, FRANCESCO
(c. 1373-1457). Doge of Venice 1423-57, the longest of all the ducal reigns. He is chiefly associated with the Venetian conquest of the mainland—Ravenna, Vicenza, Padua, Verona, Brescia—in response to the challenge of Milanese expansion under the Visconti. A center of controversy throughout his reign, he was accused by the Council of Ten of neglecting Venetian maritime interests in the East and of scheming to overthrow the Republic in favor of a personal despotism like that of the Visconti at Milan or the Medici at Florence. Forced to abdicate at the age of eighty-four, his reign may be said to have fixed the Venetian constitution in its final form. Up to his time the position of the doge was unstable: many of them were assassinated, compelled to abdicate, blinded and exiled, etc. From Foscari to the Napoleonic conquest, the Council of Ten was supreme and the Venetian government the most stable in Europe; political theorists regarded its constitution as a perfect model of oligarchical rule.

FOUCQUET, FRANÇOIS
Illuminator. Executed a copy of St. Augustine's *City of God* c. 1473: also a number of copies of *Book of Hours* and other works.

FOUCQUET, JEAN
(c. 1420-1480). Master of school of miniaturists in Tours and chief founder of the French school of painting of the fifteenth century. Commissioned to paint what is a famous portrait of Charles VII. In Rome painted Pope Eugenius IV's portrait, now lost. His best known works include a portrait of the Virgin (said to be the royal mistress, Agnes Sorel), a *Book of Hours* for the Duke of Berry, and the illuminations for French translations of Boccaccio and for Josephus' *Antiquities of the Jews.*

FOURTEEN-HUNDRED-NINETY-FOUR, "ANNO INFELICISSIMO"
The year of the French invasion by Charles VIII, seeking to make good his claims to Naples; it inaugurated the Italian wars of the sixteenth century, during which France and Spain fought over prostrate Italy; in many respects it was a resumption of the long quarrel between France and Spain (Aragon) that dated

from the thirteenth century. Italian interest in local affairs and the inability to unite gave France an easy victory. Italian defeats in 1494 and in the later invasions caused much soul searching: they were attributed to excesses—too much luxury, irreligion, and immorality, or to the lack of discipline and morale. Publicists asked themselves how these latest "barbarians" could be driven off and found their answer in the example of ancient Rome's defense against its barbarian attackers; of the same tendency as many other solutions was Machiavelli's *Art of War*, in that it called for a citizen militia that was trained, disciplined, and patriotic like those of the ancient republic. The high point of the anguish came with the merciless sack of Rome in 1527, a fatal blow to Renaissance Italy and the culmination of the invasions that began in 1494. A concatenation of factors and forces explains why Charles VIII's invasion occurred when it did, viz., the crusading character of the king who dreamed of reconquering the Holy Land and saw in the possession of southern Italy a vital stepping stone for that end, the king's necessity to engage the energies of the nobility in foreign wars so as to avoid rebellion at home, the dependence of the French crown on Italian bankers many of whom were exiles and agitated for restoration to their native cities by French might, and the ambitions of Ludovico Il Moro, the Sforza ruler of Milan: his policies led to the severance of the alliance with Naples and Florence and, in his isolation, to the alliance with France. Thus France received an invitation to interfere in Italian affairs and was ready to answer the call.

FOWLER, WILLIAM

(Late sixteenth century). Scottish poet. Attached to Stuart court. Translated *Il Principe*. Imitated Petrarch, Tasso, Ariosto in his verse collections, *The Tarantula of Love* and *The Triumph of Petrarch*.

FOXE, JOHN

(1516-1587). English clergyman. An Anglican prebendary under Elizabeth, he had taken refuge on the Continent during Mary's reign. Author of *Book of Martyrs*, published in 1559. Originally in Latin, later translated into English and greatly expanded as the *Acts and Monuments of These Latter and Perilous Days*. After the King James version of the Bible, the *Book* has had the greatest influence on the English-speaking world, ideologically and stylistically.

FOXE, LUKE
(1586-1635). English sailor. In 1631 on expedition in search of Northwest Passage in the region of Hudson Bay. Author of an account of his voyage urging his conclusion that no such passage existed.

FRACASTORO, GIROLAMO
(c. 1478-1553). Veronese physician, astronomer, astrologer, literary critic, and poet; he had studied at Padua; author of the Latin poem *Syphilis sive de Marbo Gallico*, 1531, a description of the syphilis epidemic that occurred in Naples at the time of Charles VIII's presence there, 1494-1495. Versed in Aristotle, Fracastoro took an interest in and contributed significantly to several fields. He criticized the employment of epicycles and deferents in astronomy, in geography he coined the term "pole", in medicine "syphilis", which he named for the amorous shepherd of Greek mythology who contracted the malady. A truly scientific work was his treatise of 1546, where he suggested that infection is caused by minute organisms conveyed from a diseased person to a healthy one. He served as Physician to the Council of Trent.

FRANCAVILLA, PIETRO
(1548?-1615). Sculptor. Born in Cambrai, he studied in Florence and Italianized his name from Franceville. Worked in bronze. He entered the service of Henry IV of France. He did mythological subjects, e.g., *Orpheus, Jove*, as well as depictions of his patrons.

FRANCESCO DI GIORGIO MARTINI
(1439-1502). Italian illuminator. Pupil of Il Vecchietta. Influenced by Pollaiuolo. Illuminated *De Animalibus* of Albertus Magnus: executed in 1463.

FRANCIA, FRANCESCO RAIBOLINI
(c. 1450-1517). Italian painter, goldsmith and metals artist of Bologna. Leading artist of Bolognese Renaissance. Influenced by Raphael and Perugino. Noted for *Dead Christ, Assumption, Madonna,* and other religious paintings, he also painted portraits, e.g., of Federigo Gonzaga. Symonds: "One of the most sincerely pious of Christian painters. . . For mastery over oil painting and

for charm of color Francia challenges comparision with what is best in Perugino, though he did not quite attain the same technical excellence."

FRANCIS I

(1494-1547). King of France. He fought endlessly for the control of Italy. His reign began auspiciously with his sparkling victory at Marignano and the occupation of Lombardy, 1515. Unsuccessful in election as Holy Roman Emperor. Participated in conferences with Henry VIII of England at the Field of the Cloth of Gold, in 1520. In conflict with the Holy Roman Empire from 1521 to 1525. Defeated by Charles V at Pavia and taken prisoner, in 1525. Surrendering Burgundy, he gained release in 1526. Undertook a second war: 1527-1529. Lost Italian possessions. Started a third war and a fourth. His reign marks the real onset of the Renaissance in France. He was generous in his patronage of artists and humanists (many of whom, e.g., Benvenuto Cellini, were enticed from Italy). He was more notable for his taste for magnificence and finery than for rigorous statecraft.

FRANCIS II

(1544-1560). King of France. Son of Henry II and Catherine de Medici. Weak and sickly. Unsuccessful conspiracy against his life. Married Mary Queen of Scots in 1558. Tool of his uncles Cardinal of Lorraine and Duke of Guise, who vied for control of the royal government with the Queen Regent, Catherine de Medici. Supported persecution of Protestants and thus kindled the civil and religious wars. He reigned only two years.

FRANCIS DE SALES, SAINT

(1567-1622). French noble of Savoy. Cleric. Went on mission to convert Calvinists. Helped in founding Order of the Visitation of Our Lady. Wrote *The Love of God* and *Introduction to the Devout Life.*

FRANCISCO DE PORTUGAL, FIRST COUNT OF VIMIOSO, DOM

(Died 1549). A man of action in the Portuguese tradition of the *fidalgo.* He spent his life in the royal service and as courtier to Dom Manuel. His poems, songs, sayings and moralistic reflections were long remembered and most of them published in 1605 as *Sentenças de Dom Francisco de Portugal.*

FRANCISCO MANUEL DE MELO
(1608-1666). Prolific Portuguese writer, poet, translator. He embodied the Portuguese ideal of the *fidalgo* and was as ready to wield arms as the pen, play the soldier, royal councilor, or courtier. Among his works may be mentioned the *Concordancia matemática de antigas e modernas hipótesis, Politica Militon, Fidalgo Aprendiz, Manifesto de Portugal, Mayor Pequeno* (both these last playing their part in the winning of Portuguese independence from Spain in the 1640's), *Obras Métricas, Obras Morales, Cartas Familiares,* and translations of Molière.

FRANCIS OF PAULA, SAINT
(1416-1507). Italian Franciscan monk who withdrew from the Order to live as a hermit. The community that grew up around him came to be organized as the Order of Minims in 1436, confirmed in 1474. He enjoyed the patronage of the French kings.

FRANCK, SEBASTIAN
(1499-1543). German liberal thinker of the Reformation. At first, a Catholic priest. Later, a Lutheran: finally, a champion of religious freedom. Called by Luther "The Devil's Mouth." Set up printing presses in Basel and Ulm. Expounded a humanistic mystical syncretism. Author of *Chronica,* in German: published in 1531: a universal history and his own *apologia.*

FRANCKEN
Family of Flemish painters. Hieronymus (1540-1610). Frans (1542-1616). Ambrosius (1544-1618). Frans (1581-1642). Worked in Antwerp. Subjects were religious, mythological, historical. Also portraiture. The later generation shows the influence of Rubens, but all of them, in some degree, that of Italy.

FRANCO GIACOMO
Author of *Habiti d'Huomeni et Donne Venetiane:* published c. 1610.

FRANCO, NICCOLO
(1515-1570). Minor writer, plagiarist and adventurer. Native of Benevento. He crossed swords with, among others, Pietro Aretino and fell into so many feuds that his enemies were bound to catch him eventually. He was condemned by the Inquisition for libel and blasphemy and hanged. Author of a dialogue deal-

ing with the harmony of the female body and a great deal of bellicose verse.

FRANÇOIS DE CORTETE
(1571-1655). Notable Provençal writer. Author of comedies: *Ramounet, Miramoundo*.

FRANCUCCI, INNOCENZO DI PIETRO, INNOCENZA DA IMOLA
(1481-1550). Painter of Bologna. Pupil of Albertinelli. He did chiefly religious frescoes and worked under the spell of so many painters, e.g. Raphael, Andrea del Sarto that he is an eclectic.

FRANGIPANI, THE
An ancient noble family of Rome. They sparred with emperors and popes, with Orsini and Colonna, for power and influence in Rome. By the time of the Renaissance they had established the Colosseum as their domicile and fortress, encamped there amid the brutal retainers whom they led in endless raids and petty warfare against their enemies.

FRAUNCE, ABRAHAM
(1587?-1633). English poet. Protégé of Sir Philip Sidney. Wrote *The Countess of Pembroke Yuychurch Containing an Affectionate Life and Unfortunate Death of Phillis and Amyntas*. Also songs and occasional verse.

FREDERICK II
(1534-1588). King of Denmark. In conflict with Sweden. Suppressed piracy. Efficient ruler. Most of reign was tranquil.

FREDERICK II, EMPEROR, STUPOR MUNDI
(1194-1250). The greatest of the Hohenstaufen emperors and mighty antagonist of the popes. The defeat and overthrow of his dynasty and the Empire together with the Babylonian Captivity and Great Schism of the Papacy constitute the double cancellation of authority in Italy that paved the way for the independent city-states and the Renaissance culture. Frederick himself, brilliantly gifted and accomplished, anticipates the Renaissance ruler: "Statesman and philosopher, politician and soldier, general and jurist, poet and diplomat, architect, zoologist, mathematician, the master of six or it may be nine languages, who collected ancient works of art, directed a school of sculpture, made independent researches in natural science [founded the University of

250

Naples] and organized states, this supremely versatile man was the Genius of the Renaissance on the throne of the Emperors." (Kantorowicz)

FREDERICK III, EMPEROR

(1415-1492). He was the last emperor to be crowned, 1452, at Rome. A Hapsburg, he devoted himself to the aggrandizement of his house and ancestral lands, caring little for the Empire. He marked all his belongings with the cryptic anagram AEIOU, said to mean "*Austriae est imperare orbi universo.*" The early period of his reign was graced by his brilliant humanist secretary, Aeneas Silvius Piccolomini (afterward Pope Pius II); Frederick himself, rather indolent, dabbled in astrology, alchemy, literary studies and gardening.

FREDERICK III, CALLED THE WISE

(1463-1525). Elector of Saxony. Founded University of Wittenberg in 1502. Protected Martin Luther and gave him a haven in Wartburg Castle.

FREDERICK V

(1556-1632). Elector of the Palatinate, called to be king of Bohemia by the Rebels, called The Winter King. Deposed in 1623. Spent rest of his life in exile. He is the central figure in the opening events of the Thirty Years' War.

FREE, JOHN or PHREAS

(fl. c. 1430-died 1465). English scholar. Bishop of Bath. Born in Bristol. Studied medicine, theology, Roman law in Italy. Physician, translator, (he knew Greek as well as Latin), bibliophile. Typical Renaissance figure in manifestation of wide intellectual interests. His patron was the humanist enthusiast, John Tipcroft, the earl of Worcester.

FRENCH ACADEMY

French literary institution founded in 1635 by Cardinal Richelieu. Produced *Dictionary of the French Language.* The forty members, called The Forty Immortals, supervise French grammar, syntax, orthography, rhetoric. Its purpose to fix the language as a literary vehicle is in keeping with the spirit of royal despotism and centralism of the seventeenth century, but not with the Renaissance, when the disposition to probe and to experiment was stronger.

FRENCH ART

Until after the Hundred Years' War (1337-1453) there was no single centre of art in France. In the late fifteenth century artists of Bourges composed the School of the Loire or the School of Touraine. Avignon and Aix too were art centers. Toward the end of the fifteenth century French art began to reflect Italian influences. Franco-Flemish school featured precision, realism, color. Italian influence appeared as suggested by such names as Froment of Avignon, Jean Perréal, Jean Fouquet. Image makers produced sacred statues in ivory, stone, and wood. Book illuminators flourished. Among them may be mentioned Pol de Limbourg. Under Francis I, Italian artists and scholars were invited to France—Leonardo da Vinci, Andrea del Sarto, Cellini, Bandello, Alciatus, Alamanni, and many more. The School of Fontainebleau was founded, becoming characteristically French in spirit, although it owed much to foreign artists. Notable names of the sixteenth century were Michel Colombe, sculptor: Germain Pilon, Barthelmy Prieur. Under Louis XIII (1610-1643) French art became finally unified, until then it was derivative, owing much (and about equally) to the Lowlands and to Italy.

FRENCH INVASION OF 1494, THE

The French invasion of Italy, in 1494, exercised a tremendous influence on warfare and strategic operations. Military architects, among them Leonardo da Vinci, designed fortifications intended to withstand the most violent assaults. Cannon replaced battering rams as siege engines. Mining techniques were developed.

FRENCH LANGUAGE

In the town of Villers-Cotterêts Francis I proclaimed French as the official language, in 1539.

FRENCH RULERS

Charles VII: 1422-1461. Louis XI: 1461-1483. Charles VIII: 1483-1498. Louis XII: 1498-1515. Francis I: 1515-1547. Henry II: 1547-1558. Francis II: 1559-1560. Charles IX: 1560-1574. Henry III: 1574-1589. The Bourbon line began with the ascension of Henry IV, 1589-1610, Louis XIII, 1610-1643. Dates refer to duration of rule.

FRESCOBALDI, GIROLAMO

(1583-1643) Italian composer, especially for organ, and the

252

greatest virtuoso organist of his time; "the Italian Bach," he was famed as an improvisor. He was a child prodigy, whose fame brought him the post of organist to the popes; he composed many toccatas and caprices, and was a pioneer of the fugue; he was an early master of instrumental, rather than vocal counterpoint—relatively few of his works are for voice.

FRISCHLIN, NICODEMUS
German astronomer. Wrote on astronomical subjects in opposition to astrology. His work was published in 1586.

FROBEN, JOHANNES or FROBENIUS
(c. 1460-1527). German pioneer printer and publisher. Founded press at Basle, Switzerland. Published texts of Church Fathers, Latin Bibles, works of Erasmus. Noted for taste and accuracy. Issued the Ninety-Five Theses of Martin Luther. Brought out Erasmus' New Testament in Greek in 1516. Known as "the Aldus of the North," his was one of the great publishing houses of the sixteenth century.

FROBISHER, SIR MARTIN
(c. 1535-1594). English navigator. Went in search of Northwest Passage: also gold. Discovered Frobisher Bay, Canada, in 1576. In West Indies expedition with Drake. Participated in defeat of Armada, commanding ship *Triumph*.

FROMENT, NICOLAS
(c. 1435-c. 1484). French painter. Primitive. Worked at Avignon from 1461 to 1482. Produced a *Burning Bush,* in the Cathedral of Aix, and *Resurrection of Lazarus*. His patron was René of Anjou, whom—with his wife—he painted in a diptych.

FRUNDSBERG, GEORG VON
(1473-1527). German general. He organized the force of German mercenaries known as *Landsknechte.* Fought against Swiss. Led the troops of the Swabian League. Fought at Battle of Pavia. Appears in German plays and novels. It was his troops, shortly after his death, that sacked Rome so mercilessly.

FRUSCHLIN, NICODEMUS
(1547-1590). German humanist. Neo-Latin dramatist. Professor of poetry at Tübingen. Author of satirical plays: *Julius Redivivus, Priscanus Vapulans:* attacks on barbarities of contemporary Latinity.

253

FUCHS, LEONHARD

(1501-1566). German botanist. His name is associated with the genus *Fuchsia*. Author of the compendium of edible and medicinal plants entitled, *De Historia Stirpium*: published in 1542 in Basel. This work is considered to have marked an epoch in the history of botany and long remained the standard work. He taught medicine at the University of Tübingen.

FUGGER FAMILY AS BANKERS

The Fugger family became bankers to Sigismond of Tyrol in 1487; for generations the family had been weavers.

FUGGER, JAKOB

(1459-1525). German merchant. Called Jakob the Rich. Member of family of financiers and merchants. Had interests in spice trade, mines in Hungary and Spain. Financier to Hapsburgs, Papacy. Built the *Fuggerei*, dwelling project for the poor, still in use.

FURNITURE IN THE RENAISSANCE

Furniture was one of the important minor arts in the Renaissance; a great painter such as Botticelli was not above decorating a *cassone*—the finely wrought chest which was indispensable to a fashionable bride. Renaissance furniture clearly reflects the dominant trends of the age, viz., the greater secularization of life and the use of wealth for private luxury, comfort and display. It may be added that the chair came into its own: aside from the folding chair and the backed stool, chairs were reserved for kings until the sixteenth century. In the Renaissance period in Italy, furniture exhibited general characteristics irrespective of locale, although—as in painting—there were regional schools, e.g., that of Venice, Lombardy, and Florence. In the fifteenth and sixteenth centuries ornament was sparingly used, classical in theme, mostly carved, mythological symbolism, foliage, scrolls. As the *Cinquecento* advanced, ornament became more lavish and bolder. Classical motifs were expanded. Spain succumbed to early Renaissance influence from Italy. The style was *Plateresco*.

In France, Gothic forms were modified with Italian detail. Italian workmen were engaged for interiors. French furniture of the sixteenth century was heavy and ornate.

In the Netherlands the influence was Spanish during the sixteenth century.

In Germany a Flemish-French influence appeared, although in general Gothic style persisted until very late.

In England in the sixteenth century furniture evolved from its medieval form. Italian, French, and Flemish influence appeared.

FUST, JOHN

(d.1466) German printer who perfected and refined printing devices in mid-fifteenth century. He was a goldsmith and money lender. Gutenberg's inability to pay back his loans brought the printing shop into Fust's hands. He and his son-in-law, Peter Schöffer, took over the business and made a success of it.

G

GABRIELE, ANTONIO

Seventeenth century. Apostolic delegate. Author of *Communes Conclusiones:* comprehensive legal survey, dealing with minors, inheritance, drawing up of wills.

GABRIELI, ANDREA

(1520-1586). Venetian composer, pupil of Willaert, organist at St. Marks, composer of motets, psalms, madrigals, and organ music. He was famed as a master of counterpoint.

GABRIELI, GIOVANNI

(1557-1612). Venetian composer. Nephew of Andrea Gabrieli, composer of motets, psalms, symphonies and famous for his contrapuntal style. He was a student of Lassus and became organist to St. Mark's.

GABRIELLO DE ZERBIS

(1465-1505). Italian anatomist. Flourished in Verona. Assumed title of Medicus Theoricus. Performed dissection of human subjects.

GADIO, GIOVANNI

Illuminator and miniaturist of Cremona. In 1482 he executed an antiphonary for Cremona Cathedral.

GAFORI, FRANCHINO

(1451-1522). Milanese musical theorist of harmony, priest, and choirmaster at the cathedral of Milan. He was attached to the Sforza court in the time of Ludovico Il Moro, at whose musical school he taught.

GAGUIN, ROBERT

(c. 1433-1501). French cleric, scholar, chronicler. Author of *De Origine et Gestis Francorum Compendium:* published in 1495. Translated Caesar's *Commentaries:* published in 1495. He had an influence on Erasmus during Erasmus' student days at Paris.

GAIGNY, IOANNES DE

(died 1549). Jehan de Ganay. French theologian, poet. Rector of the University of Paris. Author of commentaries, sermons, Latin poems.

GAILLARD, AUGER

(c. 1530-1595). Provençal poet. Author of rollicking but often obscene poems. He participated to the hilt in the French civil and religious wars, the passions of which are often found in his poems.

GAISSMAYR, MICHAEL

(Died 1520). Tyrolean leader. Supporter of Lutheranism. He proposed a communistic-democratic political reform, wrote at least one manifesto in behalf of his social ideal, but was assassinated.

GALATINUS, PETRUS

(c. 1460-c. 1540). Franciscan theologian. Converted Jew of Apulia. Attacked Reuchlin. Author of *Opus de Arcanis Catholicae Veritatis:* published in 1518. He also wrote a commentary on the Apocalypse that reflects the cabalistic and Joachimite traditions.

GALE, THOMAS

(1501-1587). English military surgeon. Master of the barber-surgeons guild. Author of *Certain Works of Chirurgerie:* laid down rules of conduct for surgeon. First mention of syphilis in English, which he called *morbus Gallicus.* He was best known in his time for his treatise on gunshot wounds: *Treatise of Gunshot,* 1544.

GALEOTTO, MARZIO

(1427-1497). Italian humanist. Attached to the court of King Matthias of Hungary (1458-1490). The King, stimulated by the Italian Renaissance, assembled at his court historians, philosophers, physicians, poets, astrologers. Galeotto produced *De Egregie, Sapienter et Iocose Dictis et Factis Matthiae Regis:* published between 1484 and 1487.

258

GALILEI, GALILEO

(1564-1642). Italian astronomer, physicist and mathematician. Born in Pisa. Discovered the isochronism of the pendulum and thus made possible the perfection of the clock. From the Leaning Tower of Pisa he demonstrated that bodies of different weight fall with the same velocity, although he was not the first to make the test: also demonstrated that the path of a missile is a parabola. From 1592 to 1610 he was professor of mathematics at Padua. In 1593 he invented an open-air thermometer. In 1610 he devised a telescope that magnified the diameter of objects eight times, based on models from the Lowlands. By this means he discovered mountains on the moon, moons of Jupiter, sun spots: also that the Milky Way is composed of numerous stars. At the University of Florence he was appointed professor for life: also mathematician extraordinary to the Duke of Tuscany, the ruler of Florence. His defense of the Copernican theory resulted in denunciation by the Church in 1613. His publication of the *Dialogo dei due Massimi Sistemi del Mondo* in 1632 brought him a summons to Rome and a trial by the Inquisition. He was forced to deny his belief that the earth and the planets revolve round the sun. He had a zest for polemic. He was an outspoken anti-Aristotelian. Aristotle's physics and astronomy were discredited, yet it may be said that Galileo was very much within the Aristotelian tradition of logic and methods of proof. His greatest significance lies in his development of the theory of inertia, thus paving the way for Newton's three laws of motion. He spent his last years in retirement in a villa near Florence; after 1637, in blindness.

GALILEI, VINCENZO

(Died 1591). Musician and musical theorist, member of the Florentine *Camerata* group, father of Galileo. He was a keen student of the Greek writers on music and, strengthened by his reading, initiated the reaction against counterpoint in his *Dialogo della Musica antica et moderna*, 1581.

GALLAS, MATTHIAS

(1584-1647). Count of Campo. Austrian soldier in the Thirty Years' War. Served with troops of Catholic League: also in Italy. Fought against Swedes, whom he defeated in 1634 but then lost to them by 1638. Succeeded Wallenstein.

GALLUCCI, GIOVANNI PAOLO

Sixteenth century. Author of a comprehensive scientific treatise: *Theatrum Mundi et Temporis*: published in 1588.

GALLUS, IODOCUS

(c. 1459-1517). Alsatian humanist, he taught philosophy at the University of Heidelberg. He wrote poems of edification as well as satire; his *Monopolium et Societas des Luchtschiff*, 1488, anticipates much of the popular satire by his fellow Alsatian and contemporary, Sebastian Brant.

GALVÃO, ANTONIO

(1503-1557). Portuguese chronicler. Author of an encyclopedic work on travels and discoveries from the earliest times to 1555. Had numerous other historical and geographical works. He had served as governor of the Moluccas.

GALVÃO, DUARTE

(c. 1445-1515). Portuguese historian, father of the above. At the request of King Manual I (1469-1521), wrote chronicle of Alfonso Henriques, first king of Portugal, and other works of national and royal history, but they are uniformly devoid of any critical spirit. He led an active life as ambassador and royal servant.

GAMA, VASCO DA

(1460-1524). Portuguese navigator. Starting from Portugal, he sailed around the Cape of Good Hope and in 1498 reached Calicut, in India. This was the first voyage of a Western European seaman around Africa to the East. In 1524 he acted as Viceroy of Portuguese Asia. Da Gama's first voyage is the theme of the greatest Portuguese epic, *The Lusiadas*, by Camoens.

GAMBELLO, VITTORE

(1460?-1537). Called Il Camelio. Italian sculptor. Master of the Mint in Venice. Executed funerary monuments, bas-reliefs.

GAMES AND SPORT

Among recreational diversions were falconry, staghunts, tournaments, jousting. Tennis and bowls were popular. Indoors, chess and card playing occupied many people.

260

GANDAVO, PEDRO DE MAGELHAES
Portuguese chronicler, author of *History of Santa Cruz*, i.e., of Brazil, published in 1576. He also wrote a description and defense of Portuguese as a learned and literary vehicle of expression.

GANSFORT, WESSEL
(1419-1489) Dutch humanist and theologian, educated by the Brethren of the Common Life. He wrote humanistic Biblical exegesis and is considered a forerunner of the Reformation.

Between 1479 and 1481 he published *Farrago Rerum Theologicarum*.

GARAMOND, CLAUDE
(died 1561). French type designer. Famous for his "royal Greek type." Replaced Gothic with Roman type. He seems to have taken the decisive step in forming a distinct printed type rather than an imitation of handwriting. Name now associated with various styles of type.

GARCIA DA ORTA
Sixteenth century. Portuguese pharmacist. Author of treatise on medicinal herbs, published in 1563.

GARCÍA DE MASCARENHAS
(1596-1656). Portuguese poet. Author of epic *Viriato Trágico*.

GARCÍA DE RESENDE
(1470-1536). Portuguese chronicler. Author of an account of the Portuguese in Africa.

GARCIA, VICENTE, RECTOR DE VALLIFOGONA
(1582-1623). Spanish priest and poet. He wrote religious plays, e.g., *Comédia de Santa Bàrbara*, presented in the chapel of his church during religious festivals. He was later called to the court of Philip IV, where he associated with many of the great writers of his day, e.g., Góngora and Lope de Vega. He is remembered chiefly for his religious, lyrical verse, notably the *Cant d'agonia*. He wrote in his native Catalan as well as Spanish.

GARCILASO DE LA VEGA
(1501?-1536). Spanish poet, soldier, courtier. Born in Toledo, died in Nice. Of noble family, he was trained in classical literature, equitation, fencing, music, chivalry and war. Exemplar of

the Renaissance gentleman, modeled after Castiglione's *Courtier*. Attached to household of Charles V. Served in campaigns in Austria, Africa, France. At court of Naples. Mortally wounded in a brash charge to take a castle in Provence. Often called The Spanish Petrarch. His poems were published in 1543. He produced 38 sonnets, 5 *canciones*, 3 eclogues, 2 elegies, an epistle, 8 *coplas*.

He was instrumental in the naturalization of Italian hendecasyllabics into Spanish verse. Also introduced metrical form called *lira*. The predominant theme of the poetry is love.

GARCILASO DE LA VEGA

(1539-1616). Spanish soldier, translator, historian. Born in Peru, of Spanish conquistador father and Incan princess and thus called *El Inca*. Came to Spain in 1560. Entered military service. Educated in humanities. Translated León Hebreo's *Diálogos de Amor*. Among his historical works are: *Historia General del Perú* and *Historia de la Florida*. His work on Peru is especially valuable for the conquest and the culture of the Incas.

GARDINER, STEPHEN

(c. 1483-1555). English prelate and one-time secretary to Wolsey. Bishop of Winchester. Influential at court of Henry VIII after Cromwell's fall. Later, imprisoned by Edward VI: released. Instrumental in persecution of Protestants. He became Lord Chancellor under Mary.

GARIGLIANO, BATTLE OF

In this battle the Spanish general Gonzalo de Cordova, *El Gran Capitán*, defeated the French in 1503. The result was the possession of all southern Italy by King Ferdinand of Spain.

GARIMBERTO, GIROLAMO

(died 1575). Bishop of Gallese, antiquarian, and man of letters. Wrote on scientific and philosophical problems of Renaissance: ethics, love, nature of man. Published in 1559. Translated into French. Also author of a collection of maxims on education, statecraft, learning, law, and other intellectual interests of Renaissance. He maintained a voluminous correspondence.

GARNETT, HENRY

(1555-1606). English Jesuit. Executed on the charge of participation in the Gunpowder Plot.

GARNIER, ROBERT

(1534-1590). French dramatist and poet. Wrote versified tragic plays, among them: *Porcie, Marc Antoine, Antigone;* Seneca was his chief inspiration, e.g., in *Les Juifves.*

GAROFALO, IL, BENVENUTO TISI

(c. 1481-1559). Italian painter of Ferrara. Carried on Roman style of Raphael. Noted for richness of color; confined himself almost entirely to religious subjects.

GASCOIGNE, GEORGE

(c. 1525-1577). English poet, dramatist and literary pioneer. Author of *A Hundred Sundry Flowers:* collection of poems. *The Steel Glass:* a satire. *The Supposes:* prose comedy adapted from Italian. *Jocasta:* tragedy adapted from Dolce's *Giocasta.* Noted for first translated prose from Bandello. Also *Certain Notes or Instructions Concerning the Making of Verse Rhyme in England,* the first essay on prosody to be written in English.

GASSENDI, PIERRE

(1592-1655). French philosopher, mathematician. Professor of theology at Aix. Professor of mathematics at Collège Royal of Paris. Opponent of Descartes and sharp critic of Aristotle. Author of *De Vita et Moribus Epicuri,* published in 1647. Also *Philosophiae Epicuri Syntagma,* published in 1649. He was a priest and held ecclesiastical offices throughout his life.

GASTIUS, JOANNES

(died 1553). Swiss theologian. Author of *Convivialium Sermonum Liber:* collection of anecdotes on fables, adolescents, medicine, and other miscellaneous topics: 1543.

GATAKER, THOMAS

(1574-1654). English Puritan divine and cleric. He wrote a great many miscellaneous works, usually on religious themes; the best was Biblical commentary.

GATTI, BERNARDINO

(c. 1495-1575). Italian painter of the Lombard school. Died at Parma. Executed religious themes; he was the student and imitator of Correggio.

GAZA, THEODORUS

(c. 1400-1475). Byzantine scholar who fled to the West when

his native Thessalonica was captured by the Turks in 1430. He was professor of Greek at Ferrara until called to Rome by Pope Nicholas V to be professor of philosophy and to help carry out the ambitious papal scheme of publishing the great Greek writers in Latin translation. Nicholas' death saw him depart for Naples and the service of Alfonso the Magnanimous. In the philosophical controversy raised by Plethon, he sided with Aristotle against Plato. He translated several of Aristotle's works into Latin, Cicero's *On Friendship*, etc. into Greek; his Greek grammar, said to be the first to include syntax, was a favorite among humanists, e.g., Erasmus and Budé, and remained a standard work until the nineteenth century—it was last reprinted in 1803.

GAZIUS, ANTONIUS
(1461-1528). Italian physician of Padua who traveled widely in Europe and became physician to Sigismund I of Poland. Author of *Florida Corona Medicinae;* published in 1491 at Venice, it is a manual of rules for good health. He also wrote religious tracts and was a believer in astrology.

GEBWILER, JOHANNES
(1480-1545). Alsatian humanist, logician. Wrote *Compendium, De Natura Universalium* and a chronicle of his native Strassburg. He opposed the Reformation.

GEERTGEN, TOT SINT JANS
(c. 1465-c. 1493). Dutch painter of Haarlem. Executed religious panels. Paintings include *St. John the Baptist, Adoration of the Magi, Virgin and Child, Nativity, Man of Sorrows.* His patrons, chiefly, were the Knights of St. John, as his name indicates.

GEILER, JOHANN, OF KAISERSBERG, or GEYLER
(1445-1510). Preacher and theologian of Strassburg Cathedral. He greatly admired Gerson's writing and published many of Gerson's theological works. Purpose of his racy, humorous, satirical sermons was to reform manners and morals; his *Ship of Penitence* makes him a precursor of the Reformation, as does his translation of his fellow Alsatian's satirical poem, *The Ship of Fools*, into Latin.

GELLI, GIOVANNI BATTISTA
(1498-1563). Florentine writer. Author of poems, comedies. Wrote *The Cooper's Fancies*, in 1546. Acknowledged Tuscan

basis of the Italian language in his linguistic treatise, published in 1551. He wrote a study of Circe and Odysseus.

GELLIBRAND, HENRY
(1597-1636). English mathematician. Author of *Epitome of Navigation*, works on the construction of ships, and scientific works on magnetism and mathematics. He lauded Gassendi's astronomy.

GEMMA, RANIER, FRISIUS
(1508-1555). Flemish scientist and mathematician. His system of triangulation improved maps and charts greatly; he also wrote on cosmography, anatomy and astrology. He was the teacher of Mercator.

GENEVAN PSALTER
A corpus of Calvinist hymns: published in 1562. Music by Louis Bourgeois.

GENGA, BARTOLOMMEO
(1516-1559). Italian sculptor, painter. Also worked on engineering projects, the traditional occupation of his family over several generations.

GENGA, GIROLAMO
(c.1476-1551). Italian architect, painter, sculptor of Urbino, a member of the Umbrian school. Executed frescoes of religious subjects for the Petrucci Palace at Siena; in his last years he was court architect to the Duke of Urbino.

GENOA
During the Renaissance Genoa was a great commercial republic, governed by powerful Doges. It traded with the entire Mediterranean littoral, from Spain to the Black Sea. It experienced multiple disruptions, participating in numerous conflicts, particularly with Pisa and Venice. Not until the ascendancy of Andrea Doria in the mid-sixteenth century did Genoa play any part in the cultural flowering of the Renaissance; the city was wealthy, it was dominated by its merchant class, its citizens were notorious for their Philistinism, its endless political struggles were of the most brutal sort.

GENTILE DA FABRIANO
(c.1370-c. 1427). Italian painter. He was the first important figure of the Umbrian school and is said to have been one of the out-

standing primitives; his work is characterized by the lavish use of color and of gold ornamentation. He did religious scenes, working in Florence, Venice, Brescia, Perugia, Orvieto and Rome.

GENTILESCHI, ARTEMISIA

(1590-1642). Italian artist, daughter of Orozio. She is noted for portraits. She worked sometime in England, where she was a popular artist, noted for her chiaroscuro.

GENTILESCHI, ORAZIO

(1562-1647). Italian painter. Executed religious murals, portraits. Settled in England under Charles I.

GENTILI, ALBERICO

(1552-1608). Italian Protestant who fled to England and became Regius Professor of Civil Law at Oxford. In his *De Iure Belli*, published in 1598, he advocated for Europe an international government. His *De Legationibus* (1585) was an important manual of diplomatic practice. His work in international law influenced Grotius.

GENTILIS, SCIPIO

(1563-1616). Italian jurist. Wrote treatise on law: *De Iurisdictione Libri III*: published in 1613. Also commentary on Tasso's *Jerusalem Delivered*, published in 1586. He had studied at German universities. Alberico [see above] was his brother.

GEORGE OF TREBIZOND, TRAPEZUNTIUS

(1396?-1488?) Byzantine professor. He was in Italy as early as 1418 and taught Greek and rhetoric in Venice and Florence but chiefly at Rome. An Aristotelian, entered into controversies with Platonists, especially Georgius Gemistus Plethon and Cardinal Bessarion, both of whom were his countrymen. He made a translation of Plato and Aristotle into Latin, mostly under papal patronage.

GEORGIUS BRUXELLENSIS

Logician. Wrote *Cursus Optimarum Quaestionum Super Totam Logicam*: published in Leyden in 1504.

GERALDINI, ALESSANDRO

(1455-1525). Italian priest. Lived in Spain. Wrote an account of Columbus' voyages, in Latin.

266

GERARD, JOHN

(1545-1612). English herbalist and barber-surgeon, author of *Herball* published in 1597. Botanical genus *Gerardia* derives its name from him.

GERARD, JOHN

(1564-1637). English Jesuit. Linguist. Traveled throughout England as missionary. Imprisoned in Tower of London for three years: escaped. After Gunpowder Plot, fled to continent. Wrote autobiography in Latin.

GEREMIA, CRISTOFORO DI

(c. 1430-1476). Italian goldsmith, medalist, sculptor of Mantua. Worked in Rome in the papal service as well as for the Gonzaga ducal house of his native city.

GERHARD, HUBERT

(1550-1620). Italian sculptor. Pupil of Gian Bologna; he also shows the influence of Cellini. He emigrated to Germany and worked at Augsburg, Innsbruck, etc. He is important for the transition to Baroque art in Germany.

GERHARD, JOHANN

(1582-1637). German Lutheran apologist. Professor at Jena. Ecclesiastical leader and counselor of princes. His reputation rests on doctrinal works: chiefly *Loci Theologici* (1610-1622) in nine volumes. Also *Confessio Catholica* (1634-1637) in four volumes. His devotional book, *Meditationes Sacrae,* published in 1606, was translated into most European languages. Known as the Arch-Theologian and as the "oracle of his time," he was chiefly important as a definer and defender of Lutheran orthodoxy.

GERMAN ART

German art began with the Carolingian Renaissance in the ninth century. German art of the Renaissance presents a combination of Italian tendencies and the German artistic tradition. Three phases are distinguishable:

First phase: naturalistic realism. Notable names—Master of the Life of Mary, Lucas Moser, Konrad Witz.

Second phase: called Late Gothic or Neo-Gothic. Began c.

1450. Revival of idealistic motif: e.g. in the sculptors Pacher, Veit Stosz, Tilman Riemenschneider.

Third phase: modification of the naturalism of first phase. Albrecht Dürer's paintings show the influence of the Italian Renaissance.

In architecture, the ideals of classic Renaissance were less assimilated than in the visual arts. Formal Gothic style was superseded but German tradition persisted.

GERSDORFF, HANS VON

(Late fifteenth—early sixteenth century). Prominent German surgeon. Author of *Book of Treatment of Wounds*.

GESNER, CONRAD

(1516-1565). Of Zurich, self-made and self-trained student of zoology and botany; he was the greatest figure of the sixteenth century in the development of zoology; also a physician. His *Bibliotheca Universalis*, 1545-1549, was the first systematic general bibliography to appear: it is an immense bibliographical dictionary of all Greek, Latin, and Hebrew writers, coupled with an encyclopaedia of the Arts and Sciences. He became a Lutheran minister but devoted himself to scientific studies and the writing of several books on zoology and botany. He was professor of natural history at Zurich and came to be known as the German Pliny.

GESUALDO, CARLO, PRINCE OF VENOSA

(c. 1560-1614). Neapolitan composer and murderer. A wealthy noble, he maintained a large group of musicians at his court; he was a friend of Tasso, many of whose poems he set to music. His wife's infidelity caused him to have her and her lover murdered; Gesualdo fled to the Este court at Ferrara, where he married the Princess Eleonora, 1594. Returned to Naples after a few years, he composed the dramatic madrigals for which he is remembered and founded a musical academy. He is credited with important innovations in harmony.

GÉYER, FLORIAN

(died 1525). French knight. Participated in the Bavarian War. Assassinated. Subject of novels, plays.

GHERARDI, CRISTOFANO

(1508-1556). Florentine painter, disciple of Raphael and of Vasari.

GHIBERTI, LORENZO

(1378-1455). Italian sculptor. Collaborated with Donatello. Inspired by ancients. First to imitate ancient Romans—Vasari. Executed bas-reliefs; he did the famous bronze doors for the baptistery of Florence, beating out Brunelleschi in the competition. It was these doors which Michelangelo pronounced to be worthy to open into Paradise.

GHIBERTI, VITTORIO

(1416-1496). Italian sculptor, goldsmith, son of the above. Born in Florence. Executed bronze pieces, helped his father in the execution of the famous bronze doors of the baptistery.

GHIRLANDAIO, DOMENICO

(1449-1494). Italian painter of Florence. Taught Michelangelo. Noted for frescoes which exemplify superb craftsmanship in the naturalistic tradition. Portraits include Florentine Merchant, Poliziano, Giuliano de' Medici. He did religious scenes but depicted much of Florentine daily life in all his work. Through his many pupils and disciples he was vastly influential.

GIACOMO DA FABRIANO

Italian illuminator of Rome. Had flourishing *bottega*. c. 1470-1474.

GIAMBELLI, CIPRIANO

Sixteenth century. Canon of Verona. Wrote treatise on dreams: sources, external influences, occult portents. Citations from Petrarch, Ariosto. Published in 1589.

GIAMBELLI, FEDERIGO

(c. 1530-1588). Italian military engineer. In service of Queen Elizabeth I. Aided in resisting the Armada, although he contributed very little except his great fame, but that was enough to alarm the Spanish commanders. Died in London.

GIAMBULLARI, PIER FRANCESCO

(1495-1555). Florentine man of letters. He was a militant exponent of Italian, and identified Italian with Tuscan; several of his works were defense, descriptions, grammatical and etymological studies of the native tongue in preference to Latin. He wrote a *History of Europe* from 887 to 947, studies of Dante, and a good deal of polemic. His brother, BERNARDO (1450-1529), was a poet.

GIANNOTTI, DONATO

(1492-1573). Florentine humanist and political exile in Venice. Author of a *History of Florence* and a *History of Venice*. He is the Machiavelli of his generation; he held the same posts in the Florentine Republic of 1527 as Machiavelli had held in that of 1498-1512, was imprisoned upon the restoration of the Medici, and wrote an impassioned work, *Discorso delle case d'Italia,* 1535, which constituted a vision of a powerful, united Italy, free of foreign domination. He too wrote histories; he too was fascinated by the ancient Republic of Rome and its institutions.

GIBBONS, ORLANDO

(1583-1625). English composer, organist to King James I. Wrote *Fantasies:* 1610, madrigals. Noted for sacred music. Called The English Palestrina.

GIDEON DE LAUNE

(c. 1565-1659). Apothecary to King James I. First Master of the Society of Apothecaries.

GIGGLESWICK SCHOOL

In Yorkshire, England. Public school founded in 1512.

GILBERT, SIR HUMPHREY

(1539-1583). English navigator and soldier. Abandoned law for the army. Served in Ireland, Netherlands. Twice on expedition to the New World, seeking the Northwest Passage. Planted the first British colony in America at St. John's, Newfoundland, in 1583. When his largest ship sank off Cape Breton, he sailed for England. His own ship, however, sank with all aboard.

GILBERT, WILLIAM

(1540-1603). Physician to Queen Elizabeth I of England. Author of a treatise on the magnet: published in 1600. He postulated that terrestrial magnetism and electricity were allied manifestations of the same force. Gilbert was the first to use the expressions *electricity, electric force, electric attraction, magnetic pole.* Called The Father of Electricity.

GILPIN, BERNARD

(1517-1583). English itinerant preacher. Ethics rather than doctrine were his concern. Traveled in Northern England, helping poor. Called The Apostle of the North. He had studied at Oxford, much admired the works of Erasmus, knew Greek as well as Latin, and, during the Marian persecutions, was on the Continent.

GIL POLO, GASPAR

(c. 1535-1591). Spanish poet, much admired and honored by Philip II. Died at Barcelona. Wrote *La Diana Enamorada*. Pastoral romance that appeared in 1564. Most of his works are based on classical themes.

GIOCONDO, FRA GIOVANNI, OF VERONA

(c. 1433-1515). Italian architect, scholar. Collector of ancient manuscripts and inscriptions. Edited Latin texts. In Paris, he discovered the correspondence between Pliny the Younger and the Emperor Trajan.

GIORGIO, FRANCESCO DI

(1439-1502). Italian sculptor, painter, architect and engineer. Executed in bronze: bas-reliefs, *Descent from the Cross, Judgment of Paris;* his paintings include *The Chess Players* and *The Rape of Europa;* he built fortifications and invented the military mine; he also wrote a treatise on architecture, military and civil. He is thus a good example of Renaissance versatility.

GIORGIONE

(c. 1478-1511). Or Georgio Barbarelli. Venetian painter. Worked in Venice. Noted for beauty and richness of color. Executed *Enthroned Madonna* as altarpiece: also frescoes. Among works are *The Concert* and *Champetre,* and *The Three Philosophers.* Influenced Titian. J. A. Symonds' appraisal is that he 'first cut painting altogether adrift from mediaeval moorings, and launched it on the waves of the Renaissance liberty.' He had a very great influence upon sixteenth-century painting.

GIORNICO, BATTLE OF

At this Battle the Swiss defeated the Milanese in 1478.

GIOTTO DI BONDONE

(c. 1260-c. 1337). Florentine painter and architect, one of the greatest painters of all times. He is thought to have been the pupil of Cimabue. With him the Renaissance tradition of realism and naturalism begins: his figures are highly individualized and natural, his scenes intensely dramatic. One of his most frequent subjects was scenes from the life of St. Francis, whose teachings and outlook are reflected in Giotto's work. Some of his most famous paintings are the frescoes in the Church of St. Francis at Assisi that include *The Glorification* of the Saint and ten scenes of *The Life of the Virgin and Christ,* and the thirty-eight frescoes done in the Arena Chapel of Padua on the *Life of Christ.* The bell tower of the cathedral of Florence is thought to be Giotto's work.

GIOVANNI BANDINI DELL'OPERA

(1540-1598). Florentine sculptor, did bronze casts; practically all his work shows him to have been under the spell of Michelangelo.

GIOVANNI DA PISA

(Fifteenth century). Italian sculptor. He collaborated with Donatello in several works. His own independent work was dominated by the style and method of Donatello, as was all Italian sculpture in the fifteenth century.

GIOVANNI DA UDINE

(1487-1564). Italian painter. Belongs to the school of Raphael, with whom he collaborated. He worked in the Vatican, Rome, and Udine.

GIOVANNI DE VIGO

(1460-1525). Italian surgeon of Genoa. Author of *Practica Copiosa in Arte Chirurgica,* published in Rome in 1514. Translated into English, French, Spanish, Italian, German. Invented a number of surgical instruments.

GIOVANNI BANDINI DELL'OPERA

(c. 1470-c. 1516). Giovanni delli Corniole. Pisan sculptor and gem cutter who spent most of his life in Florence, a member of the circle of Lorenzo the Magnificent. Worked in bronze. Left cameo portraits of Savonarola and Lorenzo.

GIOVANNI DI BOCCARDI

(1460-1529). Italian book illuminator. Known as Boccardino Il Vecchio. Illuminated a number of manuscripts including a *Roman Breviary, Missal, Book of Hours.* His brother FRANCESCO was also a miniaturist and illuminator.

GIOVANNI DI PAOLO

(born before 1403-1482). Italian painter of Siena. Executed a *Crucifixion, Madonna and Child, Assumption.* The Byzantine tradition is very strong in his work.

GIOVANNI VENDRAMIN DA PADOVA

Illuminator. Executed antiphonary for Ferrara Cathedral, chorales, in 1482.

GIOVIO, PAOLO

(c. 1483-1552). Italian humanist. Wrote a survey of Turkish history: published in 1540. Also treatise on fish eaten by ancient Romans: published in 1560. Author of a popular emblem book that appeared in 1574. His chief work was a *History of His Own Time,* 1494-1547, like all his works, full of errors; he was wealthy and lived in the grand style and thus had access to courts and palaces; it is knowledge thus gained that redeems his historical writings from utter uselessness.

GIRALDI, GIOVANNI BATTISTA or GIAMBATTISTA

(1504-1573). Italian dramatist. Known as Cynthius. Professor of medicine and philosophy at Ferrara. Also produced collection of one hundred tales, entitled *Ecatommiti.* It was utilized as a source book by better writers e.g., Shakespeare, who drew upon it for *Othello* and *Measure for Measure.* Leading Italian writer of mid-sixteenth century, in fiction and drama. Wrote *Orbecche:* first Italian tragedy actually performed. Produced in 1541. First printed in 1543. Horror drama, based on one of the *Ecatommiti* and modeled on Seneca.

GIRALDI, GIGLIO GREGORIO

(1479-1552). Italian humanist and papal notary. Author of numerous works, on literary, antiquarian, mythological subjects.

GITHERN

A musical instrument, similar to a guitar. A variant spelling is cithern. In use from the fourteenth to the seventeenth century.

GIULIO ROMANO or GIULIO PIPPI

(c. 1492-1546). Italian painter, architect and decorator, the most trusted disciple of Raphael, with whom he worked in the Vatican and for whom he finished many frescoes. For the last twenty years of his life he worked for the Gonzaga ducal house of

Mantua, where he built the ducal palace and rebuilt the Palazzo da Te, both decorated with his frescoes; he also reconstructed the cathedral, established an influential school of art, and did various engineering and military structures. He died in the year that the Pope designated him architect for St. Peter's.

GIUNTA or GIUNTI
Italian family of printers who flourished in the sixteenth century; the business was founded in 1497. Notable members were: Luca Antonio (died c. 1537). Established a publishing house in Venice. Filippo (1450-1517). Established a printing press in Florence. Giulio and Tommaso. Settled in Spain. Royal printers. Giacomo. Established a publishing house in Lyons in 1520. At its height the firm had offices and branches in Florence, Venice, Lyons, London, Madrid, Burgos, Salamanca, Saragossa, Medina del Campo, and Lisbon.

GIUSTINIANI, AGOSTINO
(1470-1536). Italian Oriental scholar. Professor of Hebrew in Paris.

GIUSTINIANI, BERNARDO
(1408-1489). Venetian politician, diplomat and historian. He had been educated in the humanist manner by Guarino, Filelfo and George of Trebizond, and followed the precepts of his teachers in combining action with study. In the intervals of public service he wrote a history of Venice, probing particularly into the origin of the city, in which he employed the humanist methods of cutting through the accumulations of tradition and legend.

GLAREANUS, HENRICUS or HEINRICH LORITI
(1488-1563). Swiss humanist and musical theorist. Friend of Erasmus. Wrote *Liber de Asse et Partibus eius*. Published in Basel in 1551. Also wrote on Latin writers. His principal works were on music: the *Isagoge de Musica* and *Dodekachordon*, which represent a break with earlier doctrines of modes and proportion.

GLASS
Stained glass windows were one of the supreme artistic achievements of the middle ages; this tradition tended to languish in the Renaissance. The making of glassware for domestic use greatly developed and became one of the fine arts. In the middle of the

fifteenth century Venetian glass began to assume artistic form. In the sixteenth century Venetian became the most perfect glass, artistically and technically.

In Germany, the green wine-glass, the *Römer*, was produced in the sixteenth century.

In the Netherlands, during the sixteenth century, glass factories were influenced by Venetian and German glassware.

In France, Nevers glass and enamelled glass of the sixteenth century are the most remarkable glass produced in France until recent times.

In England, in the sixteenth century, Edward VI and later Queen Elizabeth employed Venetian glass-workers in their courts.

It may be added that the sixteenth century saw improvements in the industrial production of glass, making it far more economical for artistic and also domestic use. The profusion of glass in Elizabethan homes, e.g., is suggestive of the new importance of glass for artist and architect.

GNAPHEUS, GULIELMUS

(born 1493: date of death uncertain). Original name Willem de Volder. Dutch dramatist. Taught in Holland and Germany. As Lutheran, imprisoned twice. Author of *Acolastus*: based on Biblical theme of Prodigal Son. Translated into German, French, English. Influenced English drama.

GOCLENIUS, RUDOLF

(1547-1628). German logician. Devised the Goclenian Sorites.

GODEFROY, DENIS

(1549-1622). French jurist and legal scholar. Wrote on independence of French Church in order to refute papal claims. He became a Protestant and fled to Geneva.

GODUNOV, BORIS

(1551?-1605). Tsar of Russia during the Time of Trouble, prior to the ascension of the Romanovs. During the reign of his brother-in-law, the young Tsar Fedor Ivanovich, Godunov presided over the Regency Council. Defeated the Crimean Tartars, sought to colonize Siberia, and received territory from Sweden. On the death of Fedor in 1598, he assumed the throne. He died in conflict with the boyars. Godunov is the subject of Moussorgsky's opera, based on Pushkin's drama.

GODWIN, FRANCIS

(1562-1633). English cleric, antiquary, and historian. Bishop of Hereford. Author of *Rerum Anglicarum Annales:* published in 1616, part of which was a catalogue of English bishops. Also wrote a science-fiction fantasy, *Man in the Moon:* published in 1638.

GOES, DAMIÃO or GOIS

(1501-1573). Portuguese humanist, historian, scholar, diplomat, friend of Erasmus and Bembo; his many callings, his talents as soldier and musician, and his collections of art and manuscripts make him an example of the universal man of the Renaissance. He served on diplomatic missions to the principal courts of Northern Europe. He was accused of Lutheranism and was incarcerated by the Inquisition. He translated Cicero into Portuguese and wrote several Latin works on Portuguese history; commissioned by the royal court, they were *Crónica do Serenissimo Sentiar Rei Dom Manuel* and *Crónico do Principe Dom João.*

GOES, HUGO VAN DER

(c. 1440-1482). Flemish painter of Ghent. Executed noted altarpieces, redolent, frequently, with death and anguish; he also did portraits remarkable as brilliant character studies. He was a luminary of the Flemish-Burgundian age and was greatly admired by Duke Charles the Rash of Burgundy.

GOHORY, JACQUES

(Died 1576). French physician. Professor in Paris. In 1567 published a summary of the philosophy and medicine of Paracelsus, whom he defended against his detractors. His many other works are a mixture of keen observation and fantasy.

GOLDING, ARTHUR

(c. 1536-c. 1605). English scholar and translator. Translated Ovid's *Metamorphoses* in verse: published in 1567. Also made prose translations of authors ranging from Calvin to Grosseteste.

GOLTZIUS, HENDRIK

(1558-1617). Dutch painter, etcher, and printer. Founded school of engraving in Haarlem. Engraved many portraits: also Italian prints.

GOMAR, FRANÇOIS or GOMARUS

(1563-1641). Protestant theologian. Born at Bruges. One of the leaders of rigid Calvinism. Professor of theology and Hebrew at Leyden, in which connection he participated in a revision of the Dutch Bible. Opponent of Arminianism. His supporters were known as Gomarists.

GONÇALVES, RUI
Sixteenth century. Portuguese lawyer and writer. Author of treatise proclaiming the superiority of feminine qualities. Published in 1557, it was fulsomely dedicated to Queen Caterina, wife of João III.

GONDOMAR, DIEGO SARMIENTO DE ACUÑA, COUNT OF
(1567-1626). Spanish diplomat. Ambassador to England. Prevented King James I from supporting enemies of Spain in the early stages of the Thirty Years' War.

GONFALONI, GONFALONIERI DI GIUSTIZIA
For purposes of government Florence was divided into territorial units called *Quartieri,* each of which was divided into *Gonfaloni.* Real power, however, lay with the economic organizations, the guilds; and essentially with the seven major guilds, *Arti Maggiori,* rather than with the fourteen minor ones, the *Arti Minori.* The most important institution of government was the *Signoria,* composed of eight priors representing the *Quartieri* and *Arti* and presided over by the *Gonfalonier di Giustizia,* the Gonfalonier of Justice. The Signoria was elected by lot every two months.

GÓNGORA Y ARGOTE, LUIS DE
(1561-1627). Greatest poet of late Spanish Golden Age. Born and died at Cordova. Studied canon law at Salamanca. Led dissolute and riotous life as student. Became Deacon. His poems appeared in the *Romancero General* in 1660. Became chaplain to king. Wrote ballads, popular lyrics, sonnets; also *Soledades:* unfinished poem, 1613. Originated the Baroque style of writing known as Gongorism.

GONTHIER, JEAN
(1485-1574). German Hellenist and physician. Translated the *Practica* of the sixth century Greek physician Alexander of Tralles, first parasitologist. Author of *Anatomicarum Institutionum Libri IV.* Also wrote *De Medicina Veteri et Nova.* He was a prolific author on a great range of subjects; he became a Protestant.

277

GONZAGA

The Italian ducal house which ruled Mantua from 1328 until the eighteenth century. Giovanni Francesco II (died 1519): Duke of Mantua. Federigo II (died 1540): Duke of Mantua. During his rule, Mantua became a great cultural centre. Guglielmo (died 1587). Vicenzo (died 1612): Friend of the poet Tasso. They had great difficulty preserving the independence of Mantua against Venice, Milan.

GONZAGA, FEDERIGO II

(1500-1540). Duke of Mantua. Made his court a notable centre of intellectual and artistic interests.

GONZAGA, FRANCESCO

Duke of Mantua. In command of forces of Holy League—consisting of Spain, Milan, Pope Alexander VI, Venice, Emperor Maximilian I. Awaited troops of Charles VIII of France at River Taro. Duke of Mantua's troops defeated by Charles VIII at Fornovo in 1495. His wife was the celebrated patroness, Isabella d'Este of Ferrara; in their time Mantua was at the zenith of its fame as a cultural center.

GONZAGA, SAINT LUIGI

(1568-1591). Joined the Society of Jesus in 1585. Cared for the sick during the plague of Rome. Died of plague.

GONZALES DE MENDOZA, JUAN

(c. 1540-1617). Spanish cleric. Augustinian. Sent on a mission to China. Wrote an account of the country.

GONZALO DE CÉSPEDES Y MENESES

(1585-1638). Spanish novelist. Author of a picaresque novel: *Varia Fortuna del Soldado Pindaro.* Published in 1625. Also *Historias Peregrinas Y Ejemplares:* a series of six erotic adventures. Published in 1625.

GONZALO DE CÓRDOBA

(1453-1515). Called El Gran Capitán. Spanish soldier: negotiated surrender of Granada in 1492. In 1495 was sent to aid Ferdinand II of Naples against the French: conquered the kingdom of Naples in 1503-1504. It was his organization of the Spanish infantry that laid the basis of Spanish military ascendancy in the sixteenth century.

GONZATE, DAMIAN, FILIPPO, IACOPO

(Early sixteenth century.) Italian sculptors, brothers. Executed bronze statuettes of the four Evangelists in the Cathedral of Parma.

GOOGE, BARNABE

(1540-1594). English poet. Traveled on the Continent. Author of eight eclogues, sonnets, *Cupid Conquered.* Also produced translations of Seneca and Virgil as well as anti-Papal polemic. He was a relative of Sir William Cecil and thus came to serve the government in various capacities, chiefly in Ireland.

GORGES, SIR ARTHUR

(died 1625). English poet and translator, mariner. In command of the *Wast Spite,* Sir Walter Raleigh's flagship on the Island Voyage of 1597, an expedition of which he wrote an account. First translated Lucan's *Pharsalia* into English. Published in London in 1614.

GOSSELIN, GUILLAUME

(died c. 1590). French mathematician of Caen. Author of *De Arte Magna*: on algebra. Published in 1577. Translated Nicolas Tartaglia's *General Treatise on Numbers.* His conception of mathematics is occult and mystical, being in the Pythagorean tradition. Also wrote Latin verse.

GOTTSKÁLKSSON, ODDUR

(died 1556). Icelandic Lutheran leader. Translated New Testament into Icelandic in 1540. He had studied in Germany and became a Lutheran.

GOUDELIN, PIERRE or GOUDIN

(1579-1649). Provençal poet. Used the dialect of Languedoc. Author of *Le Ramelet Moundi*: appeared in 1617. He composed a *Chant Royal* on the death of Henry IV.

GOUDIMEL, CLAUDE

(1505-1572). French musician. Composer. Born in Besançon. Victim of Massacre of St. Bartholomew. Composed many songs, five masses, and set many of the *Psalms* to music.

GOUJON, JEAN

(c. 1515-1572). French sculptor and architect. Huguenot, he was killed in the St. Bartholomew's Day Massacre. Helped to decorate the Louvre, excelled in bas-reliefs, notably the *Caryatids* of the Louvre. Also a figure of *Diana*. Executed *Nymphes de la Fontaine des Innocents*.

GOULSTON, THEODORE
(1572-1632). English scholar. Physician. Published a Latin translation of and commentary on Aristotle's *Rhetoric* in 1619 and of the *Poetics* in 1623. Also wrote on Galen.

GOULU, NICOLAS
(1530-1601). French humanist scholar. Royal lecturer on Greek and Latin; he left a great many commentaries on classical authors.

GOURMONT, GILLES DE
(1480-after 1533). French printer who set up first Greek press in Paris, in 1507. Issued *Alphabetum Graecum*. Also texts of Homer, Hesiod, and Chrysoloras' Greek grammar. He also published a Hebrew grammar.

GOYEN, JAN JOSEPHSZOON VAN
(1596-1656). Dutch painter. Noted for his landscapes and marine scenes, e.g. of harbors, canals; he delighted in typical Dutch scenes, especially winter ones.

GOZZOLI, BENOZZO
(c. 1420-c. 1497). Italian painter of Florence: also goldsmith. Executed frescoes: Biblical motifs. Pupil of Fra Angelico. Sponsored by the Medici. Interested in questions of perspective. He did the famous *Journey of the Magi* for the Medici Chapel in which he portrays several of the members of the family.

GRAF, URS or URSUS
(c. 1485-1527). Swiss artist, engraver. Influenced by art of Albrecht Dürer. Traveled: settled in Basel. As goldsmith, executed reliquary of St. Bernard. Noted for drawings and numerous woodcuts.

GRAFTON, RICHARD
(died c. 1572). English chronicler and printer. He printed Bibles, the First Book of Common Prayer, Hall's *Chronicle*, his own *Chronicle of the Affairs of England*, as well as a great deal of religious works.

GRAMINAEUS, THEODOR
Sixteenth century. Author of *Mysticus Aquilo:* an exposition of the end of the world. Associated with religious turbulence inspired by Martin Luther. Published in Cologne in 1576.

GRANACCI, FRANCESCO
(1469-1543). Italian painter of Florence. Friend of Michelangelo. He collaborated with Ghirlandaio.

GRANADA
In 1492 the city of Granada fell to the Spaniards, thus completing the reconquest of Spain from Moorish domination.

GRAND MYSTÈRE DE JÉSUS, LE
A Breton biography of Jesus. Published in 1530.

GRANGIER, JEAN
(c. 1576-1643). French cleric. Scholar. Died in Paris. Professor of rhetoric at the Collège de France, Paris. Best orator of his time. Left speeches, dissertations in Latin. Translated Dante into French, (1596-1597).

GRANJON, ROBERT
Sixteenth century. French printer, engraver, he worked at Paris, Lyons, but principally at Rome. Devised several types; he cut the first Arabic and the first Chaldaic-Syriac type for printing works in those alphabets.

GRANUCCI, NICCOLÒ
(floruit 1530). Novelist and biographer of Lucca. Author of collection of fourteen *novellae;* entitled *L'eremita, la carcere e'l diporto.* Themes are: Love and violence, against classical and oriental backgrounds, but frequently contemporary events and Renaissance personalities appear, published in 1569. He published another work of the same curious sort in 1574, *La Piacevole notte e lieto giorno.*

GRANVELLE, ANTOINE PERRENOT, CARDINAL DE
(1517-1586). Roman Catholic prelate and statesman. Under Charles V he was Secretary of State, in 1550. Prime Minister to Margaret of Parma, the Regent of the Netherlands. In 1575 appointed by Philip II of Spain as president of Council for Italian affairs.

GRAPALDI, FRANCESCO MARIA

(1465-1515). Italian poet laureate: crowned by Pope Julius II in 1512. Author of an encyclopedic work dealing with equipment belonging in a Renaissance household: together with construction of hospitals, medicinal gardens, pharmacies. Published in 1494. He also wrote on the *Psalms* and on Plautus' comedies.

GRATIUS, ORTWINUS

(1491-1542). German theologian and anti-humanist. Professor at the University of Cologne. Educated by the Brethren of the Common Life. Polemical writer. He opposed Reuchlin and was among those pilloried by Von Hutten and others in the famous *Epistolae Obscurorum Virorum.*

GRAZZINI, ANTONIO FRANCESCO

(1503-1584). Called Il Lasca. Florentine satirist and writer of comedies: e.g. *Cene* (1540-1547): a picture of the lighter side of Florentine life. One of the founders of the literary society, the Accademia della Crusca.

GRÉBAN, ARNOULD

(c. 1410-c. 1471). French dramatic poet. Born at Le Mans. Author of *Mystère de la Passion,* an enormous work centering on redemption through the purging away of original sin by Christ's intervention.

GRECO, EL

(c. 1541-1614). Cretan-born painter. Actual name was Kyriakos Theotokopoulos. Pupil of Titian. Worked in Toledo. Head of Castilian school. Pictorially expounded Spanish mysticism. Produced *Adoration of the Shepherds, Crucifixion, Ascension.* Famous for the elongation and distention of forms, as well as intense religiosity, he initiated the Baroque age in Spain.

GREEK FATHERS, THE

Part of the renewed interest in "the Christian classics" was the publication and study of the Greek Fathers in the purest texts possible. Attempts to reunite the two Churches also stimulated interest. Origen, especially, attracted scholarly interest; among the several editions of his works was a famous one by Erasmus.

GREEK SCHOLARS IN THE WEST

The influx of Greeks dates from 1438 when 500 Greeks attended the Council of Ferrara-Florence, some of whom remained in

Italy for lengthy periods, with a considerable number spending the rest of their lives in the West. They received a warm welcome, particularly in Florence; many became public lecturers or tutors, although many beat out a meager existence as translators, copyists, editors to printers. Single individuals, such as Chrysoloras, had come as early as the 1390's. They contributed to Italy the painstaking Byzantine methods of textual study and an idealization of the classical past. Among many, the following may be mentioned: Manuel Chrysoloras, died 1415; Cardinal Bessarion, 1403-1472; John Lascaris, late fifteenth century; Georgias Gemisthos Plethon, 1356-1450; George of Trebizond, late fifteenth century; Theoedore of Gaza, 1400-1475; and John Argyropulos, professor of Greek at Florence 1456-1471.

GREENE, ROBERT

(c. 1560-1592). English playwright, poet. Traveled on continent. His plays include *Friar Bacon and Friar Bungay, A Looking-Glass for London and England*. Also songs, eclogues, pamphlets and tracts. He frequently parodied the drama of contemporary playwrights, e.g. Kyd's *Spanish Tragedy*. He was a member of the group named *University Wits*.

GRÉGOIRE, PIERRE

(1540-1597). French writer of Toulouse, canonist. Author of *De Republica*: on political theory, administration of country in peace and war, remedies for religious abuses.

GREGORY XIII

(1502-1585). Pope 1572-1585. Established seminaries for Germany and England. Active in Counter Reformation and ally of Philip II of Spain. Approved plan to murder Queen Elizabeth I. Responsible for Gregorian reform of calendar. Sent missions to Asia, Africa, America.

GREGORY XIV

(1535-1591). Pope. Reigned for two years. Praised by Tasso. Saintly: led retired life. Inexperienced politically. Counter Reformation went ahead in his time, he continued to follow Spanish policy and to oppose Henry IV of France.

GREGORY XV

(1554-1623). Pope 1621-23. Supported Emperor Ferdinand II in Thirty Years' War. Founded Congregation of Propaganda in

1622: turning point in missionary history. Transferred the electorate of the Palatinate to Duke Maximilian of Bavaria. Received as gift university library of Heidelberg: Bibliotheca Palatina.

GRENVILLE, SIR RICHARD
(c. 1541-1591). Cousin of Sir Walter Raleigh. In command of fleet to colonize Virginia. Prepared defenses against Armada. In a later encounter with the Spanish, near the Azores, his ship, *Revenge,* separated from fleet by Spaniards; Grenville was fatally wounded. Appears in Charles Kingsley's *Westward Ho!* Also in Tennyson's *The Revenge.*

GRESHAM'S SCHOOL
In Holt, England. English public school. Founded in 1555 by Sir John Gresham (died 1556).

GRESHAM, SIR THOMAS
(c. 1519-1579). English financier. King's Merchant in Antwerp. Dismissed, as a Protestant, by Queen Mary. Founder of the Royal Exchange in London. Appointed by Queen Elizabeth to replace debased coinage with sound currency. He also served the Queen on diplomatic missions. He is credited with propounding the economic principle known as Gresham's Law, that cheap money drives out good money; but it was known long before his time. He endowed Gresham's College, London, the first home of the group that came to form the Royal Society.

GREVE, HEINRICH
(Born c. 1450). Professor of literature at Leipzig and German man of letters. Wrote *Parva Logicalia,* a work on logic.

GREVILLE, SIR FULKE
(1554-1628). English poet, statesman. Attached to court of Queen Elizabeth I. Friend of Sir Philip Sidney. Wrote tragedies, sonnets, life of Sidney. He was a friend of Giordano Bruno, who dedicated one of his works to him.

GREY, LADY JANE
(c. 1537-1554). Claimant to English throne. Great-granddaughter of Henry VII. Remarkably skilled in Greek, Latin, and other languages. Proclaimed Queen of England in 1553 and reigned for nine days. Imprisoned: refused to recant Protestant faith and was subsequently beheaded by Mary.

GRIBALDI, MATTHAEUS

(died 1564). Italian jurist. Author of *De Methodo ac Ratione Studendi*: a student guide to the study of law. He became a Protestant and fled from Padua, where he taught, to Grenoble.

GRIJALVA, JUAN DE

(c. 1489-1527). Spanish conquistador. Explored the coast of Mexico, on one of the expeditions that preceded that of Cortés. Gave the area the name of New Spain.

GRIMALD, NICHOLAS

(1519-1562). English poet, of Italian birth, descended from a Genoese merchant family. Contributed to Tottel's *Songs and Sonnets*. Translated parts of Cicero and Vergil. He embraced and then abjured Protestantism; most of his writings are steeped in religious feeling and deal with Christian subjects.

GRIMAUDET, FRANÇOIS

(1520-1580). French jurist. He wrote numerous works and manuals on civil law, a discourse on royal and sacerdotal power, in which he argued that laymen should be present in church councils, and works on the currency and economic matters.

GRINDAL, EDMUND

(c. 1519-1583). English Protestant Archbishop of Canterbury. Suspended by Queen Elizabeth I. Violently opposed Roman Catholicism; he had taken refuge on the Continent during Mary's reign.

GRINGOIRE, PIERRE or GRINGORE

(c. 1475-1538). French poet. Wrote satires and allegories. Among his pieces are *Jeu du Prince des Sots* and *Folles Enterprises*.

GRISONS LEAGUE

The Swiss canton which ruled the Valtelline Pass in Switzerland, which was a vital link in the lines of communication between the Spanish and Austrian Hapsburgs, especially during the Thirty Years' War. In 1620 the Spaniards seized the Pass. Resistance was made by the Swiss under George Jenatsch (1596-1639), a Protestant minister. In 1621 Spain occupied the Pass. In 1639 a treaty with Spain confirmed Spanish use of the Pass.

GROCIN, WILLIAM

(c. 1446-1519). English humanist. Not of the same stature as Colet, but important as one of the English travelers to Italy who brought back humanist methods of scholarship. They had their application, for him, to theology and church history. He was an important influence on Colet, Linacre, and More; Erasmus had high praise for his scholarship. In Italy he had mastered Greek, on which he lectured, along with theology, at Oxford in the 1490's. He had no interest in the revival of Plato, remaining an Aristotelian; he helped his friend Aldus in the publication of Aristotle's works.

GROLIER, JEAN

(1479-1565). Treasurer general of France, diplomat, and bibliophile. He accumulated a great collection of about 3,000 books, all of them beautifully bound; they belonged to him and his friends: according to the inscription, to "J. Grolerii et amicorum."

GROTIUS, HUGO

(1583-1645). Dutch jurist, classical scholar, poet, statesman, theologian, biblical exegete of Leyden. At age fifteen he was engaged on an edition of Martianus Capella, published in 1597. Moved to the Hague as advocate. Historiographer to the Netherlands. He wrote *Mare Liberum,* 1609, on international law as it applied to the seaways. His republicanism and political opposition to the stadtholder, Maurice of Nassau, as well as his agitation in behalf of the Arminians and religious toleration against the dominant, orthodox Calvinists, resulted in his condemnation to life imprisonment in 1619. Escaping in 1621 to France, he published *De Iure Belli et Pacis.* This famous treatise is the foundation of international law. He recognized fully the sovereign state, subject to no control exterior to itself and concerned only for its preservation and aggrandizement. The relations of states are governed by natural law, which he defines as synonymous with the "dictates of right reason" and which is embodied in some degree in all human laws. Under the sanction of "natural justice," he prescribes the rules for such matters as the treatment of the sick, wounded, prisoners, and non-combatants, and lays down prohibitions of pillage, massacre, and violation of truces. In the Swedish service, he acted as ambassador to France, 1635-1645. He published editions of Plutarch, Greek dramatists, Lucan and

Silius Italicus; he was the author of two Latin tragedies on Biblical themes and of two notable Latin poems.

GROTO, LUIGI

(1541-1585). Blind Italian poet. Called Il Cieco d'Adria. In youth, Groto was public speaker to Queen of Poland and Doge of Venice. He wrote comedies, tragedies, pastorals: little of it of any merit.

GRUET, JACQUES

Swiss reformer. Attacked Calvinism. Arrested; executed in 1547: a classic miscarriage of justice.

GRUFFYDD, ELIS

(fl. c. 1490-1552). Welsh copyist, translator, chronicler, soldier. Author of a *History of the World* from the creation to his own day. He enlisted in the armies of Henry VIII to fight against France; his adventures are incorporated in his *History*.

GRUMBACH, WILHELM VON

(1503-1567). German adventurer. Associated with German Knights who attempted to destroy the territorial princes. At court of Prince of Bayreuth. Plundered Würzburg and fell under the ban of the Empire. Tortured, executed. Subject of drama, novels in which he is portrayed as a national hero.

GRUNEWALD, MATTHIAS

(1470-1528). German religious painter. Except for his use of brilliant color and his technical mastery, there is little of the Renaissance in his work; working in the period of heightened religious sensibility prior to the Reformation in Germany, he painted works that carry religious feelings to the point of hysteria and depict suffering and agony in a most grim and stark manner. This is especially true of his famous *Isenheim Crucifixion*. His work thus makes the sharpest contrast with that of his Italian contemporaries such as Leonardo and Raphael, whose works convey an air of serenity and calm; it is the contrast between Gothic and Renaissance.

GRUTER, JANUS

(1560-1627). Classical scholar and philologist. Professor at Rostock, Heidelberg. Compiler of corpus of ancient inscriptions. Edited many Latin authors, e.g., Seneca, Sallust, and Tacitus.

GRYPHIUS, ANDREAS

(1616-1664). German poet and dramatist. Author of sonnets, odes, religious lyrics, epigrams, tragedies, and comedies; he wrote in Latin, German, as well as the Silesian dialect.

GRYPHIUS, SEBASTIAN

(1493-1556). Member of the family of German printers. He and his brother François established themselves in Paris, while another brother, Jean, headed a branch office in Venice. The firm flourished for several generations; their device was a griffin.

GUALTEROTTI, RAFFAELLO

(1544-1638). Italian poet at the Medici court of Florence. Wrote on the nuptials of Francesco de' Medici and Bianca, in 1579. Also an epic on the glories of Europe: written in honor of the marriage of Cosimo de' Medici and Princess Maria Magdalena of Austria, in 1608. He wrote an unfinished poem on *America*.

GUALTERUS, RODOLPHUS

(died 1577). Swiss poet. Author of Latin verse comedy, on Biblical theme, entitled *Nabal*: 1562. His father and namesake, (1518-1586) was a follower of Zwingli and a vociferous critic of the Roman Church.

GUARINI, BATTISTA

(1537-1612). Italian poet. Attached to courts of Ferrara, Florence, Urbino. Wrote sonnets and madrigals in which appear references to contemporary personal, literary, political events. Also author of a pastoral tragicomedy entitled *Pastor Fido*, published in 1590. Also wrote manual on diplomatic duties.

GUARINO DA VERONA

(1370-1460). Italian scholar and teacher. He came to Florence where he learned Greek from Chrysoloras himself and was the outstanding Greek scholar of his day. Chrysoloras returned to Constantinople, accompanied by Guarino, who remained in his revered master's house for five years. Guarino brought back to Florence a rich haul of fifty-four Greek manuscripts in 1408. He was called to Ferrara to teach the sons of the Este Marquis and founded a famous boarding school. He emphasized the classics in the curriculum, especially Greek literature, but also good manners, conduct, and the development of character. Man makes his way to learning and virtue by the study of the humanities.

He made several translations from Plutarch: a number of lives and his *De liberis educanalis* which, along with Quintilian and the *De Oratore* of Cicero, was basic to Renaissance educational theory; other translations were works of Isocrates, Lucian, and the whole of Strabo in addition to textual studies in Caesar, Cicero's speeches, and both Plinies. The University of Ferrara, founded in 1391 but languishing at the time of his arrival, responded to Guarino's inspired teaching as professor of Greek and rhetoric; by 1474 it rivaled Bologna and Padua.

GUAZZO, MARCO

(1490-1556). Italian poet, historian. Wrote account of Charles VIII in Italy down to the battle of Fornova, which he interpreted as a grand defeat for the French.

GUAZZO, STEFANO

(1530-1593). Italian man of letters and private secretary to Margaret, the duchess of Mantua. Author of manual of epistolary style: eulogistic, apologetic, complimentary. Also wrote series of letters to contemporary figures of note, among them: Spinola, Sannazaro, Guasco.

GUÉDRON, P.

(1565-1621). Composer to Henry IV and Louis XIII of France. Works include *Alcine,* a ballet, presented in 1610; *Délivrance de Renaud,* 1617, and many more.

GUELPHS AND GHIBELLINES

The Italian names for the antagonists in the medieval struggle between the popes and the Holy Roman Emperors; Guelph, derived from the Welf family and leaders of the feudal opponents of the Hohenstaufen dynasty in Germany, designated the propapalists; Ghibelline, from a Hohenstaufen castle known as Waiblingen, identified the Imperialists or anti-papalists. Traditionally Florence and Milan were Guelph, Pisa Ghibelline, and Venice neutral. By the time of the Renaissance the parties carrying these banners had little reference to the original quarrel: the Empire was feeble, the papacy in eclipse. Guelph and Ghibelline meant only the ins and the outs in the remorseless struggles for control of the municipal governments; in those cities where one party succeeded in banishing the other, the victors tended to split forming two new factions. Such was the case at Florence where the triumphant Guelphs divided into Blacks, *Neri*, and Whites, *Bianchi;* winning out, the Blacks exiled the Whites, among whom was Dante.

GUERCINO, GIAN-FRANCESCO BARBIERI
(1590-1666). Italian painter of Bologna. Head of eclectic school and was influenced chiefly by Caravaggio. Executed altarpiece, frescoes, religious genre.

GUERRERO, FRANCISCO
(c. 1527-1599). Spanish musician. Composed sacred music: masses and motets, but a few secular madrigals also.

GUEVARA, ANTONIO DE
(c. 1490-1545). Spanish historian, courtier, priest. Franciscan Order. Bishop. Noted for *Reloj de Príncipes o Libro Áureo del Emperador Marco Aurelio*. Didactic novel illustrating the perfect prince: published 1529. In English translations by Baron Berners and by Sir Thomas North, it is thought to have influenced the euphuistic style in England. Also author of letters, studies of Roman emperors.

GUICCIARDINI, FRANCESCO
(1483-1540). Florentine historian and public servant. Unlike his friend Machiavelli, he went over to the Medici upon their restoration in Florence in 1512 and thereafter became an important official of the Medici popes. Returned to Florence, he lost the favor of its Medici duke and entered upon a forced retirement which lasted until his death three years later. He was the author of two great works. The *Florentine History 1378-1509*, a work of his youth and not published until 1859; and the *History of Italy 1492-1534*, written in his years of forced leisure. His earlier history exhibits a fervent dislike of the Medici: Lorenzo the Magnificent is cited as a political huckster and tyrant; in the later work they are very favorably viewed: Lorenzo is hailed as the patriot whose diplomacy warded off the northern invaders during Italy's golden age. Both books are notable for their critical and analytical quality, and, especially the *Italy*, for a conception of human nature that emphasized egotism and man's capacity for self-deception.

GUIDACERIO, AGATHON
(Early Sixteenth century). Italian priest. Taught Hebrew in the

Sapienza in Rome. Made translations from Hebrew into Latin. Also author of a Hebrew grammar, published in 1539. He wrote a commentary on and made a Latin translation of the Song of Songs; in 1530 Francis I designated him Professor Royal of Hebrew in the Collège de France.

GUIDEO, GIACOBBE
Sixteenth century. Jewish physician. Became lecturer in medicine at Bologna in 1529.

GUIDICCIONI, GIOVANNI
(1500-1541). Italian priest, poet, diplomat. In the service of Pope Paul III. Author of sonnets.

GUIDO DE BRAY
Sixteenth century. Calvinist of Mons. Author of *The Rod of Christian Faith:* published in 1555.

GUIDO, GUIDI or VIDUS VIDIUS
(Died 1569). Italian physician. He became physician to Francis I of France, on whose death he became physician to Duke Cosimo of Florence. He wrote several works on medicine, surgery, fevers, anatomy, etc.; he translated and commented upon Hippocrates and Galen. He was a friend of Cellini.

GUILDFORD, SIR RICHARD
(died 1506). English traveler. Attached to the court of Henry VII. Made a pilgrimage to the Holy Land, in 1506, where he died; his chaplain wrote an account of the arduous trip and of the difficulties with the Mamelukes.

GUILLAUME DE BAILLOU
(1538-1614). French physician. One of the most distinguished in the Renaissance. Interested in epidemic diseases. The first to describe the epidemic of whooping cough in 1578: termed the condition *quinta*. Among the first physicians in France to rebel against uncritical acceptance of Galen and Arab medical writers. Followed methods of Hippocrates. Author of *Epidemiorum et Ephemeridum Libri Duo*. Dean of medical faculty in Paris.

GUILLAUME LE BÉ
(died 1598). French printer. Worked in Venice, Rome. Notable for his typography.

GUILLET, PERNETTE DU

(d. 1520-1545). French poetess of Lyons, learned in Greek and Latin, of noble birth. She was an accomplished musician of the lute and the spinet. Her poems, deeply Platonic in spirit, were published in 1545 as *Rymes de Gentile et Verteuse Dame Pernette du Guillet.*

GUIRAUD-DASTROS, JEAN

Seventeenth century. Provençal writer. Author of *Trinfe de la Langue Gascoune:* 1642. Contains bucolic descriptions and rural mores.

GUISE, FRANÇOIS DE LORRAINE, DUC DE

(1519-1563). French soldier, politician. Fought against Charles V. Took Calais in 1558. Hostile to Huguenots. Assassinated by Protestant fanatic, Jean de Poltrot.

GUISE, HENRI I DE LORRAINE, DUC DE

(1550-1588). Catholic leader in French civil and religious wars. Participated in Massacre of St. Bartholomew's Day in 1572. Instrumental in organization of Holy League. Assassinated by guard.

GULER DE WEINECK, JEAN

(1562-1637). Swiss military historian. Fought against Spaniards in the Valtellina Pass. Author of *Raetia:* published in Zürich in 1616 and written in German, it is an account of his canton.

GUNDULĬC, IVAN or GIOVANNI GONDOLA

(1588-1638). Yugoslav poet. Following Renaissance Italian models, he wrote dramas on classical themes: *Ariadne, The Rape of Proserpina.* Also a play entitled *Dubravka:* a eulogy of his native city, Dubrovnik (Ragusa) and the patron Saint Vlah. His greatest work is a long epic poem, *Osman,* in twenty cantos. The subject is the struggle of the Poles, and all the Slavic peoples, against the Turks, modeled on Tasso's *Jerusalem Delivered.*

GUNPOWDER PLOT

A conspiracy designed by some English Catholics who resented King James I's policy toward Catholics. They planned to blow up the Houses of Parliament in London, along with King James and his eldest son. The leader was Robert Catesby. The plot was discovered. Guy Fawkes, assigned to execute the plan, was arrested on November 5, 1605. Leaders were executed.

GUSTAVUS I

(1496-1560). Gustavus Vasa, Gustavas Eriksson. Founded Swedish royal house of Vasa. Instrumental in securing independence for Sweden in 1525.

In conflict with Christian II of Denmark. Held as hostage in Denmark in 1518-1519, but escaped. Christian beheaded many nobles, including the father and brother-in-law of Gustavus.

Gustavus organized a successful revolt against the Danes. In 1523 he was proclaimed king. Encouraged Lutheranism. Supported peasants: helped to develop economy of country.

Began construction of castle in Upsala in 1540: completed in 1611. A milestone in the history of Swedish literature and religion was the translation of the New Testament into Swedish, 1525.

GUSTAVUS II

(1594-1632). Gustavus Adolphus, King of Sweden, the Lion of the North. In many respects he was the ideal Renaissance prince: idealistic and practical, physically robust and handsome, well educated and fluent in seven languages, fond of music and poetry, skillful strategist and brave warrior, versatile in all things. In conflict with Denmark, Russia, Poland. During the Thirty Years' War fought for Protestantism and the acquisition of German domains. Extended his kingdom. Died of wounds at the Battle of Lützen in 1632. This cut short his grand design for a great Swedish empire dominating the Baltic and Northern Europe.

GUY DU FAUR

(died 1584). Seigneur de Pibrac. French jurist, poet, diplomat. Eulogized by Montaigne. Author of *De Rebus Gallicis Epistola:* published in 1573: a defense of Massacre of St. Bartholomew's Day, 1572.

GYLLIUS, PETRUS

(1490-1556). Sent to Constantinople by Francis I of France to collect manuscripts and books for the Royal Library in Paris. He wrote *De Constantinopoleos Topographia:* a treatise on history, politics and topography of Constantinople: published in 1561.

GYMNASIUM CABALLINI MONTIS

Academy founded by Pope Leo X (1475-1521), where Marcus Musurus and John Lascaris delivered lectures.

H

HABINGTON, WILLIAM
(1605-1654). English poet. Author of *Castara:* a corpus of lyrics published in 1634. *The Queen of Aragon,* published in 1641, is a tragi-comedy.

HADRIAN VI
(1459-1523). Pope 1522-3, of Dutch extraction. Had been professor of philosophy at Louvain. The last non-Italian to occupy the Holy See. He aroused hatred by a program of reform to eliminate corruption and simony. Opposed Luther. Tried to raise means to resist the Turks. Pure in motive, had high sense of duty, no interest in art. He had been the Emperor Charles V's tutor: it was his backing that made Hadrian rather than Wolsey or another Medici pope.

HAGECIUS, THADDEUS or HAJEK
(1525-1600). Astronomer. Physician to Emperor Maximilian II. Taught mathematics at Prague and was a student of eclipses, on which he wrote an important treatise. He was associated with Tycho Brahe and Kepler; he had studied at Prague, Vienna and Padua.

HÁJAK, VÁCLAV or WENCELAUS HAJEK
(Died 1553). He wrote, in Czech, a history of Bohemia down to 1527; it went through many editions, but it is devoid of the critical spirit.

HAKLUYT, RICHARD
(c. 1552-1616). English geographer, historian, Archdeacon of

Westminster. He taught geography at Oxford and sought to promote English exploration and colonization. Compiled *Principal
Navigations, Voyages, and Discoveries of the English Nation:*
published in 1589. An account of the adventures and exploits of
Elizabethan explorers and seamen. He collected the manuscript
accounts of foreigners' voyages as well.

HALL, EDWARD

(c. 1499-1547). English historian. Author of *Union of the Noble
Families of Lancaster and York.* Published in 1542. It is an
account of English history from Richard II to Henry VIII; the
whole period constitutes a single great drama in which the
crime of deposing and murdering Richard II is interpreted as the
cause of all England's disasters in the War of the Roses until
expiation is made by the rise of the Tudors and the marriage
that binds York and Lancaster together again to the great
benefit of England. Hall, basing himself on Polydore Vergil, was
the chief creator of the Tudor myth; he is the most important
source of Shakespeare's histories: Shakespeare concerned himself
with the same period, interpreted it in the same way and drew
the same moral. Many of Shakespeare's scenes are taken directly
from Hall and his portrait of Henry V as the "good king" and
Richard III as the "bad king" derives from Hall (Hall's Richard
III is a copy of Thomas More's).

HALL, JOHN

(Floruit c. 1565). English physician. Attacked quacks in numerous works in medicine and surgery. Describes a mountebank as
follows: "When anye came to him wyth urines . . . he made them
believe, that onlye by feling the weight thereof, he would tell
them of theyr diseases in their bodies, or wythout: And other-
while made them believe, that he went to aske counsel of the
devil, by going a little asyde, and mumbling to him selfe, and
then comming agayne, would tell them all and more to." He
should not be confused with JOHN HALL (1575-1635), physician
and son-in-law of Shakespeare.

HALS, FRANZ

(1580?-1666). The Elder. Dutch portrait and genre painter. Born
in Malines or Antwerp. Died in Haarlem. Ranks with Van Dyck,
Rubens, Rembrandt among the greatest Dutch painters. His
works include: *The Laughing Cavalier, Herring Vendor, Jolly*

296

Trio, Portrait of a Lady, Fool playing Lute and many more, all notable for their vivacity and naturalness, their sparkling color and accuracy in depicting everyday scenes of Dutch life. His brother DIERCK (1591-1656) and his son FRANZ (1618-1669) were painters.

HAMPTON COURT CONFERENCE OF 1605

A conference that was convened by James I of England to reconcile Puritans and Anglicans. The result was a number of liturgical changes and a decision to translate the Bible into English. This translation, published in 1611, was the King James Version of the Bible.

The king also threatened to 'harry non-conformists out of the land.' As a result, many Non-Conformists migrated to the Low Countries: then to the Plymouth Colony. James' judgment on ecclesiastical policy was summed up in the expression: "No bishop, no king"; to abolish the bishoprics, as the Puritans wished, would make it impossible for the king to rule the country.

HANMER, MEREDITH

(1543-1604). English historian, educated at Oxford. Translated Eusebius, Cassiodorus' *Historia Tripartita*, Evargius—all ecclesiastical histories of early Christianity; he wrote a *Chronicle of Ireland*, where he served as an archdeacon in various dioceses.

HAPSBURG EMPERORS

Frederick III: 1440-1493; Maximilian I: 1493-1519; Charles V: 1519-1556; Ferdinand I: 1556-1564; Maximilian II: 1564-1576; Rudolph II: 1576-1612; Matthias: 1612-1619; Ferdinand II: 1619-1637; Ferdinand III: 1637-1657.

Dates refer to length of reign.

HARDY, ALEXANDRE

(c. 1570-1631). French dramatist. Author of several hundred plays: *Marianne* is noteworthy, most of them are mediocre; at his best he may be said to bear comparison with Corneille and the French classical dramatists of the next age.

HARFF, ARNOLD VON

(1471-1505). German noble. Wrote an account of his pilgrimage to the Holy Land and of his experiences in the Near East.

HARPSFIELD, NICHOLAS

(1519-1575). English priest, scholar and theologian. Author of biography of Sir Thomas More and an ecclesiastical history of England. He opposed Henry VIII's religious changes, enjoyed favor under Mary. Upon her death he was imprisoned in the Tower until his death.

HARRINGTON, SIR JOHN

(1561-1612). English writer. Translated *Orlando Furioso* at request of Queen Elizabeth I. Banished for writing Rabelaisian satires, notably *Metamorphosis of Ajax*, 1596, *An Anatomy of the Metamorphosed Ajax* and *Ulysses upon Ajax*. Unsuccessfully attempted reconciliation of Queen and Earl of Essex. Wrote epigrams; also account of Queen's last days. His writings show the influence of Philip Sydney.

HARRIOT, THOMAS

(1560-1621). English mathematician and astronomer. Author of *Artis Analyticae Praxis*, a work on algebra. He had been Sir Walter Raleigh's tutor and was designated surveyor for Raleigh's Virginia colony; he produced an early statistical survey, entitled *A Brief and True Report on the New Found Land of Virginia*.

HARRISON, WILLIAM

(1534-1593). English chronologist and typographer and clergyman. Wrote *Description of England,* published in 1577, as part of Holinshed's *Chronicles.*

HARROW SCHOOL

English public school. Founded in 1571 by yeoman John Lyon (c. 1514-1592).

HARTUNG, JOHANN

(1505-1579). German humanist philologist. Professor of Greek at Freiburg. Author of a book of critical notes on Homer, Pindar, Hesiod, Euripides, Sophocles as well as a study of Cicero.

HARVEY, GABRIEL

(c. 1545-1630). English poet, scholar, writer and controversialist. Friend of Edmund Spenser, who depicts him as Hobbinal in *The Shepherd's Calendar*. He engaged in a famous literary quarrel with Thomas Nash and Robert Greene.

298

HARVEY, WILLIAM
(1578-1657). English physician. He had studied at Padua under Fabricius. Physician to James I of England and Charles I. Discovered circulation of the blood. In 1628 published *Essay on the Motion of the Heart and Blood in Animals*. Author of *Exercitationes in Generatione Animalium*: appeared in 1651 and was the result of his researches in embryology.

HASLOBIUS, MICHAEL
(1540-1589). German humanist poet. Wrote Latin poems in classical form on contemporary themes, especially religious subjects; he was professor of poetry at Frankfurt.

HASSLER, HANS LEO
(1564-1612). German musician and composer. He was one of the first Germans to study music in Italy; he went to Venice to study under Andrea Gabrieli. He wrote a great deal, both church and secular music. Among his patrons were Octavian Fugger and the Duke of Saxony; he is best known for his 24 Latin *canzonette*.

HATTON, SIR CHRISTOPHER
(1540-1591). English courtier. Favorite of Queen Elizabeth I. Member of Parliament. In 1587 became Lord Chancellor. He was a friend of Spenser and himself a literary amateur.

HAVERFORD WEST GRAMMAR SCHOOL
Welsh public school. Founded before 1488.

HAWES, STEPHEN
(died c. 1523). English poet. Traveler. Linguist. Produced collection of poems, *Pastime of Pleasure*, in 1509: an allegory of life. Also another allegorical poem entitled *Example of Virtue*. He often sang the praises of the Tudor dynasty in his poetry and was rewarded for doing so; he was paid a sum for his *A Joyfull Meditation* commemorating Henry VIII's coronation.

HAWKINS, SIR JOHN
(1532-1595). Or Hawkyns. Elizabethan seaman. First Englishman to traffic in Negro slaves. In 1588 he was knighted for his services against the Spanish Armada, both as re-organizer of the navy and as commander of one of the ships, the *Victory*. In 1595, along with his kinsman Sir Francis Drake, he commanded an ex-

pedition against the Spanish Main: destroyed Spanish trade in the West Indies. Died in Puerto Rico.

HAWKINS, SIR RICHARD
(c. 1562-1622). Or Hawkyns. English admiral, son of Sir John Hawkins. Prisoner in Spain for eight years, until 1602, as punishment for his pillaging of Spanish towns in the New World.

HAYWARD, SIR JOHN
(c. 1564-1627). English writer. Author of historical works: on the medieval kings of England. He was strongly monarchist in his writing, although his association with Essex and his inquiries into the deposition of Richard II brought him under royal suspicion.

HEBENSTREIT, JOHANN
Sixteenth century. German physician. Wrote on astrological subjects.

HEBRAEORUM GENS
In accordance with this Papal Bull, promulgated in 1569, Jews were expelled from the Papal States.

HEEMSKERCK, MAARTEN VAN
(1498-1574). Dutch painter who studied in Rome and was particularly influenced by Michelangelo.

HEGIUS, ALEXANDER
(c. 1433-1498). German scholar and Christian humanist. Taught Erasmus at Deventer. Studied under the Brethren of the Common Life. He did much to establish the Latin classics in the curriculum and to expel the medieval textbooks.

HEIDELBERG CATECHISM
A reformed, Calvinistic catechism drawn up by two Heidelberg professors: Zacharias Ursinus (1534-1583) and Caspar Olevianus (1536-1587) in 1562, at instance of Elector of the Palatinate, Frederick III, the Pious. Catechism intended for schools: irenic in spirit. Widely accepted by Reformed Churches within and outside Germany. Adopted as orthodox teaching of Dutch Calvinism—a disavowal of Arminianism.

HEIMERICH DE CAMPO
(died 1460). Or Heimerich de Campen. Logician. Discussed ancient and contemporary exponents of dialectics.

HEINRICH VON GORKUM

(died 1460). Logician. Wrote a treatise on logic: published in 1506.

HEINRICH VON PFOLSPEUNDT

(born 1460). German physician. Author of treatise on hygiene. Contains the first description of rhinoplastic procedure.

HEINSIUS, DANIEL, OF GHENT

(1580-1655). Classical scholar, one of the greatest of the Renaissance. Professor at Leyden. Wrote critical essays and textual studies of Greek authors, particularly Aristotle, but also Hesiod and Latin authors, e.g., Theocritus, Horace and Seneca. His exposition of Aristotle's conception of tragedy strongly influenced contemporary dramatists, e.g., Ben Jonson, Racine and Corneille.

HELMONT, JAN BAPTISTE VAN

(1577?-1644). Flemish chemist and physician. Born in Brussels. He was the first to use the term *gas*. Made chemical investigations more accurate and quantitative by means of the balance. Author of *Ortus Medicinae*, in which he suggested the physiological changes in the human body are chemically induced.

HELTAI, KASPAR

(c. 1520-c. 1575). Hungarian scholar and Protestant. Translated the Bible into Hungarian. Also wrote a chronicle of Hungarian history.

HEMMINGSEN, NIELS

(1513-1600). Danish theologian, Greek scholar, logician, and humanist education reformer. Called The Teacher of Denmark. Good Latinist. His greatest work is *The Way of Life*, written in Danish. He was a follower of Melanchthon, whose educational ideal, the *pietas litterata*, Hemmingsen did much to establish in Denmark.

HENRI DE MONANTHEUIL

(1536-1606). Professor of medicine in Paris. Also mathematician. Wrote on mathematical subjects. Translated a pseudo-Aristotelian treatise into Latin.

HENRY

(1512-1580). King of Portugal. Encouraged the Inquisition. His

301

death without direct heirs enabled Philip II of Spain to seize the throne, in 1580.

HENRY II

(1519-1589). King of France, 1547-1558. Held as hostage in Spain, 1526-1530. Married Catherine de Medici in 1533. Weak and undecisive, he was governed by the Constable, Anne de Montmorency, the dukes of Guise, and his mistress Diane de Poitiers. Seized bishoprics of Metz, Toul, Verdun, in 1552. Opposed Protestants. In conflict with England. Captured Boulogne in 1550 and Calais in 1558, from English. Made alliance with Reformers of Germany, directed against the Hapsburgs. Fought unsuccessfully in Italy and Netherlands. Died of wounds received in tournament.

HENRY III

(1551-1589). King of France 1574-1589 and Poland. During his reign the French civil and religious wars raged. Defeated Huguenots at Battles of Jarnac and Moncontour in 1569. A party to the Massacre of St. Bartholomew's Day in 1572. A dissolute ruler and a religious fanatic. Henry was stabbed to death for ordering the assassination of the Catholic League's leader, Henri, duke of Guise, by a Dominican monk, Jacques Clément. End of Valois dynasty.

HENRY IV

(1553-1610). King of France 1589-1610. Head of Protestant League. Engaged in civil and religious wars of 1568-1590's. Assumed throne after military conflicts and hostility of Catholics. Concluded War of the Three Henrys, 1585-1589, with victory at Coutras. Signed Edict of Nantes in 1598, establishing religious liberty and civil rights for the Huguenots. In 1593 renounced Protestantism for Catholicism, saying, it is said, that "Paris was worth a Mass." In 1596 ended war with Holy League. Encouraged commerce, abolished administrative abuses. Under Sully, reorganized finances. His reign was one of retrenchment; he married Marie de' Medici, and was famous for his wit and popular touch. With him began the Bourbon dynasty in France; he was assassinated by a religious fanatic, Ravaillac, when he was about to open hostilities with the Spanish and Austrian Hapsburgs.

302

HENRY IV

(1425-1474). King of Castile and Léon, 1454-1474. He was weak in the face of noble demands; during his reign the nobility determined royal policy. He was succeeded by his famous sister, Isabella of Castile, who possessed the capacity for statecraft that he so notably lacked.

HENRY VI

(1421-1471). King of England, 1415-1461, 1471. During his minority, he was under the protection of his uncles—John, Duke of Bedford, and Humphrey, Duke of Gloucester. He married Margaret of Anjou in 1445. Crowned King of France in 1431. The successes of Joan of Arc and Charles VII drove all English forces from France by 1453: Calais alone remained English. During the later years, the reign was marked by the king's periodic insanity and by economic distress. Cade's Rebellion broke out in 1450. Struggle between houses of York and Lancaster—Wars of the Roses—began: lasted from 1455 to 1485. Henry was deposed in 1461: Duke of York was proclaimed King Edward IV. Henry was imprisoned from 1465 to 1470. Rescued, restored by Warwick in 1471. Recaptured and reputedly murdered in the Tower of London.

HENRY VII

(1457-1509). King of England, 1485-1509. Founder of the Tudor dynasty. Lancastrian, on his mother's side. With an army, he landed at Milford Haven in Wales in 1485 and defeated and killed Richard III at the Battle of Bosworth Field.

Married Elizabeth, Yorkist: daughter of Edward IV. His daughter Margaret became the wife of King James IV of Scotland. Result was the creation of the Union of England and Scotland in 1603.

Henry was interested in commerce, scholarship. Promoted English trade; his most important accomplishments were the suppression of the nobility—his "over mighty subjects," and the establishment of an effective royal government and a sound fiscal system.

HENRY VIII

(1491-1547). King of England, 1509-1547. Married Catherine of Aragon, the mother of Queen Mary, 1553-1558. Joined the Holy League. In conflict with France in 1511. At the Battle of the

303

Spurs, in 1513, took command of the English troops: defeated the French. English forces defeated James IV of Scotland at Flodden Field, in 1513. Appointed Cardinal Wolsey as Lord Chancellor, in 1515. Henry's political purpose was to maintain the balance of power between France and Spain. Named Defender of the Faith by Pope Leo X for a treatise against Lutheranism: *Assentio Septem Sacramentorum.*

Imposed heavy taxation. Monasteries in England suppressed. Wolsey charged with treason: died on his way to London. Succeeded by Sir Thomas More as Chancellor, in 1529.

Henry secretly married Anne Boleyn, in 1533, declaring by enactment marriage with Catherine of Aragon was invalid. By Act of Supremacy Henry was declared head of the Church of England. Sir Thomas More, refusing to recognize the king as head of the Church of England, was executed in 1535.

Henry made enactments hostile to Protestantism as well as to Roman Catholicism. Insurrection of the Pilgrimage of Grace, in condemnation of the suppression of the monasteries: 1535.

Anne Boleyn, the mother of Queen Elizabeth, executed in 1536. Married Jane Seymour, mother of Edward VI, 1536; died. Married to Anne of Cleves in 1540. Divorced in 1540. Married Catherine Howard in 1540. Executed in 1542. Married Catherine Parr in 1543. She survived Henry.

Henry was welcomed to the throne by enthusiastic humanists as a munificent royal patron and the ideal Renaissance prince; these hopes were blighted: the Renaissance in England was arrested rather than promoted by the king's policies. England, it may be said, was too busy having a Reformation to have a Renaissance.

HENRY II

(1489-1568). Duke of Brunswick. Imprisoned for eleven years. Ally of Charles V. Opposed Martin Luther. Finally reconciled with Protestants.

HENRY THE MINSTREL

Fifteenth century. Called Blind Harry. Scottish poet. During 1490-1492, attached to the court of James IV. Author of a long poem on Sir William Wallace, Scots hero of resistance to English domination. The poem was very popular and was important as a maker and preserver of Scots national feeling.

HENRYSON, ROBERT

(c. 1430-c. 1508). Scottish poet, one of the Scottish Chaucerians. Kurt Wittig says: "In his assimilation of European subject matter, of Chaucer's conception of poetic art, and of Scottish characteristics, Robert Henryson is one of the greatest poets of the whole of Scottish literature." Author of *Testament of Cresseid*, a sequel to Chaucer's *Troilus and Criseyde*, *Orpheus and Eurydice*: collection of Aesopic fables in Scots dialect: miscellaneous minor poems.

HENSLOWE, PHILIP

(died 1616). Theatre manager. Produced plays by Webster, Marston, Dekker, Chapman, Drayton. He left a diary that is valuable to students of Elizabethan drama and stagecraft.

HERALDS' COLLEGE

Founded in London in 1461 by King Edward IV. Chartered in 1484. It is not an educational institution, but the highest authority for coats of arms and genealogies.

HERBERAY DES ESSARTS, NICOLAS D'

(died c. 1557). French scholar. Attached to the court of Francis I. Translated Spanish works into French, most notably *Amadis of Gaul.*

HERBERT, GEORGE

(1593-1633). English writer, clergyman, brother of Lord Herbert of Cherbury, one of the Metaphysical Poets. All his poetry was published after his death as *The Temple: Sacred Poems and Private Ejaculations.* He also wrote a guide for the clerical life entitled *The Priest of the Temple.*

HERESBACH, KONRAD

(1496-1576). German scholar and diplomat. Author of four books of husbandry. Published in London in 1577. He had studied philology and law in Germany, France and Italy; he penned numerous works on the classics, particularly Greek works.

HERIOT, GEORGE

(1563-1624). Scottish goldsmith and royal banker: Jeweler: attached to court of James VI of Scotland; he followed the king to London in 1603, spending most of the rest of his life there. Founder of Heriot's Hospital: now Heriot's School. Called Jingling Georgie. Appears in Sir Walter Scott's *Fortunes of Nigel.*

HERMAN, WILLIAM
(died 1548). English surgeon. Author of textbook on anatomy.

HERMANN, HUGO
Sixteenth century. German Jesuit. Author of mystical emblem book—*Pia Desideria*. Also wrote *De Prima Scribendi Origine et Universa Rei Literariae Antiquitate*: published in 1617. Deals with origin of writing, abbreviations, numerals, scribes.

HÉROËT, ANTOINE
(died 1568). French ecclesiastic and poet whose favorite themes were love and friendship; a Platonist, he wrote a commentary on the *Symposium* and translated other works into French.

HEROLD, JOANNES
One of the most popular preachers of the fifteenth century. Author of *Sermones Super Epistulas Dominicales*, published in Ulm in 1478-1480.

HERRERA, FERNANDO DE, EL DIVINO
(1534-1597). Renaissance poet of Sevillian school. Poems appeared in 1582, entitled *Algunas Obras*. Wrote History: *Relación de la Guerra de Chipre*, published in 1572: biography of Tomás Moro. Admired for his love lyrics, sonnets, and the heroic odes in which he celebrated Don John of Austria and the victory of Lepanto.

HERRERA, FRANCISCO DE, THE ELDER
(1576-1656). Spanish painter of Seville. Executed genre pieces, historical themes, mostly in Seville, where he is said to have founded the naturalistic school. Velasquez was his pupil briefly.

HERRERA, JUAN DE
(1530-1597). Spanish architect. In the service of King Philip II. Finished construction of the Escorial.

HERRERA Y TORDESILLAS, ANTONIO DE
(1559-1625). Spanish historian. Wrote an account of the Indies and one of the reign of Philip II. As official historian he had access to archives and official documents, making his histories factually reliable.

HESSUS, HELIUS EOBANUS
(1488-1540). German humanist. Latin poet. Supported Luther.

306

Translated Homer's *Iliad* and *Psalms* into Latin hexametric verse. Wrote also *Heroïdes Christianae*, and historical pieces. As professor of poetry and rhetoric, first at Erfurt and then at Marburg, he did much to popularize the new learning.

HÉTZER, LUDWIG
(died 1529). Swiss leader of Anabaptists. Translated *Prophets* into German: first Protestant version. Beheaded for heresy.

HEXENHAMMER
In Latin, *Malleus Maleficarum*, Witches' Hammer. A treatise on witchcraft by two German Dominicans—Heinrich Kramer and Jacob Sprenger. Published in 1489. Formed the basis of Inquisition's investigation and punishment of Black Arts.

HEYNLIN, JOHANN
(c. 1425-1496). Called Johannes a Lapide. Theologian and canonist. Rector of University of Tübingen. Wrote a number of monographs on logic.

HEYWOOD, JOHN
(c. 1497-1580). English dramatist, married the niece of Sir Thomas More, favorite of Queen Mary; went into exile when Elizabeth came to the throne. Wrote epigrams, proverbs. Author of *The Four P's*: a farce. Published in 1569. Also drama: *Thersites*.

HEYWOOD, THOMAS
(c. 1574-c. 1650). English dramatist and actor, educated at Cambridge. Called by Charles Lamb The Prose Shakespeare. Wrote *A Woman Killed with Kindness*. Also historical plays: *Edward IV, The Troubles of Queen Elizabeth*. Dramatized the *Metamorphoses* of Ovid. Author of masques, pageants. Among his comedies are: *The Fair Maid of the Exchange, The Fair Maid of the West*. An adventure drama: *Fortune by Land and Sea*.

HICHTUM, JOHANN VAN
(c. 1560-1628). Author of humorous wedding dialogue entitled *Woutir and Tialle:* in Frisian. Also wrote dialogue: *Ansck and Houck:* published in 1639.

HIERONIMO DA SANTO STEPHANO
Fifteenth century. Italian traveler of Genoa. Through the Red

Sea to Calicut, Ceylon, Sumatra, Maldive Islands. Wrote an account of his experiences: published in 1499.

HIERONYMUS DE MARCHO
Sixteenth century. Logician. Author of *Parva Logica:* published in Cologne in 1507.

HIERONYMUS DE NUCIARELLIS
Sixteenth century. Logician. Wrote *Sermo de Secundis Intentionibus.*

HIERONYMUS VON HANGEST
Sixteenth century. Logician. Author of *Problemata Logicalia:* published in Paris in 1516.

HIGHGATE SCHOOL
English public school in London. Founded in 1565 by Roger Cholmley (died 1565).

HILDANUS, FABRICIUS
(1560-1624). German surgeon. Called Father of German Surgery. Studied in Italy and France. Author of *Observationes Medico-Chirurgicae:* published in 1606 in Basel.

HILLIARD, NICHOLAS
(1537-1619). English miniaturist. Attached to court of Queen Elizabeth I and of James I as painter and carver and goldsmith. A self-taught, painstaking, prolific craftsman.

HINOJOSA, PEDRO DE
(1489-1553). Spanish navigator and explorer. With Pizarro in Peru. Captured Panama. Governor of Charcas. Assassinated, it is said, for his greed, arrogance and severity.

HIPLER, WENDEL
(died 1525). Chancellor of Bavaria. Died as prisoner. Subject of German drama.

HIPPOLYTUS LUNENSIS
Calligrapher who executed illuminations for Ferdinand I of Spain (1458-1494). Among his works are a copy of Onosander's *De Optimo Imperatore*, a copy of Ovid.

HOCHST, BATTLE OF
Baron of Tilly, commanding the troops of the Catholic League,

defeated Christian of Brunswick in 1622, an episode in the Thirty Years' War.

HOEFNAGEL, JORIS

(c. 1542-1600). Flemish miniaturist and illustrator, in the service of the Hapsburg Court of Rudolph II. Executed, among other works, a Roman Missal: preserved in the National Museum, Vienna.

HOFFMANN, MELCHIOR

(c. 1498-c. 1544). Itinerant Anabaptist preacher of Swabia, a furrier's apprentice who had no formal education. He evangelized in the most fanatical spirit throughout Northern Europe thinking himself God's prophet. Fell out with Luther, Carlstadt and others. Hoffmann was expelled from one city after another. Returning to Strassburg, he was imprisoned, tortured, but continued to have a great following until his death.

HOJEDA, DIEGO DE

(1570?-1615). Born in Seville. Spanish poet and Dominican monk. Prior of monastery in Peru. Author of *La Cristiada,* sacred poem published in 1611. Subject is the Passion of Christ, interspersed with theological digressions.

HOLBEIN, HANS

(1465-1524). The Elder. German painter. Born in Augsburg. Noted for altarpieces, particularly *Altar of St. Sebastian,* he also did stained glass windows and silver point drawings. His work shows the realist and naturalist influence of Renaissance Italy.

HOLBEIN, HANS

(1497-1543). The Younger. German painter. Studied under father; visited Milan in 1518. Worked in Switzerland, where he settled in 1520. His portraits include Erasmus, Melanchthon, Sir Thomas More, and Henry VIII. Made designs for wood carving: Bible illustrations: woodcuts—*Christ Bearing the Cross.* Also murals. Went to England, where he executed portraits of notable Englishmen. Court painter to Henry VIII. Died in London, of plague. Produced series of woodcuts called *The Dance of Death.*

HOLGATE, ROBERT

(c. 1481-1555). Archbishop of York. Founded three grammar schools at York, Old Malton, and Hemsworth in which Latin,

Greek, and Hebrew were to be taught. Deprived of incumbency for marrying by Queen Mary.

HOLINSHED, RAPHAEL

(c. 1525-c. 1580). English chronicler. Author of *Chronicles*, published in 1578: part of intended universal history. Furnished source material for some of Shakespeare's plays, e.g. *Macbeth*, *King Lear*. His *Chronicles* are pedestrian, much of his account of fifteenth-century England is lifted from Hall; his importance as a source book for Shakespeare has been exaggerated.

HOLLAND, HENRY

(1583-c. 1650). Son of Philemon Holland. London bookseller, compiler and publisher. Published *Baziliologia* in 1618, an illustrated chronicle of the English monarchy since 1066.

HOLLAND, PHILEMON

(1552-1637). English physician and translator. Gained reputation as most prolific English translator of his age. Translated Livy, Suetonius, Pliny the Elder, Xenophon, Plutarch, Ammianus Marcellinus; they set a standard for accuracy and readability.

HOLLAND, RICHARD

(Fifteenth century). Scottish poet. Author of *Buke of the Howlat*: a bird allegory. Published c. 1450. Also a humorous piece entitled *The Tale of Rauf Coilyear*: appeared c. 1470.

HOLLAR, WENZEL

(1607-1677). Born in Prague: died in London. Engraver and etcher. Important original engraver. Enjoyed royal favor in England; fled during the Interregnum and returned upon the Restoration of 1660.

HOLLONIUS, LUDWIG

(c. 1600). Author of allegorical play entitled *Somnium Vitae Humanae*.

HOLY LEAGUE OF 1511

This league was formed by Pope Julius II, the purpose being the expulsion of the French from Italy. At first, members of the league were the Pope, Venice, Ferdinand of Spain. Later members were the Emperor Maximilian and Henry VIII of England. The league was used as a stalking horse by Ferdinand in order to annex Navarre. The alliance ended with the defeat of the French by Henry VIII at the Battle of Spurs, in 1514.

HOLY LEAGUE AND TURKS
In 1538 Charles V, Venice, Pope Paul III, opposed the Turks. Venetians were defeated at the naval battle of Prevesa in 1540.

HOLYROOD ABBEY AND PALACE
The royal seat of Scotland, in Edinburgh. The Abbey was founded by King David I of Scotland in 1128. Holyrood Palace was begun c. 1500.

HOMELIUS, JOHANNES, or HOMMEL
(1518-1562). Professor of mathematics at Leipzig. Wrote on astronomical subjects and was associated with Tycho Brahe, who owed several important observational facts to Homelius.

HONDIUS, JODOCUS
(1563-1611). Flemish engraver. Worked in England, having fled from the terrors of the revolt going on in his homeland. Executed engraved portraits. Illustrated Drake's voyages. Among his most important works were cartographical engravings, especially a map of the world.

HONOURABLE CORPS OF GENTLEMEN AT ARMS
The royal bodyguards in Britain. Founded in 1559.

HONTERUS, JOHANNES or HONTER
(1498-1549). German humanist, schoolmaster, reformer. Printer. Studied in Basel. He wrote numerous works, most of which he himself printed, on religious reform, grammar, cosmography, and the civil law. Much of his life he spent in Poland and Hungary, where he set up the first printing press, furthering the Reformation.

HONTHORST, GERRIT VAN
(1590-1656). Prolific Dutch painter. Died in Utrecht. His trip to Italy in 1610 was decisive for his career. His specialties were portraits, genre themes, religious subjects. Chiaroscuro in the style of Caravaggio; his penchant for nocturnal scenes caused him to be known as Gherardo delle Notti.

HOOD, THOMAS
(floruit 1582-1598). English mathematician and physician, edu-

311

cated at Cambridge. Lecturer in mathematics in London. Wrote on astronomy, mathematics, navigation.

HOOFT, PIETER CORNELISZ

(1561-1647). Dutch historian, poet, and playwright. Traveled through Italy and France. Translated Petrarch. Wrote pastoral play entitled *Granida;* a comedy, *The Miser;* and tragedies, love lyrics, historical works, based on classical models. At Muiden gathered around him literary and artistic friends: called *Muiderkring*: centre of Dutch Renaissance culture. His *History of the Netherlands* in the time of the Dutch Revolt is modeled on Tacitus and a great work.

HOOGSTRAETEN, JAKOB VAN

(c. 1460-1527). Dominican monk and polemicist. Inquisitor in Mainz, Cologne. Antagonist of Reuchlin, against whom he made many charges over the Cabala and the use of Hebrew.

HOOKER, RICHARD

(c. 1554-1600). English theologian. Author of treatise: *Of the Laws of Ecclesiastical Polity,* classic defense of the Church of England as a *via media* between extremes of Rome and Geneva.

HOOPER, JOHN

(died 1555). English religious reformer. Became Protestant. Escaped persecution by flight from England; returned: Bishop of Gloucester. Lost see at instance of Queen Mary. Condemned for heresy: burned at stake.

HOREBOUT, GERARD

Flemish illuminator and painter. Executed devotional and liturgical works c. 1500, e.g., a book of the hours for Margaret of Austria. Also portraits, e.g., of Christian VII of Denmark.

HORN, PHILIP DE MONTMORENCY, COUNT OF

(1518-1568). Flemish soldier, statesman, admiral. At the court of Spain. Returning to Flanders, he opposed Spanish policies and the Inquisition. Together with Count Egmont, executed by order of Philip II of Spain. Executions help to provoke revolt of the Dutch against Spain.

HOROLOGY

The period of the Renaissance saw many improvements in timekeeping devices. Watches were invented in 1500. Peter Hele, a craftsman of Nuremberg, designed an oval watch that became known as a Nuremberg egg.

HORROCKS, JEREMIAH
(c. 1619-1641). English astronomer. First to observe Venus, in 1639. Made tidal observations. Expounded on celestial motions, describing the orbit of the moon as an ellipse. It is hard to give him due credit for his observations and discoveries because so little of his writings survived.

HORST, GREGORIUS
(1578-1638). German physician. Regarded as German Aesculapius. Wrote numerous tracts and theses on anatomy, physiology, medicine, as well as the more philosophical subject, psychophysiology.

HOTMAN, FRANÇOIS
(1524-1590). French jurist. Author of *Franco-Gallia*: a treatise against absolutism. It was based on his reconstruction of Frankish feudal institutions through the study of feudal law; he thus was a pioneer of modern historiography. Also translated Plato's *Apology* in 1548. Wrote on *Corpus Iuris Civilis*.

HOUSE OF MEDICI
Cosimo: 1434-1464. Called *Pater Patriae*. Piero the Gouty: 1464-1469. Giuliano: 1469-1478. Lorenzo the Magnificent: 1469-1492. (joint rule with Giuliano until the latter's death in Pazzi Conspiracy) Piero: 1492-1495. Lorenzo: 1512-1519.
Dates refer to duration of rule.

HOUSE OF ORANGE OF THE UNITED PROVINCES
William the Silent: 1544-1584. Philip William: 1584-1618. Maurice: 1618-1625. Frederick Henry: 1625-1647. William II: 1647-1650. Ruled as stadtholders.
Dates refer to duration of rule.

HOUSE OF RURIK (RUSSIA)
Ivan III The Great: 1462-1505. Basil III: 1505-1533. Ivan IV The Terrible: 1533-1584. Fedor I: 1584-1598. Boris Godunov: 1598-1605. Fedor II: 1605. Demetrius: 1605-1606. Basil IV: 1606-1610.
Dates refer to duration of rule.

HOUSE OF VALOIS
Charles VII: 1422-1461. Louis XI: 1461-1483. Charles VIII: 1483-

1498. Louis XII: 1498-1515. Francis I: 1515-1547. Henry II: 1547-1559. Francis II: 1559-1560. Charles IX: 1560-1574. Henry III: 1574-1589. Dates refer to duration of rule.

HOUSE OF VASA
Gustavus Vasa: 1523-1560. Eric XIV: 1560-1568. John III: 1568-1592. Sigismund III of Poland: 1592-1598. Charles IX: 1598-1611. Gustavus Adolphus: 1611-1632. Christina: 1632-1654. Charles X: 1654-1660. Dates refer to duration of rule.

HOUTMAN, CORNELIS DE
(c. 1540-1599). Dutch navigator and commercial agent. Traded with East Indies. Reached Madagascar, Cochin China, Sumatra. Killed by native sultan.

HOUTMAN, FREDERIK
(1570-1627). Dutch navigator and imperial official. While governor of the Moluccas and in other posts, he compiled the first dictionary of the Malay language and another of the language of Madagascar.

HOWARD, CATHERINE
(1520?-1542). Fifth wife of Henry VIII, niece of the powerful Duke of Norfolk. Convicted of adultery, beheaded, although political rather than moral considerations account for Henry's lack of mercy.

HOWARD, THOMAS, DUKE OF NORFOLK
(1473-1554). English statesman. Admiral. Commanded English troops at Battle of Flodden. Favorite of Henry VIII: lost royal favor. Imprisoned on charge of treason, released eventually but excluded from the king's council and friendship. Portrait by Holbein.

HOWELL, JAMES
(1594?-1666). English writer. Historiographer Royal. Author of *Epistulae Howelianae*, *A Survey of the Signorie of Venice*, and *A Treatise Concerning Ambassadors*.

HUBER, WOLF or WOLFGANG
(c. 1490-1553). German painter. Executed religious pictures, portraits. Member of the Danube school. His works are notable for their subjective fantasy and dramatic intensity; he also did woodcuts.

314

HÜBMAIER, BALTHASER

(1480-1528). Swiss Anabaptist reformer and prophet. Influenced by Luther. Organized large Anabaptist community; suffered persecution, fled to Moravia, where his movement met with great success until he was apprehended and carried off to Vienna, where he was executed.

HUDSON, HENRY or HENDRIK

(died c. 1611). English navigator. Made several expeditions, for English Muscovy Company, to discover Northeast passage to Orient. Found Greenland. Discovered Hudson River in 1609. In fourth expedition, discovered Hudson Bay. During a mutiny of his sailors, Hudson was set adrift.

HUGUET, JAIME

(1420-1490). Catalan painter of religious subjects; his works show very little of the realism and naturalism of Renaissance Italy.

HULME GRAMMAR SCHOOL

English public school. Founded in 1611 by James Assheton.

HULSIUS, FREDERICK

(Sixteenth century). Flemish engraver, associated with Theodore de Bry, spent some time in England; one of his best-known prints is an engraving of Erasmus.

HUMANISM

The term should not be used to designate the philosophy of the Renaissance. During the Renaissance the word was not used, not being coined until the nineteenth century, when it signified the preference for the classical curriculum over a scientific and technological one. It is only recently that it has come to designate one form or another of the philosophy that makes man the measure of all things. Such ideas were not lacking in the Renaissance, but they were incidental to the concerns of the humanists. Humanists (this term, as well as humanities, was employed in the Renaissance, derived from the Latin, *studia humanitatis,* humane letters) were those professors, students, lovers of the classical heritage who saw in the mastery and imitation of the ancient writers the best way to attain the lucidity, precision, and simplicity of thought and expression which was their ideal. This conception of "eloquence" became and long remained the educational ideal of the Western World.

HUMANISM IN SPAIN

In Spain, humanism took the form of Christian humanism. The unorthodox humanists: Luis Vives and Juan de Valdés, spent most of their lives abroad. Thus the Spanish humanists were eminent mainly in religious and classical scholarship: e.g. Nebrija and Cisneros. The creative writers, such as Santillana, Mena, Boscán, Garcilaso, were humanists after the Italian model. The Renaissance reached Spain between 1474 and 1504 through influx of humanists from Italy and as a result of Spaniards studying in Italy, e.g., Nebrija.

HUMANIST

In Renaissance terminology, humanist applied to one who was interested in the study of Greek and Roman culture: this was the *studia humanitatis*. This humanism stressed in particular the works and the imitation of the Latin style of Cicero. In this sense, the term humanity is still associated with the classics. The Chair of Latin, for example, at the University of Edinburgh is held by the Professor of Humanity.

HUNDT, MAGNUS

(1449-1519). The Elder. German physician, priest and logician, professor at the University of Leipzig. Commentator on Aristotle. He was the author of an anatomical study remarkable for its woodcuts and its frankness in treating pestilence, entitled *Anthropologium de hominis dignitate, natura et proprietatibus*: published in 1501. Wrote *Compendium Totius Logices*: published in Leipzig in 1511, a work on logic still in the Scholastic tradition.

HURTADO DE MENDOZA, DIEGO

(1503-1573). Spanish Renaissance diplomat, poet, historian, soldier. Born in Granada: died in Madrid. Became one of the foremost diplomats: served under Charles V and Philip II in London, Venice. Follower of Boscán. Noted writer and poet. Admired by Lope de Vega. Author of Petrarchan sonnets. Also historical work, modeled on Sallust and Tacitus: *Guerra de Granada*, about the fall of Granada and the completion of the Renconquest in 1492.

316

HUTTEN, PHILIP VON

(c. 1498-1546). German soldier of fortune. Sailed to Venezuela, in quest of El Dorado. 1536-1545. Attacked by Indians. Beheaded. Left an account of his travels.

HUTTEN, ULRICH VON

(1488-1523). German knight of humanist education and patriotic temperament. Greatly interested in the Germanic past and dreaming of a great national revival, he was fascinated by Tacitus, especially the *Germania*. He wrote *Arminius* (Herman who defeated Varus and annihilated three Roman legions in 9 A.D.) as a glorification of the Germanic past, fashioning Arminius into a national hero who warded off Roman conquest and who surpassed Alexander, Scipio, and Hannibal. He supported the Emperor Maximilian in his ambition to create a stronger monarchy; the Emperor welcomed Hutten's praises and crowned him poet-laureate in 1517. Part of Hutten's patriotism was a violent aversion for the Roman papacy; he published Valla's *Donation of Constantine* and was the chief contributor to the *Letters of Obscure Men* in the Reuchlin case. After some hesitation he joined Luther's cause. He played a role with his friend Franz von Sickingen in the Knights' War of 1522-3; defeated, he died in exile in Switzerland. His last years were embittered further by an exchange of barbs with Erasmus, whom he took to be a hypocrite for not siding with Luther.

HUTTER, ELIAS

(1544-1605). German Hebrew scholar and Orientalist, Biblical scholar. Famous for his polyglot editions of the Bible—in the ancient and modern tongues.

HUTTER, LEONARD

(1563-1616). Lutheran champion. Professor of theology at Wittenberg. Author of a *Compendium*: published in 1610.

HUTTERIAN BRETHREN

Also known as Hutterites. They were followers of Jacob Hutter (died 1536), a Swiss Brethren minister of Anabaptist persuasion. Hutterites were rigid disciplinarians and sharers in community goods. Flourished in Moravia. Persecuted, they fled to Rumania and Russia.

HUYGHENS, CONSTANTIJN
(1596-1682). Dutch poet. Secretary for half a century to the princes of the house of Orange. He wrote in Italian, French and Latin as well as Dutch. He was also a student of science and an accomplished musician.

HYMNODY
In Bohemia the followers of John Hus—Unitas Fratrum—produced a hymnbook in 1501.

HYMNS
The first Danish hymn book appeared in 1569.

I

IBN SHEM-TOV, JOSEPH
(1420-1480). Sephardic apologist. Philosopher at court of Castile. Controversialist. He was learned in Aristotle and knew the Aristotle corpus of commentators: Christian, Mohammedan (especially Averroës), and Jewish; philosophically he was part of the Cabalist tradition.

IBN YAHYA, GEDALIAH
(1515-1587). Member of distinguished Jewish scholarly family. Author of *Chain of Tradition:* a miscellany of history and legend.

ILLUMINATORS
Italian illuminators of Ferrarese school, belonging in the late fifteenth century, included Matteo da Milano and Tommaso da Modena.

ILLUSTRATED HERBAL
A herbal, illustrated with plates, made its way into Russia in 1534.

IL VIGNAIULOI
Members of a Renaissance coterie of scholars in Rome.

IMMENSA AETERNA DEI
A Papal Bull, promulgated in 1588, that reorganized pontifical administration.

IMPERIAL, MICER FRANCISCO
(died in first half of fifteenth century). Spanish Renaissance poet of Italian origin. Learned in Greek, Latin, Italian, French, Eng-

lish, Arabic. First to introduce Italian hendecasyllabics into Castilian verse. First to imitate Dante in Spanish literature: e.g. in *Dezyr a las Syete Virtudes*: allegorical poem. His superb love lyrics appear in his *Cancionero de Baena*.

IMPOSITIONS

Tariffs imposed by King James I of England, without consent of Parliament. In the case of a certain Bates, tried for refusal to pay, the imposition was upheld.

INDEX

Literary censorship sponsored by governmental or ecclesiastical agencies. The first Index is virtually contained in Plato's *Republic* with reference to the studies of prospective philosopher-kings. In 1546 the University of Louvain published an index of dangerous books. To counteract the Protestant Reformation, the Council of Trent (1545-1563) drew up an index, or catalogue of books, in two lists: *Index Librorum Prohibitorum* listed books not to be read. *Index Expurgatorius* listed permissible books after the deletion of specified passages. The printing press, which required licensing, etc., facilitated censorship by princes and ecclesiastics.

INDULGENCES, SALE OF

The Church claimed the power to remit punishment for sin after death in Purgatory on payment of a sum to the Church, which was to be used for the performance of good works. The practice, however, was so abused by many churchmen that indulgences were sold without reference to penance or repentance of error. In protest against such sales, Martin Luther posted 95 theses in Latin on the door of a Wittenberg church in 1517. He was, however, not merely attacking the sale of indulgences, but the whole system of salvation of which indulgences was a part.

INGEGNERI, MARCO ANTONIO

(c. 1545-1592). Italian church musician of Verona. Composed madrigals, masses. He was choirmaster of Cremona Cathedral; Monteverdi was one of his students.

INGHIRAMI, TOMMASO

(1470-1516). Italian humanist and classical scholar. Librarian of Vatican. Collector of ancient manuscripts. Called the modern Cicero for his Latin style; the subject of a famous portrait by Raphael.

INGLIS, JAMES

(Died 1530). Scottish prelate. Abbot of Culross. Attached to court of James IV of Scotland. Sent on mission to England. Provided dramatic entertainment for the court. Author of an attack on the clergy entitled *A General Satyre*—not extant—and possibly of *The Complaynt of Scotland*.

INGRASSIAS, GIOVANNI FILIPPO

(1510-1580). Italian physician and osteologist, studied at Padua. Critic of Galen and Vesalius, many of whose errors he corrected. He also gave the first account of sphenoid and ethmoid bones. Spent most of his life in Sicily, where he was Philip II's chief medical officer.

INNOCENT VIII

(1432-1492). Pope 1484-1492. Pontificate marked by moral laxity and nepotism. In conflict with Turks. Sanctioned Witch Bull in 1484, promoting witch-hunting and punishment in ecclesiastical courts. During pontificate Moslem rule in Spain came to an end. In 1486 Pope banned first world congress of philosophers of all religions. He gained the custody of Djem, brother and pretender to the throne of Sultan Bayazid II, and hoped thereby to force Bayazid to come to terms without a Crusade; the Pope gained an agreement that Europe would be free from Turkish attack so long as the pretender remained in prison. Innocent also made peace with the invader of Italy, Charles VIII of France.

INNOCENT IX

(1519-1591). Pope for two months. Followed the policies of Sixtus V in prohibiting the alienation of church benefices.

INNOCENT X

(1574-1655). Pope. His cautious nature caused him to be mocked as "Mr. It-can't-be-done." His sister-in-law, the notorious Olimpia Maidalchini, dominated him. On that account she was called the Papessa. His portrait was painted by Velasquez in 1650.

INTERCURSUS MAGNUS

A commercial treaty negotiated by Henry VII in 1496, between England and the Low Countries.

ISAAC, HEINRICH

(1450-1517). Flemish composer of religious and secular music, contrapuntalist. Briefly at many courts in Italy and in the North;

finally came to reside at Florence; music master to Lorenzo the Magnificent's children and set to music many of his patron's carnival songs. He composed a great amount of church music, most notably the volume of *Choralis Constantinus*.

ISABELLA I

(1451-1504). Queen of Castile and Leon. Called *La Católica*. Queen of Ferdinand V of Aragon. In reign of Ferdinand and Isabella Christopher Columbus discovered America, Granada fell, and in the interest of absolutism the expulsion of Moors and Jews began. Her famous marriage occurred in 1469. She was of a fervent crusading spirit, but she was also attuned to the new art and learning of Italy. Her children, Catherine of Aragon and Joanna the Mad, were both reared staunchly in the faith and also tutored in the new learning.

ISABELLA BOOK

Breviary of Spanish Dominican use, written in Spain, illuminated by Flemish artists. Presented c. 1497 to Queen Isabella. Breviary is now preserved in British Museum.

ISABELLA OF PORTUGAL

(1503-1539). Wife of Emperor Charles V. Mother of Philip II of Spain.

ISENBRANT, ADRIAEN

(ante 1495-1551). Painter of Bruges. His subjects were religious. Belongs to the Flemish Renaissance. "Artist of the Virgin of the Seven Sorrows" and "Jan Mostaert" are believed to be his signatures, e.g., in *The Virgin With Child* and *The Adoration of the Magi*.

ISLE OF PATMOS

Name given by Martin Luther to Wartburg Castle, where he was in exile for one year. Returned to Wittenberg in 1522. It was a reference to John the Baptist's supposed exile on the island in the Aegean.

ITALIAN ART

The Italian Renaissance covers the fifteenth and sixteenth centuries. The Renaissance interest in man and in the realities of this world were already discernible in the art of the late Middle Ages. Man became the central fact in the cosmos, and all things in life

322

and art were measured by the human standard. In the Italian art of the fifteenth and sixteenth centuries, beauty and the dignity of humanity are the keynote. Natural phenomena were explored. The Renaissance palace was a symbol of man. Painting: The first monument of Renaissance painting was the cycle of frescoes by Masaccio (1402-1428) in the Carmelite church in Florence. Masaccio, famous as the creator of chiaroscuro, was one of the first painters to abandon the medieval convention that presented color with the highest intensity in shadow. Fra Angelico (1387-1455) made certain innovations in landscape and in figures and architecture, insisting upon actual, not symbolical scale. Uccello (1396-1475) demonstrated his theories of scientific perspective. Another pioneer was Antonio Pollaiuolo (1433-1498), whose interest lay in the exploration of anatomical structure. Sandro Botticelli (1447-1510) exemplifies the Renaissance longing for classical antiquity. He was affected by Politian's Latin poetry and equally by Savonarola's eloquence. The most representative Renaissance artist is Leonardo da Vinci. Scientist, inventor, he experimented in aeronautics, in military engineering, and he was also a supreme painter, making many innovations in deep chiaroscuro, as well as a remarkable draftsman. The last and greatest of the Renaissance men was Michelangelo Buonarroti (1475-1564), sculptor and painter. The fifteenth century painters of Umbria developed landscape and spatial effects. Notable names are those of Perugino (c. 1450-1523), Piero della Francesca (c. 1416-1492), Luca Signorelli (1441-1523), the greatest of the Early Renaissance anatomists. The last great painter of Umbria was Raphael Santi or Sanzio (1483-1520), pupil of Perugino. His masterpieces are the series of frescoes in the Vatican. Andrea Mantegna (1431-1506), a passionate admirer of antiquity, is notable for his experiments in perspective and fore-shortening. The painters of Venice were concerned with recording the color and pageantry of the city. Gentile Bellini (1426-1507) exhibited the costumes and architectural atmosphere of contemporary Venice. Giovanni Bellini (1428-1516) was the first to develop color effects. He inaugurated the technique of painting in transparent oil glaze. Bellini is also noted as a distinguished landscape artist. Giorgione (1478-1510), Bellini's pupil, is noted for the sensuousness of his female figures. Titian (1477-1576) was entirely a painter of the physical beauty of man and nature. His color was probably the most beautiful of any artist of the Italian Renaissance. Titian's most famous pupil was Tintoretto (1518-1594), noted for innovations in composition and the lighting of religious scenes. The last of the Venetian Renaissance masters was Veronese (1528-1588), painter of religious themes. Correggio (1489-1534), master of Parma, continued Mantegna's experiments in perspective. Architecture of the Renaissance: Building was affected by the re-discovery of antiquity. The architects of the early fifteenth century were content with a hesitant application of classical detail to structures still essentially medieval. Only later did the architects embody the proportions and structure of antique prototypes in their buildings. The best architects of the Renaissance sought to create a style based on the ancients but suited to contemporary needs. Brunelleschi (1377-1446) was not only a designer but an engineer. His dome of the cathedral of Florence was medieval but Renaissance in the application of certain principles derived from the structure of the Pantheon. Alberti exhibited a profound knowledge of the principles and esthetics of Roman architecture, in addition to Brunelleschi's craftsman's skill. The great epic of Italian architecture in the Renaissance was the re-building of the basilica of St. Peter's in Rome, under Michelangelo's conception and execution. Donato Bramante (1444-1514) executed buildings in Rome in classical style. Palladio (1518-1580) was one of the most influential Renaissance architects, basing his classical forms on the work of Vitruvius, as did every Renaissance architect. Sculpture of the Renaissance: The history of Italian sculpture in the Renaissance in many respects parallels development in painting. The great sculptural genius of the Florentine Renaissance was Donatello (1386-1466), who in his youth had gone to Rome to study its antiquities. Luca della Robbia (1400-1482) is remarkable for his renderings of Madonna and Child. Andrea Verrocchio (1435-1488) produced the greatest equestrian statue of the Renaissance, the memorial to Colleoni, the Condottiere. Final perfection was attained by the work of Michelangelo.

ITALIAN ARTISTS

Among the outstanding Italian artists of the Renaissance were: Piero della Francesca (c. 1416-1492). Andrea Mantegna (1431-1506). Giovanni Bellini (c. 1428-1516). Gentile Bellini (c. 1426-1507). Sandro Botticelli (1444-1510). Antonio Pollaiuolo (1432-1498). Andrea Verocchio (1435-1488). Domenico Roselli (1438-1507). Luca Signorelli (1441-1523). Pietro Perugino (c. 1450-

1523). Domenico Ghirlandaio (1449-1494). Francesco Francia
(1450-1517). Lorenzo di Credi (1457-1537). Piero di Cosimo
(1462-1521). Giorgione (1477-1510). Titian (1477-1576). Andrea
del Sarto (1486-1531). Antonio Allegri da Correggio (1489-1534).
Leonardo da Vinci (1452-1519). Michelangelo (1475-1564).
Raphael (1483-1520).

ITALIAN DRAMA
The first tragedy in Italian was *Sofonisba,* by Gian Giorgio
Trissino: finished in 1515.

ITALIAN DRESS
Jacob Burckhardt, in *The Civilization of the Renaissance in Italy,*
quotes a passage in the *Forcianae Quaestiones,* by Ortensio Landi,
published in 1536. The Latin text describes the dress of the
Milanese at time of conquest of Milan by Antonio Leiva, general
of Charles V, in 1522, and the dress of other citizens: "Formerly
the Milanese used to dress very lavishly. But after the Emperor
Charles V let loose his foul and monstrous bestial forces in the
city, the citizens were so spent and exhausted that they acquired
a particular hatred for all kinds of extravagant dress: and as in
the days before Antonio Leiva's ruthlessness almost their sole
thought was directed to changes of clothing, they now think and
ponder about other matters. . . . The Neapolitans spend far too
much on dress. As for the Genoese, I consider their clothing extremely elegant. . . . I almost forgot the Venetians. They all dress
in the 'toga.' This garment suits adults. The young men, however,
—if I am any judge— rarely wear the garment commonly called
a Venetian. It is so well made that one might think it would wear
forever. . . . In the evening, when they are out wenching and
drinking, they wear Spanish cloaks. The chief concern of the
Ferrarese and Mantuans is to wear hats trimmed with gold
sequins, and as they walk they nod their head and think themselves very distinguished folk. The citizens of Lucca dress neither
extravagantly nor shabbily. In my opinion the dress of the Florentines appears ridiculous." In general, during the Renaissance,
dress became more shapely and ornamental; lavish display and
magnificence were frequent. Vespasiano da Bisticci refers to
the costly, colorful, splendid costume of several of his humanist
friends. In the use of silk, velvet, cloth of gold, brocade, lace,
etc., men outdid women.

ITALIAN HISTORIANS

Among notable historians of the Renaissance are the following: Niccolò Machiavelli (1469-1527). Jacopo Nardi (1476-1556). Francesco Guicciardini (1482-1540). Filippo Nerli (1485-1536). Donato Giannotti (1492-1572). Benedetto Varchi (1502-1565). Bernardo Segni (1504-1558). Jacopo Pitti (1519-1589).

IVAN III

(1440-1505). Vasilievich. Called Ivan the Great. Grand Duke of Muscovy. Conquered Novgorod in 1471-1478, and in 1480 threw off the Tartar yoke. Extended his domain. Married Sophia, niece of the last Byzantine emperor. Russia thus became the protector of Orthodox Christianity. Ivan twice invaded Lithuania and by treaty negotiations acquired part of the country. He added the two-headed Byzantine eagle to the Muscovite coat of arms.

IVAN IV

(1533-1584). Vasilievich. Called Ivan the Terrible. The first ruler of Russia to be called Tsar. Crushed and annexed the kingdom of Khazan in 1552. In 1556 he subjugated Astrakhan. In 1584 he conquered Siberia with an army under Yermak, Cossack chieftain. His reign was marked by war with Livonia, Poland, Sweden. Killed his own son. His reign in Russia was followed by Time of Troubles (1584-1613) after which the Romanov dynasty came to power. With the seventeenth century, secularization began, and introduction of Western influences, although Renaissance aesthetic and architectural ideas had made themselves felt, if only slightly as early as the fifteenth century.

IVRY, BATTLE OF

In this battle Henry IV of France defeated the Catholic League in 1590. It was a decisive battle in his ascent to the throne.

J

JACOBUS DE TERAMO
Author of a book on Satanic rituals: *Das Buch Beliah*: published in Augsburg in 1473.

JACOMART
(Fifteenth century). Spanish painter. His art is essentially religious and in the Flemish tradition. He was called to Naples as court painter to Alfonso the Magnanimous.

JACQUES DE BESANÇON
French illustrator and miniaturist. In late fifteenth century illuminated woodcuts for printed books.

JAGGARD, WILLIAM
(c. 1568-1623). English printer, bookseller. Printer to City of London. Published First Folio of Shakespeare's plays in 1623. The preservation of half of Shakespeare's plays is due to his edition, also the correction of many errors.

JAIME DE ENZINAS
(died 1547). Spanish heretic. Supported Erasmian views. Burned at the stake in Rome. First Protestant martyr to die in Italy.

JAMES I
(1566-1625). King of England. As James VI, King of Scots. Until 1578, dissension prevailed in Scotland among the Regents. James' policy was hostile to Catholics and Presbyterians. On the death of Queen Elizabeth I, in 1603, he assumed the English throne. James showed excessive partiality toward unworthy favorites. His reign was notorious for the sale of titles and personal scan-

dal. Sully called him the Wisest Fool in Christendom. In 1599 he published a book on demonology, and he was the author of a famous book on the divine right of kings.

JAMES II

(1430-1460). King of Scotland. During his minority, Scotland was torn by feuds of nobles. In conflict with England, as a Lancastrian in the War of Roses. Killed accidentally in Roxburgh Castle, which was in hands of English.

JAMES III

(1451-1488). King of Scotland. Son of the above. During his minority, Lord Boyd acted as governor. Later, in custody of Scottish nobles. In favor of peace with England. Nobles revolted. James was defeated and killed at the battle of Sauchieburn.

JAMES IV

(1473-1513). King of Scotland, son of the above. Though extravagant and licentious, chose reliable councillors. Assertive of independence of Scotland, in ecclesiastical sense, from Papacy. Invaded England. In Battle of Flodden, in 1513, James himself and large number of Scottish nobility killed, the defense of England having been organized by Queen Catherine while Henry VIII was in France; James was married to Henry's sister Margaret, and from that marriage derived the Stuart claim to the English crown in 1603.

JAMES V

(1512-1542). King of Scotland. During minority, Scotland split by feuds of nobles. Imprisoned. Escaped. Suppressed insurgents. Negotiated commercial treaty with Netherlands. Founded College of Justice. Supported people against barons. Hence called King of Commons. In conflict with England, his invading force was overwhelmingly defeated at Solway Moss; deserted by nobles. His only child was Mary, Queen of Scots.

JAMNITZER, WENZEL

(1508-1585). German goldsmith, born Vienna, died Nuremberg. One of the leading artists of South German school of goldsmiths. Executed table pieces, goblets, etc., for the Hapsburg emperors. He was also interested in architecture, mathematics and mechanics, as is revealed by his one book, *Perspectiva corporum regularium.*

JANNEQUIN, CLÉMENT
(died post-1560). French musician. One of the great masters of polyphonic songs. Composed: *La Guerre, Le Chant des Oiseaux, Les Cris de Paris, Le Rossignol*: published in 1537. Also *Bataille de Marignan*: 1515. His music is remarkable for its imitative or descriptive character.

JANSENISM
Calvinist movement in Catholic Church named after Cornelius Jansen, Bishop of Ypres in 1636-1638. His posthumous *Augustinus*, published in 1640, revived extreme Augustinian positions. Jansenism was associated with rigorist ethics, especially in France, where Pascal's *Lettres Provinciales* (1656-7) attacked casuistry of some Jesuit writers.

JANSSEN, ZACHARIAS
Sixteenth century. Dutch inventor. Reputedly, invented first compound microscope, c. 1590.

JANSSENS, ABRAHAM
(c. 1575-1632). Painter of Antwerp of the Flemish tradition. Noted for *Adoration of the Magi* and other religious themes; he also did historical scenes. He was influenced by Rubens, but relied more on light than on color for his special effects. Caravaggio also influenced him.

JAUREGUI Y AGUILAR, JUAN MARTÍNEZ DE
(1583-1641). Spanish poet and painter, literary enemy of Quevado and Góngora but friend of Lope de Vega and Cervantes. He wrote poetry and prose, polemical and satirical. He translated Lucan's *Pharsalia* and the *Orpheus*, and he wrote discourses on poetics and painting.

JEAN DE BILLY
(c. 1530-1580). French theologian. Translated from Greek the mystical novel of *Barlaam and Josaphat*.

JEAN DE BOURDIGNÉ
(died 1547). French cleric, doctor of law in Angers. Author of *Chronicle of Anjou*: starts with Flood. Published in 1529. Contains much legendary material: account of reign of Louis XI and Charles VIII is valuable as historical source.

JEAN DE CASTRO
(Sixteenth century). Composer of madrigals, chansons. Published in 1570. Also a Mass in three parts. Of Spanish and Portuguese descent, he passed his life in Antwerp, Vienna, and Cologne.

JEAN DE LERY
Sixteenth century. French sailor. Sailed to Brazil with a group of colonizing Huguenots in 1555. Left an account of his voyage.

JEANNE D'ALBRET
(1528-1572). Queen of Navarre, 1555-1572, Huguenot. Wrote poetry. Mother of Henry IV of France. Her mother was the celebrated patroness of poets and writers, the sister of Francis I, Margaret of Navarre.

JEHAN DE WAVRIN
Flemish historian of fifteenth century. Author of *Chronicle of England*. Illuminated copies, executed c. 1490, are preserved in the Royal Library at The Hague.

JENA UNIVERSITY OF
German university founded in 1558.

JENATSCH, GEORG
(1596-1639). Swiss political leader and pastor. Prominent during the Thirty Years' War as leader of Protestants of the Grisons. Appears in German novels and dramas.

JENKINSON, ANTHONY
(died c. 1611). English merchant, traveler, seaman. Traveled extensively at eastern end of the Mediterranean and in Russia; he made his way to Persia and to central Asia—one of the earliest Englishmen to do so. Wrote an account of the entrance of Suleiman the Magnificent into Aleppo in 1553. With Muscovy Company. In personal touch with the Tsar. Wrote descriptions of Russian life.

JENSON, NICOLAS
(died c. 1480). French pioneer printer, engraver. Associated with Gutenberg at Mainz, where he had been sent by King Charles VII, c. 1458, to learn the new art. Established press in Venice. Made improvements in typography, especially Roman type.

330

JESUIT COLLEGES
Jesuit colleges were opened in 1556 at Ingolstadt, in Prague, and in Belgium. In Rome, a Jesuit college was founded in 1550.

JESUS COLLEGE, CAMBRIDGE
Founded in 1496 by John Alcock, Bishop of Ely (1430-1500).

JESUS COLLEGE, OXFORD
Founded in 1571 by Queen Elizabeth I.

JEWEL, JOHN
(1522-1571). English cleric and writer, Bishop of Salisbury. Author of *Apologia Ecclesiae Anglicanae*, published in 1562, the earliest defense and definition of the Elizabethan Settlement and the Anglican Church. He opposed the Puritans strongly and he thought it proper for the Anglican Church to be represented at the Council of Trent. Before his involvement in ecclesiastical matters, he had been associated with Oxford, where he taught classical literature.

JEWELRY
In the fifteenth century in Italy jewelry was used as an ornament at times indistinguishable from the surface decoration of costume. Myriads of tiny pearls, for instance, were fastened to sleeves or bodices. In the *Cinquecento*, jewelry was rich and elaborate. Well known artists designed jewelry, for the canons of art applied to jewelry as to the other fine arts. Benvenuto Cellini, for instance, was more celebrated for his creations in this craft than for his sculpture. Leonardo and Dürer also designed articles for personal adornment. Elaborate chains and collars composed of massive links were worn by gentlemen of the High Renaissance: as in Titian's portrait of Pietro Aretino. Women also wore chains about the neck, usually with jewelled settings and an expansive display of pearls. Pendants and pendant brooches were popular. Titian's Isabel, Empress of Portugal, wears a large brooch that divides a heavy rope of matched pearls into two deep loops. Antique cameos also were highly esteemed.

JEWS IN ENGLAND
On the testimony of *The Wandering Jew Telling Fortunes to Englishmen*, published in 1640, there were Jews in the cities, in country districts, and even at court.

Jews are mentioned by John Lyly, author of *Euphues*, 1578.

Other references appear as follows:
The Travels of Three Brothers, by John Day in collaboration with William Rowley.
Anatomy of Melancholy, by Robert Burton, 1621.

JEWS IN ITALY

Jewish participation in Renaissance activities was associated with the scholar Azariah dei Rossi of Mantua and Abraham Colorni. Mordecai ben Abraham Finzi was a noted mathematician. Jacob de Lattes and David Pomis were physicians. Hillel of Verona and Jacob Mantino translated from Arabic into Latin. In general, it may be said that Jews played an important part in the Renaissance, particularly in Italy and—until their expulsion —in Spain and Portugal.

JOANA DA GAMA

(died 1586). Founded Franciscan convent in Évora. Portugal. Wrote *Sayings of a Nun:* published in 1555.

JOÃO DE BARROS

(1496-1570). Portuguese writer. The outstanding historian of the Portuguese Renaissance. Wrote one work of fiction: the romance of chivalry entitled *Chronicle of Emperor Clarimundo from whom Descend the Kings of Portugal.* Published in 1520: marked by exalted patriotism.

Appointed official chronicler of India.

Based his historical work on Livy. Planned a history of Portugal in Africa since the conquest of Ceuta in 1415. Planned a history of Portuguese Asia since Henry the Navigator and a history of Portuguese Brazil since Cabral. Four decades of the *Asia* were published: in 1552, 1533, 1563, 1615. He wrote numerous other works: moral dialogues, princely panegyric, grammatical and philological studies, geographical description, etc.

JOÃO DE BARROS

(Died 1547). Portuguese moralist and ecclesiastic and doctor of civil law. He is remembered for several moralizing books on marriage, notably the intriguingly illustrated and entitled *Espelho de Casados,* which went through many editions.

JOÃO DE LUCENA

(1550-1600). Portuguese chronicler and Jesuit. Author of *History of the Life of Father Francis Xavier:* published in 1600; it is still an important source for the history of the Jesuit missionary effort in India.

JOÃO DE SANTAREM
Fifteenth century. Portuguese explorer. Reached the Gold Coast in 1471.

JODELLE, ÉTIENNE
(1532-1573). French playwright. Member of *La Pléiade*. Author of the tragedy *Cléopâtre Captive*, 1552, and of the comedy, *La Rencontre*, of the same year. He was a facile versifier, very popular, and the recipient of numerous royal favors. He inaugurated the trends in drama that culminated in the seventeenth century, with Molière, Racine and Corneille.

JOHANNES ANGLICUS
Logician. Wrote commentary on Duns Scotus: *Expositiones fratris Ioannis Anglici super Quaestionibus Universalium Scoti:* published in Venice in 1492.

JOHANNES DE COLONIA
Sixteenth century. Logician. Wrote commentary on Johannes Scotus: *Quaestiones Magistrales in libros Sententiarum, Quodlibetorum, Metaphysices, et De Anima Iohannis Scoti.* Published in Basel in 1510.

JOHANNES DE STOBNICZA
Author of a treatise on geography: *Introductio in Phtholomei Cosmographiam:* illustrated with maps. Published in 1512 at Cracow, it was largely an imitation of Waldseemüller's work.

JOHANNES MAGNUS
(1488-1544). Swedish historian and archbishop of Upsala. Author of *Historia Metropolitanae Ecclesiae Upsalensis: Historia de Omnibus Gothorum Sveonumque Regibus.*

JOHANN VON GLOGAU
(c. 1430-1507). German philosopher, mathematician, and logician. Wrote *Exercitium Novae Logicae:* published in Cracow in 1511, a commentary on Aristotle, and several scientific works.

JOHANN VON GOCH
(c. 1440-1475). Dutch Cistercian monk. Postulated Bible as ultimate religious verity. Virtually, he was a forerunner of Martin

Luther. There are two men of the same name, approximately contemporaries, both Cistercian monks.

JOHN II

(1455-1495). King of Portugal, 1481-1495. Called the Perfect Prince. Imposed the royal will upon the nobles and established an efficient central government when Portugal was at the height of its power as the head of a great empire. He promoted exploration. Patron of Renaissance culture.

JOHN III

(1502-1557). King of Portugal, 1521-1557, introduced the Inquisition into Portugal. Literature flourished during his reign.

JOHN IV

(died 1656). Founded the Braganza dynasty, when he succeeded to the Portuguese throne in 1640; this marked the end of Spanish rule which dated from 1580.

JOHN AB INDAGINE

Sixteenth century. German priest. Author of *Introductiones Apotelesmaticae:* dealing with astrology, chiromancy, physiognomy.

JOHN DE BUEIL

(died c. 1478). French soldier. Served under Charles VII of France. Author of *Chronicle Jouvenal.*

JOHN OF AUSTRIA, DON

(c. 1545-1578). Spanish soldier. Illegitimate son of Emperor Charles V. Led army against Barbary pirates. Crushed Moslems in Spain. Commanded fleet of Holy League. Governor general of Netherlands, in the time of his half-brother, Philip II; his sympathy with the Dutch and his possible ambition to become the ruler of an independent state in the Lowlands led to his deposition and to the suspicion that he was poisoned by Philip. Died in camp at Namur.

JOHN OF LEYDEN

(1509-1536). John Beuckelszoon. Dutch Anabaptist. Leader of Anabaptists in Münster, where he set up kingdom of Zion, based on community of property and polygamy. Imprisoned, killed. His excesses did much to discredit Anabaptism in the eyes of contemporaries; historians, also, tend to concentrate on John's career and dismiss Anabaptism as the lunatic fringe of the Reformation.

JOHN OF SACROBOSCO or HOLLYWOOD
Thirteenth century. English astronomer, mathematician. Commented on Ptolemy's *Almagest*. Author of *De Sphaera Mundi*: most famous elementary astronomical textbook. Popular until well into the sixteenth century.

JOHN OF WESEL or JOHANN RUCHERATH
(died c. 1481). German theologian and reformer. Critic of indulgences. Confined by the Inquisition to a monastery, for life. Author of *Disputatio Adversus Indulgentias*.

JOHN VAN BATENBURG
(died 1538). Dutch preacher. Claimed to be the prophet Elias. Advocated polygamy. Executed.

JOHNSTON, ARTHUR
(1587-1541). Scottish humanist, physician, Latin poet. Patronized by James I, physician to Charles I. Translated Psalms into Latin, in 1637. Edited *Delitiae Poetarum Scotorum Hagus Alvi*, 1637, a collection of Scottish poetry.

JONES, INIGO
(1573-1652). English architect. Called "The English Palladio." Royalist during the Civil War. Built the Banqueting Hall at Whitehall, London. He had studied much on the continent and especially in Italy.

JONGELINGX, JACOB
(1531-1606). Belgian sculptor. Did tombs but more notably bronze statues, e.g., of Saturn, Venus, Diana, and also one of the Duke of Alva. He enjoyed the patronage of Philip II of Spain.

JONSON, BEN
(1573-1637). English dramatist, poet. Served in the army in Flanders. Virtually considered as the first English poet laureate. His plays include: *The Alchemist, Every Man in his Humour, Bartholomew Fair, Volpone, Sejanus.* He also produced epigrams, songs, epistles. His most famous poem is *Drink to Me only with Thine Eyes.* Wrote epigrams, epistles, songs, masques. He was richly flattered and rewarded by both James I and Charles I.

JÓNSSON, ARNGRÍMUR

(1568-1648). Prolific Icelandic historian and antiquarian. Wrote on Icelandic history and culture, in Latin; also on ancient Danish literature.

JÓNSSON, BJÖRN

(1574-1655). Icelandic farmer. Author of annals of Icelandic history.

JORISZOON, DAVID

(c. 1501-1556). Dutch leader of Anabaptists. Favored polygamy. Founder of religious sect of Davidists or Jorists, in 1536. Settled in Basel.

JOSÉ DE VALDIVIESO

(1560-1638). Spanish writer. Author of *autos*, epics. Official censor of Cervantes. Wrote poems of childlike simplicity: published in 1612. A facile author, he enjoyed a place at the court and the friendship of the great authors of the day in Spain.

JOSEPH HA-COHEN

Sixteenth century. Jewish-Italian historian. Author of *Valley of Tears*: account of persecutions of Jews from the tenth to the sixteenth century.

JOSEPH OF MONTAGNANA

Jewish writer, traveler. Author of a description of the Holy Land: published in 1481.

JOSQUIN DES PRÉS

(c. 1450-1521). Flemish composer of church and secular music. Greatest of his time. Produced masses, hymns, motets, psalms that are masterpieces of counterpoint. He entered the service of Louis XII of France; he spent much of his life in Italy where he enjoyed Sforza, Medici, and papal patronage.

JUAN DE ARGUIJO

(1567?-1623). Spanish poet. Author of sonnets: *Ariadna, Andromeda*.

JUAN DE LUCENA

(Died c. 1506). Spanish author of *Libro de Vida Beata*: published in 1643. He resided much of his life in Rome and was an intimate of the humanist Pope Pius II.

JUANA

(1479-1555). Called The Mad. Daughter of Ferdinand and Isabella of Spain. Married Philip the Handsome, founder of the Hapsburg dynasty in Spain. Juana was the mother of the Emperors Charles V and Ferdinand I. She was a delicate and sensitive person of exquisite taste and refinement; probably Philip's casual infidelities and his brutishness did much to bring on her insanity.

JULIUS

Small silver coin struck by Pope Julius II (pontificate: 1503-1513).

JULIUS II

(1443-1513). Pope. Called Il Terribile. Under his pontificate the Renaissance reached its height at Rome. He promoted the arts: patron of Raphael, Michelangelo, Bramante. Reconquered from Venice various domains in the northwest of the Papal States. Attempted to drive the French from Italy. Personally commanded troops against France. In 1508 formed League of Cambrai against Venice. In 1511 the Holy League against France was formed, the members being the Pope, Ferdinand of Spain, Venice, Henry VIII. Julius was called the savior of the papacy by the historian Jacob Burckhardt. A statue of the pope was executed by Michelangelo in 1508. In 1506 the pope laid the foundation stone of the new St. Peter's. Julius founded Swiss Guard in 1506. He patronized the papal song school, still known as the Capella Julia. Founded the first Arabic printing press in Fano.

JULIUS III

(1487-1555). Pope, 1550-1555, elected as a compromise in preference to the English Cardinal, Reginald Pole. Worldly. Devoted to carnivals, parties, hunts, bullfights. There is no significant monument to his memory, except that he succeeded in persuading Charles V to allow the Council of Trent—in abeyance since 1547—to resume in 1551.

JULIUS EXCLUSUS: JULIUS EXCLUDED FROM HEAVEN

A satire, in dialogue form, by Erasmus. Published in 1513. The subject is a debate between Pope Julius II and St. Peter. Erasmus was stimulated to write it upon witnessing the Pope's triumphal entry into Bologna in armor at the head of his victorious troops in 1508.

337

JUNG, JOACHIM or JUNGIUS

(1587-1657). German scientist, philosopher and mathematician. He is credited with having anticipated Linnaeus in his system of botanical classification by genus and specie, and also Leibnitz in his conception of the importance of mathematics for philosophical thought.

JUNIUS, HADRIANUS or ADRIAN DE JONGHE

(1511-1575). Dutch physician, humanist, poet, historian. Physician to the King of Denmark, Duke of Norfolk and many others. Wrote on philosophy, history, medicine. Corresponded with prominent contemporaries. His letters illuminate the intellectual and political atmosphere of his age. He refers in one of his works to a Laurens Castor as the inventor of printing.

JUNIUS, MELCHIOR

(Died 1604). Professor of rhetoric at Strassburg, rector of the University. Wrote treatise on art of oratory, *Methodus Eloquentia Comparandae:* published in 1585.

JUSTUS VAN GHENT

(1446-1485). Flemish religious and portrait painter. Known for his portrait of Albert Magnus. In 1469 he went to Italy and enjoyed the patronage of Federigo da Montefeltro, the Duke of Urbino.

K

KÁLDI, GEORGE

(1573-1634). Hungarian writer and Jesuit; associated with Peter Pazmany. Translated Bible into Hungarian for Catholics. Published in 1626.

KALONYMOS BEN DAVID

(Fourteenth century). French-Jewish translator of Italian descent. Translated Averroës from Latin into Hebrew. There was a Venetian physician by the same name, also a translator, with whom he is often confused.

KAPPEL, BATTLE OF, 1531

Battle between followers of Zwingli and the Catholic cantons of the interior of Switzerland; Zwingli was killed and the spread of his doctrines arrested in Switzerland.

KELLEY, EDWARD

(1555-1595). English alchemist, occultist, necromancer and imaginative charlatan; called "philosophus dubius," he was associated with John Dee, with whom he spent several years on the Continent at the court of Emperor Rudolph II. Dee eventually tired of Kelley's nonsense and some years later recorded in his diary that Kelley was killed trying to escape from Rudolph's prison.

KENNEDY, JAMES

(1406-1465). Wealthy Scottish ecclesiastic and statesman. Nephew of James I of Scotland. Bishop of Dunkeld. Opposed to the House of Douglas. As regent, ruled Scotland during minority of James III (from 1460 to 1465). Founded St. Salvator's College at St.

Andrew's. None of many writings survive; he is said to have written a *Historia sui Temporis.*

KENNEDY, WALTER
(c. 1460-c. 1508). Scottish poet and rival of the poet William Dunbar. Noted for the poem *The Flyting*, written by Dunbar and Kennedy.

KEPLER, JOHANNES
(1571-1630). German astronomer. A Protestant, he was born at Weill in Württemberg. Educated at Tübingen. He was persecuted by the Protestant faculty of Tübingen for his cosmological ideas, but found refuge with the Jesuits in 1596. In 1600 he was assistant to Tycho Brahe in Prague. He succeeded Brahe as imperial mathematician and court astronomer to Emperor Rudolph II in 1601. Kepler's Laws relate to three important discoveries of planetary motion. Kepler also wrote on optics, and was a pioneer in the field of calculus. His conception of the uniformly geometrical nature of space was basic to the later development of science.

KERLE, JACOBUS DE
(c. 1531-1591). Flemish musician. Composed motets, masses, hymns, psalms. He studied and worked in Italy and Spain, and died in the service of the Emperor Rudolph II at the court of Prague.

KET'S REBELLION
Occurred in 1549, in Norfolk, England. Rebellion led by Robert Ket against manorial lords who enclosed common lands for sheep raising. Proposed abolition of private ownership of land. Routed royal army. The rising was suppressed by Earl of Warwick. Ket was hanged in 1549. In 1582 there was published an account of the rebellion entitled *De Furoribus Norfolciensium Ketto duce liber unus.* Published by Alexander Neville.

KEYSER, HENDRIK DE
(1565-1621). Dutch sculptor, architect. Worked in Amsterdam. Designed civic buildings in Dutch Renaissance style. Also executed a statue of Erasmus.

KEYSER, THOMAS DE
(1597-1667). Dutch painter. Died in Amsterdam. Important painter of single and group portraits.

KHESL, MELCHIOR

(1553-1639). German Cardinal. Chancellor at court of Emperor Matthias (1557-1619). Subject of novel entitled *Der Dom.*

KHVOROSTININ, PRINCE IVAN ANDREYEVICH

(Died 1625). Russian author of *Prologue*, in rhymed couplets, polemical treatise against heresy. In 1622 Khvorostinin was exiled to Kirillo-Belozerski Monastery for Roman Catholic sympathy. Retracted: pardoned.

KIENING, CHRISTOPHER

Sixteenth century. German astronomer. Made a sundial in 1582.

KILIAN, LUKAS

(1579-1637). German copper engraver, noted for his engravings of the sixteenth-century Venetian masters. His work is in the Dutch tradition of engraving.

KING EDWARD'S SCHOOL

In Birmingham. English public school. Founded in 1552.

KING'S COLLEGE

In Taunton. English public school. Founded in 1293. Rebuilt in 1522.

KING'S SCHOOL

In Rochester. English public school. Reconstituted and endowed by Henry VIII in 1542.

KING'S SCHOOL

In Worcester. English public school. Established and endowed by Henry VIII in 1541.

KING'S SCHOOL

In Macclesfield. English public school. Founded by will of Sir John Percyvale in 1502. Re-established by Charter of Edward VI in 1552.

KING'S SCHOOL

In Ely. English public school. Founded in eleventh century. Reconstructed by Henry VIII in 1541.

KING'S SCHOOL

In Chester. English public school. Founded by Henry VIII in 1541.

KING'S SCHOOL
In Bruton. English public school. Founded by Richard Fitzjames, Bishop of London, in 1519. Refounded by King Edward VI in 1550.

KIRCHMAIR, GEORG
(c. 1481-1554). Austrian chronicler. Wrote an account of the Peasants' War and other historical works on the German past.

KIRKALDY, SIR WILLIAM, OF GRANGE
(c. 1520-1573). Scottish soldier, politician, and minor poet. He played an important role in the Scottish religious wars, frequently changing sides. Opposed marriage of Mary Queen of Scots to Lord Darnley. Executed. Author of *Ballad of the Captain of the Castle*, published in 1571.

KIRKE, SIR DAVID
(1596-1654). English merchant adventurer and colonial enterpriser. Attacked French in Canada. Captured Quebec. Governor of Newfoundland.

KLEBITZ, WILHELM or KLEBITIUS
(Sixteenth Cen.). Dutch polemical writer and for a while rector of the University of Münster. He began as a Lutheran but veered toward Calvinism. Engaged in violent controversy with Lutheran Hesshus in Heidelberg, in 1559. He was the author of a Dutch Confession of Faith.

KLEINMEISTER or THE GERMAN LITTLE MASTERS
German engravers and other craftsmen and artists who worked under Albrecht Dürer's influence and, through him, show the influence of Renaissance Italian art; among them were Albrecht Altdorfer, Heinrich Altgreuer, the Beham brothers and Georg Pencz.

KLING, MELCHIOR
(1504-1571). German jurist. Wrote commentary on *Institutes of Justinian, De Quattuor Institutionum Iuris Principis Iustiani Libris Ennarationes,* published in 1557. He was also a student of German feudal law.

KNIGHTS OF ST. JOHN
The Knights of the Hospital of St. John of Jerusalem, the last of the crusading orders, were installed by Emperor Charles V in

Malta in 1530, following the fall of Rhodes after a long and heroic defense to the Turks, hence they are frequently referred to as the Knights of Malta; their device was the Maltese Cross.

KNIGHTS' WAR

German knights Ulrich von Hutten and Franz von Sickingen supported the Reformation, seeing in it the means to establish a national church and German independence. They attacked the archbishopric of Trier with the intention of ending the independence of the princes and uniting Germany. Sickingen was killed in battle in 1522. Hutten fled to Switzerland, where he died in 1523. It marked the end of serious efforts in the sixteenth century to create a German national state.

KNIPHOF, CLAUS

(c. 1500-1525). Pirate. Stepson of King Christian II of Denmark. Subject of legends and poems.

KNOLLES, RICHARD

(1550-1610). English schoolmaster. Author of a *History of the Turks*, published in 1603, which was a standard work until well into the eighteenth century; it followed the classical canons for the writing of history and was extended, by various hands, to cover the seventeenth century.

KNOX, JOHN

(c. 1505-1572). Scottish reformer and theologian. Leading churchman of the Reformation in Scotland. Early came under the influence of Calvinistic doctrines. Taken prisoner to France and condemned to the galleys until 1549. On the accession of Mary Tudor, he fled to the continent. Pastor in Geneva. Returned to Scotland in 1559, he led the religious and baronial opposition to the regent, Mary of Guise, and her daughter, Mary, Queen of Scots; it was against them—and Mary Tudor—that he wrote his *Blast of the Trumpet Against the Monstrous Regiment of Women.* Instrumental in making the Presbyterian Church the established church of Scotland. Author of *History of the Reformation of Religion within the Realm of Scotland,* a great work despite its violent bias; the work reflects his own character, narrow but deep.

KOBERGER, ANTON

(c. 1445-1513). German pioneer printer and publisher, established in Nuremberg c. 1470, but with branches in other cities. He published a German Bible and the first printed book in Hungarian.

KOCHANOWSKI, JAN

(1530-1584). Polish poet. Educated in Italy at Padua. Product of the Italian Renaissance. Author of elegies in Latin, imitative of Tibullus and Propertius. Raised Polish poetry to high level. Produced metrical version of Psalms, original tragedy on Greek model—*The Dismissal of the Greek Envoys,* published in 1577. *Songs on St. John's Eve. Laments.* He is the outstanding representative of the Renaissance in Poland. His nephew, PIOTR (1566-1620), was also a poet, who wrote epics and chivalrous romances and who translated *Orlando Furioso* and *Gerusalemme Liberata* into Polish.

KOHLHASE, HANS

(Died 1540). German merchant of Berlin. Subject of plays, German novel, owing to an epic quarrel with Karsochsen.

KORAN

First Italian translation appeared in 1547.

KRAFT, ADAM

(c. 1455-c. 1509). German sculptor. Executed sepulchral statuary, e.g., *The Entombment,* in the cemetery of Nuremberg where, along the entrance way, he executed the *Seven Stations of the Cross.* Leading sculptor of the early Renaissance in Nuremberg. Continued to use some Gothic forms.

KRALITZ BIBLE

Printed in 1579-1593 on the press in Kralitz Castle of Baron von Zerotin, Bohemia. He was prominent member of Unitas Fratrum, or Moravian Church. The Bible was translated from Hebrew and Greek. It did for the Czechs what Luther's version did for the Germans.

KRANTZ, ALBRECHT

(c. 1458-1517). German historian and theologian, advocate of the reform of the Church. Rector of University of Rostock. Ambassador to France, England. Author of a *History of Saxony,* of Scandinavia, and of the Vandals.

KRATZER, NICOLAUS

(1487-1550). German humanist, astronomer and mathematician. Clockmaker. Deviser of the *King's Horologes*. Attached to the court of Henry VIII and lectured at Oxford on astronomy; he was the friend of Erasmus and of Holbein, who painted his portrait.

KRELL, NIKOLAUS or CRELL

(1550-1601). German court official, Chancellor to the Duke of Saxony. He sought to supplant Lutheranism (in the place of its birth) by Calvinism. When his protector, Duke Christian I, died, he was executed.

KULMBACH, HANS VON

(c. 1476-1522). German painter. Influenced deeply by Albrecht Dürer, of whom he may have been a student. Among his works are hagiographical scenes and *Adoration of the Magi*. He also painted many portraits. He worked chiefly in Poland, as court painter at Cracow, and at Nuremberg.

KURBSKI, PRINCE ANDREI

(1528-1583). Russian statesman. Belonged to progressive party in Russia during the reign of Ivan the Terrible. In 1564 Kurbski went over to Ivan's enemies, the Lithuanians, whose country was then part of Poland; entered service of King Sigismund. In Lithuania he became acquainted with Western culture. Wrote four letters to Ivan, revealing classical knowledge and logical argument, and accusing Ivan of cruelty and injustice to nobility. Kurbski also wrote polemics defending Orthodox faith against Catholic Poles. Author of a history of the Grandduchy of Muscovy.

KYD, THOMAS

(c. 1558-1594). English playwright. Author of *The Spanish Tragedy*, also *Cornelia*—translation from French *Cornélie* of Garnier. He was the practitioner of the "tragedy of blood" and may have been the source for some elements of Shakespeare's plays, e.g., the play-within-the-play and the ghosts of *Hamlet*.

L

LA BALUE, JEAN
(1421-1491). French cardinal, statesman. Secretary of State under Louis XI. Imprisoned by king from 1469 to 1480. Papal legate in the last years of his life. He wrote some poetry and made translations of philosophical and legal works.

LABÉ, LOUISE
(c. 1520-1566). Called La Belle Cordière. French poet. Wrote *Sonnets*, 1555, amatory poems, elegies.

LA BOÉTIE, ETIENNE DE
(1530-1568). French jurist. Friend of Montaigne. Wrote a diatribe against absolute monarchy. Also poems, translations.

LACE
About the year 1530 the Venetians began to employ the needle to create lace. The first real lace was the fine needlepoint lace known in Italy as *punto in aria*. A pattern book of laces, printed in Venice in 1560, tends to establish Italy's claim to have been the first European country to develop the making of true lace, although Flanders was a close second. Lace-making on pillows was first introduced into Germany in 1561 by Barbara Uttmann (1514-1575).

LACTANTIUS
The first book printed in Italy was the text of Lactantius, in 1465.

LADIES' PEACE
A variant name of Treaty of Cambrai of 1529. In French, *Paix*

des Dames. So called because it was arranged by Margaret of Austria, aunt of Emperor Charles V, and Louise de Savoy, mother of Francis I of France.

LAETUS, POMPONIUS or LETO

(1425-1498). Humanist teacher and antiquarian, an illegitimate scion of the Sanseverino family of Naples. For many years he was professor at the University of Rome where he lived a simple, frugal life on his farm on the Quirinal, where farming was conducted according to the agricultural treatises of Cato and Varro. His satires against the clergy and his supposed indifference in matters of religion brought him into difficulties with the anti-humanist pope, Paul II. Later popes supported Laetus and he became a celebrated teacher. He initiated the annual celebration of Rome's foundation by a literary festival at which he and his friends and students recited classical works and their own compositions: out of these ceremonies there developed the Roman Academy, of which Laetus was the chief figure until his death. He was also the director of productions of ancient plays, mostly of Plautus, at Rome. He edited and commented upon several Latin authors, e.g., Varro, Virgil, Pliny and Sallust. He made the Academy a center for the study of Plato.

LA FAYE, ANTOINE DE

(Died 1615). Huguenot cleric. Associated with Théodore Bèze at Geneva. Wrote lives of Calvin and Bèze, translated the histories of Josephus and Livy.

L'AFFAIRE DES PLACARDS

Posters, opposing Catholic ritual were placed on the doors of King Francis I, at Amboise, and in other French cities. The king was consequently forced to expel heretics, of whom many were burned at the stake, 1534. It marks the beginning of the disturbances that culminated in the civil and religious wars in France in the latter half of the century.

L'AFFAIRE PÉRONNE

At the town of Péronne, on the Somme, Louis XI of France, at a conference with Charles the Rash, the ambitious Duke of Burgundy, was forced by threats to negotiate a treaty in 1468; it was a celebrated encounter between the two antagonists and is depicted in Scot's *Quentin Durward.*

LAGUNA, ANDRES
(1499-1563). Spanish physician and humanist. Studied at Salamanca. Wrote commentaries on Galen, Aristotle, and Dioscorides as well as a great number of treatises on anatomy and on *materia medica*.

LAINEZ, JAMES or LAYNEZ
(1512-1565). Spanish theologian. Influential as papal theologian at Council of Trent, also at Colloquium of Poissy, where he debated with Huguenots. Successor to St. Ignatius Loyola as General of the Society of Jesus. He had been one of the group of friends around St. Ignatius Loyola that formed the original Society of Jesus, c. 1534.

LA MARCHE, OLIVIER DE
(c. 1426-1502). French writer, poet, chronicler, at the court of Charles the Rash, Duke of Burgundy. Author of allegorical poems and romances of chivalry that are typical of the decadent chivalry of the Burgundian court.

LAMBERTUS DE MONTE
(Died 1499). Logician. Wrote a commentary on Aristotle.

LAMBETH ARTICLES
Adopted in 1595. In nine points, the Articles stated predestination system then predominant in Church of England, never had the force of law.

LAMBINUS, DIONYSIUS or DENYS LAMBIN
(1520-1572). French scholar. Professor of Greek. He spent about ten years in Italy studying and collating manuscripts. Editor of Latin texts, among them Lucretius, Cornelius Nepos, the whole of Cicero, Horace; he also translated Aristotle's *Ethics* and *Politics* into Latin.

LANCASTER ROYAL GRAMMAR SCHOOL
English public school. First recorded mention: 1469.

LANDFRIEDENSKREISE
Ten judicial regions into which the Holy Roman Empire was organized by Maximilian I in 1512. The purpose was the maintenance of peace throughout these areas and was part of Maximilian's attempt to revise the imperial constitution. It was largely

through his policies that Roman law came to be established as the code of the Empire (except in regard to fiefs and land).

LANDINO, CRISTOFORO
(1424-1504). Italian humanist and philosopher. Wrote Neo-Platonic dialogues and commentaries on Vergil, Dante. His *Disputationes Camaldulenses* consisted of philosophical dialogues in which his former student, Lorenzo the Magnificent, and Alberti debated the virtues of the active and the contemplative life; it imitates Cicero's *Tusculan Disputationes*. Professor of poetry at Florence and a member of the Florentine Academy, whose famous proceedings he recorded.

LANDINO, FRANCESCO
(c. 1325-1397). The blind Florentine composer and organist of the *ars nova* age. He is remembered for his secular songs; the cadential formula, *Landino sixth*, takes its name from him.

LANDO, ORTENSIO
(1512-1560). Italian humanist. Produced scholarly and satirical works, in Italian and Latin. Anti-Ciceronian, he wrote *Paradossi* and *Sferza di Scrittori antichi moderna*, and translated More's *Utopia* into Italian.

LANE, SIR RALPH
(c. 1530-1603). The leader of the first English attempt to colonize North America: Roanoke Island in 1585-86. His account of the venture was incorporated in Hakluyt's *Principal Navigations*.

LANFRANCO, GIOVANNI
(1580-1647). Painter of Parma. Died in Rome. Produced frescoes, altar pictures in the Baroque style; he was a member of the school of Annibale Carracci.

LANG, JOHANNES
(1485-1565). German physician, friend of Melanchthon. In his *Epistulae Medicinales* he advocated Greek semeiology and was a pioneer in brain surgery. He was physician to four Electors of the Palatinate during forty years. Accompanied them on two occasions with their armies against the Turks.

LANG, MATHHAEUS
(1468-1540). German ecclesiastic. Archbishop of Salzburg. Opposed to Lutherans. Subject of a novel by R. Champigny.

LANGEN, RUDOLF VON
(1438-1519). German humanist. He traveled extensively in Italy in 1465 and 1486. He reorganized the Cathedral School of Münster in 1500 along humanistic lines.

LANGUET, HUBERT
(1518-1581). French publicist and violent polemicist. Author of *Vindiciae contra tyrannos*, 1579, the most thorough-going attack on royal absolutism. He was a fervent apologist of the Dutch Revolt and wrote an *Apology* for William of Orange.

LANG VON LANGENFELS, PHILIPP
(1543-1610). German converted Jew. Chamberlain and favorite to Emperor Rudolf II. Subject of German novel.

LANTERIUS, JACOBUS or LANTERI
Sixteenth century. Brescian engineer. Wrote on military fortifications.

LAOCOÖN
The statue of Laocoön, a Hellenistic sculpture of the priest of Apollo and his two sons struggling against serpents, was excavated in 1506 near the Baths of Trajan in Rome. This statue was one of the first pieces of sculpture used to establish the Vatican Museum of antiquities, begun by Pope Julius II.

LA PERRIÈRE, GUILLAUME
(1499-1565). Poet, historian of Toulouse of which he was a municipal official. Wrote chronicles of Duchy of Foix. Published in 1539; a planned chronicle of Toulouse never appeared.

LA PRIMAUDAYE, PETER DE
(1549-1619). French writer and moralist, mild apologist for his religious views. Councillor of Henry III and Henry IV of France. Author of *L'Académie françoise*, in dialogue form; it deals with education, moral concepts, war, politics; La Primaudaye was a member of the French Reformed Church. His work was highly popular in England.

LARIVEY, PIERRE
(1560-1611). French comic dramatist. Canon of St.-Étienne de

Troyes. Of Florentine parentage. He had very little originality, deriving much from Italian comedies by Aretino, Piccolomini, and Firenzuola.

LA ROCHELLE, SIEGE OF, OF 1628
One of the great strongholds of the Huguenots, proximate to the Bay of Biscay. England aided the Huguenots, under the Duke of Soubise, in resistance for fourteen months against the French, instigated by Cardinal Richelieu, who came to be known mockingly as Bishop of La Rochelle. La Rochelle was taken in 1628.

LASCARIS, CONSTANTINE
(1434-1501). Member of Byzantine imperial family of Lascaris. Greek scholar of Constantinople. On fall of city in 1453, captured by Turks, escaped and fled to Italy, where he promoted Greek studies. Tutor to daughter of Francesco Sforza, Duke of Milan. Moved to Rome. Attached to Cardinal Bessarion. Moved to Messina, where he taught Greek to, among others, the future Cardinal Bembo, until his death. Collector of manuscripts. Author of *Erotemata*, first Greek book printed in Italy, in 1476, a grammar.

LASCARIS, JANUS or ANDREAS JOANNES
(1445-1535). Greek scholar. After the fall of Constantinople, in 1453, he settled in Italy. In Florence, he was sponsored by Lorenzo de' Medici. Lectured on Thucydides, Demosthenes, Sophocles. To Paris, attached to court of Charles VIII and Louis XII. Returned to Rome. Discovered some 200 classical manuscripts. Supervised printing press and the Greek College established at Rome by Pope Leo X. In France, under Francis 1, helped to found Royal Library at Fontainebleau. Edited several of the Greek *editiones principes*, published at Florence.

LAS CASAS, BARTOLOMÉ DE
(1474-1566). Spanish prelate, historian, Dominican missionary, friend of Charles V. Called Apostle of the Indies, Father of the Indians. First priest to be ordained in New World, in Hispaniola. Preached among Indians, attempted amelioration of their condition; he espoused, and then repented, the importation of Negro slaves to relieve the Indian. Author of *Historia General de las Indias*, a mine of anthropological and historical information.

LASCO, JOHANNES

(1499-1560). Polish noble, humanist, Erasmian reformer. Embraced Reformation movement. Invited by Archbishop Cranmer to London. Formed community of Protestant refugees. Returned to Poland in 1556.

LASSO, ORLANDO DI

(c. 1531-1594). Flemish composer. His career is the culmination of the Netherlander school of counterpoint. Attached to Duke Albert V in Munich. With Palestrina he was the chief composer of the sixteenth century. Produced some 2000 pieces, masses, motets, madrigals, chansons, sacred and secular German songs. He sojourned for many years in Italy—Sicily, Naples, Rome and Milan—and probably knew Palestrina, whom he surpassed in the technical mastery of musical forms.

LASTRICATI, ZANOBI

(1508-1590). Italian worker in bronze. Made casts for Gian Bologna.

LA TAILLE, JEAN DE

(c. 1540-1608). French dramatic poet. Among his works are, *Saül,* a tragedy, and *Les Carrivaux,* a comedy; he translated Ariosto's Negromante into French.

LATERAN COUNCIL, FIFTH

Lasted from 1512 to 1517. Held at Lateran Palace of the Popes in Rome. Under Pope Julius II—whose Pontificate ran from 1503 to 1513—council was convoked to re-establish peace among Christian princes, promote war against Turks, reform Church 'in its head and members.' It was terminated under Leo X, but indecisively except to conclude the Concordat of 1516 with Francis I of France by which royal rights over the Gallican Church were confirmed.

LATIMER, HUGH

(c. 1485-1555). English Protestant martyr. Chaplain to Queen Anne Boleyn. Out of favor, he retired from the royal court to teach, preach, and write. Sent to Tower twice during Henry VIII's reign. Under Mary, in jail for one year. Found guilty of heresy, he was burned at the stake. His *Sermon on the Plough* is a vivid description of English rural society of the mid-sixteenth century.

LATIN FATHERS, THE
It should be remembered that the Renaissance was fundamentally a Christian and religious movement. The writings of the Latin Fathers were revered as Christian classics and, as with classical authors, an energetic attempt was made to peel off the medieval accretions and get back to the pure texts. Saints Augustine and Jerome were especially revered; the renewed interest in Augustine, especially, is important for the Reformation movement.

LATOMUS, BARTHOLOMEUS
(1485-1570). Ciceronian. Latinist. Professor of Latin at Royal College of Francis I.

LA TOUR, GEORGES DE
(1593-1652). French painter, court painter to Louis XIII. Noted for striking use of light in night scenes and an Italianate naturalism. Two of the very few works that are known to be his are *St. Sebastian* and *Education of the Virgin*.

LATVIAN LANGUAGE
The earliest book in Latvian was a translation of the Lord's Prayer by Grunau, appeared in 1521-1530.

LAUD, WILLIAM
(1573-1645). Archbishop of Canterbury. Chief minister to Charles I. Tried to impose High Anglicanism by force. Impeached, tried for treason, executed by the Parliamentarians.

LAUDONNIÈRE, RENÉ GOULAINE DE
Sixteenth century. French Huguenot. On expedition to America found colony in Florida. Returned when settlement was devastated by Spaniards in 1565. Wrote a *History of Florida*, published in 1586, which was translated into English by Hakluyt.

LAURANA, FRANCESCO
(1424-1502). Italian sculptor. Died in Avignon. Executed religious statuary, portrait busts, particularly a famous one of Beatrice of Aragon, the daughter of Ferrante I, the king of Naples. His work is marked by an idealizing beauty that contrasts with the realism of Donatello.

LAURANA, LUCIANO
(c. 1425-1483). Architect of Urbino, where he worked upon the famous ducal palace. He also worked in Naples.

LAUTENBACH, KONRAD

(1534-1595). German theologian and Latin and German poet. Student in Strassburg under Johannes Sturm. Librarian in Heidelberg. Lutheran minister in Frankfurt. Translated Josephus' *De Bello Iudaico* into German, published in 1571.

LAUTREC, ODET DE VOIX, VICOMTE DE

(1485-1528). Marshal of France, Governor of Milan. He fought in the Italian wars, at Marignano, 1515, La Bicocca, 1522, the reconquest of Milan, 1527, and died during the siege of Naples, 1528.

LA VALETTE, JEAN PARISOT DE

(1494-1568). Grand Master of the Knights of Malta. Resisted Turkish siege of Malta in 1565. The city of Valletta, built in 1568, was named after him.

LAX, CASPAR

(Early sixteenth century). Spanish Occamist logician, philosopher and mathematician. Author of *Termini*, published in 1512. *Obligationes*, published in 1512. *Insolubilia*, published in Paris in 1512. He had studied at the University of Paris and spent much of his mature life there.

LAZARILLO DE TORMES

Title of the prototype and the best of all Spanish picaresque novels. Anonymous. Three editions appeared in 1554. Work is an anti-clerical satire. Placed on Index. Translated into French, English, Dutch, German, Italian. Lazarillo was a character of Spanish folklore and is depicted as an ideal criminal type. Tale divided into seven treatises. Realistic and illuminating account of life in sixteenth-century Spain.

LEDESMA BUITRAGO, ALONSO DE

(1562-1623). Spanish poet. Originator of *conceptism*—mystical school of writing; it took its name from his book of religious poems, *Conceptos espirituales.*

LEEDS GRAMMAR SCHOOL

English public school. Founded by Sir William Sheafield in 1552.

LEEUW, WILLEM VAN DER

(1610-1655). Flemish engraver of Antwerp. Influenced by Rembrandt and Rubens.

LEFÈBVRE D'ÉTAPLES, JACQUES, FABER STAPULENSIS

(1455-1536). The Colet of France in that he made a journey to Italy in 1492 and was especially influenced by Ficino's and Florentine Neo-Platonism. His interest in the new learning stemmed from its application to theological studies. In his later years he was one of the greatest Biblical scholars of northern Europe. However, he never really broke out of the Scholastic philosophical mold, having been trained at its stronghold, the University of Paris; he introduced the humanist methods for the study of Aristotle and is thus called "the founder of the Aristotelian Renaissance in France". In 1509 he published the *Quintuplex Psalterium,* a study of the Psalms, and in 1512 a similar work on St. Paul's Epistles; in these two works he followed the philological and textual methods of the humanists. In the latter work he proclaimed the inefficacy of good works, concluding that man was dependent on God's grace; the book was known to Luther who undoubtedly derived his idea of "sola fide" from Lefèbvre. He strongly criticized the abuses of the Church and did much to purge them away in the diocese of Meaux, whose bishop was his friend and patron. In a manner reminiscent of Erasmus, he found that he could not accede to the Reformation, and so he remained within the Church.

LEGEND OF JULIA

According to the testimony of the Italian historians Infessura, Matarazzo, and Nantiporto, Lombard workmen dug up on the Appian Way, in 1485, a marble tomb, with the inscription: Julia, daughter of Claudius. The carved beauty of the figure appealed to the populace so intensely that Pope Innocent VIII, afraid of the effect of the pagan tomb on the orthodox faith, had the girl Julia buried secretly at night.

LEICESTER, ROBERT DUDLEY, EARL OF

(c. 1531-1588). Elizabethan courtier and literary patron. Sentenced to death for complicity in the plot to make Lady Jane Grey queen, but released. Held high office under Elizabeth I of England. He seems to have hoped to marry Elizabeth and thus become the effective ruler of England as royal consort. Involved in dubious marriages. Ineffective as commander of expedition to Low Countries and ineffective as a statesman. One hundred titles —and there are probably additional ones that have been overlooked or lost—of particular works have been traced as dedicated to him in the years 1558-1588. They range from the translators, such as Thomas Blundeville and Arthur Golding, to the historians, Richard Grafton, John Stow, Edmund Campion and Raphael Holinshed, writers on education, John Florio and Richard Mulcaster, the imaginative writers, George Gascoigne, Geoffrey Whitney, Robert Greene, Gabriel Harvey and Edmund Spenser, and much Puritan and anti-Papalist religious and political propaganda. He also organized, as early as 1559, and the first to hold a royal patent, a company of players, Leicester's Men. The group's musicians were organized, in 1582, into a separate company. He therefore played a most significant role in the literary flowering that occurred in Elizabethan England.

LEINBERGER, HANS

(c. 1470—died after 1530). German sculptor. Known to have been in Landshut and Munich from 1516 to 1530. Woodcarver and worker in bronze. A luminary of the early Bavarian Renaissance; there are still strong Gothic elements in his work.

LEIPZIG INTERIM

Issued in 1548. A modification of twenty-six articles of Augsburg Interim, by Melanchthon and colleagues. Declared the law of the land in 1548, by Maurice of Saxony, it aroused opposition among strict Lutherans. Led to the Adiaphoristic Controversy.

LE JEUNE, CLAUDE

(c. 1530-c. 1600). French composer, active in Paris where he enjoyed great notoriety. He inclined to the Huguenot party during the civil and religious wars; he suffered hardship and nearly lost his manuscripts. Remembered for his *chansons*, elegant and lyrical. He also composed religious music, motets, madrigals in the Italian manner and set psalms, e.g., those of Theodore de Béza as well as the Psalms of David, to music.

LELAND, JOHN or LEYLAND

(c. 1506-1552). English antiquary, scholar, chaplain to Henry VIII. Educated at Oxford and Cambridge. Traveled on Continent. Commissioned by Henry VIII to survey antiquities and libraries of England. Wrote account of these antiquities together with topographical and literary material that was to be used in a great history, but he went insane before he could write it; later scholars have profited greatly by the notes he compiled.

He is the first of a long line of great antiquaries in England in the 16th and 17th centuries.

LE MAIRE DE BELGES, JEHAN

(1470-1525). French poet. Author of *Les Illustrations de Gaule et Singularitez de Troyes*, historical-romantic narrative. Shows familiarity with classical writers and with contemporary Italian humanists. Published in 1533.

LE MAISTRE, GILLES

(1499-1562). French jurist and magistrate of the *Parlement* of Paris. Wrote *Décisions Notables*, deals with legal problems relating to amortization, fiefs, and vassalage. He had a reputation for severity against Huguenots.

LEMERCIER, JACQUES

(1585-1654). French architect, patronized by Richelieu. He along with several other architects of his generation developed a French style of architecture based upon the classical forms and adhering to the classical canons. He did many Jesuit churches, part of the Louvre, and the residence of Richelieu, which was later modified to become the Palais-Royal.

LEMIRE, AUDEBERT

(1573-1640). Flemish historian. Produced a biographical study of famous Flemish personalities, Erasmus, Frisius, Agricola, Chenardus, Clichtove, etc. He wrote numerous works on the political and ecclesiastical history of the Lowlands, particularly Belgium.

LEMNIUS, MARGADANT, SIMON

(1511-1550). Raeto-Romansch poet and humanist. He was involved in a literary controversy with Luther, who had no taste for Lemnius' satires and epigrams; Lemnius' defense appears in his *Apologie*. Author of *Amores*, epigrams, *De bello Raetico-Raeteis*, an epic on the Swabian Wars, and a satire, the *Monochopainomachia*. Also translated the *Odyssey* into Latin.

LE NAIN, ANTOINE; LOUIS; MATTHIEU

(1588-1648); (1593-1648); (1607-1677). French painters and brothers. Most of their work was done in collaboration. The more outstanding were Antoine and Louis, both of whom painted simple petits bourgeois and peasant genre scenes of everyday life in restrained colors, and notable for detail and realism.

LEO X

(1475-1521). Giovanni de' Medici, the son of Lorenzo the Magnificent. Pope 1513-1521. Aesthete, epicure, humanist, created Cardinal at the age of thirteen, in 1488. Prisoner of the French at the Battle of Ravenna in 1512. Escaped. Active politically. Opposed Church reforms. Conspiracy to poison him, exposed. Restored Medici rule in Florence. Tolerant, indecisive, he was not fitted by temperament to deal with Luther; he finally excommunicated him in 1520. Protector of the Jews. Drove the French from Italy, but was defeated by Francis I in 1515. Made Concordat in 1515 with Francis I. Patron of the arts. Called The Renaissance Pope. Interested in music. Published *Liber Quindecim Missarum*. The Vatican became a theatrical and literary centre. Most notable personalities attached to the papal court were Pietro Bembo and Jacopo Sadoleto, Niccolò Machiavelli, Paolo Giovio, Francesco Guicciardini, Raphael; Ariosto mentions Leo in canto seventeen of *Orlando Furioso*. Leo founded a Greek college and a printing press in Rome.

LEO XI, ALESSANDRO DE' MEDICI

(1535-1605). Great-nephew of Leo X and friend of St. Philip Neri. Pope. His pontificate lasted from April 1 to April 27, 1605. Patron of arts. The Villa Medici is named after him. His portrait was painted by Antonio Scalvati.

LEO AFRICANUS

Original name—Al Hassan ibn Mohammed Al Wezaz Al Fasi. Born in Spain. Captured, in Morocco, by pirates. Sent to Italy as a present to the Pope, Leo X. Wrote an account of Africa, published in 1550.

LEO OF ROZMITAL

Author of *Travels* through Germany, Flanders, England, France, Spain, Portugal, Italy, 1465-1467.

LEÓN, LUIS PONCE DE, FRAY

(1527-1591). Spanish Augustinian monk, mystic poet, theologian.

Educated at University of Salamanca. Entered Augustinian Order, 1544. Classical and Hebrew scholar. Professor, 1561. Denounced to Inquisition. In 1572, imprisoned for five years. Edited St. Teresa's works. Author of *De los Numbres de Cristo*, Platonic dialogue on Christ. Also *Vida Retirada*. Noted for perfection of some thirty lyric poems; he wrote in Spanish and Latin.

LEONARDO DA VINCI

(1452-1519). Italian painter, sculptor, anatomist, musician, architect, engineer, the universal man of the Renaissance, par excellence. Born, illegitimate, at Vinci, between Pisa and Florence; he went to Florence in 1466 as protégé of Lorenzo the Magnificent. From 1482 to 1499 he served Lodovico Sforza in Milan. In Florence he acted as military engineer for Cesare Borgia, in 1500. With Michelangelo he competed for a commission to paint the Palazzo Vecchio. Court painter to Louis XII of France; in Milan, in 1506. Court painter to Francis I of France, in 1516. From 1516 to his death he resided in France. Originator of science of hydraulics, made contributions to anatomy, mathematics, meteorology. Built the Mastesana Canal and military fortifications. Architect in the reconstruction of Pavia Cathedral. He began but never completed a great bronze monument to Francesco Sforza. He was the supreme Renaissance type, a wide-ranging polymath. Among his paintings are: *Mona Lisa, Adoration of the Kings, The Last Supper, Virgin of the Grotto, St. Jerome.*

LEONARDUS, CAMILLUS

Sixteenth century. Astronomer. Published a treatise on this subject in 1496. Also on gems and their properties, *Speculum Lapidum*, published in 1502.

LEONI, LEONE

(1509-1590). Milanese. Sculptor, craftsman, medalist. Executed sculptures in bronze, busts, statues, works of craft for the Emperor Charles V. His son POMPEO, (c. 1533-1608) collaborated with his father; he also helped to decorate the sanctuary of the Escorial for Philip II.

LEONICENO, NICOLO

(1428-1524). Italian physician and humanist. Traveled in Europe, resided in England for some time. Professor of medicine at Padua, Bologna, and Ferrara. Translated Aphorisms of Hippocrates.

Began Latin translation of Galen. Corrected botanical errors in Pliny's *Natural History*. Paved way for botanical science that was later developed in Germany by Mattheolus (1501-1577) and Cordus (1515-1544). Wrote treatise on syphilis. He was a friend of Ariosto. Deeply learned in the classics, he translated Dion Cassius and Lucian into Italian.

LEON OF MODENA
(Died 1648). Rabbi. Most famous Venetian Jew. Scholar, preacher, writer. Translated part of Ariosto's *Orlando Furioso* into Hebrew. Left autobiography.

LEOPARDI, ALESSANDRO
(1450-1522). Venetian architect and sculptor. Executed churches, tombs, bronze pieces; it was he who cast Verrocchio's famous statue of the Condottiere Colleoni, unfinished at the time of Verrocchio's death.

LEPANTO, BATTLE OF
Naval battle fought between Holy League, consisting of Venice, Spain, Pope Pius V, under the command of Don John of Austria, against the Turks. Turks were defeated, in 1571, a great event of the sixteenth century, much celebrated in literature—the crusading impulse was still alive.

LERMA, FRANCISCO GÓMEZ DE SÁNDOVAL Y ROJAS, DUKE OF
(c. 1552-1625). Expelled the Moriscos from Spain. Minister of Philip III, who ceded governmental control to Lerma. He was corrupt and venial and enriched himself by the confiscations of Morisco property; he fell after thirty years of power, but not before he had garnered a Cardinal's hat for himself.

LE ROY, LOUIS
(1510-1577). French humanist, professor of Greek at the Collège de France. Historian and social critic. Author of *De la Vicissitude*, a life of Budé, and numerous translations from the Greek.

LESCOT, PIERRE
(c. 1510-1578). French architect. Began on the Louvre. One of the founders of the classical school of architecture in France. His work was profoundly influenced by Renaissance Italy.

LESLIE, JOHN or LESLEY
(1527-1596). Scottish chronicler. Bishop of Ross. Supported Mary,

Queen of Scots, whose envoy to England he became; there he was arrested for his part in Mary's plotting. When he was released, he fled to France and then to Rome, where he died. Author of a ten-volume *History of Scotland,* in Latin, published in 1578.

LESRAT, GUILLAUME, SEIGNEUR DE LANCRAU
(1499-1562). French jurist. President of the *Parlement* of Mortier. Author of collection of decrees relating to Brittany.

LESSIUS, LEONARD
(1554-1623). Flemish Jesuit and theologian, professor of theology at Louvain. He played an important part in the disputes on grace in the Catholic Church, and was himself a gifted, if violent, polemicist.

LE SUEUR, EUSTACHE
(1617-1655). French painter. Born in Paris. Specialized in religious scenes. Produced series of compositions on the life of St. Bruno. Also decorator.

LEVI, GIOVANNI BATTISTA
(c. 1552-after 1605). Italian painter of Verona. Executed altarpieces.

LEVITA, ELIAS or ELIGAH
(1468-1549). Jewish poet, Hebrew scholar, and Biblical exegete. Expelled from Germany. Attached to Cardinal Egidio da Viterbo. Taught Hebrew at Padua. Author of a Talmudic Dictionary.

LEYDEN, LUKAS VAN
(1494-1533). Dutch painter, engraver: religious pictures, engravings. Belongs in early Northern Renaissance.

LEYDEN, UNIVERSITY OF
This Dutch university was founded in 1574, the oldest in the Netherlands, by William of Orange to commemorate the heroic resistance to the Spanish siege of that year. The university soon made Leyden a center of science, medicine, Protestant theology and printing.

L'HOPITAL, MICHEL DE
(1507-1573). French jurist, statesman, exponent of religious toleration. Chancellor of France in 1560. Instrumental in gaining

privileges for Huguenots. Councillor of Catherine de Medici. Dismissed in 1568. Wrote poems, speeches, in Latin.

LIBAVIUS, ANDREAS
(1540-1616). German physician, naturalist. Professor of poetry and history. Participated in contemporary controversial issues. Author of treatises on physics and occultism. Author of *Alchymia:* published in 1597. Wrote on chemistry in relation to medicine, iatrochemistry, a subject in which he was the next great name after Paracelsus; he was very critical of Paracelsus and credited himself with having rid the subject of Paracelsian magic, superstition and fantasy. For all that he still believed in the Philosopher's Stone and all the hocus pocus of alchemy.

LIBER DISTILLANDI
This treatise was published by Hieronymus Brunschwig of Strassburg in 1500. It deals with the extraction of quintessences by means of steam distillation.

LIBER GNOMAGYRICUS
First Greek book printed in France. Published in 1507, in Paris.

LIBER JORDANI DE PONDERIBUS
A treatise on statics. Published in 1533.

LIBERTINES
(1) A sixteenth century pantheistic sect in France and the Netherlands. Also known as *Les Spirituels.* They denied the distinction between good and evil.

LIBERTINES
(2) A group in Geneva that, from patriotic and other motives, resisted the discipline imposed by the Councils under Calvin's influence. Also called Perrinists, after Ami Perrin, the leader from 1546. The group disintegrated in 1555.

LIBERUM VETO
After 1466 the Polish Diet consisted of noblemen as representatives. Enacted laws and elected king, but for all decisions a unanimous vote was necessary. One member, exercising his *liberum veto,* free veto, could block action.

LIBRI, GIROLAMO DAI
(1474-1556). Painter and miniaturist of Verona. Executed lyrical

altarpieces. His father, Francesco, was also an artist and chief teacher of his son.

LIBRO DE MONTALVO
This expression refers to the codification of Spanish law, in 1485.

LIÉDIT, LYOSET
Flemish illuminator. From 1460 to 1478 he worked at Hesdin and Bruges. Became member of Guild of Illuminators of Bruges, in 1469.

LIGORIO, PIRRO
(1493-1580). Architect. Died in Ferrara. Belongs in the Roman Renaissance. Of Neapolitan origin, he was a notorious fabricator of Latin inscriptions which he brazenly passed off as authentically Roman.

LILY, WILLIAM, or LILLY, LYLY, LYLE
(c. 1468-1522). English scholar. Associated with More, Linacre, Colet. Traveled in Italy, Jerusalem. Headmaster of St. Paul's School. Reputedly, first to teach Greek in London. Collaborated in producing the long-standard Eton Latin Grammar. Also wrote Latin verse.

LIMOUSIN, LÉONARD
(c. 1505-c. 1577). French painter of Limoges, the most famous of a family of enamel artists. Attached to court of King Francis I and Henry II, for whom he did some 2,000 enameled vases, goblets, medallions, and portraits. His work shows Italian influences.

LINACRE, THOMAS
(1460-1524). Early English humanist who had studied medicine and the humanities in Italy, spending about twelve years there. He translated several of Galen's treatises into Latin. He was a friend of Aldus, for whom he edited Proclus' *On the Sphere;* he also had a hand in the Aldine *editio princeps* of Aristotle. Returned to England, he was called to the royal court as tutor to Prince Arthur, apparently a position of honor rather than responsibility; he was a member of the circle of English humanists that included Colet, Grocin, and More. He was the author of *De Emendata Structura Latini Sermonis Libri Sex.* Also produced Latin grammar. Helped to found College of Physicians in 1518.

LINDSAY OF PITSCOTTIE, ROBERT

(c. 1500-c. 1565). Scottish chronicler. His *Chronicles of Scotland* covers the period from James I to Mary, Queen of Scots, 1430-1565; a large part of it, especially the part on the fifteenth century, contains much that is fabulous.

LINSCHOTEN, JAN HUYGEN VAN

(1563-1611). Dutch cartographer and traveler in the Portuguese and Spanish domains in the New World and the Far East. Author of an *Itinerary*, a travelogue that included many exceptionally good maps; translated into Latin, English, German, French. Used as a mariners' manual for many years.

LINTHOLZ, JOHANN

(died 1535). German logician, one of the last German scholastics. Wrote treatise on Universals: published in Leipzig in 1500. In 1509 he published a major work of commentary upon Aristotle's logic, physics, metaphysics, and ethics.

LIPPERSHEY, HANS or LIPPERSCHEIM

(c. 1570-1619). Dutch optician. Putatively, invented telescope in 1608.

LIPPI, FILIPPINO

(1458-1504). Florentine artist. Son of Fra Filippo Lippi. He executed frescoes in Rome and Florence, and painted *The Virgin* and *The Saints*, *The Vision of St. Francis*, *The Adoration of the Magi*. He completed Masaccio's frescoes in the Brancacci Chapel; the chief influences upon him were his father and Botticelli, but these tended to give way to Masaccio.

LIPPI, FRA FILIPPO

(1406-1469). Florentine painter. Carmelite monk. Protégé of Cosimo de' Medici. In the Prato Cathedral his frescoes include *Life of St. John the Baptist* and *Life of St. Stephen*. Among his paintings are: *Madonna with Saints, Annunciation*. His work is characterized by the serene religiosity of his scenes and figures, a feature shared with his master, Fra Angelico.

LIPPI, LORENZO

(1606-1665). Florentine painter and poet. Author of burlesque *Malmantile Regained*: published in 1676. Uses chivalric material satirically. He painted portraits, including a memorable self-portrait.

LIPSIUS, JUSTUS
(1547-1606). Dutch classical scholar. Studied in Italy. One of the greatest Latin scholars of his day. Professor at Jena, Leyden, Louvain. Edited a monumental Tacitus, Seneca, Pliny the Younger. Also produced a Menippean satire.

LITHGOW, WILLIAM
(c. 1582-c. 1645). Scottish traveler. Wandered for twenty years through Britain, Europe, Africa, Asia. Left an account of his travels, *The Totall Discourse,* which was widely read and went through twelve editions.

LITHUANIAN LANGUAGE
The rise of written Lithuanian literature dates from the period of the Protestant Reformation. In 1547 Martinas Mosuidius (died 1560) published in Königsberg a Lutheran catechism. In 1595 Canon Mikolajus Dauksa (died 1613) published a Roman Catholic catechism in Lithuanian.

LITTLETON, SIR THOMAS or LYTTLETON
(1422-1481). English jurist. Noted for treatise *Tenures:* earliest printed monograph on English law: published in 1481. Used as legal textbook for centuries, because it was a thorough and authoritative statement of the law, written in concise and simple language, (low French).

LLWYD, MORGAN or LLOYD
(1619-1659). Welsh writer. Pastor. Translator. Wrote in Welsh and English. Author of *Book of the Three Birds:* an allegory derived from the German mystic, Jakob Boehme, some of whose works he translated from English into Welsh.

LOBELIUS, MATTHIAS DE or L'OBEL
(1538-1616). Flemish botanist. Physician to King James I of England. His name is associated with the genus *Lobelia.* He attempted a classification of plant forms based on the configuration of leaves.

LOBO LASSO DE LA VEGA, GABRIEL
(1559-1615). Spanish poet. He wrote tragedies, romances, bur-

lesques, and historical poems, one of which, *Cartas Valerosos,* celebrated Cortés' conquest of Mexico.

LOBO, RODRIGUES

(1580?-1622). Prominent Portuguese poet. Author of eclogues, lyrics. Called the last significant poet of the age of Camoens. His poem *Condestabre,* published in 1609, describes the conflict between Portugal and Spain.

LODGE, THOMAS

(c. 1558-1625). English poet, playwright, trained in law and medicine at Oxford and Avignon. Plays: *Wounds of Civil War* and *A Looking Glass from London and England.* Also produced poems, pamphlets, a satire entitled *A Fig for Momus.* He carried on a defense of the liberal arts in a protracted controversy with Stephen Gosson. His euphuistic works, such as *Scillaes Metamorphosis* and *Rosalynde* were sources for Shakespeare's *Venus and Adonis* and *As You Like It.* A trip to South America is reflected in his *A Morganite of America.* He wrote a work on the plague and other medical treatises.

LODI, PEACE OF, 1454

Ended the war between Venice and Milan over the succession of Francesco Sforza to the Milanese duchy. Florence and Naples had lent their support to Sforza, while the papacy backed Venice; by the settlement Sforza was recognized as duke of Milan and the Venetians gained additional territory on the mainland. There was also proclaimed—under the aegis of the papacy—the "Most Holy League" for the preservation of the peace of the peninsula for twenty-five years; it was subsequently renewed and ran down to its *de facto* nullification by the French invasion of 1494. Although there were at least six Italian wars in the period 1454-1494, the League succeeded by and large in restricting them to short durations and restoring the *status quo.* The League's history testifies to the existence of some national sentiment in Italy; but it was still an age when the state could think only of itself, and so much so that united action in defense of Christendom against the Turk (the ostensible purpose of the League) was impossible. Historians of diplomacy have found in the age a classic study in the balance of power, heralding that of Europe after 1648.

LODOVICO PATAVINO
Patriarch of Aquileia. Possessed 200,000 ducats: c. 1460. Called 'perhaps the richest of all Italians.'

LOISTS
A religious sect that developed in Antwerp. The members embraced a number of Manichean concepts. Their property was confiscated in 1531.

LOLLIO, ALBERTO
(1508-1568). Ferrarese humanist. Published a series of orations on England, the Papacy, the Tuscan language, civility, and a pastoral comedy, *Aretusa*, all in Italian.

LOMBARD ILLUMINATORS
Among fifteenth century Lombard illuminators were: Giovanni Pietro da Birago, Andrea Solari. Giovanni Pietro, between 1471 and 1474, executed eighteen chorales.

LOMBARDO, ANTONIO
(1458-1516?). Italian sculptor and architect. Worked in bronze; worked upon many of Venice's palaces and churches.

LOMBARDO, PIETRO
(c. 1435-1515). Italian sculptor, architect, father of Antonio and Tullio. They emigrated from Lombardy to Venice, where they did—mostly in collaboration—all their work. Their work helped to initiate the Venetian Renaissance in architecture; several other members of the family were also artists. Executed sepulchral sculptures: among them, Dante's tomb at Ravenna.

LOMBARDO, TULLIO
(c. 1455-1532). Italian sculptor, architect of Venice. Executed sculptures and buildings in picturesque style. Produced an Adam, choir chapel, marble angels, a Madonna.

LONGOMONTANUS
(1562-1647). Christian Severin. Danish astronomer. Assisted Tycho Brahe. Established an observatory at the University of Copenhagen, where he was professor of mathematics. He wrote several works on astronomy and mathematics.

LONITZER, ADAM
(died 1586). German botanist. Gave his name to the genus *Lonicera*.

LOPE DE RUEDA

(c. 1510-1565). Spanish dramatist and herald of Spain's Golden Age. He was actor, manager, playwright and traveled with his itinerant company, converting the wagon into a stage. He wrote witty comedies and farces which depict the life of common people, utilizing their idiom. He developed the dramatic form known as the *paso;* among his plays were *Paso de las Aceitunas, Eufemia* and *Los Engañados.*

LOPE DE VEGA CARPIO, FÉLIX

(1562-1635). The greatest of the Spanish dramatists. He wrote, in verse, a prodigious number of plays, ranging from farce and comedy to history and tragedy; he possessed an inexhaustible wit, a genius for dramatic situations and effects, and a capacity to depict human character which rivals, if it does not equal, Shakespeare's. He had little formal education and thus was quite free to ignore the classical rules of drama; his own life was as full of escapades as one of his plays, and in the end he entered holy orders but never stopped writing dramas.

LOPES, FERNÃO DE CASTANHEDA

(Fifteenth century). Portuguese historian, who wrote chronicles of the reign of Peter I, Ferdinand I and John I, and probably the *Condestabre de Portugal,* the story of Portuguese expansion. His works are remarkable for their accuracy and their vigorous and colorful style.

LOPEZ (DR.)

Jewish physician to Queen Elizabeth I. Tried and executed in 1594.

LOPEZ DE GOMARA, FRANCISCO

(c. 1510-1572). Spanish historian. He was chaplain to Hernan Cortés and, in writing the history of the conquest of Mexico, he verged on adulation of the conquistadores. It was Lopez de Gomara's misrepresentations that prompted Bernal Diaz del Castillo, in part, to set forth the truth in his own famous account. Lopez de Gomara was no participant in the events he described.

LOPEZ DE VILLALOBOS, FRANCISCO

(c. 1473-1549). Spanish humanist, physician, and poet. Specialist in syphilis. Author of first book on syphilis in Spanish, *Tratado Sobre Las Pestiferas Bubas.* In the form of a poem of seventy-two stanzas, each of ten lines. In 1514 became court physician to King Ferdinand, later to the Emperor Charles V. Participated in wars of Charles V in Italy. He wrote a good deal of satirical and humorous verse.

LORD MAYOR'S SHOW
London. First organized as Sir Christopher Draper's pageant in 1566.

LORENZI, STOLDO DE GINO
(1534-1583). Italian sculptor. He belonged to a family of sculptors of Settignano that flourished in the sixteenth century; it included his brother ANTONIO DI GINO (died 1583) and BATTISTA DI DOMENICO (1528-1594). Stoldo is best known for his statue of Neptune at Florence, Battista for his work on Michelangelo's tomb. They worked also at Pisa and Milan.

LORENZO DI CREDI
(1459-1537). Florentine painter and sculptor. Schooled by his father, he became an assistant to Verrocchio, Perugino and Leonardo. His own best work was done for the altarpiece in the Cathedral of Pistoia.

LORENZO DI PIETRO, IL VECCHIATTA
(c. 1412-1480). Italian painter, sculptor and goldsmith of Siena. Executed *St. Peter and St. Paul,* in marble; *St. Catherine of Siena; Cristo Risorto,* and a series of frescoes for the hospital at Siena. He executed several highly wrought reliquaries in gold.

LORINI, BUONAIUTO
(c. 1540-c. 1611). Italian engineer in the service of Venice. Author of treatise on architectural fortifications, published in 1607. Illustrated by engravings by the Flemish artist, Theodore de Bry (1528-1598).

LORRAIN, CLAUDE
(1600-1682). French painter of landscapes; he worked chiefly in Rome.

LORRAINE, DUCHY OF
Claude I (1496-1550), member of the Guise family of Lorraine, the baronial house which led the militant Catholic party during the French religious and civil wars. First Duke of Guise. François de Lorraine: Le Balafré (1519-1563). Soldier, statesman. Per-

370

secuted Huguenots. Assassinated. Charles de Lorraine (1524-1574). Prelate. Reintroduced the Inquisition into France. Henri I de Lorraine (1550-1588). Participated in the Massacre of St. Bartholomew. Assassinated. Louis II of Lorraine (1558-1588). Assassinated. Louis III of Lorraine (1575-1621). Cardinal. Charles of Lorraine (1554-1611). Fought in the Huguenot Wars. Charles of Lorraine (1571-1640). In exile. Henri II of Lorraine (1614-1664). Imprisoned by the Spaniards.

LOTICHIUS, PETRUS SECUNDUS
(1528-1560). German Neo-Latin poet, humanist, and physician. Professor of medicine at Heidelberg. Wrote elegies, eclogues imitative of Ovid, Vergil, and Sannazzaro; his poems are characteristically melancholy.

LOTTI, LORENZO IL LORENZETTO
(1490-1541). Florentine sculptor and architect. He worked briefly with Verrocchio at Pistoia; at Rome he was an assistant to Raphael. He carved a *Madonna with Child* for Raphael's tomb; he did the sculpture for the Chigi tomb and chapel.

LOTTO, LORENZO
(c. 1480-1556). Venetian painter. Executed frescoes, altarpieces, paintings with religious themes; he did many very fine portraits, unusual for their precise expression of character and individuality.

LOUIS XI
(1423-1483). King of France 1461-1483. Made an attempt to wrest the throne of his father, Charles VII. When king, destroyed the power of the nobles. In successful conflict with Charles the Bold, Duke of Burgundy, from 1467 to 1477. Aroused the Swiss and the Flemish against Charles. Acquired Burgundian territory, Provence, Anjou, Maine. Founded absolute monarchy in France. Established three universities. His last years were filled with terrors and the fear of death. During his reign close economic relations prevailed between France and Italy, particularly Florence. Louis, having resolved matters satisfactorily for the royal power in France, was several times on the verge of interfering in the affairs of the peninsula, but such schemes came to nothing. The new culture of Italy began to have an impact upon France in Louis' reign.

LOUIS XII

(1462-1515). King of France 1498-1515, just and humane rule. His marriage to Anne of Brittany, made possible by the annulment of his first marriage, assured the union between Brittany and France. Louis occupied Milan and spent most of his reign engaged in Italian wars, which ended disastrously for him. He humbled Venice in 1509. When the Holy League was organized against him, he was driven from Italy and defeated by Henry VIII and the Emperor Maximilian at the Battle of the Spurs in 1513.

LOUIS XIII

(1601-1643). King of France, 1610-43. Throughout his reign, royal policy was dominated by Richelieu. Involved in the Thirty Years' War: 1618-1648. In his reign occurred the rising of the Huguenots: 1622-1628.

LOUVRE, THE

Museum in Paris. Designed in 1546-1578 by French architect Pierre Lescot (c. 1510-1578). It was built as a royal fortress and palace by Philip II in the thirteenth century. In the course of the sixteenth century it was redesigned by several architects but principally by Lescot, and greatly expanded. It did not become a museum until Napoleon's time.

LOYOLA, SAINT IGNATIUS DE

(1491-1556). Spanish founder of Society of Jesus in 1534. At court of Ferdinand. Saw military service: wounded. Renounced arms. In 1522 made pilgrimage to Jerusalem. Dedicated to missionary work. From 1540, resided in Rome. Author of *Spiritual Exercises:* on training of Jesuits.

L'OYSELEUR DIT DE VILLIERS, PIERRE

(1530-1590). Chaplain to William of Orange (1533-1584). Wrote *Apology:* life and career of William: appeal to Dutch to free Holland from Spanish rule.

LUCARIS, CYRIL

(1572-1637). Greek theologian. Patriarch of Constantinople. Sent the *Codex Alexandrinus,* fifth century Bible manuscript, to England. He had studied in Italy and accepted many Protestant ideas, which he incorporated in his *Confession of Faith;* his ecumenicalism led him to send novices to seminaries in the West and to correspond with many religious leaders of Western Europe. His ideas were subsequently condemned in synod. Charged with treason, executed by Sultan.

LUCAS VAN LEYDEN
(1494-1533). Dutch historical and genre painter and engraver, the conscious rival of Dürer. He did religious and secular subjects, treating both realistically; his work is notable for painstaking detail and chromatic power. Among his paintings—about 20 survive—are *The Chess Player, Lot and His Daughters*, and *The Last Judgment.*

LUCENA, VASCO DE
(Late fifteenth century). Portuguese scholar at the court of Charles the Rash, duke of Burgundy. Translated into French Quintus Curtius Rufus: *Faictz et Gestes d'Alexandre le Grand* and Xenophon's *Cyropaedia.*

LUCY, SIR THOMAS
(1532-1600). English squire. Traditionally, prosecuted Shakespeare for deer-stealing. Reputedly, prototype of Shakespeare's Justice Shallow in *Merry Wives of Windsor* and *Henry IV,* Part II.

LUDOLFUS DE SAXONIA
Author of a Life of Christ. Published in Lyons in 1519.

LUFFT, HANS
(1495-1584). German printer of Marburg. Called The Bible Printer. Issued the first edition of Luther's Bible in 1522. He printed also for the English market, e.g., one or two works by Tyndale.

LUINI, BERNARDINO
(c. 1480-1532). Italian painter of Lombard school. Died in Milan. Member of circle around Leonardo. Executed easel pictures and frescoes with religious motifs. Works include *Herodias, Birth of Christ, Jesus among the Doctors.* Two of his masterpieces are *The Martyrdom of St. Catherine* and *Christ after the Flagellation.* Symonds: "Appropriated his teacher's type of face, and, in oil-painting, his refinement . . . genius more simple and idyllic than Da Vinci's. . . . None, perhaps, of all the greatest Italian *frescanti* realized a higher quality of brilliance, without

gaudiness, by the scale of colors he selected and by the purity with which he used them in simple combinations. . . . His feeling for loveliness of form was original and exquisite."

LUIS DE GRANADA

(1504-1588). Spanish preacher, writer, mystic, and Dominican monk. Wrote on religious and devotional subjects, in Latin, Spanish, Portuguese. Works translated into many languages. He translated the *Imitation of Christ* into Spanish; he was deeply learned in the Latin Church Fathers but also in Cicero.

LUNGHI, MARTINO or LONGHI

(Died 1591). Roman architect. He worked chiefly in Rome from 1540 on, where he did the Borghese Palace. Architect of transitional period immediately before Baroque era. His son, ONORIO (c. 1569-1619), and grandson, MARTINO THE YOUNGER (1602-1660), also were architects.

LURDAN

A loafer, a vagabond. A term used from the thirteenth to the eighteenth century.

LURIA, ISAAC BEN SOLOMON ASHKENAZI

(1534-1572). Hebrew mystic and Cabalist, who led the life of a hermit during which he experienced many visions. He had a large following of fellow mystics, in the writings of one of whom, Hoyim Vital, Luria's philosophy is expounded.

LUSATIAN

The language of the smallest of the Slavonic group, the Lusatian Serbs or Wends, who lived in Saxony and Prussia. The New Testament was translated into Lower Lusatian in 1548. First printed book was a hymnal by Möller and a *Lutheran catechism*: in 1574. In 1597 appeared an Upper Lusatian translation of the *Small Lutheran Catechism*.

LUSCINIUS, OTTOMAR or NACHTIGALL

(1487-1537). German organist, musical theorist and theologian. Author of *Ioci et Sales Miri Festivi*. He was organist at Strassburg; his chief work of musical theory was *Institutiones musicae*.

LUSKIN

A lazy, idle fellow. A term used from the fourteenth to the seventeenth century.

LUTHER, MARTIN

(1483-1546). Religious reformer. Born in Eisleben, Germany. He became an Augustinian monk and in 1507 was ordained a priest. On a pilgrimage to Rome during 1510-1511 he observed the unfavorable conditions in the Church. From 1511 to 1546 he was professor of Biblical exegesis at Wittenberg University. Attacking the sale of indulgences, he nailed ninety-five theses to the door of Wittenberg Church in 1517. This act he publicly defended before Augustinians, and appeared before Cardinal Legate Cajetanus in 1518. In Leipzig, in 1519, he publicly debated with Johann Eck, denying papal supremacy. In support of his theses, he published a number of pamphlets, one of them being *An Address to the Nobility of the German Nation*. Basically, his doctrine was justification by faith. This made the priesthood an unnecessary intermediary between God and man. Luther was excommunicated by Pope Leo X in 1520: but Luther publicly burned the bull of excommunication. At the Diet of Worms he appeared before the Emperor Charles V, in 1521. The promulgation of the Edict of Worms placed Luther under the ban of the Empire. Luther secured asylum in the Castle of Wartburg during 1521-1522, with the aid of Frederick the Wise, the duke of Saxony. There Luther translated the New Testament into German. Returning to Wittenberg in 1522, he dedicated himself to organizing his Church and translating the Old Testament into German. In 1525 he married Katherine von Bora, a former nun. His opposition to the Peasants' War of 1524-1525 diminished his popularity. After 1530, the Lutheran Church passed into the control of Protestant princes.

LÜTZELBURGER, HANS

(died 1526). German wood engraver whose work is so finely wrought that he is designated one of the greatest wood engravers who ever lived. He engraved Holbein the Younger's *Dance of Death;* another work remarkable for its size and detail is the perplexing *Peasants Fighting with Nude Men in a Wood.*

LÜTZEN, BATTLE OF

Fought in 1632 between the Swedes and Imperial troops, one of the great battles of the Thirty Years' War. It pitted King Gustavus Adolphus of Sweden against the imperial general and adventurer, Wallenstein. The Swedes won the battle, but lost their king and subsequently had to withdraw from Germany.

The subject has inspired many German poets, most notably Schiller, who in his dramatic trilogy makes a national hero of Wallenstein.

LUXEMBOURG, PALACE OF

In Paris. Built between 1615 and 1620, for Marie de Medici. Under direction of Solomon de Brosse. Rubens and Nicholas Poussin contributed to decoration.

LYLY, JOHN

(c. 1554-1606). English writer. Author of *Euphues:* didactic romance, with social and educational implications, an early form of the novel. Lyly's highly rhetorical and contorted style known as Euphuism. Also wrote comedies, dramas based on mythological and classical motifs: *Sappho and Phao, Midas, Galatea.*

LYNDSAY, SIR DAVID or LINDSAY

(1490?-1555). Scottish poet. Lyndsay of the Mount. Attached to court of King James IV, Queen Margaret, James V. On missions to Netherlands, Denmark. Encouraged acceptance of Reformation. Author of *Satire of the Three Estates:* satire on abuses in Church and State; *Dialogue between Experience and a Courtier:* a versified history of world; *History of Squire Meldrum:* a versified romantic biography. Also many shorter pieces.

M

MABUSE, JAN DE

(c. 1478-c. 1533). Flemish painter. Attached to Philip of Burgundy with whom he traveled to Italy in 1508. Worked in Utrecht. Specialized in portraits, historical scenes. Works include a number of *Madonnas*, *Agony in the Garden*, *Neptune and Amphitrite*. All his work after 1508 shows the profound influence of the Italian Renaissance masters, whom he had studied diligently.

MACAULT, ANTOINE

Translated into French Diodorus Siculus: *Les Trois Premiers Livres de L'Histoire*. Published in Paris, 1535, Cicero's *Speeches*, 1548. He was *valet de chambre* to Francis I and dedicated his first work to the king.

MACHAUT, GUILLAUME DE

(c. 1300-1371). French composer, poet, and priest. He composed one of the earliest polyphonic masses; his music—motets, rondeaux, ballads—is conceived strictly in the style of the *ars nova*.

MACHIAVELLI, NICCOLÒ

(1469-1527). Florentine practitioner and theorist of politics, remembered for his famous *Prince*, 1513. This work is not consistent with his more considered and longer *Discourses on Livy*, *Art of War*, or *History of Florence*. He had been a high civil servant and diplomat in the republican government of Florence that came into power on the fall of Savonarola in 1498 and fell to the Medici in 1512. He suffered imprisonment, torture, and forced retirement, in the first months of which he wrote the *Prince* in a blaze of revulsion. If it is a serious work it must be taken as supplementary to his other writings, its precepts applicable in crisis or desperate circumstances that are comparatively rare; if not serious, as a satire, and its dedication to the Medici as ironical. Much of what he says is a sardonic description of the political practice of his own day and not a recommendation of such practice; Machiavelli, in his own practice as secretary and diplomat, was not "Machiavellian". Cesare Borgia, the supposed hero, was, after all, a colossal failure; a warrior prince not mentioned by Machiavelli, Federigo da Montefeltro of Urbino, kept his word faithfully and was a notable success in ruling his duchy without trouble for forty years. Finally, the political, economic, and military means necessary to achieve Machiavelli's patriotic ends were not then available in Italy. His greatest importance is that he was the founder of a modern school of political science, emphasizing power and how it is gained and held, not what should be done to fulfill a providential scheme.

MACHUCA, PEDRO
(Sixteenth century). Spanish architect, sculptor and painter. He was the chief builder of Charles V's palace at Granada, finished by his son LUIS, died 1579. The father had studied in Italy and adhered closely to Italian precepts on proportion, etc.

MACIP, VICENTE JUAN or JUAN DE JUANES
(c. 1500-1579). Spanish religious painter, a member of the Valencian school. He also painted portraits. His style is a fusion of Renaissance Italian modes with the medieval Spanish tradition; he is designated as one of the Spanish mannerists.

MACROPEDIUS, GEORGIUS
(1475-1558). Dutch neo-Latin poet and playwright. Author of Biblical plays, comedies: also *Hecastus*, an adaptation of *Everyman*.

MADERNA, CARLO
(1556-1629). Italian architect. Died in Rome. Important architect in the transition to Baroque. He worked chiefly in Rome—for Pope Paul V. His work is suggestive of the Baroque.

MADERNA, STEFANO
(1571-1639). Italian sculptor. He worked in Rome, particularly for Pope Pius V. His work is suggestive of the Baroque.

MADRID, TREATY OF

Francis I of France was defeated and taken prisoner at the Battle of Pavia in 1525 by the forces of Charles V. Francis was held captive in Spain until he signed the Treaty of Madrid, in 1526, whereby he surrendered Burgundy, rights to Artois and Flanders, claim to Italian territory. Charles V's sister, the widowed Queen of Portugal, was to marry Francis. On his release, Francis broke his pledge: renewed the war. The French ultimately lost Naples and Milan.

MAECENAS, GAIUS CILNIUS

(Died 8 B.C.). Roman statesman, contemporary and intimate of the Emperor Caesar Augustus, patron of letters. He is associated with the circle of Vergil and Horace; in the Renaissance his name was frequently invoked as the paragon of the perceptive, wealthy, generous patron.

MAESTLIN, MICHAEL

(1550-1631). German astronomer. Teacher of Kepler.

MAESTRI, ADRIANO DI GIOVANNI DEI

(died 1499). Called Adriano Florentino. Italian worker in bronze. Cast the *Bellerophon* of Bertoldo, according to the inscription: "*Expressit me Bertoldus, conflavit Hadrianus.*"

MAFFEI, GIOVANNI CAMILLO

(Sixteenth century). Italian philosopher. Author of treatise on natural philosophy.

MAFFEI, RAPHAEL, OF VOLTERRA

(1450-1521). Italian scholar and historian. Author of voluminous encyclopedia, *Commentariorum rerum urbanarum*, in thirty-eight books, published in 1530. The subjects cover geography, mathematics, history, music, zoology, arts, voyages to India, America, and the circumnavigation of the Cape of Good Hope.

MAFFEIUS, IOANNES PETRUS

(1535-1603). Jesuit historian. Wrote life of St. Ignatius Loyola, a history of the pontificate of Sixtus V, and other works of ecclesiastical history.

MAGDALEN COLLEGE

Oxford University. Founded in 1458 by William of Wayneflete (1395-1486).

MAGDALIUS, JACOBUS

(died 1520). Scholar and theologian of Gouda in the Netherlands. Dominican. Author of works on biblical interpretation. He was a notable Greek and Hebrew scholar whose biblical exegesis helped prepare the way for Reuchlin and the next generation of scholars. He also wrote Latin religious poetry.

MAGDEBURG, BATTLE OF

In this battle the Imperial troops of Ferdinand II were defeated by Swedish forces under Torstenson, in 1645.

MAGELLAN, FERDINAND or MAGALLANES

(c. 1480-1521). Portuguese navigator who joined the Spanish service, 1517. One of his ships first circumnavigated world (1519-1522). To India, Spice Islands, South America. Discovered Philippine Islands in 1521. Killed by natives. He was one of the great navigators of the age, combining courage and determination with intelligence and knowledge. His journey was made the more memorable by the first-hand account written by the Italian traveler, Antonio Pigafetta.

MAGGI, BARTOLOMEO

(1516-1552). Italian physician. Professor of anatomy and surgery at Bologna. Physician to Pope Julius III. He made important contributions to the treatment of battle wounds.

MAGISTRI, JOHANNES

Logician. Author of *Quaestiones:* on Aristotle's *Organon.* Published in 1488. Also a commentary on Petrus Hispanus: published in 1490.

MAGNUS, OLAUS

(1490-1558). Swedish humanist, historian and cartographer. After the Reformation, he lived in Rome. Author of *Historia de Gentibus Septentrionalibus*: published in 1555, and of the *Carta marina*, 1539, one of the finest cartographical works of the day. His brother, JOHANNES (1488-1544), was the last primate of Sweden. He fled with his brother to Rome; he too was an historian and wrote a history of Sweden and of the archdiocese of Upsala.

MAGNUS

(1540-1583). King of Livonia. Son of King Christian III of Denmark. In conflict with King Frederick II of Denmark and Ivan the Terrible of Russia. Subject of German drama.

380

MAGRO, GUGLIELMO GIRALDI DI GIOVANNI DEL
Fifteenth century. Known as Il Magri. Italian illuminator. Worked on copy of Aulus Gellius, Bible, psalter. His masterpiece is the Borso and Ercole Bible.

MAICLER, GEORG KONRAD
(1574-1647). German Latin poet, poet laureate. Wrote eulogy of Lucas Osiander, Stuttgart reformer: *Panegyricus de Vita et Obitu Reverendi Patris Lucas Osiandri*, published in 1606. He was a minister and most of his poetry was on spiritual and sacred subjects.

MAIDSTONE GRAMMAR SCHOOL
English public school in Kent, founded in 1547.

MAINARDI, SEBASTIANO
(c. 1460-1513). Italian painter, collaborated with Ghirlandaio in practically all the more famous painter's works; with the death of his master, 1494, Mainardi seems to have stopped working.

MAIN GAUCHE
A left-hander. This was a French dagger especially used in duels in the sixteenth century.

MAINZ
In 1450 Gutenberg the printer opened a workshop in Mainz. This city was pillaged by Adolph of Nassau in 1462. Printers were dispersed over Europe.

MAIR, JOHN or MAJOR
(1470-1550). Scottish historian and theologian. Professor of Scholastic philosophy at Paris, where he was educated and spent most of his life, at Glasgow, and St. Salvator's at St. Andrew's. All his works were in Latin; he is remembered for the first critical history of Scotland in his *Historia Majoris Britanniae*.

MAITLAND, SIR RICHARD
(1496-1586). Scottish statesman, poet, collector of ancient Scottish poetry. Lord Privy Seal. Author of poems on Scotland. He supported the cause of Mary, Queen of Scots.

MAITLAND, WILLIAM
(c. 1528-1573). Scottish statesman. Secretary of State. Supported Mary, Queen of Scots but collaborated in murder of Lord Darn-

ley and David Rizzio. Died in prison. He had hoped to unite Scotland and England by bringing Mary to the throne of England.

MAÎTRE PATHELIN
The French farce of *Maître Pathelin* appeared in 1470.

MAKARII, METROPOLITAN
(1482-1563). Metropolitan of the Russian Church in 1542, Makarii was associated with several important, national literary projects. He directed the *Cheti Minei*, completed in 1552: a collection of almost all extant Russian Church literature. Also: *The Book of Degrees*: genealogy and history of Russian princely lines, and a *Calendar* of the saints of the Orthodox Church.

MALATESTA, SIGISMONDO PANDOLFO
(c. 1417-1468). Tyrant of Rimini. Convicted of rape, murder, sacrilege, perjury, incest, adultery. Patron of scholarship and art. He was the most famous of his family, the rulers of Rimini, since the thirteenth century; they were overthrown by Cesare Borgia, their domains becoming part of the Papal States in the sixteenth century. Malatesta absolutism, brutality, patronage of the arts and learning, and role as condottieri made them typical of Renaissance Italian rulers.

MALER, HANS
(c. 1540-1603). German painter, medalist and goldsmith of Nuremberg. Worked until c. 1530 in Ulm, then at Nuremberg in the service of the Emperors Maximilian II and Rudolph II. He painted portraits of his imperial patrons but also of the cobbler poet, Hans Sachs.

MALFANTE, GIOVANNI
(c. 1410-c. 1450). Italian traveler of Genoa. Visited Nigeria in 1447. Wrote an account of his travels.

MALHERBE, FRANÇOIS DE
(1555-1628). French poet and literary critic. Attached to courts of Henry IV and Louis XIII. Author of epistles, sonnets, odes, lyrics; also translations. Influential in shaping an unadorned, lucid style for French literature; it was as a critic rather than as a poet that he had a profound influence upon French literature, paving the way for the classicism of the age of Louis XIV.

MALORY, SIR THOMAS

(Died c. 1471). English writer. Life obscure; he probably wrote in prison, where he died. Author of *Morte d'Arthur*, Arthurian romance. Written in a vigorous English prose, it was published by William Caxton in 1485, who edited the work, changing it considerably and giving it the title by which it is generally known.

MALPIGHI, MARCELLO

(1627-1694). Italian anatomist. Professor at Pisa, Messina, Bologna. Physician to Pope Innocent XII. Pioneer in the use of microscope for anatomical and biological research. Wrote a series of treatises on his discoveries. He made the full and final proof of Harvey's theory of the circulation of the blood.

MALTA

During the sixteenth century Malta was used as a base for the activities of Spanish pirates. It was besieged by the Turks in 1565, but resisted. Turks retired. Charles V established the Knights of the Hospital of St. John of Jerusalem there in 1530; they came to be known as the Knights of Malta and held the island until Napoleon's time.

MANARDI, GIOVANNI

(1462-1536). Italian physician. Follower of views of the French medical reformer Pierre Brissot (1478-1522). He was professor of medicine at Ferrara, physician to King Ladislas II of Hungary, and dabbled in astrology. He wrote on pathology and syphilis among other subjects.

MANCHESTER GRAMMAR SCHOOL

English public school, founded by Hugh Oldham, Bishop of Exeter, in 1515.

MANDER, KAREL VAN

(1548-1606). Flemish painter and humanist. Author of a *Painters' Book*, biographical studies of Lowland painters. He also wrote dramas on Biblical subjects and translated several classical authors. He traveled extensively, especially in Italy.

MANDERSTOWN, WILLIAM

(Early sixteenth century). Scottish philosopher. He was educated at St. Andrew's and at Paris and associated with John Mair. He wrote on moral philosophy, on Aristotle's *Nicomachean Ethics* and on alchemy.

MANESS
A term used in the sixteenth and seventeenth centuries to designate the feminine of man.

MANETTI, ANTONIO
(1423-1497). Florentine architect, scientist, man of letters. He wrote a life of Brunelleschi.

MANETTI, GIANOZZO
(1396-1459). Florentine. Humanist scholar, learned in Latin, Greek, and Hebrew: a pioneer in the study of Hebrew and the collection of Hebrew manuscripts. Of a deeply religious turn of mind and temperament. He served his native Florence in many public offices and on embassies; political enemies compelled him to leave Florence for Rome, where he became secretary to Pope Nicholas V, whose life he wrote. Upon retirement from the papal service he went to Naples in his last years. There he translated the *Nicomachean Ethics* of Aristotle, and wrote a tract against the Jews, which was the chief use he made of his Hebrew learning. Long before Pico's famous oration, Manetti wrote a tract *On the Dignity and Excellence of Man*, 1452. He also wrote studies of Dante, Petrarch, and Boccaccio.

MANOEL I
(1469-1521). King of Portugal. Called The Great, The Fortunate. During his reign Portugal was noted for intense activity in exploration. Issued code of law. Expelled Jews. Sent expeditions headed by Cabral, Albuquerque, Tristão da Cunha, Vasco da Gama.

MANRIQUE, GÓMEZ
(c. 1415-c. 1490). Spanish statesman, poet, man of letters. Participated in revolts in the reign of John II. Wrote satires, lyrics, dramatic pieces, and a treatise on politics entitled *Regimiento de Principes*.

MANRIQUE, JORGE
(1440-1479). Spanish lyric poet. Of distinguished lineage, he was a professional soldier. Killed in action fighting for Ferdinand and Isabella. Lyrics appear in the *Cancionero General*: 1511. Man-

384

rique is noted particularly for his immortal elegy on his father's death, *Coplas*, which was translated into Latin and English by Longfellow; his other poetry is undistinguished.

MANSION, COLARD
(died c. 1484). Belgian scholar and printer. Translated Ovid's *Metamorphoses*: published in 1484, and Boccaccio, 1476, both in French.

MANTEGNA, ANDREA
(1430-1506). Italian painter. Born in Vicenza. In 1460 settled in Mantua, where he spent most of his life, in the service of the ducal family, the Gonzaga. Head of Paduan school. Worked also in Rome. Executed frescoes, murals, nine tempera pictures entitled *Triumph of Caesar*, engravings: *Adoration of the Magi, Flagellation of Christ, Entombment*. In addition, Mantegna was a sculptor, architect, poet. His technical skill exercised a deep influence on Italian art. J. A. Symonds: "His inspiration was derived from the antique. The beauty of classical bas-relief entered deep into his soul and ruled his imagination."

MANTINO, GIACOBBE
(1490-1549). Italian Jewish physician. Practiced in Venice. Physician to cardinals: also to Pope Paul III. Professor of medicine at Bologna, in 1529. Also lectured at the Sapienza in Rome in 1539. Translated philosophical and medical treatises from Hebrew into Latin.

MANTUA
The city was kept in perpetual turbulence by the Guelph-Ghibelline struggle until the Gonzaga house gained control there in 1328. For military services and diplomatic support rendered to the emperors, the Gonzaga attained the title of marquis in 1432, of duke in 1531. With the marriage of Francesco Gonzaga (died 1519) to Isabella d'Este of Ferrara (1474-1539), the Mantuan court—long a famous artistic and literary center—reached its zenith. Francesco was commander of the League's forces that defeated the French in the Battle of Fornovo of 1495; he and, after his death, Isabella utilized every diplomatic counter to preserve Mantua from absorption by its larger neighbors. They succeeded, and, with the backing of the Emperor Charles V, their son and successor Federigo (1500-1540), had little trouble maintaining his domain. So too his successors, down to 1708, when the ducal

house died out. Ercole Gonzaga (1505-1563), second son of Francesco and Isabella, was a cardinal of the Church, regent of the duchy after his brother's death, a munificent patron of the arts and learning, and an important figure at the Council of Trent.

MANUEL, NICHOLAS ALEMAN or NIKOLAUS DEUTSCH

(1484-1530). Swiss artist, poet, woodcarver. Died in Berne. In French military service. Studied under Titian. Supported Reformation. Wrote comedies, polemics. Executed a series of frescoes entitled *Dance of the Dead*. Also religious paintings, woodcuts, stained-glass windows. Represents, by his versatility, the Renaissance type of *uomo universale*.

MANZOLI, PIER ANGELO or MARCELLUS PALINGENIUS STELLATUS

(c. 1500-c. 1543). Italian Neo-Latin poet, whose Latinized version of his name is his anagram. He was prosecuted for heresy under Pope Paul III, chiefly for his poem *Zodiacus vitae*, in which he expresses his strong anti-clerical sentiments in a satirical vein; his positions on morals, metaphysics and astronomy did not commend themselves to the Pope either. His poems became popular in Protestant countries.

MANZOLUS, BARTHOLOMAEUS

Sixteenth century. Scholastic logician of Bologna. Author of *Dubia super Logicam Pauli Veneti:* published in 1523.

MAP OF ITALY

Reputedly, Petrarch inspired the drawing of the first map of Italy. Cartography enjoyed a great age, artistically and scientifically, in the Renaissance. Until the 1530's Italy was the great center for map-making, thereafter it was the Netherlands.

MARBECK, JOHN

(c. 1523-1585). English composer, organist. Calvinist. Condemned to stake but pardoned. Author of earliest English Bible *Concordance*: published in 1550. Also *Boke of Common Praier Noted*: in which the traditional plain chant was adapted to the liturgy Edward VI established in 1549.

MARCANTONIO MAJORGIO CONTI
or MAJORAGIUS, MARCANTONIUS

(1514-1555). Italian humanist. Professor in Milan. Author of *Antiparadoxon,* in dialogue form: published in 1546. It was an attack upon Cicero's *Paradoxes;* he also wrote commentaries on Aristotle's *Rhetoric.*

MARCANTONIO, RAIMONDI

(c. 1488-1534). Italian goldsmith, engraver of Bologna. Worked in Rome. Engraved Raphael's works.

MARCELLUS II

(1501-1555). Pope for less than a month. Church reformer, scholar in many fields of knowledge. Supported art and literature. On his death, the poet Faustus Sabaeus wrote: "It is not the grave which honors the ashes, but the ashes which honor the tomb." As scholar and Apostolic Librarian before his pontificate, he promoted historical and archaeological knowledge, and greatly expanded the Vatican Library. Palestrina wrote his most famous mass in memory of Marcellus.

MARCI, JOHANN MARCUS

(1595-1667). Physician, scientist and anatomist of Kronland. He was physician to Emperor Ferdinand III and professor at the University of Prague. He wrote treatises on embryology, optics, mathematics and natural philosophy.

MARCO DA GAGLIANO

(c. 1575-1642). Florentine composer and priest. He was *maestro di cappella* in San Lorenzo and to the dukes of Tuscany. He composed church music, e.g., motets and madrigals, and founded the *Accademia degl'Elevati* for musicians, patrons and music devotees; he is remembered chiefly for his *Daphne,* 1602, a milestone in the development of the operatic form—it was performed in Mantua in 1608.

MARCO D'OGGIONO

(c. 1470-1530). Italian painter. Belongs to the school of Leonardo, and worked in the service of Lodovico Il Moro at Milan. His work is striking for its wild, bizarre beauty.

MARENZIO, LUCA

(1553-1599). Italian musician. Composed motets, masses and madrigals, for which he was famous in his day, especially in England. He was appointed to the Papal Chapel, was music master to Cardinal d'Este, and served at the court of Sigismund III of Poland.

MARGARET OF ANJOU

(1429-1482). Married Henry VI of England. Virtually the ruler

387

of England. In the Wars of the Roses, she was defeated at the Battle of Tewkesbury in 1471 and imprisoned in the Tower for four years. Ransomed by Louis XI of France. Unlike her royal spouse, she was resourceful, intelligent and courageous.

MARGARET OF AUSTRIA

(1480-1530). Daughter of Maximilian I. Regent of the Netherlands for her nephew Emperor Charles V. In 1529 she arranged the Treaty of Cambrai between France and the Empire, negotiating with Louise of Savoy.

MARGARET OF FRANCE

(c. 1532-1574). Margaret of Savoy. Daughter of Francis I of France. Patron of the arts. Friend of the poet Ronsard.

MARGARET OF NAVARRE

(1492-1549). Margaret of Angoulême, Queen of Navarre, sister of Francis I of France. She advocated religious liberty and a mild reform of the Church. Patron of literature; among her beneficiaries were Rabelais, Dolet and Marot. Held brilliant courts. Author of poems, letters and *Heptaméron*: a collection of Boccaccian tales, seventy-two in number, on erotic themes. The most striking feature of the collection is the pervasive sense of ribaldry, the disdain of all moral restraints, the sardonic humor.

MARGARET OF PARMA

(1522-1586). The natural daughter of Charles V. Able and decisive Regent of the Netherlands during 1559-1567. Instrumental in the recall of the unpopular Cardinal Granvelle. On violent outbreak of Dutch nationalists, she was persuaded to turn against the leaders: Count Egmont, Count Horn, and William of Orange. Resigned the Regency on the arrival of the Duke of Alva in Brussels, in 1567. Her correspondence with Philip II is extant and reveals her cautions against Alva's harsh methods.

MARGARET OF VALOIS

(1533-1615). Daughter of Henry II and Catherine de' Medici. First wife of Henry IV of France. Wrote her memoirs late in life, after her marriage was annulled and she maintained a small court and literary circle at Usson and then at Paris.

MARGARET TUDOR

(1489-1541). Queen of James IV of Scotland and mother of

James V. She was caught in the vortex of intrigue that enveloped the Scottish Crown; her married life was nearly as checkered as that of her brother Henry VIII. It was by this marriage that the Stuarts became related to the English royal house and could claim the English throne in 1603.

MARIANA, JUAN DE
(1536-1624). Spanish humanist, historian, and political economist. Jesuit. Educated at Alcalá. Traveled to Rome, Paris, Flanders, teaching and lecturing. Author of Latin *Historiae de Rebus Hispaniae libri XXX*, which he himself translated into Spanish. Ranges from earliest times to 1516. Translated into many languages. Also author of *De Rege et Regis Institutione*, 1598, in which he defended tyrannicide and for which he was condemned by the Order.

MARIGNANO, BATTLE OF
Fought between King Francis I of France and Swiss for the possession of Milan. Swiss heavily defeated, in 1515.

MARINELLA-VACCA, LUCREZIA
Venetian poetess. Wrote sacred poetry. Lives of Saints Francis, Justina, Caterina: prose and poetic versions. Published in 1602.

MARINEO, LUCA
(1444-1533). Italian humanist and historian. Author of *De Rebus Hispaniae Memorabilibus*. In 1486 he settled in Spain teaching in the University of Salamanca; he became official historian to Ferdinand and then to Charles V, to whom he dedicated his monumental work.

MARINER'S MIRROR
(or *Spiegel der Zeevart*). Was the first collection of marine maps and charts to be printed, 1584-85, and was translated into English in 1592. It went through many editions and was translated into several languages. From its compiler, the Dutchman Lucas Janszon Waghenaer, it came to be known in English as the *Waggoner*.

MARINO, GIAMBATTISTA or MARINI
(1569-1625). Italian poet. Served at the French court. Under the patronage of Maria de' Medici. Author of *La Adone*: published in 1622. His name is associated with the florid, extravagant style,

akin to Euphuism, known as *Marinismo*. His followers, who carried his style into Baroque elaboration, were Girolamo Preti (1582-1626), Claudio Achillini (1574-1646), G. B. Manso (1561-1654).

MARION, SIMON

(1540-1605). French jurist. Author of collection of pleas relating to prominent statesmen: published in 1620. He was famed in his day as a jurist of the *Parlement* of Paris; he was a favorite of Henry IV.

MARIOTTO, ALBERTINELLI

(1474-1515). Italian painter. Partisan of the Medici. Deserted painting for innkeeping. Worked for many years with Fra Bartolommeo. Practically none of his work is known to have survived.

MARISCHAL COLLEGE

In Aberdeen, Scotland. Founded in 1593 by George Keith, Earl Marischal (c. 1553-1623).

MARKHAM, GERVASE

(c. 1568-1637). English writer, poet, dramatist who wrote on country life, horses, etc. He wrote the *Tragedie of Sir Richard Grinvelle, The Danube Knight* as well as the manual on *A Way to Get Wealth*.

MARLIANI, GIOVANNI

(died 1483). Italian physicist. Author of *De Proportione Motuum in Velocitate*.

MARLIANO, BARTOLOMEO

(Died 1569). Italian archaeologist. Wrote and compiled monumental studies of classical antiquity and topography, particularly for the site of Rome.

MARLOWE, CHRISTOPHER

(1564-1593). English poet, dramatist, educated at Cambridge. Wrote "The Passionate Shepherd to his Love." Translated Ovid, Lucan. Author of seven plays, among them *Tamburlaine, Doctor Faustus, The Jew of Malta*. Also chronicle play: *Edward the Second*. He was stabbed to death in a tavern brawl in London.

MARMION, SHACKERLEY

(1603-1639). English dramatist. Fought in Low Countries.

Author of an epic entitled *Cupid and Psyche*. Also wrote three comedies, of which *The Antiquary* is the most notable. His work was well received at the court of Charles I.

MARMION, SIMON
(died 1489). Painter, illuminator, miniaturist of Valenciennes. Called by contemporary poet *prince d'enlumineurs*; all his work shows Flemish influence. Executed notable miniatures, *Book of Hours.*

MARMITTA, IL
Sixteenth century Italian artist. Worked in Parma and Rome as painter, engraver, illuminator and miniaturist. Executed missal, *Book of Hours.*

MARNIX, PHILIP VAN
(1538-1598). Baron Sainte-Aldegonde. Flemish statesman, poet. Friend and apologist of William of Orange. Participated in the war of liberation of the Netherlands. Author of the violently anti-Catholic pamphlet, *The Beehive of the Roman Faith*: Dutch, English, German, Latin and French versions. Wrote *Wilhelmus-lied*: national anthem.

MARPRELATE, MARTIN
Unidentified pseudonym of writer of Puritan pamphlets issued between 1588 and 1589. These violent pamphlets stemmed from anti-prelatical movement in England and stirred up a lengthy controversy.

MARRANOS
Also known as Conversos. Spanish Jews who were forcibly converted to Christianity during the fifteenth and sixteenth centuries, but remained crypto—Jews. The word passed over into Italian and came to mean a person who failed to live up to the code of chivalry; as such it is used by Ariosto.

MARSTON, JOHN
(1576-1634). English satirist, poet, playwright; literary antagonist of Ben Jonson. Took holy orders in 1607, renouncing the stage and playwriting. Author of a lewd work entitled *The Metamorphosis of Pigmalion's Image*. A series of satires: *The Scourge of Villanie*. His tragedies include: *Antonio's Revenge, Sophonisba, Antonio and Mellida, The Dutch Courtesan*. Among his com-

edies are: *What You Will, Parasitaster*. He had collaborated with Ben Jonson, George Chapman, and John Webster in producing several of these works.

MARSUPPINI, CARLO

(1398-1453). Italian humanist, born at Genoa but came to Florence as tutor to the Medici; he succeeded Leonardo Bruni as Chancellor of Florence. He was a great Greek scholar and gave public lectures on the language and literature at Florence; at the request of Pope Nicholas V he translated the *Iliad*. He wrote numerous Latin lyrics, much of them in praise of the Medici.

MARTIN

A term used in the sixteenth and the seventeenth centuries to designate a dupe, a fool.

MARTÍNEZ, ALFONSO, DE TOLEDO

(1398-1470). Spanish satirical novelist, biographer, historian. Chaplain of Juan II of Castile. Wrote religious biographies: history of Spain. His best work is a realistic prose satire called *El Corbacho*, published in 1495. Contains violent excoriation of the female sex.

MARTINUZZI, GEORGE

(1482-1551). Cardinal. Hungarian statesman. Councillor to John Zapolya, King of Hungary. In conflict with Queen Mother Isabella. Assassinated.

MARTIUS, JOHANNES FRANCISCUS

Italian book illuminator. For King Matthias Corvinus of Croatia he executed three manuscripts containing parts of Livy's *Roman History*, c. 1475.

MARTORELLI, BALDO

(died 1475). Preceptor to children of Duke Francesco Sforza of Milan. Illuminator. Collector of theological and classical works.

MARTYRS' MIRROR

The martyrology of the religious sect known as Mennonites.

MARULIC, MARCO

(1450-1524). Dalmatian poet. He had studied at Padua. Author of Latin poems, sermons, and treatises on religious and moral subjects.

MARULLUS, MICHAEL TARCHANIOTA

(1453-1500). Greek scholar, poet, soldier. Born at Constantinople. Educated in Florence. Under patronage of Lorenzo de' Medici. Author of *Epigrams* and *Hymni Naturales,* in four books. Influenced by Lucretian studies.

MARY I

(1516-1558). Mary Tudor, Queen of England. Daughter of Henry VIII. Scholarly, devout, a good linguist. When her mother, Catherine of Aragon, was divorced, she forcibly signed a declaration that her mother's marriage was illegal. Assumed the throne in 1553. Resolved to restore Catholicism, she made her reign notorious for religious persecutions. Acquired the name of Bloody Mary. Among her victims were Ridley, Latimer, and Archbishop Cranmer.

Married her cousin, Philip II of Spain, an unfaithful husband who involved England in war. By the Treaty of Cateau-Cambrésis England lost Calais in 1559.

MARY, QUEEN OF SCOTS

(1542-1587). Mary Stuart. Became queen when six days old. Educated in France, married Francis II of France in 1558. On his death in 1560, she returned in 1561 to Scotland, where her Catholic religion caused distrust. In 1565 she married her cousin, Lord Darnley, a Catholic. Their son became James VI of Scotland. She tried to impose Catholicism on Scotland. After Darnley was murdered with her connivance, she was implicated in intimacies with the musician Rizzio. Married the Earl of Bothwell. The marriage provoked Scottish nobles to rebellion. Defeated at Langside by the Earl of Moray, in 1567, Mary fled to England, supplicating Queen Elizabeth for mercy. Mary was imprisoned; implicated in Catholic plots against the Queen; beheaded.

Appears in dramas by Schiller, Swinburne.

MARY OF BURGUNDY

(1457-1482). Wife of Maximilian of Austria, Holy Roman Emperor. Heiress to the lands of Duke Charles the Rash of Burgundy, her marriage brought her domains to the Hapsburgs.

MARY OF FRANCE

(1496-1533). English Princess. Queen of Louis XII of France. Daughter of Henry VII and Elizabeth. Betrothed to Charles, who became Charles V, she secretly married Duke of Suffolk, much to Henry VIII's anger.

MARY OF GUISE
(1515-1560). Mary of Lorraine. Married James V of Scotland. Mother of Mary, Queen of Scots. As regent of Scotland, she opposed John Knox and the Protestants, but not successfully.

MARY OF HUNGARY
(1505-1558). Queen of Hungary. Regent of the Netherlands. Administered the Netherlands for twenty years.

MASACCIO, TOMASO GUIDI
(1401-1428). Florentine painter, celebrated for his frescoes in the Brancacci Chapel at Florence; he represents the next great development in painting after Giotto. His work radiates the humanism of the fifteenth century: he may be said to have done for painting what his friends Brunelleschi and Donatello did, respectively, for architecture and sculpture. He invented chiaroscuro; close student of the human form and of perspective, he carried his art to new heights of naturalism in the treatment of human figures and landscapes. Not long after his death, the Brancacci Chapel became a place of pilgrimage for the painters of Italy and thus his ideas and practices were disseminated.

MASCARDI, AGOSTINO
(1591-1640). Italian scholar and historian; he was the first Jesuit to be expelled from the Order. Wrote account of Count Luigi Fieschi, the Genoese, and his defeat by galleys of Andrea Doria. Published in 1629; his most important work was *L'Arte Storica*, a treatise on "storiografia del secolo."

MASSA, ANTONIO
Italian writer. Sixteenth century. Wrote against duelling as an immoral and uncivilized practice: *Contra L'Uso del Duello*. Published in 1555.

MASSA, NICOLA
(1504-1589). Italian physician. Specialized in syphilis and typhoid. Author of *De Morbo Gallico*. First writer to point out that syphilis is a cause of mental disease. He taught anatomy at Padua.

394

MASSINGER, PHILIP

(1583-1640). English dramatist. Author of some forty plays recorded or ascribed to him. Eighteen extant. Works include: *The Virgin Martyr, The Bondman, The Roman Actor, The Fatal Dowry.* Also comedies. He collaborated in several instances with John Fletcher and others, possibly on *King Henry VIII*, with Shakespeare.

MASSON, JEAN PAPIRE

(1544-1611). French historian. Wrote biographies of Dante, Petrarch, Boccaccio and the history of France; he engaged in a controversy with François Hotmon over the nature of the French legal tradition.

MATSYS, QUENTIN or MASSYS

(c. 1466-1530). Flemish painter. Belonged to school of Antwerp. Subjects include Biblical motifs, genre pieces, portraits: *Erasmus, The Money Changer, The Alchemist.* His sons Jan, 1509-1575, and Cornelis, died c. 1580, were also artists.

MATTEO DA BASCIO

(c. 1495-1552). Italian monk. Founded Capuchin Order in 1529 as a reform movement of the Minorites of the Franciscan Order.

MATTEO DE' CONTUGI DA VOLTERRA

Late fifteenth century. Italian copyist and calligrapher. Worked for dukes of Urbino. Decorated copy of Libanius and other volumes.

MATTEO DI GIOVANNI

(c. 1430-1495). Italian painter of religious subjects of the Sienese school. His pictures include *Slaughter of the Innocents* and are notable for their bright colors and refinement of line.

MATTHEW DE GRADIBUE

Italian physician of Gradi, near Milan. Composed series of treatises on anatomy: published in 1480.

MATTHIAS

(1557-1619). Holy Roman Emperor 1612-1619. In 1606, after Hungarian Protestant revolt, he was declared head of the House of Hapsburg. Tried unsuccessfully to reconcile Protestants and Catholic League. In 1618 an uprising in Prague initiated the Thirty Years' War, for which he, irresolute and weak, was partly responsible.

MATTHIAS I CORVINUS

(1458-1490). King of Hungary—Croatia. Reign marked by conflict with Turks. Protector of people. Proverb that 'with passing of Matthias, justice passed out.' A true Renaissance prince, he was an absolute despot, patron of learning and art, and the builder of a great library at Buda.

MATTIOLI, PIETRO ANDREA

(1501-1577). Italian physician and botanist of Siena. Studied at Padua, Perugia, Rome. At Trent he became a friend of Bishop Bernardus Clesius. Because of efficient work in an epidemic, his fame spread rapidly. Among the first in Italy to liberate pharmacology from Arab traditions.

Author of a commentary on Dioscorides: published in Venice in 1554. The best work on pharmacology of this period. This book served as a textbook for two centuries. Encyclopedia of Renaissance Pharmacology. Mattioli died of the plague in Trent.

MAURITIUS HIBERNICUS

(died 1513). Also known as Mauritius de Portu Hibernico. Logician. Author of *Epitomata in Scoticas Formalitates*: published in Venice in 1501.

MAURO, FRA or MAURA

(Fifteenth century). Italian cartographer and monk. His world map, of 1457-59, is over six feet in diameter; in the medieval tradition of the *mappaemundi*, it includes much legend and Dantesque cosmography; it includes, however, much of Africa, based on the Portuguese explorations, and Scandinavia; its Asiatic portion is based upon Marco Polo. Renaissance Italy, as in so much else, was the center of the art and science of map-making.

MAUROLYCO, FRANCESCO

(1494-1575). Italian mathematician, architect, and scholar. Wrote on optics. Published Latin editions of Archimedes, Apollonius, Diophantus. Produced first published work on geometrical analysis of lenses and a great number of miscellaneous writings. He was the son of a Byzantine who had fled the Turks to take refuge in Sicily.

396

MAUSSAC, PHILIPPE JACQUES DE

(1590-1650). French classical scholar. Lexicographer.

MAXIM GREK

(1480-1556). Greek monk who studied in Italy, came under Renaissance influence. Moved to Russia in 1518 to correct corrupted Russian church books. His activities brought condemnation. In 1525 he was imprisoned for heresy, remained in prison until 1551. Wrote tracts criticizing Russian superstition and governmental injustices. Also produced didactic treatises and textbooks.

MAXIMILIAN I

(1459-1519). Holy Roman Emperor 1493-1519. Author of treatise on hunting. Patron of the arts. Re-organized the administration of justice and did much to establish Roman law as the code for the Empire. He laid the basis of the Hapsburg ascendancy in Europe.

MAY, THOMAS

(1595-1650). English dramatist. Author of comedies, dramas, poems: *The Heir, The Old Couple*. Translated Vergil's *Georgics* and Lucan's *Pharsalia*. Wrote *History of the Parliament of England*: published in 1647.

MAYORS, JOHN

(c. 1640-1679): English chemist. Physiologist. Investigated the chemistry of combustion.

MAZARIN BIBLE

This Bible was printed by Johann Gutenberg (c. 1398-1468) in 1456 at Mainz; it was the first printed Bible and got its name because it was found in Mazarin's library in the seventeenth century.

MAZOCHI, JACOPO

Sixteenth century Italian, bookseller and printer in Rome. Collected and preserved antique Roman inscribed tablets, arranged and deciphered them. This collection formed the basis of the monumental *Corpus Inscriptionum Latinarum*. He was official librarian to the Sapienza of Rome, and he wrote and published numerous scholarly works.

MAZZONI, GUIDO

(1450-1518). Il Modanino. Italian sculptor. Twice in France, first at the court of Charles VIII and later of Louis XII. Executed tomb of Charles VIII, a *Pietà*. He began his career as a fashioner of masks and director of public festivals; his work is characterized by simplicity and realism, especially his religious groups, e.g., the *Pietà* and the *Deposizione*.

MEDICI FAMILY OF FLORENCE

The virtual rulers of Florence after 1434, when Cosimo (1389-1464) came to power. The Medici made their fortune as merchants and bankers; their ascendancy in Florentine affairs marked the triumph of the financial magnates over the older merchants whose power stemmed from their dominance of the guild organizations. Exiled by the Albizzi faction, Cosimo returned within less than a year and soon gained full power. Although he rarely held an official post and permitted many of the republican institutions to function as before, he controlled the public finances so closely as to be in an unassailable position. In diplomatic matters he broke off the long-standing ties with Venice in favor of the Sforza of Milan. He is chiefly remembered for his vast patronage. He spent enormous sums of his own money (the distinction between his private wealth and the public funds had virtually disappeared) on Florence for state purposes, charity and above all on art and learning. Artists who enjoyed his patronage include Brunelleschi, Donatello, Ghiberti, Luca della Robbia; he was the founder of the Florentine Platonic Academy and was a chief figure in the revival of Greek studies. He was voted the title of *Pater Patriae* posthumously. His son and succesor, Piero (1416-1469), was sickly and died after only five years of rule. The inevitable reaction in the name of Florentine liberty came against him; the conspiracy was led by the Pitti family, but was crushed by Piero, who dealt with his enemies relatively mildly. His son and successor was the celebrated Lorenzo the Magnificent (1449-1492), who presided over Florence in its most brilliant age. Although the family banking business began to falter under his direction, he was a particularly astute politician and diplomat, a munificent and discriminating patron of art and literature and humanistic learning, and a fine poet and scholar in his own right. He and his brother Guiliano were set upon in the Pazzi Conspiracy of 1478, but Lorenzo managed to escape injury and to retain power, although his brother was killed. After the crisis of the conspiracy and the war that followed it had passed, Lorenzo practiced with consummate skill

398

the role of maintaining the balance of power in Italy. Thus peace generally prevailed in Italy until his death in 1492. It is debatable whether his diplomatic capacity could have preserved the status quo and have averted French interference that began in 1494. He procured a cardinal's hat for his son Giovanni, later Pope Leo X. Among the outstanding artistic and literary figures associated with him were Botticelli, Ficino, Filippo Lippi, Ghirlandaio, Michelangelo, Pico, Politian, Pulci, Verrocchio and many more. His son Piero (1471-1503) succeeded to his position at the head of Florentine affairs, but was exiled for his weakness before the French invasion of 1494; the democratic tide of opposition to the Medici brought the restoration of the Republic and the ascendancy of Savonarola. The future Pope Leo X was instrumental in the overthrow of the Republic and the return (1512) of his family; actually, as Leo X, he ruled Florence from Rome, although he did so through his nephew Lorenzo (1492-1519), the Medici prince immortalized by the tomb executed for him by Michelangelo in the Church of San Lorenzo. Lorenzo was the father of Catherine de' Medici (1519-1589), who married Henry II of France and was regent to her sons during the French civil and religious wars, which were made the more frightful by her vacillating policies. Lorenzo was succeeded by his son Alessandro (1511-1537), although the real ruler continued to be Leo X and after him the second Medici Pope, Clement VII. The Medici were again expelled in 1527 and a Republic proclaimed once more. But with the aid of the Emperor Charles V, Clement crushed the Republic and reestablished his family, now as dukes. Alessandro was duke until his assassination in 1537 by his kinsman Lorenzino. Thereupon another kinsman, Cosimo I (1519-1574) became duke; he was granted the title Grand Duke of Tuscany by Pope Pius V in 1569, the title under which his descendants ruled the moribund city until 1737. Cosimo I was a ruthless and resourceful despot. He succeeded in expanding his domain considerably, conquering, e.g., the ancient enemy of Florence, Siena. He stimulated economic growth and prosperity in his dominions and was a patron of the arts in the period of Florence's cultural senescence. Cellini was the chief artist to enjoy his exasperating patronage. Cosimo's son and successor was Francesco, whose daughter was Marie de' Medici (1574-1642), the wife of Henry IV of France, the regent of their son Louis XIII and the antagonist of Richelieu. Pope Leo XI too was a Medici.

MEDINA SIDONIA, ALONSO PÉREZ DE GUZMÁN EL BUENO DUKE OF

(1550-1615). Spanish Armada commander, by order of Philip II of Spain. Defeated by English. Lost Cádiz in 1596 to English. He was a military commander and the premier nobleman of Spain; much against his will he accepted the command of the Armada upon the death of the original commander and experienced admiral, Santa Cruz. The tradition of his bungling is largely unfounded.

MEDWALL, HENRY

(Late fifteenth century). English writer and protégé of John Morton, Archbishop of Canterbury. He wrote several plays, which were performed before Henry VII at the court.

MEIT, KONRAD

(c. 1480-1550). German sculptor. Native of Worms. Apprentice in the shop of Cranach. Produced marble sculptures, statuettes made of various materials, portrait busts, tombs. His study tour of Italy had a lasting effect upon him; he shows the influence of Cranach and of Dürer.

MELANCHTHON, PHILIPP (SCHWARZERT)

(1497-1560). German religious reformer and classical scholar; the grand-nephew of Reuchlin. Collaborated with Martin Luther in the Protestant Reformation. Professor of Greek and theology at Wittenberg. Drafted the *Augsburg Confession,* in 1530. Author of *Loci Communes Rerum Theologicarum*: published in 1521. First important Protestant treatise on dogmatic theology. He was also, an educational reformer and did much to establish the classical tradition in German education.

MELISSUS, PAULUS SCHEDE

(1539-1602). German poet and humanist. Wrote Latin poems in classical form, on contemporary themes. He was ennobled and made poet laureate by the Hapsburgs; having been converted to Calvinism, he became librarian at Heidelberg. He had spent several years in Italy.

MELOZZO DA FORLI

(1483-1494). Italian painter of Umbria. Worked in Rome. Specially known for perspectives. Executed murals, ceiling pictures in the Vatican for Sixtus IV, that already show traces of *trompe l'oeil.* A famous painting is his *Sixtus IV* with his nephews at the installation of Platina as librarian of the Vatican collection.

MELVILLE, ANDREW

(1545-1622). Scottish scholar. Successor to John Knox and organizer of the independent Presbyterian Church in Scotland. Principal of Glasgow University: then principal of Theological College at St. Andrews. Led fight against royal efforts to establish Episcopalianism in Scotland. Imprisoned. Spent last eleven years of his life as professor at Sedan, where he wrote a number of Latin poems.

MELVILLE, SIR JAMES

(1535?-1617). Scottish courtier and diplomat. Attached to Mary Queen of Scots in France. On missions to Queen Elizabeth I and Palatinate. Wrote his *Memoirs,* which are a principal source for the history of Scotland in his life time.

MELZI, FRANCESCO

(1493-c. 1570). Italian painter. Attached to Leonardo da Vinci, whom he followed to France. His subjects were mythological, *Leda, Vertumnus and Pomona.*

MEMLING, HANS

(c. 1430-1494). Flemish religious and portrait painter. Worked in Bruges. One of the great figures of the Flemish Renaissance, he was a disciple of Roger van de Weyden and the van Eycks; his works exhibit the spirit of religious calm, the minute detail and the brilliant coloring of the Flemish tradition, although there is a tinge of conventionality in his religious works that suggests that the great age was coming to an end.

MENA, JUAN DE

(1411-1456). Spanish Renaissance poet and scholar. Called *El Genio Español.* Life obscure. Educated at Cordova, Salamanca, Rome. In Italy, influenced by classical study. First translator of *Iliad* into Spanish. Latin secretary and historian to Juan II. Noted especially for long poem *El Laberinto de Fortuna:* 1445. He is an important figure in the diffusion of the new learning of Italy.

MENCEVIC, SISKO, SIGISMONDO MENZE

(1457-1527). Croatian poet. Made attempt to reform Croatian language on the basis of Italian models and to adopt Italian metres; he was especially attracted by the works of Petrarch.

MENDOZA, ANTONIO DE

(c. 1490-1552). Spanish imperial official, rival of Hernan Cortés. First viceroy of New Spain. Viceroy of Peru. Promoted the welfare of the Indians. At the behest of Bishop Zumárraga, he introduced the first printing press to America, in 1535.

MENDOZA, CARDINAL PEDRO GONZÁLEZ DE

(1428-1495). Spanish prelate, statesman. Archbishop of Seville. Helped Isabella to secure the throne of Castile. In the name of Ferdinand and Isabella, Mendoza occupied Granada in 1492.

MENGHUS, FAVENTINUS BLANCHELLUS

(died after 1492). Physician. Logician. Wrote text on logic entitled *Expositio*. Also *Quaestiones*.

MENNO SIMONS

(1492-1559). Dutch reformer. Leader of branch of Anabaptists called Mennonites. They were of two independent origins: Swiss and Dutch. The Swiss group, at first called Brethren, were nicknamed Anabaptists. In 1525 Swiss Mennonites were founded under leadership of Zurich scholar Conrad Grebel (c. 1498-1526). Grebel was first a follower of Zwingli, but broke with him. The first Anabaptist Confession, the *Schleitheim Articles*, the creed of the Brethren, appeared in 1527.

The Dutch Dordrecht Mennonites issued their *Confession* in 1632.

MENTELIN, JOHANN

(c. 1410-1478). German printer and bookseller. Worked with Gutenberg. First to set up printing press in Strassburg.

MERCATI, MICHELE

(1541-1593). Italian metallurgist, physician, naturalist, amateur archaeologist. Author of *Metallotheca Vaticana*, an important work in mineralogy. He had studied at Pisa under Cesalpino, was an intimate of several popes who made him keeper of the archives, director of the botanical garden, etc., and wrote an archaeological work on Roman obelisks.

MERCATOR, GERARDUS

(1512-1594). Flemish geographer, mathematician and cartographer, developer of the projection that bears his name. His world atlas, completed by his son and published in 1594, was long a standard work. His career marks the end of Italian and the beginning of Dutch supremacy in the art and science of map-making. He also wrote several important treatises on his subject, particularly on the application of mathematics to geography and cartography.

MERCENARIUS, ARCHANGELUS
Sixteenth century. Professor of philosophy at Padua. In 1574 he published a commentary on Aristotle.

MERCERS' SCHOOL
In London. Founded by Mercers' Company in 1542.

MERCHANT TAYLORS' COMPANY
London livery company. First chartered by King Edward III in 1327: again, by Henry VII, in 1503.

MERCHANT TAYLORS' SCHOOL
In Crosby, England. Founded by the merchant tailor John Harrison of London, in 1620.

MERCHANT TAYLORS' SCHOOL
In Middlesex, England. Public school: founded by the Company of Merchant Taylors in 1561.

MERCURIALE, GIROLAMO
(1530-1606). Physician and professor of medicine at Padua, Bologna, and Pisa. Essentially a psychiatrist. Expounded that the frequency of melancholia was due to luxury and pleasure. Author of *De Morbis Puerorum*: published in 1583. On medical gymnastics: *De Gymnastica*: published in 1569. *De Morbis Cutaneis*: published in 1572, on dermatology. He also translated Greek medical authors into Latin, e.g., Hippocrates.

MERIAN, MATTHAUS, THE ELDER
(1593-1650). Swiss engraver, bookseller. Worked in Frankfurt. Produced engravings for Martin Zeiller's topography and for several important cartographical works. Also original etchings: landscapes, battle scenes, biblical scenes.

MERSENNE, MARIN
(1588-1648). French mathematician, Minorite Franciscan, theologian and musical theorist. Friend of Descartes and many of the great scientists of his day; he also translated Galileo into French.

Taught in convent schools. Wrote on music, philosophy, physics, mathematics.

MERULO, CLAUDIO

(1533-1604). Italian musician and music publisher. Organist at St. Mark's. Composed madrigals, toccatas, masses, motets. He is important in the development of instrumental music, while his *La Tragedia*, 1574, was an early form of the opera.

MESCHINOT, JEAN

(1415?-1491). French poet. Author of *Les Lunettes des Princes*.

MESTA, LA

A Spanish sheep-herding combine. Throughout the sixteenth century, particularly in the reign of Philip II (1556-1598), the mesta had royal preference over other agricultural activities, although it contributed to the economic decline of Spain by causing erosion.

METALWORK

In the Renaissance metalwork achieved artistic heights. The quatre-foil grilles and lanterns for corners of city palaces indicate the skilled use of iron. In cathedral accessories, in locks and chests, German craftsmen wrought with equal skill. In Renaissance Spain iron work was revived in the monumental screens in churches. Iron was also used artistically for church furniture: as in the case of pulpits, and in domestic architecture, even in nail heads.

METHWOLD, WILLIAM

(died 1653). In the service of the East India Company. Traveled in India. First Englishman to visit the diamond mines of Golconda, in 1622. Wrote an account of his travels.

METIUS, ADRIAN

(1571-1635). Dutch mathematician. Wrote on astronomy, mathematics, particularly geometry. He taught mathematics and medicine at the University of Franeker. Both his father and brother were naturalists.

METLINGER, BARTOLOMAEUS

Fifteenth century. German physician. Author of treatise on rules for maintaining health, on diet, nursing, published in Augsburg in 1473.

METLINGER, PETER

(Died 1491). German printer. He was one of the first to carry the new art of printing to France; he established himself in Dijon and other French cities in the 1480's.

MEURS, JAN DE or JOANNES MEURSIUS

(1579-1639). Dutch classical scholar and historian. Professor of history and Greek at Leyden. Called The True and Legitimate Mystagogue to the Sanctuaries of Greece. Wrote on Greek antiquities, festivals, mysteries of Eleusis. Author of *Eleusiana, Panathenaea*: published in 1619, and edited Lycophron, Plato and Cato. He went to Denmark at the invitation of Christian IV as official historian. He wrote historical works on Denmark as well as on his native Holland.

MEXIA, PERO

(c. 1497-1552). Spanish historian and scholar. At the instance of the Emperor Charles V he wrote a history of this reign: not published. Mexia enlarged the work to include Roman Emperors to Maximilian, Charles V's predecessor: published in 1545. Translated into Latin, English, German. This history is actually a history of civilization, includes political history, philosophy, arts, science. He was a friend of Erasmus and of Vives.

MICHAEL OF BRESLAU

Sixteenth century. Logician. Taught in Cracow. Author of *Introductorium Dialecticae:* published in 1515.

MICHAEL PARISIENSIS

Sixteenth century. Logician. Taught in Cracow. Author of *Proprietates Terminorum:* a commentary on Petrus Hispanus: published in Cracow in 1512.

MICHEL DE TOURS

French scholar. Translated Vergil's *Bucolics* in 1516. Apuleius' *Metamorphoses* in 1517. Vergil's *Georgics* in 1519.

MICHELANGELO

(1475-1564). Michelangelo Buonarroti. Great Italian sculptor, painter, architect, he was also a poet and engineer. Apprenticed to painter Ghirlandaio, Michelangelo attracted the attention of Lorenzo the Magnificent. Young Michelangelo was taken into Lorenzo's household and urged to study Lorenzo's collection of antiques. He did the famous tomb of the Medici Chapel.

In 1496 Michelangelo traveled to Rome, where, until his death, he resided, except for visits to Florence. Among his statuary are: *David, Pietà, Moses, The Bound Slaves*. The ceiling of the Sistine Chapel is adorned with his frescoes, also in this chapel is the fresco: *The Last Judgment*. Michelangelo was the architect of St. Peter's and of the Roman Capitol. His work conveys a towering monumentality and strength; his depiction of the human figure was idealized in the classical tradition rather than minutely realistic and detailed. The beginnings of the Baroque style may be seen in his work; Baroque may almost be defined as the narrow, excursive and inferior imitation of Michelangelo's work by lesser men.

MICHELOZZI, MICHELOZZO

(1396-1472). Italian sculptor, architect, goldsmith, assistant to Donatello and Ghiberti. He became architect and confidant of Cosimo de' Medici, for whom he built the Riccardi Palace, a chapel at Croce, and the redesign of San Marco; he is one of the formative influences in the development of Renaissance style of architecture and decoration.

MICROBES

Postulated as agents of disease in 1546 by Italian physician Fracastoro (1483-1553).

MIDDLETON, THOMAS

(c. 1570-1627). English playwright and pamphleteer. Wrote satires, paraphrases. Chronologer to City of London. Imprisoned. Voluminous dramatist. Author of *The Changeling, The Mayor of Queenborough, The Witch, A Fair Quarrel, A Game of Chess*, which has reference to Spanish diplomacy: the black knight was Gondomar the Spanish ambassador who is accused of plotting conspiracies; by the time of the play, 1620's, diplomacy had indeed become a game of chess.

MIDWIVES

The prejudice against men engaging in obstetric practice, except to perform Caesarian sections, was so strong and widespread that in 1522 a certain Dr. Wartt of Hamburg, having assumed a woman's dress to attend a case of labor, was burned alive for the offense.

MIEREVELT, MICHIEL JANSZOON VAN

(1567-1641). Dutch painter. Worked at The Hague. He was court painter to the House of Orange, many of whose portraits he painted.

MILAN

Milan was the chief city of fertile and productive Lombardy. Its ruling dukes made it one of the most powerful city-states, and the name of the Visconti dynasty, particularly that of Gian Galeazzo, was equated with the dominant though clamant status of the city.

The Sforza family succeeded the Visconti, and continued to promote the prosperity of the city. Lodovico Sforza encouraged industries and trade, agriculture and the arts.

In poetry and philosophy and engineering and sculpture Milan became pre-eminent. And over all towered the name of Leonardo da Vinci.

Whatever the political conditions might be at any given time, however secure and stable they might appear, there were always brusque and violent disruptions, undercurrents of revolt, horrific cruelties, bloody vendettas, vast immoralities.

The major industry of Milan was armor making, in which there was a flourishing export trade as well. In addition, lace was a profitable Milanese export.

MILAN CATHEDRAL

Consecrated in 1577.

MILANESE, LUDOVICO

Italian composer. Organist in Lucca from 1514 to 1537. Composed *laude*.

MILE

English statute mile was established by law in 1593.

MILICH, JACOB

(1501-1559). German humanist, physician, astronomer, astrologer. Taught at Wittenberg where he was associated with Melanchthon. Author of *Oration on the Dignity of Astrology*.

MILLES DE NORRY

French writer. In 1567 he abjured Protestantism. Author of text on commercial arithmetic: published in 1574. Also produced poems, tragedies, sonnets, and an astronomical-astrological poem entitled *L'Univers:* published in 1583.

MINERBETTI, ALESSANDRO
Sixteenth century. Florentine noble and academician. Delivered eulogy on young son of Ferdinand I de' Medici. Published in 1614.

MINES
Renaissance inventions relating to mining apparatus included pumps, boring machines, adits, blast furnaces, windlasses.

MINI, PAOLO
Sixteenth century. Florentine physician. Author of treatise on works of notable Florentines, including artists and sculptors. The work was published in 1577. He also published a *Discourse on Wine* and "its proper use".

MINO DA FIESOLE or MINO DI GIOVANNI
(1431-1481). Italian sculptor. Executed busts, sepulchral statuary, at Fiesole, Rome, and Florence. His work is characterized by grace and delicacy but tends to lack vigor.

MINSHEU, JOHN
(fl. 1617). English lexicographer. Author of a book descriptive of life in Elizabethan age, entitled *Pleasant and Delightful Dialogues in Spanish and English, profitable to the learner and not unpleasant to any other Reader:* Published in 1599. He compiled learned dictionaries and grammars of Spanish.

MINTURNO, ANTONIO SEBASTIANO
(Died 1574). Italian man of letters, classicist and Bishop of Ugentino. He was the author of one of the many treatises on the *Art of Poetry* which appeared in Italy beginning in the 1530's that were based on Aristotle's *Poetics.* His, which appeared in 1559, helped to establish the dramatic principle of "the unity of time," which he asserted was part of the Aristotelian canon and which came to be a very important literary doctrine, e.g., in seventeenth-century France.

MIRROR FOR MAGISTRATES, A
A composite work, ostensibly a continuation of Lydgate's *Fall of Princes;* it is written in the form of monologues in verse spoken by the ghosts of English statesmen and kings of the period—in

the most popular edition—from Richard II to Henry VIII. The verse monologues are interspersed with prose comments by the authors, who pose as a literary club. The principal authors were William Baldwin, Thomas Churchyard and Thomas Sackville, Lord Buckhurst. Most of their figures, incidents and interpretations are drawn from Hall's *Chronicles*. The *Mirror* urged a morality of obedience to properly constituted authority, although revolt against a "tyrant" is condoned. A tyrant is one who usurps power, usually by violence and war, and then cruelly misuses that power; the prime example given is Richard III. The emphasis of the *Mirror* is upon the necessity of obedience to princes and magistrates, who are designated God's deputies, and on the horrors that rebellion and civil war bring. Each monologue constitutes an historical example for the edification of princes and all who possess authority. First published in 1563, it was considerably expanded in the editions of 1578 and 1587; it was very popular during Elizabeth's reign and had a fundamental influence upon Spenser's *Faerie Queene*, Sidney's *Arcadia* and Shakespeare's histories. The three authors had a common political purpose in the works mentioned.

MISSAGLIA, THE
Milanese family of armorers, famous in the fifteenth century; they enjoyed the patronage of popes, the Visconti, and the Este in Italy as well as Louis XI of France. Throughout the Renaissance Milanese armor was highly prized all over Europe, for armor making, too, had become one of the fine arts in Italy.

MOCENIGO, THE
Noble family of Venice, eminent as doges, military leaders, diplomats, ecclesiastics and writers in the affairs of their homeland from the fourteenth until the early eighteenth century. The most famous of them was TOMMASO (1343-1423), who was doge from 1414. He was a proponent of the maritime empire and of naval strength; he opposed the policy of his successor, Foscari, of expanding on the mainland to meet the threat of Milanese expansion. Under Tommaso Venice attained the height of her prosperity and strength.

MOCQUET, JEAN
(Born 1575). French traveler, apothecary to the court of Henry IV. He made five great journeys—to Africa, India and South

America between 1601 and 1612. Wrote an account of his travels, published in 1617 and lavishly illustrated. He returned with a great many artifacts for the curious court.

MODERNO, IL

(Early sixteenth century). Pseudonym of Italian engraver. He was probably from Padua, and worked in Venice and Rome, where he engraved papal bulls. He did several bronze bas-reliefs of scenes from the life of Christ as well as mythological subjects.

MOHÁCS, BATTLE OF

This battle was fought by Hungarians and Croatians against Turks, in 1526. Turks were victorious, with the result that most of Hungary was conquered.

MOHAMMED II, SULTAN

(1429-1481). The conqueror of Constantinople in 1453 and the subject of a famous portrait by the Venetian painter Giovanni Bellini. His achievements as as conqueror and statesman, his intellectual attainments and interests, and his capacity for tolerance make him one of the most fascinating rulers of the age. He laid the foundations of the Turkish Empire for centuries to come by his conquests, his organization of the military and administrative system (the janissaries were his innovation), and his establishment of a great palace school for the training of the governing class. By the time of his death he had extended his conquests into the Balkans and inflicted severe defeats upon the Venetian maritime empire, and was engaged in the conquest of the island of Rhodes and of Otranto in southern Italy. His successors went on with conquests to the East and in North Africa; Christian Europe thus was not gravely imperilled until the reign of Suleiman the Magnificent, 1520 and after. Mohammed's mother was a Serbian, Christian princess.

MOLENFELT, MARTIN

Fifteenth century. Logician of Livonia. Wrote *Tractatus Obligatoriorum.*

MOLINA, LUIS

(1535-1600). Portuguese Jesuit, theologian, theorist of international law. He lectured at Coimbra but then went to Spain, where he spent most of his life and is usually reckoned a Spaniard. He was the originator of the doctrine of *Molinismo* in his *Concordia* of 1589. He sought to reconcile man's dependence on divine grace, so much emphasized in Protestant theological thought, with human free will. He was also a luminary of the Spanish school of international law; he wrote *De justitia et iure,* 1590's.

MOLINET, JEAN

(1435-1507). French poet, chronicler. Author of *Le Temple de Mars,* published c. 1480. Also wrote panegyrics in verse: *La Mort Frédéric Empereur, Lamentables Regrets pour le Trépas de Monseigneur Albert.* He was historian to Charles the Rash, Duke of Burgundy, for whom he wrote a chronicle of the ducal house.

MOLINISM or MOLONISMO

A religious system that attempts to reconcile the doctrine of divine grace and man's dependence on it with the doctrine of free will. Luis de Molina (1535-1600), Spanish Jesuit, first developed system. This was modified by Leonard Lessius (1554-1623), Flemish Jesuit. Molinism was postulated by Molina in his *Concordia,* in 1589. It led to a bitter theological dispute between the Jesuits and the Dominicans, who espoused the older Thomistic view.

MOLZA, FRANCESCO MARIA

(1489-1544). Italian lyric poet and humanist. Nobleman of Modena. Wrote sonnets, elegies, amatory pieces. Wrote in Latin and Italian. Author of *La Ninfa Tiburina* and other elegant pieces. He lived a riotous life.

MOMPER, JOOS DE

(1564-1634). Dutch painter of Antwerp, painted landscapes and sea scenes. Other members of the family were also painters.

MONARDES, NICOLAS

(1512-1588). Spanish physician and botanist. Wrote on medicinal plants of West Indies: *Dos Libros de todas las Cosas de Indias Occidentales*: published in 1565. Contain mention of tobacco, describing its "uses" and "virtues." He also wrote on medicine, particularly on infirmities of the tongue and throat.

MONMOUTH, HUMPHREY

(died 1537). Wealthy London draper, sheriff, knight. Helped to publish Tyndale's translation of the Bible. Committed to the

Tower of London on charges of heresy in 1528 but was later released.

MONMOUTH SCHOOL
British public school. Founded by William Jones in 1615.

MONTAGNA, BARTOLOMMEO
(c.1450-1523). Italian painter. Founder and greatest figure of the school of Vicenza. Executed frescoes, always of religious subjects, especially Madonnas; his work is characterized by a stately dignity and severity.

MONTAIGNE, MICHEL EYQUEM, SEIGNEUR DE
(1533-1592). French essayist born of a wealthy Catholic father and a Protestant, Portuguese Jewish mother. His position was a humorous neutrality and skeptical tolerance in the age of the French civil and religious wars; he was essentially a *politique*. His career best suggests the link between the Renaissance and the Enlightenment. He exemplies Renaissance individualism and introspection: his own inner self was really the subject of his famous *Essays*. With him the Renaissance scholar no longer engages fully in the life of his time as had the humanists of an earlier day so notably done. Montaigne retired from the hurlyburly of public life—he was trained as a lawyer, had served as a judge, and been mayor of Bordeaux—and withdrew to the quiet of his study. Nor does he place antiquity nearly so high as his humanist forebears had done, as may be seen in his treatment of "barbarian": for the humanists' barbarian was a pejorative term bestowed upon those outside the pale, but Montaigne finds the "savage" lives closer to "nature" and thus is superior to those within the pale. His barbarian is the "noble savage" of the Enlightenment. In the John Florio translation of the *Essays*, Montaigne came to exert a profound influence upon English literature and thought.

MONTAÑEZ, JUAN MARTÍNEZ
(c. 1570-1649). Spanish sculptor, architect. Died in Seville. Executed realistic, colorful wood sculptures of common life and religious subjects, especially Crucifixions. His portrait was painted by Velásquez.

MONTCHRESTIEN, ANTOYNE DE
(1575?-1621). French poet and economist. He coined the term

political economy. Author of *Traicté de L'Oeconomie Politique,* published in 1615. An important work of economic analysis and history: covers commerce, manufacture, navigation, trade with America. It influenced Colbert and later economists. Montchrestien also produced a number of historical and biblical tragedies, one on Mary, Queen of Scots, ancient Carthage, etc.

MONTE, GIOVANNI BATTISTA DE

(1498-1551). Italian physician, man of letters, and numismatist. Born in Verona: died in Padua. Taught at Naples, Ferrara, Padua. Translated Hippocrates, Avicenna and Galen. Author of *Expectatissimae in Aphorismos Hippocratis Lectiones:* published in Venice in 1553-1555. He is said to have first introduced clinical methods in the teaching of medicine at Padua.

MONTEJO, FRANCISCO DE

(c. 1473-c. 1548). Spanish conquistador. Twice attempted the conquest of Yucatan. His son, Francisco, completed the conquest by 1546.

MONTEMAYOR, JORGE DE

(1520?-1561). Portuguese poet and musician at the court of Philip II of Spain. Founder of pastoral novel in Spain. Born in Portugal: died in Italy. Musical tutor to the Infanta Juana. Killed in duel in Italy. Author of first pastoral romance in Spain, entitled *Diana enamorada* 1559. Achieved great popularity. Novel in prose interspersed with lyrics. Influenced Sir Philip Sidney, Honoré d'Urfé. Source of material in Shakespeare's *Two Gentlemen of Verona.*

MONTEVERDI, CLAUDIO

(1567-1643). Italian composer and first great figure in history of opera. Born in Cremona. Attached for many years to the Gonzaga court of Mantua, where he composed his masterpiece, the opera *Orfeo,* 1609. *Maestro di capella* at St. Mark's, Venice, from 1613 on. Composed sacred music, operas, madrigals, motets: used harmonic in place of polyphonic style, said to have invented tremolo and pizzicato. "The Beethoven of Baroque."

MONTGOMERIE, ALEXANDER

(1556?-1610?). Scottish poet. Captain. Attached to court of James VI of Scotland. Helped to introduce Italian form of sonnet. Imitated Ronsard. Author of long allegorical poem: *The Cherrie and the Slae.* Seventy sonnets, miscellaneous poems.

MONTJOSIEU, LOUIS DE

(Late sixteenth century). French classical scholar and archaeologist. He taught at the Palace Academy in Paris and, in 1583, took one of his noble students on a tour of Italy. Among his works are a study of the "new cosmology," a commentary on Plato, a study of Roman Gaul and a description of ancient art.

MONTLUC, BLAISE DE

(1501-1577). French soldier. Served in Italy and against the Huguenots. Marshal of France. Left *Memoirs of his Military Life*. Called by Henry IV of France *The Soldiers' Bible*.

MONTMORENCY, ANNE, DUC DE

(1493-1567). French statesman and soldier. Constable of France, opposed to Emperor Charles V. Banished in 1541. Restored. Taken captive by Spanish. Fought against Huguenots from 1551 to 1567. Defeated at St. Quentin in 1557. Drove English from Le Havre. Fatally wounded at Battle of St. Denis during the French civil and religious wars.

MONTORSOLI, FRA GIOVANNI ANGELO

(1507-1563). Italian sculptor and architect. Pupil of Michelangelo, whom he assisted in several works. Pope Clement VII designated him to restore the classical statues recently excavated, the *Laocoön* and the *Apollo Belvedere*.

MOORS IN SPAIN

In 1502 an edict ordered the expulsion from Spain of non-converted Moors.

MORAIS, FRANCISCO DE

(c. 1500-1572). Portuguese writer at the court of John III; wrote romances and was poet and moralist. Author of chivalric romance entitled *Palmeirim de Inglaterra*. The most widely read work of its kind in Portugal in the sixteenth century. A highly imaginative work, it was translated into Spanish and provided materials and inspiration for several later authors.

MORALES, CRISTOBAL

(c. 1500-1533). Spanish composer of church music. He was brought to Rome to sing in the papal choir and there mastered the new contrapuntal style. He composed cantatas, magnificats, motets, and masses; he spent his last year as chapelmaster at Toledo.

MORALES, LUIS DE

(c. 1509-1586). Called *El Divino*. Spanish painter. Attached to court of Philip II of Spain. Subjects are religious, among them: *Pietà, Ecce Homo, Master Dolorosa*, depicting suffering and melancholy.

MORALITY

The beginning of the sixteenth century coincided with the supreme achievements of the Renaissance. That period, at the same time, notably in Italy, presented a decline of morality, a profound indifference to traditional mores, to personal, social, religious restraints. "We Italians," said Machiavelli, "are corrupt above others." Profligacy and licentiousness, debauchery, moral and sexual perversions in multiple variety, were prevalent among peasantry and princelings alike, in all levels of society among spiritual guides and secular rulers. Hand in hand with the greatest cultural, humanistic, artistic achievements went violent passions, embittered and sanguinary enmities, murder and revenge. Assassination, too, became one of the fine arts: for the prince it was frequently a necessary practice, a by-product of the prevailing illegitimacy of despotic rule. Corruption ranged all the way from cheating at games, even when a Cardinal was a participant, to bloody *vendette* practiced equally by duke and ploughman. Perjury was notorious. The *ius talionis* provoked retaliation to the ultimate degree. The chivalric love of the Middle Ages, the ideals of knighthood sung by trouvère and minnesinger had evolved into total lust, unbridled libidinousness, passionate voluptuousness directed to the desecration of marriage. In a lesser degree, but in a no less reprehensible sense, acts of burglary were common occurrences. Thefts from the Church, destruction of private homes, public indecencies and brigandage all contributed to the widespread laxness, both social and moral, that marked these dichotomous times. Lax morality is often the concomitant of individualism: the new freedom may be for evil as well as for good. Nevertheless, there was also a powerful stream of moral idealism in the Renaissance.

MORE, SIR ANTHONY or MOR or MORO

(c. 1512-c. 1576). Flemish painter at court of Emperor Charles V and then at court of King Philip II of Spain. In England executed portrait of Queen Mary, 1553, at the behest of Philip II, who wished to see what his future wife looked like. More did many portraits and was in fact one of the greatest portrait painters of the century.

MORE, SIR, SAINT THOMAS

(1478-1535). English humanist. Student at Oxford for two years, he turned to the common law which he studied at Lincoln's Inn. His diplomatic success in negotiating the peace of Cambrai, 1529, led to his appointment as Lord Chancellor upon Wolsey's fall. His opposition to the divorce of Queen Catherine was the occasion of his resignation; his inability to accept Henry VIII— an intimate friend who frequently had dropped in on More's famous household at Chelsea—as supreme head of the Church caused him to be imprisoned in the Tower and executed. He was the friend of Colet, Lily, Linacre, Vives, Bishop Fisher, and Erasmus; in the Prince of Humanists More found a kindred spirit, one who also hoped for the restoration of piety by good letters. With More the real issue between Henry and the Church was at last clear: anti-clerical and humanist though he was, More could not envision any reform of the Church not consistent with the preservation of the traditional *res publica Christiana;* he could not recognize the sovereign state or the absolute prince. He wrote the *Utopia,* 1516, in Latin; it is a combination of Plato's *Republic,* a well run Benedictine monastery, and a conception of the noble savage's life in the New World. His *History of Richard III* was the principal source for Shakespeare's play.

MOREL, FÉDÉRIC, THE ELDER

(1523-1583). French Hellenic scholar and printer. Translated Clement of Alexandria. Also wrote number of hymns. The printing firm that he founded was continued by his sons, who were classical scholars in their own right. FÉDÉRIC THE YOUNGER (1558-1630) was professor of Latin at the Collège de France and edited several classical texts. Other members of the family were Claude, Gilles and Charles. Under royal patronage, they published the Church Fathers in seventeen volumes.

MORETTO, ALESSANDRO BONVICINO

(1498-1554). Painter. Died in Brescia. Leading artist of Renaissance in Brescia, where he decorated a great number of churches and produced altarpieces, notable, as is all his work, for the use of color; in addition to religious paintings he also did portraits.

MORISCOS

The Moriscos were Christianized Moors in Spain. Alarmed at their increase in number, the Duke of Lerma, Philip III's chief minister, ordered their expulsion. Since they controlled commerce, mechanical skills, and agriculture in Southern Spain, their departure was a great economic loss. The expulsion occurred in 1609-1610.

MORITZ DER GELEHRTE (THE LEARNED)

(1572-1632). Landgrave of Hesse-Cassel. Founded academy called Collegium Adelphicum Mauritianum in 1599. He was a generous patron of learning and music, the Collegium was intended to prepare noble sons for the university.

MORLEY, THOMAS

(1557-1603). English composer, music publisher, and musicologist and outstanding figure in the English school of madrigalists. Epistler and Gospeller at Chapel Royal. Produced numerous madrigals and canzonets, anthems, ballets, motets. Also music for lute and virginal. Author of a treatise on modal music entitled *Plaine and Easie Introduction* which is still valuable for the history of music in England.

MORNAY, PHILIPPE DE, SEIGNEUR DU PLESSIS-MARLY

(1549-1623). French statesman. Became Protestant. French leader of Huguenots. Called Pope of the Huguenots. Retired from court life to writing. Author of Mémoires in four volumes and of numerous religious works.

MORONE, DOMENICO

(c. 1442-post 1517). Italian painter of Verona. Executed religious themes and scenes of chivalry. Influenced by Mantegna. His son FRANCESCO, c. 1470-1529, was also a painter. Father and son worked in Venice.

MORONI, GIOVANNI GIAMBATTISTA

(c. 1510-1578). Italian painter. Belonged to Brescian school as portraitist. Among his studies are those of Bartolommeo Bonga, Bernardo Spina, and Antonio Novagero.

MORTON'S FORK

An expression associated with its inventor, John Morton, Archbishop of Canterbury, Chancellor under Henry VII. The Fork was a method of royal extortions. Those who lived lavishly were forced to pay large sums on the basis of their evident wealth. Those who lived simply were liable to similar extortion on the ground of their assumed hoarding. The whole thing may be apocryphal, for it cannot be traced further back than Bacon's famous biography of Henry VII.

MORYSON, FYNES
(1566-c. 1614). English traveler. Traveled through England, Scotland, Europe, Holy Land, Levant. Author of *Itinerary:* published in 1617.

MOSCOW CATHEDRAL
The Cathedral of the Annunciation was constructed in Moscow during the years 1482-1490; its architect was the Italian, Aristotle Fieravanti, of Bologna.

MOSCOW, PATRIARCHATE OF
In 1589 the Patriarchate of Moscow was established. This occurred when the head of the Greek Orthodox Church, the Patriarch of Constantinople (which was in Turkish hands) visited Moscow and was tricked or compelled to establish the Patriarchate of Moscow, independent and coequal with his own see. Thus it marked the beginning of the Russian Orthodox Church as well as the beginning of the tradition by which Moscow could claim to be "the third Rome" (ecclesiastically).

MOSCOW, SCHOOL OF
By 1570 Moscow became the capital of Russian art. Architecturally, Moscow combined Oriental elements with Renaissance Italian. Similarly in art, the late Italo-Byzantine influences combined with Western European trends. Italian artists and architects who went to Russia in the late fifteenth and early sixteenth century, and are connected with the Kremlin, were Aristotle Fieravanti, P. A. Solario, Marco Ruffio and Aloisio da Milano.

MOSES DA CASTELLAZZO
Sixteenth century. Jewish painter. Lived in Italy. Executed portraits, engravings, medallions. Friend of Cardinal Bembo.

MOSTAERT, JAN
(c. 1475-c. 1556). Dutch painter. Principal themes were Biblical, although several of his paintings depict mythological subjects. Also executed portraits. He was court painter to the Archduchess Margaret of Austria.

MUCAGATA, PHILIPPUS
Italian logician. Wrote treatise on logic: published in Venice in 1494.

MULCASTER, RICHARD
(c. 1530-1611). English educator, Greek and Oriental scholar. Headmaster of Merchant Taylors' School, London. Author of Latin poems and several pedagogical works on the education of children.

MULLINER, THOMAS
(Fl. mid-sixteenth century). English musician. Organist of Corpus Christi College, Oxford, from 1563 to 1564. His *Commonplace Book* contains organ arrangements, dance music, plainsong, anthems. He collected pieces for virginals.

MULTSCHER, HANS
(c. 1410-c. 1467). German painter and sculptor of the Swabian school. Produced portraits and paintings in late Gothic style. He worked in Ulm where he decorated the Town Hall and high altar of the Cathedral.

MUN, THOMAS
(1571-1641). English merchant. Director of the East India Company. Wrote on economics: *England's Treasure by Foreign Trade*, in which he argues along mercantilist lines for a "Balance" of trade.

MUNDAY, ANTHONY
(c. 1560-1633). English dramatist. Ex-Jesuit seminarian. Informer against Jesuits. Wrote plays, pamphlets on crimes and executions. Voluminous translator of Spanish chivalric romances; he also edited and expanded Stow's *Survey of London*.

MUNDY, PETER
(1600-1667). English traveler. Visited Constantinople, Spain, India during the years 1630-1634. Left an account of his travels. Also visited China and Japan.

MÜNSTER, SEBASTIAN
(1489-1552). German scholar and geographer. Author of *Cosmographia Universalis*: published in Basel in 1544 and translated into several languages. He edited a Hebrew Bible, 1534-5, and taught theology at Heidelberg and later at Basel.

MUNZER, THOMAS

(c. 1489-1525). German reformer. Anabaptist. Leader of peasantry during Peasants' War against nobles and clergy, who were the principal landowners. Beheaded along with other leaders of the Peasants' War.

MURETUS, MARCUS ANTONIUS or MARC-ANTOINE MURET

(1526-1585). French humanist, poet, exegete, priest. He was first associated with *La Pléiade* group and embarked on a great career as professor at Paris, when he was accused of heresy and had to flee to Italy, where—in Venice and Rome—he spent the rest of his life. He edited numerous classical texts, e.g., Aristotle, Horace, Terence, Catullus, Propertius, most of which were published by the Aldine Press of Venice.

MURMELIUS, JOHANNES

(1480-1517). German humanist. Head of Cathedral School of Münster, where the curriculum had been modified along humanist lines. He wrote many textbooks for teaching the classical languages.

MURNER, THOMAS

(1475-1537). German poet and priest of Strassburg. Member of Order of Franciscan Minors. Author of *Logica Memorativa*: published in 1509. An introduction to logic in the form of a card game, *cartiludium*. Wrote satirical attack on Luther. Also treatise on law, and an attack on astrology. Translated Vergil's *Aeneid*.

MURRAY, SIR DAVID, OF GORTHY

(1567-1629). Scottish poet. A favorite of Prince Henry, the son of James I. His best known poem is entitled *The Tragical Death of Sophonisba*.

MURULLUS, MICHAEL TARCHANIOTA

(c. 1450-1500). Greek scholar. Born at Constantinople. After capture of city by Turks, taken to Italy. Studied in Florence. Under patronage of Lorenzo de' Medici. Wrote on Lucretius: four books of hymns, epigrams. Died by drowning.

MUSCOVITE CULTURE

During the reign of Ivan the Terrible (1533-1584) Muscovite literature attained its height. Many compilations appeared: *Cheti Minei:* an encyclopedic collection of all Russian religious literature. Also: *Illustrated Chronicle* of 1560's and 1570's, unfinished history of the world.

MUSICAL INSTRUMENTS
Among musical instruments that were in popular use in the Renaissance were: the lute, trombone, pipes, drum, harp, organ, virginal, viola da gamba, recorder, trumpet, bugle.

MUSIC PRINTING
First complete collection of part-songs, printed from movable type, issued c. 1498 by Ottaviano de Petrucci (1466-1539).

MUSSATO, ALBERTO
(Early fourteenth century). Italian grammarian and poet who received the poet's crown of laurel in 1314 from the city of Padua, twenty-six years before the famous coronation of Petrarch.

MUSURUS, MARCUS
(c. 1470-1517). Cretan classical scholar who studied Greek under Lascaris at Florence. He taught Greek at Venice and made it "a second Athens." Helped Aldus Manutius in publishing Greek texts, e.g., Aristophanes, Euripides, Plato and Pausanias. Edited *Etymologicum Magnum*, published in 1499.

MUTIANUS, RUFUS or CONRAD MUTH
(1471-1526). German humanist and scholar. Associated with the University of Erfurt. Platonist. He had a hand in composing the *Epistolae Obscurorum Virorum* in defense of Reuchlin. He was acquainted with many of the famous humanists of his day and had studied in Italy. As a canon he devoted himself to "God and the Saints and the study of all Antiquity," which may be taken as a perfect characterization of the Northern Renaissance.

MUZIANO, GIROLAMO
(c. 1530-1590). Italian painter. Noted for landscapes, mosaics. Participated in foundation of Academy of St. Luke in Rome. His style was eclectic, drawn from Michelangelo, among others. He did principally religious scenes for ecclesiastical patrons who included Pope Gregory XIII. He worked at Orvieto, Loreto, Ferrara and Rome.

MUZIO, GIROLAMO
(1496-1576). Italian diplomat, scholar. Wrote on poetry, state-

421

craft, education, the use of Italian as a literary and scholarly vehicle, conduct and functions of chiefs of state. Also theological polemics on the Reformation in Italy. He was variously a courtier of the Emperor Maximilian I, the Duke of Ferrara and the Duke of Urbino.

MYCONIUS, FRIEDRICH

(1495-1546). German Lutheran theologian. Friend of Martin Luther and onetime Franciscan monk. Author of *Historia Reformationis*.

MYCONIUS, OSWALD

(1488-1552). Swiss cleric and Zwinglian theologian. Associated with Zwingli. Wrote a biography of Zwingli, 1532.

MYSOS, DEMETRIUS

(1519-1570). Deacon. Sent in 1557 by Greek Patriarch to Würtemberg, to study Protestantism. Stayed with Melanchthon over a year.

MYSTÈRE DE SAINTE BARBE, LE

A Breton religious biography. Published in 1557.

MYTENS, DANIEL

(c. 1590-c. 1648). Dutch painter. Specialized in portraits. Born at The Hague. Lived in England for twenty years. King's Painter to Charles I of England. Subjects include Duke of Hamilton, Earl of Arundel.

N

NANCY, BATTLE OF

In this battle, in 1477, the Swiss defeated Charles the Rash of Burgundy: death of duke. The end of the supremacy of Burgundy. It was a cultural turning point because it marked the end of the attempt of the Burgundian ducal house to create a "middle kingdom." The lands, extensive, prosperous and culturally advanced, were divided between France and the Hapsburgs, and the Flemish-Burgundian Renaissance came to an end.

NANINI, GIOVANNI MARIA

(c. 1545-1607). Italian musician of Tivoli. Composer. Established the first public school of music in Rome, with the help of his friend, Palestrina. Chapel master in Sistine Chapel. Composed motets, canzonets, madrigals. He was a great contrapuntalist. His brother, GIOVANNI BERNARDINO (1560-1623), was also a composer and contrapuntalist; he was one of the first to utilize organ accompaniment in church music.

NANTES, EDICT OF

Most important manifesto on religious tolerance in sixteenth century. Issued in 1598 by Henry IV of France: granted religious and civil freedom to the French Huguenots. Also admission to hospitals, opportunities to found schools, publish books, hold public office, and govern their own towns which they could fortify and garrison. It was revoked by Louis XIV.

NAPIER, JOHN

(1550-1617). Laird of Merchiston. Scottish mathematician. Invented logarithms: expounded in his *Mirifici Logarithmorum*

Canonis Descriptio, published in 1614. He also did pioneer work in the use of the decimal system. Designed various methods of calculation.

NARVÁEZ, PÁNFILO DE
(c. 1480-1528). Spanish explorer. Sent on mission from Cuba by its governor, Diego de Velásquez, to arrest Cortés. His mission failed, for he was defeated and imprisoned by Cortés; most of his men then joined Cortés who was thus enabled to conquer Mexico. Returned to Spain. On expedition to conquer Florida, which he reached in 1528. Died at sea while attempting to reach Mexico.

NASH, THOMAS or NASHE
(1567-1601). English writer. Satirist, pamphleteer. Author of novel entitled *The Unfortunate Traveler:* published in 1594.

Cooperated with Marlowe in tragedy entitled *Dido, Queen of Carthage.* Also wrote play—*Will Summer's Testament.*

NASI, DON JOSEPH, DUKE OF NAXOS
(died 1579). Spanish Jew who fled to Constantinople. Friend of Selim II, Turkish ruler. In 1570 encouraged Selim to attack Venetians, when a great fire broke out in the Venetian Arsenal; as a result the Venetians lost Cyprus to the Turks. He then sought to be made king of Cyprus.

NASI-MENDES, GARCIA
Sixteenth century. One of the notable Jewish women of the Renaissance. Marrana of Portugal. Lived in Antwerp. Moved to Italy. Belonged to banking house of Mendes. Patron of scholars. Her daughter Reyna married the above.

NATIONAL ARMY
In 1534 an attempt was made to form a national army in France.

NAUSEA, FREDERICK
(c. 1480-1552). Blanciampianus. German Catholic theologian. Preacher in Mainz. Bishop of Vienna. Author of *Liber Mirabilium Septem*: published in 1532. Deals with determination of future by examination of rare phenomena. Illustrated with woodcuts by Anton Woensam. He sought to reconcile Lutherans and Catholics, going so far as to propose communion in both kinds to the laity and the marriage of the priesthood.

NAVAGERO, ANDREA

(1483-1529). Italian poet, librarian of St. Mark's, official historian of Venice. On embassy to Spain. Wrote elegies, epigrams and other verse in imitation of Catullus, Vergil, Ovid. Poems published in 1530. Also orations. His brother, BERNARDO (1507-1565), was a humanist, diplomat, theologian and cardinal.

NEBRIJA, ELIO ANTONIO DE, NEBRISSENSIS

(1444-1522). The first great humanist of Spain. He had spent ten years studying in Italy and brought back to his homeland a mastery of the humanities as well as great zeal for their dissemination in Spain. His wide scholarly interests bore fruit in grammatical and lexicographical works, editions of and commentaries upon several Latin authors, the formulation of a set of rules for the pronunciation of Greek, and humanist studies of Spanish antiquity and history. His greatest interest was biblical exegesis, but here he came into conflict with the authorities of his university, Salamanca, and was forced to relinquish his chair. He was promptly invited by Ximénes to Alcalá de Henares, where he lectured on the classics and had a hand in the completion of the Complutensian Bible.

NECKER, OLIVIER

(c. 1440-1484). Called Olivier le Diable. French barber. Privy Councilor of Louis XI. After death of king, he was hanged. Appears in Sir Walter Scott's *Quentin Durward*.

NEGROLI, THE

Milanese family of armorers of the sixteenth century. Among their clients were the Emperor Charles V and the French kings. Their work is characterized by a classical elegance of design and a luxurious ornateness of detail. A shield for Charles V features an elaborately sculptured Medusa; an embossed casque for Francis I, the crest of which is a female figure rising from amid coiling foliage with the long tresses of a gorgon's head in her hands, is one of the great masterpieces in metal work. Delicately worked armor was a necessary part of the accouterment of gentlemen and courtiers for the splendid court ceremony of the age.

NEMI SHIP, THE

A very large Roman galley of the first century A.D. discovered in the lake of Nemi, 1446-1447. It spurred interest in archaeology.

NEO-LATIN PLAYS
Such plays are characteristic of the Renaissance. To turn out plays was a talent expected of the gentleman and courtier of the Renaissance; Seneca was the model for tragedy, Plautus for comedy. Some were based on Biblical themes, and had a didactic purpose. Many others were humorous, ribald, earthy. Jakob Locher wrote a play based on Plautus' *Asinaria*: published in 1505. Nicholas Grimald was the author of a religious drama entitled *Christus Redivivus*: published in 1543. Livinus Brechtanus wrote a *tragoedia Christiana* entitled *Euripus*: Jesuit piece, published in 1556.

NEROCCIO DI BARTOLOMEO DI BENEDETTO DE' LANDI
(1447-1500). Italian painter, sculptor of Siena. Produced in his studio more than seventy paintings and sculptures: altarpieces, Madonnas, several mythological figures.

NEUENAR, HERMANN
(1481-1530). German nobleman, prelate and humanist. Chancellor of University of Cologne. Author of *De Gallia Belgica Commentariolus*: published in 1584: it is a history of Roman Belgium. He was learned in Greek as well as Latin, and was a defender of Reuchlin, writing an appeal to Rome in his behalf.

NEVEU, PIERRE or NEPVEU
(died c. 1542). French architect. Executed many châteaux, e.g., Chambord, Amboise, and Blois.

NEVILE, ALEXANDER
(1544-1614). English Latinist and classical scholar. Composed Latin prose and verse. He was secretary to Matthew Parker, the Archbishop of Canterbury.

NEWCASTLE-UNDER-LYME HIGH SCHOOL
English public school. Founded in 1602.

NICCOLI, NICCOLÒ
(1364-1437). Florentine humanist and connoisseur, famous in his day for his classical learning and for his collections of things ancient and contemporary: paintings, mosaics, sculptures, vases, precious stones, coins, medallions, and, above all, manuscripts. He lived in the grand manner, and wielded a caustic pen that made him many enemies. Yet he retained the friendship of Co

imo de' Medici, who paid for many of Niccoli's acquisitions. By his death his library boasted a total of 800 manuscripts, half of which he bequeathed to Cosimo; they now form part of the Laurentian Library.

NICE, TREATY OF
Charles I of Spain had invaded Provence in 1536, but a peace settlement was arranged between France and Spain in 1538.

NICHOLAS, HENRY
Sixteenth century. Dutch religious fanatic and preacher, favored polygamy, organized the "Family of Love," making the pretension that he was a new prophet and superior to Christ.

NICHOLAS V, TOMMASO PARENTUCELLI, POPE
(1398-1455). His ascent to the papacy marks the triumph of humanism in Rome; Italy's humanists flocked to Rome hailing him joyfully as the "heaven-sent" pope. The long protracted shame of Rome was at last to end; the Eternal City would resume her rightful place among the cities of the world. Hence his munificent patronage of the building arts and of humanist learning. He rebuilt the city's walls and much of the Capitol, restored half a dozen great churches, inaugurated the building anew of St. Peter's, and made many additions to the Vatican. Aqueducts, bridges, and municipal buildings were renovated, while great boulevards were laid out. His patronage of scholarship was on a grander scale: he called to Rome a host of humanists who were commissioned to make translations or to author new works, meanwhile enjoying generous stipends from the papal treasury. Among those who had answered Nicholas' call to make Rome magnificent were Alberti the architect, the painter Fra Angelico, and the humanists Manetti, Guarino, Valla, Filelfo, and the Greeks Bessarion and Theodore Gaza. Nicholas' last years were clouded by the fall of Constantinople and Stefano Porcaro's conspiracy. Nicholas had been born at Sarzana but spent a number of years as tutor to the sons of wealthy families in Florence and thus had gained entry to its humanist circles. Most of the learned men who followed him to Rome were Florentines with the result that the Renaissance at Rome had a distinctly Florentine character at the start.

NICOLAY, NICHOLAS DE
(1517-1583). French chronicler. Wrote accounts of travels all over

427

Europe and Scotland, the Far East, Constantinople. He was a gifted linguist and made several translations, e.g., of a navigational manual from the Spanish, and was a courtier of Henry II. His travel books are illustrated by his own engravings.

NICOT, JEAN

(c. 1530-1600). French scholar and diplomat. Introduced tobacco into France upon his return from an embassy to Portugal, c. 1560. The term *nicotine* is derived from his name. He was secretary to King Henry II; he compiled a dictionary of French.

NIEUWELANDT, WILLIAM VAN DEN

(1584-1635). Dutch engraver, painter. Author of plays on classical themes entitled *Livia* and *Nero*. His father Adrian, died 1601, was a painter of landscapes and seascapes; his brother Jan, born 1579, was also a painter of landscapes.

NIGRI, PETRUS

Fifteenth century. Logician. Author of *Clipeus Thomistarum*, published c. 1475.

NIFO, AGOSTINO

(c. 1473-c. 1546). Italian philosopher of Sessa. Professor at Padua and then at Rome where he enjoyed the patronage of Leo X. He edited the complete works of Averroës, 1495-7. Wrote commentaries on Aristotle's *Physics, On the Soul*: also on Ptolemy's astronomy. Author of treatise on witchcraft—*De Demonibus*. Treatise on meteorology: published in 1540. Also wrote *De Infinitate Primi Motoris Quaestio*.

NIKITIN, AFANASII

(died 1472). Russian merchant of city of Tver. Journeyed to Turkey, Persia, and India—1466 to 1472. Left an account of his trip, interesting for colorful descriptive details; geographical and ethnological information.

NIZOLIUS, MARIUS or NIZZOLI

(1498-1566). Italian humanist, philosopher. Professor at Parma. Ciceronian scholar. Author of *Observationes in M. T. Ciceronem*, published in 1536. *Thesaurus Ciceronianus*. Also wrote philosophical treatises.

NO BISHOP, NO KING

During the reign of James I of England (1603-1625) the divine

428

right of kings and the divine right of bishops were asserted in this dictum. It was the king's response to the demand of the Puritans, at the Conference of Hampton Court, that the bishops be abolished; he meant that the bishops were an important part of the royal government, that without them the king could not rule.

NONHEMIUS, IOANNES
Sixteenth century. German physician. Author of *Elements of Physiology*, published in 1542, under the Latin title of *Elementorum Physiologiae Libri IV*.

NOORT, ADAM VAN
(1557-1641). Flemish painter, a gifted colorist. Master of Rubens. His father, LAMBERT, born 1520, was also a painter.

NORTH, SIR THOMAS
(c. 1525-c. 1601). English translator. Noted for translation of Plutarch: published in 1579. Served as material for Shakespeare's plays, *Julius Caesar*, *Coriolanus*, and *Antony and Cleopatra*. He made the translation from the French translation of Amyot. From the Spanish, he translated *The Diall of Princes* by Guevara, and from the Italian, *The Moral Philosophie* of Doni.

NORTON, THOMAS
(1532-1584). English poet, lawyer. Actively opposed to Catholicism. Translated Calvin's *Institutes*. Collaborated with Thomas Sackville, one of the authors of *A Mirror for Magistrates*, in tragedy of *Gorboduc*: published in 1561. *Gorboduc* is something of a political morality play. It enjoins obedience on the ruled to the ruler and develops some of the horrors that rebellion and civil disturbance bring; it concerned itself specifically with the problem of the succession and the anarchy that ensues when the heir to the throne is undesignated. As such it has definite reference to Queen Elizabeth.

NORWICH SCHOOL
English public school. Refounded in 1547.

NOSTRADAMUS
(1503-1566). French astrologer of Jewish extraction. Physician to Charles IX and favorite of the Queen-regent, Catherine de' Medici. Author of versified predictions entitled *Centuries*, pub-

lished in 1555. Many of his prophecies have reputedly been fulfilled.

NOTKE, BERNT
(c. 1435-1509). North German sculptor and painter. More of his work was done at Lübeck and may be characterized as a superb example of late Gothic realism.

NOTTINGHAM HIGH SCHOOL
English public school. Founded by Agnes Mellers in 1513.

NOVAGERO, ANDREA
(born 1488). Poet. Health undermined by excessive studying. On mission for Charles V. Died of fever at Blois, at age of forty-six.

NOVARA, DOMENICO MARIA
(1454-1504). Italian astronomer, physician. Taught mathematics and astonomy at Bologna from 1483 to 1504. He was associated with Copernicus, first as a student, later as a colleague.

NUMAN, PHILIP
(1550-1617). Dutch poet. Wrote in Dutch and in Latin.

NUMMI BRACTEATI
Thin silver coins, stamped on one side only, in use during Middle Ages and until seventeenth century.

NÚNES, PEDRO
(1492-1577). Portuguese mathematician and cosmographer, professor at Coimbra. Invented measuring instrument known as *nonius*, for use in astronomy. Wrote on terrestrial navigation and on algebra.

NUNES DE LEÃO, DUARTE
(1530-1608). Portuguese historian and scholar. Edited the chronicles of Rui de Pina, published in 1600 and 1642; wrote histories of Portugal and her kings, and wrote on Portuguese spelling and the character of the language.

NUÑEZ CABEZA DE VACA, ALVARO
Early sixteenth century. Spanish explorer. Member of Florida expedition led by Pánfilo de Narváez, 1528: described in *Naufragios*: 1542. Also explored Paraguay. His experiences were published by his scribe Pedro Hernández.

NÚÑEZ DE GUZMÁN
(c. 1478-1553). Spanish humanist. Edited many classical texts.

O

OAKHAM SCHOOL
In Rutland, England. English public school founded by Archdeacon Johnson in 1584.

OBRECHT, JAKOB
(c. 1430-c. 1505). Flemish musician, composer. He was a prolific composer of motets, masses, songs, hymns, and other church music. He had visited Italy twice, residing first at Florence and then Ferrara; as a contrapuntalist he was important for establishing that form of musical composition in Italy.

OBSOPAEUS, VINCENTIUS
(died 1548). German humanist and rector of school in Ansbach. Friend of Melanchthon. Wrote amatory poetry. Famous for his *De Arte Bibendi:* written in Ovidian imitation.

OCAMPO, FLORIÁN DE
(1495?-1558). Spanish chronicler. Court chronicler to Emperor Charles V. Canon of Zamora. Edited Alfonso X's *Crónica General:* source of epic themes for writers from sixteenth to nineteenth century. Chief work is *Los Cuatro Libros de la Crónica General de España:* 1543. Begins with Creation and extends to Romans. Contains invented anecdotes, fantastic legends woven together with authentic narrative.

OCHINO, BERNARDINO DE
(1487-1564). Italian reformer. Franciscan, later Capuchin. Confessor of Pope Paul III. Preached at Augsburg: also in England at the invitation of Cranmer. In 1553, fled to Zurich, then Po-

land. Died in Moravia. Author of theological treatises. He had belonged to the circle of learned and pious persons associated with Juan de Valdés in Naples—in the 1530's.

OCKEGHEM, JEAN DE or OKEGHEM

(c. 1430-1496). French-Flemish school. Composer. Musician, first to Charles the Rash of Burgundy, then to Charles VII of France. Author of masses, motets, polyphonic songs. Master of counterpoint. He was the teacher of Josquin des Prés.

OCLAND, CHRISTOPHER

(d. 1590?) Latin poet and controversialist, English schoolmaster in Cheltenham. Author of Latin patriotic epic on wars and exploits of English kings, from Edward III to Edward VI. Poem became school history text. Entitled *Anglorum Proelia ab Anno Domini 1327 usque ad Annum 1558*. Published in 1582. Also an epic on the reign of Queen Elizabeth I.

O'CLERY, MICHAEL

(1575-1643). Irish historian. Franciscan friar, he studied at Louvain. Collected Irish manuscripts. In 1630 produced Royal List. Chief work: *Annals of the Four Masters*, 1632-1636, a history of Ireland, of its great families and clans, and of the Church in Ireland. He also wrote on the Irish martyrs.

OECOLAMPADIUS, JOHANNES

(1482-1531). German religious reformer. Greek name means Candlestick. Original German name was Heussgen. Born in Württemberg. Assisted Erasmus in publishing Greek New Testament. Associated with Zwingli, and contested in his behalf against Luther, although Luther also had a profound influence upon him. Became reformer of Basel.

OFFREDUS, APOLLINARIS

Sixteenth century. Logician of Cremona. Wrote commentary on first book of Aristotle's *Posterior Analytics*. Published in Cremona in 1581. Also *Quaestiones*.

O'HUIGINN, TADHG DALL or O'HIGGIN

(died 1591). The Blind. Irish poet. Descended from long line of poets. One of the best known and most accomplished Irish poets of the sixteenth century.

432

OLDENDORP, JOHANNES

(1488-1567). German jurist and Lutheran propagator. He studied at Cologne and Bologna, and then taught law at Cologne, Marburg and Frankfurt. He wrote extensively on the nature, history and philosophy of law.

OLEARIUS, PAULUS

Author of *De Fide Concubinarum:* a series of speeches satirizing clerical vices. Published in 1540.

OLEVIANUS, KASPAR

(1536-1587). German theologian and professor at Heidelberg. Founded German Reformed Church. Participated in drawing up Heidelberg Catechism at the instance of Frederick III, Count Palatine.

OLIVER, ISAAC, THE ELDER

(c. 1556-1617). French-born miniature painter. Worked in England and noted for his fine miniature portraits. His sons, Isaac the Younger and Peter, collaborated with him.

OLIVIER, AUBIN

(died 1581). French engraver of wood and metals. He was head of the royal mint. Died in Paris. Executed *Médaille de Henri II.*

OLIVIERI, MAFFEO

(1484-1534). Sculptor. Executed medallions: candelabra of St. Mark's.

OLIVIER VON SIENA

Physician. Logician. Wrote *Tractatus Rationalis Scientiae:* published in 1491.

OPITZ, MARTIN

(1597-1639). German poet, critic, and would-be reviver and refiner of German as a literary language. Fled to Holland to escape plague. Died of plague. Translated classical tests. Also wrote didactic poems, pastorals, translations, hymns. Founded first Silesian school of poets. Historiographer to King Ladislas IV of Poland. Author of *Aristarchussive de contemptu lingual teutonicae* in Latin: on the German language. Published in 1617. His translation into German of the libretti of *Daphne* by Rinuccini and of *Giuditta* by Salvadori is of the first importance for the history of German opera.

OPERA

The first composer to stamp his work indelibly on opera was Claudio Monteverdi (1567-1643). His major contributions were an increase in the effective use of harmony, the use of thematic material for scenic and histrionic description, and the introduction of a form of mezzo-recitativo.

First real opera, *Daphne,* libretto by Rinuccini, music by Caccini and Peri, was performed in 1597. These three men belonged to a circle of artists, musicians, and poets at Florence known as the Camerata, who reacted against the contrapuntalists and sought a remedy in Greek drama. The Camerati pondered Plato's words on music, and especially Aristoxenus' treatises, from which they derived a notion of music conveying the same sentiment as the words, a notion almost of program music. The recitatives and monody—as employed in *Daphne* and in opera ever since—were modeled on the declamation and monophony characteristic of Greek drama; the creation of the opera, the *"dramma per musica,"* by these musical Hellenists is a striking example of the creative power of the reborn classics.

ORATORIANS

A religious Order. Founded at San Girolamo, a parish church in Rome, in 1575, by St. Philip Neri (1515-1595). The Order consists of independent communities of priests living under obedience to a rule but without vows. The central objective is the salvation of souls by prayer, preaching, and administration of the sacraments.

ORATORIO

The first oratorio is considered to have been composed in 1600 by Italian composer Emilio del Cavaliere (c. 1550-1602) and was entitled *La rappresentazione di anima e di corpo.* The form grew out of the preacher St. Philip Neri's efforts to give dramatic force to his lectures and sermons on biblical history by the singing of lauds and hymns composed for the occasion; his sermons were delivered in the 1560's in the Church of San Girolamo, and the full designation of the new form is *rappresentazione per il oratorio.*

ORDÓÑEZ, BARTOLOMÉ

(died 1520). Spanish sculptor. Born at Burgos. Studied in Italy. Executed sepulchral statuary for the tombs of Cardinal Ximénes de Cisneros and of King Philip I (died 1508). He was an important link between Spain and the new art of Italy.

ORIENT
Among travelers to the Orient during the sixteenth century were these Portuguese: António Tenreiro, Frei Pantaleão de Aveiro (who traveled in the Holy Land), Pedro Paris, Manuel Barradas, António de Andrade.

ORLANDO FURIOSO
Ariosto's poem of *Orlando Furioso* produced, for some two centuries, many imitations and adaptations: notably the *Girone Cortese* of Luigi Alamanni, published in 1548, and the *Amadigi* of Bernardo Tasso (1493-1569), published in 1560.

ORLEY, BERNARD VAN
(c. 1490-1542). Flemish painter. Visited Rome twice. Introduced Italian artistic taste and style to Brussels. Imitated Michelangelo and Raphael, while retaining Flemish minute exactitude. Executed religious portraits, designs for tapestries, stained-glass windows. He also did many secular paintings, especially when he was court painter to Margaret of Austria and then Mary of Hungary, for whom he did many portraits.

ORRENTE, PEDRO
(c. 1570-1644). Spanish painter. Noted for the exact and detailed depiction of animals in his paintings, most of which are of religious subjects, also for his landscapes. Called the Spanish Bassano.

ORSINI FAMILY, THE
The ancient noble family of Rome that had played a foremost role in the political life of the city from the thirteenth through the sixteenth centuries; traditionally pro-papal and Guelph, the Orsini were the relentless antagonists of the Colonna. The two frequently plunged the city into blood baths. The family produced several popes, numerous ecclesiastics, soldiers, and statesmen; it still survives.

ORTA, GARCIA DA
Sixteenth century. Portuguese physician. Published, after years of medical practice in Goa, a study of medicinal plants of India in 1563. He was the first European to see and describe cholera.

ORTELIUS, ABRAHAM
(1527-1598). Abraham Ortel. Flemish cartographer: of German

parentage. Born at Antwerp. Author of *Theatrum Orbis Ter-rarum:* published in 1570. This atlas was used for a long time as a geographical source book. His friend and inspiration was the celebrated Mercator. He was appointed royal geographer by Philip II of Spain. He also wrote a *Thesaurus Geographicus.*

ORZECHKOWSKI, STANISLAW

(1513-1566). Polish humanist, statesman, and Roman Catholic priest. Author of political tracts defending Polish nobility, of one attacking priestly celibacy—although he was a zealous defender of the Church in Poland. He had studied both in Italy and Germany.

OSIANDER, ANDREAS

(1498-1552). German humanist, astronomer and religious reformer. In 1522, introduced Reformation in Nuremberg. Published Copernicus' *On the Motion of the Heavenly Bodies,* in 1543. Professor at Königsberg. Expounded his views on justification: resulting in Osiandrian controversy in Lutheran Church. Controversy spread from clergy to people. Finally settled on Formula of Concord, in 1577.

OSIANDER, LUCAS

(1534-1604). German Lutheran theologian, musician and propagandist at the court of Ludwig of Württemberg. He wrote an *Epitome* of the ecclesiastical history of the sixteenth century. He adapted polyphonic music for the services of the Lutheran Church in his book of chorales of 1586. It has been called the first German chorale book.

OSORIO, JERONIMO, BISHOP OF FONSECA

(1506-1580). Portuguese historian, theologian, called the Portuguese Cicero. He was educated at Paris and at Bologna. Author of *De Rebus Emmanuelis,* an account of the reign of King Manuel of Portugal. Published in 1571, it is vigorous in style and impartial in its point of view.

OSTROGSKI, KONSTANTIN VASILI

(1526-1608). Established first printing press in Poland and patronized the first Slavonic translation of the Bible, in 1581. Called Ostrog Bible.

OSTRORÓG, JAN

(1436-1501). Polish humanist and political writer. His subjects were universal military service, royal power, reforms. He had studied in Germany and Italy, to which he made several later visits.

OSUNA, FRANCISCO DE
(Died 1540). Spanish mystic. Franciscan. Author of *Tercer Abecedario*, published in 1527. Postulates self-denial and prayer as the way to union with God. He served as an official of the Spanish Empire, but found time to write a great number of pious and edifying works.

OUNDLE SCHOOL
English public school. Founded before Reformation. Endowed in 1566 by will of Sir William Laxton, Lord Mayor of London. Taken over by Grocers' Company in 1573.

OUWATER, AELBERT VAN
(died c. 1475). Dutch painter. Died in Haarlem. His work was chiefly religious, notable for its depiction of landscapes; he also did portraits. Only one of his works, *The Resurrection of Lazarus*, survives.

OVERBURY, SIR THOMAS
(1581-1613). English courtier and writer, favorite of James I. Associated with Earl of Somerset. Sent to Tower. Author of *Characters*: a collection of character sketches imitative of Theophrastus. Also: *Wife*, a poem, and *Crumbs Fallen from King James' Table*: a collection of sayings of the king. Fallen from favor, he was imprisoned in the Tower, where he was poisoned by his enemies.

OWEN, JOHN
(1560-1622). Welshman. Scholar and schoolmaster. Fellow of New College, Oxford, England. Called the British Martial. Noted for his Latinity. Author of *Epigrammata*: published in 1603-1613. They were translated into English, French, Spanish and German, and were best sellers in the early seventeenth century.

OXFORD, EDWARD DE VERE, EARL OF
(1550-1604). English poet. Courtier. In disfavor with Queen Elizabeth I. Author of miscellaneous poems and plays; he was both actor in and producer of plays as a member of the court circle of writers. He had traveled extensively in Italy.

P

PACCHIAROTTO, JACOPO
(1474-1540?). Italian painter of Siena. Implicated in a plot, he was forced to flee from Siena, but was subsequently allowed to return. His work is a fusion of many styles, e.g., of Perugino and Signorelli, which gives his painting a disparate character.

PACCIANTE, MICHELE
Author of *Catalogus Scriptorum Florentinorum*. Published in Florence in 1589.

PACE, RICHARD
(c. 1482-1536). English Dean of St. Paul's, friend and correspondent of Erasmus. On mission to Swiss in behalf of Henry VIII. Wrote an account of his embassy.

PACHECO, FRANCISCO
(c. 1564-1654). Spanish portrait and religious painter, father-in-law of Velásquez, author of an account of contemporary art and artists, *Arte de la pintura*.

PACHECO PEREIRA, DUARTE
(Late fifteenth—early sixteenth century). Portuguese explorer, conqueror, imperial official, geographer. Known as the Portuguese Achilles for his exploits in establishing the Portuguese Empire in India and China. He wrote a treatise on navigation along the West African coast, *Esmeraldo de Situ Orbis*, c. 1506, long used as a mariner's manual.

PACHER, MICHAEL

(c. 1440-1498). German painter, sculptor. Died in Salzburg. Leading artist of East Alpine Gothic school. Executed easel pictures, carvings for huge winged altars. His work shows Italian influence, particularly that of Mantegna.

PACIOLI (PACIOLA), LUCA

(c. 1450-1520). The greatest Italian of the age in the field of pure and applied mathematics, a Franciscan monk. The author of numerous works in mathematics; his treatise of 1494 was the first mathematical work to be printed. Enjoying Sforza patronage at Milan, Pacioli was the revered friend of Leonardo, who illustrated his book on *The Divine Proportion*. A more influential work was a treatise on the system of double entry bookkeeping. Pacioli's career at Milan testifies to the regard for mathematics and science there in contrast to the mystical and Platonic interests characteristic of Florence.

PACK, OTTO VON

(1480-1537). German diplomat and conspirator of Saxony who in 1528 forged a letter implying an attack on the Duke of Saxony by Catholic princes.

PADILLA, MARIA

(died 1531). Wife of Spanish revolutionary Juan López de Padilla. After death of husband, defended Toledo. When Toledo fell, she fled to Portugal. Appears in Spanish drama.

PADUA, UNIVERSITY OF

The greatest university of the age, traditionally a center for the study of medicine based on Galen. It became the citadel of Aristotelianism and nourished the development of science and scientific method; it was especially important in the evolution of astronomy, anatomy, and mechanics. While the Scholastic curriculum largely continued at Padua, as at almost all the universities of Europe, humanist methods of historical and textual criticism were soon known and practiced there. Associated with it as students or professors—and in many instances both—were Vesalius, Nicholas of Cusa, William Harvey, Copernicus, Galileo, Pomponazzi, and Zabarella. Padua was conquered by Venice in 1404; from then until the Counter Reformation the university enjoyed a remarkable degree of freedom from ecclesiastical supervision.

440

PAETUS, LUCAS
Sixteenth century. Italian jurist. Author of treatise on Roman law: *De Iudiciaria Formula Capitolini Fori:* published in 1587.

PAEZ XARAMILLO, PEDRO
(1564-1622). Portuguese chronicler, Jesuit. Missionary to Abyssinia. Author of a *History of Ethiopia;* important as account of Ethiopian history, geography, and languages.

PAGANISM IN THE RENAISSANCE
That there were pagan elements in the Renaissance is undeniable. It is, however, by no means typical or dominant, even in Italy. Much that is taken to be paganism was little more than anti-clericalism and was not new or peculiar to the Renaissance. Petrarch himself had a vision of a fusion of Christianity and the classical spirit. His followers may have ignored that aspect of his teaching in their concentration on the classics, but the humanists could hardly be designated as anti-Christian; the strongest construction that can be put on their position is that they insisted on one world at a time. In northern Europe the moral and Christian character of the Renaissance—typified by Erasmus—is obvious. The notion put forth by Gilson that the Renaissance is the middle ages minus God will not stand analysis; he had his mind on the present age and its dilemmas or shortcomings, not on the past. At present the tendency in historical studies is often to the other extreme, viz., to deny pagan elements in the Renaissance entirely by explaining away the lusty paganism of Boccaccio, Poggio, Valla, Aretino, Pulci, Rabelais, etc.

PAINTER, WILLIAM
(c. 1540-1594). English compiler of *Palace of Pleasure*: a miscellany consisting of the chief French and Italian novels, e.g., Boccaccio. Published in 1566-1567. It was a source book of plots for English dramatists, including Shakespeare.

PAINTING OF THE FIELD OF CLOTH OF GOLD
This painting was executed by Hans Holbein (1497-1543). Canvas preserved in the Museum of Versailles.

PALEARIO, AONIO
(1503-1570). Italian humanist, professor of Greek and Latin literature at Lucca, then at Milan. Imbued with Lutheran-Zwinglian ideas, he was accused of heresy, tried by the Inquisition, and

burnt at the stake. Author of didactic poem, *De Immortalitate Animarum,* published in 1536.

PALESTRINA, GIOVANNI PIERLUIGI DA

(c. 1525-1594). The greatest composer of the century, the genius of vocal counterpoint. He spent most of his life as organist and choirmaster to various churches in Rome, under papal patronage. A prolific composer of religious music, including masses, motets, madrigals, and settings for *The Song of Solomon,* his works are notable for their simplicity of construction and profound religiosity of feeling. Not an innovator, he rather sums up the development of polyphonic music that had gone on in the century-and-a-half preceding his birth. His preference for simplicity and religious purity was stimulated partly by the Council of Trent; during the Counter Reformation it was felt that all ecclesiastical music had to be purged of profane or secular elements. There were Trentine decrees to that effect. The Council frowned upon intricate polyphonic music, but in the end did not issue any decree on the subject. The complexity and sensuousness of Palestrina's earlier compositions are not to be found in those of his later years.

PALISSY, BERNARD

(c. 1509-1589). French ceramic artist. Invented Palissy ware c. 1545. Wrote autobiography. Also wrote on scientific, agricultural, religious subjects. He set out deliberately to refashion ceramics, both artistically and technologically; hence his scientific studies as well as his study of classical ceramic art. He enjoyed the patronage of the French court.

PALLADIO, ANDREA

(1518-1580). Italian architect. Based his work on ancient Roman principles, particularly those of Vitruvius in his *De Architectura,* and those he derived from his study and sketches of surviving Roman structures. The Palladian style may be characterized as one of classical grandeur and restraint; its cardinal principle being perfect symmetry. He was the most influential architect of the last four centuries in Europe and America; his *Villa Rotonda* of Vicenza was the model and archetype for public and private buildings from Inigo Jones and Sir Christopher Wren to Jefferson's *Monticello* and the Columbia University *Rotunda.*

PALMA, JACOPO, IL VECCHIO

(c. 1480-1528). Italian painter. Belonged to Venetian school. Works include *The Three Sisters, Sleeping Venus, Adam and Eve*. Noted for altar figures, half-figure painting, mundane women, religious genre. Made significant use of color. His son and namesake, Il GIOVANE, 1544-1628, was also a painter of religious subjects. He was influenced by Michelangelo and Titian.

PALMIERI, MATTEO

(1406-1475). Florentine humanist and exponent of humanist education, public official. In the course of his life he held practically every office in the Florentine government and served frequently on embassies. He wrote several historical works, including a history of the world to 1446, of Florence, of the Pisan war of 1406. He also wrote a dialogue on the good citizen and a doctrinal poem, *La citta de vita*, where he fell into theological error by following Origen on the nature of Christ. He ran into difficulties with the Church on those grounds. He typifies the humanist concern to fuse the active and the contemplative life.

PALSGRAVE, JOHN

(c. 1480-1554). English humanist and grammarian. Compiled French-English dictionary and grammar, one of the first intended for English readers, published in 1530. He translated a number of Italian works into English.

PÄMINGER, LEONARD

(1495-1567). Austrian musician and composer of polyphonic music; his four volumes of motets cover the cycle of the liturgy for one year of the Lutheran Church. He wrote German and Latin songs and hymns.

PÄMINGER, SOPHONIA

(1526-1603). Austrian poet, son of the above. Author of poems of local Italian and German events and celebrities: on music, oracles, epigrams, enigmas, epitaphs, lyrics. Collection of poetry, *Poematum Libri Duo*, published in 1557. He was a schoolmaster of Ratisbon, where he carried out a reform of the teaching of Latin along humanist lines. He published his father's music.

PAMPILION

A fur used for trimming garments. The expression was in use in the fifteenth and sixteenth centuries. In the sixteenth century pampilion also meant a *coarse woolen fabric*.

PANGIAROLA, FRANCESCO
Sixteenth century. Cleric of Milan. Wrote account of death of Cardinal Carlos Borromeo of Milan (died 1584).

PANION
An abbreviated form of *companion*. A term in use in the sixteenth century.

PANNONIA, SONG OF THE CONQUEST OF
A Hungarian narrative poem. Appeared in 1526.

PANNONIUS, JANUS
(1434-1472). Hungarian poet and humanist. Achieved wide recognition as one of the finest Latin poets of the Renaissance. He had studied at Ferrara, as one of Guarino's students, and at Padua. He knew Greek and made several translations of Greek authors. He is one of the earliest and most important figures for the introduction of humanist learning into Hungary.

PANTOJA DE LA CRUZ, JUAN
(c. 1550-1608). Spanish painter. Court painter to Philip II and Philip III. Painted religious subjects, portraits. Executed a *Nativity* and a portrait of Philip II.

PAPON, JEAN
(1505-1590). French jurist and humanist. Master of Petitions under Catherine de' Medici. Compiled collection of decrees relating to French civil and criminal law. He wrote a work in praise of "two princes of eloquence," Demosthenes and Cicero.

PARACELSISTS
Adherents to the medical theories of Paracelsus were, in Germany: Adam von Bodenstein (died 1576), Michael Schutz, Michael Doring (died 1644): in Italy, Peter Severinus (1540-1570).

PARACELSUS, THEOPHRASTUS BOMBASTUS VON HOHENHEIM
(c. 1493-1541). Self-taught and self-made physician, born in Zurich where he studied under his father. He was an indefatigable and inquisitive traveler who, in the course of his wanderings, took a degree at Ferrara, 1515. Anti-medieval and anti-Greek, he was the iconoclast *par excellence* of the older scientific traditions; he aroused strong distrust and criticism by his bombast and arrogance, going so far, when he was physician to

the city of Basel, as to publicly burn the works of Galen and other authorities, including the Arabs. Championing observation and empirical methods, he did much to point the way to the application of chemistry to medicine and to the development of homeopathic medicine; there are, however, some medieval cobwebs and oddities peculiar to his medical theories. He is chiefly important for having cleared the way for the development of medicine beyond the limits attained by the ancients; by his time the ancients had taught all they could to Europe, and reverence thereafter for their texts could only hinder medical science. His Latinized name may refer to his birthplace or have been intended to boast his superiority to the ancient Greek medical authority, Celus. Rubens painted his portrait.

PARADIN OF CUYSEAULX
(died 1573). Author of emblem book. Deals with emblems of monarchs and political leaders, among them Henry II and Louis XII of France, and Philip of Burgundy. Published in 1563.

PARÉ, AMBROISE
(c. 1519-1590). Prominent French barber-surgeon. Worked in military surgery. In 1545 he published a treatise on the care of gunshot wounds in which he described his use of ligatures and dressings instead of the usual cauterization by fire; he knew no Latin and therefore was less influenced by the texts. He utilized Vesalius' *De Fabrica* extensively. It was still somewhat novel to insist that a surgeon know anatomy. Called the Father of Modern Surgery. Greatest surgeon of the Renaissance. Surgeon to Henry II and Francis II and Charles IX. His *Deux Livres de Chirurgie* appeared in 1573. His fame spread throughout France. He had many critics and wrote his *Déverse Places* as an apologia.

PARKER, MATTHEW
(1504-1575). English cleric, scholar, court chaplain, Archbishop of Canterbury. Tried to reconcile the religious left and right to the *via media* of Anglicanism. Made a revised translation of the Bible called Bishops' Bible, published in 1572. Edited early English chronicles, e.g., Matthew of Paris. Author of *De Antiquitate Britannicae Ecclesiae,* which assumes an "Anglican Church" in the Middle Ages.

PARKHURST, JOHN
(1512-1577). Bishop of Norwich. Author of Latin epigrams.

PARMIGIANO, IL, FRANCESCO MAZZOLA

(1503-1540). Italian painter and etcher, member of the Lombard school and profoundly influenced, first, by Correggio and then Raphael. The sack of Rome in 1527 caused him to flee to Bologna and then to his native Parma, where he lived out his life in poverty. He did religious frescoes and portraits and is credited with having introduced etching to Italy.

PARR, CATHERINE

(1512-1548). Sixth wife of Henry VIII. Actively attempted elimination of religious persecution and interceded in behalf of his daughters, Mary and Elizabeth, whom he pronounced illegitimate. She is said to have been accomplished in Greek, Latin and modern languages.

PARR, THOMAS

(c. 1483-1635). Called Old Parr. Said to have been longest-lived Englishman.

PARRASIO, AULO GIANO

(1470-1534). Italian humanist scholar. Discovered many classical manuscripts, including some of Dracontius, Charisius, Sedulius, and Prudentius, in the monastery of Bobbio and another monastery near Milan. Author of text on rhetoric, including survey of classical orators: *Breviarium Rhetorices*: published in 1509.

PARREUT, JOHANNES

(died 1495). German philosopher, physician of Bayreuth. Associated with University of Ingolstadt, where he was professor of medicine. Author of *Textus Veteris Artis*: published at Ingolstadt in 1492, it is a commentary on Aristotle's *Organon*.

PARSONS, ROBERT

(1546-1610). English Jesuit. Associated with Cardinal Allen and Edmund Campion. Conspired to restore England to Papacy. Fled to Continent. Founded Catholic seminaries in Spain, France for the training of English priests. He has a place in the history of political thought, for he urged the rights of the governed against the governor.

PASQUIER, JEAN

(1529-1615). French antiquary, poet, student of Roman law, and friend of Montaigne. Wrote on French archaeology, literature, religious institutions, politics: *Recherche de la France*.

PASQUINADE
Name given to lampoons and satires on public figures in Italy; these vilifications were fastened to an antique statue in Rome that had been given the name Pasquino, an outspoken schoolmaster. Pietro Aretino's first scourgings of princes were pasquinades mocking the Cardinals of the Church.

PASQUINO DI MATTEO DE MONTE PULCIANO
(Born c. 1435). Italian sculptor. The tomb of Pope Pius II is attributed to him. His work shows the influence of Donatello.

PASSAROTTI, BARTOLOMEO
(1530-1592). Painter and engraver of Bologna. Noted for his portraits, he also did religious paintings.

PASSERAT, JEAN
(1534-1602). French classical scholar and poet, held the Chair of Eloquence at the Collège de France. Member of *La Pléiade*. Wrote poems on classical subjects, eulogies of France, edited and commented upon Catullus, Tibullus and Propertius.

PASSI, PIETRO
(Sixteenth century). Italian writer. Author of an assertion of the existence of natural magic, Passi was a member of the Order of the Camalotese. The book was largely a repetition of arguments put forward in the 1490's by Pedro García to contradict Pico's position. It was assumed that magic existed but could be used only by demonic powers. Passi's work was published in Venice in 1614.

PASTON, JOHN
(1421-1466). English country gentleman. His family associated with village of Paston, in Norfolk. Collection of their letters and family papers reveals social and domestic conditions in fifteenth-century England. Other members of the family were his father, WILLIAM (1378-1444), "the Good Judge," who established the family fortune, and the son, SIR JOHN (1442-1479), letter-writer and Yorkist courtier.

PASTORAL NOVEL
One of the best pastoral trilogies was written by the Portuguese Francisco Rodrigues Lobo: *Spring*, published in 1601, *Pilgrim Shepherd*, in 1608, *Disillusioned*, in 1614. Poems are interpolated in the narratives.

PATENT
World's first patent was granted in Venice to German printer John of Speyer in 1469.

PATER PATRIAE
Title conferred on Cosimo (1434-1464), member of the Medici family.

PATINIER, JOACHIM
(c. 1475-1524). Flemish painter. He was a friend of Dürer, who painted his portrait. Died in Antwerp. Executed religious paintings with broad landscape backgrounds. He was chiefly concerned with landscapes and he succeeded in conveying the sense of great vistas sweeping over vast expanses; so much was he concerned with landscape that his figures are frequently dwarfed by it—many of them he did not paint himself but had them inserted in the scenes he had executed.

PATRICIUS, FRANCISCUS or PATRIZZI
(1413-1492). Bishop of Gaëta, and humanist. Friend of Aeneas Silvius Piccolomini. Wrote Latin poetry; *De Institutione Reipublicae Libri Novem*: moral-political analysis of education of princes: encyclopedic in character. Published in 1518. He is chiefly important for his *Epitome* of Quintilian.

PATRIZZI, FRANCESCO
(1529-1597). Ferrarese humanist, philosopher, mathematician, historian, soldier, orator and poet; he was educated at Padua. Wrote on Roman military theory and practice: a synthesis of Polybius, Livy, and Dionysius of Halicarnassus. Published in 1583. Entitled *La Militia Romana*. His chief work was *Discussiones Peripateticae* in which he attacks the life and writings of Aristotle, for Patrizzi was an ardent Platonist and expounded Plato's philosophy as professor of the Sapienza at Rome. He took up the cudgels again in his *Della Poetica,* in which he attacks the *Poetics* and in the course of his polemic wrote a pioneer work of literary history and criticism.

PAUL II
(1417-1471). Pope 1464-1471. In conflict with Turks. Supported Skanderbeg, defender of Western Christianity. During his pontificate attempt was made to unite Russian Orthodox and Roman Catholic Churches. Without classical culture, he was neverthe-

less interested in art and printing. Founded papal publishing house, Libreria Editrice Vaticana. He sought to make the papal court a center of splendor and magnificence. His fears of paganism and suspicion of humanists or republicans led him to abolish the Roman Academy, 1468; it was restored by his successors.

PAUL III, ALEXANDER FARNESE
(1468-1549). Pope 1534-1549. In many respects he was a typical Renaissance pope: nepotist, luxurious liver amid the splendor of his magnificent Farnese Palace, and sly and opportunistic prince more skilled in politics and diplomacy than pious works. However, by initiating the Council of Trent, sanctioning the Society of Jesus and spurring the investigations of the Inquisition, he can be said to be the first of the Counter Reformation popes. He had sought to include the Lutherans in the Council.

PAUL IV
(1476-1559). Pope, 1555-1559. As Cardinal Carafa he had been the leader of the Reform Party within the College of Cardinals. He was austere in his private life and purged the Roman hierarchy of unworthy men, including his own nephew. In conflict with Spain. Opposed to Queen Elizabeth I. Suppressed simony. Ruthlessly gave free rein and support to Inquisition. His suspicions caused intellectual activities and arts to languish. Banned Ariosto's *Orlando Furioso*. He had founded Order of Theatines.

PAUL V
(1552-1621). Pope. Pious, but reputation damaged by nepotism. Provoked hostility of England, France. In conflict with Venice. Increased Vatican Library. Accused by James I of England of organizing Gunpowder Plot in 1605.

PAULUS PERGULENSIS
Fifteenth century. Logician. Author of a *Compendium:* published in Venice in 1498.

PAVISE
A shield large enough to protect the entire body. In use during the fourteenth, fifteenth, sixteenth centuries.

PÁZMÁNY, PETER
(1570-1637). Hungarian cleric, Jesuit. Leader of Counter Reformation movement in Hungary. With Hapsburg backing, he was successful in restoring Catholicism after Calvinism had made

449

great headway in Hungary. He founded many monastic and educational institutions in Hungary, and was a tireless propagandist.

PAZZI CONSPIRACY OF EASTER SUNDAY, APRIL 26, 1478

Took place in the cathedral of Florence against Medici rule. The plot grew out of the territorial ambitions of Pope Sixtus IV who sought to bestow the strategic Imola (in the Romagna) on his nephew. Lorenzo the Magnificent's opposition angered the pope, and around him, if not with his active involvement, the plot was woven. The principals were the pope's nephew, Girolamo Riario, the Florentine Pazzi family, rival bankers of the Medici, and Archbishop Salviati of Pisa. At the raising of the Host during the Mass, Lorenzo and his brother, Giuliano, were attacked; Giuliano was killed, Lorenzo managed to escape. Efforts to seize the government palace (Palazzo Vecchio) and to rally the people against the Medici failed. Spontaneously the people took up the cause of Lorenzo and inflicted the severest reprisals on the plotters: the Archbishop and Francesco Pazzi were hanged from the windows of the Palazzo and others were done to death in the most brutal fashion by mobs. Sixtus followed by excommunicating Lorenzo, imposing an interdict on Florence, and, with his ally Naples, invaded Tuscany. Florence's allies, Milan and Venice, were involved in difficulties of their own and so Florence stood alone. Two desperate years passed before Lorenzo succeeded in detaching Naples—he himself went secretly to Naples —from the papal alliance and making peace with each party separately. Thereafter Lorenzo's position was unchallenged and the Medici ascendancy strengthened.

PEACHAM, HENRY

(c. 1576-c. 1643). English writer, painter, musician. Author of *Graphice*: on art techniques. Published in 1606. His best known book is in the tradition of the Renaissance man of many talents and accomplishments and the courtier of many graces; it is entitled *The Compleat Gentleman*.

PEASANTS' WAR

The Protestant Reformation aroused great hope, especially among the depressed peasantry of Central Europe. The peasants converted the spiritual Reformation into an economic and social protest. In Bavaria, unorganized revolt against the German feudal system broke out, spreading through Southern Germany to

Franconia and Swabia. The peasants proposed Twelve Articles, which called for the end of serfdom and manorial dues. Revolt suppressed with violence, after extreme excesses on the part of the German nobles. The peasants were defeated at Königshofen in 1525. Luther, who detested rebellion and revolution against what he took to be the divinely ordained state, urged the princes to put the peasants down, that "Whoever can, should smite, strangle, or stab, secretly or publicly." The war arrested the spread of Lutheranism with the result that south Germany remained predominantly Catholic.

PECOCK, REGINALD, BISHOP OF CHICHESTER
(1395?-1461?). Welshman. Author of *The Repressor of Over Much Blaming of the Clergy*. Preached against church reform, against Lollards. Recanted in 1457. Died while confined in abbey. His historical studies led him to conclude that the Apostles' Creed was not authentic, that the Donation of Constantine was a fraud.

PEDERSEN, CHRISTIAN
(1480-1554). Danish scholar. Wrote in Danish a *History of Denmark*. He studied in Paris; compiled a Danish-Latin dictionary. He managed a printing press at Malmo where he published the *Chronicle of Holger Dansk* and other works. Translated the Psalms of David and the New Testament. Co-editor of a first translation of the Bible into Danish, under the auspices of King Christian III.

PEDRO DE MEDINA
(Born c. 1493). Spanish cosmologist and cartographer. *The Art of Navigation,* an illustrated manual, published in 1545, was the most famous of his many works; it was translated into English, Italian, and German, and went through many editions.

PEELE, GEORGE
(c. 1558-c. 1597). English dramatist, poet. Author of *King Edward I:* chronicle play. *Arraignment of Paris:* masque. *Sir Clyoman and Sir Clamydes. David and Bethsabe*: in blank verse and prose. *The Old Wives' Tale. Battle of Alcazar*. He was a member of the circle known as the University Wits that included Marlowe and Nashe.

PEIRESE, NICHOLAS CLAUDIUS FABRICIUS
(1580-1637). French scientist and disciple of Galileo under whom

he studied at Padua. Aside from important work in astronomy and its use in determining longitude, he was learned in the humanities and particularly interested in numismatics. He was one of the most learned men of his day. At his death, eulogies in forty languages were published in his memory, in 1638. The languages employed included Chaldaic, Syriac, Hebrew, Arabic, Persian, Turkish, Georgian, Ethiopian, Coptic, Greek, Russian, Hungarian, Provençal, Portuguese.

PELBART DE TEMESVÁR
(c. 1435-1504). Hungarian Franciscan friar. Preacher. Author of ecclesiastical works in Latin.

PELETIER DU MANS, JACQUES
(1517-1582). French humanist, poet. Produced many translations, among them Horace's *Ars Poetica*, in 1545; it has been said that literary criticism in France has its beginning only with the publication of this translation. Friend of Ronsard and *La Pléiade*. Also a mathematician. Wrote text on algebra: published in 1554.

PELLEGRINO DA MARIANO
(Died 1492). Italian painter, illuminator. His *Chorales* are preserved in the Piccolomini Library in Siena.

PELLEGRINO DA MODENA
(c. 1463-1523). Italian painter of Modena who worked there, in Ferrara and Rome. He worked principally in churches, religious frescoes.

PELLEGRINO DA MONTICHIARI
(Born c. 1520). Italian lutanist and lute maker of Brescia; he is credited with the earliest conception of the violin.

PELLEGRINO DA SAN DANIELE
(c. 1467-1547). Italian painter. He painted the frescoes of the *duomo* of his native Udine. He also worked at Farrara. His paintings are almost exclusively religious in subject matter and devout in execution.

PEMBROKE COLLEGE
Oxford University. Founded in 1624 and named for George Herbert, Third Earl of Pembroke, who was Chancellor of Oxford at the time.

PEMBROKE, MARY HERBERT, COUNTESS OF

(1561-1621). Patroness of poets, e.g., Jonson and Spenser. Sister of Sir Philip Sidney; he dedicated his *Arcadia* to her. She wrote one volume of poems, *Antonius*.

PEMBROKE, WILLIAM HERBERT, FIRST EARL OF

(c. 1501-1570). Governor of Calais. Influential in diplomatic circles. Wife was sister of Catherine Parr, Henry VIII's last wife.

PEMBROKE, WILLIAM HERBERT, THIRD EARL OF

(1580-1630). Son of Mary, Countess of Pembroke, and nephew of Sir Philip Sidney, courtier and poet. Scholars have identified him as the "Mr. W. H." to whom Shakespeare dedicated his sonnets, and his mistress, Mary Fitton, as the Dark Lady of the Sonnets.

PENA, JEAN

(c.1527-1558). French mathematician. Royal professor in Paris. Attached to French court. Wrote on optics. Edited Euclid's text on optics, with Latin translation. He asserted that interplanetary space was an empty void, still a rather daring position in his time.

PENCZ, GEORG

(c. 1500-1550). German painter, engraver, assistant to Dürer. Born in Nuremberg. Died in Leipzig. Executed portraits, allegorical subjects, mythological pieces, copperplate engravings; he did a remarkable set of engravings of scenes from the Old Testament. His work shows Italian influence, viz., Bronzino and Giulio Romano.

PENDASIUS, FEDERICUS

(Died c. 1604). Professor at Padua and Bologna. Mantuan philosopher. Wrote *De Natura Corporum Coelestium*, published in 1555. On planets, motion of earth, meteors; it is interesting in that it shows no knowledge (not even mention) of Copernicus or any of the newer cosmological ideas.

PENDULUM

Isochronism observed in 1582 and time-keeping mechanism based upon it was invented in 1641 by Galileo Galilei.

PENNI, GIANFRANCESCO

(c. 1488-c. 1528). Italian painter. Pupil of Raphael, whom he assisted in frescoes for the Loggia and Stanze of the Vatican. He later worked with Giulio Romano; he never achieved greatness.

PENRY, JOHN
(1559-1593). Welsh pamphleteer. He became an ardent Puritan while at Oxford and Cambridge. He was probably the chief author of the *Martin Marprelate* pamphlets, 1588-89; they were a defense of Presbyterianism and a strong attack upon the Anglican clergy. He was accused of treason and hanged.

PERERIUS, BENEDICTUS
(1535-1610). Jesuit of Valencia. He was the author of two important treatises, *De Magia* and *De communibus omnium rerum naturalium principiis*, on magic, astrology, alchemy, divination by dreams; while he denied astrology any efficacy, he acknowledged existence of magic and thought transmutation of metals was possible. His second work had particular reference to Aristotle's *Physics* and was probably used as a textbook in teaching Aristotelian science in the Jesuit schools. It was reprinted many times after its publication in 1562.

PERESVETOV, IVAN SEMONOVIC
(First half of the sixteenth century). Russian publicist who came to Muscovite Court, c. 1538. During the 1540's, he was active as a writer. Produced political tracts advocating strengthening the power of the Tsar at the expense of nobility. He anticipated some of later reforms of Ivan the Terrible.

PÉREZ DE HITA, GINÉS
(1544?-1619?). Spanish historian, poet, novelist. Life obscure. Participated in war against Moors: 1568-1571. Wrote versified adaptation of the Trojan War entitled *Bello Troyano*: 1592. Chief work is *Historia de los Bandos de los Zegríes y Abencerrajes:* usually called *Guerras Civiles de Granada*. One of first historical novels in Spanish literature and one of first Moorish romance cycles, it is the story of the fall of Granada in 1492. Popular in Spain and abroad. Inspired Mlle. de Scudéry; Mme. de la Fayette, Chateaubriand, and Washington Irving.

PERI, JACOPO
(1561-1633). Florentine composer, singer, and member of the Camerata group, the circle round Court Bardi that reacted

against the overly intricate polyphonic music; inspired by ancient Greek drama, he and Caccini created the first opera, *Daphne*, 1597, the libretto of which was by Rinuccini. His opera *Euridice* appeared in 1600.

PERINO DEL VAGA

(1499-1547). Italian painter. Belongs to school of Raphael, whom he assisted in painting the Loggia of the Vatican. With the sack of Rome of 1527 he fled to Genoa, where he decorated the palaces of the Doria, rulers of the city, but returned to Rome in the time of Paul III.

PERION, JOACHIM

(1499-1559). French classical scholar and philologist. Benedictine father. Professor of theology at the University of Paris. Made attempts to improve the Latinity of contemporary theological literature, modeling himself on Cicero. Author of *De Rebus Gestis Vitisque Apostolorum Liber*, a study of the origin of French, and numerous theological and religious works, and a great many translations, e.g., of Aristotle, Demosthenes, St. John of Damascus, etc.

PERKINS, WILLIAM

(1558-1602). English theologian of Christ's College, Cambridge. Author of *Armilla Aurea*, a theological treatise that went through fifteen editions and was translated into Spanish and Dutch. He was strongly Calvinist.

PEROTTI, NICCOLO

(1430-1480). Italian humanist, classical scholar, ecclesiastic. Translated Polybius and Epictetus and edited Pliny the Elder, Martial, Varro, Sextus Pempeius and Nonius Marcellus. Produced first modern treatise on Latin prosody, entitled *Metrica*. Also modern Latin grammar: *Rudimenta Grammatices*, published in 1468. He was also an excellent Greek scholar, having studied under Guarino and Bessarion.

PERRÉAL, JEAN or JEAN DE PARIS

(c. 1455-c. 1528). French painter, miniaturist. Worked in Lyons, Moulins. Royal painter to Charles VIII, Louis XII, Francis I. Noted for fresco of *The Liberal Arts*. He is thought to have followed Charles VIII's army into Italy in 1494 and been charged by the king to paint a series on the principal battles; he is thus one link between the new art of Italy and France.

PERSE SCHOOL
Cambridge, England. Founded by the will of Stephen Perse (c. 1548-1615).

PERUGINO, PIETRO VANNUCCI
(1446-1524). Italian painter. Headed Umbrian school in early Renaissance period. Taught Raphael. Worked in Perugia, Florence, Rome. Works include frescoes, portraits, *Crucifixion*, *Pietà*, *Vision of St. Bernard*. He was a close student of perspective, as may be judged by his fresco of *Christ presenting the Keys to St. Peter;* he was one of the earliest Italians to paint in oils.

PERUZZI, BALDASSARE
(1481-1536). Italian painter, architect. Attached to court of Pope Leo X. Worker mostly at Rome, where he built palaces and villas. One of these was the Farnese Palace, built for the banker, Agostino Chigi, in which he sought to follow the description of the palace of the sun in Ovid's *Metamorphoses;* his Massimo Palace is notable for its curved façade, coinciding with the bend of the street.

PESARO
Italian centre of book illumination during Renaissance. Produced codices for dukes of Urbino, who were its rulers until it passed into the control of the papacy. Pesaro was also a ceramic center.

PÉTAU, DENYS
(1583-1652). French scholar. Latinized name: Dionysius Petavius. Theologian. Jesuit. Professor of theology at Paris. Wrote *Opus de Doctrina Temporum:* published in 1627.

Author of some fifty works on theology, history, philology; he was chiefly important for his editions of the later Greek Fathers.

PETER OF ALCANTARA, SAINT
(1499-1562). Spanish cleric, mystic and monastic reformer. Founded the Alcantarines, branch of the Franciscan Order, that spread from Spain to Portugal and Kingdom of Naples. He wrote a manual on prayer and meditation.

PETER SYMONDS SCHOOL
In Winchester. English public school. Founded by the London merchant Peter Symonds in 1607.

PETRARCA, FRANCESCO or PETRARCH

(1304-1374). Italian scholar and poet, "the first humanist". He was born in Arezzo of Florentine parents; his father was a friend and political colleague of Dante, to whom Petrarch was presented at least once in childhood. Exiled at the same time as Dante, 1302, the family took refuge in Arezzo, Pisa, and finally Avignon when the father joined the papal service. Petrarch thus grew up in southern France; his father intending him for the law, he went to the University of Montpellier and later continued law studies at Bologna. In 1326 his parents died and he (and his brother Gherardo) was free to do as he pleased: this was the end of his law studies: he gave himself up to the Latin classics and to poetry. Living the life of an amorous young blade, and probably employed in the papal service, he saw Laura at Mass, 1327, and his famous obsession began. To distract himself he traveled—to Rome, the Lowlands, Germany, possibly England; he went on nature hikes and became the first great Alpinist. The love of nature shines forth in much that he wrote. Laura, ignoring his pleas to the end, died in the plague of 1348; by then Petrarch had entered minor orders (chiefly to assure himself of an income), fathered two illegitimate children (whom he educated, provided for, and had legitimized), and poured forth his love for Laura in his immortal Italian sonnets, the *Canzoniere*. These songs were the first thing to bring him fame, signified by his coronation as poet laureate by a Roman Senator in 1341; he proceeded to exploit his fame as poet in order to gain celebrity for his personality and his ideas. Thus his European acclaim (and his persuasive Latin style) insured a sympathetic reception for his ideal of "eloquence," his conceptions of virtú, fama, individuality, and personal glory as well as his exaltation of the classics and the ancient Roman world; it also assured a widespread imitation of his efforts to collect ancient manuscripts, coins, and inscriptions as well as of his devotion to Cicero; and it also would bring eager agreement with his condemnation of philosophy and dialectic, medicine, science, and law as they were then understood, his commendation of the study of Greek, and his lyric apologies for the life of the scholar and man of letters. Not only did this culture hero gain an ardent welcome for these ideas and practices, but he shaped them into a single movement that came to dominate the culture of the age: to have established the vogue and ideology of classical antiquity and humanistic studies was Petrarch's most

457

significant achievement. In this sense he was "the founder of the Renaissance".

Petrarch has been called variously the first modern man, scholar, and literary artist; that such estimates are exaggerated, that instead he was the Italian Janus, may be concluded from this statement in his *Secretum*—his introspective spiritual autobiography in the form of a dialogue that pits Petrarch against a censorious St. Augustine: "There is a certain justification for my way of life. It may be only glory that we seek here, but I persuade myself that, so long as we remain here, that is right. Another glory awaits us in heaven and he who reaches there will not wish even to think of earthly fame. So this is the natural order, that among mortals the care of things mortal should come first; to the transitory will then succeed the eternal; from the first to the second is the natural progression." His works include the unfinished Latin epic celebrating the Roman victory over Carthage, *Africa;* his biographical essays on famous Romans, *Lives of Illustrious Men;* his letters to ancient authors, e.g., Homer, Cicero, Vergil, and Livy; his personal *Letters,* which are numerous and of great importance as historical sources; and his treatises *On Solitude, On Contempt for the Worldly Life,* and *On his own Ignorance and that of Many Others.* Among his patrons were Cardinal Colonna, the Visconti of Milan, and the city of Venice; but for the most part he remained a free-lance scholar and poet. It was he who designated the Avignon papacy as "the Babylonian Captivity", urging the Popes to return to Rome; his classical enthusiasms led him to support Cola di Rienzi's republican revolution at Rome.

PETRAMELLARIUS, IACOBUS or GIACOMO PIETRAMELLERA
(Early sixteenth century). Professor of astronomy and astrology at the University of Bologna, apologist for astrology.

PETRI, BERNARDINUS
Sixteenth century. Logician. Belongs to Sienese school. Wrote commentary on Hentisberus: published in Naples in 1514.

PETRI, LAURENTIUS
(1499-1573). Became the first Lutheran Archbishop of Sweden, in 1531. He sought to resist royal encroachments on the liberties and prerogatives of the Church. Contributed homiletical and devotional material, Bible translation, hymns, liturgies to the development of the Lutheran Church in Sweden.

PETRI, OLAVUS

(1493-1552). Spiritual leader of Reformation in Sweden. Introduced reforms in Swedish Church and state, with the backing of King Gustavus Vasa. Produced devotional literature, Bible translation, apologetic treatises, Swedish Mass, Swedish Hymn Book, historical works. Exerted great influence on succeeding generations in Swedish Lutheran Church. Author of prose history of Sweden.

PETRUCCI, OTTAVIANO DE

(1466-1539). Italian, the first printer of music. He was established at Venice and Rome, and was noted for the beauty and accuracy of his editions.

PETRUS BRUXELLENSIS

(died 1514). Logician. Author of *Quaestiones:* on Aristotle's *Organon.* Published in Paris in 1514. Also *Quodlibeta:* a commentary on Petrus Hispanus.

PETRUS DE AQUILA

Sixteenth century. Logician. Author of *Scotellus:* a commentary on Petrus Lombardus: published in Paris in 1585.

PETRUS MANTUANUS

Fifteenth century. Logician. Author of *Logica:* published in Venice in 1492.

PETRUS PEREGRINUS

Author of *Epistula de Magnete.* Published in 1558.

PETRUS TARTARETUS

Late fifteenth century. Logician. Wrote commentary on the *Physics* and *Ethics* of Aristotle. Published in Paris in 1494.

PETTIE, GEORGE

(1548-1589). English writer of romances, and translator. Author of *A Petite Palace of Pettie his Pleasure.*

PEUCER, KASPAR

(1525-1602). German humanist, physician and philosopher. Wrote on divination, oracles, lot-casting, chiromancy: *Commentarius de Praecipuis Divinatonum Generibus,* published in 1593. He was professor at Wittenberg and succeeded to Melanchthon's position of leadership among the Lutherans upon the latter's death.

PEUERBACH, GEORG VON

(1423-1469). Austrian astronomer, mathematician, and humanist. Professor at Vienna. Author of *Theoricae Novae Planetarum*, published c. 1472. Also wrote on trigonometry. He traveled extensively in Italy—and studied at Padua—France and Germany; in addition to his scientific specialties he lectured on Horace, Juvenal, and the *Aeneid*. His student was Regiomontanus, and they have been said to have been "the first to expound the Latin poets in Vienna," and thus did much to establish the vogue of classicism in Germany.

PEUTINGER, KONRAD

(1465-1547). German antiquary, historian, geographer. Owned famous copy of ancient Roman military map: called *Peutingerian Table;* it is twenty-one feet in length. He was an enthusiastic collector of manuscripts, coins, and inscriptions; he was instrumental in the publication of an anthology of Greek and Latin inscriptions that appeared in 1534. Wrote *Sermones de Germaniae Antiquitatibus*. He served the Fuggers as a legal adviser.

PEY DE GARROS

(c. 1500-1581). Provençal satirical poet and literary critic. Translated Psalms into Gascon in 1565. In 1567 he published a volume of his poems, *Poesies Gasconnes*, dedicated to the King of Navarre; it includes a series of eclogues on ancient personages, e.g., Hannibal and Julius Caesar.

PFEFFERKORN, JOHANN

(1469-1521?). Converted Jew of Nuremberg. Attacked Judaism, proposing destruction of all Jewish books except Bible and the forcible conversion of Jews. He initiated the violent dispute with Reuchlin over the study of Hebrew and of Hebrew texts, such as the Cabala.

PFISTER, ALBRECHT

(c. 1420-c. 1466). German pioneer printer. Reputedly, printer of *Pfister Bible* and the first to print illustrations from woodcuts.

PFOLSPEUNDT, HEINRICH VON

(Fifteenth century). German physician. Author of *Buch der Bundth-Artzeney:* on temperance and hygiene. Published in 1460.

PHAER, THOMAS or PHAYER

(c. 1516-1560). English physician. Jurist. Made verse translations of part of the *Aeneid*. He wrote several medical works, on the plague, diseases, children's maladies, etc.

PHARMACOLOGY

The discovery of America exercised an appreciable influence on pharmacology. Among newly introduced vegetable remedies were guaiac wood, in 1508; China root, in 1525; sarsaparilla, in 1530.

PHARMACOPOEIA

The word derives from the Greek meaning *making of medicines;* in the sense of an official list of drugs and the regulations governing their use, etc., the first known pharmacopoeia appeared in Nuremberg in the 1540's.

PHILIBERT EMANUEL

(1553-1580). Ruler of Savoy. Efficient administrator. Organized army.

PHILIP I

(1478-1506). King of Spain. Called The Handsome. Son of Emperor Maximilian II. Married Juana, daughter of Ferdinand and Isabella. Philip and Juana became joint sovereigns of Castile (1504-1506). Philip founded the Hapsburg dynasty in Spain. Reputedly, he was poisoned.

PHILIP II—FELIPE EL PRUDENTE

(1527-1598). King of Spain. Married four times: Maria of Portugal, Mary I of England, Elizabeth of Valois, Anna, daughter of the Emperor Maximilian I. Ruler of Naples, Sicily, Milan, Netherlands. In conflict with France. He suppressed a Morisco revolt. Sent out Armada against England: defeated. Conquered Portugal. Defeated Turks in 1571 in the battle of Lepanto. Patron of art, built royal palace, Escorial, near Madrid, in 1563-1584. His costly wars, industrial and commercial policies induced Spanish decline. His reign saw the commencement of *El Siglo de Oro.*

PHILIP III

(1578-1621). King of Spain 1598-1621. Indifferent ruler. Entrusted government to favorites. He was devout in religion and a discriminating patron and connoisseur of the arts; in his reign Spain reached the zenith of its cultural great age.

PHILIP IV

(1605-1665). King of Spain 1621-1665. During his rule the economy of the country declined. He was much like his father, Philip III, viz., incompetent to govern, genuinely pious, devoted to the arts, which in the form of painting and drama continued to flourish in his reign. Country disrupted by internal revolts. In 1648 Holland gained independence from Spain by the Treaty of Westphalia; it concluded the Thirty Years' War, an unmitigated disaster for Spain.

PHILIP DE MAZEROLLES

(Died 1479). Illuminator, court painter of Charles the Rash. Executed *Book of Hours, Prayerbook.*

PHILIP NERI, SAINT

(1515-1595). Florentine religious reformer and founder of the Congregation of the Oratory. He was attached to the Church of San Girolamo in Rome, where he built over the church an oratory as a place for religious instruction and the recitation of portions of the Bible, especially of the Old Testament, in what became a semidramatic presentation. His use of music on these occasions to help convey the meaning of the sacred text gave rise to a musical form, the oratorio.

PHILIPPUS OF LEYDEN

Sixteenth century. Author of *De Republica:* published in 1516.

PHILOPONUS, IOANNES

Sixteenth century. Neo-Platonic philosopher. Wrote commentary on Aristotle's treatise on meteorology.

PHINOT, DOMINICO or PINOT

(c. 1510-c. 1555). French composer of chansons, motets, masses, chiefly of church music.

PIAZZA DEL CAMPIDOGLIO

This area was designed by Michelangelo in 1538. It surmounts the Capitoline Hill that overlooks Rome.

PIBRAC, GUY DU FAUR, SEIGNEUR DE

(1529-c. 1584). French jurist, diplomat, poet, humanist who wrote extensively, in Latin and French, on political matters. At his death, Montaigne wrote his eulogy. Author of *De Rebus Gallicis Epistola et Responsio:* a legalistic defense of the Massacre of St.

Bartholomew: published in 1573. Also wrote *Quatrains Moraux:* inspired by both Stoic and Christian sentiment: published in 1574.

PICCINO, NICCOLÒ
(c. 1380-1444). Italian condottiere. Famous in his day as an adroit opportunist and leader of one of the largest bands of cut-throats in Italy. One of the memorable occasions was his attack, which failed, on Florence at the command of the Duke of Milan, 1440. It meant that Medici rule would last. His attempts to carve out an independent domain for himself in Umbria and the marshes failed. He is depicted on a well-known medallion by Pisanello.

PICCOLOMINI, ALESSANDRO
(1508-1578). Italian scholar. Professor of moral philosophy at Padua. Archbishop of Siena. Wrote philosophical treatise on nature of man, the universe, logic, ethics. It is a compendium of Renaissance philosophy. Published in 1542. He also made translations from Vergil, Ovid, and Xenophon, and wrote a commentary on Aristotle.

PICO, COUNT OF MIRANDOLA, GIOVANNI
(1463-1494). Italian humanist and philosopher. The most famous figure, with Ficino, of the Florentine Academy, whose learning was a strange bouquet of profound scholarship and recondite lore drawn from Plato, Plotinus, Hermes Trismegismus, Arabic writers, the Jewish Cabala, and the Scholastics. His esoteric eclecticism may be seen in his celebrated *Oration on the Dignity of Man* and the nine hundred theses to which it was a preface; he comes very close to a conception of natural religion. When a number of his theses were found to be heretical, he thought it better to take refuge in France, 1484-1488; his French sojourn was vital for the naturalization of Italian humanism north of the Alps. He was a pioneer Hebraist and was central to the Hebrew and Oriental revival of the Renaissance. He was among the first to dismiss astrology as entirely false, a part of his conception of man's freedom and power of creation. He was the "noblest of the erudite and the most erudite of the nobles," according to a contemporary.

PICTORIUS, GEORG VON VILLINGEN
(c. 1500-1569). German philosopher. Professor of medicine.

Wrote on medical subjects, natural science, divination, astrology, witchcraft. Also author of a series of poems on man, animals, plants.

PIERIN DEL VAGA or BUONACCORSI

(c. 1500-1547). Italian painter. He worked in Rome assisting Raphael in the Loggia of the Vatican. He fled to Genoa at the time of the sack of 1527 and decorated the palace of the Doria with mythological and historical frescoes. Later he returned to Rome under the patronage of Pope Paul III. He did interior decorations as well.

PIERO DELLA FRANCESCA

(1420?-1492). Italian painter. Pupil of Domenico Veneziano. The scientist as painter; he was a close student of perspective; he also is noted for his use of architectural background in many of his paintings and his depiction of light. He wrote two dissertations on painting: *Libellus de corporibus regularibus* and *De prospectiva pingendi*. His most famous painting is the *Madonna with Saints, Angels and Federigo da Montefeltro*.

PIERO DI COSIMO

(1462-1521). Italian painter of Florence. Master of Andrea del Sarto. Executed mythological subjects, portraits, and religious scenes, *Perseus delivering Andromeda, Destruction of Pharaoh's Host*.

PIERRE DE BUR

(c. 1427-1505). Neo-Latin poet. Author of *Moralium Carminum Libri IX*.

PIERRE DE MANCHICOURT

Sixteenth century. Franco-Flemish composer. Author of masses and motets: published in 1539. He also composed secular songs.

PIETAS LITTERATA

The educational ideal of an informed and eloquent piety, characteristic of the later Renaissance. In contrast with Petrarch and the fifteenth-century Italian humanists, Erasmus and his later followers saw in the classics an educational instrument for nurturing good Christians and citizens. In the course of the sixteenth century from Erasmus, d. 1536, through Melanchthon, d. 1560, Cordier, d. 1564, Sturm, d. 1589, and the pedagogical expositions of the Jesuits (to whom the classics were "hooks to draw souls"), the subordination of the classical curriculum to religious and civil ends became more complete. By an increasingly narrow selection of texts and expurgation of authors, the classics became handmaids of Christianity, Protestant or Catholic. The ideal of the *Pietas litterata*, in various forms, was to hold its own in Western educational theory and practice to the end of the nineteenth century.

PIETRO MARTIRE VERMIGLI

(1500-1562). Peter Martyr. Florentine Protestant theologian. Fled to Zurich and became professor of theology. He was invited to England by Edward VI. Professor of theology at Oxford. Friend of Cranmer. Collaborated in the *Book of Common Prayer*. With accession of Mary he returned to Zurich and published Biblical commentaries and expositions of Calvinism.

PIGAFETTA, ANTONIO

(1491-1534). Italian traveler of Vicenza. Accompanied Magellan. In service of Portugal, France. Wrote for Charles V an account of his voyage around the world, entitled *Le Voyage et Navigation fait par les Espaignols ès Isles de Mollusques.*

PIGAFETTA, FILIPPO

(1533-1603). Papal chamberlain and writer. He wrote an account of Africa based on the experiences of the Portuguese explorer Duarto Lopes, who dictated them to Pigafetta. It was the best geographical treatise on its subject and was translated into English by Hakluyt as *A Report of the Kingdom of Congo.*

PIGHIUS, ETIENNE WYNANTS

(1520-1604). Dutch classical scholar and antiquarian. Author of *Hercules Prodicious Seu Principia Iuventutis Vita et Peregrinatio*, published in Cologne in 1609. A survey of princely qualifications and training in the form of an eulogy of Charles Frederick, son of the Duke of Cleves. He spent eight years in Italy in humanist circles; he edited Valerius Maximus and wrote the *Annales Romanorum;* while on his first trip to Italy he made a collection of sketches of Roman monuments.

PILGRIMAGE OF GRACE

In 1536 there was a rising in Lincolnshire, England, protesting Henry VIII's religious changes. As the Pilgrimage of Grace, the rising spread to Yorkshire, where 40,000 men took up arms.

The Pilgrimage was a protest of the Catholic peasantry as much against economic exploitation as against religious changes. With the execution of the leader, Robert Aske, a lawyer, the rebellion subsided.

PILON, GERMAIN
(c. 1537-1590). French sculptor. Born and died in Paris. Appointed royal sculptor in 1568. Controller General of Mint. Executed realistic tomb sculptures for the sepultures of Francis I and Henry II. Also produced *Three Graces*, monuments, portrait busts, medals.

PINA, RUI or RUY DE
(c. 1420-1521). Portuguese historian and statesman. He was a prolific author of historical works, writing chronicles of the Portuguese kings from Sancho I to Manuel I, although the works on the earlier reigns may not be from his pen. He was designated royal chronicler, archivist and librarian by Manuel I, whom he served as ambassador and courtier. His works include detailed treatment of Portuguese explorations and empire-building.

PINTO, FERNÃO MENDES
(c. 1509-1583). Portuguese traveler. Wrote about his travels through the Far East. He was the first European to write on Japan from actual experience. Called Prince of Liars, for the fantastic adventures that he records in his *Peregrinacam*: in his wanderings of twenty years he was shipwrecked several times, held prisoner thirteen times, and sold into slavery seventeen times.

PINTO, HEITOR
(1528?-1584) Portuguese religious writer and Hieronymite monk. Author of *Image of Christian Life*, published in 1563. In dialogue form. He also wrote a commentary on Biblical prophecy.

PINTURICCHIO, BERNARDINO DI BETTO, IL
(1454-1513) Painter. Executed easel pictures, religious and historical frescoes. In the 1490's he came to Rome and enjoyed papal patronage; he painted the Borgia apartments in the Vatican for Alexander VI; he did chiefly Biblical scenes, but in the frescoes he did for the Piccolimini Library at Siena he painted contemporary scenes and portraits, including one of Pius II.

466

PINZON, MARTIN ALONSO
(c. 1440-1493). Spanish navigator. With Columbus' expedition, in command of *Pinta* in 1492. Discovered Haiti.

PIRAMO, REGINALDO
Italian calligrapher. His work shows Flemish influence. Late fifteenth century.

PIRCKHEIMER, WILLIBALD
(1470-1530) German humanist. Friend of Albrecht Dürer, who did his portrait, and Reuchlin. He was a patron of humanist scholars, an enthusiast in archaeology and a translator of several Greek works into Latin.

PISANO, VITTORE, IL PISANELLO
(c. 1380-c. 1455) Italian painter and medalist. Early Renaissance artist in northern Italy. Decorated ducal palace in Venice. He was in the service of many Italian princes in the course of his life, most notably Alfonso the Magnanimous of Naples. Known for animal drawings, portraits and the portrait medals for which he is celebrated—among these are studies of Piccinino, Francesco Sforza, Sigismondo Malatesta, and Alfonso the Magnanimous.

PISTOLS
First manufactured by Camilo Vetelli of Pistoia (hence the name), c. 1540.

PITHOU, PIERRE or PETRUS PITHOEUS
(1539-1596) French jurist, humanist. Converted to Catholicism after narrowly escaping death in the St. Bartholomew Massacre. Author of legal works in Latin and an exposition of Gallicanism. He edited several Greek and Latin texts: Juvenal, Persius, Phaedrus, Salvianus and Petronius. He had one of the finest private libraries of his day and was probably the outstanding classical scholar of France at the end of the sixteenth century.

PIUS II, AENEAS SYLVIUS PICCOLOMINI, POPE
(1405-1464) One of the most effective humanist writers and perceptive minds of his century. He had been secretary to the Emperor Frederick III, who had made him poet-laureate; he played an important role in introducing the new learning and outlook of Italy to Germany. His cosmographical writings were

known to Columbus, who utilized them in formulating his geographical conceptions. Pius may be said to represent the Renaissance papacy at its best even though he was not exempt from the fault of nepotism. The threat of the Turks caused him to preach a crusade, but his efforts to organize an expedition to set out from Ancona by sea (depicted in a famous fresco by Pinturicchio at Siena) came to nothing; Pius died awaiting the Venetian fleet. Throughout the fifteenth century, especially after 1453, and down to the Reformation, the papacy sought to persuade the European powers to cooperate in crusades against the Turks, but to no avail. Pius left a fascinating autobiography, his *Commentaries,* which is also a mine of historical information, judgments, insights, and reflections on the events and personages of his day. His pontificate ran from 1458 to 1464.

PIUS III

(1439-1503). Pope for less than a year. Patron of arts. Left to Cathedral Library of Siena frescoes depicting life of Pius II, painted by Pinturicchio. Commissioned Michelangelo to carve fifteen statues for Siena Cathedral altar: not executed. Condemned nepotism, he was earnest about the reform of the Church.

PIUS IV

(1499-1565). Pope 1559-1565. Active politically. Unlike his predecessor, Paul IV, he followed a pro-Spanish policy. He helped to bring the Council of Trent to conclude its work in a final session; the most influential person during his pontificate was his nephew, St. Charles Borromeo. Promoted building and patronized artists. Only pope who appears in an opera, in Hans Pfitzner's *Palestrina.*

PIUS V

(1504-1572). Pope 1566-1572. Sought to depose Queen Elizabeth I. Encouraged French Catholic hostilities toward Huguenots. Formed Holy League in 1570, with Venice and Spain: directed against Turks. Holy League, under Don John of Austria defeated Turks at naval battle of Lepanto, in 1571. Battle celebrated by artists: Titian, Paolo Veronese, Tintoretto. He took steps to carry out and make permanent the decrees of the Council of Trent. Saintly and otherworldly, he was the last pope to be canonized.

PIZARRO, FRANCISCO

(c. 1475-1541). Spanish conquistador of Peru. He had accompanied Cortés in the conquest of Mexico and Balboa when he discovered the Pacific. Two expeditions, 1526-28 and 1532-35, resulted in the exploration of northwestern South America and the conquest of Peru. He was greatly assisted by his brothers, Gonzalo (c. 1506-1548) and Juan (died 1536), and his half-brother, Hernando (died c. 1565). Pedro Pizarro (c. 1514-1571), a cousin, also participated. He wrote an account in his *Relación del descubrimiento y conquista de los reynos del Perú,* 1571.

PIZZOPASSO, FRANCESCO

(Died 1443). Bishop of Dax and Pavia, Archbishop of Milan. Possessed important library of theological, liturgical and classical works and manuscripts. Of his sixty-five manuscripts now in the Ambrosian Library, one of Donatus and one of Probus' *Notae Juris* were especially important for the scholarship of his day.

PLADE, PEDER or PALLADIUS

(1503-1560). Danish cleric. First Lutheran bishop of Zealand. Participated in translation of Bible, known as Christian III's Bible, 1550. Translated Luther's *Smaller Catechism.* Wrote *Handbook for Pastors.* His chief work was the *Book of Pastoral Visitation.*

PLANTIN, CHRISTOPHE

(1514-1589). French printer and publisher. Set up press in Antwerp. Noted for beauty of typography. He was one of the great publishers of scholarly and scientific works, e.g., he published Vesalius, Ortel and Guicciardini. He was famed for his classical, Hebrew and liturgical texts. For Philip II of Spain he published the famous *Polyglot Bible,* in eight volumes. The firm continued to flourish until well into the nineteenth century.

PLATINA, BARTOLOMMEO, SACCHI

(1421-1481). Italian humanist. He was one of the leading lights of the Roman Academy and participated in its productions of the plays of Plautus, until the pontificate of Paul II, whose distrust of the pagan spirit caused him to abolish the Academy and to imprison Platina, 1468-69. Sixtus IV, however, revived the Academy and loaded Platina with honors: he became the librarian of the Vatican collection. His installation is the subject of a famous fresco by Melozzo da Forli, where he appears with Sixtus and his four nephews. He wrote numerous works, principally the *History of the Popes, The Prince* and *True Nobility*.

PLATONIC ACADEMY OF FLORENCE
Held in Lorenzo de' Medici's villa at Careggi, in Florence. One of members was Cristoforo Landino (1424-1504). Commentator on Horace and Vergil: also translated Pliny the Elder; he wrote interesting accounts of the debates on, e.g., the active vs. the contemplative life. The leading members were Marsilio Ficino, Pico della Mirandola, and Lorenzo the Magnificent himself. Attempted reconciliation of Platonism and Christianity. Academy continued until 1522. Suppressed on occasion of conspiracy against Giulio de' Medici. Under name of Florentine Academy, revived by Duke Cosimo in 1540.

PLATTER, FELIX
(1536-1614). Swiss physician and anatomist. Studied in France. Professor of anatomy at University of Basel for forty years. Ordinary physician to Margrave of Baden. In his *Praxis Medica* (1602-1608) he classified diseases.

PLATTER, THOMAS
(1499-1582). Swiss humanist, educator and printer of Basel. He wrote pedagogical works and an autobiography, which is an important document for the historian of sixteenth-century culture.

PLÉIADE, LA
The circle of French writers (fl. 1550 and after) inspired by Italian humanist ideals and dedicated to fashioning French into the highest literary language, a constellation of seven luminaries modeled on a group of poets in Alexandria of the third century B.C. The members were the poet Pierre de Ronsard, 1525-c. 1585, who, as he said, was "the first who in all France had ever Pindarized"; Joachim Du Bellay, 1522-1560, poet and author of the group's manifesto, *The Defense and Ennoblement of the French Language,* that they will "loot the Roman city and the Delphic temple" in enriching the national language and literature; Jean Dorat, 1502-1588, Ronsard's mentor, one of the great teachers of the age, learned in the classics and possessed of a sensitive literary taste; Antoine de Baïf, founder of the *académie de poésie et musique*; Estienne Jodelle, the dramatist whose tragedies and comedies followed Roman models, particularly

his *Captive Cleopatra;* Remy Belleau; Pontus de Tyard. If the *Pléiade* fell short of achieving its vaunted aims, their fulfillment may be seen in the great dramatists of the next century, Racine, Corneille, Molière.

PLETHON, GEORGIUS GEMISTUS
(c. 1356-1450) Byzantine classical scholar and Neo-Platonic philosopher. He was a member of the Byzantine delegation to the Council of Florence, 1430's, and there gave a famous discourse on Plato; it was the beginning of the Platonic revival in the Renaissance, for his words are said to have inspired Cosimo de' Medici to found the Platonic Academy of Florence and to sponsor Ficino in a lifetime of study, translation and exposition of Plato. Plethon drew up a work while in Florence that recounted the differences between Aristotle and Plato, and this stimulated great interest in Plato; if not the first, it was a significant step in unseating Aristotle from his sovereign position in European thought.

POCKLINGTON SCHOOL
In Yorkshire. English public school. Founded in 1514 by Dr. John Dolman.

POCULARY
An ecclesiastical pardon or indulgence for drinking.

POELENBURGH, CORNELIS VAN
(1588-1667). Dutch painter. Died in Utrecht. Executed idyllic Italian landscapes with religious and mythological figures. He had sojourned at Rome for six years.

POGGINI, DOMENICO
(1550-after 1589) Italian medalist and sculptor. Pupil of Michelangelo. Died in service of papacy after having worked for Duke Cosimo I of Florence. Executed in bronze, statuettes: a *Pluto, David, Apollo* and busts of his patrons.

POGGIO BRACCIOLINI FIORENTINO
(1380-1459) Humanist scholar, translator, and manuscript detective. He became apostolic secretary at Rome and went to the Council of Constance, from which he went out to northern monasteries searching for manuscripts; his office gained entry for him. He recovered a number of Cicero's works, the entire works of Quintilian (on rhetoric and central to the humanist

ideal of learning and education), Vitruvius, Lucretius' *De rerum natura,* and other Latin manuscripts. He knew Greek but was far from perfect in it. He had a taste and capacity for invective, relishing lampooning ecclesiastics as well as fellow humanists, such as Valla and Filelfo. After fifty years at Rome he was called to his native city to become Chancellor; his sharp tongue kept him in political broils, but the friendship of Cosimo de' Medici preserved him from exile. In retirement in his last years, he wrote a history of Florence, largely a continuation of Bruni's history; earlier he had written a sheaf of Boccaccian stories, the popular *Facetiae*. His own life was Boccaccian: he fathered fourteen illegitimate children and at the age of fifty-five was so graceless as to marry a young girl, forgetting his faithful mistress and mother of his children.

POISON AND ASSASSINATION

Rare in the Middle Ages, assassination was practiced with the skill of a fine art in the Renaissance. Paid assassination, especially murder by poison, was a far from rare means of eliminating rivals and enemies, political, papal, personal. The Borgias were notorious for their use of powders and sweet-tasting draughts, poisoned daggers, fatal philtres. Onufrio Panvinio, official historian of the Papacy, in his *Epitome Pontificum,* mentions three cardinals—Orsini, Ferrerio, and Michael, who were poisoned by Pope Alexander VI. Of all cities, Naples held life the cheapest commodity; the humanist Jovianus Pontanus says: Nec est quid Neapoli quam hominis vita minoris vendatur: *There is nothing sold more cheaply in Naples than human life.* Princes and governments hired assassins to liquidate obnoxious or hostile personalities. As aids to destruction, there were poisoned letters, mineral and herbal concoctions and potions; acids, secret weapons, even magic were brought under sinister contribution.

POLANUS VON POLANSDORF, AMANDUS

(1561-1610). Czech theologian. Professor of Old Testament at Basel. Rector of University. Author of *Syntagma Theologiae Christianae.*

POLE, CARDINAL REGINALD

(1500-1558). Catholic prelate. Archbishop of Canterbury under Mary. Friend of Sir Thomas More. Papal legate. He possessed royal blood, and so he and the members of his family were targets of Henry VIII; with Henry's religious revolution, the devout Pole was in greater danger and, after several efforts by Henry to bring him over to the royal side, he fled to Rome. He had been educated at Oxford, Paris and Padua; in 1536, while still a layman, he was made Cardinal; after his failure to organize a league against England, he participated in the Council of Trent. In 1549 he narrowly missed being elected pope, while in 1553 he joined Mary in the attempted restoration of Catholicism in England. In this they failed, both he and Mary dying on the same day in 1558. He belonged to the moderate party in the Church hoping for reform and seeking reconciliation with the Protestants.

POLE, MARGARET, COUNTESS OF SALISBURY
(1473-1541). Daughter of Duke of Clarence. Henry VIII's hostility to her son Reginald caused her execution.

POLIGRAFI
In the sixteenth century there arose a group of men associated with printing. They performed the functions of editors, proofreaders, hack writers, and were known as *poligrafi*. Among them were Lodovico Dolce, Girolamo Ruscelli, Ortensio Lando (1512-1553), Anton Francesco Doni (1513-1574), and Pietro Aretino.

POLISH ART
The Italian Renaissance was introduced in Poland by King Sigismund I (1506-1548) often called the Cracow Renaissance. The king entrusted the rebuilding of his medieval castle in Cracow to an architect called Franciszek Wloch: that is, Francesco the Italian. Between 1502 and 1516 he constructed a three-story colonnade of arcades around the castle courtyard. Another Italian, Berecci, built the Sigismund Chapel (1517-1533) in Cracow Cathedral. Polish nobles and town officials summoned architects from Italy to erect castles and town halls in the Renaissance style. Polish Renaissance sculpture appears in sepulchral monuments. An Italian sculptor working in this genre was Giovanni Padovano. The best Polish sculptor was Jan Michalowicz of Urzedow, active from 1533 to 1582. He was called the Polish Praxiteles. During the first half of the sixteenth century the guilds produced many paintings and sculptures. A notable instance is the St. Martin in an altar in Poznan Cathedral, executed in 1628 by Krysztof

Boguszewski. The best known of the Polish artists who attained success abroad was Jan Ziarnko of Lwow, known as Il Grano. He was both a draftsman and an engraver: active toward the end of the sixteenth and the beginning of the seventeenth century.

POLIZIANO, ANGELO AMBROGINI, Anglicized as POLITIAN
(1454-1494) Florentine humanist scholar and poet. The greatest poet and classical scholar, Latin and Greek, of his age. He is remembered for his attack on the slavish imitation of Cicero; such imitation was the abrogation of personality and the negation of style; his principal antagonist in the quarrel, which divided humanists more than any other issue, was Pietro Bembo. Of more permanent significance, perhaps, were Politian's contributions to textual criticism; his was a rare combination of critical method and sensitive taste. His masque, *Favola di Orfeo*, 1470's, was a forerunner of the opera. Among his translations were Homer, Herodian, Epictetus, Hippocrates, and Galen.

POLLAIUOLO, ANTONIO DEL
(c. 1429-1498). Italian artist of Florence: engraver, sculptor, goldsmith. Sponsored by the Medici. Specially noted for his bronzes. Executed work in niello: paintings, statuary, sepulchral monuments, bronze groups. Pioneer in anatomical studies as artistic ancilla, he is said to have been the first artist to practice dissection. His workshop was one of the most influential in the development of Florentine art; his brother, PIERO (1443-1496), worked with him, but was a painter in his own right. Their nephew, SIMONE (1457-1508), was an architect.

POLLICH, MARTIN
(died 1513). Logician of Melrichstadt. Wrote commentary on Aristotle: published in 1512.

POLYGLOT PSALTER
The Genoa Polyglot Psalter was published in 1516.

POMIS, DAVID DE
(1525-1588) Italian-Jewish physician, rabbi, Talmudic scholar. Studied medicine in Perugia. His *Apology for the Jewish Physician*, in which he enumerated the many popes served by eminent Jewish physicians, and his personal intercession with Pope Sixtus V caused the Pope to rescind several of the prohibitions by which Jews were restricted in the practice of medicine.

Aside from a number of medical treatises, he compiled a Talmudic dictionary in Hebrew and Aramaic and with Latin and Italian explanations of the terms.

POMPONAZZI, PIETRO
(1462-1525) The great Aristotelian philosopher and author of *On the Immortality of the Soul*. He was trained at Padua and taught philosophy at Bologna, and for periods at Padua and Ferrara. Knowing no Greek, he depended on humanist translation of the texts and other source material; he passed over Scholastic commentary and interpretation of Aristotle in favor of the earlier Alexandrian commentators, particularly Alexander of Aphrodisias. As the Alexandrians, so Pomponazzi asserted that Aristotle denied the immortality of the soul, adding that there was no evidence of any kind to demonstrate its immortality and that such proof was beyond the human mind. His views thus undermined the theological system of St. Thomas—largely based on Aristotle—and threatened a fundamental dogma of the Church. Assailed by the Inquisition, Pomponazzi's life was saved by the intervention of Bembo, papal secretary and later Cardinal, with Pope Leo X, both of whom were men of humanist sympathies and outlook. Before his death he made several attempts to reconcile his views with Christian teachings. There is in his works—as in those of the Platonists of the Florentine Academy and in contradistinction to the Averroist school of Aristotle—an emphasis on the dignity and worth of the individual soul and on a more personal conception of human nature. Pomponazzi's career indicates that Aristotle was largely exempt from the anti-Scholastic reaction: the Aristotelian corpus continued to be read despite the growing vogue of Plato.

PONCE, PEDRO DE
(c. 1520-1584). Benedictine monk. Born in Spain. The first to teach deaf mutes.

PONT, TIMOTHY
(c. 1560-1630). Scottish cartographer. Author of a *Survey of Scotland and its Islands*, the first Scottish atlas. He was a mathematician and utilized that specialty in drawing up his maps.

PONTANUS, JOANNES JOVIANUS
(1426-1503). Italian humanist, poet, diplomat. Secretary to Ferdinand I of Naples. Wrote didactic poems, epigrams, Latin verse,

erotic pieces, elegies, idylls, *Eridanus.* Also he wrote on various aspects of Neapolitan history, e.g., the reign of Ferdinand I and the invasion of Charles VIII. He was a central figure in the Academy of Naples.

PONTIUS, SIMON

(1495-1554). Italian physician and philosopher. Wrote *De Coloribus Libellus:* published in 1548. On the nature of color, light and shade, application of color to art. Also *De Coloribus Oculorum:* published in 1550. A contribution to ophthalmology.

PONTORMO, JACOPO CARRUCCI

(1494-1556). Italian painter. Belonged to Florentine school. Studied under Leonardo da Vinci. Works include: *The Deposition, Adam and Eve, Venus and Cupid.* Also portraits.

POOR LAW

The English Parliament passed the first Poor Law in 1601, when England was 'full of paupers and sturdy beggars.'

POPE, SIR THOMAS

(c. 1507-1559). Privy Councillor and philanthropist. Attached to court of Queen Mary, then to Queen Elizabeth I. Founded and endowed Trinity College, Oxford University.

POPOLO GRASSO

In Renaissance Italian towns and cities, "the fat people" or those newly rich commercial and industrial enterprisers who sought and often succeeded in dominating the political as well as the economic life of their town. They were the most dynamic class in Italy; the culture of the Renaissance can be said to have been in their image.

POPOLO MINUTO

In Renaissance Italian towns and cities, "the little people" or proletarians who were excluded from any role in the political life of their city; their demands and agitation for political rights explain a good deal of the strife that was so characteristic of the Italian city-states.

PORCARO, STEFANO

(Died 1453) Republican revolutionary; inspired by the memory of ancient Rome, his "humanist" plot—resembling closely that of Cola di Rienzi—featured the seizure of the pope and cardinals and proclamation of himself as "Tribune". Pope Nicholas V's humanist sympathies had led him to tolerate Porcaro's fulminations against pope and clergy, but when the plot was discovered he ordered Porcaro's death and he was hanged from the parapet of Castel Sant'Angelo. His career stands as a reminder that the classical revival inspired revolutionaries as well as sustained despots; the assassination of two Visconti dukes of Milan is another example that Brutus as well as Caesar was honored by imitation.

PORCELLIS, JAN
(1584-1632). Dutch painter. Died in Leyden. He was a painter of tempestuous sea scenes.

PORDENONE, GIOVANNI ANTONIO DA
(c. 1483-1539). Italian painter of Venice. Executed frescoes based on Biblical motifs in a grandiloquent style that suggests the Baroque. He decorated many Venetian palaces.

PORTA, FRA GUGLIELMO DELLA
(c. 1510-1577). Italian sculptor. Executed sepulchral statuary, principally the tomb of Pope Paul III.

PORTA, GIACOMO DELLA
(1539-1604). Italian architect and sculptor. Designed churches. Belongs in the first phase of Roman baroque. Executed villas, fountains, and the cupola of St. Peter's, Rome.

PORTA, GIOVANNI BATTISTA DELLA
(1538-1615). Italian scientist, alchemist. Author of *Magiae Naturalis Libri IIII*, published in 1615. Treatise on natural magic, cosmetics, chemical experiments, secret writing, love philtres. He founded the *Accademia dei Secreti* at Naples as a center of occult lore. Experimented wih *camera obscura* and helped lay the foundation of scientific optics.

PORTORO ROYAL SCHOOL
In Northern Ireland. Founded in 1618. Irish public school.

PORZIO, CAMILLO
(c. 1528-1580) Neapolitan historian, poet laureate of Pisa. Author of a *History of Italy*, published c. 1568, and an account of the Kingdom of Naples.

PORZIO, SIMONE

(1496-1554) Italian philosopher and scientist, father of the above. Author of *De coloribus Libellus,* a treatise on color theory, based on Aristotle, published in 1548. He supported Pomponazzi's position on the human soul, following the Alexandrine school of interpretation of Aristotle. Unlike Pomponazzi, he could and did read Aristotle and the early commentators in the original Greek.

POSSEVINO, GIOVANNI BATTISTA

(1520-1549). Author of a treatise on the qualities of a gentleman and a courtier, entitled *Dialogo dell' Honore.* Edited by his brother Antonio, Jesuit scholar and diplomat. Published in 1559.

POST-CAMONEAN CYCLE

Imitators of the Portuguese poet Camõens constituted a cycle, beginning with Luiz Pereira Brandão, author of *Elegiad,* published in 1588. Others of this group, and their works, are as follows: Vasco Mousinho de Quevedo Castelo Branco: *Afonso Africano,* Dom Francisco Child Rolim de Moura (1572-1640): *Dos Novissimos do Homem,* Francisco de Sá e Meneses (died 1664): *Malaca Conquistada:* published in 1634, Manuel Tomaz (1585?-1665?) *Insulana,* Gabriel Pereira de Castro (1571-1632): *Ulissêa,* published in 1636, Braz Garcia de Mascarenhas (1596-1656): theme of Variatus, Lusitanian leader who fought against Romans.

POSTEL, GUILLAUME

(1510-1581) French Oriental scholar, philosopher and eccentric. Author of *De Orbis Terrae Concordia.* On his travels in the Near East he acquired many documents that bear on the history of Christianity. He probably participated in the publication of the Syriac New Testament, c. 1555.

POSTHIUS, IOANNES

(1537-1597) German poet and physician. Wrote Latin verse in classical style but covering wide range of contemporary themes. He traveled extensively, particularly in Italy. Besides humanist and religious verse, he wrote on medicine and translated an Arabic work into Latin as *Thesaurus Sanitatis.* He was also a good Greek scholar.

POTTINGAR

In the fifteenth, sixteenth, seventeenth centuries, a term meaning an *apothecary.*

478

POURBUS, FRANS, THE ELDER

(1545-1581) Flemish painter. Died in Antwerp. Executed religious and historical paintings, portraits.

POURBUS, FRANS, THE YOUNGER

(1569-1622) Flemish painter, son of the above. He was famed for his portraits. He was essentially a court painter, having worked at the courts of Brussels, Innsbruck, Mantua and Naples, before he settled at Paris at the court of Marie de' Medici.

POURBUS, PIETER

(c. 1520-1584) Flemish painter. Died in Bruges. He was celebrated for his religious paintings.

POUSSIN, NICOLAS

(1594-1665). French painter. Worked largely in Rome. Influenced by Titian and Venetian colorists. Exerted marked influence on painting in seventeenth century. Among his works are: *Bacchanales, Et in Arcadia Ego.*

POYNINGS' LAW

To establish English rule in Ireland, Henry VII sent Sir Edward Poynings (1459-1521) as Lord Deputy. A law was passed that no Irish Parliament should convene and make laws without the consent of the English Privy Council, known also as the Drogheda statutes and part of the attempt to Anglicize the Irish government. It was not repealed until 1782.

POZZO, MODESTA

(1555-1592) Venetian poetess. Wrote under pseudonym of Moderata Fonte. Author of romantic, chivalric epic entitled *Tredici Canti del Floridoro di Mad,* 1581, and a cycle of religious poems, 1582-92. She was a prodigy of learning, accomplished in music and skilled in drawing; she was in fact one of that band of women in the Renaissance remarkable for their gifts and talents.

PRAETORIUS, MICHAEL

(1571-1621). German musician, composer, historian of music. Author of *Musae Sioniae: Syntagma Musicum,* an historical account in three volumes; the second volume is a basic source for the musical practices and conceptions as well as the musical instruments of the day. He was a prolific composer, was organist

and conductor at the courts of Saxony, Brunswick and Magdeburg.

PRESTON, THOMAS

(1537-1598). English dramatist. Wrote blood-and-thunder tragedy
entitled *Life of Cambises*: appeared in 1569; it was an important
herald of the historical drama, such as Shakespeare was to write.
He was associated all his life with Cambridge: as master of Trinity Hall, fellow of King's College, and as vice-chancellor of the
University.

PRICE, HUGH

(c. 1495-1574). Founder, in 1571, of Jesus College, Oxford University.

PRIEUR, BARTHÉLEMY

(1570-1611). French sculptor, sculptor to Henry IV. Executed
tombs, large-scale sculptures, and worked on the fountain of
Diana of Fontainebleau.

PRIMATICCIO, FRANCESCO

(1504-1570). Italian painter, sculptor, architect. Died in Paris.
Founded school of Fontainebleau. Worked in France for Francis
I. Decorated the chateau at Fontainebleau. Court architect to
Catherine de' Medici. Executed large-scale decorations. His
figures show the elongation and contortion that came to characterize the Baroque; there is a profusion of decoration in his works
that also suggests the Baroque. Among the important influences
upon him was that of Michelangelo.

PRINTING

The invention of printing is credited to Johann Gutenberg of
Mainz, c. 1450, although there are several others who may merit
that honor, most notably Lourens Coster of the Lowlands. The
chief reason that so little can now be known of the beginning of
printing is that the invention and improvements in techniques
were assiduously kept as trade secrets. The printing press was a
powerful factor in promoting the Renaissance. In 1470 Michael
Freyburger, Ulrich Gering, Martin Grantz, German printers,
established printing press within area of Sorbonne. In 1466 two
German clerics and printers, Conrad Schweinheim and Arnold
Pannartz, brought printing, 'the holy art,' to Italy. They opened
their workshop in the monastery of Santa Scholastica in Subiaco.

Press is still preserved. In 1467 they moved to Rome and received help from Pope Paul II and several cardinals. It was first established in Naples in 1474, in the reign of Ferdinand I, King of Naples (1458-1494). In France printing was established in 1470. The first edition of Villon's poems dates from 1489. It was brought to England by William Caxton in 1476 and to the New World (Mexico City) by Juan Pablos in 1536. By 1500 some 5,000 books had been printed in Italy alone. The first known printer's device was that of Fust and Schoeffer (who took over the bankrupt Gutenberg's shop) in the *Mainz Psalter* of 1484. Two famous ones were Aldus Manutius' and Johannes Froben's.

PROCACCINI, THE
A family of painters of Bologna that flourished in the sixteenth and seventeenth centuries. ERCOLE THE ELDER (1515-1595) was a mannerist painter of religious subjects, e.g., *The Conversion of St. Paul,* and the founder of the family tradition. His sons were CAMILLO (c. 1551-1629), who did religious paintings and a series of frescoes on the life of the Virgin for the *duomo* at Piacenza; GUILIO CESARE (c. 1570-1625), the most original and gifted of the family, noted for his composition, use of colors and chiaroscuro; and CARLO ANTONIO (c. 1555-c. 1605), a painter of landscapes and flowers. The latter's son ERCOLE THE YOUNGER (1596-1676) and two other members of the family, GIUSEPPE, who worked in Pavia, and FRANCESCO SIGISMONDO (1548-1626), were also painters.

PROFESSORSHIPS
In early Renaissance, in Italy, chairs were limited to civil law, canon law, medicine. Gradually rhetoric, philosophy, and astronomy received similar status. Salaries were at times in form of a fixed sum. In the course of the Renaissance, competition among academic institutions resulted in increased appreciation of professors and of more distinguished incumbents. Tenure was on rare occasions for life: usually, for a year or half year. Scholars consequently were forced to travel in search of positions. Medicine and law received largest salaries.

PSCHLACHER, KONRAD
Sixteenth century. Logician of Freistadt. Wrote commentary on Petrus Hispanus: *Parvorum Logicalium Liber:* published in Vienna in 1516.

PUERSTINGER, BERTHOLD

(1465-1543). Bishop of Chiemsee. Author of *Tewtsche Theology:* first Catholic dogmatics, in German. A systematic presentation of Catholic doctrine. Published in Munich in 1528.

PULCI, LUIGI

(1432-1484). Italian poet. The protégé of Lorenzo the Magnificent and the friend of Politian and Aretino. He wrote *Morgante Maggiore*, 1483, a humorous and satirical retelling of the chivalrous legends of Roland; the story carries him to the land of the paynims in the company of a Rabelaisian giant named Morgante. There is some notion of a natural religion and of the beneficence of all religions in the work which mixes the sublime and the ludicrous indiscriminately. Two brothers, BERNARDO (c. 1425-c. 1496) and LUCA, were also poets; Bernardo also made a translation of Vergil's *Bucolics*.

PULGAR, HERNANDO DEL

(1430?-1493?). Spanish historian, classicist, biographer, and court chronicler to Juan II and Enriquez IV, wrote *Claros Varones de Castilla*: 1486: biographies of notable men. As Spanish ambassador to France, wrote *Crónica de los Reyes Católicos*: translated into Latin. Also epistolographer.

PUPPER, JOHANN or GEPUPPER or GOCH

(died 1475). Dutch theologian. Educated under the Brethren of the Common Life. Studied also at the University of Cologne. Based religious life on Scripture. Author of *De Libertate Christiana*: published c. 1474.

PURCHAS, SAMUEL

(c. 1575-1626). English cleric, compiler, editor, popularizer of books on geography. Works include *Purchas, his Pilgrimage*: a miscellany on religions. Also *Hakluytus Posthumus;* an anthology of the literature of travel and exploration, drawn in part from Hakluyt's papers.

PUTTENHAM, GEORGE

(died 1590). English writer. Reputedly, author of *The Arte of English Poesie*: published in 1589; although it may have been written by his elder brother, RICHARD, c. 1520-c. 1600, also a writer.

482

PYNSON, RICHARD

(died 1530). Normandy-born pioneer printer in England. In 1509 he introduced Roman type into England. He was designated as king's printer on the accession of Henry VIII.

Q

QUARLES, FRANCIS
(1592-1644). English poet. Chronologer to the City of London. Prolific writer in prose and verse. Held positions in civic and ecclesiastical fields. Author of *Emblems*: a volume of morally and spiritually edifying verse, *Enchiridion*, a manual of sayings and dicta. *A Feast of Worms*, a paraphrase of the Bible story of Jonah; *The Virgin Widow*, a comedy. According to Saintsbury, "He would versify anything from the *Arcadia* to the *Lamentations*."

QUARTON, ENGUERRAND or CHARONTON
(Born c. 1410). French painter, influenced by the Van Eycks and the Flemish school. He worked at Avignon, and is known for religious work depicting the life of the Virgin. His work is notable for the treatment of drapery, light and landscape, and also for nude studies.

QUEBEC, MISSIONS TO
Four French friars founded missions in Quebec in 1615.

QUEEN'S COLLEGE
Cambridge University. Founded in 1448 by Queen Margaret of Anjou. Refounded by Elizabeth Wydeville, consort of King Edward IV, in 1465.

QUESNEL, THE
French family of painters and engravers that flourished in the sixteenth and early seventeenth centuries. PIERRE (died c. 1575) worked at the court of James V of Scotland. His sons were

485

FRANÇOIS (1573-1619), a court painter for Henry III and Henry IV of France, notable for his portraits, and NICHOLAS (died 1632), who did many engravings, working chiefly at Paris.

QUEVEDO, FRANCISCO DE
(1580-1645). Francisco Gómez de Quevedo y Villegas. Spanish satirical poet and novelist. Critic of court corruption. Viceroy of Naples. Orphaned while young, he was educated by Jesuits. Classical scholar. Author of *Flores*: published in 1605. Collection of poems. Secretary of Philip II. As a result of a duel, fled to Italy in 1611. In the service of the Spanish Viceroy, Duke of Osuna. Disgraced, he returned to Spain. Imprisoned for four years in monastery. Died, broken in health. Author of noted picaresque novel—*Vida del Buscón*: published in 1626. *Sueños*: published in 1627. A series of visions of hell. Also wrote philosophical and theological treatises and polemical works. He was, in literary style and conception, an antagonist of Gongorism, which he regarded as deformity and decadence. He was one of the luminaries of the *Siglo de Oro*.

QUICK PENNY
Also called Hearth Tax. By Spanish edict of 1585, Flemings were ordered to pay this tariff, an assessment that created widespread indignation.

QUIRINAL PALACE
Papal Palace in Rome. Designed in 1574 by Italian architect Domenico Fontana (1543-1607). In 1870 it became the residence of the kings of Italy; since World War II it has been the home of the Italian presidents.

486

R

RABBINICAL BIBLE
First published between 1516 and 1517 by Christian printer Daniel Bomberg (died 1549).

RABELAIS, FRANÇOIS
(1494-1533). French satirist and comic genius. Son of a provincial, bourgeois lawyer, he was successively a friar, monk, and secular priest; his medical studies at Montpellier were, for lack of patience, not completed, although he did publish learned works in medicine and also archaeology; he made several trips to Italy. In his famous works *Pantagruel*, 1533, and *Gargantua*, published a year later, are to be found all the literary trends—humanist, heroic, realist—of the day. Interpretations of his career are manifold: the last of the medievals, first of the moderns, ardent believer in one religious dispensation or another, etc. Without doubt he was the greatest comic and satiric genius of the Renaissance, a lover of humanity despite its faults, possessed of a remarkable faith in unspoiled human nature and a gusto for words and verbal extravagance. In his description of the Abbey of Thélème and the riotous lives of its inmates who follow the rule "Do what thou wilt", he may be said to have done for medieval monasticism what Cervantes' *Don Quixote* did for medieval knighthood: laughed it off the stage.

RADZIWILL, NICHOLAS or MIKOLAJ
(1515-1565) Polish prince of Lithuanian descent and opponent of the dynastic union of the two countries. His family was very wealthy and influential in Polish affairs; it was at his expense

487

that a Protestant translation of the Bible—the Radziwill Bible—was published in 1553.

RAFFAELLO DA MONTELUPO
(c. 1505-c. 1567) Italian sculptor and architect. Pupil of Michelangelo. He worked at Rome until compelled to flee by the sack of 1527. He did religious figures but also a few mythological ones; much of his work consists of sepulchral monuments.

RAIMONDI, MARCANTONIO
(c. 1480-c. 1534). Italian engraver of Bologna and Rome. Principal Renaissance engraver. Works include: *Judgment of Paris, Death of Dido, Quos Ego,* subjects inspired by the *Aeneid.*

RAINOLDS, JOHN
(1549-1607). English scholar and clergyman. It was he who suggested to James I that a new English translation of the Bible be prepared; the result was the King James Version, one portion of which was Rainolds' work.

RALEIGH, SIR WALTER
(1552-1618). English navigator, historian, courtier, poet. Attached to the court of Queen Elizabeth I, whose favor secured for him estates, monopoly in wine, patents to lands in America. Named the American territory Virginia, in honor of the Queen. Colonized Roanoke Island in 1585. Introduced tobacco and the potato into England and Ireland. Patron of the poet Edmund Spenser. Banished by Queen for four years, during which he went on an expedition against Cadiz in 1596 and the Azores in 1597. On the death of Elizabeth, he was charged with a plot against James I and was imprisoned in the Tower of London in 1603. In captivity, he composed a *History of the World.* Released to lead an expedition for gold on the Orinoco banks. The expedition was abortive. Returning to England, he was beheaded by order of the king, and on the insistence of the Spanish ambassador Gondomar, for preying on Spanish shipping and territories. Also wrote poems: accounts of his voyages. His *Travels* to *Virginia* comprised a series of American scenes: fishing, sailing ships, Indians, published in 1607.

RAMUS, PETRUS or PIERRE DE LA RAMÉE
(1515-1572) French humanist and logician. Mathematician. His *Animadversions on Aristotle* of 1543 was a milestone in the

critical revaluation and rejection of much of Aristotle's scientific thought. Killed in Massacre of St. Bartholomew's Day. Author of *Basilae*, source for intellectual life of Renaissance in Switzerland. His adherents were known as Ramists.

RAMUSIO, GIANBATTISTA

(1485-1557). Venetian editor, classical scholar, diplomat. Compiled an encyclopedic work on voyages and travels in Asia, Africa, Europe, America, *Delle navigationi e viaggi*, that brought together many firsthand accounts, e.g., Marco Polo's, Magellan's etc. The Italian Hakluyt. For the Aldine Press, he edited Quintilian and Livy.

RAMUSIO, GIROLAMO

(1450-1486). Venetian physician, father of the above. Translated Avicenna from Arabic into Italian. Died at Damascus. The Ramusio were one of the great families of Venice in the sixteenth century, producing numerous scholars and public servants.

RANDOLPH, THOMAS

(1605-1635). English poet. Dramatist. Friend of Ben Jonson. Author of poems, six plays, among them: *Aristippus, The Conceited Pedlar, The Jealous Lovers*. They show the influence of the classics both directly and through Jonson.

RANINA, DINKO, or DOMENICO RAGNINA

(1536-1607). Yugoslav poet. Adapted metres of Italian forms and attempted to reform the Yugoslav language on the basis of Italian models as a literary vehicle.

RANTZOVIUS, HENRICUS or RANTZAU

(1526-1598). Danish statesman and Latin poet. He wrote, under the pseudonym Cilicius Cimber, a Latin poem on the conquest of Dithmarschen, in which his son, Johan, was the victorious commander.

RAO, CESARE

Italian scholar. Author of burlesques, diatribes, and skits on public affairs, pedantry, academies, literature. His *L'Argute* was published in 1567.

RAPARD, FRANCIS

Sixteenth century. Dutch physician who practiced in Bruges.

Author of *A Great and Perpetual Almanach*: published in 1551. He denied the value of astrological prediction to medical science.

RAPHAEL

(1483-1520). Raffaello Santi or Sanzio. Italian painter. Born in Urbino. In the service of the popes—Julius II and Leo X. Principal architect of St. Peter's 1514-1520. Chief conservator of excavations in Rome: 1520. Works include *Apollo and Marsyas, St. George and the Dragon, Holy Family,* numerous madonnas, many frescoes in the Vatican, portraits; perhaps his most famous painting is the *School of Athens.* His father, GIOVANNI (died 1494), was court painter and poet to Duke Federigo da Montefeltro of Urbino; he was his son's first teacher, but upon his death Raphael entered the workshop of Perugino, who had a lasting influence upon him. Another influence in his development was his sojourn, 1504-1508, in Florence, from where he went to Rome. Nevertheless, all his work bears the stamp of his distinctive genius, placid and serene, harmonious and delicate. Unlike Leonardo who worked endlessly on a single work and left most of his paintings unfinished, Raphael was a prolific artist who worked, seemingly, without effort. Both for his vision of human beauty and his technical mastery, he is one of the supreme masters of Renaissance art.

RAPICANO, NICOLA

Late fifteenth century. Italian calligrapher. His work shows Flemish influence.

RAPICIUS, GIOVITA RAVIZZA

(1476-1553). Italian grammarian, and man of letters. Author of *De Numero Oratorio Libri Quinque*: on Latin style. Also a book on education, *De instauratione scholarum.*

RAPPRESENTAZIONE DI ANIMA E DI CORPO

Musical composition by Emilio de' Cavalieri (1550?-1602). Considered the first oratorio.

RATALLER, GEORGE

(1528-1581) Dutch classical scholar and philologist, lawyer, Neo-Latin poet, of noble birth. He rounded out his studies in the Lowlands and France by a trip of sight-seeing and study in

Italy. Author of *Epigrams*. He edited and translated into Latin Hesiod, Sophocles and Euripides.

RATDOLT, ERHARD
(c. 1443-c. 1528) German pioneer printer. Issued works on mathematics, astronomy, liturgy. Ornamented with numerous wood engravings in several colors, his works are notable for their greaty beauty. He was active in Venice from 1476 to 1485, returning to Germany thereafter; his illustrations and decorations show the influence of Italian art.

RATICHIUS, WOLFGANG or RATKE
(1571-1635) German educator. Introduced into several German cities a new method of teaching languages and founded, at Magdeburg, an experimental public school. He wrote extensively on education and pedagogy; the goal that he sought for Germany was "a common language, a common government, and a common religion."

RATIO STUDIORUM
The academic curriculum drawn up by the Jesuits in 1584-85.

RAULIN, JOHANNES
(Sixteenth century) Logician. Wrote on Aristotelian logic.

RAUW, JOHANN or RAVIUS
(Died 1600). German theologian, geographer and musician. His *Cosmographia*, in German, with maps and illustrations, was published in 1597. He published a German songbook, many of the songs being Luther's hymns which Rauw set to music; it has had an important place in German church music.

RAUWOLF, LEONHARD
(Died 1596) German physician, botanist and traveler. His botanizing—seeking rare specimens and especially those mentioned by Pliny, Galen, Dioscorides and the Arab writers—took him on extensive travels in Italy and the Near East. His findings were compiled and carefully described in *Aigentlishe Beschreibung der Raiss*, 1582, a work which is a milestone in the development of botanical science. A large portion of the work was translated into English in the seventeenth century.

RAVAILLAC, FRANÇOIS
(1578-1610). Assassin of Henry IV of France.

491

RAVENNA

In northern Italy. This city was the chief residence of Roman emperors in fifth century; of Byzantine exarchs from sixth to eighth centuries. Ceded to Papacy by the Carolingian dynasty. Dante spent most of his exile there, during the ascendancy of the Da Polenta family. In the fifteenth century Ravenna fell under Venetian control until it was regained by Pope Julius II in 1509. It played no significant role in the Renaissance; most of its art (it is famed for its mosaics) and architectural monuments date from the classical and Byzantine periods.

RAVENSCROFT, THOMAS

(c. 1592-c. 1640). English composer of catches, songs, roundelays, madrigals and compiler of musical collections: *Melismata*, published in 1609, a miscellany of songs, ranging from three- to ten-part music; *The Whole Book of Psalms*, published in 1621, known as *Ravenscroft's Psalter*—about half the compositions were his own.

RAVESTEIJN, JAN ANTHONISZ VAN

(c. 1570-1657). Dutch painter. Died in The Hague. Paintings of marksmen, regency pieces, portraiture. His brother ANTHONY (1580-1669) was also a painter.

RAYMOND, JOHN

Author of *A Voyage made through Italy in the Years 1647 and 1648*.

RECORDE, ROBERT

(c. 1510-1558). English mathematician, physician. Professor at Oxford, Cambridge. Physician to Edward VI and Queen Mary. Died in a debtors' prison. Published a textbook on arithmetic: *The Ground of Arts*: appeared in 1551. He also wrote on algebra, astronomy, and is said to have introduced algebra into England.

REGIOMONTANUS, JOHANN MÜLLER

(1436-1476). German mathematician, astronomer, and humanist. He spent several years at the University of Vienna where he lectured on Latin poetry. He departed for Italy to master Greek under Cardinal Bessarion and to study at Padua; upon his return, he settled at Nuremberg where he established a printing press and a school of mathematics and astronomy. Made bishop of Ratisbon, he was called to Rome to participate in a reform of the

492

calendar but died within the year. He translated into Latin the works of Ptolemy, the *Conics* of Apollonius of Perga, and other scientific treatises.

REGNIER, MATHURIN
(1573-1613). French satirical poet. Canon of Chartres Cathedral. He wrote *Le Mauvais Repas, La Folie est Générale, Macette;* he followed the literary canons established by the *Pléiade* group, but also shows the influence of Ariosto.

REICHLE, HANS or REICHEL
(1570-1641). Sculptor and architect of Augsburg. Influenced by Gian Bologna, under whom he studied at Florence; he worked principally in Italy.

REICHSREGIMENT
German for "the government of the Empire" and translated as the Council of Regency. Made up of about twenty members, it was to constitute, with the emperor, the executive power of the Holy Roman Empire and was part of the constitutional changes that occurred under Maximilian I, c. 1500. It was revived by Charles V, who was persuaded to do so at the Diet of Worms, 1521. He allowed the Council no power except in his absence from Germany. Neither emperor had any interest in making the experiment work, and preferred to let it die, as it soon did. It met the last time in 1524. It was seen as the instrument by which Germany would become a national state comparable to England and France, but neither of the emperors was a German nationalist or patriot; their chief interest was Hapsburg dynastic and territorial ambitions.

REINHOLD, ERASMUS
(1511-1553). Astronomer, astrologer, and mathematician. Author of astrological tables. Professor of mathematics at Wittenberg.

REIS, PIRI
Turkish cartographer. Produced a world map in 1513.

REISCH, GREGOR
(c. 1467-1525). German humanist, monk, friend of Erasmus, inspired by Aristotle's works. Author of *Margarita Philosophorum:* an encyclopaedia of the liberal arts in dialogue form; published in 1496 and frequently reprinted until 1583.

REJ, MIKOLAJ

(1505-1569). Polish writer. Supporter of the Reformation. First to undertake seriously the adaptation of the Polish language to literary needs. Inaugurated the Golden Age of Polish Literature. Wrote a *Short Conversation*: between a lord, a bailiff and a priest; it is brilliant satire and social criticism, appeared in 1543. Also wrote poems: didactic, moralizing and religious plays: *The Zoological Garden, The Mirror, The Life of an Honest Man*: idealistic work with literary examples.

RELIGIOUS and CIVIL WARS IN FRANCE

From 1562 to 1589 eight wars occurred between Catholics and Huguenots. They ended on the accession of the Bourbon Henry IV of France, who, declaring reputedly that "Paris was worth a mass," was converted to Catholicism and subsequently proclaimed religious tolerance in the Edict of Nantes, 1598.

REMACLE D'ARDENNE

(1482-1524). French Neo-Latin poet. Author of comedy, *Palamedes*. Also *Amores*, epigrams.

REMONSTRANTS

Forty-five Dutch ministers, defenders of the views of Arminius (1560-1609). They signed the Remonstrance in 1610. A conflict between the Remonstrants and the Contra-Remonstrants, who supported the theologian Gomarus, created violent religious dissension in Holland. In 1619 the Remonstrants were deposed from the ministry and later sentenced to banishment. Among the victims of the conflict was Jan Barneveldt, who was executed, and Hugo Grotius, who fled.

RENAISSANCE, ART OF

Giorgio Vasari (1511-1574) in the Introduction of his *Life of the Painters*, published in 1550, used for the first time the expression *rinascità*—Renaissance. The French term *Renaissance* was chosen as the title by Jules Michelet for the seventh volume of his *Histoire de France*, published in 1855. The term became universal in use through Jacob Burckhardt's *The Civilization of the Renaissance in Italy*, published in 1860.

Architecture: Architects of the Renaissance replaced ornamental system of Gothic with that of the antique. Notable names in this field are those of Brunelleschi, Michelangelo, Leone Battista Alberti, and Bramante. Vitruvius' work of the first century, *On Architecture,* had a profound influence upon Renaissance architecture.

Sculpture: Emphasis on the exact depiction of anatomy and the human form. Equestrian statues appeared. Bronze statues. Themes from classical mythology. Notable names include Donatello, Verrocchio, Michelangelo.

Painting: Similar characteristics applied to painting. Portraits were in vogue: fresco painting. Mythological themes. Outstanding masters were Masaccio, Uccello, Correggio, Ghirlandaio, Giovanni Bellini, Mantegna. Masters of the High Renaissance were Leonardo da Vinci, Giorgione, Titian, Raphael, Michelangelo.

French Renaissance: The Italian Renaissance came to France under Francis I (1515-1547). Construction of castles decorated in Renaissance style. The outstanding master was Philibert de L'Orme (c. 1515-1570). Jean Goujon (1510-1568) and Germain Pilon (1537-1590) expressed the new ideals in sculpture. Florentine artists brought classic form to France: Leonardo Rosso, Primaticcio, and Cellini.

In general, the French Renaissance yielded to Mediterranean form and classical proportion.

English Renaissance: Hans Holbein, the German artist, brought the Renaissance to the English court. The English Renaissance remained dominantly a court affair, stimulated by occasional visits of Italian sculptors and painters. During the sixteenth century, architecture and the decorative arts adhered to late Gothic. On occasion, there was also added Italian ornamentation, introduced by Pietro Torrigiano (1472-1528) and Benedetto da Rovezzano (1474-1552). Inigo Jones (1573-1652) brought Palladian classicism to its height in England, as in the Banquet Hall of Whitehall.

German Renaissance: Developed under the guidance of Albrecht Dürer (1471-1528). He made the graphic arts the most powerful medium for new conceptions in form and thought. His contributions in perspective, anatomical, humanistic themes extended the scope of Northern European art for centuries. Between 1500 and 1530 most of the German painters were affected by the Renaissance. Hans Holbein, the foremost portraitist of this period, carried the specific forms of the German Renaissance to Switzerland and England. Matthias Grünewald and Hieronymus Bosch are Gothic in spirit, but show a mastery of the Italian techniques, perspective, use of color, etc. But Lucas Cranach, Hans Burkmair, Albrecht Altdorfer show the direct influence of the Italian Renaissance.

In sculpture and architecture the blend of northern heaviness and love of ornamentation with Italian classicism is manifested. Among sculptors may be mentioned Konrad Meit (c. 1480-1551), Peter Vischer (1488-c.1549), Peter Floetner (c. 1490-1546).

The German Renaissance in architecture is most typically represented in castles, town halls, dwellings: as in the instance of Elias Holl's (1573-1646) city hall of Augsburg.

Flemish and Dutch Renaissance: In Flemish countries Matsys, Mabuse, Van Orley, Lucan van Leyden and Jan van Scorel were Romanists. Antonis Mor was internationally recognized as a portraitist. Pieter Aertsen was a still life artist. Pieter Brueghel the Elder added to the Late Renaissance interpretation of human life and nature.

In architecture, the Gothic style continued longer than in painting and sculpture. Jacques Dubroencq (c. 1505-1584) may be considered as the initiator of an Italianate style in Holland. Cornelis Floris' (1514-1575) city hall of Antwerp represents the mannerism of the late Renaissance.

Spanish Renaissance: Italian artists were instrumental in disseminating Renaissance forms. The combination of Renaissance forms with Spanish-Moorish ornamentation was called the Plateresco style. Among the outstanding examples are the cathedral and the city hall of Seville by Diego de Riaño and Martin de Gainza. Throughout the sixteenth century Italian artists made their way to Spain, bringing the new art with them, while many Spanish artists spent their apprenticeship in Italy.

Sculpture: Pietro Torrigiano (1472-1528) brought the terra cotta style of Northern Italy to Spain. Alonzo Berruguette (1480-1561) adapted Michelangelo and Sansovino to Spanish forms.

RENAISSANCE CLUBS

One of the features of the Renaissance was the proliferation of literary and social clubs. Some were of brief duration, while others endured and even acquired European reputations. At Bologna, for example, there was the Viridario. It was interested in the correction of printed texts. The Sitibondi studied law. The Desti took the subject of chivalry as a theme. Other clubs in Bologna were: Sonnacchiosi, Oziosi, Desiosi, Storditi, Confusi, Politici, Instabili, Umorosi. Bologna was typical of the towns and cities of Renaissance Italy; similar coteries flourished north of the Alps.

RENAISSANCE COMEDY

Among notable comedies of the Italian Renaissance are the following: Machiavelli's *Mandràgola*, published c. 1513, G. Bruno's *The Candle-maker:* 1580, *Calandria:* 1513, by Bernardo Dovizi of Bibbiena (1470-1520), *Aridosia:* 1536, of Lorenzino de' Medici (1514-1548), *Straccioni:* 1544, of Annibal Caro (1507-1560), Seven comedies by Il Lasca, produced between 1540 and 1550, and the comedies of the Florentine Giovanni Maria Cecchi (1518-1587).

RENAISSANCE CONCEPTS

Period of intellectual revival, especially in Italy and Europe during fifteenth and sixteenth centuries.

Term coined by French historian Michelet and developed into historical concept by Swiss historian Jacob Burckhardt: 1860.

Renaissance thought was a period of transition from medieval theological interpretation of reality to modern, scientific views.

Renaissance also gave significance and stress to man and his place in the cosmos, and rejection of medieval attitudes to science.

RENAISSANCE ENTERTAINMENTS

As recreational and cultural activities in the Italian Renaissance, there was participation in jousts, tournaments, social diversions, carnival processions, dramatic performances, masked balls, duck hunts, concerts, declaiming Latin poetry.

RENAISSANCE EPIC POETRY

The vogue of classical literature, particularly the fame of Homer and Vergil, during the Renaissance caused many humanists and poets to attempt the epic form. Petrarch marked the first notable attempt in his Latin epic on the Punic Wars, *Africa.* Most epics were written in the vernacular, and it seemed to be conceived as the most appropriate literary form in which to express the spirit of a people. Most notable among the national epics was Camôes' *The Lusiads;* others were Tasso's *Jerusalem Delivered,* Ariosto's *Orlando Furioso,* Boiardo's *Orlando Innamorato,*

Spenser's *Faerie Queene* and what is in many respects the culmination of the Renaissance concern to write epics inspired by the classical models: Milton's *Paradise Lost.*

The epic poetry of the sixteenth century was continued in the seventeenth, but there arose a stream of imitations based on Ariosto and Tasso. Among these epics were: *The Recovery of the Cross:* published in 1611 by Francesco Bracciolini (1560-1647). *Conquest of Granada:* published in 1650 by Girolamo Graziani (1604-1675).

Mock heroic epic is represented by the *Mockery of the Gods:* published in 1618-1624 by Francesco Bracciolini, and *The Rape of the Bucket:* published in 1622 by Alessandro Tassoni (1565-1635).

RENAISSANCE FARCE

Italian farce was broad in humor, uninhibited in morals, usually acted in local dialects, and often partly improvised on a fixed scenario. Jacopo Sannazzaro (1458-1530) and P. A. Caracciolo wrote farces in the Neapolitan dialect. Giovanni Giorgio Alione (1460-1521) wrote in Piedmontese.

Among other such writers were the Sienese Niccolò Campani, the Paduan Angelo Beolco (1502-1542), called Il Ruzzante, and the Venetian Andrea Calmo (1510-1571). Artisans and members of lower classes formed clubs for acting these popular plays. One such club was the Congrega dei Rozzi at Siena. These groups were the predecessors of professional companies of actors, the first of which played at Mantua in 1567. From these activities developed the *commedia dell'arte.*

RENAISSANCE HISTORIANS

Niccolò Machiavelli (1469-1527); Jacopo Nardi (1476-1556); Francesco Guicciardini (1482-1540); Filippo Nerli (1485-1536); Donato Giannoti (1492-1572); Benedetto Varchi (1502-1565); Bernardo Segni (1504-1558); Jacopo Pitti (1519-1589).

RENAISSANCE HUMOR

Risibility, whether frank and spontaneous or wry and satirical, was promoted by humorous anecdotes, by the professional jester —*l'uomo piacevole*—and by collections of witty apothegms and *dicta* in the manner of Plutarch. Humorous instigations included practical jokes—*burle* and *bèffe.* A certain Dolcibene was considered the king of Italian jesters. Two famous jesters of the mid-fifteenth century were Arlotto (1483), a priest near Florence, and Gonnella, the court fool of Ferrara. In a more literary sense, poets and satirists produced skits and parodies, pastiches and caricatures of well-known poems or trends. Teofilo Folengo (c. 1520) composed an *Orlandino,* ridiculing chivalric heroism. Under the name of Merlinus Coccaius, he produced a macaronic poem on the allusive Alexandrian type of epic.

RENAISSANCE IN SPAIN

In Spain, the Renaissance—*Renacimiento*—began in late fifteenth century. Already perceptible in Italian and humanistic influences on Santillana and Mena. In reigns of Ferdinand and Isabella (1471-1516) and Charles V (1516-1556), when the Renaissance took root in Spain and reached its zenith in the reigns of Philip II, III, and IV (1556-1665). Period marked by Spain's predominance as a world power, and achievement of political, religious, linguistic unity, *El Siglo de Oro.* Varied influences are apparent: humanism, Platonism, Erasmus, Petrarch. Because of religious orthodoxy, secular features of Renaissance are comparatively minor.

In art the *plateresco* style was prevalent—the architectural style in which delicate, rich decoration was concentrated on doorways and windows, the rest of the structure remaining spare. Interiors were treated lavishly, utilizing arabesques, twisted scrolls and the *rejas* or elaborate screens and grillwork of wrought iron.

In lyric poetry, Petrarch introduced into Spain by Juan Boscán and Garcilaso de la Vega. Interest in popular poetry and ballads demonstrated by publication of *cancioneros.*

In drama, great achievements by Tirso de Molina, Lope de Vega, Calderón. Also development of new types of prose fiction: chivalric romances and picaresque tales.

RENAISSANCE JOURNALS

Among periodical publications devoted to Renaissance studies in various phases are the following:

Renaissance News: Quarterly publication of the Renaissance Society of America. This Society also publishes an annual volume of *Studies in the Renaissance.*

Rinascimento (Italy)

Traditio: Fordham University. Not exclusively devoted to Renaissance studies.

Revue Belge de Musicologie (Belgium)

Kunstchronik: German, monthly devoted to history of art.

Bibliothèque d'Humanisme et Renaissance: annual (Switzerland)

Zeitschrift für Kunstgeschichte: annual, devoted to history of art. (Germany)

RENAISSANCE POPES

The papacy was in no position to play the role of patron of the arts and learning during the Babylonian Captivity and the Great Schism. With the restoration marked by the ascension of Martin V to the papal throne, the papacy began to cultivate the new art and learning. However, the first who could be called rightfully a Renaissance pope came a generation later in the person of Nicholas V (1448-1455), who had previously moved in humanist circles at Florence and who called many Florentine artists and humanists to Rome with him; he was himself an enthusiastic collector of classical manuscripts. Pius II (1458-1464). Scholar and writer. Produced poems, dialogues, letters, a novel, a history, and a geography that reputedly influenced Columbus. He was one of the great figures of his generation and represents the Renaissance papacy at its best. Sixtus IV (1471-1484) typifies the popular conception of the Renaissance papacy: lavish in its patronage of art and scholarship, steeped in luxury and worldly vices, practiced in intrigue and political maneuver. His nephew, the warrior pope, Julius II (1503-1513), was the patron of Michelangelo. Leo X, the Medici pope at the time of Luther's revolt, was one of the most munificent of all Renaissance patrons; by his time, and in part owing to him, the center of the Renaissance had shifted from Florence to Rome, where it flourished until the sack of 1527. Not long after, the Counter Reformation papacy came into being; for it the Renaissance was synonymous with paganism and worldliness and hence suspect.

RENAISSANCE STATE, THE

The medieval period held to a conception of the *res publica Christiana,* the Christian Commonwealth; it is the period of the Renaissance that saw the development of a single, coherent, sovereign governmental apparatus called the state, replacing the welter of authorities that typified the middle ages, feudal, ecclesiastical, dynastic, municipal, and guild. "State" was first used in the new sense by the English political writer Thomas Starkey, c.

500

1535; Machiavelli was both builder and describer of the state, the Leviathan as Hobbes was to call it. The institutions of modern diplomacy—the means of contact between the new entities—have their origin in the Renaissance era. The first part of Burckhardt's *Civilization of the Renaissance in Italy* is a famous description of "The State as a Work of Art."

RENAISSANCE STYLE IN ART

The first phase of Renaissance art, in Italy, extended from c. 1420 to c. 1560. In the Netherlands, from c. 1450 to c. 1600. In other European countries, from the 1490's to c. 1600.

In Italy the first stages were marked by a return to classical antiquity and the inspiration of natural forms. In France and Germany the reliance on antiquity was, if anything, stronger, but only in a restricted circle of artists and scholars.

The Italian Renaissance was imitated in other European countries. In architecture, the Renaissance rejected the Gothic forms, and returned to the long basilican and central plans, adding the harmonious use of ornaments based on antique models. Among secular buildings, the city dwellings received their modern forms and standards of habitability. In Italy, magnificent country villas began to appear, and in Germany and France the modern domestic château.

Early Renaissance period: 1420-1500. North of Alps: 1490's-1540.

High Renaissance: 1500-c. 1540. North of Alps: to c. 1570.

Late Renaissance: to c. 1560. North of Alps: to c. 1610.

RENAISSANCE WOMEN

Love and beauty fascinated many a Renaissance artist, poet, philosopher; it was the age when the term "Platonic love" was coined, but also an age of great sensuality and sexual immorality. Woman was apostrophized, eulogized, carved in stone, painted, molded in bronze. She was the object of passionate adoration, both Platonic and carnal. Beauty, as in ancient Greek philosophy, came to be regarded as the proper criterion for many, if not all, aspects of life; even ethics and morality were subordinated to this aesthetic norm in the sense that beauty was truth, including moral truth.

Prostitution was not only rampant, but accepted as a phase of this passion, stripped of any moral implications. In Venice alone some 12,000 harlots were registered professionally. In some respects, these harlots were the direct descendants of the ancient Greek hetaerae, for they possessed, apart from their physical attractions, intellectual interests and were frequently skilled in drawing and music, in Latin and painting.

Not all woman, of course, were licentious and lascivious. There were devoted mothers, saintly nuns, faithful wives, some of them living in placid obscurity; others, by virtue of their ways, are recorded in the chronicles and memoirs and letters of their contemporaries.

The Renaissance was a period of greater prosperity and hence of leisure for those women whose households could afford servants. Many more women than in the middle ages, free from kitchen drudgery and the nursery, could and did give themselves over to education and the polite intercourse of court and salon. Some were educated in the same way and on the same subjects as men; several of the Renaissance tracts on education give special attention to the education of women. While they were still used at men's convenience in the chess game of forming family alliances, the glorification of love—so prominent in the age— would seem to have caused them to be held in higher esteem than earlier. Among some of the notable women may be mentioned Beatrice and Isabelle d'Este for their artistic tastes, intellectual attainments, and political astuteness; the redoubtable Caterina Sforza, wife of Girolamo Riario, for her defense of her lands against her husband's murderers and for a time against Cesare Borgia; Vittoria Colonna the poetess and confidante of Michelangelo; Elisabetta Gonzaga, the bluestocking duchess of Urbino whose court was a school of manners, the scene of Castiglione's *Courtier;* Marguerite of Navarre, the sister of Francis I of France, for her accomplishments as a writer and her enlightened patronage of, among others, Rabelais; Catherine of Aragon whose humanist attainments decidedly surpassed those of her famous husband; and the bluestocking daughters of Sir Thomas More.

RENASCENTES LITTERAE
The rebirth of literature. A Latin expression used contemporaneously during the Italian Renaissance to designate the renewed knowledge, understanding and reverence for ancient civilization, particularly its literature; it also referred to the production of many new and great literary works by contemporary authors.

RENAUDOT, THEOPHRASTE
(1586-1653). Physician. Publicist. Noted for public disputes on medicine and science. Founded *Gazette de France:* first issue appeared in 1631. The first French periodical publication. It carried news of the court and of Paris and the kingdom as well as of Europe; it enjoyed the patronage of the government, while Renaudot enjoyed the protection of Richelieu and then of Mazarin.

RENÉ I
(1409-1480). The Good. Angevin. Claimant to the throne of Naples and rival of Alfonso the Magnanimous. Returned to Aix-en-Provence. Produced romances, poetry. Called Last of the Troubadours.

RENÉE OF FRANCE
(1510-1576). Daughter of Louis XII of France. She had been betrothed to many of the great princes of Europe, e.g., Charles V and Henry VIII, but finally married Hercules d'Este of Ferrara; upon his accession she became Duchess of Ferrara and the center of a group of humanists, poets, artists and religious leaders. She embraced Calvinism, was deprived of her children, thrust into prison and made to conform to her husband's views. She returned to France on the death of her husband and made her court a center of Calvinist propaganda. Her Italian court had considerable importance for the introduction of Protestant ideas into Italy.

RENGIFO, JUAN DÍAZ
(Sixteenth century). Spanish Jesuit writer and teacher. Author of important manual of Spanish versification: *Arte Poética Española.* Published in Salamanca in 1592. It is a manual for readers and students and has been said to testify to a decline of the literary standards that had prevailed earlier in the century.

RENI, GUIDO
(1575-1642). Italian painter. Died in Bologna. Chief representative of the idealistic trend in the Bolognese-Roman Baroque movement. His specialty was religious themes, mythological subjects, frescoes; his most famous work is the *Aurora* fresco in the Rospigliosi Palace of Rome done for Pope Paul V. In it he made perfect use of the grandeur and the gold and silver color tones that may be seen in his most characteristic works.

REPTON SCHOOL

In Derbyshire. English public school. Founded in 1557 under the will of Sir John Port.

RESENDE, GARCIA DE

(1470-1536) Portuguese poet and chronicler, secretary to Kings John II and Manuel I. Compiled a corpus of poems entitled *Cancioneiro Geral,* many of which are his own. Also versified contemporary chronicles.

RES PUBLICA CHRISTIANA

The Christian Commonwealth of the middle ages, the ideal—to a remarkable extent achieved—of a single great society in Europe under the spiritual headship of the papacy and, theoretically at least, the temporal headship of the Holy Roman Emperors. What was still left of the *Res Publica* was shattered in the sixteenth century by the forces unleashed during the Reformation.

REUCHLIN, JOHANN

(1455-1522). The greatest German humanist, professor at Heidelberg. As a young man he had traveled and studied in both Italy and France, and was the friend of Pico, who stimulated his interest in Hebrew and the Cabala, the corpus of Jewish theosophy. He published a Hebrew grammar and dictionary: Hebrew, along with Greek which he had also mastered but in which he was no pathfinder, was an adjunct to the study of the Old Testament. He was drawn into endless controversy in which he defended the study of Hebrew and the use of humanist methods of textual criticism in Old Testament studies; accused of heresy by the Inquisition, his case dragged on for six years and became the *cause célèbre* of the era. Practically all the humanists rallied to his support; Reuchlin published their pledges and salutes as *Letters of Eminent Men* in 1514. One gambit of his friends was the *Letters of Obscure Men,* purporting to be the opinions of Reuchlin's antagonists; it was in fact a satire in which were exposed the bad learning, foul motives, and evil lives of clerical opponents; the work helped to deepen the sense of outrage with which ecclesiastical abuses were regarded in Germany. The case appealed to Rome, Reuchlin was finally acquitted by Pope Leo X.

REUSNER, NICOLAS
(1545-1602). German scholar and jurist. He was the author of some eighty works, most on the civil law, but including political works, histories, philosophy, literary studies and a great deal of poetry that followed classical models. He was greatly honored by the Emperor Rudolph II, who crowned him poet laureate and made him ambassador, etc.

REY, JEAN
(c. 1582-c. 1650). French chemist and physician who adapted an instrument to measure water temperature, 1632. He was a student of the nature of burning.

RHEGIUS, URBANUS or RIEGER
(1489-1541) German Lutheran, preacher at Augsburg, friend of Luther and humanist writer. He penned over a hundred works including the Latin verse for which he was made orator and poet laureate by the Emperor. He renounced the priesthood, became a Lutheran propagandist and wrote most of his works on religious and ecclesiastical subjects.

RHENANUS, BEATUS
(1485-1547) German humanist scholar. Friend of Erasmus, whose works he published and whose biography he wrote. Published editions of Latin texts, e.g., of Velleius, Seneca and Tacitus.

RHENISH LITERARY SODALITY
A noted German society in the fifteenth century comparable to the Italian academies. Among those associated with this coterie was the humanist John Trithemius (1462-1516).

RHETICUS, GEORG JOACHIM VON LAUCHER
(1514-1576) German mathematician, astronomer, professor at Wittenberg. Worked with Copernicus, whom he prodded into allowing the publication of *De Revolutionibus Orbium Coelestium*.

RIBALTA, FRANCESCO DE
(c. 1555-1628). Spanish painter of religious scenes. Noted for his treatment of chiaroscuro. Belongs to the Valencian school. He had studied in Italy, coming under the influence of Carracci.

RIBAUT, JEAN
(1520-1565). French navigator. Pioneer colonist in North Amer-

ica. Reached Florida in 1562. Founded colony in South Carolina in 1564. Colony destroyed by Spaniards. Ribaut's ship wrecked. Himself captured and killed by Spaniards. Author of *The Whole and True Discovery of Terra Florida:* published in London in 1563.

RIBEIRO, BERNARDIM

(1482-1552). Portuguese bucolic poet. Author of five eclogues, and the mixed pastoral and chivalrous romance *Menina e moça,* or *Young and Youthful.*

RIBERA, JOSÉ

(c. 1588-c. 1652) Called Lo Spagnoletto. Spanish painter and etcher. Lived most of his life in Naples after having studied in Rome. Prominent in Neapolitan school. Among his works are *Descent from the Cross, Assumption, Martyrdom of St. Bartholomew, Adoration of the Shepherds.* His forte was harshly realistic religious paintings. Also single portraits, earthy chiaroscuro; his studies of old men who are worn and emaciated are famous as examples of extreme realism over which a quality of dignity and of beauty has been cast.

RIBERO, DIOGO or RIBEIRO

(Died 1553) Portuguese cartographer. Produced an atlas, the *Carta Universal,* 1529. He spent much of his life in the service of Spain.

RICCI, MATTEO

(1552-1610) Italian Jesuit mathematician, scholar and man of letters. Missionary in India, China. Established mission in Peking. Introduced Christianity in many cities. Wrote on Chinese geography, history, and under the name of Lie-ma-tu, enjoyed great notoriety at the Emperor's court, where he discoursed on European technology and mathematics.

RICCIUS, JACOBUS

Logician of Arezzo. Wrote commentary on *Summula* of Paulus Venetus: published in 1488.

RICH, BARNABE

(c. 1540-c. 1620) English soldier, author of pamphlets, romances in the manner of Lyly's *Euphues* and reminiscences. In military service in the Low Countries, in France. Author of *The*

Adventures of Brusanus, published in 1592. Shakespeare drew upon his *Farewell to Military Profession* in *Twelfth Night.*

RICH, RICHARD
(Early seventeenth century.) English soldier. Made voyage to Virginia. Wrote an account entitled *News from Virginia:* published in 1610.

RICH, SIR RICHARD
(c. 1496-1567) Lord Chancellor of England, political opportunist. He served under Henry VIII, Edward VI and Mary in turn, prosecuting religious groups as expediency suggested.

RICHARD III
(1452-1485). King of England, Yorkist, brother of Edward IV, called Crouchback. On death of Edward IV proclaimed himself Protector and then king on the grounds that Edward IV's sons, "the princes in the tower," were illegitimate. In ensuing rebellion, was defeated at Bosworth Field, in 1485, and killed in battle. Appears in Shakespeare's historical play *Richard III.* Also in other English and German plays. Throughout the sixteenth century in England, particularly by the Elizabethan poets, he was regarded as the tyrant *par excellence,* against whom rebellion is justified and necessary; in recent years scholars have sought to rejuvenate his reputation, explaining away his infamy as a part of the Tudor myth.

RICHER, EDMOND
(1559-1633). French theologian. Wrote on pedagogy: *Obstetrix Animorum:* published in 1608. Also treatise on relationship between Papacy and French state: *De Ecclesiastica et Politica Potestate Libellus:* published in 1612; it is a defense of Gallican Church and an assertion of the superior authority of a Church council to the papal power. He reissued the works of Gerson, publishing them with a commentary of his own.

RICHIER, LIGIER
(c. 1500-1567) French sculptor of Lorraine. Executed sepulchral statuary, particularly for the tomb of René de Châlons, where a skeletal Death appears that is notable for its anatomical exactitude, as if it were a model for medical students, and also for its ghastly dramatic character. As a Protestant he was forced to flee to Geneva.

RICHELIEU, ARMAND JEAN DU PLESSIS, DUC DE

(1585-1642) Called *Eminence Rouge*. French cardinal, states-man. One of the greatest French statesmen. Chief minister of Louis XIII. Virtually in charge of French foreign and domestic policy. Frustrated the attempts to dismiss him by the Queen Mother, Marie de' Medici. He is remembered for carrying on the wars with the Hapsburgs of the Empire and of Spain, and thus laying the foundation of French hegemony in Europe; the creation of a powerful and efficient royal government; the forced submission of the Huguenots to the royal government and administration; and the establishment of the French Academy, intended to establish literary canons, correct usage, spelling, etc., for the French language.

RIDEMAN, PETER

(1505-1556). German member of Hutterian Brotherhood of Ana-baptists. Author of *Our Religion, Doctrine, and Faith.*

RIDLEY, NICHOLAS

(c. 1500-1555). Bishop of London. Protestant reformer. Chap-lain to Henry VIII. Collaborated in Cranmer's Prayer Book. Pro-moted Protestantism. Supported Lady Jane Grey as claimant to throne. Excommunicated as heretic, burned at stake under Mary.

RIDOLFI, ROBERTO DI

(1531-1612). Florentine merchant who settled in England. Con-spired against Queen Elizabeth and plotted to set Mary Queen of Scots on the English throne in 1570. He derived from the Floren-tine family of bankers, Ridolphi di Piazza, which was prominent in the economic and political life of Florence from the thirteenth to the seventeenth centuries, and had intermarried with the Me-dici.

RIEMENSCHNEIDER, TILMAN

(1460-1531). German sculptor. Died in Würzburg. Sculptured in stone. Also produced wood carvings. Important German sculp-tor in the period of transition from Gothic to Renaissance art. For showing opposition to the Bishop, he was imprisoned during the Peasants' War. He executed large figures, altar sculp-ture, single figures, architectural sculpture on portals, sepulchral statuary, and an *Adam and Eve*. The imperial tombs of Henry II and Kunigunde at Bamberg are his work and are in the full tide of the Renaissance.

RIESE, ADAM

(1492-1559). German mathematician. Author of one of the most famous texts on arithmetic, the *Rechenbuch:* published in 1522. He and the school he founded at Annaberg, Saxony enjoyed great fame among contemporaries. Believed to have devised the radical sign for indicating square roots.

RIGAULT, NICOLAS

(1577-1654). French Jesuit scholar. Edited the Christian Latin writers, Tertullian and Cyprian; in keeping with the outlook of the Counter Reformation, Catholic, and particularly Jesuit, classical scholars devoted themselves to the Christian rather than pagan classics.

RINCON, ANTONIO DEL

(1446-1500). Spanish painter. Very little is known about his life and the attribution of several works to him is little more than supposition. It is thought that he studied in Italy and thus was an important figure in introducing the new Italian modes to Spain.

RING, THE

German family of painters associated with Münster. The father, LUDGER (1496-1547), was architect and printer as well as painter of religious subjects and portraits, including his own very fine self-portrait. His sons, HERMANN (1521-1597), LUDGER THE YOUNGER (1522-1583) and HUBERT (born in 1524), also did religious subjects and portraits, but show more definitely Italian influence, particularly that of Michelangelo.

RINKART, MARTIN

Early seventeenth century. Author of noted German hymn: *Nun danket alle Gott.*

RINUCCINI, OTTAVIO

(1562-1621). Italian poet and librettist of Florence. Member of the *Camerata* group, also known as the Bardi Academy. Followed Marie de' Medici to France. He wrote the libretto for the first opera, Peri's *Daphne;* for the same composer he wrote *Euridice,* and was librettist to Monteverdi, Coccini and Gagliano.

RIOJA RODRIGUEZ, FRANCISCO DE

(1583-1659). Spanish poet and literary critic. Enjoying the patronage and protection of the Duke of Olivares, he wrote literary criticism, on oratory, law, philosophy and theology; he wrote sonnets and songs of a profound religious sense.

RISNER, FREDERICK
Published an edition of Al Hazen, Arab scientist, in 1572.

RISPETTI
In the Italian Renaissance, these were songs associated with the country side; they were a popular form of love lyric and adhered to a set verse form.

RIVAIL, AYMAR DU
(1490-1560). French jurist. Wrote the first full-scale history of ancient Roman law, including lives of famous jurists: *Civilis Historiae Iuris Commentariorum Libri Quinque*: published in 1515. It includes also some treatment of canon law.

RIVIUS, JOHANNES
(1500-1553). German classical scholar, teacher, theologian, of Saxony. Wrote on dreams, divination, condemnation of witchcraft. Author of *De Familiari Cuiusque Genio*: on guardian angels. Published in 1537. His edition, 1539, of Sallust was unusually accurate and complete.

RIZZIO, DAVID
(c. 1533-1566). Italian who became French secretary to Mary Queen of Scots. Negotiated marriage of Darnley and Mary. His influence over the queen provoked enemies, including Darnley, to drag him from Holyrood Palace and stab him to death.

ROBBIA, LUCA DELLA
(c. 1400-1482). Florentine sculptor and ceramist. Also goldsmith: originated the Robbia workshop. Produced series of panels called *Singing Galleries*. Also many reliefs on church doors: also Madonnas. He was the inventor of glazed or enameled terra cotta, the medium in which he did most of his work; it permitted him the vivid colors so characteristic of his work—particularly the greens and what came to be known as the "della Robbia blue." The shop continued to flourish until the 1540's under his descendants, ANDREA (1435-c. 1525), LUCA II (c. 1480-c. 1520), GIOVANNI (1469-c. 1530) and GIROLAMO (1488-1566), who was also an architect and spent most of his life in France at the royal court.

ROBERTELLI, FRANCESCO

(1516-1567). Italian classical scholar, professor at Venice, Padua and Bologna. He edited Aristotle's *Poetics*, correcting the text, translating it into Latin and adding a commentary on it; he also edited Aeschylus and *editio princips* of *On the Sublime*, which he attributed to Longinus. His work on *The Art of Textual Criticism* was long a standard manual for Latin manuscripts, treating handwriting, the various sources of error and corruption of the text and laying down the rules for restorations and emendations.

ROBSART, AMY

(c. 1532-1560). Wife of Robert Dudley, Earl of Leicester. Found dead: believed to have committed suicide. Reputedly, Dudley and Queen Elizabeth connived at murder. She frequently appears in the literature of the period and later.

ROCCATAGLIATA, NICCOLÒ

(Died after 1636). Italian sculptor of Genoa, but worked chiefly in Venice. Executed figurines of child with flute, child with violin, child with drum. He was called *el maestro dell putto* or the master of the child's figure.

ROCCHI, CRISTOFORO

(died 1497). Italian architect and sculptor. Pupil of Bramante. Worked in Pavia, where he designed and initiated the construction of the cathedral.

RODRIGUEZ DE FONSECA, JUAN

(1451-1524). Spanish cleric. Chaplain to Ferdinand and Isabella. Hostile to Columbus and later, as bishop of Burgos in the time of Charles V, to Cortés.

ROE, SIR THOMAS

(c. 1580-1644). English ambassador and courtier. Envoy to West Indies and many European courts. He traveled to Judea, Persia and the Ottoman Empire. Wrote memoirs of his embassies and left much of his correspondence.

ROGER OF VENRAY

(1451-c. 1507). Rutgerus Sycamber. Dutch monk. Attached to monastery of Hagen. Associated with humanists Arnold Bost, Johannes Trithemius. Wrote *Dialogus de Quantitate Syllabarum*: published in 1502. Also poems.

ROGERS, JOHN

(c. 1500-1555). English Catholic priest who became Protestant. Assisted in Coverdale's and Tyndale's rendering of the Bible which he published in 1537 under the pseudonym of Thomas Matthews. He contributed marginal notes and an introduction. On return to England, preached against Catholicism, was imprisoned and burned at the stake under Mary.

ROHAN-GIÉ, HENRI, DUC DE

(1579-1638). French Huguenot leader. Led the Huguenots in 1627-1628 against Richelieu. Attached to German Protestant forces. In favor with Henry IV of France. Opposed Imperial and Spanish troops. Fatally wounded at Rheinfelden. He translated and edited Caesar's *Gallic Wars* as *The Complete Captain*, and wrote his *Mémoires* and other works.

ROI DE BOURGES

A contemptuous designation of Charles VII (1422-1461), for he was confined to Bourges during the period of the Hundred Years' War when England controlled northern France.

ROJAS, FERNANDO DE

(c. 1465-c. 1541). Spanish writer; he was of Jewish descent and had studied law at Salamanca. On the basis of an acrostic that spells out his name, the famous novel in which life is realistically depicted, *La Celestina*, is attributed to him. It was translated into English by John Rastell, c. 1525.

ROJAS VILLANDRANDO, AUGUSTÍN DE

(1572-1635). Spanish novelist, adventurer. Called *el caballero del milagro*. Led picaresque life: fought in France, where he was imprisoned, joined a privateer, was a fugitive from justice, and strolling actor. Author of theatrical prologues and one play, *El Natural Desdichado*. Satire on government—*El Buen Repúblico*. Chief work: Picaresque novel: *El Viaje Entretenido*, which appeared in 1603. This is a series of adventures against theatrical background. Had literary influence on Calderón, Scarron, Shakespeare, Goethe.

ROJAS ZORRILLA, FRANCISCO

(1605-c. 1650). Spanish dramatist. Practically nothing is known of his life beyond the fact that he was dubbed a knight of Santiago. His best play was *Del Rey Abajo Ninguno*. Several of his works provided plots and materials for other dramatists, e.g., Corneille.

ROLFE, JOHN

(1585-1622). English colonist in Virginia. Established the cultivation of tobacco in Virginia. Married Pocahontas, daughter of Indian chief. Reputedly, killed by Indians.

ROLLOCK, ROBERT

(c. 1555-1599). Scottish scholar, theologian. First Regent of Edinburgh University. Author of theological treatises in Latin.

ROMAN ACADEMY

Founded by Pomponius Laetus (1425-1498). Members assumed Roman names, performed Plautine plays. In 1468, by order of Pope Paul II, the members of the Roman Academy were arrested and put to the torture and the academy dissolved. It was re-established by Sixtus IV and greatly favored by Leo X.

ROMANIAN BOOKS

In 1540 a Calvinist *Catechism* was printed in Romanian at Sibiu. In 1560 Deacon Coresi published in Transylvania a Romanian translation of the Gospels: first major book in Romanian. In 1564 *Tâlc al Evangheliilor*, a Calvinist book of homilies, appeared.

ROMANINO, GIROLAMO DA ROMANO, IL

(c. 1485-1566). Italian painter. Died in Brescia. Executed altarpieces, portraits; the chief influence upon him was Titian.

ROMAN TYPE

First used in England by Norman-born printer Richard Pynson (died 1530).

ROMBOUTS, THEODOOR

(1597-1637). Dutch painter, engraver. Executed genre themes. He traveled and worked extensively in Italy.

ROME

Rome was the ancient *alma mater*, the fountain and source of the Italian Renaissance. As the *caput mundi*, it had endured for centuries, a city of great contrasts, of licentiousness and asceticism, of paganism and Christianity, of poverty and luxury and splendor. It was the seat of the Papacy in the Renaissance and a focal centre for political and intellectual activities. It was continuously exposed to attack, assault, sack, coveted by foreign powers, undermined by insidious forces. Yet, under the Popes, who were statesmen as well as prelates, it withstood all those subversive challenges.

In the Renaissance, the humanists were fired with a passion for the culture of the classics. Search for Greek and Roman manuscripts became a primary purpose in life. Poets and sculptors, historians and philosophers thronged to examine the treasures stored in the Vatican. They surveyed the Roman Forum, the triumphal arches, the decayed temples and baths that recalled the glories of antiquity. First Petrarch and Poggio, Brunelleschi and Donatello, then Botticelli and Ghirlandaio, Michelangelo and Perugino rescued the heritage of the ancients, or copied and adapted to contemporary use whatever was still resplendent, still memorable.

The first phase of the Renaissance centered in Florence, but by 1500 it had shifted to Rome.

ROME, SACK OF, 1527

The culmination of the disasters inflicted upon Italy that began with the French invasion of 1494, the conquest and sack of the city by the Imperialists—an army that included a large contingent of German Lutherans—destroyed the Roman world of learning, literature, and art that flourished there since the days of Nicholas V. Many a scholar and artist lost his life to the sword, torture, or disease; others ended their days in obscurity, poverty, suffering. The peace of 1530 between Pope Clement VII and the Emperor Charles V was the shroud thrown over the Italian corpse: the Medici were restored to Florence, the ascendancy of Spain in the peninsula was permanently established, the papacy itself was virtually the prisoner of the Emperor. Within a decade there emerged the Counter-Reformation papacy that had nearly as little taste for humane learning and art as it had for Protestantism. Contemporaries as well as later historians confirm the horror and completeness of the catastrophe; by then however the Renaissance had migrated north of the Alps.

RONDELET, GUILLAUME

(1507-1566). French physician, ichthyologist, and professor of medicine at Montpellier. Author of *De Piscibus Marinis;* published in 1554, it was profusely and accurately illustrated, and was a milestone in the study of marine life.

514

RONDINELLI, NICCOLÒ

(c. 1450-c. 1510) Italian painter of religious scenes. He was a follower of Giovanni Bellini and is notable for his vivid colors.

RONDINELLUS, IOANNES

(Sixteenth century). Italian scholar. Delivered funeral oration on Charles IX of France. Published in 1574.

RONSARD, PIERRE DE

(c. 1524-1585) French poet, chief figure of *La Pléiade*, courtier, of noble birth. Considered founder of French lyric poetry. Wrote odes, elegies, eclogues, sonnets and songs following classical models, most notably Pindar and Horace, and also Petrarch. His attempt at a great national epic, *La Franciade*, was never finished. He became poet royal in 1563. The works and critical linguistic views of Ronsard and *La Pléiade* circle point to the French classicism of the seventeenth century.

ROOVERE, ANTHONIS DE

(Died 1482). Flemish poet. He contributed a poem on the death of Philip the Good to the *Chronicle of Flanders* by André de Smet. Author of grimly humorous, satirical poems descriptive of social conditions of his time.

ROPER, MARGARET

(1505-1544). Daughter of Sir Thomas More, the "Meg" of More's letters. Her portrait, now lost, was painted by Holbein. She translated a work of Erasmus, who greatly admired her and dedicated a treatise in her honor. Noted for her devotion, affability and charm, scholarly achievements and linguistic accomplishments. Her husband, WILLIAM ROPER (1496-1578), wrote More's biography; as the work of an ardent Catholic it is especially memorable for the passages reporting the conversations of father and daughter in the Tower before his execution in 1535.

RORE, CYPRIEN DE

(1516-1565). Flemish musician, who spent most of his life in Italy, a pupil of Willaert, whom he succeeded as choirmaster at St. Mark's, Venice. Composed madrigals, psalms, motets, masses, and was especially important in the development of the Renaissance madrigal.

ROSINUS, JOHANN OF EISENBACH or ROSSFELD

(1551-1626). German Protestant theologian and scholar. Author

515

of *Antiquitatum Romanorum Corpus Absolutissimum,* a compendium of Roman antiquities, first published in 1585. It was corrected and expanded by other hands in the early seventeenth century.

ROSSELLINO, ANTONIO
(1427-c. 1479). Italian sculptor. Inclined to manner of Ghiberti. Executed sepulchral sculpture. Nativity group, monument to Cardinal di Portogallo. He was for a number of years at the Este court of Ferrara and also at Parma. He carved a famous portrait bust of the humanist Matteo Palmieri.

ROSSELLINO, BERNARDINO
(1409-1464). Italian sculptor, architect, brother of the above, with whom, and three other brothers, he opened an important workshop in Florence. Executed tombs, architectural sculptures and similar works. His best-known sculpture is the tomb of the humanist Leonardo Bruni; as architect he is remembered for the Rucelli Palace at Florence and the Piccolomini Palace at Siena. He was called to Rome by Pope Nicholas V to begin the reconstruction of several great churches there, including St. Peter's, his design for which was adopted in part by his successor, Bramante.

ROSSETTI, BIAGIO
(c. 1447-1516). Italian architect who served the Este house of Ferrara, where he worked on the Schifanoia Palace and other structures, including fortifications.

ROSSI, AZARIAH
(c. 1513-1578). Jewish writer of Mantua. Critic of Hebraic and other literatures. Chief work: *Light of the Eyes,* on Jewish chronology and archaeology.

ROSSI, SALOMONE DE'
(c. 1565-c. 1628). Called L'Ebréo. Rabbi of Mantua. Composer. Attached to the Gonzaga court at Mantua. Composed madrigals, sonatas, synagogical music, and some of the music for a religious play, *Maddalena.* He was one of the important composers of instrumental music of his time.

ROSWEYDE, HERIBERT
(1569-1629). Dutch scholar of Utrecht. Jesuit. Projected hagiographical series of *Acta Sanctorum,* in which the critical methods of humanist scholarship would be applied to sources and docu-

ments of Christian antiquity. The project was suppressed by the Bollandist Jesuits. Rosweyde did publish several works in the field, however, viz., *Martyrologeum Romanorum* and *Vitae Patrum*.

ROTROU, JEAN DE

(1609-1650). French dramatist and poet. Member of *L'Étoile*, group of five poets. Author of many tragicomedies of which *Venceslas* and *Saint Genest* are the best, frequently on historical subjects.

ROTTENHAMMER, JOHANN

(1564-1625). German painter. Died in Augsburg. His themes are religious and mythological. During his stay in Venice he was profoundly influenced by Titian.

ROWLEY, WILLIAM

(1585?-1624?). English playwright and actor. He wrote *A New Wonder, A Match at Midnight* and *All's Lost by Lust*. His best works were produced in collaboration with Thomas Middleton and include *A Fair Quarrel* and *The Changeling*.

ROYAL CHARTER

In 1609 under Rudolf II of Germany, a Royal Charter was issued granting religious freedom to the nobility, knights and free cities.

ROYAL COLLEGE OF PHYSICIANS

Founded in London in 1518. The humanist Thomas Linacre was the chief figure in its founding.

ROYAL EXCHANGE

In London. Founded between 1566 and 1571 by English financier Sir Thomas Gresham (1519-1579).

ROYAL GRAMMAR SCHOOL

In Newcastle-upon-Tyne. English public school. Founded at beginning of sixteenth century by Thomas Horsley. Royal Charter granted by Queen Elizabeth in 1600.

RUBENS, PETER PAUL

(1577-1640). Flemish painter, the greatest figure of the Flemish school. He spent eight years in Italy at the court of Mantua; upon his return he opened a great and enormous studio at Antwerp, which, with students flocking in to learn from him, became a great art center. Something resembling mass production methods were used in which the design was Rubens but the execution his assistants'. Worked in Paris, Madrid, London. Work includes portraits: Philip IV of Spain; religious, mythological, historical subjects, landscapes. Noted for rich coloring and roseate, sensuous nudes. Two famous canvases are *Rape of the Sabines* and *Descent from the Cross*.

RUBIO, ANTONIO

(1568-1615). Spanish Jesuit. Wrote commentaries on almost all of Aristotle's works. When the Jesuit Fathers became teachers in 1570 at the University of Mexico, founded in 1551, Rubio was among them. His commentaries are the first such to have been written in the New World. He has been called a "dissident Thomist."

RUCELLAI, BERNARDO

(1449-1514). Florentine humanist. Leader of Platonic Academy; place of meeting of members was known as *Orti Oricellari*, the older Latin form of Rucellai. One of its members was Machiavelli. The family had been rich and prominent in Florentine affairs since the thirteenth century; it had produced 14 gonfaloniers and 85 priors. The famous Palazzo Rucellai was its residence.

RUCELLAI, GIOVANNI

(1475-1525). Italian dramatist, poet, son of above. Took holy orders. Lived in Rome. Attached to the court of Pope Leo X. Among the first poets to use blank verse. Author of *Le Api*: published in 1524. Imitative of Vergil's *Georgics*. Author of classical tragedy *Oreste*: appeared in 1525. Imitative of Euripides. Also wrote *Rosmunda*. He also wrote a treatise on the use of the vernacular Italian tongue.

RUDOLPH

(1576-1608). King of Croatia. Became king at age of twenty-four. Had spent some time at court of Spain. Interested in arts, science, astrology. Abdicated: retired to Prague, establishing museum of arts and antiquities.

RUDOLF II

(1552-1612). Holy Roman Emperor 1576-1612. King of Hungary. King of Bohemia. Educated in Spain by Jesuits. Son of Maxi-

518

milian II. As Emperor, he determined to eradicate Protestantism. When revolts broke out in Hungary, in 1608, he created his brother Matthias King of Hungary, in 1611 of Bohemia. Had astrological interests, patron of Tycho Brahe and Kepler, he is said to have locked up alchemists with the command to produce gold for him.

RUGBY SCHOOL
English public school. Founded by Lawrence Sheriff in 1567.

RUGGLE, GEORGE
(1575-1621). English playwright. Fellow of Clare College, Cambridge. Author of highly popular comedy entitled *Ignoramus:* first printed in 1630; writen in Latin, it was a satire on lawyers and their technicalities.

RUIZ DE ALARCÓN Y MENDOZA, JUAN
(c. 1581-1639). Spanish classical dramatist, born in Mexico. Held governmental and commercial positions. He wrote, typically, what might be called comic morality plays in which the characters symbolize virtues and vices; thus his *La Verdad Sospechosa* is the comedy of the habitual liar, *Las Parades Oyen* of the gossiper, etc. Fame became European. As a writer of comedies in which the humor depends upon character, he influenced Corneille, Molière, Goldoni.

RULERS OF ARAGON
Alfonso V, the Magnanimous, King of Aragon, Sicily, Naples: 1416-1458; John II. King of Aragon and Sicily: 1458-1479; Ferrante I, King of Naples: 1458-1494; Ferdinand II, King of Aragon: 1479-1516. (Dates refer to duration of rule.)

RULERS OF DENMARK
Christian I: 1448-1481. John: 1481-1513. Christian II: 1513-1533. Christian III: 1534-1559. Frederick II: 1559-1588. Christian IV: 1588-1648.
Dates refer to duration of rule.

RULERS OF DENMARK AND NORWAY
Frederick I: 1523-1533. Christian III: 1534-1559. Frederick II: 1559-1588. Christian IV: 1588-1648.
Dates refer to duration of rule.

RULERS OF ENGLAND
Edward IV: 1461-1483. Edward V: 1483. Richard III: 1483-1485. Henry VII: 1485-1509. Henry VIII: 1509-1547. Edward VI: 1547-1553. Mary: 1553-1558. Elizabeth: 1558-1603. James I of England: 1603-1625.
Dates refer to duration of rule.

RULERS OF MILAN
The family of the Sforza. Francesco: 1450-1466. Galeazzo Maria: 1466-1476. Gian Galeazzo: 1476-1479. Ludovico (Il Moro): 1479-1500.
Dates refer to duration of rule.

RULERS OF POLAND
Casimir V: 1445-1492. John Albert: 1492-1501. Alexander: 1501-1506. Sigismund I: 1506-1548. Sigismund II: 1548-1572. Stephen Bathory: 1575-1586. Sigismund III: 1587-1632. Vladislav VII: 1632-1648. John Casimir: 1648-1668.
Dates refer to duration of rule.

RULERS OF PORTUGAL
Alfonso V: 1438-1481. John II: 1481-1495. Manuel I: 1495-1521. John III: 1521-1557. Sebastian I: 1557-1578. Cardinal Henry: 1578-1580. Philip I: 1580-1598. Philip II: 1598-1621. Philip III: 1621-1640. John IV: 1640-1656.
Dates refer to duration of rule.

RULERS OF RUSSIA
Ivan III: 1462-1505. Basil IV: 1505-1533. Ivan IV: 1533-1584. Theodore: 1584-1598.
Dates refer to duration of rule.

RULERS OF SPAIN
"The Catholic Kings," Ferdinand and Isabella: 1474-1504. Ferdinand lived to 1516, ruling officially only Aragon after the death of Isabella in 1504. Philip I: 1504-1506. Charles I: 1516-1556. Philip II: 1556-1598. Philip III: 1598-1621. Philip IV: 1621-1665.
Dates refer to duration of rule.

RULERS OF SWEDEN
Charles VII: 1448-1457. Christian I of Oldenburg. 1457-1481. Sten Sture The Elder: 1470-1503. John II: 1497-1501. Svane

520

Sture: 1503-1512. Sten Sture The Younger: 1512-1520. Christian II: 1520-1523. Gustavus Vasa I: 1523-1560. Eric XIV: 1560-1568. John III: 1568-1592. Sigismund: 1592-1604. Charles IX: 1604-1611. Gustavus II Adolphus: 1611-1632. Christina: 1632-1654.

Dates refer to duration of rule.

RULMAN, ANNE
(1583-1639) French jurist, antiquarian, Huguenot. He wrote a "secret history" of the religious disorders of his time, but is remembered for his exhaustive work on Roman antiquities in southern France; he also compiled a collection of speeches and pleas by prominent French jurists and statesmen.

RUSCELLI, GIRALAMO
(Died 1566) Italian scholar. He came to Rome, where he founded the *Accademia dello Sdegno*, but then settled in Venice. He made a translation of Ptolemy's *Geography*, compiled an anthology of classic Italian works that included critical estimates, e.g., of Boccaccio, and wrote discourses on Italian philology, poetics, etc.

RUSCHI, FRANCESCO
(1610-1670) Italian painter of Venice. Influenced by Caravaggio. Executed religious themes, largely Old Testament scenes.

RUSCONI, GIOVANNI ANTONIO
(Died c. 1590) Italian architect. He is remembered for his translation of Vitruvius, illustrated by many woodcuts, which was the chief edition of the work used in the late Renaissance. No structures designed by him are now known to exist.

RUSSIAN ASSEMBLY
The first national assembly was convened by Ivan IV of Russia in 1549.

RUSTICI, GIOVANNI FRANCESCO
(1474-1554) Italian sculptor. Pupil of Verrocchio. Worked in Florence and for Francis I of France. Executed in bronze *John the Baptist Preaching*, with collaboration of Leonardo da Vinci in 1511. Also a *David*, a *Mercury* for the Cardinal de' Medici and a bust of Boccaccio.

RUTHVEN, THE RAID OF
In 1582 William Ruthven, Baron Ruthven (c. 1541-1584) carried

off boy-king James VI of Scotland to Castle Ruthven. This kidnapping known as Raid of Ruthven. Ruthven beheaded in Sterling.

RUTILIUS, BERNARDUS
(died 1537). Italian scholar. Wrote legal biographies entitled *Iuris Consultorum Vitae:* published in 1538.

RUZAEUS, ARNULF or RUZÉ
(c. 1480-1541) French jurist, ecclesiastic, chancellor of the University of Orleans. Wrote on functions of the crown, regalia, apostolic mandates, limits of lay authority.

RUZZANTE, IL, ANGELO BEOLCO
(1502-1542) Italian popular dramatist, actor and producer. His comedies and farces, written in the dialect of Pavia, are notable for their artless art and their ingenuous personages. They include *Parlamento de Ruzzante, Piovana, Fiorina, Maschetta,* and *Vaccaria.* They are remarkable for their intellectual and psychological sophistication, suggesting that Il Ruzzante was an actor-dramatist of refined rather than popular culture.

RYCKE, JOSSE DE
(1598-1627) Flemish scholar and Latin poet, Catholic ecclesiastic. Born in Ghent. Professor at Bologna. Author of archaeological and historial description of Rome.

S

SABAEUS, FAUSTUS
Sixteenth century. Custodian of Vatican Library. Wrote epigrams: *Epigrammatum Libri Quinque:* published 1556.

SABELLICO, MARCANTONIO COCCI
(c.1436-1506). Italian humanist, historian. Author of history commissioned by the state of Venice: *Historiate Rerum Venetarum,* which was continued later by Bembo. Also a universal history in 92 books. He had been a member of the Roman Academy with Pomponius Laetus and Platina, and later became head of the Library of St. Mark's at Venice.

SABINUS, ANGELUS or SABIN
(Fifteenth century) Italian humanist and Neo-Latin poet. Wrote versified letters to the figures of Ovid's *Heroides,* e.g., Odysseus and Penelope. He was the first editor of the Roman historian Ammianus Marcellinus.

SABINUS, GEORGIUS
(1508-1560) German philologist and Latin poet, diplomat. Wrote account of election and coronation of Charles V: *Electio et Coronatio Caroli V.* Published in 1550. Wrote elegies and other pieces. He was educated at Wittenberg; a Lutheran, he married Melanchthon's daughter Anna. He became professor of rhetoric at Frankfurt on the Oder. He sojourned several times in Italy, where he was welcomed into several humanist circles and became a close friend of Bembo. He published editions of Cicero's *Orations* and Ovid's *Metamorphoses.*

SACCHI, ANDREA

(1599-1661) Painter. Died in Rome. He specialized in religious paintings, persevering in the classical tradition of the Renaissance and ignoring the contemporary Baroque schools. He greatly admired Raphael. Executed *The Miracle of St. Gregory, The Vision of St. Romualdo.*

SACHS, HANS

(1494-1576). German shoemaker, the cobbler-poet. Leader of the guild of *Meistersinger* of Nuremberg. Wrote more than 4000 Master-songs. Also farces and Shrovetide plays. Joined cause of Reformation. Wrote poem addressed to Luther, calling him the Nightingale of Wittenberg. Appears in Wagner's opera *Die Meistersinger von Nurnberg.* Many of the melodies of his songs were adapted for Lutheran hymns.

SACKVILLE, THOMAS, EARL OF DORSET and BARON BUCKHURST

(1536?-1608). English playwright, poet. Contributed poems to miscellany called *A Mirror for Magistrates*: *The Induction, The Complaint of Henry Stafford.* Collaborated in drama, *Gorboduc*, with Thomas Norton. *Gorboduc* and the *Mirror* were two of the most popular and influential works of the Elizabethan age.

SÁ DE MIRANDA, FRANCISCO DE

(c. 1481-1558) Portuguese writer who is of the first importance in introducing the new Italian literary forms to his country, after having spent five years in Italy. He introduced the new metrical forms: the Italian sonnet, *canzone* of Petrarch, tercets of Dante, *ottava rima of* Boiardo, eclogues of Sannazzaro, etc. His two comedies, *Foreigner* (1528) and *Vilapandas* (1538), laid the foundations for the Portuguese national theatre. His *Cleopatra* was the first Portuguese tragedy to follow the classical canons.

SADLER, SIR RALPH

(1507-1587). Scottish diplomat. Jailer of Mary Queen of Scots. His papers are a source for Scottish history and were edited by Sir Walter Scott.

SADOLETO, JACOPO

(1477-1547) Italian humanist, Ciceronian Latinist, friend and colleague of Bembo in the papal service, Cardinal. Among the moderate Catholic reformers who sought a reconciliation with the Protestants; his extensive correspondence shows him to have been a friend or admirer of Erasmus, Melanchthon and even Calvin. Inspired by Cicero, he wrote treatises entitled *De Gloria* and *De laudibus philosophiae;* his dialogue on education emphasized the study of Greek. His poem celebrating the Laocoön statue, excavated in 1506, was one of the most popular works of the age.

SAFTLEVEN, CORNELIS
(1608-1661) Dutch painter. Died in Rotterdam. His subjects were genre, landscapes, still life. His brother HERMAN (1609-1685) was also a painter, notable for his landscapes and his Italianate manner.

SAGE, DAVID or LESAGE
(Born toward the end of the sixteenth century). Poet and lawyer. Author of *Las Foulias d'aôu Sage de Mountpelie,* appeared in 1650. Little is known of his life except that it was one of debauchery and difficulty over debt; his work—epigrams, satires, sonnets, elegies—is notable for its obscenity.

SAHAGÚN, BERNARDINO DE
(d. 1499-1590) Spanish Franciscan monk. Missionary and historian of Mexico. He wrote a history of the Spaish New World, missionary works, a dictionary of Latin, Spanish and Aztec, and compiled an Aztec grammar.

ST. BARTHOLOMEW'S DAY, MASSACRE OF
Huguenots in France, during the Religious Wars, were massacred on August 24, 1572. Instigation came from the Queen-Mother, Catherine de' Medici, the Duke of Guise, and his brother the Cardinal of Lorraine.

In Paris, massacre lasted two days and nights: spread to rural areas.

Murder of Huguenots continued until the middle of October. Reactions in other countries included laughter from Philip II of Spain: a commemorative medal struck by the pope: mourning at the court of Queen Elizabeth.

ST. BEE'S SCHOOL
Cumberland. English public school. Founded in 1583 by Edmund Grindal, Archbishop of Canterbury.

ST. CAMILLUS DE LELLIS
(1550-1614). Founder of the Order of the Fathers of a Good Death.

ST. CATHARINE'S COLLEGE
Cambridge University. Founded in 1473 by Robert Woodlark, Provost of King's College.

SAINT-GELAIS, MELLIN DE
(1491-1558). French poet in Latin and French. Attached to court of Francis I and then Catherine de' Medici. Friend of the poet Clément Marot. Author of lyrics, epigrams, rondeaux. Credited with introduction of Italian sonnet into France. His verse and his life recall those of Villon.

ST. JAMES' PALACE
London, built by Henry VIII: 1532-1533. It was the official court of the monarchy and hence ambassadors were accredited to "the Court of St. James".

ST. JOHN'S COLLEGE
Oxford University. Founded in 1555 by Alderman Sir Thomas White (1492-1567).

ST. JOHN'S COLLEGE
Cambridge University. Founded in 1508 by Lady Margaret, Countess of Richmond and Derby, the mother of Henry VII; her advisor in this and other educational foundations was Bishop John Fisher.

ST. MARK'S, RECONSTRUCTION OF
The reconstruction of St. Mark's, in Venice, was begun by Michelozzi (1396-1472) in 1437. It was completed in 1452. The chief changes were in the façade, to which Gothic elements were added.

ST. OLAVE'S AND ST. SAVIOR'S GRAMMAR SCHOOL
London. Founded by bequest of merchant Henry Leeke in 1561.

ST. PAUL'S SCHOOL
London. English public school. Founded in 1509 by John Colet, Dean of St. Paul's (1467-1519). It was the first school in England to follow the humanist precepts in teaching the classical languages and literatures.

526

SALAMONE DA SESSO
(born c. 1465). Italian goldsmith. In service of the duke of Ferrara. Produced swords, daggers.

SALAS BARBADILLO, ALONSO JERÓNIMO DE
(1581-1635). Spanish picaresque novelist. Playwright, poet. Born and died in Madrid. Attempted business, law. Author of verse, short plays, novels. Friend of Cervantes, whose *Don Quixote* he imitated in *Caballero Puntual*. Contributed to program of Madrid literary academies. Repeatedly fined: exiled for satirical attacks on officialdom. His greatest work is *La Hija de Celestina*: published in 1612. Influenced Scarron, Molière. Also wrote *El Sutil Cordobés, Don Diego de Noche,* in epistolary form.

SALESBURY, HENRY or SALISBURY
(c. 1561-c. 1637) Welsh writer, grammarian, physician, educated at Oxford. Author of a Welsh grammar, the *Grammatica Britannica,* apeared in 1593.

SALISBURY, WILLIAM or SALESBURY
(c. 1520-c. 1584) Welsh scholar and translator, learned in Greek, Latin, Hebrew and many modern languages; he had studied at Oxford. Author of a dictionary in English and Welsh, appeared in 1547, and possibly the first work to be printed in Welsh. By commission of Queen Elizabeth, he translated, with Richard Davies, *The Book of Common Prayer* and the Bible into Welsh.

SALM, NIKLAS, COUNT
(died 1530). In conflict with Turks at the siege of Vienna in 1529. Subject of legends and ballads.

SALMERÓN, ALPHONSO
(1515-1585). Spanish Jesuit, theologian, exegete. Influential at the Council of Trent. Published commentaries on the Gospels, Acts of the Apostles, Epistles of St. Paul.

SALMON, JEAN
(1490-1557). French Neo-Latin poet. Called The French Horace. He was a courtier to Francis I; most of his poetry was addressed or dedicated to noble patrons. His best work was his classical odes.

527

SALUTATI, COLUCCIO

(Died 1404) One of the early humanist scholars; he became head of the chancellery of Florence, one of the permanent posts in the government, most of which ran for six months or a year. In charge of the city's foreign correspondence, he drew up state papers that were models of classical elegance and style, so much so that Florence's enemy, the Visconti duke of Milan, is supposed to have said that one of Salutati's state papers was of the weight of a thousand horse in the political scales. His career illustrates the serviceability of the new learning to princes and states.

SALVIATI, LEONARDO

(1520-1572). Italian painter, engraver, illustrator. Employed by Venetian printer Marcolini.

SALVIATI, LEONARDO

(1540-1589) Florentine scholar and literary critic, born of a family long prominent in the political affairs of Florence. He was the principal founder of the *Accademia della Cresca.* He wrote verse and two comedies, but is remembered chiefly as a linguistic scholar. He had a remarkable knowledge of the Italian dialects, favoring the establishment of Tuscan as the proper literary vehicle for Italian writers of the vernacular. It was largely his linguistic views that led him, in a famous dispute, to declare Ariosto superior to Tasso. He wrote philological studies of Petrarch's and Boccaccio's works, and also a paraphrase and commentary in Italian upon Aristotle's *Poetics.*

SAMPSON, THOMAS

(1517?-1589). English Puritan writer. Author of a *Supplication* addressed to Queen Elizabeth in behalf of the Puritans as well as other religious writings. He collaborated in the translation of the Geneva Bible, 1560.

SAMUEL DE CASINENSIS

Italian Franciscan of Milan. Logician. Author of *Liber Isagogicus,* published in Milan in 1494. An introduction to Aristotle and Duns Scotus. He opposed the prevalent belief in witchcraft.

SÁNCHEZ, FRANCISCO

(1557-1632). Spanish physician and skeptical philosopher. He was a penetrating critic of Aristotelian science. In 1581 published *Quod mihi scitur.* Also produced *Opera medica.*

528

SÁNCHEZ COELLO, ALONSO

(c. 1531-1588). Spanish court painter to Philip II. He did numerous portraits of princes and courtiers. His work shows Flemish and Venetian influences.

SÁNCHEZ DE LAS BROZAS, FRANCISCO, EL BROCENSE

Spanish humanist. A follower of Erasmus, he applied Erasmus' canons to the study of the four Gospels and was prosecuted by the Inquisition. He is said to have declared that all things were subject to scrutiny except faith, but he seems to have been desirous of examining faith also. He was learned in Greek and Latin, published grammatical works for both languages, and edited the poems of Garcilaso de la Vega. He was an antagonist of Aristotelianism; his iconoclastic and turbulent spirit is probably best revealed in his *Paradoxes,* 1581. He published editions with commentary of Horace, Vergil, Ovid, Perseus and Politian.

SANCTORIUS

(1561-1636). Latinized name of Santro, Santrio. Representative of medical school of physiology. Professor at Padua. He was a pioneer in the application of chemical and physical concepts to the biological study of man, as is suggested, e.g., by his experiments and investigations to ascertain the gain in weight of the body from the consumption of food and expulsion of waste; thus he helped to initiate precise quantification in biology. Author of *Ars Statica Medicinae,* published in 1614. Laid the foundation of the study of metabolism.

SANDERS, NICHOLAS or SANDER

(c. 1530-1581). Lecturer on canon law at Oxford. Ordained priest. Died in Ireland. Author of some fourteen works, notably *De Visibili Monarchia Ecclesiae,* published in 1571. He remained a Catholic, opposed Queen Elizabeth and went to Spain and Ireland in attempts to overthrow her. Associated with William Allen.

SANDOVAL, PRUDENCIO DE

(c. 1553-1620). Spanish historian. Benedictine. Bishop of Tuy, Royal Chronicler to Philip III. Chief work: *Historia de la Vida y Hechos del Emperador Carlos V.* Also produced other chronicles and histories relating to Spain. While he had the advantage of free access to the archives, he did not make good critical use of the materials he found there.

SANDYS, GEORGE

(1578-1644). English poet, official in Virginia and treasurer of the Virginia Company. Traveled in Europe, Near East. Translated Ovid's *Metamorphoses* and a Latin poem by Grotius on *Christ's Passion*. Also wrote an account of his travels, *Relation of a Journey*.

SANGALLO, ANTONIO DA, THE ELDER

(1455-1534). Italian architect. He was noted chiefly for military structures and fortifications, but also did churches, e.g., the Church of S. Biagio at Montepulciano, and palaces, e.g., the Palazzo Tarugi.

SANGALLO, ANTONIO DA, THE YOUNGER or CORDIANI

(c. 1485-1546). Italian architect, nephew of the above. Associated with Bramante, then with Raphael in building of St. Peter's. He was the most gifted of the family; he designed the great Farnese Palace at Rome, many churches for Florence and Rome as well as gates and fortifications for the two cities. His son FRAN-CESCO (died 1576) was a sculptor and architect.

SANGALLO, GIULIANO DA

(1445-1516). Italian architect, uncle and brother to the above. He worked in Florence, where he collaborated in the design of the Strozzi Palace, and Rome, where he contributed to St. Peter's. He worked for about five years in France. He did many churches and fortifications.

SANMICHELI, MICHELE

(1484-1559). Military architect of Verona. Died in Corfu. Designed palaces, heavy fortifications. Wrote on architectural theory. Builder of five palaces for the nobles of his native city, most notably the Palazzo Pompei; he also did the city gates for Verona and Venice, where he built the Grimani Palace on the Grand Canal.

SANNAZARO, JACOPO

(1458-1530). Italian poet, courtier to Frederick III of Naples, whom he followed into exile to France, and member of the Academy of Naples. He is remembered chiefly for his pastoral romance in Italian prose and verse, *Arcadia*, which had a great influence on Italian literary style but which also inspired Sir Philip Sidney's pastoral romance of the same name. He wrote much Latin verse, idylls inspired by the Neapolitan landscape, and a poem on the birth of Christ, *De partu Virginis*, which caused him to be called the Christian Vergil. In France he discovered a lost poem of Ovid and a few other minor classical works.

SANO DI PIETRO

(1406-1481). Italian painter, miniaturist. Born in Siena and associated with city throughout his life. In 1455, when famine ravaged city and divine aid saved it, Sano was commissioned to paint picture commemorating incident. Executed religious themes, panels, scenes in life of St. Jerome.

SAN PEDRO, DIEGO DE

(Late fifteenth century). Spanish Renaissance poet and novelist. His life is obscure. His poems appear in the *Cancionero General*. Wrote novel: *Tratado de Amor*, 1491. Chief work: *Cárcel de Amor*, 1492, most popular *novela sentimental* of Renaissance. In epistolary form. Influenced by Dante and Boccaccio. Highly popular, for there were twenty translations and some twenty-five editions of this work. Influenced Rojas, Cervantes. Novel became a kind of *breviario de amor*.

SANSOVINO, ANDREA CONTUCCI DA

(1460-1529). Florentine sculptor and architect; he did much of his work at Rome in the form of tombs, statues and reliefs for church interiors.

SANSOVINO, FRANCESCO

(1521-1586). Venetian scholar, editor, publisher and printer, translator, versifier and author of rhetorical, historical works as well as commentaries upon classical authors. Compiled speeches of noted Renaissance orators—Bembo, Varchi, Trissino, published in 1569. Produced collection of satires of Ariosto, Alamanni and others, in 1573. Wrote treatise on utopias, with reference to More's *Utopia;* also critical life of Emperor Charles V.

SANSOVINO, JACOBO or TATTI

(1486-1570). Florentine sculptor and architect, father of the above, protégé of Andrea, whose name he took. Most of his work was done at Venice, where he designed the Library of St. Mark's and other notable buildings such as the Palazzo Cornei.

SANT'AGATA, FRANCESCO DA

(floruit c. 1520). Italian sculptor of Padua. Goldsmith. Executed a *Hercules* in wood.

SANTA HERMANDAD

A Spanish term meaning *Holy Brotherhood*. This was a league of towns and cities established in Castile in 1476 for the maintenance of public order and the suppression of crime and violence, especially in rural areas.

SANTI, GIOVANNI

(c. 1440-1494). Italian painter and poet in the service of the dukes of Urbino and Mantua. Father of Raphael. Executed frescoes, altarpieces. Belongs in the early Umbrian Renaissance. He wrote the *Cronaca rimata* on the life of his patron, Duke Federigo da Montefeltro of Urbino.

SANTO MARIANO

(c. 1490-c. 1550). Italian surgeon, lithotomist. He served as military surgeon in the wars of Charles V against the Turks, contributed improved techniques to the development of surgery and published several manuals on the surgeon's art. In later years he practiced at Rome and Venice.

SANTOS, FREI JOÃO DOS

(Died 1622). Portuguese Dominican and missionary to India. He wrote several accounts of his travels and activities in the East, among them *Ethiopia oriental* and *Relacão do descobrimento das minas de prata de Chicova* and other works of descriptive geography.

SANUDO, MARINO

(1466-1536). Venetian humanist scholar, historian, statesman, collector of rare manuscripts. He was a prolific author of historical works on Venice and Italy, e.g., *Lives of the Doges* and *The Expedition of Charles VIII*. He is remembered chiefly for his *Diaries,* covering the years 1498 to 1533 in fifty-eight volumes and a mine of information about Venetian, Italian and European political events.

SAPIENZA

Name of University of Rome. Under Leo X, in 1513, there were eighty-eight lecturers. It dated from the reign of Pope Boniface VIII in the early fourteenth century.

532

SARAVETIUS, MICHAEL
(Sixteenth century). Logician. Thomist. Author of *Quaestiones*, published in Rome in 1516.

SARBIEWSKI, MACIEJ KAZIMIERZ or MATTHIAS CASIMIR SARBIEVIUS
(1595-1640). Polish Jesuit priest, Neo-Latin poet and professor of rhetoric and theology at Vilna. Author of odes and lyrics imitative of Horace. Called the Polish Horace. His family was of Italian origin; he himself spent some time in Rome engaged in ecclesiastical matters, but also archaeological and literary studies.

SÄRKILAHTI, PETER
Introduced Lutheranism into Finland 1517-1522; he was a pastor and educator, and had been educated in Germany.

SARPI, PAOLO
(1552-1623). Venetian prelate, councillor to the Venetian government, Brother Paul of the Servite Order. His interests included philosophy (which he taught at Venice), science and medicine (he is said to have discovered the contractibility of the iris), and oriental languages; but he is best known for his *History of the Council of Trent,* 1619. There he takes a moderate position with regard to the Protestants; he had hoped for a doctrinal compromise and their return to the Church; his interpretation of the Council is as a tragic victory of papal absolutism and centralism. His anti-papalism and anti-clericalism were well within the Venetian tradition concerning ecclesiastical matters.

SARRAZIN, JACQUES
(1592-1660). French sculptor. One of the founders of Academy of painting and sculpture. Worked on the Louvre. Executed sepulchral statuary. He studied and worked for about twenty years at Rome.

SARTORIUS, JOHANNES
(c. 1500-1570). Dutch humanist and Lutheran theologian of Amsterdam. He wrote many theological works, was learned in Latin, Greek and Hebrew. His linguistic and philological learning had application in the study of the Bible. He compiled a Latin dictionary and other linguistic works.

SAULI, STEFANO
Fifteenth century Genoese noble. Author of Ciceronian treatise on Christian hero. The family, originally of Lucca, was long

prominent in the economic and political life of Genoa; commercial magnates, they gave the Republic 29 senators and three doges.

SAUMAISE, CLAUDE DE

(1588-1643). Latinized name, Salmasius. French classical scholar, professor of Latin at Leyden, commentator on Pliny the Elder. Also wrote treatises on Greek and Roman texts and edited several minor classical authors. Wrote Latin defense of Charles I of England, which was refuted by John Milton. He also wrote a treatise defending usury.

SAVILE, SIR HENRY

(1549-1622). English classical scholar, philanthropist. Tutor in Greek and Latin, secretary to Queen Elizabeth I. Translated Tacitus: edited Xenophon. On committee responsible for Authorized Version of Bible. Founded chairs of astronomy and geometry at Oxford University. He was a friend of Sir Thomas Bodley, whom he aided in establishing the famous library.

SAVIN, PAOLO

(floruit c. 1510). Italian sculptor of Venice. Worked on chapel of San Marco.

SAVOLDO, GIAN GIROLAMO

(c. 1480-c. 1548). Italian painter. Known to have worked in Brescia between 1480 and 1548. His subjects are religious themes, portraits. His work shows the influence of Giovanni Bellini and Titian and is remarkable for its luminous color.

SAVONAROLA, GIROLAMO

(1452-1498). Born in Ferrara, of an ascetic and mystical disposition, he was nurtured on the Scholastic works, especially those of St. Thomas, and became a Dominican monk at twenty-three. He gained great fame as a preacher and at the express wish of Lorenzo the Magnificent was sent to the convent of San Marco at Florence. He inaugurated a great religious revival and, with the expulsion of the Medici as a consequence of the French invasion of 1494, played a decisive role in the reestablishment of a republic in Florence. He held no political office, but he was identified with the democratic (relatively) government and exercised a vast influence on public opinion. Thus those who sought to overthrow the government in favor of oligarchical or Medicean rule, had to dispose of the Friar. With the aid of the infamous Borgia pope, Alexander VI, Savonarola's enemies brought him down; found guilty of heresy, he was hanged and burnt in the public square. He had a lasting influence on Pico, Botticelli, and Michelangelo. In his fanatical spirit and fiery eloquence, in his flaying of abuses within the Church and his thundering call for reform, he is reminiscent of Luther.

SAVORY, ROELANDT

(1576-1639). Dutch painter. Died in Utrecht. His subjects are fantastic landscapes: storms, waterfalls between beetling cliffs, stark mountains, etc. with powerful light effects. He also did animal figures, many of them being strange creatures out of mythology.

SAVOY, HOUSE OF

Among the members of this oldest ruling family of Europe, dating from the eleventh century, were: Philibert I (1464-1482); Charles I (1468-1490); Charles Emmanuel I, The Great (1580-1630).

SAXTON, CHRISTOPHER

(floruit 1570-1596). English topographer, educated at Cambridge. Made a geographical survey of England and Wales. Began his *Atlas* in 1574, completed in 1579. It included almost all the counties of England and Wales. His maps are remarkable tor their beauty as well as accuracy.

SCAINO, ANTONIO

(Sixteenth century) Author of treatise on playing games, published in 1555 at Venice and entitled *Trattato del giuoco della palla;* it includes descriptions of soccer and lawn tennis, which are traced back to antiquity.

SCALIGER, JOSEPH JUSTUS

(1540-1609). French classical scholar and chronologist. Protestant, descendant of an Italian family of Verona, and son of Julius Caesar Scaliger. He was one of the greatest classical scholars of the century; he carried textual criticism and emendation to a new height of sophistication, and, highly critical of the mere imitation of Latin literary style, set an example of the profound study of the contents of the classics and of their historical background; he thus established what is still the basis of ancient chronology

535

in his *De emendatione temporum* and his *Thesaurus temporum*. He studied first under his father, taught himself Greek—not to know which, he said, was "to know nothing"—studied Roman law under Cujas, enjoyed the patronage of the nobleman Louis Charteigner, but finally fled France and the turbulent religious wars for a chair at the University of Leyden. His editions of classical authors include Ausonius, Festus, Catullus, Tibullus, Propertius, Apuleius, Caesar, Polybius and Eusebius.

SCALIGER, JULIUS CAESAR
(1484-1558). Italian-born classical scholar and physician who became a French subject and physician to the bishop of Agen. He is remembered chiefly as the violent partisan of Cicero and Ciceronianism against the strictures of Erasmus. He wrote an exposition of the character of Latin, *De Coucis Latinae linguae,* and an important work on prosody and metrics, the *Poetica,* in which he follows Aristotle's *Poetics* closely and reverently, calling the Greek "our perpetual mentor on everything good in the arts." He wrote commentaries on the medical and botanical works of Aristotle, Hippocrates and Theophrastus.

SCALZA, IPPOLITO
(c. 1532-1617). Italian sculptor and architect of Orvieto, where he did almost all his work. He helped to decorate the cathedral and designed the Buzi palace. His brothers were LODOVICO, an architect and sculptor, and FRANCESCO, an architect and mosaicist.

SCAMOZZI, VINCENZO
(1552-1616). Italian architect, architectural theorist and disciple of Palladio. Executed monuments, designed the communal palace of Vicenza; and the proscenium of the Olympic Theatre of Vicenza, begun by Palladio and first significant edifice designed for dramatic performances.

SCANDINAVIAN ART
In Sweden, during the Renaissance, artists and craftsmen, particularly German and Flemish, were imported into the service of the nobility.

SCANDINAVIAN RULERS
Christian I of Oldenburg (1448-1481). King of Denmark, Norway, Sweden.

Charles VIII: 1449-1457. King of Sweden. Driven from throne. Replaced by Christian I.

Frederick I: 1523-1533. King of Denmark and Norway.

Dates refer to duration of rule.

SCÈVE, MAURICE or SÉVE

(c. 1510-c. 1564). French poet of Lyons. Author of amatory sequence entitled *Délie, objet de plus haute vertu*: published in 1544. *Délie* was probably Pernette du Guillet, poetess of Lyons. He was the chief figure of a literary circle at Lyons, which anticipated in some respects the *Pléiade* group of a later date. He may have been of Italian extraction.

SCHARDT, JOHANN GREGOR VAN DER

(1530-after 1581). Sculptor of Nuremberg. Influenced by Giovanni da Bologna. He worked in Denmark for some time, doing a magnificent fountain for the courtyard of the royal castle of Kronborg on the island of Zealand.

SCHAUMBURG, OTTO VON, COUNT

(Died 1640). Participated in Thirty Years' War. Subject of German poem, ballad.

SCHEDEL, HARTMAN

(1440-1514). German physician, humanist, enthusiastic collector of humanist works, thanks to which a part of the writings and sketches of Cyriac d'Ancona were preserved. His *Liber de Antiquitatibus* is an important collection of ancient inscriptions and his history of the world, the *Nuremberg Chronicle*, shows some traces of the humanist conception of history; this last was published in 1493 with woodcut illustrations by Wohlgemut, the father-in-law of Dürer. He is chiefly important as one of the early German humanists who established the vogue of the new learning.

SCHEIDT, SAMUEL

(1587-1654). German composer, organist and choirmaster of Halle. Wrote pieces for harpsichord, *Tabulatura Nova*: c. 1624, a great work for organ, and vocal works. He did much to develop the chorale.

SCHEINER, CHRISTOPHER

(1575-1650). German Jesuit and astronomer. He contended with Galileo for priority in the discovery and over the nature of sun spots.

SCHENCK, JOHANN

(1531-1598). German physician of Strassburg. Author of treatise on medical subjects, published in seven volumes, 1584-1597. Learned in Greek and Latin, and basing himself on Hippocrates, he wrote what was long a standard work, especially for pathological anatomy.

SCHETUS, CASPAR or SCHETZ

(Died 1580). Dutch humanist and financier. Financial agent of Philip II at Brussels. Author of *Dialogus de Pace*, published in 1579. Discusses Spanish and Flemish relations. He also wrote Latin verse.

SCHEURL, CHRISTOPH

(1481-1542). German jurist, statesman and humanist of Nuremberg. Author of a history of Nuremberg. Also wrote book against the Reformation. He was active in the government of his native city and in the diplomatic service of the Emperor Charles V and Francis I of France.

SCHIAPPALARIA, STEFANO

Sixteenth century. Genoese scholar. Used ancient Roman history for contemporary analogies in governments of Italy, France, Holy Roman Empire.

SCHIAVONE, ANDREA

(c. 1500-1563). Italian painter and engraver, born at Zara. Worked in Venice. Executed *Holy Family, Adoration of the Magi* in oils, and many frescoes in the palaces and churches of Venice; his work shows the influence of Titian and Tintoretto.

SCHICKHARDT, HEINRICH

(1558-1634). German architect. Designed castles, churches, towns. Belongs in the late Renaissance.

SCHIFANOIA

A famous Renaissance summer palace of the Este in Ferrara. Adorned with remarkable frescoes by Cosimo Tura (died 1495) and Francesco Cossa (died 1477), in which the months are alegorically depicted along with scenes picturing the court life of the ducal house.

SHMIDT, ULRIC or SCHMIDEL

(Sixteenth century). German soldier, traveler, associated with the Spanish effort, by expeditions led by Pedro de Mendoza, to explore and colonize the Plate and Paraguay river valleys. Advanced to the coast of Brazil. Left an account of his travels in South America: *Warhafftige Beschreibunge*: published in 1567 and frequently republished.

SCHÖFFER, PETER

(c. 1430-c. 1502). German pioneer printer. Developed printing techniques, type, matrices, printing in colors. He was the son-in-law of Johann Fust, who acquired Gutenberg's shop when the latter went bankrupt. Schöffer and Fust were partners until Fust's death, in 1466, whereupon Schöffer, carried on until his own death. He was the first to use Greek type.

SCHÖNER, JOHAN

(1477-1547). Mathematician of Nuremberg. He wrote numerous works on astronomy, astrology, geography, mathematics and medicine, but is chiefly remembered for the four globes he constructed, 1515-1533, which indicate a Southwest and Northwest Passage; his work was based to a considerable extent on the maps of Waldseemüller. Schöner was a friend of Copernicus and of Melanchthon; he renounced the Catholic priesthood to become a Lutheran and to devote himself to mathematics, which he taught at Nuremberg.

SCHONGAUER, MARTIN

(c. 1430-1491). German painter, engraver. Worked in Colmar, Alsace. Produced easel pictures, with religious motifs, of the late Gothic school. Important as a pioneer in copperplate engraving. Albrecht Dürer worked in his studio for some time. Few of his paintings survive, and it is for his engravings that he is known. His work is in the Flemish tradition and is notable for its detail and the great number of persons crowded into his scenes; he confined himself to religious subjects.

SCHOOLS

In Renaissance Italy, every town, however small, taught Latin, which, with reading, arithmetic, and writing, was considered a necessary element of instruction. Sometimes schools were under church sponsorship. Sometimes the municipality controlled them. On occasion, there were also private establishments.

SCHOON OF GOUDA

Author of six Latin plays, imitative of Terence, but based on Biblical themes. They include: *Nehemias, Saulus, Juditha.*

SCHOUTEN, WILLEM CORNELISZOON

(c. 1567-1625). Dutch navigator. In service of the East India Company. The first to double Cape Horn, in 1616, which he named for his home town. Wrote a journal, *Diarium*: published in 1619 in Amsterdam; it recounted his trip and also reported that there was no great southern continent, divided by a strait from Africa, as the best cartographers had assumed up to then.

SCHREVELIUS, CORNELIUS or SCHREVEL

(1615-1664). Dutch scholar. Rector of Leyden University. Author of *Lexicon Graeco-Latinum et Latino-Graecum*: published in 1654. Also edited classical texts.

SCUDO

Italian coin of small denomination; part of Cesare Borgia's fearsome reputation was the ease with which he could bend it double in the palm of his hand.

SCHWEIGGER, SOLOMON

(1551-1622). German Protestant preacher and traveler. Chaplain of German Embassy in Constantinople. Worked for union of Greek Orthodox and Lutheran Churches. Traveled in Near East, gathering information about the Greek Orthodox Church and the Sultan's government, which he incorporated in his travel book *Neue Reisebechreibung aus Deutschland nach Constantinopel und Jerusalem*. He claimed to have translated the Koran from Arabic into German, but actually based his work on an Italian version.

SCHWEINICHEN, HANS VON

(1552-1616). German noble. Accompanied Duke Heinrich XI of Liegnitz in travels through Bohemia, Poland. Left autobiography and diary: useful as historical sources, especially for the social habits and customs of his time.

SCHWENCKFELD VON OSSIG, CASPAR

(1489-1561). German reformer. Mystic, a central figure in the reform movement in Silesia. Opposed to Luther on certain doctrinal points. Persecuted by Catholics and Lutherans. Author of

Letters and *Treatises*: published in 1524-1530. Established community of Schwenckfeldians. He himself appears in a German novel entitled *The Schwenckfeldians*, by F. Sommer.

SCIOPPIUS, KASPAR or SCHOPPE
(1576-1649). German theologian, classical scholar. Renounced Protestanism, which he consistently attacked but also flayed the Jesuits. Author of philological and literary studies: *Grammatica Philosophia*: published in 1628. *Paradoxa Litteraria*: published in 1628. His endless theological and scholarly quarrels caused him to be known as the snarling scholar, "canis grammaticus." He compiled a Latin grammar and edited Varro, Symmachus and several works of other classical authors.

SCOREL, JAN VAN
(1496-1562). Dutch portrait and religious painter. Visited Holy Land, Venice and Rome, where he became supervisor of the Vatican gallery. Mabuse and Dürer were the principal influences upon him. He was important in introducing the Italian humanistic forms in Holland, to which he returned not long after the death of his fellow countryman and protector, Pope Adrian VI.

SCOTT, ALEXANDER
(c. 1525-c. 1584). Scottish poet. Author of some thirty-six brief pieces. Many of them are amatory, with some satirical, sacred, and occasional poems. Notable are: *The Lament of the Master of Erskine, Welcome to Queen Mary, Christ's Kirk on the Green.*

SCOTT, REGINALD
(c. 1538-1599). English writer, educated at Oxford. Wrote on hop culture, the earliest work of its kind in England. Also a demonographer, in that he wrote *The Discovery of Witchcraft*, published in 1584, a work intended to show what witchcraft really was and so save simple persons and children from unjust persecution; Shakespeare is said to have drawn upon the work in his depiction of witches in *Macbeth*.

SCOTUS, JOHANNES ANTONIUS
Sixteenth century. Logician of Naples. Author of *Quaestio de Demonstratione Potissima.*

SCOURGE OF PRINCES
A designation given to Pietro Aretino (1492-1556).

SCRIVERIUS, PETRUS or SCHRYVER
(1576-1660). Dutch classical scholar, Latin poet. Author of *Saturnalia*: eulogy of tobacco. He published editions of Martial, Seneca, and Apuleius.

SCULTETUS, TOBIAS
(fl. c. 1590). German poet. Wrote Latin poems in classical form on contemporary themes.

SEA ATLAS
The first printed sea atlas was Lucas Waghenaer's *Spieghel der Zeevaert*. It appeared in Leyden in two volumes, in 1584-1585. It was long a standard work, appeared in many editions, and was translated into several languages.

SEBASTIAN
(1554-1578). King of Portugal. During minority, grandmother was Regent: also Cardinal Henry. In command of troops in Morocco, where he was killed in Battle of Alcázarquivir, the worst disaster in Portuguese history. The belief that he was captured and would return gave rise to the messianic legends of Sebastianism and made him a literary character. His death without heirs opened the way to Portugal's annexation by Spain in 1580.

SEBASTIANO DEL PIOMBO or SEBASTIANO LUCIANI
(c. 1485-1547). Italian painter of Venice. Worked in Rome, Venice. Friend of Michelangelo. Executed altarpieces, portraits, mythological scenes. His works are notable also for their landscape backgrounds. His best-known portraits include the doge of Genoa, Andrea Doria, Cardinal Reginald Pole, and Christopher Columbus. In 1531 he was made keeper of the papal seals, whence *piombo.*

SEBRIGHT SCHOOL
English public school in Worcestershire. Founded in 1620 by William Sebright, Town Clerk of London.

SECOND HELVETIC CONFESSION
A document that enunciated the common faith of the Swiss Protestant Churches. Promulgated in 1566. Adopted throughout Switzerland and also in Scotland, Hungary, France, Poland.

SECRETS OF MASTER ALEXIS OF PIEDMONT
A popular Italian pharmacopoeia containing secret medical prescriptions, culinary recipes, and advice on health. Ascribed to G.

Ruscelli: also to Hieronimo Rossello. Translations exist in Latin, English, French, German.

SECUNDUS, JOHANNES or JAN EVERAERTS

(1511-1536). Dutch poet, jurist. Author of Latin elegies, epigrams, odes, and especially the amatory *Basia*, which was very popular to judge by the numerous editions. He was a close imitator of Catullus.

SEDBURGH SCHOOL

English Public school. Founded in 1525 by Provost of Eton, Dr. Roger Lupton (died in 1540).

SEISENEGGER, JAKOB

(c. 1505-1567). Painter of Vienna, from Styria. Court painter. Executed portraits, historical subjects.

SELDEN, JOHN

(1584-1654). English jurist, classical and historical scholar, member of Parliament. He was one of the greatest pioneers in English legal and parliamentary history in his *England's Epinomis, Jani Anglorum, Analecton Anglo-Britannicon, Titles of Honour, History of Tithes* and *Privileges of Baronage.* His conversations were interestingly recorded and preserved by his secretary, in the *Table Talk.*

SEMPILL, ROBERT

(c. 1530-1595). Scottish soldier. Ballad writer. Author also of poems with political themes.

SENNERT, DANIEL

(1572-1637). German physician and naturalist. He sought to reconcile the scientific knowledge and conceptions of his time with the views of the ancient scientific writers, whom he did not believe to be obsolescent. One of his chief concerns was to reconcile the Democritan "corpuscular" or atomic theory with the traditional conception that was based on Aristotle.

SEPTEMBER TESTAMENT

The New Testament, translated by Luther into German. Published in September, 1522: hence called the September Testament.

SEPÚLVEDA, JUAN GINÉS DE

(c. 1490-1574). Spanish humanist, philosopher and theologian, historian, the Spanish Livy. He studied at Alcalá de Henares but also under Pomponazzi at Bologna; he was fifteen years in Italy, where he was engaged in a revision of the Greek New Testament and in translations and commentaries upon the works of the early Aristotelian commentator Alexander of Aphrodisius, before he returned to Spain to enter the service of Charles V and then Philip II. He became historian to Charles V and wrote *De rebus gestis Caroli V* and later *De rebus gestis Philippi II*, both humanist works that sing the praise of the prince. He crossed swords with Las Casas, asserting the Spanish right to suppress and exploit the Indians.

SERLIO, SEBASTIANO

(1475-1554). Architect and architectural theorist. Died at Fontainebleau in the service of the French monarchy. Designed palaces, mostly in Venice, which resemble those of Palladio and Sansovino. His work in eight volumes, *Trattato di architettura*, reflects his study of Roman antiquities as well as the Venetian architectural tradition; published between 1540 and 1575, the treatise was important in the formation of the classical ideal of the succeeding age.

SERMONETA, ALEXANDER

(Early sixteenth century). Physician. Logician. Wrote commentary on the *Consequentiae* of Strodus.

SERVETUS, MICHAEL or MIGUEL SERVETO

(1509-1553). Spanish scientist, unitarian theologian, physician. Went to Italy, Germany. Met Luther. Arrested by Inquisition, he was condemned but managed to escape. Editor of Ptolemy. Also postulated pulmonary circulation of blood. Author of treatises: *De Trinitatis Erroribus, Dialogorum de Trinitate, Christianismi Restitutio*. Tried at Geneva, one of his prosecutors being John Calvin. Burned at the stake as a heretic.

SEVERINO, MARC AURELIO

(1580-1656). Italian anatomist and surgeon. Author of a treatise on comparative anatomy: *Zootomia Democritaea*, published in 1645. Performed the first operation of tracheotomy in diphtheria in 1610, during an epidemic in Naples. His novel ideas on the treatment of incurable diseases brought him into conflict with the

544

Inquisition and led to his imprisonment. He wrote several other works on his various specialties and was an outstanding practitioner.

SEVERO DA RAVENNA
(Late fifteenth and early sixteenth century). Italian sculptor. He worked principally in Padua, where he did a *St. John the Baptist* for the façade of the Chapel of St. Anthony of Padua. He did many bronzes, particularly a series of Neptunes. His work is distinguished by its naturalism and grotesqueness, which place him in the tradition of Donatello.

SEVERINUS, PETRUS
(1542-1602). Danish physician, studied and practiced at Venice, and became royal physician upon his return to his homeland. He was an important figure in the Paracelsan revival. His *Idea of Philosophic Medicine,* 1571, urged that the methods of Paracelsus (died 1541) be used to supplement and correct those of Galen and Hippocrates. His work was quite influential, reissued as late as 1660.

SEYMOUR, EDWARD, EARL OF HERTFORD and DUKE OF SOMERSET
(c. 1506-1552). Lord Protector of England at the outset of the reign of Edward VI, a minor. In service of Henry VIII, brother of Henry's third wife. Lord Great Chamberlain. Led army in France. Assumed Protectorate of England on death of Henry VIII. Defeated Scots at Battle of Pinkie, in 1547. Inaugurated Protestant reforms. Indicted, deposed, pardoned. Then condemned on charge of felony, executed at behest of rival, John Dudley, Duke of Northumberland.

SFORNO, OBADIAH
(1475-1550). Jewish-Italian physician, philosopher, Biblical exegete and Talmudic scholar. Taught Reuchlin Hebrew. Among his books were *Luce delle nazioni,* an attack on the philosophy of Aristotle and of Maimonides.

SFORZA BOOK OF HOURS
Famous illuminated book executed by Milanese school: c. 1490.

SFORZA, FRANCESCO
(1450-1466). The successful condottiere whose marriage to Bianca, the daughter of the last Visconti, enabled him to acquire

the Duchy of Milan, although it required all his diplomatic and military skill to fight down a Milanese attempt to re-establish a republic. With his accession a revolution in Italian alliances occurred: Medici Florence broke its long-standing ties with Venice in favor of Milan. With Naples, this triple alliance was basic to the peninsula's stability until 1494, although Naples frequently deserted these ties for the papal alliance (as in the Pazzi conspiracy of 1478), whereupon war resulted. Francisco's son and successor was the coldly efficient GALEAZZO (1466-1476), who was assassinated in a personal quarrel. His heir was the seven-year-old GIAN GALEAZZO (1476-1494), whose uncle, LUDOVICO IL MORO (1494-1500), usurped the ducal throne as regent. It was he and his brilliant wife, Beatrice d'Este of Ferrara, who inaugurated the most magnificent age of Milan, when its court was the most brilliant in Italy and there was great prosperity. Diplomatic complications, stemming from his usurpation, led to an alliance with France; the result was the French invasion of 1494 and the downfall of the Sforza. Ludovico ended up in a French prison in 1500 and spent the rest of his life there. Milan became a bone of contention between France and Spain.

SHAKESPEARE, WILLIAM
(1564-1616). Greatest dramatic poet. Born in Stratford-on-Avon. Actor-playwright. Lived in Stratford and London. Produced comedies, histories, tragedies: *Henry V, Richard III, Antony and Cleopatra, Tempest, Twelfth Night, As You Like It, Comedy of Errors, Othello, Hamlet, Macbeth, King Lear.* Also sonnets, poems; *Venus and Adonis, Rape of Lucrece.* First Folio, containing thirty-six plays, published in 1623.

SHELTON, THOMAS
(floruit 1612-1620). First English translator of Cervantes' *Don Quijote;* it was commissioned by Theophilus Howard, second earl of Suffolk.

SHERBORNE SCHOOL
English public school. Origins uncertain—probably eighth century. Refounded by King Edward VI in 1550.

SHERLEY, SIR ANTHONY
(c. 1565-1635). English traveler and adventurer. On expedition to the West Indies in 1596. Envoy to Persia in 1599. In the service of Philip III of Spain, in 1609. He wrote an account of his travels

in Persia, *Relation*, 1613. It is a mark of English interest in Persia that at least two other books were written about the same time on his trip and on the adventures of his brothers, Thomas and Robert, in Persia and elsewhere.

SHIELDS
After c. 1550 shields were rarely used in battle. In siege operations, however, and in reconnaissances, shields continued in use until late in the seventeenth century.

SHIPTON, MOTHER
English witch and prophetess. Reputedly, born c. 1487 as Ursula Shipton. Died in 1561. A figure of popular legend, there is no documentary evidence for her life earlier than 1641.

SHORE, JANE
(c.1445-c. 1527). Mistress of King Edward IV of England. Her beauty and wit enabled her to influence him greatly. Accused of sorcery by Richard III and arrested and compelled to do penance. She died in obscurity and poverty. Subject of one of Percy's *Ballads*: also appears in drama entitled *Jane Shore*, by Nicholas Rowe: published in 1714.

SHORTHAND
The modern system with c. 500 signs was invented in 1588 by Englishman Dr. Timothy Bright (1551-1615). French and German systems did not appear until the seventeenth century.

SHREWSBURY SCHOOL
English public school. Founded by King Edward VI in 1552. Refounded by Queen Elizabeth I in 1571. Its most famous alumnus was Sir Philip Sidney.

SIBERCH, JOHN
German printer, probably from Cologne. Set up first printing press in Cambridge, England, in 1521. Within first year issued ten books.

SICKINGEN, FRANZ VON
(1481-1523). German Knight. Attached to court of Charles V. Played major part in the spread of the Reformation. He was associated with Ulrich von Hutten in the Knights' War, a patriotic attempt to end the existence of the ecclesiastical princes and fashion a German national state. He lost the support of Charles;

his defeat and death symbolize the strength of the German princes and the impotence of the knights. He became a legendary figure and appeared as a national hero in German literature.

SIDNEY, SIR PHILIP

(1554-1586). Elizabethan courtier, poet, soldier, author, ambassador, friend of Edmund Spenser. Among his works are *Arcadia,* a pastoral romance; *Astrophel and Stella,* a cycle of love sonnets, and *The Defense of Poesie* and *An Apology for Poetry,* his influential critical writings. He died of wounds sustained in the Netherlands fighting the Spanish.

SIDNEY SUSSEX COLLEGE

Cambridge University. Founded under will of the Lady Frances Sidney, Countess Dowager of Sussex, in 1596.

SIEGE OF VIENNA

Vienna was besieged by the Turks in 1529. The Hapsburgs, however, succeeded in repulsing the enemy. It was besieged a second time by the Turks in 1683.

SIENA

This Italian city was prominent in book illumination in the fifteenth century. Graduals, missals, hymnals, and other devotional works were produced in abundance. Illuminators included Sano di Pietro (1401-1481), Pellegrino di Mariano (died 1492), Liberale da Verona (1445?-1529), Girolamo da Cremona (died 1483), Francesco di Giorgio Martini (1439-1502). Siena, famed in the Renaissance for its mystics and pageants, was during the fourteenth and fifteenth centuries a prominent art centre, producing, however, works that still retained medieval characteristics. The true Renaissance painters of Siena were Domenico di Bartolo (floruit 1428-1447) and the engineer Francesco di Giorgio (1439-1502), who rivalled Botticelli in mastery of line and beauty of figures: Neroccio dei Landi (1447-1500), Lorenzo di Pietro (1412-1480), Matteo di Giovanni (1435-1495). By the end of the fifteenth century the Sienese school was an exhausted tradition. In the sixteenth century the painters of note were Il Sodoma (1477-1549) and Domenico Beccafumi (1486-1551). Traditionally the city was an archenemy of Florence for the hegemony of Tuscany. It was ruled by the typical Renaissance despot, the Petrucci family (1487-1523), whereupon it became a pawn in the struggle between France and Spain. The city fell

548

to Charles V in 1554; he bestowed it upon the Medici dukes of Florence and Tuscany.

SIGISMUND I
(1467-1548). King of Poland. In conflict with Russia and Moldavia. Reformed currency. Fought against Turks. Introduced Lutheranism. Made peace with Teutonic Order.

SIGISMUND II
(1520-1572). King of Poland. In conflict with nobles. Reformation spread into Poland. Sigismund II was last of Jagellon line.

SIGISMUND III
(1566-1632). King of Poland. Also king of Sweden. During his reign, chaotic conditions in Poland. In Thirty Years' War, fought against Protestants.

SIGLO DE ORO, EL
The Golden Age of Spanish literature (ca. 1492-ca. 1681), representing the artistic and religious apogee of Spain. This period, also called the *Edad de Oro,* was long and rich, declining during the first years of the reign of Carlos II (1665-1700). The sixteenth century coincides with Spain's dominant role in European military and political affairs. The distinguishing features of the *Siglo de Oro* are: awareness of the classical heritage, national grandeur, Neo-Platonism, and mysticism. Notable authors and works in the various literary genres are: Garcilaso de la Vega (1501?-1536): *Eglogas;* Fray Luis de Granada (1504-1588): *Introducción del símbolo de la fe;* Santa Teresa de Jesús (1515-1582): *El castillo interior o las moradas;* Fray Luis de León (1527-1591): *De los nombres de Cristo;* San Juan de la Cruz (1542-1591): *Subida del monte Carmelo; Lazarillo de Tormes* (anonymous, 1554); *Romanceros* (collections of short poems, partly narrative, partly lyrical); Miguel de Cervantes (1547-1616): *El ingenioso hidalgo Don Quijote de la Mancha;* Luis de Góngora (1561-1627): *Soledades;* Lope de Vega (1562-1635): *Fuenteovejuna;* Gillen de Castro, (1569-1631): *Las mocedades del Cid;* Tirso de Molina (1583?-1648): *El burlador de Sevilla;* Juan Ruiz de Alarcón (1581?-1639): *La verdad sospechosa;* Calderón de la Barca (1600-1681): *La vida es sueño.* The Golden Age of Spanish literature closes with Calderón's death. The foregoing writers and representative works reflect the mature realization of the potentialities of Spanish genius.

SIGNORE

Roughly equivalent to *tyrant* or *despot;* the term often had a neutral, rather than pejorative, connotation, as *dictator* or *tyrant* had in antiquity. The *Signore's* success in ending the rife factional disputes and bitter feuds of the fourteenth and fifteenth centuries was often a real boon to the city; sometimes he gained the lordship (*signoria*) of the city by election of the people, more usually by guile and violence. It was the illegitimate origin and the difficulty of maintaining his power that made the typical *signore* a lavish patron of the arts and learning, and his state, in Burckhardt's phrase, necessarily "a work of art".

SIGNORELLI, LUCA

(1441-1523). Italian painter of the Umbrian school, the scientist as painter. He is remembered for his religious paintings and especially for his nudes. He spent much time in the study of anatomy, dissecting the human body—in secret—in order to study the pattern of muscles and the skeletal structure; these studies enabled him to render correctly the organic movement of the body. Apart from its exact anatomical depiction, his work is characterized by a pervading melancholy and austerity, and by great dramatic force. Michelangelo was impressed by Signorelli's work, and the affinity between the two men appears in the *End of the World,* a work suggestive of Michelangelo's *Last Judgment.* The *End of the World* is one part of the frescoes, his best-known work, which Signorelli did for the New Chapel in the Cathedral of Orvieto; he also worked in the Cathedral of Perugia.

SIGONIUS, CAROLUS or SIGONIO

(c. 1524-1584). Italian classical scholar of Modena. Professor at Venice, Padua.

SIGURDSSON, EINAR

(1539-1626). Icelandic poet and Protestant minister. Leading poet of the Reformation period in Iceland.

SILOE, DIEGO

(c. 1495-1563). Spanish architect and sculptor. Leader of Italian Renaissance ornamentation in art upon his return to Spain after a sojourn in Italy. He is associated chiefly with the construction of the cathedral of Granada. His father, GIL, was a sculptor but strictly within the older Gothic tradition; he did the tombs of Juan II of Castile and Isabella of Portugal at Burgos.

SILVATICUS, GIOVANNI BAPTISTA
(1550-1621). Physician of Milan. Wrote on syphilis and the use of the unicorn's horn, precious stones, etc. in the cure of human maladies.

SILVESTER, ANTONIUS
(died 1515). Logician. Wrote a treatise on Buridar's *Summulae*: published in 1511.

SILVESTER MAZOLINUS DE PRIERIA
(died 1523). Logician. Author of a *Compendium Dialecticae*. Also an *Apologia:* published in Bonn in 1499.

SIMEONI, GABRIELE
(1509-1575). Florentine writer and scholar. He went to seek his fortune in France at the court of Francis I, where he served for a while as part of the Florentine diplomatic staff. He is credited with helping to introduce the new classical learning in France. He wrote much verse and satire in the manner of Francesco Berni; in his *Dialogo pio e speculativo,* 1560, he sought to identify Gergovie as the site of the tower vainly besieged by Julius Caesar in the Gallic Wars—its identification was a cause of much discussion in the sixteenth century.

SIMNEL, LAMBERT
(c. 1475-c. 1534). English pretender. Crowned in 1487, in Dublin, as King Edward VI. Landed in England with Irish and German troops. Defeated, pardoned, taken into royal service as falconer or scullion boy in the kitchen by Henry VII.

SIMON DE LENDENARIA
Sixteenth century. Logician. Author of *Recollectae Supra Sophismatibus Hentisberi.*

SIMON DE PHARES
(Fifteenth century). French astrologer to King Charles VIII, physician, botanist. Author of book on famous astrologers, *Recuil des plus célèbres astrologues,* which includes an autobiographical sketch. He was condemned as a diviner by the *Parlement* of Paris and many of his books were burned.

SIMON, MARMION
Fifteenth century. French painter, miniaturist.

SIMONY
Simony was so rampant in the papacy during the Renaissance in Italy that the statement was made that 'our churches, priests, altars, sacred rites, our prayers . . . are purchasable.'

SIRECTUS, ANTONIUS
Logician, author of *Formalitates Moderniores De Mente Scoti:* published in 1505.

SIXTUS, IV, POPE 1471-1484
(1414-1484). The Renaissance prince on the papal throne, of the della Rovere family, a Franciscan monk, a nepotist among nepotists. His chief policy was the consolidation of the Papal States, not that they be ruled directly from the Vatican, but that local despots and vicars be replaced by the papal nephews. His attempt to establish his nephew Girolamo Riario as lord of Imola and Forli was opposed by Florence; it embroiled the peninsula in war and led to the Pazzi conspiracy against the Medici. In the manner of a secular prince he sought to beautify Rome by building projects of all sorts, one of which was the Sistine chapel; he was a collector of manuscripts, art and archaeological objects; he opened the first museum for the public and organized the celebrated Sistine chapel choir; he was the patron of several writers, e.g., Platina whom he made librarian of the Vatican collection and commissioned to write the important *History of the Popes,* the Greek scholar John Argyropulos, and Pomponius Laetus of the Roman Academy. He is most memorable as a patron of painting (as his nephew Julius II was to be); Pinturicchio, Signorelli, Botticelli, Ghirlandaio, Roselli, Perugino were all called upon to decorate the Sistine chapel; Sixtus himself appears with four of his nephews and his librarian Platina in a superb fresco by Melozzo da Forli in the Vatican library.

SIXTUS V
(1521-1590). Pope 1585-1590. Although the two men were markedly similar in many respects, Sixtus and his predecessor, Gregory XIII, were mortal enemies; during the latter's reign, the future Sixtus busied himself with the pursuits of a scholar, particularly Biblical studies. This work bore fruit in the Septuagint, published in Rome by his order in 1587. A similar authoritative edi-

tion of the Vulgate was cut short by his death. Built Lateran Palace, Vatican Library, completed the dome of St. Peter's. Gave sanction for the Spanish Armada to attack England in 1588. Encouraged agriculture and commerce in the Papal States, where he moved rigorously to stamp out lawlessness.

SKARGA, PETER

(1536-1612). Polish Jesuit, preacher at the court of Sigismund III and writer. Contributed to the restoration of Catholicism in Poland and the union of the Ruthenians with Rome, in 1596. He proposed, in his most important work, *Sermons to the Diet*, 1597, a fundamental change of the Polish constitution: absolute monarchy, reduction of the powers of the Diet and the privileges of the nobility. He furthered the reform of the Church in Poland.

SKELTON, JOHN

(c. 1460-1529). English poet. Protégé of Henry VII. Under disfavor of Cardinal Wolsey. Author of *The Crown of Laurel, The Bowge of Court, Speak Parrot, Against the Scots, Ware of Hawke!* Also a rollicking piece entitled *The Tunning of Eleanor Rumming*. He was at his best as a satirist, his favorite target being the clergy; his verse form—repeating the same rhyme through several couplets and utilizing short lines—is called Skeltonic.

SLEIDANUS, IOANNES

(c. 1506-1556). German humanist, historian, diplomat, Protestant reformer. Author of *On the State of Religion and Government under the Emperor Charles V*, 1555, a history of the reign in twenty books.

SMITH, CAPTAIN JOHN

(1580-1631). English soldier, colonizer. Served in France under Henry IV, against Turks. By dint of his energy and resourcefulness he saved the Virginia colony in the grim year of 1607-8, an account of which he gave in *A True Relation*, written in Virginia and published in England in 1608. In it he tells of his role in the colony, his dealing with the Indians, of his capture and danger of death at their hands, but makes no mention of Pocahontas. It is only in his *General Historie*, 1624, that the gallant intercession of Pocahontas in his behalf, among other embellishments, appears. His *Map of Virginia*, 1612, and *Description of New Eng-*

land, 1616, were the earliest geographical surveys of those areas. New England, the Charles River, Plymouth, Cape Anne all owe their designation to this second work. In these two works and other pamphlets he was a persuasive promoter of colonization. *The True Travels,* 1630, is a superb narration of his career.

SMITH, SIR THOMAS

(1514-1577). English statesman, scholar. He studied at Paris and at Padua after taking his degree at Cambridge. From 1535 to 1540 he was reader in Greek at Cambridge and was associated with Sir John Cheke in an attempt to reform the pronunciation of Greek in England, speaking it according to the principles laid down by Erasmus. Served on diplomatic mission for Queen Elizabeth. Author of *De Republica Anglorum,* a basic source for the English constitution in the Tudor period.

SMOTRITSKY, MELETY

(1578-1633). Ukrainian writer and ecclesiastic. Author of a *Grammar,* published in 1619. It is a polemical as well as a linguistic work.

SNYDERS, FRANS

(1579-1657). Flemish painter of Antwerp. He traveled extensively in Italy in the early part of his career. Noted for still lifes, hunting and animal scenes; he served his apprenticeship as an assistant to Brueghel the Younger.

SOCIETY OF JESUS

This Society was founded in 1534 by St. Ignatius de Loyola and approved by Pope Paul III in 1540.

SOCINIANISM

The Italian theologians Fausto (1539-1604) and Lelio (1525-1562) Sozzini founded the sect of the Socinians. It postulated the humanity of Christ, divinely endowed. It denied the Trinity and a personal devil, the natural depravity of man, vicarious atonement, eternal punishment. Socinianism is also called Old Unitarianism. Of all the sects spawned in the age of the Reformation, Socinianism probably embodied in greater degree the humanism and rationalism of the Renaissance.

SODERINI, PIERO DI TOMMASO

(1452-1522). The principal leader, as gonfalonier for life, of the Florentine republic from 1502-1512. As a typical Florentine bur-

554

gher, he was eminently acceptable for political office, although he had no talent for leadership or courage. He was deposed and fled in 1512 in the face of the restoration of the Medici by Spanish bayonets. Upon his death in exile, Machiavelli wrote this contemptuous epitaph on his former chief and colleague, "The night that Piero Soderini died, his soul arrived at the mouth of Hell; and Pluto shouted at him: Silly soul, Hell's not for you, go on to the Limbo of babies."

SODOMA, IL, GIOVANNI ANTONIO BAZZI
(c. 1477-1549). Italian painter of Siena. Of the Lombard school, he was the most gifted of Leonardo's disciples. Worked also in Rome for Pope Julius II. Produced a *Nativity, Leda and the Swan, Flagellation of Christ, Marriage of Alexander and Roxane* and *Alexander in the Tent of Darius*, the last two for the Farnese palace of the banker Agostino Chigi.

SOLARI, GUINIFORTI
(1429-1481). Italian architect. Born in Milan. Began the façade of the Charterhouse, La Certósa, of Pavia in 1473.

SOLARI, PIETRO ANTONIO
(Died 1493). Italian architect and sculptor, son of Guiniforte. He worked in Milan and Alexandria; he is remembered chiefly because he entered the service of Ivan III, for whom, collaborating with other Italians, he built a palace and portions of the Kremlin.

SOLARIO, ANDREA
(ante 1470-post 1522). Italian painter. Produced portraits, religious paintings. Belonged to circle associated with Leonardo da Vinci at Milan; his stays of several years in Venice and then in Flanders left their influence upon his work. For a number of years, also, he was painter to the French Cardinal d'Amboise.

SOLARIO, CRISTOFORO
(c. 1460-1527). Italian sculptor, architect, brother of Andrea. Called Il Gobbo, The Hunchback. Executed statues for Milan Cathedral—*Adam and Eve*. He was called by Lodovico Il Moro from Venice to work on La Certósa of Pavia; he did the tombs there of Lodovico and his wife Beatrice d'Este as well as a statue of Duke Gian Galeazzo Visconti. His work shows the influence of Leonardo and Bramante.

SOLIGO, CRISTOFORO
Fifteenth century. Venetian cartographer. Published maps in 1489.

SOLIHULL SCHOOL
Origins uncertain of this English public school. First recorded mention occurs in 1560.

SOLWAY MOSS, BATTLE OF
In this battle James V of Scotland was defeated by Henry VIII, King of England, in 1542. James died in the same year and was succeeded by his infant daughter, Mary, Queen of Scots.

SOMERS, SIR GEORGE
(1554-1610). Helped to found South Virginia Company. Discovered Somers Islands, known now as Bermudas, in 1609. His shipwreck and stay there were described by a companion, Silvester Jourdain, in *A Discoverie of the Bermudas, otherwise called the Isle of Divels,* a work in which Shakespeare found some raw materials for *The Tempest.*

SONCINAS, PAULUS
(died 1494). Logician. Author of *Quaestiones Metaphysicales.* Also *Expositio:* published in Venice in 1499.

SONCINO or SONCINATI
Jewish family of printers who took their name from the town, near Cremona, where they established their press in 1483. The firm moved several times—Naples, Brescia, Rimini—and finally to Constantinople in 1547. They produced the best Hebrew editions of the day; among them were a Bible and Petrarch, 137 altogether. The chief figures were JOSHUA SOLOMON, who established the firm, and GERSON BEN MOSES.

SONG OF THE CONQUEST OF PANNONIA
A Hungarian narrative poem, published in 1526.

SORIANO, FRANCESCO or SURIANO
(1549-1620). Italian composer, singer, musician. He studied under Palestrina and was the last important member of the Roman school of polyphony founded by Palestrina. He was choirmaster of St. Peter's and a prolific composer of religious and secular music, including masses, motets, madrigals, psalms—for as many as sixteen voices—and a *Magnificat* and *Passione.*

SOROLAINEN, ERIC
(1546-1624). Finnish bishop. Published an ecclesiastical handbook and other religious works. Under his leadership work was resumed to complete Finnish translation of the Old Testament; it appeared in 1642. He worked energetically in behalf of the Protestant cause in Finland.

SOUSA, FREI LUIS DE
(1555-1632). Portuguese writer and Dominican monk. He was a prisoner of the Moors in Algeria, where he came to know Cervantes. He wrote about his exploratory trips in Spanish America (he entered the Spanish service with the annexation of Portugal to Spain), as well as a work on Antarctica. He also wrote ecclesiastical biography and history.

SOUTHAMPTON, HENRY WRIOTHESLEY, THIRD EARL OF
(1573-1624). Soldier, patron of Shakespeare and other poets. Attached to court of Queen Elizabeth. A friend of Essex and implicated in the plot, he was first sentenced to death and then to life imprisonment; James I released him and made him a privy councillor. Member of Virginia company. Died on way to serve in Netherlands.

SOUTHWELL, ROBERT
(c. 1561-1595). English poet and Jesuit priest. Imprisoned and executed as traitor. Author of poem *The Burning Babe*. Also religious pieces.

SOZZINI, FAUSTO
(1539-1604). Italian theologian, nephew of Lelio Sozzini. Established the system known as Socinianism. Denounced by the Inquisition, he fled to Switzerland and then Poland, where he organized the Polish Brethren. Author of theological treatises, among them *De Auctoritate Sanctae Scripturae*.

SOZZINI, LELIO
(1525-1562). Italian theologian. He fled to Switzerland from the Inquisition. He traveled widely and met many of the Protestant leaders, including Luther and Calvin. As a formulated doctrine, Socinianism owes more to his nephew than to him; his writings, however, were the starting point of that doctrine as it was developed by the younger man.

SPADA, LEONELLO

(1576-1622). Italian painter. Executed religious frescoes in churches, e.g., in the cathedral of Reggio and oil paintings such as *The Concert* and *Aeneas and Anchises*. He signed his works with an L over a sword (*spada*).

SPAGYRIC

Alchemy. A term invented by Paracelsus (1493-1541). The expression was common in the sixteenth century. An alchemist was known as a spagyrist or a spagyrite.

SPALATIN, GEORG

(1484-1545). Lutheran. Acted as intermediary between Duke Frederick the Wise of Saxony and Luther. Court chaplain. Negotiated hearing of Luther in Germany rather than at Rome. Many of Luther's letters were addressed to him. His *Annales reformationis* describes many of the events and personages of the Reformation from, as it were, the inside.

SPANISH ART

Architecture: The plateresque style belongs to the latter decades of the fifteenth century through the sixteenth. End of Gothic period and advent of the Renaissance, although both phases overlapped and the same architect could produce work in each style. In fact, Spain was the crossroads where the artistic influences and traditions of Flemish-Burgundian art, Italian art and the native Moorish-Spanish art met and mingled; the great flowering of art, architecture, literature and music in the Spain of Philip II, III, and IV cannot be understood or appreciated apart from these three traditions. But the history of Spain's cultural great age that takes proper account of these three traditions, and of their fusion and interpenetration, has yet to be written. It will be noted that Spanish ties with Italy stemmed from the Aragonese acquisition of Sicily in the late thirteenth century and the conquest of southern Italy in the 1440's by Alfonso the Magnanimous, who established his court at Naples. With the Lowlands the connection dated from the reign of Philip the Handsome, 1506-1508, and, more definitely, of his son, the Emperor Charles V, 1516-1556. Thus, during the age under consideration, there was a continuous cultural interplay among these areas: Spanish artists sojourned in Italy and the Lowlands, Flemish and Italian artists were called to the Spanish court, etc. Some of the leading architects were: De Egas, Güas, Alonso de Covarrubias, Francisco de Colonia.

High Renaissance: Last three quarters of the sixteenth century. In the area around Granada, Renaissance motifs were sometimes applied to Gothic plans. In general, Andalusia in the Southwest, Central Spain around Toledo and Madrid, and Northeast Spain reflected Italian Renaissance trend.

The Escorial represents a stream-lining of the High Renaissance principles. Other representative buildings are the Cathedral of Granada, the Cathedral of Valladolid, the Palace of Charles V in Granada.

Renaissance painting: The end of the fifteenth century and the sixteenth century. The influences were Italian of the Early and High Renaissance, and Flemish impacts. Spanish founders of the Renaissance style include Bartolomé Bermejo (c. 1440-1495), Pedro Berruguette (died 1504), Rodrigo de Osuna the Elder (active between 1464 and 1484).

A heightening of Renaissance characteristics appeared early in the sixteenth century, influenced by Pedro Campagna (1503-1580). Portraiture was developed by Alonso Sánchez Coello (1515-1590). Domenikos Theotocopoulos (1541-1614), El Greco, achieved the fullest expression of Spanish temperament combined with inventive genius.

Other important Spanish painters include:

Luis de Vargas (1502-1568), Francisco de Herrera the Elder (1576-1656), Juan de las Rolas (1559-1625), Fernández Navarrette (1526-1579).

SPANISH FICTION

Sixteenth century themes dealt with Spanish and Moorish relationships and sentimental subjects: e.g. Antonio de Villegas' *Del Abencerraje*: published in 1551. Alonso Núñez de Reinoso— *Clareo y Florisea*: published in 1553.

Most typically Spanish of all Renaissance prose fiction was the picaresque novel, in which the protagonist, a rogue, passes through a series of loosely connected episodes, stratagems, dubious encounters.

SPANISH FURY

The sack and pillage of Antwerp by Spanish soldiers under the duke of Alva during the Wars of Dutch Independence: Nov. 3, 1576.

SPANISH LYRICS

During the Renaissance in Spain, Spanish poets who studied classical and Italian poetry still retained feelings for the popular poetry of Spain. Such poetry—ballads, *romances fronterizos*—is illustrated in the *Romanceros* of Nucio (1550) Nájera (1550), Fuentes (1550), Sepúlveda (1551), Timoneda (1573).

SPANISH PLAYS ON BIBLICAL THEMES

Plays, based on Biblical themes, were popular in sixteenth century Spain and were the starting point for the great age of Spanish drama. Among such plays were: *Auto de Caín y Abel,* by Jaime Ferruz. *Tragedia llamada Josefina,* published in 1535 by Micael de Carvajal. *Entremés de Noemi y Ruth,* by Sebastián de Horosco (1510-1580).

SPANISH THEATRE

The greatness of Renaissance Spain lies in her theatre. The nativity plays of Gómez Manrique (1412-1490) were developed in conformity with the Italian Renaissance by Juan del Encina (1469-1529), who abandoned Biblical shepherds for pagan pastoral themes: e.g. in his *Cristino y Febea.* Bartolomé de Torres Naharro (died after 1530) produced *The Soldiery, The Kitchen Staff, Comedia Jacinta.* The Portuguese-Spanish playwright Gil Vicente (1465-1539) used mythology, humorous elements, lively technique, criticism of the Church, e.g. in *Amadís, Templo de Apolo* (1526). These efforts culminated in the works of the greatest master of Spanish drama, Lope de Vega.

SPATARO, GIOVANNI

(c. 1460-1541). Italian musician and musical theorist. He was choirmaster of San Petronio in Bologna, wrote much church music in that connection, and several theoretical works and not a few polemical ones, e.g., on *The Errors of Franchino Gafori.*

SPEE, FRIEDRICH VON

(1591-1635). German Jesuit, poet, professor of philosophy and theology at Cologne and Trier. Active in Counter Reformation and in suppression of witchcraft, on which subject he wrote a Latin treatise. His lyrical religious verse, written in German, is in the German mystical tradition.

SPEED, JOHN

(c. 1552-1629). English cartographer and historian. He wrote

History of Great Britain. In 1627 he published his *Prospect of the Most Famous Parts of the World,* the first printed general atlas by an Englishman. He is best known for *Theatre of the Empire of Great Britain,* 1611, with a separate map for each county of England, Wales and several for Ireland; they are remarkable for their accuracy (he had the habit of correcting them in subsequent editions) as well as their beauty. On the reverse sides he printed an account of the special features and events peculiar to that county. He was a friend of many of the leading scholars of the day, e.g., Camden and Cotton, and, with them, a member of the Society of Antiquaries.

SPELMAN, SIR HENRY

(c. 1564-1641). English scholar, antiquarian, historian. Served in Ireland. Wrote on juristic subjects. Compiled a dictionary of Latin and Old English: *Glossarium Archaeologicum.* His researches into England's feudal past, especially his study of *Tenures by Knight Service,* made him a pioneer of modern historiography: he showed how Parliament's origin must be sought in the feudal past and did not antedate 1066. Since his findings tended to support the king's claims and not those of Parliament, his works were ignored and his profundity unrecognized until relatively recently.

SPENSER, EDMUND

(c. 1552-1599). English poet. Attached to House of Leicester. Secretary to Lord Deputy of Ireland. Lived in England and Ireland. Author of *The Shepherd's Calendar.* His major work, the *Faerie Queene,* is an allegory on England and its queen, "Gloriana." One of the greatest masterpieces in English literature. Also composed sonnets, hymns, an *Epithalamium.*

SPERANDIO DA MANTOVA

(1425?-after 1504). Italian sculptor and medalist of Mantua. In the service of Borso d'Este at Ferrara and the Gonzaga at Mantua. Executed medallions, bas-relief—*Flagellation.* Executed many portrait busts, two famous ones being that of Eleanor of Aragon and that of Ercole I d'Este. He was famous as a portrait-medalist; examples are his studies of Andrea Bentivoglio and Duke Federico da Montefeltro of Urbino.

SPERONI, SPERONE

(1500-1588). Italian man of letters and jurist of Padua. Author of *Canace,* a tragic drama in Italian in which he set himself to follow strictly the rules laid down by Aristotle. For nearly half a century he was the great authority on literature and wrote numerous works on Dante, Ariosto, Virgil, etc., as well as on literary style and the use of the vernacular. Something of a feminist, he wrote dialogues *Della dignità delle donne* and *Dell'amore.*

SPICES
Spices were used as condiments for flavoring foods and as preservatives of meats. The spice trade involved caravans that crossed the Asiatic deserts, or from Egypt brought their cargoes to the European ports of Marseilles, Genoa, Constantinople. The principal spices imported to Europe were cardamon, saffron, pepper, ginger, nutmeg.

SPIDER, THE UNIVERSAL
A term applied to Louis XI or France (1423-1483), for his skill and persistence in weaving diplomatic webs in every court of Europe and for his utter contempt for the chivalrous ideal of the warrior king.

SPIEGHEL, ADRIAAN VAN DER or SPIGELIO
(1578-1625). Dutch physician who spent most of his life in Italy. Professor of anatomy at Padua. He wrote several works on anatomy and medicine. He was a pioneer in brain surgery.

SPINETTI, GIOVANNI
(Late fifteenth century). Venetian maker of musical instruments. Invented spinet, an offspring of the harpsichord, from which it differed in being smaller and having only one string for each note.

SPINOLA, AMBROGIO DI
(1569-1630). Italian general, of a famous noble family of Genoa, chief general in service of Spain during the Thirty Years' War.

SPRANGER, BORTOLAMÄUS
(1546-1611). Flemish painter. Specialized in mythological subjects, portraits. He traveled and studied extensively in Italy, especially at Milan and Rome; he subsequently became painter to the court of Vienna and then of Prague. Perhaps this explains why his work belonged to no particular school or national tradition, but was "international mannerist" in character.

SPRINGAL

Also sprynhold, springold. A catapult used in hurling heavy missiles. In use during the fifteenth and sixteenth centuries.

SPURS, BATTLE OF

At Guinegate, Henry VIII of England defeated French in 1513. Descriptive name of battle reputedly stems from the flight of the French cavalry, who left much of their accouterment scattered about the field.

SQUARCIONE, FRANCESCO

(1397-1468). Italian painter. Taught Andrea Mantegna. Founder of Paduan school. Traveled in Italy, Greece, making drawings, copying, taking casts, collecting material on antiquity. Said to have taught some 137 pupils, especially in perspective.

STADE OF HESSE, HANS

(Sixteenth century). German soldier and explorer in the service of Portugal. Made two voyages to Brazil, in 1547 and 1555. Captured by cannibal Indians. Author of a history of Brazil, published in 1557, the *Warhafftige Historia;* its hair-raising descriptions of life among the natives of Brazil made it very popular and it went through many editions. In another version it was illustrated by de Bry's engravings.

STAMFORD SCHOOL

English public school. Founded in 1532 by William Radcliffe of Stamford.

STANYHURST, RICHARD

(1547-1618). Irish scholar, educated at Oxford. Translated part of Vergil's *Aeneid* and published Latin commentaries on Porphyry. Also wrote a *History of Ireland* and a *Description of Ireland* which were incorporated in Holinshed's *Chronicles.*

STANZIONE, MASSIMO

(1585-1656). Italian painter. Died in Naples. He was a prolific painter of religious and mythological subjects; his work shows the influence of the Bolognese school, to which his masters belonged; he worked principally in Naples and was a forerunner of "Neapolitan Baroque."

STAPLETON, THOMAS

(1535-1598). English theologian, Roman Catholic. Wrote in

Latin. Author of *Tres Thomae,* biographies of St. Thomas More, and Beckett. Also translated Bede's *History* into English.

STAR CHAMBER, COURT OF

Prerogative Court of the English Government. In 1487 Henry VII of England established a court consisting of members of the Privy Council plus two judges. The court had jurisdiction over riots and unlawful assemblies. In time, the number of members was increased. The court became a judicial session of the entire Privy Council plus two judges. The court was used as a means of oppression, political and ecclesiastical. It was abolished in 1641. It was known as the Court of the Star Chamber because it met in a chamber in Westminster Palace whose ceiling was decorated with stars. The term has now acquired a pejorative significance, implying an unjust or secret court.

STARKEY, THOMAS

(1499?-1538). English cleric. Chaplain to Henry VIII. Author of a *Dialogue* on religious reform, a *Treatise against Papal Supremacy,* and the suggestion that the King's divorce be referred to a council of the Church. He traveled, in the company of Reginald Pole, in Italy; perhaps that trip helps to explain how it was that he was the first to employ "state" in its modern sense rather than its older meaning, e.g., "The king lives in state."

STARTER, JAN JANSZOON

(c. 1594-1626). Poet, born in England but of Dutch descent; he spent most of his life in the Lowlands. Author of *Frisian Paradise,* appeared in 1621. Written largely in Dutch; contains Frisian poems.

STATES-GENERAL

Summoned in Paris in 1614. The last assembly before the French Revolution in 1789; it had not met since the Hundred Years' War before 1610, although there were some sessions of bodies calling themselves by that name during the Civil and Religious Wars of the latter part of the sixteenth century.

STATES OF ITALY

In the fifteenth century, the five chief states of Italy were the Republics of Florence and Venice, the Kingdom of Naples, the Papacy—the states of the Church, the duchy of Milan, known officially as the Patrimony of St. Peter, and the Duchy of Milan.

STAUPITZ, JOHANN VON
(died 1534). German theologian and mystic. Vicar-General of Augustinian monastic order in Germany at the beginning of the Reformation. Taught and advised Martin Luther. In 1512 he relinquished his chair at the University of Wittenberg to Luther. Initially he supported Luther, to whose religious travail he had been a witness; he soon attacked and condemned him.

STEELYARD
German merchants of the Hanse who lived in London in an area known as the Steelyard or German House. The merchants were expelled by Queen Elizabeth I in 1597.

STEENWIJCK, HENDRIK VAN, THE ELDER
(c. 1550-c. 1603). Flemish painter, father of below. Worked in Germany. He was noted for paintings featuring complex architectural designs such as palaces and church interiors, executed with minute details.

STEENWIJCK, HENDRIK VAN, THE YOUNGER
(c. 1580-c.1649). Flemish painter. Most of his work was of the interior of churches; he frequently completed the paintings of other artists by adding architectural elements.

STEPHANUS DE MONTE
Carmelite monk. Logician. Taught in Pavia. Author of *Ars Insolubilis: Docens de Omni Scibili Indifferenter Disputare*: published in 1490.

STERNHOLD, THOMAS
(died 1549). Groom of the Robes to Henry VIII. He and John Hopkins published their versifications of the Psalms, dedicated to Edward VI, in 1548, 1549 and 1561; in the last and longest edition forty Psalms appear. Done into ballad metre, the Psalms were readily singable and Sternhold seems to have sung his own creations.

STEVENSON, WILLIAM
(died 1575). English cleric. Putative author of comedy: *Gammar Gurton's Needle*.

STEVINUS, SIMON
(1548-1620). Flemish mathematician. In 1585 he published a treatise describing his invention, the decimal system, and pro-

claimed its application to weights and measures. As a student of mechanics he contributed much to statics and hydrostatics; he too mounted a tower and dropped objects of different weight (possibly before Galileo) in an attempt to prove Aristotle's laws of motion wrong: air resistance, however, caused the lead to fall faster than the wood and thus Aristotle seemed to be confirmed. His studies of terrestrial magnetism resulted in improvements in navigation. He served as military engineer to Maurice of Nassau and wrote on fortifications, bookkeeping, and other matters of applied mathematics and science.

STIFEL, MICHAEL
(1485-1567). German mathematician. An Augustinian monk, he became a Lutheran. His *Arithmetica integra* was an important exposition of algebra and made it widely known in England. His study of exponents contributed to the development of logarithms.

STIGELIUS, IOANNES
(1515-1562). German poet, professor of rhetoric at Wittenberg, friend of Melanchthon and Luther, designated poet laureate by Charles V. Wrote Latin lyrics in classical style but covering a wide range of contemporary themes.

STIRLING, WILLIAM ALEXANDER, EARL OF
(c. 1567-1640). Scottish poet. Traveled extensively in France, Spain and Italy. Secretary of State for Scotland. Author of *Aurora*, a corpus of sonnets, elegies, madrigals, published in 1604. Wrote the long epic poem *Doomsday*. He assisted the king in the King James Version of the Psalms. He also wrote *An Encouragement of Colonies* (he had been granted an estate in Canada) and *Four Monarchicke Tragedies: Croesus, Darius, Alexander the Great and Julius Caesar*.

STOCKPORT GRAMMAR SCHOOL
English public school. Founded in 1487 by Lord Mayor of London, Sir Edmond Shaa (or Shaw).

STOGLAV
Record of decisions of the Russian Synod of 1551, which ruled on matters of religious dogma and morals.

STORNELLI
In the Italian Renaissance, these were songs associated with the country-side.

566

STOSS, VEIT

(c. 1440-1533). German woodcarver and sculptor. Died in Nuremberg. Leading artist in late Gothic and early Renaissance period in Nuremberg. His representation of figures was dramatic and realistic, suggesting Italian influence. Chief works: Wing altar and tomb of Casimir V in Cracow Cathedral, 1492, tomb of Archbishop Olesnicky, 1493, both done in stone. Other altar pieces in Cracow and other Polish cities. In Nuremberg: *Rosary and Annunciation, Crucifixion, St. Anna, St. Jacob,* relief of the Passion. His best known wood carving is the *Annunciation,* done for the Church of St. Lorenz in Nuremberg.

STOW, JOHN

(c. 1529-1605). English antiquary. Collector of manuscripts. Chronicler. Among his writings are *Summary of English Chronicles, The Annals of England,* and *A Survey of London*: published in 1598, an invaluable source for the wealth of information on Tudor London. Stow is among the most accurate and trustworthy chroniclers of the period.

STRADA, FAMIANUS

(1572-1649). Roman Jesuit, classical scholar, historian, author of *Prolusiones Academicae,* a great miscellany of Latin scholarship in which he deals with rhetoric, oratory, history and politics; his essential concern was with good Latin style: how to judge it in the classical poets and authors, and how to attain it in one's own writing. He was professor of rhetoric at the Roman College; he wrote an important history of the Revolt of the Lowlands against Spain, 1555-1590, entitled *De bello belgico.*

STRAPAROLA, GIOVANNI FRANCESCO

(c. 1495-c. 1557). Italian writer. Author of a collection of seventy-three tales called *Facetious Nights.* Source from which Shakespeare and later playwrights derived material.

STRODE, WILLIAM

(1598-1645). English poet. Author of a tragi-comedy, *The Floating Island,* which, with music by Lowes, was performed before Charles I; he also wrote miscellaneous poems—elegies and lyrics.

STROMAYER, CASPER

Sixteenth century. German surgeon. Author of *Practica Copiosa:*

published in 1559. Noted for high standards of technique and ethics.

STUBBES, PHILIP

(Late sixteenth century). Puritan social critic and zealot. Author of *Anatomy of Abuses*: published in 1583; it was an attack on the lavish mores of the times. Thomas Nashe replied with his *Anatomy of Absurdity*.

STUMPF, JOHANNES

(1500-c. 1577). Swiss geographer and historian. He was the author of a voluminous history of Switzerland, called briefly *Eidgenossenschaft*, 1546, and a history of the Council of Constance. In the earlier part of his life he had been an active follower of Zwingli.

STURE, STEN, THE ELDER

(c. 1440-1503). Swedish noble. Regent of Sweden. In conflict with Danes. Instrumental in founding University of Uppsala, 1477, the oldest university in Sweden.

STURM, JAKOB

(1489-1553). German reformer and statesman. He was a protagonist of religious tolerance. Associated with Strassburg, where he founded the Protestant Gymnasium in 1538.

STURM, JOHANNES

(1507-1589). German classical scholar and educator. He was the head of the Strassburg Gymnasium, referred to above, for forty-three years, where he instituted many educational innovations, particularly the graded readers for the study of Latin. His Christian ideal of education and his pedagogical principles are set forth in his *De puerorum ludis recte operiendis*. He was the most influential schoolmaster of the century; his school became the model for many Gymnasia all over Germany, his Latin text books were widely used, his pedagogical works widely read, and he attracted brilliant students who imitated his methods when they became schoolmasters. He was much admired by Roger Ascham, who refers to him in *The Scholemaster*.

STYMMELIUS, CHRISTOPHER

(1525-1588). German poet and Protestant minister. Author of a drama of student life in the sixteenth century that recalls the Goliardic spirit. The play is called *Studentes sive Comoedia de*

568

Vita Studiosorum. First published in 1549. Another Latin comedy was *De immolatione Isaac.*

SUAREZ, FRANCISCO
(1548-1617). Spanish Jesuit theologian, political theorist, and ethical jurist who taught in Spain and Portugal, and at Rome. He has been called the last of the Scholastics. In *De Defensione Fidei* he argued that kings are responsible to their subjects and that government is established to promote the common good. His *Tractatus de legibus* made him the luminary of the Spanish school of international jurisprudence; he defines natural law as the sanction controlling the relations of sovereign states; the *Tractatus* was much esteemed by Grotius; it owed much to Vittoria.

SUBMARINE
First navigable submarine invented in 1620 by the Dutch scientist Cornelia Jacobszoon Drebbel (1572-1633), who lived in England.

SUCKLING, SIR JOHN
(1609-1642). English Cavalier poet. Author of plays, lyrics, amatory pieces. Noted for *Ballad of a Wedding.* Reputedly poisoned himself in Paris. Saintsbury: "Everything in Suckling turns to a ripple of merriment."

SULEIMAN or SOLYMAN, I or II
(1496-1566). Called The Magnificent. Ottoman Sultan of Turkey. He annexed Belgrade, Budapest, Rhodes, Algiers, Aden, Bagdad. In his reign Ottoman power reached its greatest height and threatened Christian Europe. It was a great cultural age. He decreed far-reaching educational and legal reforms; he is Suleiman the Lawgiver to the Moslem world. He was a munificent patron of the arts, of literature, and of science; he was the patron of Sinan, the greatest of all Turkish architects.

SULK
Plough. A term used of a ship cutting through the waves. A sixteenth century expression. Derived from the Latin sulcus, *a furrow, a trail,* Vergil: Infundunt sulcos—*They cut furrows* (through the waves).

SULLAM, SARA COPIA
(c. 1590-1641). Jewish scholar and poetess of Venice. Versed in

Greek, Latin, Hebrew, Italian, Spanish. Held a literary salon. Only a few sonnets and her *Manifesto,* an apologia, survive.

SULLY, MAXIMILIEN DE BÉTHUNE, DUKE OF, BARON DE ROSNY
(1560-1641). French statesman. Protestant. Attached to Henry of Navarre, who became Henry IV. Sully became Finance Minister in 1597: also held other offices. He re-organized French finances: encouraged agriculture: built bridges, roads, canals. On death of Henry, he was forced into retirement.

SUPREMACY, ACTS OF
These Acts of Parliament separated Anglican from Catholic Church. Signed by Henry VIII of England in 1534, and by Queen Elizabeth I in 1559, after Mary had repealed them.

SURGETUS, JOHANNES
Sixteenth century. French jurist of Soissons. In the service of Juan de Cardona. Author of *Militaris Disciplinae Enchiridion*: published in 1512. On the art of war, but advocating European peace. Published at a critical time, when the Holy League had been concluded.

SURIANO, MICHELE
Sixteenth century. Ambassador to Venice. Wrote on missions to France and Spain.

SURREY, HENRY HOWARD, EARL OF
(c. 1517-1547). English poet, son of the Duke of Norfolk. He, with Wyatt, introduced the Italian sonnet and other verse forms into England; in his early poems he imitated Petrarch closely. His translation of part of the *Aeneid* is notable for his use of blank verse. He had begun to emancipate himself from his Italian models and to show promise as a truly great poet, when he was accused of treason—for introducing the royal insignia on his coat of arms and advising his sister to become the king's mistress—and executed. His death is an indication of the disastrous impact on England's cultural life of Henry VIII's reign.

SUSINI, ANTONIO
(died 1624). Florentine sculptor. Traditionally, executed *Centaur and Deianira, Horse,* and some figures for the cathedral of Pisa.

SUSINI, FRANCESCO
(died 1646). Florentine sculptor, nephew of the above. Executed a *Hercules and Wild Boar*, according to traditional attribution.

SUSIO, GIOVANNI BATTISTA
(Sixteenth century). Italian writer. Author of treatise on duelling: condemns it, but presents lucid appraisal of the practice.

SUSSANAEUS, HUBERTUS
(1512-after 1550). French humanist, poet, jurist, physician. Member of Rabelais Circle of Lyons. Author of collection of epigrams and poems: *Ludorum Libri*: published in 1538. He produced editions of Cicero and Horace.

SUTTON VALENCE SCHOOL
English public school. Founded in 1576 by English merchant and philanthropist William Lambe (1495-1580).

SWEELINCK, JAN PIETERSZOON
(1562-1621). Dutch composer. Organist in Amsterdam. He was the first to make independent use of pedals, in fugues. Composed sacred music: *Cantiones Sacrae*.

SWISS ACADEMY
The Academy of Geneva, under the direction of Theodore de Bèze, was established in 1558.

SWORDSMANSHIP
Italian schools of swordsmanship were highly popular in the Renaissance. Among notable Italian fencers was Vincenzo Saviolo, described by John Florio as the most perfect fencer of his time. Saviolo, whose patron was the Earl of Essex, wrote a *Manual of Practice*.

SYLBURG, FRIEDRICH
(1536-1596). German classical scholar. Edited the whole of Aristotle, the Greek Fathers Clement of Alexandria and Justin Martyr, Dionysius of Halicarnassus, and the *Scriptores historiae Romanae;* his editions were remarkable for their thoroughness and accuracy. He was one of the great Greek scholars of his day and contributed to the Greek *Thesaurus* of Henri Estienne, one of his teachers. In the last years of his life he was librarian at Heidelberg.

571

SYLVESTER, FRANCISCUS

(died 1525). Logician of Ferrara. Wrote commentary on *Posterior Analytics* of Aristotle.

SYLVESTRE

In 1648 the Hieromonakh Sylvestre prepared in Rumanian a New Testament collated with Greek and Hungarian Calvinist versions.

SYLVIUS, JACOBUS

(1478-1555). Latinized form of Jacques Dubois. French physician. Anatomist. Teacher of Vesalius. He was one of the pioneers in the study of the venous valves; their action suggested the circulation of the blood by the heart to Harvey.

SYRLIN, JÖRG, THE ELDER

(c. 1425-1491). German sculptor, woodcarver. Work chiefly in Ulm; the Cathedral and in market place. His work is characterized by its rich fantasy.

SYRLIN, JÖRG, THE YOUNGER

(c. 1455-c. 1521). German sculptor, woodcarver, son of the above. His work resembles that of his father but is inferior to it.

SZABACS, BATTLE OF

A Hungarian narrative poem. Appeared in 1476.

SZLACHTA

A Polish term for the Polish nobility.

SZYMONOWICZ, SZYMON

(1558-1629). Polish poet. He helped to organize the humanist Academy of Zamosc and wrote much Latin verse; his best work was in Polish, the *Idylls* of village life, inspired by Theocritus and Virgil.

T

TABOUROT DES ACCORDS, ÉTIENNE

(1549-1590). French poet. Author of series of essays and *facetiae;* his verse was highly artificial and complex; he was a friend of Ronsard and the *Pléiade* group.

TABULA PEUTINGERIANA

The Peutinger Table. A world-map: so called because it was acquired by Konrad Peutinger (1465-1547), antiquary, scholar, and author of, among other works, *Inscriptiones Romanae*: published in 1520. He was also keeper of the archives in his native city of Nuremberg.

The Peutinger Table is a roll of parchment in twelve sections. It was intended to serve as a portable road map. Land is painted in buff color, the sea in green, roads in red, and rivers in blue. The map extends from Britain to the mouth of the Ganges. The main roads, about 500 cities, distances from each city, chief mountains and rivers are indicated.

The map is generally believed to have been a twelfth or thirteenth century copy of a much earlier map. This prototype is variously dated in the second to the fourth century A.D. Other authorities attribute the map to Castorius, a Roman grammarian who lived c. 340 A.D.

TACCA, PIETRO

(1577?-1640). Florentine sculptor. Worked in France. Began a monumental *Centaur and Deianira*. Influenced by Gian Bologna, to whom he had been an assistant. His most famous work is the *Four Moors*, part of a monumental work by Bondini in Livorno;

the chained writhing figures were inspired by Michelangelo. He also did a monumental equestrian statue of Philip IV of Spain. His son Ferdinando was also a sculptor.

TAEGIUS, FRANCISCUS
Sixteenth century. Logician. Thomist. Wrote *Lectura in libellum Thomas Aquinatis de Fallaciis:* published in Pavia in 1511.

TAFUR, PERO
(c. 1410-c. 1484). Spanish writer and traveler. Traveled through Europe, Greece, and the Middle East, which he narrated in his credulous travelogue, *Andanzas e viajes.*

TAGLIACOZZI, GASPARO
(1546-1599). Italian professor of surgery at Bologna. Noted for his plastic nasal surgery. His work raised the suspicion of ecclesiastical authorities and he was prevented from advancing surgery as he might otherwise have done.

TALIATION
Repayment. Equated with retaliation. A term in use in the fifteenth, sixteenth, and seventeenth centuries.

TALLIS, THOMAS
(c. 1510-1585). English musician. Attached to Chapel Royal under Henry VIII, Edward VI, Queen Mary, and Elizabeth I. He composed many of the earliest musical settings for the Anglican liturgy or service. He and Byrd were together organists to the chapel. Much of their music was jointly published. One of his songs is the essence of polyphonic complexity; it calls for eight five-voice choruses, in forty parts.

TALMUD
Rabbinical thesaurus. Recension completed during fifth century. First complete edition published 1520-1523 by Christian printer Daniel Bomberg (died 1549).

TANSILLO, LUIGI
(1510-1568). Italian poet. Author of religious epic, lyrics, didactic pieces. His experiences fighting against the Turks are reflected in his poetry. His best work is his lyrical poems of love, sorrow, spiritual yearning and idyllic nature.

TARLTON, RICHARD

(died 1588). English actor. Clown at court of Queen Elizabeth. Corpus of *Tarlton's Jests* attributed to his authorship. He may be the original Yorick of *Hamlet*.

TARTAGLIA, NICCOLÒ

(c. 1500-1557). Italian mathematician. Reputedly, invented gunner's quadrant. Also found solution of cubic equation. He produced the first Latin edition (fairly complete) of Archimedes, 1543, a work which had a very great importance for mechanics and quantification in science.

TASSO, BERNARDO

(1493-1569). Italian poet. Father of Torquato Tasso. Corresponded with Bambo Tolomei the historian, Pope Clement VII. His letters, published in 1585, reflect spirit and conditions of his age. His most important work was a long epic of chivalry, an Italian reworking of the Spanish poem *Amadis of Gaul*, entitled *Amadigi*.

TASSO, TORQUATO

(1544-1595). Italian poet. Born at Sorrento. Led wandering life. In 1560, studied law at Padua. Here his first book was published —*Rinaldo*, a romantic poem. Wrote poem—*Amintas*, a superb pastoral drama, presented at Ferrara, to which court he was attached. Lost mental balance. Confined for seven years, during which he produced poems, philosophical dialogues. Noted for epic *Jerusalem Delivered*: completed in 1575; the theme is the capture of Jerusalem during the First Crusade, presented from a thoroughly Christian and medieval point of view. He was the agonized soul whose fate typifies the dilemma of the arts and learning in the Counter Reformation.

TASSONI, ALESSANDRO

(1565-1635). Italian poet. Author of a mock heroic epic entitled *Secchia Rapita: The Rape of the Bucket*.

TAUSEN, HANS

(1494-1561). Bishop of Viborg, professor of Hebrew at Copenhagen. Wittenberg student. From 1524 on, he preached Lutheranism in Denmark. In 1526 Tausen became chaplain to King Frederic I (1523-1533).

Called The Luther of Denmark. Translated the Pentateuch

from Hebrew into Danish. Also wrote polemical work in allegorical form: *The Lie and the Truth.*

TAVERNA, GIULIANO
(Sixteenth century). Milanese engraver and gem and glass cutter, associated with Annibale Fontana.

TAVERNER, JOHN
(c. 1495-1545). English organist, choirmaster at Oxford, composer of sacred music: masses and motets. He also wrote some secular music.

TAVERNER, RICHARD
(c. 1505-1575). English reformer. Supported Reformation. Made revision of Bible, in 1539: called Taverner's Bible. He wrote several religious works and made translations from Erasmus.

TAVERNIER, JEAN LE or JOHANNES DE
(Fifteenth c.) Flemish illuminator of Oudenaarde in the service of Philip the Good, duke of Burgundy. In 1458 he illuminated a copy of *Les Conquêtes de Charlemagne.* Much of his work was historical; he was something of an historian and seems to have illustrated some of his own historical writings.

TAYLOR, JOHN
(1580-1653). Called The Water Poet, because he held the post of Thames waterman. English minor poet. Participated in the siege of Cadiz. Traveled from England to Scotland, Germany. Wrote accounts of his wanderings. Author of *Penniless Pilgrimage,* which like most of his work is a mine of information for the social historian.

TEBALDEO, ANTONIO or TEBALDI
(1463-1537). Italian poet. Author of Latin epigrams, sonnets in the manner of Petrarch, and pastoral eclogues. He spent some time at the courts of Ferrara—in the service of Isabella d'Este and then Lucretia Borgia—and Mantua. He went to Rome at the invitation of Leo X and remained there until driven into penury and exile by the sack of 1527.

TEIXEIRA, PEDRO
(1575?-1640). Portuguese traveler. Twice to India. Considered the first to go around world from West to East. Wrote an account of his voyage in 1610; the *Relaciones,* in Spanish, which concen-

576

trate on his overland treks in Syria, Persia and Central Asia. Served in Brazil. On expedition to the Amazon.

TELESCOPE
Putatively, the telescope was invented in 1608 by Hans Lippershey, a Dutch spectacle maker.

TELESIO, ANTONIO
(1482-1534). Italian humanist of Milan, learned in Greek as well at Latin. Author of Latin lyrics, speeches, treatise on *emblemata* published in 1531. Also a play entitled *Imber Aureus*.

TELESIO, BERNARDINO
(1509-1588). Renaissance philosopher of nature and experimental science. Founder of *Accademia Cosentina* at Naples. Opposed medieval Aristotelianism. Scientific empiricist. Author of *De Rerum Natura iuxta Propria Principia*. He was the nephew of Antonio, his first teacher; he also studied at Padua.

TÉLLEZ, GABRIEL or TIRSO DE MOLINA
(c. 1584-1648). Spanish dramatist. Prior of monastery. Author of some 300 pieces: comedies, interludes, *autos*. One of the great dramatists of the Spanish golden age, he is remembered chiefly for his *El burlador de Sevilla*, the earliest literary treatment of the Don Juan theme. He was a master of characterization and a superb wit.

TEMPERATURE
Reputedly, Galileo invented an instrument for measuring temperature: c. 1600.

TENIERS, DAVID
(1582-1649). The Elder. Flemish painter. Noted for paintings of peasant and religious scenes. His work shows the influence of Rubens. His halfbrother, JULIEN (1572-1615), was also a painter. Together they were the founders of the family's artistic tradition, which flourished until the end of the seventeenth century.

TERESA DE JESÚS, SANTA, DE ÁVILA
(1515-1582). Spanish mystic of Counter Reformation. Of noble lineage. In childhood, had visions and religious ecstasy. At age of seven, ran away to seek martyrdom. She and St. John of the Cross were responsible for a reformation of the Carmelite Order; their branch of the Order is known as the Discalced or Barefoot

Carmelites. Canonized in 1622. Wrote *Libro de las Fundaciones* in 1573. Also collection of some 400 letters. Produced introspective autobiography: *Libro de su Vida*, 1562-1565. Her greatest mystical work is *Las Moradas*, published in 1588. Also *Camino de Perfección*: a guide for nuns, published in 1585.

TESTI, FULVIO

(1593-1646). Italian poet of Ferrara. Imitated Horace. An anti-Spanish patriotic motif pervades his poetry, much of which is dedicated to Duke Charles Emmanuel of Savoy. He was a strict classicist, as may be seen in his drama *L'Isola di Alcina*.

TETRODE, WILLEM

(Sixteenth century). Flemish architect and sculptor. He was active in Italy—in Florence and Rome—and was there known as Guglielmo Fiamingo. Active between 1542 and 1575. Worked in Cologne, in bronze. Influenced by Giovanni da Bologna. He also worked in London.

TETZEL, JOHANN

(c. 1465-1519). German Dominican monk. Sold indulgences—to raise funds for the building of St. Peter's, Rome. His methods and the conception of the indulgence aroused Luther to promulgate Ninety-Five Theses. Tetzel retorted with 106 theses. Rebuked and abandoned by Catholics. Tetzel appears in a drama entitled *Tetzelocramia*, published in 1617. The putative author is H. Kielman.

TEXTOR, JEAN

(c. 1480-1524). French humanist. Seigneur of Ravisi. Rector of the University of Paris, where he did much to establish the classical curriculum. He wrote numerous pedagogical works, manuals and treatises on classical antiquity and letters and epigrams.

THEATRES, PERMANENT

Unknown in the middle ages when productions were in the open air or in churches; the attempt to provide appropriately classical stages and theatre settings for productions of the classical playwrights, or plays modeled on the ancients, was greatly abetted by the publication of Vitruvius in 1484, and attained its summit—with regard to resonance and acoustics, scenography, perspective and dignity—in the Olympic Theatre at Vicenza begun by Palladio. The opera house is the culmination of this effort. In the development of the theatre, as well as of drama, the Este family of Ferrara has an honored place. The first permanent English theatre was opened in London in 1576 and called the Theatre. The Globe opened in 1599.

THENAUD, JEAN
(Late fifteenth-early sixteenth century) French writer, Franciscan monk. Traveled in Orient. Wrote an account of his travels.

THEURDANK
A poetic allegory. Inspired by the Emperor Maximilian I (1493-1519).

THEVET, ANDRÉ
Sixteenth-century French traveler. Geographer royal of France and Franciscan friar. Sailed to Brazil in 1555 with colonizing Huguenots; he wrote an account of the settlement entitled *Les Singularités de la France anarctique.* It included much geographical information and, in an English translation, it was an important work to English navigators in the last quarter of the sixteenth century.

THOMAS À KEMPIS
(c. 1379-1471). German theologian. Entered Augustinian monastery in 1407. Author of famous *De Imitatione Christi,* the greatest pious and literary monument of the *devotio moderna* of the Netherlands.

THOMAS, PETRUS
Franciscan. Logician. Author of *De Conceptu Entis,* published in Venice in 1515.

THOMESSEN, HANS
(1532-1573). Editor of collection of hymns, first Danish hymnbook, published in 1569, entitled *Den danske Salmebog.*

THORLÁKSSON, GUDBRANDUR
(1542-1627). Bishop of Iceland. He translated much of the Old Testament of the Gudbrand Bible, named for him and published in 1584; this edition was based in large part on the 1540 translation by Oddur Gottskálksson. The translation into Icelandic of 1584 is, however, "the great Reformation edition." Also author of *Vísnabók,* a collection of Icelandic poetry, published in 1612.

THORNE, ROBERT

(Died 1527). English merchant and geographical writer. Business caused him to reside in Spain; prompted by the Spanish example of overseas enterprise, he wrote an expostulation to Henry VIII and to the English ambassador to Spain proposing that England engage in the same activity. His two letters were published as *The Book of Robert Thorne*, in 1582 by Hakluyt, after circulating in manuscript for half a century.

THOU, JACQUES AUGUSTE DE

(1553-1617). French statesman, historian and bibliophile. Participated in drawing up Edict of Nantes in 1598. Author of a *Historia Sui Temporis*, 1604. His library was one of the greatest of the age, having a total of 8,000 and more books.

THYNNE, WILLIAM

(Died 1546). English scholar. He was the first editor of Chaucer; his edition was published in 1532 and dedicated to Henry VIII.

TIBALDI, PELLEGRINO

(1527-1596). Pellegrino da Bologna. Italian painter, sculptor and architect. He worked in Milan, Rome, Bologna, Ferrara and Spain, where he did a cycle of frescoes for the Escorial. Executed easel pictures, frescoes, architectural work. In the latter part of his career he was chiefly engaged in architectural work in which his use of shadowed and lit surfaces—as with his use of shade and light in his painting—suggests the Baroque style.

TICHBORNE, CHIDWICK

(c. 1558-1586). English Catholic conspirator. Executed for his part in the Babington Plot to assassinate Queen Elizabeth.

TIMONEDA, JUAN DE

(1490?-1583). Spanish dramatist, author of romances, poet, bibliophile, scholar. Author of comedies, farces. Also *Rosa de Romances*: collection of ballads: 1573. Best known work: collection of stories entitled *El Patrañuelo*: 1567: first successful Spanish imitation and adaption of Italian *novela* form.

TINCTOR, NICOLAUS

Logician. Wrote commentary on Petrus Hispanus: *Dicta Tinctoris Super Summulas Petri Hispani*: published in 1486.

TINODI, SEBESTYEN

(c. 1510-1556). Hungarian poet. He wrote a versified Hungarian chronicle of the events of 1540-57, which includes his own compositions, many of which came to be regarded as Hungarian folk melodies. He was himself a gifted musician, a wandering singer and flute player.

TINTORETTO, JACOPO ROBUSTI, IL

(1512-1594). Italian painter of Venetian school. He sought to combine the design of Michelangelo with the color of Titian, and succeeded to a remarkable degree. Works include *The Last Judgment, Crucifixion, Marriage of St. Catharine, Abraham's Sacrifice, The Miracle of St. Mark;* also portraits. Called the Thunderbolt of Painting.

TIPTOFT, JOHN, EARL OF WORCESTER

(c. 1427-1470). English humanist enthusiast and statesman, one of the first Englishmen to be acquainted with Italian learning. Called the Butcher of England for his cruelty in disposing of Lancastrian antagonists during the ascendancy of his own party, Edward IV and the Yorkists. Held high political office: Treasurer of the Exchequer, ambassador to Mantua, Lord High Constable. On pilgrimage to Jerusalem and traveled and studied in Italy from 1458 to 1461. He was the translator of Buonaccorso's *Declaration of Nobleness,* printed by Caxton in 1460. Also translated Cicero's *De Amicitia.* He was a customer of the Florentine bookseller, Vespasiano, who wrote a sketch of him in his *Memoirs;* there he says that the Earl had studied Latin at Padua and Greek at Florence. He reports how he was captured and beheaded by the Lancastrians in 1470 when Edward IV was temporarily driven from England; the pious Vespasiano said he made a good end, requesting the executioner to decapitate him with three strokes in honor of the Holy Trinity.

TIRANT LO BLANCH

One of best known Spanish romances of chivalry. First three parts written by Johanot Martorell. Fourth part by Martí Johán de Galla. Begun c. 1460. First appeared in 1490. Influenced by English romance *Guy of Warwick:* also by Dante, Petrarch, Boccaccio. Theme: exploits of Admiral Roger de Flor. Contains realistic, obscene, burlesque elements.

TIRSO DE MOLINA
The pseudonym for the Spanish dramatist, Gabriel Téllez.

TISSARD, FRANÇOIS
Early sixteenth century. French scholar. Traveled in Italy. Author of Hebrew and Greek grammar: published in Paris in 1508. He was an important pioneer of Greek studies in France.

TISSERAND, JEAN
(died 1494). French Franciscan friar. Died in Paris. Putative author of popular Easter hymn: *O filii et filiae.*   ..

TITIAN or TIZIANO VECELLIO
(c. 1477-1576). Italian painter. The greatest figure of the Venetian school and one of the great masters of all time. His most brilliant achievement was as a colorist. His long and prolific life may be divided into three phases, viz.: the first when he was more strictly within the colorist tradition of the Venetian school and chiefly influenced by Georgione and Giovanni Bellini; the second when his work became more notable than before for the sense of design and for its domestic and monumental qualities and when Michelangelo was his inspiration; and the third phase—the last quarter-century of his life—when his technical mastery and luminous coloring were brought to new heights and joined to an intense personal spirit and mystical emotion. State painter in Venice. Sponsored by Alfonso d'Este, Duke of Ferrara. Court painter to Charles V and then to his son Philip II. Executed frescoes, portraits, paintings with religious motifs, mythological episodes. His works include: *Assumption of the Virgin, Rape of Europa, Bacchus and Ariadne, Ecce Homo, Holy Family.*

J. A. Symonds' testimony is that "In his masterpieces thought, color and sentiment, and composition—the spiritual and technical elements of art—exist in perfect balance."

Again: "Titian gave to color in landscape and the human form a sublime yet sensuous poetry no other painter in the world has reached."

He adds: "Titian, the Sophocles of painting, has infused into his pictures the spirit of music, the Dorian mood of flutes and soft recorders, making power incarnate in a form of grace."

Among other notable works of Titian are: *Portrait of a Lady, Portrait of Pietro Bembo, Portrait of Aretino, Venus Anadyomene, Diana and Actaeon.*

TOLLAT VON WOCHENBERG, JOHANN

(c. 1450). Physician. Under the pseudonym of The Mystic he wrote a book entitled *The Triumphal Chariot of Antimony:* recommended use of this emetic compound in treating fevers.

TOMÁS DE VILLANUEVA, SAINT

(1488-1555). Spanish Augustinian monk, preacher at the court of Charles V, archbishop of Valencia. His sermons meet the Renaissance canons of style and eloquence; many of them were published in collections, e.g. *Sermón de amor de Canciones Sagradas;* other works of religious edification include *Opúsculos* and *Soliloquio*—all in Spanish.

TOMÉ DE JESÚS

(1529-1582). One of the great Portuguese mystics. Augustinian monk. Author of *Works of Jesus,* appeared in 1602, which he wrote in prison having been captured in Africa at the Battle of Alcázarquivir; he had accompanied King Sebastian on the expedition. He wrote many more works of mystical experience and pious edification.

TOMITANO, BERNARDINO

(1506-1576). Italian scholar, philologist and physician. Wrote on Tuscan language, use of vernacular in poetry, prosody, with references to Dante, Petrarch, Boccaccio, Michelangelo, entitled *Della lingua toscana.* He also wrote *Contraditionum solutiones in Aristotles et Averrois dicta,* and medical treatises on the plague, syphilis, etc.

TONBRIDGE SCHOOL

English public school. Founded by Sir Andrew Judd in 1553. Chartered by King Edward VI in 1553.

TONNAGE AND POUNDAGE

The grant of custom duties assigned to kings of England since the time of Edward III.

TORO, BATTLE OF

This battle, fought in 1476, made Ferdinand and Isabella of Spain victors over the Portuguese. The issue was the challenge to Isabella as Queen of Castile.

TORQUEMADA, TOMÁS DE

(c. 1420-1498). Dominican monk. First Inquisitor General for

Spain. Later, Grand Inquisitor: 1487. Reorganized Inquisition in Spain as an instrument of the Crown. Gained notoriety for ruthless punishment of those convicted by Inquisition. He was the chief figure in the expulsion of the Jews which began in 1492.

TORRE, MARCANTONIO DELLA
(c. 1483-1512). Italian physician. Professor of anatomy at Pavia.

TORRES NAHARRO, BARTOLOMÉ DE
(died post 1530). Spanish dramatist, poet. Life obscure. Priest. Fluent in Latin, French, Italian, Portuguese. In youth, as soldier, captured by pirates: sold into slavery in Algiers. Ransomed, went to Rome. Sponsored by Pope Leo X. First play: *Comedia Trofea*. Also dramatic satire: *Comedia Tinelaria*: attacked corruption of Roman society. Best play: *Comedia Himenea*: first 'cape and sword' play in Spanish literature. He expounded his dramatic principles, contributed to development of secular drama in an influential treatise, *Propalladia*.

TORRICELLI, EVANGELISTA
(1608-1647). Italian physicist and mathematician. Assistant to Galileo for a few months before the latter's death, Torricelli succeeded him as professor at the Florentine Academy. His major contribution to hydromechanics was the invention, in 1643, of the barometer from an inverted column of mercury. He also discovered that water will not rise above thirty-three feet in a suction pump. He made improvements on the telescope, constructed a primitive microscope, and worked on the cycloid.

TORRIGIANO, PIETRO
(1470-1528?). Florentine sculptor. Migrated to England, where he did a famous bust of King Henry VII in terra cotta and the tomb of Henry in Westminster Abbey. In England he was known as Peter Torrysorry. He spent the last decade of his life in Spain. Executed figurines in bronze for Florentine citizens. Like his fellow Florentine Cellini, he had a violent temper. Cellini did not accompany him to England because he broke the nose of Michelangelo, whom Cellini idolized, in a squabble. He was sentenced to death for blasphemy when he smashed a *Madonna and Child* which he had done for a Spanish duke; the duke did not pay what the artist thought he should.

TORY, GEOFFREY
(c. 1480-1533). French calligrapher, type-designer, book-binder, printer royal to Francis I. Influential in establishing Roman type in place of the Gothic. Executed *Book of Hours* in 1506. He traveled in Italy and became an admirer of Italian art and learning. His humanist sympathies led him to publish several Italian works, most notably Alberti's, and several classical authors. He is considered to have been an early important link between Italy and Renaissance France.

TOSCANELLI, PAOLO DEL POZZO
(1397-1482). Florentine scientist, friend of Brunelleschi, Alberti, Nicholas of Cusa, and Regiomontanus. He wrote treatises on perspective and meteorology, but was better known as an astronomer and geographer. He founded a school of geographers; some of its maps—those of Francesco Berlinghieri—were the first to be printed. The tradition that Toscanelli played a decisive role in helping Columbus is now regarded as apocryphal.

TOTTEL, RICHARD
(died 1594). English publisher. Compiled first English poetic anthology: *Tottel's Miscellany*: published in 1557. Contributors included Wyatt, Surrey, Heywood, Tourneur, Rochford, Bryan.

TOUCHET, MARIE
(1549-1638). Born in Orléans. Mistress of King Charles IX of France and said to have been a beauty of keen intelligence.

TOULOUZE, MICHEL
Author of first printed book on dancing: *L'Art et Instruction de bien Danser*. Published in Paris in 1490.

TOURNEUR, CYRIL
(c. 1575-1626). English playwright and poet. His dramas include *The Atheist's Tragedy*, *The Revenger's Tragedy*. Also the *Transformed Metamorphosis*. His works are prevailingly gloomy and violent.

TOURNIQUET
Invented by German surgeon Fabriz von Hilden (1560-1634), who was one of the earliest physicians to deny the virtue of precious stones in stopping the flow of blood and in healing fractured bones.

585

TRAPEZUNTIUS, GEORGIUS or GEORGE OF TREBIZOND

(1395-1484). Byzantine classical scholar, a native of Crete, came to Venice c. 1430 and taught Greek there, then at Florence and finally and chiefly at Rome. His harsh words on Plato led him into controversy with Plethon and Bessarion; he made numerous translations, e.g., the *Rhetoric* and *Problems* of Aristotle, whose side he espoused in the controversy referred to above.

TRAVERSARI, AMBROGIO

(died 1438). General of the Carmelite Order; one of the relatively few Italian scholars concerned to repossess the Christian classics and to translate the Greek ones into Latin. He was to the Christian Renaissance what Petrarch was to the classical revival. His outlook is suggested by his reluctance in agreeing to translate Diogenes Laertes for Cosimo de' Medici: he did not want to be distracted from the work of restoring the pure texts of the great Christian writers and was afraid to corrupt himself in such a task as translating a pagan author. In his desire to make Greek theology again available to the Latin world, he translated works of Saint John Chrysostom, Dionysius the Pseudo-Areopagite, Aeneas of Gaza, and many more.

TREMELLIUS, EMANUELE or TREMELLIO

(1510-1580). Italian Hebraist and Reformer. Born at Ferrara. Converted to Catholicism under the influence of Cardinal Pole who brought him to England during Mary's reign. Regius Professor of Hebrew at Cambridge. Traveled in Europe. Taught at Heidelberg. Translated the Bible in collaboration with F. Du Ion (or Junius), his French son-in-law, from Hebrew and Syriac into Latin: 1579.

TRENT, COUNCIL OF

(1545-1563). Council of Roman Catholic Church that defined its position against the Protestants. First session was held in 1545 at Trent: lasted two years; then moved to Bologna. Second session was held in 1551: lasted two years. Among Catholic doctrines and traditions reaffirmed were: papal sovereignty over the Church, original sin, justification by good works, transubstantiation and the seven sacraments, historic tradition, and the pre-Reformation interpretation of Scripture.

However, the Council was not held until a quarter-century had passed from the time when its necessity had first appeared; the heated dissension and rancor of the intervening period made the original purpose — smoothing out the difficulties with the Lutherans — difficult or impossible to achieve. The Council was never free of the fierce rivalry of France — opposed to the Council — and Spain — strongly favorable to it. The Emperor Charles V was the chief protagonist of reconciliation with the Lutherans, but by the late date of 1545 compromise could command little backing among churchmen or anyone else with the exception of a few humanists. Additional difficulties stemmed from disagreement over the nature of a council and papal fears of a revival of the conciliar movement.

Once in session—it was twice interrupted for four and ten years respectively—the Council considered its purpose to be an uncompromising affirmation of Christian dogma and the reform of abuses in the Church. This purpose it did achieve. Several of the Council's actions had profound effects upon European culture. It considered and then left to papal discretion the translation of a new Latin Bible, a revision of the Breviary and Missal, the writing of a catechism and the Index of prohibited books. It took steps to insure the careful education at seminaries of candidates for the priesthood, formal provision for which had never been made.

The Council's concern with church music marked the beginnings of a reaction in Europe against excessively elaborate polyphony, for it insisted that the music be subordinate to the words, that music was not an end in itself but an aid to concentration and devotion. A proposal to expel polyphony from the Church was defeated, largely, it is said, because the Emperor Ferdinand I protested that much polyphonic music was of a deeply religious nature. As it was, the Council did initiate a trend toward greater simplicity and religiosity in church music. It also issued a decree abolishing profane music in church services: "All music in which anything lascivious or impure is mixed, whether for the organ or for the voices, is to be kept out of the churches. Likewise all profane actions, worldly conversations, walking about, noise or shouting, in order that the house of God may be truly a house of prayer." Such requirements were eminently suitable to the genius of Palestrina.

The opening sessions of the Council were dominated by Cardinal Reginald Pole, the later ones by Cardinal Charles Borromeo.

TRIBOLO, NICCOLO PERICOLI
(1485-1550). Florentine sculptor who worked in his native city, Bologna, and Rome. Executed superb fountains, most notably the exquisite and graceful Fontana della Villa della Petraia at Florence. *Young Satyr* attributed to him. The monument to Pope Adrian VI at Rome was his work.

TRICASSO DA CERASARI, PATRICIO
(1491-1550). Italian chiromancer of Mantua. Author of works on chiromancy that were placed on the Index.

TRINCAVELLI, VETTORE or TRINCAVELI
(1496-1548). Italian classical scholar, publisher and philosopher at Venice. Physician. Aristotelian. Taught at Padua. He printed Arrian, 1535, and several Greek medical works, and edited Aristotle's *Poetics*, the famous Greek text of 1536; it is with this edition that the enormous influence of the *Poetics* over the next three or four centuries begins—the same year saw the publication of an improved Latin translation by Alessandro de' Pazzi. Thus while Aristotle was losing ground in philosophy he was gaining it in literature.

TRINITY COLLEGE
Cambridge University. Founded by Henry VIII in 1546.

TRINITY COLLEGE, OXFORD
Founded in 1555 by Sir Thomas Pope (died 1559).

TRINITY SCHOOL OF JOHN WHITGIFT
English public school. Founded by Archbishop of Canterbury, John Whitgift (1530-1604).

TRISMOSIN, SOLOMON
Author of alchemical work entitled *Splendor Solis*: published in 1582.

TRISSINO, GIOVANNI GIORGIO
(1478-1550). Italian scholar, poet, imitator of the Pindaric ode. Sponsored by Popes Leo X and Clement VII. Aristotelian. Proposed reform of Italian language, orthography, grammar, etc., and was a proponent of a national Italian tongue. He translated Dante's *De vulgas apostrophe*. Author of the epic historical poem *L'Italia Liberata dai Goti*, 1547-1548, based upon Procopius' account of the Byzantine reconquest of Italy under Justinian and following Aristotle's canons for writing epics.

TRITHEMIUS, JOHANNES

(1462-1516). German humanist, historian, member of the Rhenish Sodality of Literature. He did much to establish the vogue of humanism in Germany. He edited and compiled many historical works, although they are not particularly notable for following rigorously the humanist canons of textual analysis and historical study; among his works on history are *Catalogus scriptorum ecclesiasticorum, De viris illustribus Germaniae, Chronicon ducum Bovariae*, etc. Like so many of his contemporary German humanists, he was an ardent patriot; as such he was particularly attracted to Tacitus. It is in fact with Trithemius that Tacitus' *Germania* took its place as the single most important classical work in German classical studies and historiography, a place which it retained until the twentieth century.

TRITONIUS, PETRUS or PETER TREIBENREIF

(Late fifteenth to early sixteenth century). German composer and humanist. He was a student of Konrad Celtes at Ingolstadt but had also studied in Italy at the University of Padua before he settled at Vienna as a teacher of voice and instrumental music. He set Horace's *Odes* and other Latin poems to music, the best-known collection being the *Harmoniae Petri Tritonii super odis Horatii Flacci*, 1507; their publication was a milestone in music printing.

TROMBONCINO, BARTOLOMEO

(Died post 1535). Italian musician of Verona, composer of polyphonic music. Attached to the court of Mantua and then that of Ferrara. He composed some church music but is remembered for his *frottole* or popular songs, many of which were published by Petrucci, 1504-8. He is said to have murdered his wife and her lover, with what punishment, if any, is unknown.

TROMPETA, ANTONIUS ANDREAS

(Died 1518). Italian logician in the tradition of the Scotists. Wrote *Quaestiones Quodlibetales*, published in Venice in 1493.

TROTZENDORF, VALENTIN

(1490-1556). German scholar and educator. His career parallels that of Johannes Sturm at Strassburg. He became a Protestant and head of the Goldberg School in Silesia. He was an exponent of the humanist-inspired classical curriculum as the best means to nurture good citizens and pious men. He wrote several works setting forth the methods and organization of the school. The *Leges scholae Goldbergensis*, promulgated by Duke Henry VI of Silesia in 1563, were based largely on Trotzendorf's *Schulordnung* and followed by several other schools.

TRUBER, PRIMUS or PRIMOZ TRUBAR
(Died 1586). Carinthian who promoted Protestantism in the southern domain of the Hapsburgs and had to flee to Germany; there worked on his translation of part of the New Testament and sought to promote Protestantism in his homeland by publishing tracts and pamphlets at the printing press at Urach (near Tübingen). A complete Slovene Bible, based on Luther's German edition, was published, 1584, by his colleague, Jurij Dalmatin.

TRUTVETTER, JODOC
(Died 1519). German theologian, man of letters and logician. Taught Luther. Author of *Summulae Totius Logicae,* published in Erfurt in 1501. Also *Epitome Seu Breviarium,* published at Erfurt in 1512.

TSAR
The title of the ruler of Russia. It was first assumed officially by Ivan IV in 1547.

TSCHUDI, AEGIDIUS
(1505-1572). Swiss historian, member of a family prominent in Swiss history since the sixteenth century, antagonist of the Reformation. Considered Father of Swiss History. Author of *Chronicon Helveticum,* from year 1000 to 1470, which is rich in documents and inscriptions, ardently patriotic, and the chief source of materials for the William Tell legend.

TUCHER, HANS
(Fifteenth century). German traveler, brewer of Nuremberg, friend of Albrecht Dürer. Made a pilgrimage to the Holy Land in 1479, of which he wrote an account.

TUKE, SIR BRIAN
(Died 1545). English official. Magister Nuntiorum—Master of the Posts, 1533, and secretary to Henry VIII. He was a patron of learning, the friend of Leland who sings his praises; Holbein painted several portraits of him.

TUNSTALL, CUTHBERT

(1474-1559). English prelate, statesman, scholar, learned in Latin, Greek and Hebrew. Master of the Rolls. Bishop of Durham. Friend of Sir Thomas More, Erasmus. Sent on diplomatic missions by Henry VIII. Roman Catholic adherent, but supported royal supremacy over Church. Opposed to Tyndale, whom he prohibited from publishing translation of the New Testament. Tunstall himself played a part in the publication of the Great Bible of 1539. Deprived of office under Edward VI, restored by Mary. Deprived again by Queen Elizabeth I.

TURA, COSIMO

(c. 1430-1495). Italian religious painter, muralist. He was a leading figure of the Ferrarese school and was patronized by Borso and Ercole d'Este. Executed a *Pietà, Christ Crucified, Madonna with Child;* he also did mythological works and portraits, e.g., his *Primavera, Portrait of a Man* and (probably) the portrait of Duke Borso.

TURBERVILLE, GEORGE

(c. 1540-c. 1610). English poet, secretary to Thomas Randolph, the ambassador to Russia. Translated prose and verse from classics, e.g., Ovid. Author of a collection of poetry called *Epitaphs, Epigrams, Songs, and Sonnets,* in which he followed Italian models and verse forms. His *The Booke of Faulconrie* was published in 1575; he also published *Poems Describing Russia,* 1568.

TURKISH RULERS

Mohammed II: 1451-1481; Bayazid II: 1481-1512; Selim I: 1512-1520; Suleiman I: 1520-1566; Selim II: 1566-1574; Murad III: 1574-1595; Mohammed III: 1595-1603; Ahmed I: 1603-1617; Osman II: 1618-1622; Mustapha I: 1622-1623; Murad IV: 1623-1640; Ibrahim I: 1640-1649.

Dates refer to duration of rule.

TURNEBUS, ADRIANUS

(1512-1565). French humanist, Greek scholar, royal reader in Greek at Paris, and director of the Royal Press. Edited and translated Greek texts, including Aeschylus, Sophocles, Cicero, Philo and Appian, commentaries on Varro and Pliny the Elder. One of the most prominent personalities in the French Renaissance. He was a master of textual criticism, especially of the Greek writers; in his *Adversaria* he proposed many interpretations and emendations that came to be accepted in many instances. Montaigne admired him greatly.

TURNER, WILLIAM
(1510-1568). English cleric. Botanist, physician. Author of *Libellus de Re Herbaria Novus*: published in 1538. His *Herbal* was the first scientific botanical study in English: published in 1551. For all his common sense and scientific spirit, there is much in his work that is sheer fantasy, nonsense, and superstition.

TURQUET DE MAYERNE, THEODORE
(1573-1655). Swiss physician. Exponent of bedside study of disease. He was placed under a ban by the Faculty of the University of Paris for using antimony. He wrote several works on pathology, a treatise contra-Hippocrates and Galen, and a *Description* of France, Spain, Italy, Germany.

TUSSER, THOMAS
(c. 1524-c. 1580). English musician, poet, farmer. Author of *Five Hundred Points of Good Husbandry*, 1573, an expansion of the *One Hundred* of the edition of 1557. Many English proverbs derive from this work, written in popular verse. He was educated at Eton and Cambridge and was musician to William Paget, one of Queen Mary's best councillors.

TWYNE, JOHN
(c. 1501-1581). English schoolmaster and writer. Headmaster of Canterbury Grammar School. Member of Parliament. Noted antiquary. Author of *De Rebus Albionicis, Britannicis atque Anglicis Commentariorium Libri Duo*: published in 1590. An examination of British history, with archaeological and linguistic arguments confirming his views.

TYARD, PONTUS DE or THIARD or THYARD, SEIGNEUR DE BISSY
(c. 1521-1605). French poet and scholar. Bishop. One of the leaders of poetic Renaissance in France. Member of La *Pléiade*. Wrote on philosophy, theology. Author of *Livres des Vers Lyriques*, published in 1555; also *Oeuvres Poétiques*, published in 1573. He was competent in Oriental languages, which he would seem to have used to satisfy his curiosity about alchemy, astrology, etc. His *Mantice* is a discourse on the "truth" of astrology.

TYE, CHRISTOPHER

(c. 1497-1572). English musician. Composer. Translated part of the Acts of the Apostles into English verse. Organist at Chapel Royal. Composed Anglican church services, anthems, which were an important influence on the later Elizabethan composers.

TYNDALE, WILLIAM

(c. 1494-1536). English translator of New Testament, Pentateuch. Translated New Testament from Greek into vernacular. Met many frustrations, refusals of aid, difficulties in publication. Translation published at Worms: smuggled into England. He antagonized everyone: Henry VIII because he opposed the divorce, Sir Thomas More because he defended the English Reformation, etc. Betrayed while in Flanders: imprisoned, strangled and burned at stake as a heretic.

U

UBALDINI, PETRUCCIO

(c. 1524-c. 1600). Italian writer, illuminator, of Florence. Went to England: participated in Scottish Wars. Author of *Vita di Carlo Magno Imperatore,* the first Italian book printed in England, in 1581. Also author of a description of England, an account of the Spanish Armada, biographies of English and Scottish women, poetic pieces, etc.

UBERTINI, FRANCESCO called BACHIACCA

(c. 1494-1557). Florentine painter. Noted for his historical, mythological and religious themes. Patronized by the Medici.

UCCELLO, PAOLO or PAOLO DI DONO

(c. 1396-1475). Italian artist of Florence. Experimented in perspective. Executed stained-glass windows, mosaics. Portraits of contemporaries, artists, the condottiere John Hawkwood, and the series of battle scenes for which he was best known in his day and which were studied by artists for their mastery of lineal perspective, the *Battle of San Romano.*

UDALL, NICHOLAS

(c. 1505-1556). English schoolmaster, translator, playwright. Translated *Apothegms* of Erasmus. Wrote *Ralph Roister Doister,* earliest known English comedy, based on Plautus. Also Latin plays on religious subjects. He collaborated with Leland in making translations from Terence. He was headmaster of Eton and then Westminster School.

UGOLETO, TADDEO

Italian humanist. Royal Librarian at the court of King Matthias Corvinus of Hungary (1458-1490). His brother ANGELO was a printer at Parma, active 1482-1500, of classical works.

UGONI, GIOVANNI ANDREA

Sixteenth century. Brescian courtier, scholar. Wrote dialogue on nature of man, mortality, ethics, Platonism: published in 1562. Also treatise on philosophy of names: discusses classical, oriental name origins and derivations. Published in 1562.

ULLOA, ALFONSO

(Died 1570). Spanish writer, scholar, who settled in Venice early in life. Author of a history of Ferdinand I, a life of the Emperor Charles V, of Francesco Gonzaga of Mantua, a history of Europe 1564 to 1566, and an account of the Dutch Revolt. Translated Alonso de Fuentes' dialogue on physics into Italian and a great many more Spanish and Portuguese works into Italian.

ULMER, JOHANN KONRAD

(1519-1600). German theologian and devotional poet. Author of lyrics of early Lutheran hymnal, *Kirchengesang*, 1569, 1599.

UNGNAD, JOHN, COUNT

(Sixteenth century). Southern Slav who fled his Hapsburg homeland for Germany. Lutheran. Set up printing press at Urach, Württemberg, where parts of the Bible and religious tracts and pamphlets in Slavonic were published.

UNIVERSITY PRINTING

University presses grew out of the medieval *stationarii*, who were licensed, as early as 1276 at Cambridge University, to "publicly avouch the sale of staple-books." Many of these establishments were also copyists and binders, and it was thus an easy transition for them to the University Press in the age of printing. One of these *stationarii* was a Garrett Godfrey, early in the sixteenth century; he was the friend of Erasmus with whose blessing printing began at Cambridge, c. 1520, under the imprint of John Siberch. The first printing press was set up at Oxford as much as half a century before John Siberch became the first Cambridge printer, but it was not until the close of the sixteenth century that printing was permanently established at the two Universities. Later both Presses were granted monopolies by royal charter on certain works, e.g., the Bible and the *Book of Common Prayer.*

URBAN VII
(1521-1590). Pope. On second day after election as Pope, he fell ill and died after a few days.

URBAN VIII
(1568-1644). Pope 1623-1644. Literary connoisseur. Pontificate marked by extensive nepotism. Throughout his pontificate the Thirty Years' War raged, but he had little influence on its course. The rather strict guidelines he set down for determining the validity of miracles are still followed in large part. During his pontificate, trial of Galileo Galilei by Inquisition took place. Interested in music. Poet. Beautified Rome by extensive building program. His portrait was painted by Van Dyck, the statue of him that is part of his tomb was done by Bernini.

URBINO
During fifteenth and sixteenth centuries this city was a famous center of art and literature. Federigo da Montefeltro and other dukes of Urbino were patrons of the arts, architecture, learning and music, all of which was financed by the earnings of the dukes as condottieri. Federigo's famous library, assembled for him by Vespasiano, went to the Vatican Collection when the duchy was taken by the papacy; it contains some of the finest examples of the book illuminator's art. Castiglione's *Courtier* takes the Montefeltro court for its setting.

URECHE, GRIGORE
(1590-1646). Moldavian historian. He wrote a history of Moldavia, the first to be written in Rumanian; he was the first to assert the Roman origin of Moldavia and to claim Rumanian to be a Romance language.

URFÉ, HONORÉ D'
(1567-1624). French writer. Author of pastoral romance entitled *Astrée.* His work shows the influence of Ronsard, Petrarch, Sannazzaro and Tasso, whom he studied diligently; the *Astrée* contains many sentimental episodes which made it a favorite work of La Fontaine and Rousseau.

URSINUS, KASPAR VELIUS
(1493-1539). German humanist, historian. He was a fine Greek

scholar, studied and traveled for several years in Italy. Author of *De Bello Pannonico Libri X*, which has reference to the wars against the Turks fought by the Hapsburgs, his patrons. His account of the Battle of Mohács, 1526, does not survive.

URSINUS, ZACHARIAS

(1534-1583). German theologian and Reformer. One of two authors of the *Heidelberg Cathechism*, published in 1562. This epitome of the Reformed faith owes much to Ursinus, who was a member of the University of Heidelberg. The co-author was Olevianus, a popular preacher in Heidelberg.

URSULINE ORDER

Order of Nuns: Founded in 1535. Founder was St. Angela de Merici of Brescia, Italy. Purpose was to educate young women. The first female teaching order, it soon opened convents in France and Germany.

USHER, JAMES or USSHER

(1581-1656). Irish scholar, Anglican bishop in Ireland, theologian. He devised a system of dating events since the creation which he set at 4004 B.C.—a system which was long followed in the English-speaking world. He had a great reputation for erudition in his day and was a prolific writer.

USQUE, SAMUEL

(born c. 1492). Portuguese Jew. Author of *Consolation for the Tribulations of Israel*. Published in Ferrara in 1553, it holds an honored place for its style in the literature of sixteenth century Portugal.

UTENHEIM, CHRISTOPH VON

(Died 1527). German ecclesiastic, humanist enthusiast, bishop of Basel. He was a friend of Erasmus and many of the outstanding humanists of his day; initially he favored Luther and worked for the reform of the Church; but when Luther withdrew from the Church and threatened ecclesiastical unity, he turned against him.

V

VADIANUS, JOACHIM or VON WATT
(1484-1551). Swiss scholar. Friend of Zwingli. Supported Martin Luther. Before his involvement in the Reformation he had been designated poet laureate by the Emperor Maximilian I and was rector of the University of Vienna. He wrote much literary, theological and historical material, including a history of the Abbey of St. Gall.

VADISCUS
A satire against the clergy, issued in 1520 by Ulrich von Hutten.

VAET, JACOBUS
(1535-1567). Flemish musicologist and contrapuntalist. Kapellmeister to Emperor Maximilian II at Vienna. Composed over seventy motets and other church music as well as secular music.

VALCKENBORCH, LUKAS VAN
(c. 1530-1597). Dutch painter. Died in Nuremberg. He produced large-scale landscapes with many figures, mainly rustic; his work is characterized by its refinement and meticulous detail. His brother MARTIN (1535-1612) was also a painter of landscapes. Their sons were also painters.

VALDÉS, ALFONSO DE
(died 1532). Spanish humanist and satirist. Most prominent Erasmian of his time. One of the 'heterodox' figures of Spanish Renaissance. Corresponded with Erasmus and Melanchthon. Condemned clerical venality. Latin Secretary of Charles V.

Wrote anti-clerical political tract in defense of sack of Rome by Charles V: *Diálogo de Lactancio*. Also wrote satire on European politics. Imitated style of Greek satirist Lucian.

VALDÉS, JUAN DE

(died 1541). Brother of the above, Spanish humanist, literary critic, Erasmian reformer, theologian whose doctrines suggest those of the Unitarians and Socinians. Studied Latin, Greek, Hebrew. Absorbed techniques of Greek satirist Lucian. Protestant: fearing Inquisition on account of his unorthodox *Diálogo de la doctrina Christiana*, went to Italy where he formed a circle of learned and pious friends at Naples, also stayed at the Gonzaga court at Mantua. His unorthodox religious views appeared in his *Ciento y Diez Consideraciones Divinas*: 1539. Chief work: Dialogue on Spanish language and literature entitled: *Diálogo de la lengua*. He and his brother wrote a satire in the manner of Erasmus' *Familiar Colloquies*, entitled *Dialogue of Mercury and Cain*.

VALENTE, FRANCESCO DI ANTONIO DEL

Sixteenth century. Italian sculptor of Padua. Worked in bronze. Followed the tradition of Donatello, with whom he collaborated.

VALENTIN DE BOULOGNE

(1594-1632). Painter, the son of an Italian painter who had gone to the Lowlands. Died in Florence. Specialized in realistic genre pieces: soldiers, gypsies. Harsh lighting effects. He also did historical paintings.

VALENTINE, BASIL

Putative author of works on alchemy. Believed to have lived in Germany in the fifteenth century. Author of *The Triumphal Chariot of Antimony*, although the attribution is by no means certain.

VALERAND DE LA VARENNE

(fl. c. 1500). Neo-Latin poet. Author of epic on Joan of Arc: *De Gestis Joannae Virginis*.

VALERIANO, PIERO or GIOVAN PIETRO DELLA FOSSE

(1477-1560). Italian humanist, Neo-Latin poet, imitator of Horace. He was a favorite of Popes Leo X and Clement VII, who made him professor of eloquence. He wrote antiquarian works, a *Dialogo sopra le lingue volgari*, which closely follows Trissino's, and an account of the sorrows which befell the scholars of his day, where he gives a graphic picture of the horrible sack of Rome of 1527, and a compendious book of literary and artistic symbols, *Hieroglyphica*.

VALLA, GIORGIO

(c. 1430-c. 1499). Italian humanist, probably a cousin of Lorenzo. He taught rhetoric at Padua, Genoa and Venice. He translated Ptolemy, Galen, Alexander of Aphrodisias and Aristotle into Latin; his translation of Aristotle's *Poetics*, 1498, though imperfect, was the first into Latin and marked the beginning of its vast influence on European literature.

VALLA, LORENZO

(c. 1405-1457). Italian humanist scholar who proved the *Donation of Constantine* a forgery. His *The Falsely Believed and Mendacious Donation of Constantine* has reference to Alfonso the Magnanimous—to whom Valla was secretary at the time—and his attempt to acquire Naples by overthrowing the Angevin house and denying the pope's claim as feudal overlord. The Emperor Frederick II, died 1250, had suspected the *Donation* was a fabrication but had offered no proof, Nicholas of Cusa had come close to demonstrating its falsity, the English bishop Reginald Pecock had concluded it was a forgery. By the same methods and in the same iconoclastic spirit, Valla derided the apostolic authorship of the Creed and demonstrated the spuriousness of the writings attributed to Dionysius the Areopagite. He was called to Rome by Nicholas V to make translations of Homer, Thucydides, and Herodotus, of which the last was cut short by his death. He wrote two books of great importance: his *Annotationes* on the New Testament in which he applies the humanist methods of textual analysis and thus detects many errors and mistranslations from the Greek. Known only in manuscript, it was found by Erasmus and published by him in 1505. Erasmus acknowledged its fundamental influence on him. A second work also had a profound influence on Erasmus and many humanists: the *Elegantiae*, the foremost manual of Latin style and usage. A pagan spirit, Valla was bitter and hostile against the clergy and Church abuses; his *De voluptate* attacks chastity as a false ideal and the work has been called an essay in Christianized Epicureanism.

601

VALLE, PIETRO DELLA
(1586-1652). Italian traveler and explorer. Learned in Oriental languages. Author of an account of his travels in Turkey, Persia, India: in epistolary form. It is an interesting account of the ways of life and the geography of these areas, buttressed by historical knowledge which he derived from the ancient classical authors.

VALLENSIS, ROBERTUS
Sixteenth century. French scholar. Author of treatise on grammar: *De Corrupti Sermonis Emendatione Libellus:* published in 1534.

VALOIS LINE OF FRANCE
Charles VII: 1422-1461; Louis XI: 1461-1483; Charles VIII: 1483-1498; Louis XII: 1498-1515; Francis I: 1515-1547; Henry II: 1547-1558; Francis II: 1558-1560; Charles IX: 1560-1574; Henry III: 1574-1589.
Dates refer to duration of rule.

VALTELLINE PASS
Link between Austrian and Spanish possessions in the Alps. Under the Grisons League. In 1621 the pass was seized by Spain, despite resistance by Protestants; its control was one of the critical questions throughout the Thirty Years' War.

VALVERDA, JUAN
(Sixteenth century). Spanish anatomist. Wrote, in 1554, on the circulation of the blood.

VAN DE VELDE, JAN
(1568-1623). Dutch artist. Noted for his wood engravings, especially portraits. He and his brother established the family tradition as artists. Its great fame came in the time of their sons in the late seventeenth century. They include JAN II (1593-1641), painter of portraits and landscapes, and ESAIAS (died 1630), who did rather foreboding landscapes.

VANINI, GIULIO CAESARE LUCILIO
(1585-1619). Italian philosopher. Priest. Expounded mechanistic philosophy. Condemned as magician and atheist. Burned at stake.

VAN SOMER, PAUL
(1576-1621). Dutch painter of Antwerp. Specialized in portraits. Attached to court of King James I of England after 1606, where he was a great favorite.

VARCHI, BENEDETTO
(1503-1565). Florentine humanist and historian. Lectured at the
Florentine Academy. Wrote erotic treatises, a history of Florence
and a treatise on poetry. He was a republican and hence opposed
to the Medici dukedom established in Florence by Charles V in
1530; he was an adherent of the Strozzi, whom he followed into
exile to Venice. The pangs of exile are reflected in his history,
which covers the period 1527-1538, but he is fair, nevertheless, to
his political enemy, Duke Cosimo I.

VARENIUS, BERNARDUS or VAREN
(c. 1622-c. 1650). Dutch geographer with a thorough training in
mathematics, physics and the humanist disciplines. Author of a
basic *Geographia universalis,* published in 1650. It was an exceptionally good work and long remained a standard manual.

VAROLI, COSTANZO
(c. 1543-1575). Italian anatomist and surgeon. Described the
pons Varolii, nerve fibers in brain, in his chief work, *De nervis
opticis.* He taught anatomy at the Sapienza and enjoyed papal
patronage.

VAROTARI, DARIO
(1539-1596). Italian painter, sculptor, architect who worked
principally in Padua and Venice. He was of German descent, his
father having fled the religious disturbances of his native Augsburg and settled in Verona; their original name was Weyrother.
He did historical paintings for the palace of the Podestá at Padua
and executed various commissions to decorate the palaces and
lay out gardens, etc., for the Venetian families, the Mocenigi and
the Pisani; in addition, he decorated several Venetian churches.
His daughter, CHIARA (died post-1600), was a portrait painter
and poetess; she wrote *An Apology for the Female Sex.* Her
brother, ALESSANDRO, called IL PADOVANINO (1590-1650),
was the greatest artist of the family. He was notable for his female
figures—historical, mythological, hagiological—which show the
influence of Titian. His work shows the characteristics of the
Venetian school to which he belonged, viz., rich coloring, an atmosphere of splendor and affluence, and superb draftsmanship.

VARTHEMA, LODOVICO DE
(c. 1475-1517). Italian traveler, "a gentleman of Bologna." His
Itineraro, 1510, was one of the most popular travelogues of the

sixteenth century and he himself enjoyed the fame of a Marco Polo or Columbus. He masqueraded as a Moslem and so made his way to Mecca, from there he went overland to Persia, India, Ceylon, Siam and the Malay Peninsula and East Indies, and returned by sea, around Africa, to Lisbon in 1508.

VASARI, GEORGIO

(1511-1574). Born in Arezzo but reared and educated at Florence; humanist, architect, painter, and art critic, called "the father of art criticism"; he was well fitted by his temperament, travels, and humanist education—and also lived at the opportune time—to write his *Lives of the Great Painters, Sculptors, and Architects,* 1550, the work that remains the starting point for all histories of Renaissance art and which embodies a full conception of the age from Cimabue to Michelangelo (Vasari's life-long friend) as the rebirth, *"rinascita"* of the fine arts. He was the architect of the Uffizi Palace which now houses the National Library and the celebrated Uffizi Gallery.

VATICAN LIBRARY

The Vatican Library dates unofficially from the period of the restoration of the papacy to Rome by the Council of Constance; officially founded by Nicholas V at the mid-fifteenth century as part of his conscious policy to bring the Renaissance to Rome. Many popes contributed to the library, none more than Sixtus IV, who made it a public collection and appointed its first director, Platina, who did much to catalogue its holdings and make them available. In the sixteenth century the famous collection of Duke Federigo da Montefeltro of Urbino was added—the spoils of war; Leo X and Clement VII greatly added to it. From its beginning it has been essentially a manuscript collection; the Vatican Archives constitute a separate collection. In establishing the Vatican Library the papacy was following a lead given long before by the princely houses, who had great collections that were frequently open to scholars, e.g., that of the Gonzaga of Mantua, the Visconti of Milan, the Este of Ferrara and the Medici of Florence.

VAUGELAS, CLAUDE FAVRE DE

(1595-1650). French grammarian. He composed a treatise directed toward a common standard of French with regard to pronunciation and vocabulary, entitled *Remarques sur la langue française.* He was a proponent and then a member of the French Academy.

VAUQUELIN DA LA FRESNAYE, JEAN, SIEUR DES YVETEAUX

(1536-c. 1608). French poet. Imitator of Horace, disciple of Ronsard and *La Pléiade* group. Author of satires, epistles, idylls. His treatise on *Art poétique français* is the most important work of literary criticism between that of Du Bellay and Boileau.

VAUX, THOMAS, BARON OF HARROWDEN

(1510-1556). English poet. Author of religious and chivalric pieces. Contributed to Tottel's *Miscellany.*

VECCHI, ORAZIO

(c. 1550-1605). Italian musician, composer, at the ducal court of Modena and chapelmaster at the cathedral. Noted for *L'Amfiparnasso*, 1594, a prototype of the opera. He was a composer of madrigals and many aspects of *L'Amfiparnasso* recall the madrigal form. He called his piece, performed at Modena in 1594, a *"commedia harmonica"* and it does suggest the *commedia dell' arte*, which he, as it were, set to music.

VEDEL, ANDERS SORENSEN

(1542-1616). Danish preacher, poet, historian, archaeologist. Wrote extensively in all these fields. Collected old Nordic folk songs. Translated Saxo Grammaticus' *Gesta Danorum* into Danish and accumulated many documents and materials for a continuation of the chronicle, but never completed his task. He was the teacher of Tycho Brahe and did much to reanimate the humanist movement in Denmark after the travail of the Reformation. In 1591 he published the earliest collection of popular Danish songs.

VEEN, OTTO VAN

(1556-c.1629). Dutch painter. Teacher of Rubens. His subjects were Biblical and historical. Worked in Antwerp. He had spent five years studying and working in Rome, during which he worked out his own mannerist style.

VELÁZQUEZ, DIEGO DE

(c. 1465-c. 1522). Spanish conquistador. Accompanied Columbus to New World. Founded Santiago, Havana, governor of Cuba, antagonist of Cortés during the latter's expedition to Mexico.

VELÁZQUEZ, DIEGO RODRÍGUEZ DE SILVAY

(1599-1660). Spanish painter. Chief painter of Spanish school. Studied in Italy. Court painter to Philip IV who had a high regard all his life for Velázquez and was the subject of many of his portraits. Exercised greatest influence on European painting until late nineteenth century. Among his works are portraits, historical scenes, genre pieces, mythological and religious themes: *Surrender of Breda, Adoration of the Magi, Crucifixion, Mars, Venus and Cupid*, Philip IV, Cardinal Borgia, Pope Innocent X, *The Drinker, The Carpet Embroideress*, Count Olivares who was his first patron and had introduced him to the royal court. His palette was a "cool" one, balancing his brilliant coloring with much grey.

VÉLEZ DE GUEVARA, LUIS

(1579-1644). Spanish dramatist and picaresque novelist. In military service in Italy. Had distinguished patrons at the royal court, but existence was impecunious. He was a disciple of Lope de Vega. Specialized in sensational *teatro de ruido*. Reputedly wrote some 400 plays. Known for his picaresque novel *El Diablo Cojuelo*: social satire. Among his plays, by turns bitter and humorous, including religious and historical plays, are *Santa Susana, Reinar después de morir, La luna de la sierra*.

VELHO, ÁLVARO

Sixteenth century. Putatively, the Portuguese author of the day-to-day narrative of Vasco da Gama's first voyage: appeared in 1497-1499. Entitled *Roteiro*, it is an indispensable source for the historian of European expansion.

VELUANUS, ANASTASIUS

Reformer. Author of *The Laymen's Guide:* published in 1554. It attacked the Catholic Church.

VENICE

Venice was the great commercial cosmopolitan emporium of the Italian Renaissance. The wealth of the city was conditioned by her ships, by the cargoes they imported and by their exports: from Alexandria to Crete and Constantinople, from the Adriatic to the Black Sea, from the Mediterranean littoral to the Orient.

As a cultural and mercantile centre, it brought together East and West, Moslems and Jews, mariners and poets, merchants and wandering scholars. The Venetian government, wealthy citizens, and ecclesiastic patrons, promoted music and painting, statuary and bronzes, pageants and bookbinding. It was a city of banquets and parades, and its argosies brought endless wealth to its citizens. Bellini, Giorgione and Carpaccio, Titian and Veronese stand out as the great Venetian masters. The Venetian school of painting—characterized by its rich coloring, a luxurious sense of opulence, and a gay acceptance of the sensuous world—would seem to be the perfect expression of the life of the city. Intellectually, it boasted the greatest university of the Renaissance, Padua, which enjoyed great freedom of inquiry in a society where anticlericalism and resistance to ecclesiastical pretension were age-old traditions.

There never arose the despotic dynasty in Venice that was so typical of the constitutional evolution of other Italian states. The merchant oligarchy ruled supreme; the communal institutions of Venice sufficed. Emphasis has always been placed upon the ruthlessness with which the oligarchy suppressed independence or opposition; yet without the loyalty and public-spiritedness which inspired her citizens, suppression, no matter how ruthless, would not have sufficed. Her insular position, similar in many respects to that of England at a later date, helps to explain her relative immunity to despotism and political broils, as it does also her safety in the face of military attack and her acquisition of a far-flung maritime empire. In the late fourteenth century Venice sought to expand on the mainland in order to meet the threat of Milanese expansion and to compensate for losses sustained in the eastern Mediterranean in wars against the Turks. The conquest of *terra firma* entailed a constitutional struggle, in the course of which the doge's power was greatly reduced and the Council of Ten became the dominant institution of government. By 1450 the Venetian constitution was fixed; it lasted until the Napoleonic conquest and was the most stable in Europe.

VENIER FAMILY, THE

Eminent in the political history and cultural life of Venice from the twelfth through the sixteenth century, ANTONIO (died 1400), FRANCESCO (1490-1556) and SEBASTIANO (1496-1578) were doges. The last was important as the organizer of the Venetian fleet that participated in the Battle of Lepanto, 1571; his portrait was painted by Tintoretto. DOMENICO (1517-1582) was a versifier of Petrarchan and Bembist poetry, but was more important for his house, which he made the home of a

Venetian literary coterie. LORENZO (1510-1556), brother of Domenico, was a man of letters, author of scurrilous prose and poetry that could be confused with the barbs unleashed by Pietro Aretino; and MAFFEO (1550-1586), son of Lorenzo and archbishop of Corfu was also a facile versifier, but an anti-Petrarchan and also a dramatist.

VENUSTI, MARCELLO

(c. 1515-c. 1584). Italian painter. Worked chiefly in Rome. Executed *Holy Family, Annunciation* and *Pietà*. Influenced by Michelangelo, who was a close friend and for whom he named his son Michelangelo (c. 1560-1642). The son gave up painting for military architecture.

VERA, JUAN ANTONIO DE

(1588-post 1620). Spanish diplomat, classical scholar, soldier, courtier, and lesser poet. He is remembered chiefly for his two-volume *El Embajador*, 1620, the most influential treatise of the age on diplomacy and the perfect ambassador. It was quickly translated into French and Italian, and went through many editions. In the sixteenth and early seventeenth centuries, the Spanish was the most fully developed and efficient diplomatic service in Europe.

VERE, SIR FRANCIS

(c. 1560-1609): English soldier. In command of forces in the Netherlands. Participated in Battle of Breda. In Cadiz expedition of 1596. His *Commentaries* is an autobiographical record of his adventurous career; he was a benefactor of the Bodleian Library, now at Oxford.

VERGERIO, PIER PAOLO

(1370-1444). Italian humanist and education theorist. His pedagogical treatise *De ingenuis moribus et liberalibus studiis* urged that pride of place be given in the curriculum to the Latin classics and in a way that recalls Petrarch, placed primary emphasis on "style" and "eloquence"; in keeping with this ideal of education he wrote the first introduction to the study of Quintilian. He extolled Cicero and the Latin Father of the Church in whom later humanists frequently found a mirror of themselves, St. Jerome. He went to Florence to learn Greek under Chrysoloras, attended the Council of Constance as a papal secretary and left

608

in the train of the Emperor Sigismund for Hungary where he remained until his death. He also wrote a work on prosody.

VERGIL, POLYDORE, OF URBINO
(c. 1470-c. 1555). Humanist, historian, priest; he studied at Bologna and Padua, entered the service of the duke of Urbino and then of Pope Alexander VI who sent him as a collector of Peter's pence to England, where he gained the patronage of Henry VII and stayed on for most of the rest of his life. His humanist history of England banished as so much medieval darkness the tradition of Britain's foundation by Brutus and his Trojan descent; he did help to create, however, the Tudor legend or "myth." He introduced the new historical methods of Italy, treating the Round Table in a manner reminiscent of Valla's critique of the Donation of Constantine. Thus his career is an important bridge between England and Renaissance Italy.

VERHEIDEN, JACOBUS
Sixteenth century. Dutch divine. Author of biographical anthology containing sketches of Protestant reformers, humanists, preachers. Among them are: Hus, Wyclif, Luther, Erasmus, Savonarola, Knox, Calvin. Illustrated with portraits. Published in 1603.

VERHEIDEN, WILLEM
(1568-1596). Dutch historian. He wrote, from a Protestant point of view, a history of the Dutch Revolt, in Latin and following the humanist model, *De jure belli belgici adversus Philippum;* he saluted England's victory over the Armada in his oration, *In classem Xerxis Hispani oratio,* 1589.

VERINO, UGOLINO
(1438-1516). Florentine poet who sought to fuse the classical and Christian traditions in his work. He wrote *Flametta,* a cycle of 82 elegies on love, a vision of heaven entitled *Paradisus,* the *Carliade,* which was inspired by Charlemagne as an ideal Christian type and heroic defender of the Church, and *De illustratione* or *De gloria urbis florentinae,* an apotheosis of his home town as well as a remarkably detailed description of its civic life and citizenry. His son MICHELE (died c. 1514) was a child prodigy, author of the *Disticha moralia,* in which he discourses on love, wisdom, sin, avarice, patriotism, etc.

VERNIER, PIERRE

(1580-1637). French soldier, mathematician, inventor. He devised the small sliding scale adapted for minute precision readings which takes its name from him.

VERONESE, PAOLO CALIARI

(1528-1588). Italian painter of the Venetian school. Produced easel pictures, frescoes, murals, paintings with a great sense of beauty and narrative force. Exerted deep influence long after his death. Among his works are *Jesus and the Centurion of Capernaum, Marriage at Cana, Martyrdom of St. George, Esther Before Ahasuerus, Feast at the House of Simon.* He painted many secular and mythological works commissioned by the Venetian state, e.g., *Venice Ruling with Justice and Peace*, the *Triumph of Venice* and *The Rape of Europa*. In 1573 he was called before a court of the Inquisition sitting at Venice to be queried about *The Supper at the House of Simon*, which he had rendered for a monastery refectory. Artistic considerations had caused him to fill out his painting with a servant with a bloody nose, a jester with a parrot on his wrist, two halberdiers lurking in the background, etc.; he had also depicted St. Peter and the Apostles as little more than ordinary human beings engaged in mundane matters, e.g., carving the roast, picking one's teeth with a fork, etc. Such secularism and concern for aesthetic perfection were typical of much Renaissance art, although rarely carried to such an extreme as in the instance of Veronese. Reflecting the spirit of the Council of Trent and the Counter Reformation, the court required Veronese to "correct" his painting, which, however, he seems never to have done.

VERRAZANO, GIOVANNI DA

(c. 1485-c. 1528). Italian navigator of Florence. In French service. Explored North American coast in 1524. Discovered New York Bay. Killed by natives on an expedition to West Indies.

VERROCCHIO, ANDREA DEL

(1435-1488). Florentine sculptor, painter, goldsmith and engineer; student and disciple of Donatello. His greatest achievement was his sculpture. Among his famous statuary are *David, Doubting Thomas, Beheading of John the Baptist,* and his equestrian representation of the condottiere *Bartolomeo Colleoni*. His works as goldsmith have been lost, as have most of his paintings.

VERSOR, JOHANNES

(died 1480). Logician. Wrote a commentary on Aristotle's *Organon* and on Petrus Hispanus.

VERSTEGAN, RICHARD or RICHARD ROWLANDS

(died c. 1635). Printer, scholar. Born in London. Of Dutch origin. Settled in Antwerp. Author of *Theatrum Crudelitatum Haereticorum*, published in 1567, with illustrations of Catholic martyrdoms; it was a work directed against Elizabeth's treatment of Catholics. He also wrote and published *Antiquities Concerning the English Nation*.

VESALIUS, ANDREAS

(1514-1564). Born in Flanders, he studied at Louvain, Paris, and Padua where he took his medical degree and taught surgery. His *Seven Books on the Structure of the Human Body*, 1543, remarkably systematic, detailed, and complete, owed much of its fame and influence to its illustrations; their draughtsman is not known, spurring suspicions that they are plagiarisms of Leonardo's work in anatomy, which they resemble closely. Vesalius' anatomy is still cast, to some extent, in the mold of Galen, some of whose errors he repeats; most notably is this true in his description of the circulation of the blood. He accepted the doctrine of the "septum", the wall dividing the heart, as porous and thus facilitating the passage of the blood from the veins to the arteries; it was not until William Harvey that this great hurdle to the development of anatomy, physiology, and medicine was overcome. For reasons that are not clear, Vesalius gave up his research to become a military physician and then physician to the Emperor Charles V.

VESPASIANO DA BISTICCI

(1421-1498). Florentine bookseller and manuscript dealer, the most famous of his day. Among his patrons were Cosimo de' Medici, Popes Eugenius IV and Nicholas V, King Alfonso the Magnanimous of Naples, Alessandro Sforza, and Duke Federigo da Montefeltro of Urbino, for whom he assembled one of the finest libraries of the age. It later found its way into the Vatican Library. Bookselling then involved the high adventure of locating copies of manuscripts as well as directing a corps of copyists and designing bindings. In 1480 Vespasiano sold out, unhappy with the commercialization of the trade that came in the wake of the printing press. He then dedicated himself to writing, among other works and all in Italian, the memoirs: *Lives of Illustrious Men of the Fifteenth Century* and a companion volume on eminent women. It was his reading of the *Lives* that inspired Burckhardt to write *The Civilization of the Renaissance in Italy.*

VESPUCCI, AMERIGO

(1451-1512). Florentine geographer and cartographer. He developed a very accurate method for calculating latitude. Participated in several expeditions to New World, in 1497, 1499, 1501, 1503. In last voyages, explored Darien area. Also wrote account of the New World which was utilized by Waldseemüller in drawing his famous map of 1507; largely because Vespucci had shown the southern continent to be distinct from Asia, Waldseemüller designated it "America." Since the Waldseemüller chart was a remarkable advance over earlier ones, it was long used by navigators and hence the name stuck.

VETERANI, FEDERICO

(Fifteenth century). Noted copyist and calligrapher. Executed a Livy and an Appian.

VIADANA, LODOVICO

(1564-1645). Italian musician, kappelmeister at the Cathedral of Modena and later at Rome, composer of church and secular music: madrigals, masses, motets, canzonetti, and what he called *concerti ecclesiastici a 1, 2, 3, 4 voci con il Basso continuo per sonar nell'organo.* He was the first to make use of the *basso continuo,* played in this work by the organ.

VIAU, THÉOPHILE DE

(1590-1626). French poet, writer, one of the Libertines, he was condemned to death, sentence commuted, banished. Author of tragedy *Pyrame et Thisbé;* also lyrics—odes and idylls—depicting country life.

VICARY, THOMAS

(Died 1562). First surgical master of the English corporation of barber-surgeons, which was founded in 1540 and helped to establish semiprofessional standards by requiring examinations to be successfully passed and by making instruction in anatomy available to its members. Royal chirurgeon to Henry VIII. First known surgeon of St. Bartholomew's Hospital, London. First to write a book on anatomy of the face: *The Englishman's Treasure or The True Anatomy of Man's Body*, published in 1548.

VICENTE, GIL

(1470?-1536?). Portuguese dramatist and lyric poet. He wrote frequently in Spanish as well as Portuguese, sometimes mixing the two languages in the same work. Life obscure. Dedicated his work to Kings Manuel I and Juan III. Author of devotional works, comedies, farces; religious allegorical plays, many of which show the influence of Erasmus; tragic comedies based on chivalric romances, e.g., *Don Duardos*. Primarily, Vicente was a court poet, but also used popular lyric forms in which the common man figured, e.g., in his *Monologue of the Herdsman*. First printed in 1502, the play marks the beginning of the poetic theatre of Portugal.

VICENTINO, NICOLA

(1511-1572). Italian musician, composer, musicologist and priest. Invented *archiorgano* and *archicembalo*, instruments intended to produce Greek modes, even half and quarter tones. His treatise on *L'Antica musica ridotta alla moderna prattica* was published in 1555; it has reference to the court of Ferrara, one of the musical (as well as dramatic) centers of Italy.

VICO, ENEA

(1523-1567). Italian engraver and numismatist. First writer on numismatics in Italy. Brought to Florence by Duke Cosimo de' Medici. Engraved paintings of Michelangelo and other artists, noted especially for portraits. Author of book on ancient coins entitled *Le immagini delle donne auguste*.

VICTORIA, TOMÁS LUIS DE

(c. 1540-1611). Spanish composer. Friend of Palestrina, under whom he studied. Chapelmaster in Rome. Wrote motets, masses, magnificats, hymns, utilizing all the newer contrapuntal techniques, but all his music is intensely Spanish and mystical. His last and most productive years he spent in Spain.

VICTORIUS, PETRUS or PIERO VETTORI

(1499-1585). The greatest Greek scholar of his age. He opposed the Medici and, with the fall of the Florentine Republic by 1530, retired to the family estate, San Casaciano; Duke Cosimo I enticed him to return to Florence (from Rome where he had fled upon Cosimo's ascension in 1537) to be professor of Latin—later of Greek and philosophy. He is remembered for his surpassing editions, with extensive commentary and explication, of classical works. They include Cicero's *Letters* and *Philosophical Works,* Cato, Varro, Terence, Sallust, Aristotle's *Rhetoric, Poetics, Politics, Nicomachean Ethics,* Sophocles' Oedipus trilogy, the *editio princips* of Euripides' *Electra,* the first complete edition of the *Agamemnon,* and miscellaneous writings of Plato, Xenophon, Porphyry, Dionysius of Halicarnassus, Demetrius' *De Elocutione.* In addition, there are his own voluminous writings—*Letters, Orations* and critical and textual studies. He led a simple, spare life, completely dedicated to classical scholarship. Unsurpassed as a teacher, he attracted students from all over Europe. His portrait was painted by Titian.

VIDA, MARCO GIROLAMO or MARCUS HIERONYMUS
(c. 1490-1566). Italian humanist, Neo-Latin poet, bishop, the greatest Christian poet of his age. Wrote long didactic poems— on silkworms, chess. His *Christias* in six books is an epic poem on the life of Christ. His *De Arte Poetica,* a treatise in the form of a didactic poem, was highly regarded for a long time as an excellent guide for the writing of poetry; he followed the literary principles of Horace's *Ars Poetica* and extolled Vergil's *Aeneid* as the finest example of epic verse and the model to be imitated.

VIERI, FRANCESCO DE'
Sixteenth century. Italian scholar. Called Il Verino Secundo. Wrote on humanistic philosophy, immortality, and other metaphysical subjects.

VIÈTE, FRANÇOIS
(1540-1603). French mathematician, astronomer, attached to the court of Henry III and Henry IV. Founder of modern algebra: related algebra to geometry, trigonometry, and astronomy. Called Father of Algebra because he established the use of letters to stand for unknown quantities.

VIEZZE, ANDREA DELLA
Italian illuminator. Executed copy of Procopius. Fifteenth century.

VIGNOLA, JACOPO, IL BAROZZI
(1507-1573). Italian architect who worked at Rome, Bologna

and, briefly, in France for Francis I. He succeeded Michelangelo as architect for St. Peter's. He was secretary to the Roman society known as the *Accademia Vitruviana*, where discussions, inspired by Vitruvius' encyclopedic work, of the orders of architecture were held. Vignola wrote two works of architectural theory and practice which are among the earliest works to justify the profuse architectural decoration that came to characterize Baroque style. They are entitled *Regola delli cinque ordini d'architettura*, 1563, and *Due regole della prospettiva pratica*, 1583.

VILLAMEDIANA, CONDE DE

(1582-1622). Satirist and dramatist. Of noble lineage. Attached to court: involved in many escapades. Exiled to Naples. Killed by assassin. Noted for epigrams, longer poems in baroque style, sonnets. Also play: *La Gloria de Niquea*.

VILLANI, GIOVANNI

(c. 1275-1348). Florentine merchant and public official; his attendance at Pope Boniface VIII's jubilee of 1300 stimulated him to write his famous chronicle of Florence. The spirit of his history is conveyed by this quotation, "Rome is sinking; my native city is rising, and ready to achieve great things, and therefore I wish to relate its past history, and hope to continue the story to the present time, and as long as my life shall last." This is a trumpet announcing a new age. He died in the famous plague of 1348, the point at which the *Cronica* stops, having made the grand sweep from Biblical times to the rise of Florence to greatness. The work was carried down to 1363 by his brother MATTEO and another year added by the latter's son FILIPPO, who is better known for his *Book concerning the Famous Citizens of Florence*. Dedicated largely to the history of art and literature, it posits a long bleak period from the fall of Rome to the revival of art by Cimabue and Giotto and of letters by Dante. Later humanists followed Villani closely, except that they substituted Petrarch for Dante, since he used the vernacular, while Petrarch wrote Ciceronian Latin. At any rate all the heroes of the rebirth were Florentines.

VILLON, FRANÇOIS

(born 1431-died after 1463). French poet. Student in Paris. Led debauched, irregular life. In 1455 he fatally stabbed a priest. In 1462 he was arrested for theft and brawling. He was sentenced to death, but the sentence was commuted to banishment: 1463. Most

615

of his work deals with the seamy, bawdy underworld of Paris. *Le Petit Testament* and *Le Grand Testament* are long poems. In addition, he wrote some forty ballades and rondeaux. One of the earliest and greatest French lyric poets.

VINCENT DE PAUL, SAINT
(1576-1660). French priest, chaplain to the galley slaves. Noted for charitableness. Founder of Congregation of the Priests of the Mission: called Lazarists, or Vincentians and also founded the Sisters of Charity.

VINCENT, RAYMOND
French artist. In 1549, he was appointed by Pope Paul III as illuminator. Influenced by Raphael and Michelangelo. Executed psalter.

VINCI, PIERINO DA
(1522?-1554). Italian sculptor. Nephew of Leonardo da Vinci. Worked in bronze. According to Vasari, he began a *Samson* after seeing Michelangelo's sketches. He spent his apprenticeship in Rome, as was *de rigueur* for young artists by the sixteenth century; he was called back to Florence by the Medici duke, Cosimo I, who commissioned several works of him, few of which were finished. He died in the prime of life when his earlier promise seemed about to be realized.

VINCKEBOONS, DAVID
(1576-1629). Flemish painter who established himself in Amsterdam and did much to introduce the later Flemish tradition of painting there. Genre painter, pictures of manners and landscapes. His three sons have a place in the history of culture also, as painters, engravers, cartographers and architects.

VIRET, PIERRE
(1511-1571). Swiss religious reformer. Converted Lausanne to Protestantism. Meeting with opposition, he withdrew to Geneva. Aided Guillaume Farel in spreading Calvinism in Switzerland.

VIRTÙ
Roughly *talent, genius,* and *competence;* it was the temper of mind and spirit extolled by Petrarch and greatly admired in the Renaissance. It has nothing to do with morality or virtue, but refers to supreme excellence and creativity, the capacity for great achievement. Virtuoso derives from the term, but has little rele-

vance to the Renaissance conception of the man of *virtù*, who was
no specialist but *l'uomo universale*.

VISCHER or FISCHER

Family of sculptors and brass founders of early Renaissance period in Germany. Their workshop, which flourished throughout
the fifteenth and sixteenth centuries, was located at Nuremberg.
Most famous of them was Peter Vischer the Elder (c. 1457-1529).
Executed tombs, religious bronzes and contributed the statues
of Arthur and Theodoric the Ostrogoth to the celebrated Hapsburg tomb at Innsbruck. His five sons carried on the family tradition; their work represents a fusion of German and Italian
styles: two or three of the sons had traveled in Italy and thus
brought the new conceptions of art back with them.

VISCONTE, BARTOLOMEO

(1402-1457). Bishop of Novara. Patron of illuminators. Commissioned many decorated books, among them: two copies of Suetonius, executed in 1434 and 1444: *Historia Augusta*, Lactantius.

VISCONTI, THE

The despotic dukes of Milan. GIAN GALEAZZO (1378-1402)
trapped his uncle and cousins by a famous stratagem and thus
cleared the way for his personal rule. He purchased the title of
duke from the Emperor Wenceslaus and aimed to attain a royal
Italian crown. He nearly succeeded, capitalizing on the factional
quarrels and weaknesses of his neighbors, the preoccupation of
Venice with the Levant and the decadence of the papacy. Only
Florence, isolated, seemed to stand in his way. The plague carried him off in 1402, and thus Florentine independence and Italian disunity were preserved. Neither the would-be king nor his
adolescent successor could make use of the royal crown which
Gian had ordered of his craftsmen. His son, GIOVANNI MARIA
(1402-1412) was assassinated and succeeded by his brother
FILIPPO MARIA (1412-1447). He restored and greatly expanded Milan, but was stymied by a Florentine-Venetian alliance. He had married his daughter to the condottiere Francesco
Sforza, who succeeded, in default of Visconti heirs, to the duchy
by 1450, but not before an attempt to establish a republic, the
Ambrosian, failed.

VITAL CALABRESE, HAYYIM or CHAIM

(1543-1620). Rabbi of Jerusalem, born in Safed, Palestine, died

617

in Damascus. Cabalist. Disciple and perpetuator of the mystical and ascetic teachings of Isaac Luria. Author of *Tree of Life*.

VITÉZ, JOHN or JANOS

(c. 1408-1472). Hungarian archbishop, royal chancellor, patron of Hungarian humanism, mentor of Prince, later King, Matthias Corvinus. Inspired by Italian models, he founded an academy and a public library.

VITONI, VENTURA

(1442-1522). Italian architect. He was born and worked chiefly in Pistoia, a builder of churches and monasteries. He worked in the tradition of Brunelleschi, seeking to initiate a return to his principles and away from the tendency toward profuse decoration.

VITRUVIUS

Roman architect of the first century A.D. whose ten-volume *De architectura* covered everything from town planning to interior decoration; the massive work was first printed in 1484 and in an illustrated edition in 1511. Aside from providing detailed information on Roman and Greek architectural forms and engineering, he had a vast influence on Renaissance theories of art. Beauty could be achieved only by interrelating the size and shape of all parts to each other and to the whole in such a way that harmony and proportion were achieved. The harmony and proportion were those of the human body—itself, as the handiwork of God, a reflection of the perfect harmony and proportion of the universe. Hence the "module" or basic unit of measurement, e.g., the width of a pilaster or diameter of a column in architecture, all other dimensions being a multiple or division of that unit. Cardinal Ippolito de' Medici founded a club in Rome, whose purpose was the study of Vitruvius. The club was called *Le Virtù*: fifteenth century; in the sixteenth century there was an *Accademia vitruviana* at Rome; many Italian cities and towns boasted similar societies. The manuscript of Vitruvius had been found in the Swiss monastery of St. Gall in 1414.

VITTORIA, ALESSANDRO

(1525-1608). Venetian portrait sculptor and medalist. Executed portrait busts, tombs, for the doges and wealthy personages of Venice; he also executed religious works, e.g., *John the Baptist*.

VITTORIA, FRANCISCO DE

(1480-1546). Spanish Dominican friar, ethical jurist, and professor at the University of Salamanca. He was the founder of the great Spanish school of international jurisprudence that included Domingo De Soto, Luis de Molina, and Francisco Suarez, and which flourished in the sixteenth and early seventeenth centuries. His *De Potestate Civile* is one of the earliest works to revise the medieval concept of a law of nations, *ius gentium*, governing the relations of individuals and corporations within the framework of Christendom, in the direction of the modern idea of a system of law governing the relations of sovereign states, *ius inter gentes*. So far did he go in recognizing the existence of equal sovereign states that he could assert that Spanish discovery of America conferred no more rights of possession than "discovery" of Spain would have brought to a canoe full of Indians; nevertheless his work is couched in medieval terms, assuming a community of nations in which "the will of the majority (of states) should prevail". He had a profound influence on Grotius.

VITTORINO DA FELTRE

(1378-1447). The most famous schoolmaster of Renaissance Italy. He was trained at Padua and later learned Greek under Guarino. He was summoned to Mantua by the Gonzaga to be tutor to their four children. Given a free hand and liberal support, Vittorino established a famous boarding school. Conscious of the importance of environment and of daily exercise in the lives of the young, he chose a pleasant site for his school, *La Giocosa*, surrounded by green prospects and playing fields. Latin was taught as the mother tongue, for the vernacular was considered unworthy. Basing his teaching on the humanist theory of Vergerius, Alberti, Guarino and others, he utilized the classics to prepare his pupils for lives of moral virtue and cultivated leisure. Aside from a wide range of Latin and Greek authors, there were lessons in music, mathematics, and, above all, declamation. Noble children and gifted paupers, boys and at least a few girls were taught together. Many of his pupils came from northern Europe, including a surprising number from England; his most famous pupils were Lorenzo Valla and Federigo da Montefeltro of Urbino. An exemplary Christian in his own life, his school was a Christian nursery of humanism. His brilliant success was a personal one, deriving from his charm and warmth, his sympathy and single-minded dedication; in a larger sense, he succeeded in meeting the educational needs of a new society.

VIVARINI FAMILY, THE

Family of painters and founders of a workshop at Murano near Venice. In Murano the Byzantine artistic tradition was still strong, and the works of the family represent a fusion of the Byzantine modes with the humanistic art of Italy. They did altarpieces. Members of the family include ANTONIO (c. 1415-c. 1480); his brother BARTOLOMEO (c. 1430-c. 1500), who worked in Venice and painted in oils, perhaps the first to do so in Venice; and Antonio's son, the most gifted, famous in his day as a religious painter, ALVISE (c. 1448-c. 1505).

VIVES, JUAN LUIS

(1492-1540). Spanish humanist, educator, and social reformer. He was a cosmopolite who spent most of his life in France, England, and the Lowlands. Until he was muscled out of the realm by Henry VIII for his support of Catherine of Aragon's side in the divorce case, Vives was a dear friend of the Queen, tutor to her daughter Mary, and a member of the circle of English humanists that included More. He was one of the most original figures of the later Renaissance in his concern for social problems; *On the Help of the Poor*, 1526, outlined a system of relief and charity for the "worthy" poor that they may live useful lives; the book is notable for its criticism of the Church's failure to help the poor sufficiently and for his argument that municipal governments accept responsibility for the poor. In education his most important work was *De tradendis disciplinis*, 1531, where he followed the tradition of Vittorino and the Italian humanists, although he insisted strongly on the mastery of the vernacular as well as Latin and Greek, and that education was for a Christian life.

VIZINHO, JOSEPH

Fifteenth century. Portuguese-Jewish cartographer, under King John II of Portugal. He probably wrote the *Regimento do estrolobio y do quadrante*, c. 1509, the most important manual of navigation produced in the Renaissance.

VIZISCH, JOSEPH

Physician to John II of Portugal (1481-1495). Member of commission appointed by the King to examine Columbus' request for ships.

620

VOITURE, VINCENT
(1597-1648). French writer, poet. Attached to court of the marchioness of Rambouillet. Author of letters, poems, noted for their elegance and artificiality.

VOLOKOLAMSKY, SAINT JOSEPH or VOLOCSKY
(c. 1440-1515). Russian theologian. Author of *Illuminator*, first formal piece of Russian theological writing. He was a prolific writer of religious and ecclesiastical works; their tendency is conservative, submissive to the power of the state.

VOLTERRA, DANIELE DA, IL BRAGHETTONE
(1509-1566). Italian painter and sculptor of Tuscany. Executed religious frescoes, a *David Killing Goliath, Moses on Mt. Sinai, Descent from the Cross*. He greatly admired Michelangelo, many of whose designs he utilized for his own work. His sobriquet, "the breeches-maker," is owing to his commission from the pope to paint clothes upon the nudes in Michelangelo's *Last Judgment* of the Sistine Chapel; the popes of the Counter Reformation regarded art quite differently from their predecessors of the late fifteenth and early sixteenth centuries.

VOLUSENUS, FLORENTIUS
(c. 1504-1547). Scottish humanist, friend of George Buchanan. He spent most of his life on the continent. Notable for his Latinity. Headmaster of school in Provence. Author of *De Animi Tranquillitate*, a Ciceronian dialogue that reflects its author's Christian and humanist outlook and temperament.

VONDEL, JOOST VAN DEN
(1587-1679). Holland's greatest poet. Born in Cologne. Moved to Amsterdam. Influenced by French poetry. Wrote lyrics: *Greetings, Songs of the Prince*. Author of satirical verse: *The Rumbler of the Roosters-run, The Curry-Comb*. Elegies. In 1641, converted to Catholicism: celebrated conversion in a poem—*The Glory of the Church*. Also wrote plays, Biblical, historical: *Lucifer, Adam in Exile*. He made many translations into Dutch: from Italian, Tasso; from Latin, Vergil, Ovid, Horace, Seneca, and portions of the Bible; from Greek, Sophocles and Euripides.

VOS, CORNELIS DE
(1585-1651). Flemish painter, died in Antwerp. Known for portraits, altarpieces. His brother PAULUS (c. 1600-c. 1655) was

also a painter, notable for his depictions of animals and hunting scenes.

VOS, MARTEN DE

(c. 1535-1603). Flemish painter who studied at Antwerp and, for seven years and chiefly under Tintoretto, at Venice. Upon his return to Antwerp he established an influential art school, a center of Venetian and Italian art forms. His own work reflects the grandiose and colorist traditions of Venetian art. Much of his work (religious) was destroyed during the Dutch Revolt and after.

VOSSIUS, GERARD JOHN

(1577-1649). Dutch classical scholar, professor at Leyden. Specialized in grammar, rhetoric, history of literature, mythology. Published Latin grammar and histories of Greek and Roman literature. *De Historicis Latinis,* 1627, *De Historicis Graecis,* 1624, and an *Ars Rhetorica,* 1647.

VOUET, SIMON

(1590-1649). French painter, engraver. Born and died in Paris. Worked for Louis XIII and Richelieu. Noted for lavish decorative style. Executed portraits, historical and religious themes. He first gained a reputation as a portrait painter at Rome; upon his return to France he established an influential art school in Paris.

VRELANDT, WILLEM

(Died 1481). Burgundian illuminator. In 1467-1468 he executed miniatures in *Histoire du Haynaut* and was chief figure of a school of illuminators patronized by the dukes of Burgundy.

VRIES, ADRIAEN DE

(1560-1627). Dutch sculptor. Born at The Hague, died in Italy. Executed portrait busts, mythological subjects, e.g., *Mercury, Triton, Hercules and the Hydra,* decorative sculptures. He studied in Florence and worked in Prague, Nuremberg and Vienna, enjoying the patronage of the Emperor Rudolf II.

VRIES, HANS VREDEMAN DE

(1527-1604). Dutch engraver of architectural works, paintings, decoration, etc. His engravings, issued in anthologies, did much to establish the decorative manuscript style in the Lowlands. He wrote several treatises on the arts, the *Architecture,* in which he followed Vitruvius, and the *Perspective.*

VROOM, HENDRIK CORNELISZOON
(1566-1640). Dutch painter of seascapes, also a ceramics decorator.

VULCANIUS, BONAVENTURA or DESMET
(1538-1614). Dutch classical scholar of Bruges. Professor at Leyden. Editor of Arrian's *Expeditio Alexandri Magni,* published in 1575, and of Callimachus and Apuleius.

VULPIUS, MELCHIOR
(c. 1560-1615). German composer of church music, chorals, oratorios, wedding hymns, etc. He also wrote a work of musical theory. He was cantor at Weimar, where he spent most of his life.

VULTEIUS, REMENSIS
(Died 1542). French Neo-Latin poet. Author of *Xenia,* epigrams.

VYSHENSKY, IVAN
(1550-1620). Ukrainian publicist, author of polemical works that opposed union with the Latin church of Poland. His poetical and rhetorical works, written in a non-ecclesiastical, popular Ukrainian dialect, helped to fix the literary language of Ukraine.

W

WADDING, LUKAS
(1588-1657). Franciscan friar, historian of the Franciscan Minorites, and author of a life of Duns Scotus. He was of Irish birth but spent his life in Spain and at Rome, where he founded St. Isidore's College for Irish students.

WADHAM COLLEGE
Oxford University. Founded in 1612 by bequest of Nicholas Wadham (died 1609).

WAKEFIELD GRAMMAR SCHOOL
English public school. Founded by Royal Charter in 1591.

WALDBURGER, HANS
(c. 1573-1630). German sculptor. Died at Salzburg. Executed sacred and secular sculpture. He worked at Innsbruck and Salzburg; he probably made a trip to Italy. His characteristic work (altarpieces) combined Gothic and Renaissance elements. His father and namesake (c. 1543-1622) was also a sculptor and chief teacher of his son.

WALDIS, BURKARD
(c. 1490-c. 1556). German poet, proponent of the Reformation. Franciscan monk, became Lutheran. Imprisoned. Translated Aesop and wrote a religious drama entitled *De parabell vam verlorn Szohn*. He also produced versions of the Psalms.

625

WALDMANN, HANS

(died 1489). Swiss political figure. Burgomaster of Zurich in 1483. Notorious for his ruthless character. Fought against Charles the Bold of Burgundy. Appears as a character in a number of nineteenth century German dramas.

WALDSEEMÜLLER, MARTIN

(c. 1470-c. 1522). German cartographer and humanist. His *Cosmographie introductio*, 1507, included two exceptionally good maps, a theoretical and scientific treatise on geography as well as Amerigo Vespucci's account of his explorations in the New World. It was Waldseemüller who first designated the New World as America, justifying that name in the work of 1507. He and his circle of humanist friends in Alsace published a new edition of Ptolemy, 1513.

WALLASEY GRAMMAR SCHOOL

English public school. Origins uncertain. First recorded mention occurs in 1595.

WALLENSTEIN, ALBRECHT VON

(1583-1634). Bohemian general in the service of the Hapsburgs during the Thirty Years' War. Gained victory in Denmark. Removed from command. Assassinated by Irish and Scottish officers. A figure of legend and literature, he was fashioned into a great national hero and patriot by Schiller in his famous dramatic trilogy.

WALTER, FRIAR

(Sixteenth century). Dominican monk of Utrecht. Preached Lutheranism in Holland. Died in Strassburg.

WALTHER, JOHANN

(1496-1570). German musician, singing master to the duke of Saxony, friend of Luther, with whom he cooperated in producing the "German Mass," c. 1524. Wrote sacred music, religious songs. Published first Protestant songbook.

WARBECK, PERKIN

(1474-1499). French-born pretender to English throne. Claimed identity of Richard, Duke of York, son of Edward IV. Aided by Charles VIII of France and Emperor Maximilian I. In 1499, in Cornwall, proclaimed himself king. Taken prisoner. Admitted imposture. Hanged in Tower of London by Henry VII.

626

WAR OF THE THREE HENRYS

French civil and religious wars of the last third of the sixteenth century. The participants were Henry III of Valois, Henry of Navarre, Henry of Guise. Henry III, last of the Valois kings, supported Protestants, in fear of power of Henry of Guise. The king was driven from Paris by Catholic adherents of Guise: 1588, on the Day of Barricades. Guise was murdered by henchmen of the king. In the following year, Henry III was murdered by fanatical monk. Henry of Navarre then assumed throne of France as Henry IV. All three Henrys were assassinated.

WARS OF THE ROSES

Civil war between House of York and House of Lancaster for English throne. Symbol of York was a white rose: badge of Lancaster, a red rose. After twelve major battles, Henry Tudor, of the House of Lancaster, became king: married Yorkist princess and thus ended the conflict. As a result of war, English nobility was depleted. Among the battles were: Battle of St. Albans, in 1455, where the Duke of Beaufort was killed: Battle of Northampton, in 1460, the Yorkists being victorious: Lancastrians defeated at Mortimer's Cross in 1461: Lancastrians victorious in 1461 at Second Battle of St. Albans: Henry, Earl of Richmond, defeated the Yorkist King Richard III at Bosworth Field in 1485. Duration of Wars: 1455-1485. Throughout the Tudor period, and especially during Elizabeth's reign, much literature was written about the wars, which were almost always depicted as the occasion of unmitigated disaster and suffering for the body politic. The moral that emerged was the political one that rebellion initiates a chain reaction of calamities that continue over many generations until the original "crime" is expiated by suffering; Kings were sent of God and rebellion against them was seen to be contrary to the order and harmony of the universe. With Bosworth Field and the Tudor dynasty the cycle of disaster was closed. The fear of civil war, however, was a constant in England after Henry VIII's religious changes. The Gloriana cult of Elizabeth and many great works of literature, e.g., *A Mirrour for Magistrates, Spenser's Faerie Queene, Sidney's Arcadia*—the theme of which is civil war—and Shakespeare's histories—running from Richard II, when things first went awry, to Richard III, when England's disasters culminated—all reflect a political concern and take a cautionary stance.

WARWICK, RICHARD NEVILLE, EARL OF

(1428-1471). Yorkist leader in Wars of the Roses. The King Maker. Defeated at Battles of St. Albans and Wakefield. In 1461 however he took London and proclaimed Edward IV king. Imprisoned Henry VI in Tower of London. Warwick later deposed Edward IV and set Henry VI on throne. In 1471, Edward, regaining power, killed Warwick at Battle of Barnet. Warwick was a skilled politician and diplomat: greatest landowner in England.

WARWICK SCHOOL

English public school. Probably founded c. 914. Refounded by Henry VIII in 1545.

WATSON, THOMAS, BISHOP OF LINCOLN

(1513-1584). English ecclesiastic and humanist, educated at Cambridge. He opposed the religious changes and was imprisoned frequently. He wrote a Latin tragedy entitled *Absolom* and did some few translations from the classics.

WATSON, THOMAS

(c. 1557-1592). English poet and classical scholar. In 1581 translated into Latin Sophocles' *Antigone* and the *Aminta* of Tasso; also Italian madrigals, *The first Sett of Italian Madrigalls Englished*. Author of *Hecatompathia or Passionate Century of Sonnets*, a cycle of sonnets that Shakespeare knew closely. Also *Tears of Fancy*.

WAYNFLETE, WILLIAM OF, or WAINFLEET

(c. 1395-1486). Bishop of Winchester. Founder in 1458 of St. Mary Magdalen College, Oxford University. Attached to the court of Henry VI and then an adherent of Edward IV. He also founded a grammar school at Wainfleet, 1484.

WEAPONS AND ARMOR

Renaissance weapons included: the espadon or two-handed sword, the hilt being elaborately decorated and often studded with precious stones: rapier, cutlass, sabre, malchus, civic sword: dagger: musket: crossbow, used largely for hunting: caliver: match-lock guns, wheel-lock pistols: hunting gun: halberd and other pole arms: stone bow or prodd: culverin. The estoc was a sword hollowed out or grooved throughout its length. The arquebus was invented in Spain in first half of sixteenth century. From the time

628

of Louis XI to that of Francis I of France (1461-1547), the halberd and pike were used almost exclusively by Swiss infantry. Armor was used for man and horse. Helmet and breastplate were often gilded or silvered, heavy with ornamentation. The salade was a light open helmet.

WEBSTER, JOHN
(c. 1580-c. 1625). English playwright. Collaborated frequently with other authors: Drayton, Middleton, Thomas Dekker, *et al.*, all of whom were exploited by the theatrical manager, Philip Henslowe. For this reason, probably, only a few of his works rise above mediocrity. Those few are sufficient, however, to place him in the first rank of Elizabethan dramatists. Wrote *The White Devil, The Duchess of Malfi;* also, putatively, *The Devil's Law Case, Appius and Virginia.*

WECKHERLIN, GEORG RUDOLPH
(1584-1653). German poet. A native of Stuttgart, he settled in London and became an assistant to John Milton, who was then Latin Secretary. Author of lyrics, sonnets, in German and in English.

WEDDERBURN, JAMES
(c. 1495-1553). Scottish poet, Protestant. Author of ballads, many of which are satirical of the papacy and Catholic Church. He wrote two plays, which are also satirical.

WEELKES, THOMAS
(c. 1575-1623). English musician, organist at Chichester Cathedral. Composed madrigals, anthems and instrumental music.

WEIGEL, VALENTIN
(1533-1588). German mystic in the tradition of Eckhart and Tauler. Neo-Platonist. He wrote numerous works on the nature of Christianity, the human understanding and the interior life.

WEISSKUNIG, DER
The White King. An account of the achievements of the Holy Roman Emperor Maximilian I (1459-1519) dictated by himself.

WELLINGBOROUGH SCHOOL
English public school. Founded in 1478.

WELSER, PHILIPPINE
(1527-1580). Secret wife of Archduke Ferdinand. Daughter of the great German house of merchants and bankers. Her morganatic marriage and her two sons by it are subjects of several German plays and novels.

WELSH BIBLE
First complete version was finished in 1588, by William Morgan and Edmund Prys. The New Testament in Welsh had been published by Richard Davies in 1567. Queen Elizabeth had directed that a Welsh version of the Bible be made and also the Book of Common Prayer.

WERNER, JOHANNES
(1468-1528). German astronomer and mathematician. Author of *Canones de Mutatione Aeris,* a work on weather prediction, published in 1546. He contributed to the development of trigonometry by his study of spherical triangles. He also dabbled in astrology and mixed much nonsense with his science.

WESENBECKIUS, MATTHIAS
(1531-1586). Belgian jurist. Wrote poem decrying St. Bartholomew's Day Massacre: *Aenigma Timorumenon in Latum Sanguine Maceratum:* published in 1572. He wrote several treatises on Roman law.

WESSEL, JOHANN
(1419-1489). Early Dutch humanist. Called *Lux Mundi*—Light of the World. Educated by the Brethren of the Common Life. Studied Greek, Hebrew, theology. Head of nunnery in Groningen. Wrote treatise on logic: published in Groningen in 1614. He had gone to Italy to study Greek and later taught Greek at Paris, where Reuchlin was among his students.

WESTMINSTER SCHOOL
English public school. Origins uncertain. First recorded mention in 1339. Finally chartered by Queen Elizabeth I in 1560.

WESTPHALIA, PEACE OF, OF 1648
Treaties that concluded the Thirty Years' War. The preliminary negotiations lasted four years. The French, Swedish, and the Emperor Ferdinand III were involved. Sweden received West Pomerania and the Bishoprics of Bremen and Verden. France retained the Bishoprics of Toul, Metz, Verdun: also Alsace. The eccle-

siastical map was redrawn as of 1624. Bohemia was retained by the Emperor. Calvinism acquired same status as Lutheranism. German princes granted new sovereign rights. Brandenburg acquired East Pomerania and four bishoprics. Switzerland and the Dutch Netherlands were declared sovereign, free states. Hesse-Cassel received the Abbey of Hersfeld and part of Schaumburg. Mecklenburg received the Bishopric of Schwerin and Ratzeburg. The *Jus reformandi* was retained by the overlords: 1648.

WEYDEN, ROGIER VAN DER

(c. 1400-1464). The rival and successor of the Van Eycks as the leader of the Flemish school. He was official painter to the city of Brussels, which he left only to visit Italy, 1447, which, however, seems not to have influenced him perceptibly. His art reflects rather the quickened religiosity of the *devotio moderna* and is characterized by movement and a somber, dramatic intensity; as such his work contrasts with the Van Eycks' which tends to be static and serene, exhibiting a more conventional religiosity. He depicted the suffering of Jesus often, the *Descent of the Cross* being a subject he chose to depict several times. He also did portraits, e.g., of Duke Charles the Rash of Burgundy and Lionello or Meliaduse d'Este; his portraits exhibit the same sense of tragedy and emotional intensity. Aside from works commissioned by the city of Brussels, he served churches, guilds and wealthy individuals, among them the ducal house of Burgundy.

WEY, WILLIAM

(c. 1407-1476). Englishman who made a pilgrimage to the Holy Land twice, in 1458 and 1462 and one to Santiago de Compostella in Spain; he wrote descriptions (unpublished) of his journeys.

WHITGIFT, JOHN

(1530-1604). Anglican prelate, Archbishop of Canterbury under Elizabeth I. Rigorous in maintaining religious uniformity and hence attacked in the Puritan-inspired *Martin Marprelate* pamphlets. Collaborated in Lambeth Articles, the statement of Anglican doctrines which most shows Calvin's influence.

WIDMANN, JOHANNES

(1440-1524). Physician of Tübingen. Wrote on medical subjects, especially syphilis. Adherent of Avicenna's principles.

631

WIEDERMANN, JACOB

Anabaptist. Settled in Austerlitz in 1528. His followers practiced community of property.

WIER, JOHANN

(1515-1588). German physician, student of epidemics—the plague, malaria, etc. Author of *De Praestigiis Daemonum et Incantationibus ac Veneficiis,* 1563, on witchcraft and the black arts, which he opposed and decried; his work is a milestone in the war on superstition.

WILLAERT, ADRIAN

(c. 1489-1562). Flemish musician and composer, the greatest master of contrapuntal music of his day. After a career at various courts, he became chapelmaster at St. Mark's, Venice, 1527 on. There he developed the madrigal and the antiphonal use of two or more choirs. He is important for introducing to Italy the more advanced musical theory of the Netherlands; he was the founder of the Venetian school of composers which included his most famous disciple, Gabrieli.

WILLAERTS, ADAM

(1577-1664)). Dutch painter of Utrecht. Noted for marine subjects, fires, genre. He belonged to the mannerist school; his three sons were also painters.

WILLIAM I OF ORANGE

(1533-1584). Called William the Silent, although not known as such in his lifetime, and not known to have been taciturn. Founder of the Dutch Republic: first Stadholder. Prince of Orange, Count of Nassau. In 1555 he was Commander of the Imperial armies. Refused to attend Council of Blood: 1567. In conflict with Henry II of France. Led War of Independence against the Duke of Alva and the Spanish forces: 1568-1576.

United seven northern provinces against the Spanish. By the Union of Utrecht, in 1579, the independence of Holland was declared. Assassinated at Delft by Balthasar Gerard, who was in the pay of Philip II.

WILLIAM OF SELLING or CELLING

(died 1494). English Benedictine monk. First Englishman who studied Greek in the early modern period. Studied in Italy for three years at Bologna, Padua, and Rome; he made two more trips to Italy and brought back classical manuscripts. Teacher of Thomas Linacre.

WILLOUGHBY, SIR HUGH
(died 1554). English navigator. In search of Northeast Passage to the Orient. In command of expedition that sailed from Deptford in 1553. Reached the coast of Norway, Russian Lapland. Died there.

WILSON, ARTHUR
(1595-1652). English historian and dramatist. Author of a history of the reign of James I. His only play that survives is *The Inconstant Lady*.

WILSON, SIR THOMAS
(c. 1525-1581). English humanist. He studied with Cheke at Padua. He made the first English translation of Demosthenes' three *Olynthiacs*, 1570. He also wrote a manual of style, *The Art of Rhetoric*.

WIMPHELING, JAKOB
(1450-1528). German humanist, professor at Heidelberg. Author of *Germania*, published in 1501, and *Epitome Rerum Germanicarum*, published in 1505; works which radiate patriotism. He also wrote grammatical manuals and influential works on pedagogy. He was famous as a teacher. He was a harbinger of humanism in Germany and a would-be reformer—along humanist lines —of education; although his attempt to found a university to accommodate the new learning came to nothing, he did establish several literary and humanist societies in several German cities, e.g., Strassburg. These were of importance in creating the vogue of the new learning. He was for a while distinctly sympathetic to Luther.

WIMPINA, KONRAD
(1460-1531). German theologian, logician and religious controversialist. He was rector of the University of Frankfurt on the Oder and an opponent of Luther. As a logician he was in the Scholastic tradition and wrote *Congestio Nova Proprietatum Logicalium*.

WINSHEIME, VITUS
(1501-1570). Physician of Wittenberg. Professor of Greek. Trans-

lated into Latin Thucydides' *History of the Peloponnesian War*: published in 1569.

WISHART, GEORGE

(1513?-1546). Scottish reformer and preacher, teacher of John Knox. He had fled to the Continent upon being accused of heresy for teaching, as a schoolmaster, the Greek New Testament. He was at Cambridge briefly and then returned to Scotland. Taken prisoner, strangled and burned at St. Andrew's.

WITHALS, JOHN

Sixteenth century. English lexicographer. Produced an English–Latin lexicon for beginners which was long in use.

WITHER, GEORGE

(1588-1667). English poet. Imprisoned for attack on Parliament: *The Abuses Stript and Whipt*: published in 1613. Also pastoral poems; *The Shepherds Hunting, Motto, Fidelia, Fair Virtue*, many of which were written in prison. He fought on the Puritan side in the English Revolution.

WITHINGTON, NICHOLAS

English navigator. In the service of the East India Company. On a mission to India in 1613. Wrote an account of his travels in Western India.

WITZ, KONRAD

(c. 1405-c. 1445). German painter who did altarpieces. He was reared in the Lowlands and studied in Burgundy and/or France; his work is notable for a departure from the Gothic tradition. His naturalistic depiction of the human figure suggests the influence of the Van Eycks.

WIVALLIUS, LARS

(1605-1669). Swedish lyric poet. A restless spirit and a vagabond, he traveled throughout Europe. Wrote his best poems while in prison; they are by turns erotic, courtly, idyllic.

WOHLGEMUT, MICHAEL or WOLGEMUT

(1434-1519). German painter, woodcarver and engraver of Nuremberg, where he headed a large workshop. His work, which shows Flemish influence, included religious pieces, e.g., altarpieces and retables, as well as portraits; he also did woodcuts for books. He is best known as the master of Dürer, whose father-in-law he was.

634

WOLF, HIERONYMUS
(1516-1580). German classical scholar, translator, schoolmaster, student of Melanchthon. Edited Demosthenes, Isocrates, and Byzantine chroniclers. Wrote dialogue on astrology, commentaries on astrological texts. For a while he was secretary and librarian to Jacob Fugger, but renounced that calling to become head of a *Gymnasium* at Augsburg.

WOLMAR, MELCHIOR
(Sixteenth century). German Greek scholar and schoolmaster of Rattweil. Friend and teacher of Calvin. Taught him Greek and directed his study of the New Testament in the original Greek.

WOLSEY, THOMAS, CARDINAL
(c.1475-1530). English prelate and statesman. Served under Henry VIII: advanced rapidly. Archbishop of York: 1514. Lord Chancellor: 1515. Papal Legate: 1518. Candidate for Papacy: 1521. In his foreign policy, Wolsey tried to maintain balance between Francis I of France and Emperor Charles V. His domestic policy promoted royal power.

Wolsey founded College of Ipswich and Christ Church, Oxford. He lost royal favor for inability to secure Henry's divorce from Queen Catherine at Rome. Incurred public hostility by forced loans. Indicted for securing bulls from Rome, he was charged with treason but died on his way to trial in London. He was the last of the great medieval ecclesiastical statesmen of England.

WONSIDEL, ERASMUS
Sixteenth century. Logician. Wrote a commentary on Aristotle's *Organon*. Published in Leipzig in 1511.

WOODALL, JOHN
(c. 1566-1643). English surgeon. Surgeon General to the East India Company and author of works on surgery.

WOODVILLE, ANTHONY, EARL RIVERS, BARON SCALES or WYDVILLE
(c. 1442-1483). Defender and Director of Papal Causes in England. In service of Edward IV. Author of compilation: *Dictes and Sayings of the Philosophers*. Published by William Caxton. Beheaded by Richard III.

WORCESTER ROYAL GRAMMAR SCHOOL
English public school. Origins uncertain. Earliest recorded

mention occurs in 1290. Granted charter by Queen Elizabeth I in 1561.

WORDE, WYNKYN DE or JAN VAN WYNKYN

(died c. 1534). Alsatian pioneer printer in England. Apprentice to William Caxton, who, on his death, left his business to him. Developed type cutting. Published more than 400 works.

WORLD CONGRESS OF PHILOSOPHERS

Pico della Mirandola proposed such a congress: comprising philosophers of all nations. He intended to deliver famous speech *On the Dignity of Man* and to debate the five hundred theses he had formulated. Congress banned by Pope Innocent VIII in 1486 on the grounds that several of the theses were heretical.

WORMS, DIET OF

Charles V, Holy Roman Emperor, held first diet at Worms, in 1521. Martin Luther, summoned to appear, refused retractions of his doctrines and published writings. On May 26, 1521, Edict of Worms was issued, outlawing Luther as heretic. With aid of friends, Luther escaped to Castle of Wartburg where he lived during 1521-1522, engaged upon his translation of the Bible into German.

WOTTAN, EDWARD

(1492-1555). English physician and naturalist. Educated at Oxford. Physician to Henry VIII. Wrote *De Differentiis Animalium*, published in 1555, a scientific attempt to classify animals. He studied medicine at Padua, was learned in Greek and held a readership at Oxford.

WOTTAN, SIR HENRY

(1568-1639). English traveler, scholar, poet. Spent many years on the Continent. On mission to James VI of Scotland, to Venice, to Germany. Author of letters, tractates, poems. Among other miscellaneous writings may be mentioned his *Elements of Architecture* and the *Character of a Happy Life*.

WOTTON, THOMAS

(1521-1587). English country squire of Kent. His *Letter-Book*, covering years 1574-1586, shed light on private life in Elizabethan age.

WUJEK, JAKOB

(1540-1597). Polish Jesuit priest. Translated Bible into Polish.

636

Called Wujek's Bible. He was active in the Counter Reformation in Poland and also wrote theological and homiletic works.

WÜRTZ, FELIX or WIRTZ
(c. 1518-1574). Swiss surgeon. Author of *Practica der Wundartzeney*: published in 1563. Friend of Paracelsus and Gesner. His text went through thirty editions in one century.

WYATT, SIR THOMAS
(c. 1503-1542). English poet, diplomat, courtier, friend of the poet Surrey. Translated sonnets of Petrarch. Introduced, with Surrey, the sonnet into English literature. Also wrote satires, lyrics, rondeaus. His son and namesake, 1521-1554, conspired against Queen Mary and was executed.

X

XAVIER, SAINT FRANCIS

(1506-1552). Jesuit missionary in Goa, Ceylon, Japan. He was Spanish (Basque) and born of a noble family. Called Apostle of the Indies. Instrumental in the founding of the Jesuit Order.

XIMÉNES DE CISNEROS, CARDINAL FRANCISCO or JIMÉNES

(1436-1517). Of noble birth, confessor to Queen Isabella, the Wolsey of Spain in his many benefices and great power. For a time he had been in the papal service at Rome; in this connection he underwent a profound religious experience that led to his departure from the secular priesthood to become an Observant Franciscan and a devotee of the ascetic life. Returned to Spain, he became archbishop of Toledo (primate of Spain), provincial of the Franciscan Order, Grand Inquisitor as well as the most trusted adviser of Ferdinand and Isabella. After the monarchs he was the most powerful person in Spain and thus could carry out a reform of the regular and secular clergy. By his founding of the University of Alcalá de Henares, 1508, and his patronage of the new learning in the form of biblical scholarship, he illustrates the Christian humanist ideal of the restoration of piety through good letters. He conceived of the university as a training ground for a new ecclesiastical élite, men equally learned and pious; the Biblical languages, Latin, Greek, Hebrew, and even Aramaic, were taught there, and it produced the great Complutensian Bible, 1522. An understanding of Ximénes' career goes far in explaining why the Reformation had little appeal in Spain; his limitations as a humanist are suggested by the holocaust he made of Arabic manuscripts on the grounds that they were anti-Christian.

XYLANDER, WILHELM HOLTZMANN

(1532-1576). German classical scholar. Professor of Greek and librarian at Heidelberg. Edited Marcus Aurelius, the *editio princeps*, and also Plutarch, Strabo, and Pausanias, the last being completed by Sylburg.

Z

ZABARELLA, JACOBO
(1532-1589). Italian philosopher and logician, professor of philosophy at Padua, and a later follower of Pomponazzi. He knew Greek and was thoroughly acquainted with Aristotle and his ancient commentators: Zabarella was one of the greatest and most penetrating Aristotelian commentators of all times. His treatises *De Rebus Naturalibus, De Regressu, Opera Logica* have an important place in the development of scientific method; in these writings he anticipated the methods of analysis and proof associated with Galileo. He set off the methods of proof appropriate in the natural and mathematical sciences from the rhetorical methods of oratory and from the system of legal pleading in courts, thus contributing to the specialization of the sciences and their separation from the humanities. He was, in fact, the emancipator of the sciences.

ZACCARIA, ANTONIO MARIA
(1500-1539). Founder of Order of Regular Clerks of St. Paul: also called Barnabites. Final approval was given to the order by Pope Clement VII.

ZACCONI, LODOVICO
(1555-1627). Venetian musicologist and composer, Augustinian monk and chapelmaster of his order's church in Venice. Author of an encyclopedic treatise on modes, musical instruments, counterpoint, etc., the *Prattica di musica*, 1592, 1619.

ZACUTO, ABRAHAM
Fifteenth century. Spanish-Jewish cosmographer in the service of King John II of Portugal. Author of *Almanach Perpetuum*, trans-

lated from Portuguese into Latin in 1496, it was an important table for calculating latitude.

ZACUTUS, ABRAHAM or LUSITANUS
(1575-1642). Portuguese physician, pathologist. Born in Lisbon. Practiced medicine for thirty years. Voluminous writer. In 1629, he published *Medicorum Principum Historia*.

ZAINER, JOANNES or ZEINER or ZEYNER
(Died c. 1495). First printer in Ulm. Active from 1468 to 1478, he published the first German translation of Boccaccio's *Decameron*. His brother GUNTHER (died 1478) was also a pioneer printer.

ZANCHI, BASILIO
(1501-1558). Italian humanist scholar and poet. Compiled dictionary of Latin epithets. Wrote Latin poems: *De Horto Sophiae* and others. He resided at Rome, enjoying the patronage of Pope Leo X, at the beginning of his career. He later entered an order and studied and wrote upon theology.

ZARLINO, GIOSEFFO
(1517-1590). Venetian musical theorist, Franciscan monk, learned in humanities and science. He had been a student of Willaert and wrote important treatises on counterpoint and harmony; he was especially concerned—following Plato—about the consonance of words and music in songs and choral music.

ZASIUS, JOHANN ULRICH or ZÄSI or ZASY
(1461-1536). Swiss humanist, jurist. Wrote compendium of Roman law entitled *Catalogus Legum Antiquarum*: published in 1578. Also a collection of his legal *Consilia*: published in 1538. He admired Luther but adhered to the Church.

ZBYLITOWSKI, ANDRZEJ
Polish Neo-Latin poet. Author of occasional verse: sixteenth century.

ZEEUSCHE NACHTEGAEL or ZEELAND'S NIGHTINGALE
Famous Dutch song book, containing the work of some twenty poets. Illustrated. Published in 1623.

ZEITBLOM, BARTHOLOMÄUS
(c. 1450-c. 1520). German painter. Died in Ulm. Executed lyrical altarpieces, notable especially for their luminous, bright coloring.

ZELL, ULRICH

(died after 1507). German printer. Set up first printing press in Cologne. His *Cologne Chronicle*, 1499, is an important source for the beginnings of the art of printing and in giving the city of Haarlem and Lourens Coster priority for the invention over Mainz and Gutenberg.

ZENO, CATERINO

(Fifteenth century). Venetian merchant. Sent on mission (1471-1474) to Persia to align Persians with Venetians against Turks. His *Relazione* to the Venetian government may still be read. His father, Dragon, had traveled to Damascus and Mecca, c. 1450.

ZERBIN, GASPARD

Provençal writer. Author of popular comedies: *La Perlo deys Musos et Commedies Prouvensalos* (1655). He was a follower of Claude Brueys.

ZIMARA, MARCANTONIO

(1470-c. 1537). Taught philosophy at Padua. Lectured at Naples. Wrote commentaries on Aristotle, in which he followed the Averroistic school, strong at Padua, in interpreting Aristotle's philosophical works. His son TEOFILO (1515-1587) was a philosopher and physician.

ZINANO, GABRIELE

(c. 1560-1635). Italian man of letters. Author of dialogue on literary topics: allusions to Homer, Plato, Aristotle, Tasso, Dante and many other works; his poetry is modeled on that of Tasso.

ZLATARIC, DINKO

(1558-1609). Yugoslav poet. Rector of the University of Padua. Attempted to reform the Yugoslav literary language on the basis of Italian models. Adopted Italian meters in his love lyrics, where he followed Petrarch closely.

ZOË

In 1472 Ivan III of Russia married Zoë, the niece of the last Byzantine emperor of Constantinople, Constantine XIII. Byzantine court customs, ceremonials and dress were established at Moscow. Moscow claimed to be the "third Rome."

ZOO

The Renaissance produced contacts and interests in a variety of directions. The animate world around man became an object of curiosity and investigation. Private zoos, for instance, and menageries—*serragli*—were considered among the requisites of courtly entertainment. Among animals that were so collected or received as gifts from foreign potentates were lions, cheetahs, falcons, zebras, giraffes, elephants. For much the same reasons, botanical gardens became popular also.

ZOPPINO, NICOLO DI ARISTOTILE DE' ROSSI

(fl. 1503-1541). Italian printer, editor, librarian of Ferrara. He established his firm in Bologna and printed many works by Italians, e.g., Boiardo, Pietro Aretino, Ariosto, Vittoria Colonna, etc.; classical works in Italian translation, e.g., Vergil and Apuleius, and also popular religious works. He also worked at Venice, Milan, Perugia.

ZOUCHE, RICHARD

(1590-1661). English jurist, Regius Professor of Civil Law at Oxford. Author of *Elementa Jurisprudentiae*: Also treatise on international law.

ZRINYI, MIKLOS, COUNT

(c. 1620-1664). Hungarian statesman, poet. Ruler of Croatia. In successful conflict with Turks. Author of lyrics, many of them on his experiences as a passionate crusader against the Turks. He also wrote a number of treatises on war and politics.

ZUCCARO FAMILY, THE or ZUCCHERO

Roman family of painters that flourished in the sixteenth century. The family tradition began with OTTAVIANO (born c. 1505), who was no great artist but was the teacher of his two sons. TADDEO (1529-1566) decorated the Mattei Palace in Rome and, on the strength of that work, became painter to Popes Julius III and Paul IV. Among his paintings are *Diana, Meeting of Charles V and Alexander Farnese at Worms, The Dead Christ* and *Christ in the Tomb.* FEDERIGO (1543-1609) worked long with his brother. A squabble with his patron, Pope Gregory XIII, led him to depart for the Netherlands and England, where he painted Queen Elizabeth and Mary, Queen of Scots. He also sojourned in Spain, where he executed decorative work in the Escorial for Philip II. He painted *The Golden Age* and *Christ Descends into Limbo;* wrote a treatise on art; founded at Rome the St. Luke Academy.

ZURBARÁN, FRANCISCO DE

(1598-c. 1662). Spanish painter. Court painter to King Philip IV. Specialized in religious and monastic paintings. His early work shows Renaissance Italian influence, but he reverted to the native tradition and evolved his own style, which is characterized by his reserved use of color, simplicity of design and restrained realism. Leading artist of seventeenth century national school of painting in Spain. Executed *Crucifixion, Life of Saint Peter, Carthusian Monk Reading*.

ZURITA Y CASTRO, JERÓNIMO

(1512-1580). Spanish historian. Author of *Anales de la Corona de Aragón* from the earliest times to 1516; it is rich in state documents, to which he had access as secretary to Philip II.

ZWILLING, GABRIEL or DIDYMUS

(c. 1487-1558). An Augustinian friar. He was one of the first of his order to go over to Luther. He became a famous preacher, for which he was much praised by Luther.

ZWINGER, THEODOR

(1533-1588). Swiss physician, scholar. Professor of Greek at Basel, also professor of medicine. His encyclopedia *Theatrum vitae humanae* went through several editions; it is more notable for its superstition than its science, especially in regard to astronomy.

ZWINGLI, HULDREICH

(1484-1531). Swiss religious reformer. Studied at University of Vienna. He had been educated on the classics and influenced by the teachings of Pico and Erasmus. Taught classics at Basel. Ordained at age of twenty-two. Parish priest. Opposed use of Swiss as mercenary troops: also criticized French alliances. Priest at Einsiedeln. Opposition to Papacy developed. In 1518, preached on New Testament: beginning of Reformation in Zurich. Attacked abuses of Roman Church. Produced sixty-seven theses against Pope. Organized Swiss Protestantism. Met Luther: led in 1529 to Colloquy of Marburg. Differences between Zwingli and Luther were never reconciled.

Zwingli foresaw war with the Swiss cantons of the interior, which broke out in 1531. Protestants were defeated at Battle of Kappel. Zwingli was killed.

His theological system appears in his sixty-seven theses and the First Helvetian Confession. Postulated supreme authority of the Bible and denied the validity of the historic tradition of the Church. Zwinglianism, among the major Reformation sects, embodied most fully Erasmus' theological views and ethical teachings.